More than anything else, the church of Jesus Christ needs pastors. It is, of course, essential to have preachers explaining and applying the Bible to those listening. We thank God for these, praying that they will continue to be provided and used for His glory throughout the world. But a pastor, though never less, is more than a preacher, for, as "pastor" means, he is a "shepherd" of God's people, caring for them in all their spiritual needs, guiding, upholding, protecting and healing the needy and lovable humans whom the Lord has entrusted to his care. After more than half a century of such service Al Martin is a widely experienced shepherd now providing the first of three volumes of pastoral theology for the profound blessing of Christ's church.

From various angles these chapters come before us enriched. The pastor who has written them, having devoted himself to many years of caring for his people, has also deepened his understanding by drawing widely from an extensive library of books on the subject, feeding this material through his own thinking into the lectures. These have then been given several times to students, on each occasion re-shaped, deepened and clarified.

In listening to Pastor Martin since the late 1960s, I have been blessed by scores of his sermons yet appreciated particularly his lectures for pastors. Over the last 30 years, as he and I have spent many hours together, it has been fascinating to see him, as it were, thinking aloud and shaping treatments of various pastoral issues. To recommend now this treasure of pastoral theology is for me a real privilege. Many have already been greatly helped through hearing these lectures, but with all my heart I pray and, trusting in the Lord's activity, believe that many more will now have the opportunity of reading, digesting and applying these gems of truth for themselves and their people. Glory to God.

—**Edward Donnelly**, retired Pastor of Trinity Reformed Presbyterian Church, Newtownabbey, Northern Ireland, and Emeritus Professor of New Testament at the Reformed Theological College, Belfast, Northern Ireland

The first thing I did on my first day of ministry over twenty years ago was to start listening to Pastor Martin's pastoral theology lectures on cassette tape (yes, that long ago). These addresses not only set my ministry on a biblical course but actually saved my ministry (and my sanity) more times than I can count. I've waited a long time to see this material in print and am so glad that present and future generations of pastors can benefit from it as I did (and still do).

—**Dr. David Murray**, Professor of Old Testament and Practical Theology, Puritan Reformed Theological Seminary, Grand Rapids, Michigan

Dr. Al Martin poured a lifetime of study into lectures on the pastor and preaching. He delivered them annually to his Academy of theological students who met at the meeting place of his congregation in Montville, New Jersey. While he taught them he was engaged week by week in the dynamics of a growing and demanding pulpit ministry. The teaching was further honed and improved as the years passed within the Trinity lecture rooms themselves. Access to this teaching was made available through over a hundred cassettes, and some men transcribed those lectures in collections of well-thumbed and underlined home-made syllabi. Years of contemplation passed and finally the author was convinced, along with a number of his colleagues more eager than he, that the time had come for the contents of those lectures to be pervasively refined and presented to the Christian church for its verdict, evaluation and benefit. There is scarcely a more long-awaited event in the publishing world than the appearance of those volumes. There is certainly a cry from a million hearts that today's preaching should know more of the breath of heaven. These are not great days anywhere in the world for mighty preaching. May these volumes do much good all over the globe to assist the renewal of awakening ministries.

—**Dr. Geoff Thomas**, Pastor (Retired) Alfred Place Baptist Church, Aberystwyth, Wales. Visiting Professor of Historical Theology, Puritan Reformed Theological Seminary, Grand Rapids, Michigan

I remember rummaging around in the seminary library in Portland, OR and stumbling across a box loaded with cassette tapes from the Trinity Pulpit. These tapes were the complete set of pastoral theology lectures from Pastor Albert N. Martin. I checked out the maximum number and took them along with my Walkman to my janitorial job. I would listen to each one 2–3 times. It was a feast. It was filet mignon compared to the other pastoral theology I was getting. Pastor Martin's lectures have made a tremendous impact on my life and ministry. But Pastor Martin himself has made a bigger impact. I wrote my doctoral project on his theology of preaching and it started a wonderful friendship. I am so thankful that these lectures are being put in print. They represent the choicest fruits of his labors. All glory be to Christ.

—**Dr. Brian Borgman**, Pastor, Grace Community Church, Minden, Nevada. Author of *My Heart for Thy Cause: Albert N. Martin's Theology of Preaching* (Mentor) and *Feelings and Faith: Cultivating Godly Emotions in the Christian Life* (Crossway)

The unique value of this book series is found not so much in its printed pages, but in the heart and life of its author, and the hearts and lives of many of us he pastored and mentored over roughly half a century. The pages were born of lectures; but the lectures were born of pastoral labors—those of a real man of God, his own study of Scripture enriched by writings and examples of other godly men, striving to follow the hand of Scripture wherever it leads, in heart, life, and ministry. May God use this printed means to increase His glory in Christ's church (Ephesians 3:21).

—**Eugenio Piñero**, Pastor, Iglesia Bautista Reformada, North Bergen, New Jersey

Nothing has shaped my personal and public pastoral life more than Pastor Martin's Pastoral Theology. I was privileged to hear these messages as a seminary student and have shared them numerous times throughout the years with others aspiring to the gospel ministry. Whether you have been in the ministry for decades or are just beginning, the truths expounded by this faithful brother ought to become a near and dear companion till you face the Chief Shepherd.

—**Jim Savastio**, Pastor, Reformed Baptist Church of Louisville, Kentucky

I first encountered Pastor Martin's lectures on pastoral theology in 1997, the year before I entered seminary. I listened to the full set of audio cassettes over the course of that year and they proved to be an ideal preparation for my formal ministry training. They provided me with an excellent in-depth treatment of all the various aspects of pastoral ministry. Pastor Martin seemed not only to have read every significant work relating to pastoral theology and to have mined them for every gem of wisdom they had to offer, but to have distilled their riches and woven them throughout his lectures. These lectures are very far from being a mere digest of the past, however—they are the fruit of his own thinking, stimulated by the best of the old writers. No matter what the topic—preparing a sermon, the call to the ministry, conducting weddings and funerals, the Pastor's personal reading, his family responsibilities—Pastor Martin provides counsel that is biblically faithful and practically wise.

But these lectures are suffused throughout with a vitality that only comes with intimate experience of the things taught. Every word of these lectures has been painstakingly hammered out on the anvil of pastoral experience over decades faithfully serving the same congregation and acting as a "Pastor of Pastors" to countless men all over the world who have looked to Pastor Martin for biblical counsel in a vast array of situations. These lectures were lived before they were taught—and each one of them provides a window into Pastor Martin's own life and ministry; for with a consistency that I have rarely witnessed, he has sought to practise every word he teaches. It has been a privilege over the last 12 years to get to know the man behind these lectures a little and to see the fruit of his teaching in the church he pastored for 46 years. His character and his work are the highest commendation I can think of for these volumes, which I pray will be as great a blessing to others as they have been to me.

—**Warren Peel**, Pastor, Trinity Reformed Presbyterian Church, Newtownabbey, Northern Ireland, and Professor of New Testament Language and Literature at the Reformed Theological College, Belfast, Northern Ireland

These lectures have influenced my life profoundly. As a seminary student, they were meat and drink to my soul and equipped and furnished me for the Master's use. As a workman in the mission field, these lectures provide a biblical blueprint for the construction of God's temple filled with "living stones." As an instructor, like Elisha's servant, I have borrowed an iron axe from Pastor Martin's "tool box" to help establish and strengthen churches for the glory of Christ.

—**Thomson Chung**, Pastor, Trinity Church of Hong Kong, Reformed Baptist

THE MAN OF GOD
His Calling and Godly Life

Pastoral Theology

○────────────────○

ALBERT N. MARTIN

Volume 1: *The Man of God: His Calling and Godly Life*
Volume 2: *The Man of God: His Preaching and Teaching Labors*
Volume 3: *The Man of God: His Shepherding, Evangelizing, and Counseling Labors*

THE MAN OF GOD
His Calling and Godly Life

ALBERT N. MARTIN

TRINITY PULPIT PRESS
Montville, New Jersey

Pastoral Theology, Volume 1: The Man of God: His Calling and Godly Life
© 2018 by Albert N. Martin

Trinity Pulpit Press
160 Changebridge Road
Montville, NJ 07045
973-334-5045
office@tbcnj.org
www.trinitypulpitpress.com
www.trinitymontville.org

ISBN 978-1-943608-11-9 (hardcover)
ISBN 978-1-943608-14-0 (e-pub)

Cover design by Joseph Dunlap.

Printed in the United States of America.

DEDICATION

To the Members of Trinity Baptist Church whose noble Berean spirit made our united journey into truth a blessed experience for 46 years, and created the context within which these lectures were initially constructed and subsequently, continually refined.

> Are we beginning to commend ourselves again? Or do we need, as some do, letters of recommendation to you, or from you? You yourselves are our letter of recommendation, written on our hearts, to be known and read by all. And you show that you are a letter from Christ delivered by us, written not with ink but with the Spirit of the living God, not on tablets of stone but on tablets of human hearts.
>
> —2 Corinthians 3:1–3

The life of the minister is the life of his ministry.

Table of Contents

Unit One: The Call of the Man of God

Unit Two: The Life of the Man of God

Foreword

When I was a young minister, I came across a series of audio recordings by Pastor Albert Martin that proved to be a gold mine of wisdom. Opening the Holy Scriptures and leaning on the solid teaching of classic writers, these lectures both clarified God's calling and motivated God's servants to take it up with renewed vigor so as to preach God's Word and shepherd His flock in accord with the whole counsel of God. Well organized, theologically grounded, and carefully stated, these materials represented a high-water mark of reflection on the pastor's service to his Lord. Despite my meager financial resources at that time, I purchased the entire set of these cassettes, listened to them all diligently and prayerfully, and benefitted greatly from them—especially those addresses on the calling and life of a faithful pastor and on the content and form of the sermon and the act of preaching. About a decade later, when called upon to teach several courses in pastoral theology in the newly begun Puritan Reformed Theological Seminary in Grand Rapids, Michigan, I listened to most of these lectures again and found them even more profitable the second time through. It is, therefore, a great joy for me that Pastor Martin has reworked this material in his senior years and that now these highly esteemed lectures are finally appearing in book form to instruct, encourage, challenge, and exhort present and future generations of ministers, just as they have done for so many of us in recent decades.

Eminently practical on the one hand, *Pastoral Theology* avoids the pitfall of the American "how-to" mentality that reduces ministry to administrative and motivational skill—the very opposite of Zechariah's watchword, "Not by might, nor by power, but by my spirit, saith the LORD of hosts" (Zech. 4:6). On the other hand, there is no vague mysticism here, but Bible-based, Spirit-anointed, experiential insight into the what and how of God's calling to the ministry, the life of a faithful pastor, sermon preparation and the act of preaching, spiritual shepherding, evangelism, and pastoral counseling.

The scope of this multivolume's set of instructions is encyclopedic. By systematically studying these pages, especially under the mentorship of a wise pastor, those men aspiring to the ministry will receive the equivalent of several seminary courses in pastoral theology. New ministers who discover themselves lacking in some practical skill can turn to the relevant chapter and find sage advice. Veteran warriors of the Lord will find help to sharpen their swords, heal their wounds, and find a renewed understanding of their Commander's strategy.

The first volume of *Pastoral Theology* sets the stage for the rest. The pastor must be truly called by God to the ministry, and Martin sheds great light both on what a true call to ministry is and what it is not. But then he goes on to provide an important emphasis on the pastor's life, particularly his personal holiness—a crucial component in light of Paul's exhortation, "Be thou an example of the believers, in word, in conversation, in charity, in spirit, in faith, in purity" (1 Tim. 4:12). We also find help here in the often-neglected topic of a pastor's stewardship of his physical life, a concern also reflected in Paul's teachings (1 Tim. 5:23; 2 Tim. 4:13).

It might be asked why we should devote so much attention to the man of God. Martin makes abundantly clear that Scripture posits a cause-and-effect relationship between the character of a man's life as a Christian and his fruitfulness as a Christian minister (Matt. 7:17–20). The fruitfulness of a minister's work is usually proportional to the sanctification of his heart toward God. *Pastoral Theology* rightly stresses that we as ministers must therefore seek grace to build the house of God with the hand of sound preaching and doctrine, as well as with the hand of a sanctified life. Our doctrine must shape our life, and our life adorn our doctrine. As John Boys wrote, "He doth preach most who doth live best." We must be what we preach and teach, not only applying ourselves to our texts but applying our texts to ourselves. Our hearts must be transcripts of our sermons. Otherwise, as John Owen warned, "If a man teach uprightly and walk crookedly, more will fall down in the night of his life than he built in the day of his doctrine."

Perhaps Robert Murray M'Cheyne put it best when he famously said, "A minister's life is the life of his ministry.... In great measure, according to the purity and perfections of the instrument, will be the success. It is not great talents that God blesses so much as likeness to Jesus. A holy minister is an awful weapon in the hand of God." I am grateful that Martin marinated his work in the spirit of M'Cheyne's (and Paul's) invaluable emphasis on the minister's life.

Though pastor-preachers are jars of clay, their ministry holds a unique place in God's spiritual economy whereby He dispenses the treasures of saving grace to the world. This is not to sanction ecclesiastical imbalance or arrogance. Christ is the only head of the body, and every member must contribute his or her part to its growth (Eph. 4:15, 16). But Christ gives pastors and teachers to the church to proclaim the Word until the glory of the Lord fills the earth (vv. 10–12). It is primarily through the ministry of the Word that God builds up the church in doctrinal and practical maturity (vv. 13, 14).

Therefore, the training of ministers occupies a central place in the mission of the church. Paul not only told Timothy to "preach the word" (2 Tim. 4:2), but "the same commit thou to faithful men, who shall be able to teach others also" (2 Tim. 2:2). Whether or not our lives are being poured out at this moment like a drink offering, pastors are all but a vapor. Every one of us is one step away from the need of a replacement in the pulpit. And how many communities have no gospel preacher to declare the way of salvation?

Christ reflected this divine priority when His heart swelled with compassion for the lost sheep of fallen mankind. The Lord Jesus instructed His disciples, "The harvest truly is plenteous, but the labourers are few; pray ye therefore the Lord of the harvest, that he will send forth labourers into his harvest" (Matt. 9:37, 38). Pray, therefore, for laborers. With every chapter of this book that you read, pray for God to inculcate its biblical principles into men of God. Pray them into your own life, and pray them into your colleagues and the young men you mentor. Pray with the urgency of knowing that only God can make a minister. Pray with the confidence that the Lord promised, "And I will give you pastors according to mine heart, which shall feed you with knowledge and understanding" (Jer. 3:15).

A pastor does not have to agree with every sentence in this massive work on pastoral theology to reap enormous profit from it by the Spirit, using it to grow and maintain deep levels of mutual love and fellowship along with shared convictions concerning the heart of a biblically framed ministry. If you are a pastor, or wonder if you are being called to be a pastor, get *Pastoral Theology*, read it slowly and prayerfully, take ownership of it by marking it up, and come back to it repeatedly throughout your years of ministry. You and your flock(s) will be the beneficiaries of it and, by the Spirit's grace, will be the better for it.

Finally, I must also confess how good it is to see Al Martin continuing to use his pen in his senior years to leave behind a rich legacy of a lifetime ministry to future generations. About a decade ago, I visited him while he

was still living in New Jersey to strongly urge him to put a heavy emphasis on writing in his senior years. At the time, he tried to distance himself
from my persistence by asserting that he had no gifts to write, no computer
skills (or computer for that matter!), and no idea how to go about the whole
publication process. I told him these were just excuses—that he should get
a computer, learn how to use it, and, with the help of editors and publishing houses, he would soon learn that he had gifts for writing that he did not
know he possessed. To my surprise, he followed my advice, has since written
several books, and often thanks me for, in his words, "helping me discover a
gift that I didn't know I had"! And here I am, a decade later, having the honor
of concluding this foreword to Al Martin's magnum opus—an invaluable
multivolume work on pastoral theology! Marvelous is our God; His ways are
past finding out. May this set of books be eminently useful to the pastors and
church of Jesus Christ until our Lord returns on the clouds.

—Joel R. Beeke

Preface

Imagine with me a man who is a diesel mechanic by training and trade. He is browsing the book shelves and display tables in a well-stocked bookstore. His eyes light upon a book with this title, *An Encyclopedia of Diesel Engine Repairs*. What would be the first question raised in his mind if he were considering the purchase of that book? Would it not be, "What technical knowledge and practical experience does the author bring to this subject that I should consider purchasing his book?"

As you hold the first of several volumes of my *Pastoral Theology Lectures* in your hand, you may well be asking the same question of me. Let me respond to this question as it relates to my knowledge and experience in the field of pastoral theology. For forty-six years it was my privilege to fulfill the office and responsibilities of an elder set apart to "labor in preaching and teaching" (1 Tim. 5:17) within the life and ministry of Trinity Baptist Church (TBC). During twenty of those years, the church maintained a church-based pastoral training center called the Trinity Ministerial Academy (TMA). While enrolled in the Academy, students embarked on a program which embodied a classic seminary curriculum. From the beginning of this endeavor the elders requested that I teach all the courses in pastoral theology, eventually covering a wide range of pastoral issues which I taught sequentially in eight units in a four-year cycle. Each academic week concluded on Friday with my delivering two hours of lectures, followed by discussion and interaction between the students and me. This arrangement meant that every four years every lecture would undergo a careful review, often resulting in significant alterations or additions to my hand-written lecture notes from which I lectured and preached the material contained in them.

When it became known that these lectures were being recorded and made available through the Trinity Pulpit Tape Ministry, they began to be widely circulated in various parts of the world. Many men who had completed a standard seminary or Bible college course communicated to me that the subjects addressed in the recorded lectures were filling up a large vacuum left in their previous ministerial training. These encouragements were often accompanied with entreaties to produce the lectures in book form. After the closing of TMA in 1998, requests for the cassette and CD recordings of the lectures continued, along with appeals to put this material into print.

The elders of TBC periodically discussed whether specific efforts should be made to print the lectures. They became convinced that a very concrete step in moving forward to pursue that possibility, would be for me to upgrade and revise the lectures and deliver them one more time to a group of pastors and ministerial students while recording them in a DVD (video) format. From 2007 to 2012, all eight units were reworked, delivered, and professionally recorded at TBC in a five-day module format before 20 to 30 men. These recordings, along with a CD containing detailed outlines and printed copies of all the lengthier quotations, were attractively packaged and made available to the Christian public through Trinity Book Service (and these lectures are still available in that format from Trinity Book Service). Subsequently, the eight units of lectures were transcribed, with a view to publishing them in book form sometime in the future.

The next step was to take these transcriptions and put them into publishable form. In 2012 initial efforts were made to begin this massive task. For several very specific reasons this effort was terminated.

Meanwhile, the leadership of TBC decided that the church should establish a self-publishing ministry under the title of Trinity Pulpit Press (TPP). Early in 2016 efforts were made again to pick up and pursue the task of bringing these Pastoral Theology Lectures into print. In a very wonderful way, God began to bring together a team of brethren functioning as joint laborers under the oversight of the trustees of TPP. God willing, their labors will eventually result in a three-volume set of books entitled *Pastoral Theology Lectures*. You, dear reader, hold in your hands the first of these anticipated volumes.

As an ordinary rule, effective oral communication will always involve elements that do not constitute good literature if carried over directly from the oral into the written format with only minimal changes. For example, the recapitulation and judicious repetition which are essential elements of effective oral communication, would, for the most part, be tedious and unnecessary in a written format of the same material. Furthermore, there are some aspects of effective oral communication that bring into play the manifold para-linguistic tools of communication that simply cannot be reproduced in a written text, i.e., a frown, a smile, a raised eyebrow, hand motions to illustrate a point, the raising and lowering or pacing of one's voice, etc. Since most of these para-linguistic elements cannot be converted into words, words must be chosen and framed in an effort to supply what originally was conveyed by the para-linguistics.

These lectures were never delivered in a word-for-word reading of a fully prepared manuscript. Rather, they were delivered by me using a detailed outline as my written text, while allowing myself the liberty and freedom of a preacher in their actual delivery, including many aspects of those para-linguistics which are part and parcel of my natural preaching and teaching style.

During the many years that the recorded Pastoral Theology Lectures were in circulation, and as the many appeals to put the lectures into print continued to be made, I found it difficult to believe that their contribution was of such significance as to warrant the amount of time, labor, and financial outlay that would be necessary to put them into print. However, since my retirement from the pastoral office in June of 2008 and my subsequent relocation to Western Michigan, my ministerial opportunities, and my wider exposure to a broad spectrum of contemporary evangelical church life and ministries, have served to convince me that many of the distinctive contributions of these lectures desperately need to be heard and heeded. I have become persuaded that at this stage of my earthly pilgrimage, it is my God-given stewardship to make every legitimate effort to see these lectures put into print before the Lord takes me home. This recently born conviction has imparted to me, a man now in my mid-80s, a fresh baptism of zeal and holy joy as I rivet myself to my computer desk hours on end, in order to do my part in producing these volumes.

The emerging conviction that it was God's time for me to apply myself to this endeavor was reinforced when God brought together a team of brethren to labor with me in this project. Their shared vision, professional competence, and Christian grace, have made it a delight to be laborers together with them.

Since TMA was a ministry of a confessional church, holding to *The Second London Baptist Confession of Faith of 1689* (the "second child" of *The Westminster Confession of Faith*), the theological, ecclesiastical, and practical instruction and counsel given in these lectures is decidedly and unashamedly Evangelical, Calvinistic, Reformed, Experiential, and Baptist. However, I trust that the lectures breathe a spirit of catholicity and that this fact will make the Lectures useful to all Bible-believing, Christ-loving men who desire to have every facet of their pastoral labors conformed to the precepts, precedents, and principles of the Scriptures (Isa. 8:20).

Furthermore, since almost all of the subjects addressed in these lectures cover issues with which I had to wrestle in my forty-six years at TBC, the lectures present many definitive, as opposed to broad or general, perspectives on the ministry. In this regard, I have found that the following comments of D. Martyn Lloyd-Jones, extracted from the preface of his classic book entitled *Preaching and Preachers*, very accurately express my own thoughts.

> Some may object to my dogmatic assertions; but I do not apologize for them. Every preacher should believe strongly in his own method; and if I cannot persuade all of the rightness of mine, I can at least stimulate them to think and to consider other possibilities.[1]

As you delve into the pages of these lectures it will not be long before you discover how much I have gleaned from writers of past generations. My reasons for including even some lengthy quotes from these eminent servants of Christ are given in the lectures themselves. In order to whet the reader's appetite for such choice spiritual food, I close this Preface with the very words with which Thomas Murphy concluded the preface to his book entitled *Pastoral Theology*, first printed in 1877.

> If my work, which is now finished, shall be so blessed by the kind providence of the Great Head of the Church as to find its way into the hands of a goodly number of those who are already in the gospel ministry or who are expecting soon to enter that sacred office; if it shall help them to a riper preparation for the pastoral work; if it shall cheer them ever so little under their many discouragements and help them to solve some of their many difficulties; if it shall assist in making their toils more easy and pleasant; if it shall aid in giving greater efficacy to the efforts which they may put forth in the cause of human redemption; especially if it shall contribute anything through them to the promotion of the glory of Christ our King,—if it shall accomplish these objects, even in the smallest degree, then there will be more than a recompense for the years of labor and of prayer which have been devoted to its pages.[2]

Albert N. Martin
Jenison, Michigan, January, 2018

---

1. D. Martyn Lloyd-Jones, *Preaching and Preachers* (Grand Rapids: Zondervan, 1972), "Preface."

2. Thomas Murphy, *Pastoral Theology, The Pastor in the Various Duties of His Office* (Philadelphia: Presbyterian Board of Publication, 1877), 6.

Acknowledgments

With deepest appreciation for each one whom God graciously added to the team of workers who labored with a shared vision and serious commitment to see these Lectures finally "embalmed in printer's ink" (A. W. Tozer's words). With special thanks

- To Mr. and Mrs. Eugenio Piñero whose vision "jump started" this project;
- To the Office Bearers of Trinity Baptist Church for their support and encouragement;
- To the First Editors who undertook the daunting task of converting the transcribed lectures into a first draft in manuscript form, Pastor John Reuther, (who also fulfilled the role of a General Editor and Biographer), and Pastor Alan Dunn;
- To the meticulous technical editor, Pastor D. Scott Meadows;
- To our competent professional proofreader, Susan Carter;
- To our talented graphic artist, Joseph Dunlap, designer of the captivating dust jacket;
- To the project managers, Pastor Bart Carlson and Pastor Jeff Smith;
- To Linda den Hollander, typesetter par excellence, and gracious advisor concerning publishing protocols;
- To Gary den Hollander, final proofreader, whose thoroughness and precision of work are deeply appreciated;
- To the students who attended the Academy, and whose subsequent lives and ministries assure us that our labors to impart a biblical view of the Christian ministry and of biblical churchmanship were not in vain.

Biographical Sketch of
Albert N. Martin

Preface

Forty-four years have passed since I first became acquainted with Pastor Albert N. Martin. I was enrolled as a music student at Montclair State College, and there, for the first time, heard the gospel of God's grace in Christ from classmates who faithfully witnessed to me. One of these was a member of a church in Pequannock, New Jersey, and I began to attend church with him. I was thrilled with my new life in Christ and my new church family. I grew under the ministry of a godly pastor, and a faithful Sunday School teacher who took me under his wing. He said to me one day, "You should listen to Pastor Albert Martin in Essex Fells." He gave me a set of three introductory cassette tapes which the Trinity Pulpit offered at that time, which consisted of a topical sermon on the fear of God, an expository sermon on John 6, and a character study. I was encouraged and inspired by those expositions.

I had switched schools in the fall of 1973 and enrolled as a student at Northeastern Bible College in Essex Fells, New Jersey. The Bible college was just around the corner from Trinity Baptist Church where Pastor Martin was one of the pastors. I visited the church occasionally with some friends from my church. In 1977, I married Wendy, also a student at Northeastern, and we became members at Trinity in 1978.

I now have the privilege of telling you a little about Albert N. Martin. Some of the history of his life found in this sketch is as he has recounted it to me. In addition, I write as one whose life and ministry have been significantly impacted by his and by the personal interest he has taken in me throughout the years of my pilgrimage.

Youth and Conversion

Albert was born into a home where Scripture was revered as the Word of God. His father, George Albert, of Scottish origins, and his mother, Mildred

Sophia Sandquist, a daughter of Swedish immigrants, were both earnest Christians. Albert was the second of eleven children, one of those dying in infancy. At the time of his birth on April 11, 1934, his father was an officer in the Salvation Army, "stationed" in Alexandria, Virginia. A few months after Albert's birth, as a matter of conscience with respect to certain emphases of the Salvation Army, his father resigned as an officer and relocated to Stamford, Connecticut, making the local Salvation Army corps the religious home for his family.

Albert was not catechized or given structured teaching from Scripture, but it was clear to the children that what the Bible says, God says, and what God says is the final word concerning the truth of every issue addressed in Scripture. The children were not required to read the Bible on their own, but they were made to memorize portions of Scripture, especially some of the Psalms and Proverbs. Even in his pre-conversion years, just shy of his eighteenth birthday, he never doubted that the Bible was the Word of God. However, there were times of doubt and periods of confusion with respect to what the Bible actually teaches.

Once every quarter, the Salvation Army designated a particular Sunday as Decision Sunday. At the end of the service on these days, those who made no profession of faith were encouraged to come to the penitent-form, an object much like a kneeling bench, at the front of the meeting place. There they were encouraged to pray a decisional prayer, but without any biblical instruction concerning the basic gospel. Because Albert had been carrying a sense of his sinfulness and need of God's forgiveness with him from his early childhood, he often went forward in those services, prayed the appropriate prayer, and sang this chorus:

> *Into my heart, Into my heart;*
> *Come into my heart, Lord Jesus.*
> *Come in today; Come in to stay;*
> *Come into my heart, Lord Jesus.*

Since the same organization taught that one could be repeatedly saved and lost, Albert made several "decisions" as a youth, and sought to live as a Christian. He knew that a true Christian would read his Bible at least once a day. Hence, he developed a ritual in which he read Psalm 117, the shortest chapter in the Bible, before going to bed, in order to put some salve on his conscience that he had read a chapter in the Bible!

When he was sixteen, his family left the Salvation Army and began to attend The First Baptist Church of Stamford. They were exposed for the first time to a pastor who made an effort to preach the scriptures. There too, he met Joseph Mahady, who had come from Scotland with his wife to pursue careers as professional dancers. They were converted and eventually God changed their occupational pursuits. This young Scottish man was a bold personal evangelist. At that time Joseph began to speak to Albert and the other youth in that church concerning their spiritual needs. Joseph Mahady's ministry was a major factor leading to Albert's conversion.

Albert was converted somewhere between late 1951 and early 1952, and then he became passionate about obeying the Lord Jesus and speaking to others about Him. His long-experienced fear of death, judgment, and hell were gone. He had peace and joy in believing that his sins were forgiven, and an insatiable thirst for the Word of God. He experienced great delight in secret prayer, along with a sensitive conscience toward God and man. His siblings testified that it was quickness to confess his own sins against them and seek their forgiveness that persuaded them that he was a child of God. He also loved to be with other Christians.

Christian Growth and Service

Albert worked part-time for the local Western Union telegraph company delivering telegrams. He used his sister's old blue balloon-tire bicycle as his means of transportation. When he delivered a telegram, he would often attach a gospel tract to it. One day, when he reported to work at the Western Union office, he was told that the manager wanted to speak to him. He thought that someone had complained about this, and was fearful that he was about to be reprimanded or fired. After establishing that it was Albert, the manager told him why he wanted to speak to him. He informed him that during the previous night someone had submitted an article to the *New York Times* about a religious movement that was going on in the Stamford High School led by Albert Martin. The manager commended him for doing something good and worthwhile when so many young people were wasting their time with useless or unlawful activities.

Around this same time Albert became aware of the *Thompson Chain Reference Bible*, which he found to be an exciting tool for Bible study. He saved money from his thirty-five cents an hour bicycle-pedaling job and ordered one. When it arrived in the mail, he literally hugged it close, thankful that he now had a Bible that would help him dig into its treasures. He often sat at the dining room table, while other family members were engaged in different activities or had gone to bed, and traced out the references in the chain reference system. Over the next few years, that Bible became well marked. He began to use one of the "through-the-Bible" reading programs that were available. On his eighteenth birthday, his uncle gave him the *Strong's Concordance*. This, with the chain reference Bible, gave him his initial convictions concerning such truths as sin, repentance, salvation, and other teachings of the Word of God. With his Bible and concordance, God was laying the foundation in his heart for a life and ministry in which he was determined to know, believe, obey, and share with others all that God says in His written Word.

One of the first influential books that he read after his conversion was *The Divine Conquest* by A. W. Tozer. This was his first introduction to someone who wrote with prophetic insight warning of the weaknesses of evangelicalism with its low view of God, carnal methods, and man-centered views of ministry and worship. Seeds were planted in his heart by that book which flowered into some of the things which he found himself emphasizing during the five-year itinerant ministry which followed his graduation from Bible college.

Another book which he read during those early days as a Christian was the autobiography of Charles G. Finney. That book filled his mind with perspectives which were very attractive to him as a young believer. However, some years later, after subsequently reading Finney's *Systematic Theology*, he realized that in many areas Finney was not a safe guide to understanding Scripture. As he began to grow in his understanding of Scripture, those early perspectives imbibed from Finney's autobiography were gradually purged from his mind, albeit not without some deep mental and spiritual struggles.

Early Preaching Opportunities

In God's providence, several of the young men of First Baptist became aware of the Stamford Gospel Mission, where there were two older men who had been praying for years that God would pour out His Holy Spirit in converting grace and power upon the young people of Stamford. They found themselves beginning to attend that mission with its Sunday afternoon service followed by a fellowship meal. They also conducted Tuesday and Thursday night services. Some in that group were baptized at First Baptist, and they continued attending there on Sunday mornings. They also began regular attendance at the mission for the Sunday afternoon service and fellowship meal. The two older men, the directors of the mission, were a great means of grace in the lives of the young men. Their theological orientation was Wesleyan. They were godly, praying men who recognized the work of God in the hearts and lives of the younger men. These older men were willing to become unofficial spiritual shepherds.

Rather than put a damper on the youthful zeal of the younger men, they encouraged them to expand their ministries. They encouraged them to hold street meetings two or three times a week. They also asked some of the young men to begin preaching at the Tuesday- and Thursday-evening services which were held at the mission. Mr. Scofield (not the famous one), the mission superintendent, sat in the superintendent's chair off to the left of the pulpit, and while the young men were preaching, he would sit with his arms crossed with one hand on his forehead, eyes closed, listening to what they were saying. Periodically, he would express his affirmation with a very substantial "Amen," sometimes followed by the words, "If that's not the gospel I do not know what is." At other times, if they said something that was particularly searching, he would say out loud, "Lord, help me!" The example of how these two older men of God treated the zealous young men made a profound impression on Albert's heart. It has always made him quick to draw near to encourage and help guide young men whose zeal may greatly outstrip their knowledge. Their example has also been a prod to him to be patient in dealing with such young men, when he remembers more than a few unwise things he and his fellows did in those early days in their uninstructed zeal.

The mission hall was on the second floor of a commercial establishment. The first floor was occupied by a tavern. There were times when Albert and his friends would go into that bar, sit on the bar stools, and begin witnessing to the customers. Sometimes they would pass out tracts, one of which began with these words: "A bar to heaven, a door to hell, whoever named it, named it well."

The profound influence which these two older men had on them kept Albert in later years from harboring a sinfully negative attitude to truly godly men of evangelical Arminian persuasion.

In those early days of Christian experience and preaching the gospel on the streets of Stamford, it was Scripture that they sought to expound, declare, and apply, and some would stop long enough to listen. In his book *Preaching in the Holy Spirit*, Pastor Martin gives an account of how significant that first street preaching event was in his spiritual life, as well as laying a strong foundation for his understanding of preaching.

> It was a Thursday night in February of 1952, and I was approaching my eighteenth birthday. I left my house to walk the one-and-a-half miles to the main business area in the town of Stamford, Connecticut. In those days all the stores remained open until 9:00 p.m. on Thursdays. I knew that many of my high school buddies would be hanging around ("chilling out") in front of Liggette's Drug Store on the main street. That spot was the place where I and several other recently converted young people scheduled to meet and conduct our first open-air street meeting. Several old white-haired men of God who had been brought into our lives urged us to venture forth with our newfound faith in this way. After lustily singing several hymns and choruses, the time came for me to step forward in that little semicircle of young people in order to give my testimony and to preach the gospel. With my recently acquired leather-bound New Testament with Psalms in hand, I stepped forward, opened my mouth, and began to speak. Much to my surprise, although I was a natively timid and fearful young man, I was made conscious of the presence of dynamics that profoundly influenced what I said and how I said it on that memorable night. In a real sense, that night was my "coming-out party" in openly and boldly confessing my attachment to Christ before my peers. It was also my "spoiled-for-life party," in that I experienced on that occasion what I now know to be the immediate agency and operations of the Holy Spirit in the act of preaching.[1]

Many of the fundamental principles and convictions that have shaped his views concerning the act of preaching were being formed during those early months of his preaching experience. For example, he was learning about the necessity for the immediate agency of the Holy Spirit when preaching. Stepping out on a street corner without a fixed audience made him very conscious that if the Holy Spirit did not cause people to stop and listen by giving him utterance to speak the truth accurately and convincingly, he would preach in vain and be utterly frustrated in his attempts to preach outdoors. Another was the necessity of speaking in such a way as to engage and hold the attention of the hearers. He had to contend with the roaring of buses and with young guys driving by in cars with dual-exhaust systems, revving their engines and blowing their horns. All they wanted to do was to

---

1. Albert N. Martin, *Preaching in the Holy Spirit* (Grand Rapids: Reformation Heritage Books, 2011), vii, viii.

distract people. To gain a hearing, the young preacher had to speak loudly and distinctly to his hearers, without giving them the impression that he was screaming at them.

Another foundational principle was the necessity of quoting Scripture in the open-air sermon. In his own personal experience of preaching, he learned that there is a particular power and authority in the Word of God when it is quoted. This convinced him of the necessity of memorizing Scripture so that he might be able to quote verses in the preaching. Finally, the principle of the proper and effective use of his vocal apparatus was something which he was learning. Albert explains:

> I can remember times when my stomach muscles began to cramp, after I had been preaching for fifteen or twenty minutes on the wide sidewalk. I do not remember my vocal cords ever giving out on me, because I was instinctively speaking from my diaphragm, using the full range of the speaking apparatus given to me by God.

During that time, a Christian and Missionary Alliance pastor from Port Chester, New York, had heard about God's working in the lives of the young men. His name was Andrew Berkner. The young preachers were drawn to him by his godly, Christ-like life and spiritual wisdom, and he was drawn to their youthful zeal and spiritual passion. He took them under his wing and sought to teach them from Scripture how they should live and serve to please the Lord. Andrew used to say wise things like, "In ministering the Word of God to the souls of men, we are called upon to be skillful surgeons, not butchers." He obviously saw that, in their zealous reaction against the shallow easy-believism of the churches from which they had come, there were times when their preaching was more the work of young butchers than budding surgeons!

Throughout Albert's ministry, God brought the sagacious words of Andrew Berkner to mind for stirring his own prayers to be a skillful surgeon in handling the Word of God and apply it to the consciences of the hearers. What a lasting influence the few words of a mature man of God can have on a sincere young man!

Pastor Berkner asked Albert if he would preach at a midweek prayer service in his home church in Port Chester. Albert reminisces:

> I will never forget that first experience of preaching a sermon in a duly-constituted church setting. As I prayed and waited upon God for guidance, I was drawn to Psalm 37. I can well remember as I pored over

that chapter that I circled all of the verbs in the first section and structured my sermon based on that observation.

Later in life he found outlines of some of the first sermons that he preached. He saw in those outlines an effort to open up Scripture in a clearly structured manner with close and searching application to the consciences of his hearers. He had not been exposed to that kind of preaching before, but as he read his Bible and saw how the prophets, our Lord, and the apostles preached, he was persuaded that if he were to please God in his preaching, he had to make these men his models.

Formal Studies

Less than a year after his conversion he was enrolled as a freshman at Bob Jones University in Greenville, South Carolina, in the fall of 1952. Shortly after arriving at the university, he was informed by some students that the first hurdle he would face was a two-semester, five-hour course in elementary Greek. He was determined to obtain a grasp on elementary Greek, so that he might better know what God had said in His Word. He had been privileged to have an eighth and ninth-grade English teacher by the name of Miss Reynolds who "intimidated" him and his fellow students into mastering the elements of English grammar. She was preparing one of her students to pursue some competence in grasping the essentials of New Testament Greek. Men who enrolled with aspirations for the work of the ministry were also placed in the "preacher boys' class." These were just two of the highlights of his new course of study.

During his sophomore year at Bob Jones he joined a team of students to conduct ministry in a small mission work in Augusta, Georgia. They drove there early each Lord's Day morning, a distance of about one hundred ten miles and two and a half hours on the road each way. The mission was located in an economically depressed area of the city which was called the "white trash" section. The administrator was a home missionary in that spiritually needy section of Georgia. She had been in touch with the university to seek students to help in that work. The team taught Sunday School classes of various age groups, conducted the morning worship services, and preached around the city in the open air in the afternoons, before driving back to the university. This ministry was exhausting. However, there were many times when, driving back to the university, they were filled with joy in the Holy Spirit, and sang praises to God at the top of their lungs. They all learned the biblical truth that in losing our lives, we gain them.

Albert's parents expected him to return to Stamford for the summer of 1954 where a construction laborer job was waiting for him. However, in his devotional reading he came across passages in Jeremiah and Ezekiel where God pronounced woes on unfaithful shepherds who did not feed and protect the flock. He came across these words, "Woe to my worthless shepherd, who deserts the flock!" (Zech. 11:17). As he contemplated his plans to return home for the summer, this verse haunted him so much that he could not maintain a good conscience about returning. He was convinced that he ought to remain with that small flock in Augusta. Though he was not officially called to be their pastor, he was fulfilling a pastoral role to them. That experience solidified biblical principles concerning the pastor-flock relationship which helped him at other points in his ministerial life when he faced decisions whether to leave a church or to remain.

This early experience underscored for him that if he were to have the ears of the people as he preached, he had to win their hearts and persuade them that he was genuinely concerned for their spiritual and general well-being. Since they were accustomed only to having "preacher boys" come down on the Lord's Day and minister to them, the idea of having a resident pastoral ministry was entirely new to most of them. It was in that setting that he began to form scriptural views concerning why God had ordained qualified shepherds for His sheep. These dear brethren had no conception of what it was to be properly constituted as a church and function according to the New Testament in church life.

In the summer of 1954, Albert transferred to Columbia Bible College in South Carolina for the fall semester. He continued to drive down on the Lord's Day to minister to the people in the Augusta mission. He also made what had become a one-hundred-fifty-mile round trip every Wednesday in order to conduct a Bible study and prayer meeting. It was in that mission ministry that he engaged in some of his first efforts in the consecutive exposition of Scripture. He prepared sermons with his Greek New Testament open to the book of Romans. They had never experienced that kind of ministry, and it was there that he learned he had to guide them into patterns of mental exertion if they were to learn what Scripture teaches.

Albert learned other lessons from his ministry in those days. He learned that questions, even as he was preaching, were a catalyst to serious thinking. Occasionally a visiting preacher would be pleasantly surprised, when, having asked a rhetorical question in the sermon, he got an immediate audible response from the people.

He also saw the tragic results of "decisional evangelism" in the lives of those who had been "decisioned" by some of the former preacher boys. Those people were some of the most resistant to the Word of God because they were resting on their previously made decisions, while lacking any tangible fruit as evidence that they had been truly regenerated and genuinely converted.

Another lesson Albert learned relates to the delivery of the sermon. In an Easter sermon, he was planning to describe the death and burial of Christ in subdued tones, and to follow it with a dramatic description of His resurrection. He planned to have his voice drop to a whisper when preaching about His death, and then burst forth with a thunderous voice when he announced the fact of His resurrection. On that Lord's Day morning, while he was preaching, he actually did what he had planned to do, but as he did it he felt unclean because he realized that he had brought into the pulpit the work of the actor and emotional manipulator. As a result of that experience, he determined that he would never again calculate beforehand how he would use his voice when preaching a sermon. His heart abominated such preaching throughout the decades of his ministry. He had pre-scripted a precise use of his voice for dramatic effect, not allowing the manner of preaching to flow naturally from the matter and urgency of the content, which is always to be guided by the Holy Spirit in the act of preaching.

His first two years of college-level study concentrated on liberal arts courses and language study. He spent the last two years at Columbia Bible College concentrating on biblical, theological, and church history courses. At the time, the interpretive hermeneutic at Columbia was non-dispensational. One of his courses had the title, "The Onward Flow of God's Redemptive Plan and Purpose." Albert was indebted to a professor who taught him the essential unity of Scripture. The plot line unfolds from creation, through the fall, leading to the history of redemption, to ultimate consummation in the new heavens and the new earth. This perspective of the unity of Scripture was new to many of the students who had come from churches where they were taught, for example, that the Ten Commandments were solely for the nation of Israel. A mini-revival occurred in that Old Testament class when Dr. Sells began to expound the Ten Commandments!

The instructors at Columbia Bible College were older, spiritually mature, genuinely godly men who set a standard for him of the kind of life a true servant of God must live. Albert graduated in May of 1956, *magna cum laude*, and he was asked to join the staff of Columbia Bible College for the academic year 1956–1957.

Marriage and Itinerant Ministry

Albert met Marilyn Hart in the spring of 1952 during a visit he made to Concord, New Hampshire, shortly after his conversion. He had been asked to preach to a group of young people in the First Baptist Church of Concord. "She was an attractive brunette and he said, 'When I saw her I freaked out!'"[2] Prior to meeting each other, they had both been accepted as students for the 1952 fall session at Bob Jones University. After spending one year together there, they courted by mail and telephone calls over the next three years while Marilyn completed her education at the Providence Barrington Bible College in Rhode Island. They were married on June 30, 1956, in Concord, New Hampshire. During the summer of 1956 they took up residence in Columbia, South Carolina, where he took up his duties at the Columbia Bible College in the fall in the position of the assistant to the dean of men.

After the academic year of 1957, unusual providences moved him into an itinerant evangelistic Bible teaching ministry for the next five years. Marilyn had a miscarriage several months after they were married, and they were not able to conceive children for the next three and a half years. Marilyn generally travelled with him in these itinerant ministries which were concentrated primarily in the Midwest and on the East Coast. Although childlessness was a source of deep grief to both of them, having her accompany him in his ministry gave her a better understanding of his ministry and his commitment to the theological changes taking place in his life. It also enabled her to see the sad state of many of the churches in which he ministered. As Brian Borgman wrote,

> In this itinerant ministry he saw first-hand many of the serious deficiencies caused by the gospel of easy-believism, the carnal Christian theory and the separation of repentance from faith. He himself never preached that kind of gospel....
>
> On one particular occasion, a friend lined up a speaking engagement at Wheaton Graduate School chapel. Albert stood and challenged these young "cream of the crop" academicians. With no intimidation from his prestigious surroundings, with passion and directness, he

---

2. Brian Borgman, *My Heart For Thy Cause* (Ross-Shire, U.K.: Christian Focus Publications, 2002), 16.

appealed to them to be people of courage, like John the Baptist. The devil didn't care about their Wheaton degree, or the education, but what he would tremble at would be their godliness and zeal for Christ. After the chapel service, an elderly man with a shock of white hair came up, took his hand and simply said, "Thank you young man. As you preached, the text came to mind, 'He was a burning and shining light.' When you preached there was light and heat." That man was Merrill Tenney, and the heat and light has continued to burn from that day to the present.[3]

During this course of his itinerant ministry, Albert and Marilyn were on their way by train to Alberta, Canada, where he was scheduled to preach at a conference at the Prairie Bible Institute. They had the opportunity to meet Dr. Tozer in his study during the long layover in Chicago, when Tozer was still ministering in the Alliance Church in Chicago. After counseling with the young couple for close to an hour, Albert and Marilyn knelt at a narrow couch in Dr. Tozer's study while Tozer prayed. In that meeting he had mentioned to Dr. Tozer the name of the Bible college from which he had graduated and served. Since Tozer knew that the college was known for its "deeper life" teaching, he prayed this way: "Lord, save my young brother from pride, save him from women, and save him from the hierarchy of the 'deeper life,' Grubb, Fleece, Tozer, and the whole bunch of us; save him and keep him fresh."

While Albert was engaged in this itinerant ministry, he began to wrestle with some crucial theological issues. Having come to clear biblical convictions about the new birth and the relationship of repentance and saving faith to union with Christ as Lord, he began to pray that God would help him see how all of these things fit together. His regular Bible reading led him to passages in John 6, John 17, Romans 9, and Ephesians 1, which made these truths clearer to him. Since he had no responsibilities as a pastor or a father, he looked on this situation as God's gracious way of calling him to serious theological reflection. Often, several weeks passed between preaching engagements, and that time was used for serious study.

He was thrilled to read the reprint of Baxter's *Call to the Unconverted*, and Joseph Alleine's *An Alarm to the Unconverted*. Those two books confirmed his convictions regarding the nature and fruits of true conversion,

---

3. Brian Borgman, *My Heart For Thy Cause* (Ross-Shire, U.K.: Christian Focus Publications, 2002), 17.

truths that he was regularly preaching, and for which he would often receive opposition, even from pastors in the churches where he was ministering. Thomas Boston's *Human Nature in its Fourfold State* came into his hands. While reading that book convictions were settled in his mind, such as the true state of the sinner by nature, the transformation that comes by grace alone, and the glorious realities that await the people of God in the consummation.

He visited a used bookstore in Lancaster, Pennsylvania, where he and Marilyn were living at the time. There he purchased William Shedd's *A History of Christian Doctrine*. As he carefully read those two volumes, he was conscious that he was wrestling with basic issues of revelation. The margins of those books by Shedd were scribbled with Pastor Martin's notes as he was "debating" with Dr. Shedd, particularly regarding the doctrines of grace. At one point, after he had matured in his understanding of these truths, he was tempted to erase these notes in the margins of those books. However, he decided to leave them as a reminder for the future of how gracious God is to lead us in our understanding if we maintain a teachable spirit.

At this time he remembered that one of his former teachers at Columbia Bible College, a church history professor who held to Calvinistic soteriology, taught on the theology of the Reformation and asserted that Luther and the other Reformers believed that repentance and faith were not the cause of our regeneration, but rather the results of that sovereign work of God. This was the first time he had ever heard anyone assert such a notion in public teaching. He did not immediately embrace these things as God's truth because there were certain passages in the Word of God that seemed to him at the time to teach otherwise. However, he had read enough Christian biography to know that men whom he had been taught to esteem as godly and useful believed these things, and they were not fools.

During this time, a resurgence of interest in the historic confessions of the Protestant Reformation began to arise on both sides of the Atlantic. Gradually, the writings of men whose names had all but been forgotten were once more being read and studied. The books which had flowed from the pens of the Reformers, the Puritans, and the men of the Great Awakening were rediscovered and found to be not the dry and tedious stuff they were long presumed to be, but storehouses of nourishing spiritual food delightful to the taste of truth-hungry men and women, especially pastors. In Great Britain, God raised up The Banner of Truth Trust, which in 1955 began to reprint the Puritan classics and other books setting forth the doctrines of grace. Other publishers also began putting Calvinistic writings on the market and did brisk business in books, which a generation earlier, almost no one would buy. Pastor Martin began to devour these books as the Banner published them.

He also had to settle in his mind the biblical teaching concerning the efficacious nature of the atonement. Four or five texts were exerting pressure on his mind, drawing him to embrace the Reformed position. The Banner published one of the major treatises of volume 10 of John Owen's works, *The Death of Death in the Death of Christ*. This masterful book was published as a separate book with an incisive foreword by Dr. James I. Packer. After reading Packer's essay and carefully absorbing Owen's treatise on the nature and extent of the atonement, he confessed that he embraced those truths which are known as the doctrines of grace. God used this introduction to the writings of John Owen to begin a lifelong appreciation for that prince of English theologians.

It was not long after this that he read John Murray's masterful treatise, *Redemption Accomplished and Applied*. A book on pastoral theology that exerted a profound influence in his life on pastoral theology was Charles Bridges' *The Christian Ministry*. This volume was drawing him into a deeper understanding of the nature and calling of the Christian ministry. At the same time, because Bridges quotes freely from the old masters, Albert was being introduced to a whole new world of authors who would subsequently leave an indelible mark on his life, and eventually upon his teaching. Around the same time that Bridges came into his possession, he obtained a copy of Spurgeon's *Lectures to My Students*. Needless to say, these lectures had a profound and life-long impact on his life and ministry.

Call to the Local Church

Albert left the itinerant ministry and accepted a pastoral call in the summer of 1962. There were several issues which precipitated this decision. First, in the summer of 1960 they were delighted to discover that Marilyn was pregnant! Albert knew that he could not fulfill his parental role while spending the majority of time away from home preaching across the country. He began to pray that God would bring him into a settled pastoral ministry. He only shared this with Marilyn, and they made it a matter of earnest prayer.

The second issue which contributed to his desire to seek a settled ministry had to do with the state of most of the evangelical churches in which he had been ministering. He was beginning to come to a biblical understanding of what a healthy local church should be and could be if God's design for the church were wisely and prayerfully implemented. When he attempted to share that vision with the pastors of the churches in which he was ministering, he was often met with a negative and defeatist attitude. He prayed that, if indeed he were an "idealistic dreamer" who thought the church could be something that it never will be this side of heaven, that God would put him in a situation where he would be forced to confront such a reality. Hence, he began to pray that God would open a door of opportunity either to prove Him, or expose the folly of his "radical biblical idealism" (as some labeled it). He was convinced that if God were opening a door of pastoral ministry for him it would be in a setting where he had established a relationship of trust and mutual respect.

By this time, Albert had come to the conviction that the typical evangelical way in which men "candidate" for the ministry was at best totally inadequate, and at worst unbiblical. How can the preaching of one or two sermons and the exposure of a man to a flock and the flock to the man over two weekends enable all involved to determine whether a man meets the biblical requirements for the office, and is suited to a particular congregation?

During his five years of itinerant ministry, there were times when he had no preaching commitments, and so he would study more during those times. He would also work more to pay the bills. Once he was asked by a pastor friend whether he was willing to drive to Chester, New Jersey, where this pastor was engaged in a church-planting endeavor. The group he was working with had purchased the property of a Roman Catholic retreat center which they were converting for use in their church-planting work. He was offered a generous wage for the common labor of scraping dried dung off of a concrete floor in an old barn on the property. He welcomed this opportunity to accumulate some money for his next month's rent. While he was there, the pastor apprised him that his home church in North Caldwell, New Jersey, was without a pastor. He asked Albert whether he would be willing to minister to them and he accepted the invitation. After that Lord's Day of ministry in North Caldwell, the church asked him to stay on for two weeks of evangelistic and Bible-teaching ministry, as well as six more weeks of preaching on the Lord's Day. During that six-week commitment the existing leadership began to put out overtures to him as to whether he would consider a call to become the pastor of the church.

In order to be issued a call by that church he had to obtain the approval of the denominational executive committee. He had two meetings with them to be examined regarding his doctrinal beliefs, at which time he apprised them that there were two points of doctrine upon which he differed with the Alliance. The first was the official teaching of the Alliance that physical healing is a blessing purchased in the atonement of Christ to be appropriated and enjoyed by faith and prayer in this life. The other difference was with their "second work of grace," or "subsequence" doctrine which they apply to sanctification and empowerment for service. He was unsure that the committee would approve him, but they did, and he was given official credentials as an acceptable candidate within that denomination.

Several weeks later, in the late summer of 1962, he received a unanimous call from the congregation to be their pastor. In September of that year, he, Marilyn, and their eighteen-month-old son Joel, moved from Lancaster, Pennsylvania, to take up residence in the parsonage next door to the church in North Caldwell.

During the eight weeks of ecclesiastical courtship with that church, he made it clear to them that if he were to be their pastor he would be a man who was determined to believe and obey anything and everything which Scripture made clear regarding the life, ministry, and function of a biblically ordered church. His years in the itinerant ministry were in a real sense his personal graduate school. He came to the church in North Caldwell with convictions concerning the church and pastoral ministry, some of which he began to implement immediately.

It was during those early days that a distinct pattern emerged in his own thinking regarding how to lead a congregation wisely, graciously, and gently, into new paths of biblical obedience. First, assuming that the church is blessed with a plurality of elders functioning as true shepherds, those who are leading the people of God must be certain in their own minds that there is sufficient biblical warrant for whatever changes are to be proposed or implemented. Second, there must be given clear, convincing, and patient biblical instruction, telling them why this or that change should be made. It was during those early days that the congregation affirmed their willingness to "go wherever the hand of Scripture will take us."

This meant that Albert was being forced to consider what God's Word teaches on vital church issues. "What comprises God-honoring biblical worship?" "How should a prayer meeting be conducted?" "What does the Bible teach concerning the roles and functions of elders and deacons?" "What are the biblical requirements for church membership, and the maintenance of good standing within the church?"

It was in the crucible of reforming the life and ministry of that congregation that many of his convictions on the issues that lie at the heart of his views of pastoral theology were being formed, patiently taught, and gradually implemented. At the same time, He was immersing himself in those books and confessions of faith which sought to address ecclesiology in a biblical and systematic way. The works of Douglas Bannerman[4] and James Bannerman[5] on the church of Christ had been recently reprinted and were very helpful in confirming many previously unsure perspectives. At the same time, it was his careful consideration of these classic Presbyterian works that was steadily drawing him to what he saw to be a more biblical view of the nature, membership, and government of the New Covenant community. This influenced Pastor Martin to settle his mind concerning the proper subjects of baptism, and the autonomy of local church government by a plurality and parity of biblically qualified elders. Consecutive biblical exposition was the stuff of the weekly preaching ministry at the church. The Spirit of God blessed this practice to bring the majority of the members to the place where their love for and commitment to Scripture was deepened. More and more of the life and ministry of the congregation was taking on the practical contours of this enriched understanding of Scripture.

Departure from the Alliance

After four and a half years of ministering to the saints in that assembly it became clear to Pastor Martin that if he were to engage in ongoing biblical reformation he could no longer ethically remain within the denomination. There were now several other areas in which he had come to convictions that differed from the official doctrinal position of the denomination. He conveyed these facts to the denominational leaders in that area, but they did not feel that the issues were significant enough to warrant him leaving the denomination. Some of these leaders even suggested that he consider becoming the pastor of another prestigious Christian and Missionary Alliance Church.

About this same time, a church in Pennsylvania where Pastor Martin had ministered in his itinerant ministry put out overtures to him to become

---

4. D. Douglas Bannerman, *The Scripture Doctrine of The Church* (Grand Rapids: Baker Book House, 1976).

5. James Bannerman, *The Church of Christ,* 2 volumes (Edinburgh: T. & T. Clark, 1960). A Banner of Truth edition was published in 2015.

their pastor. Having come to the conviction that he could no longer stay in the Christian and Missionary Alliance, and that he did not want to be part of a church split, he felt that the only alternative was to relinquish his pastoral labors in North Caldwell and pursue the ministry in Pennsylvania.

There were several reasons that made this alternative very attractive. During those early years in North Caldwell, he had begun to have a ministry to men who were attending Westminster Theological Seminary. Several of the faculty members whom he had come to know were praying that God would bring him closer to the seminary in order to have an increased ministry to the students. This particular church also had a radio ministry to which he could contribute. However, when he made the decision that he must resign his pastoral role in North Caldwell, and submitted his resignation to the church board, they refused to accept it! Several of the elders and deacons took the lead in discerning whether or not he would be willing to consider remaining with the congregation should they desire to maintain their existing pastoral relationship. These men gathered the congregation and sought their suffrage concerning his resignation.

By a count of sixty positive and two negative votes, the congregation expressed its desire to retain him as their pastor. They fully understood that this decision, were he to respond positively to it, would most likely result in their giving up the church building in which they met, along with the parsonage in which he lived. However, they had tasted the joy of coming to a new understanding of God's Word, and could not be satisfied with any framework of personal church life other than, "We are ready to go wherever the hand of Scripture will take us."

They made every effort to make their severance with the denomination as honorable and gracious as possible. In turn, the denomination allowed the Martin family to live in the parsonage until they could find a suitable home. The formal break with the denomination came in January 1967. The congregation decided that they wanted to dissolve the membership and have each office-bearer relinquish his office so that the church could re-establish its membership and officers by a biblical process.

The people expressed their desire that Pastor Martin give them biblical teaching on all of the vital church issues found in Scripture. After their severance with the denomination in 1967, he taught for about nine months on these issues. The congregation agreed that the time had come to constitute as a church. Securing the assistance of pastors from other churches who were sympathetic to their church-planting endeavor, they constituted with forty-four members in a special meeting held in September of 1967, calling themselves The Trinity Church of West Essex. They adopted the *Second London Baptist Confession of Faith of 1689* as the official doctrinal standard of the church. They also adopted a modest constitution which spelled out how they were proposing to conduct their congregational life according to the precepts and principles of Scripture and the Confession of Faith. Pastor Martin then preached a brief series of sermons on the eldership and the diaconate in preparation for guiding the congregation in the process of recognition. When the time came, Pastor Albert Martin and Pastor Don Dickson were selected as elders, along with three men for the diaconate, and then ordained to their respective offices.

The Trinity Church of West Essex was now one of the first Reformed Baptist churches. Hundreds of churches committed to Reformed and Baptistic doctrine have been planted, which are at least in part the fruit of the ministry of Pastor Albert Martin and his work in those early years. Ronald Jones wrote about this:

> In the late 1960s and early 1970s, those of us who were Baptists and whose eyes were being opened to Reformed truth, felt much as Elijah likely did as recorded in 1 Kings 19. We were isolated and somewhat alone. But just as God encouraged Elijah in his day, so he also encouraged us. In our time of need he raised up a handful of men whose powerful writings and expository preaching were critical to the growth of the modern Reformed Baptist movement. Arguably the most influential of those men was our brother Al Martin. My own pilgrimage from Anabaptism to Dispensationalism and finally to a decidedly Reformed Baptist position was greatly facilitated by his tape ministry. Our family was first blessed by his public ministry when we heard him preach a three-sermon series on sanctification at a family conference in 1970. Now, more than forty-three years later, I can still recall those sermon titles, though I made no intentional effort to do so.[6]

A Reformed Baptist Church

Pastors Martin and Dickson decided that in order to be faithful to their calling and meet the needs of the flock, they would need to meet every Saturday morning. The elders and the congregation were learning how the church

---

6. *A Tribute to Pastor A.N. Martin: Eightieth Birthday Celebration*, Chet Jelinski, ed. (Self-published: Whiting, NJ, 08759), 150.

should function, with the elders and the deacons performing their respective tasks. In those early days, they had a combined meeting of the elders and the deacons once a month in order to identify more clearly each other's tasks and make a commitment to fulfill them in a manner consistent with their responsibilities.

Neither he, the other leaders, or the congregation, entertained romantic thoughts that there is anything approaching a perfect church this side of the consummation. However, they did believe that, by the grace of God and the power of the Holy Spirit, through a meticulous concern to be obedient to Scripture, they could so order their life together that God would be pleased with them, that Christ would be exalted and honored, and that the cause of the gospel would go forward through the church, impacting their own Jerusalem, and even the ends of the earth.

The Cracker Box & Montville Buildings

The summer of 1970 was an exciting time for Trinity Baptist Church. The church had been praying in their special Saturday morning prayer meetings that God would provide them with a permanent meeting place. God answered that prayer by bringing to their attention that the local Elks club building in Essex Fells was for sale. The building accommodated approximately one-hundred-eighty people. With the passing of time, as God began to fill that building to overflowing, someone named it "The Cracker Box" and that nickname stuck.

As a result of the steady growth of the church, the congregation outgrew The Cracker Box. They began renting the auditorium of a local Junior High School in Caldwell, New Jersey. During this time, they continued to use the church building in Essex Fells for various church meetings and ministries such as the Trinity Book Service, the Trinity Pulpit, and the Trinity Ministerial Academy. The church also purchased a six and a half-acre plot in Montville, New Jersey, upon which they eventually built their present facilities.

An important part of this building program was an eight-part sermon series which Pastor Martin delivered to the congregation entitled "A Godly Building Program." He also presented to the congregation a study entitled "A Theology of Church Architecture."[7] Those were days when the church saw

---

7. Pastors have testified that these studies were very helpful in thinking through issues that often go without much thought. You can find them on sermonaudio.com under Albert Martin. See footnote 22 below for other websites.

unusual answers to prayer as God enabled them to undertake these large financial projects. Within just a couple of years of completing the construction, the church was completely debt-free. Pastor Martin always sought to establish every church endeavor on the bedrock of Scripture and carry the congregation's conscience with biblical principles.

International Ministries

The contacts with students and some of the faculty of Westminster Theological Seminary eventually led Pastor Martin into a fruitful sphere of ministry in the United Kingdom. This was the result of Pastor Martin's friendship with Professor John Murray at the seminary, who was also a trustee of The Banner of Truth Trust along with Iain Murray, one of the main founders of the Trust.[8] It fell to Professor Murray and Iain Murray, with several others, to arrange the schedule, subjects, and preachers for the annual Banner of Truth Ministers' Conference held in Leicester, England. This conference began in 1962 out of the burden of the organizers for a renewal of preaching that was marked by solid exposition and doctrinal precision joined with pastoral and evangelistic passion and urgency.

Iain Murray writes of Pastor Martin's relationship to the Leicester Conference and Professor Murray's regard for him:

> One particular fear for the Leicester Conference had been that Baptist and paedo-baptist brethren would not remain harmoniously together. The invitation to the Conference of a younger friend of John Murray's, Pastor A. N. Martin of Essex Fells, New Jersey, to the 1967 Conference was to prove a major influence in preventing any such developments. The two men took different positions on baptism but possessed the highest regard for one another. In a letter to the present writer,[9] John Murray replied in the following terms to an invitation that he should take three evening services at the 1967 conference:
>
> "If Al Martin is to be there I really think he should be asked to take the three evening services you propose for me. He is one of the ablest and moving preachers I have ever heard. In recent years I have not heard his equal. My memory of preachers goes back sixty years. So,

---

8. Pastor Martin was on the editorial staff of The Banner of Truth Magazine for many years.

9. Iain Murray is John Murray's biographer. See footnote below.

when I say he is one of the ablest, this is an assessment that includes very memorable preachers of the past and present."[10]

This counsel was followed, and with such evident helpfulness in its results that thereafter Al Martin became the most frequent visiting speaker from the United States.[11]

The flip-side is Pastor Martin's life-long indebtedness to Professor Murray. Iain Murray wrote of this as well:

If John Murray erred in anything it was in underestimating the aid which his written work brought to others. He was slow to believe that anything he had written justified publication. It is questionable whether he offered anything to publishers, and he is known to have refused to allow the publication of material which publishers wished to have. His attitude was characteristically revealed in 1970 when Al Martin wrote to him to express gratitude for the great help which his books had proved in his own life and ministry. To this Professor Murray responded on November 26, 1970.

"I received your letter of the 19th yesterday. It is not possible for me to give adequate expression to my appreciation. Furthermore, I have been filled with surprise. For I could not have thought that my writings could have been to you what you have so kindly stated. And that you should have taken the time to write at such length adds to my sense of indebtedness to you. So, my friend, thank you."[12]

In the initial ministry at Leicester, Pastor Martin was asked to bring three addresses on pastoral issues from 1 Timothy 4:16. Professor Murray had heard Pastor Martin preach messages on this text at a retreat for Westminster Seminary students. He requested that Pastor Martin preach those messages at the conference. The conference was Pastor Martin's first exposure to a British gathering. It formed the basis of some lifelong friendships, and in the ensuing years provided many subsequent opportunities

---

10. Iain Murray has this footnote after this paragraph: "Such was Al Martin's closeness to John Murray that at one of the Leicester Ministers' Conferences he allowed himself the liberty of mimicking the Professor's best-known gesture—the gaze turned downwards to the fingernails of a half-clenched hand—his object being to illustrate in an address in preaching how easily we can fall into the mannerisms of those we esteem. John Murray was chairing that session and sitting with his usual grave countenance, which slowly gave way to a smile!"

11. *Collected Writings of John Murray, Volume three, Life of John Murray, Sermons & Reviews* (Edinburgh: The Banner of Truth Trust, 1982), 134.

12. *Collected Writings of John Murray, Volume three, Life of John Murray, Sermons & Reviews* (Edinburgh: The Banner of Truth Trust, 1982), 136, 137.

to minister the Word of God in churches and at conferences throughout England, Scotland, Wales, and Northern Ireland. Pastor Ted Donnelly of Northern Ireland wrote,

> We first met forty-four years ago, at the Banner of Truth ministers' conference in Leicester, England. "We met" is perhaps overstating at first—what happened is that I was thrilled and truly blessed by his preaching. It was interesting to learn, years later, that the same conference was where another rich friendship began, of which you can read in the following pages.[13] Every several years we would speak to each other at these gatherings, coming closer together as time passed. It was, however, in 1988 that the elders of TBC invited me to come over to New Jersey to teach a course to the pastoral students there. Ten days spent in his home were the real beginning of more than a quarter of a century of friendship—time together talking, sharing, praying, travelling, preaching, helping and being helped, walking, listening to music, shedding tears, laughing—close affection between two brothers in Christ, ever deepening and enriching.[14]

One of the men who attended the Leicester Conference was Achille Blaize, and he shared his thoughts about it.

> I first met Pastor Albert N. Martin at the Banner of Truth Ministers' Conference in Leicester, UK, in the spring of 1970. Whilst sitting and waiting for one of the meetings to begin, someone came in and sat to my right, leaned over and said, "What is your name?" I said, "Achille Blaize." I then asked him, "What's your name?" He simply answered, "Al." I said to myself, "This man must be the biggest phoney or 'an Israelite indeed in whom there is no guile.'" When he rose to speak, I was struck by the title of his sermon: "The History of God's Dealings in the Past is our Encouragement for the Present and Our Incentive for the Future." His preaching was so Spirit-filled, authoritative, bold and convincing that I was greatly moved. Afterwards, I remained in my seat reflecting on the sermon. To my surprise, after having returned to the hall and seeing me seated there all alone, he came up to me and asked, "Do you want to pray?" I responded positively; so we went to his room where it was quiet and there wrestled with Almighty God in prayer. There on our knees we established a friendship that by the grace of

---

13. Achille Blaize and Pastor Martin.
14. *A Tribute to Pastor A.N. Martin: Eightieth Birthday Celebration*, Chet Jelinski, ed. (Self-published: Whiting, NJ, 08759), 4, 5.

God has grown deeper and richer to this day. In 1973, Trinity Baptist Church, then meeting in Essex Fells, New Jersey, invited me to come as associate pastor with Pastor Martin.... Pastor Martin and I met every Friday between 2–5 p.m. to read, pray, discuss and study. It was during these times that he helped me to be more consistent in the craft of sermon construction: exposition, division, and application. Another most instructive and immensely valuable area of church life was our weekly elders' meetings. These were held on Saturday evenings. It was among Trinity's eldership that I saw and learned how elders are to function in the church of Christ: graciously, honestly, seeking always to do that which is pleasing to God.[15]

The relationships that had been forged between Pastor Martin, pastors in the United Kingdom, and The Banner of Truth's ministries, placed him at the forefront of the Reformed faith and Baptists in the United States. Sam Waldron, a pastor and Baptist historian, wrote,

It is likely that a small minority of Baptists, especially in the southern United States retained Calvinistic convictions in a more-or-less direct line from the 19th Century. The name of Charles Haddon Spurgeon, his writings, and continuing influence did much to project Particular Baptist influence into the 20th Century. Even among Baptist circles increasingly hostile to Calvinism, Spurgeon's name was honored and the Particular Baptist theology he preached, sometimes almost unconsciously, imbibed. Also, deserving mention as preserving Particular Baptist theology during the dark years of the early 20th Century is A. W. Pink and his writings.

Other important influences were from circles not specifically Baptist. Westminster Seminary, the re-incarnation of old Princeton, took up the biblical and Reformed heritage of its fallen predecessor. Under the leadership of J. G. Machen and its deservedly famous early faculty (Murray, Van Til, Young, Stonehouse, Kuiper, and others) many Baptist students who attended that Seminary came into contact with their Reformed heritage. The Banner of Truth Trust, a publishing house dedicated to making available experimental, Puritan, and Reformed literature, has produced a flood of Puritan and Reformed books over the last 30 years. Since this work was determined to maintain sympathies with all those who identified with the heritage of Reformed

---

15. *A Tribute to Pastor A.N. Martin: Eightieth Birthday Celebration*, Chet Jelinski, ed. (Self-published: Whiting, NJ, 08759), 11, 12.

Christianity, it was the means of bringing many Baptists to Reformed convictions over the years.

As a result of such influences several Reformed Baptist churches and pastors surfaced in the northeastern U. S. in the 1960s. These gave leadership to the emerging Reformed Baptist movement in America. Through the books written by their pastors and their cassette tape ministries, they have had (and continue to have) a national and even world-wide influence.[16]

Family Conferences

A major channel of ministry which Pastor Martin and other Reformed Baptist pastors had for several decades were the summer family conferences held by Reformed Baptist churches around the country. God used these conferences to strengthen families and edify the people of God in the churches with heart-searching preaching.

Pastor Edward Donnelly describes an amazing scene which occurred at the Southeastern Reformed Baptist Family Conference in the summer of 1990 at William Jennings Bryan College:

> The main auditorium was filled with six or seven hundred people and he was preaching on Jesus in Gethsemane. Towards the close of his sermon, all the lights went out and Pastor Martin finished preaching in the dark. As he led in prayer at the end, the lights came on again. It was discovered that the building was equipped with a motion sensor system for switching off the lighting when there was no-one in the auditorium. The large audience had been so gripped by the preaching that there was, literally, not a single movement among them. The engineers had not calculated that it would be possible for people to sit so motionless and the instruments were calibrated accordingly. When Pastor Martin had announced the closing prayer, we must have leaned forward in our seats and triggered the lighting. It was a startling example of the power of the Word![17]

---

16. Samuel E. Waldron, *Baptist Roots in America* (Simpson Publishing Company, 1991), 35, 36.

17. Brian Borgman, *My Heart For Thy Cause* (Ross-Shire, U.K.: Christian Focus Publications, 2002), 10.

Tape Ministry

In the mid-sixties, several people in the congregation urged Pastor Martin to begin recording his sermons so that those who had to miss the church services for sickness or travel could consistently follow the preaching ministry. This was the humble beginning of what became the Trinity Pulpit tape ministry. This ministry grew exponentially over the next few years. Borgman wrote in 2002,

> Since 1971, Trinity Pulpit has sent out more than 750,000 tapes throughout many parts of the world. They have never put copyrights on the tapes, and so the actual number of taped sermons is incalculable.[18]

Coupled with this explosion of the tape ministry, Pastor Martin began to receive repeated invitations to preach at various ministers' conferences in the United States and around the world. This led to increased correspondence and phone calls from men whom Pastor Martin met at these conferences, men who looked to him for advice concerning their own ministries. During the mid-1970s, and through the late-1980s, it was not uncommon for Pastor Martin to dictate and send out fifteen to twenty-five letters each week, many of them to pastors seeking counsel regarding distinctively pastoral issues. One of the beneficiaries, Richard Pike, wrote about it.

> As a pastor to a pastor, he has been on many occasions a source of wisdom and strength to me. In response to one of my "cry for help" letters, he wrote, "I am pleased that you felt at liberty to unburden yourself on paper, and I do not take lightly the stewardship of your expressions of present distress and spiritual trauma." Elsewhere he said, "My heart shares with you the grief which you feel in the face of those who are opposing the truths of the Word of God which you hold so dear." Elsewhere he wrote, "Needless to say, your continuing trials of faith are not regarded lightly by us, and we do seek to enter into those trials, especially when bearing you before the Throne of Grace. May the Lord give the confidence of His own love and concern for you in the midst of this period of darkness."[19]

Pastor Martin was not only becoming recognized as a preacher, but a pastor and church-builder. God was using him to bring reformation in these

---

18. Brian Borgman, *My Heart For Thy Cause* (Ross-Shire, U.K.: Christian Focus Publications, 2002), 22.

19. *A Tribute to Pastor A.N. Martin: Eightieth Birthday Celebration*, Chet Jelinski, ed. (Self-published: Whiting, NJ, 08759), 142, 143.

areas, not only to the church in Essex Fells, but to the church at large. The church in New Jersey was becoming well instructed in its basic understanding of how a church should function under the rule of Christ, and others were looking to Pastor Martin for help in becoming established in biblical churchmanship.

Dr. Joel Beeke is representative of the kind of help that Pastor Martin afforded many men in the ministry over the years.

> Over the last 45 years, I have listened with considerable profit and conviction to many of your sermons. Particularly when I was a young minister, I benefited from listening to the entire series of addresses that you gave to young pastors.[20] They were a huge help in forming my own ministerial habits and way of thinking. Then, I listened to most of them a second time when I became a theological teacher about 27 years ago, and they seemed even better to me![21]

You can still hear Pastor Martin preach the Word of God in the thousands of recordings available on the Internet. [22]

Honorary Doctorate

In June of 1976, Geneva College, the official denominational college of the Reformed Presbyterian Church of North America (RPCNA), in Beaver Falls, Pennsylvania, conferred on Pastor Martin the honorary degree of Doctor of Divinity (D.D.). The degree was conferred in recognition of the significant contribution being made by Pastor Martin to the present and ongoing return to Reformation theology and practice in the 1970s, especially the ever-widening circle of influence being exerted by Pastor Martin's recorded sermons.

When the initial contact was made by Geneva College inquiring whether or not Pastor Martin would accept this degree, he immediately sought the counsel of his fellow-elders and his inner circle of trusted confidants. Their counsel was overwhelmingly positive. They believed that accepting this degree would afford a wonderful opportunity for a representative of Reformed Baptist theology and practice to demonstrate genuine catholicity

---

20. He is referring here to these pastoral theology lectures.

21. *A Tribute to Pastor A.N. Martin: Eightieth Birthday Celebration*, Chet Jelinski, ed. (Self-published: Whiting, NJ, 08759), 82.

22. Sources for listening to his sermons are: sermonaudio.com; godswordtoournation .org; heraldofgrace.org; almartin.org; trinitypastorsconference.org.

with those who held to the classic biblical and Reformed confessional understanding of the Word of God.

Before he left for the commencement exercises, he spoke to the members and friends of Trinity Baptist Church, explaining exactly why he was accepting this degree. He stated that he was accepting this degree in his identity and capacity as Pastor Martin, and that he was returning after the conferral of the degree with this same identity and plan to retain the title "Pastor."

Ministry to Students

Calvinistic convictions had been appearing in religious circles which for generations had been isolated, even immunized, from this understanding of the Word of God. Among young people in particular, there was a growing interest in Calvinism and the Reformed faith. Large numbers of them, converted from Roman Catholicism, religious liberalism, and even agnosticism, were interested, not only in reading and talking about the doctrines of grace, but in putting them into practice in daily life and witness, as well as church life.

The church building in Essex Fells was just around the corner from Northeastern Bible College, and students from the school began to attend the church. Trinity sought to be a blessing to the school in different ways, and one way they were able to do this was to donate theological books and biographies to the college library. Many of the students were enriched by the ministry of Pastor Martin and Trinity Baptist Church. Additionally, there were some Westminster and Reformed Episcopal Seminary students who began to undertake the two-hour drive from Philadelphia each Lord's Day morning to spend the day in worship and fellowship with the people of God, who would invite them to their homes for the midday meal.

As he sought to be sensitive to this special providence in the course of the weekly preaching ministry, Pastor Martin frequently drew from the biblical texts he was expounding to express particular applications for pastors and future pastors. Some of these students expressed an interest in having further input and instruction regarding matters relating to the work of the ministry. Meanwhile, among Baptists of Calvinistic persuasion in other places, God had begun to lay His hand on young men and put into their hearts a desire to receive more specific preparation for the gospel ministry. As these men looked for schools where they might receive solid, biblical, ministerial training, they found that their only option was to attend seminaries which, although Reformed in theological perspective, did not share their deep appreciation for the experimental theology in large measure derived from our great Puritan heritage, and much less for our Baptist distinctives.

Many more young men were coming to deep convictions concerning Reformed theology, but were not comfortable with the idea of receiving their training in a framework other than one that held to the *1689 London Baptist Confession of Faith*. Furthermore, as men considered the seminaries that might attract them because of their clear and unashamed commitment to historic Reformed theology, they were concerned that solid Reformed and Baptist churches were not within reasonable distance of such seminaries. These men were convinced that they should not be detached from the visible local church during the most critical period of their development as they prepared to be leaders in the church of Christ. Investigations were made into the possibility of placing an academically qualified and pastorally experienced man of Baptist persuasion on the faculty of one of the non-Baptist Reformed seminaries. For various reasons, this possibility was never realized in those days. It also became increasingly evident that these faculties would continue to be divided and inconsistent among themselves in regard to Puritan theology and experimental Calvinism.

Trinity Baptist was petitioning God to raise up a school where men who gave some appreciable evidence of having the necessary graces and gifts could be further prepared for the work of the ministry (1 Tim. 3:1–7). Trinity was not alone in this concern; it was shared by the three or four Reformed Baptist churches in existence that had established a measure of pastoral and ecclesiastical communion with one another. Grace Baptist Church in Carlisle, Pennsylvania, under the leadership of Pastor Walter Chantry, was foremost among the churches in giving encouragement regarding the establishment of a ministerial academy. Out of that growing consensus came wrestling with the Word of God and interaction with the churches. In the spring of 1970, Pastor Martin addressed a meeting of Reformed Baptist pastors on *A Theology of Ministerial Training*. This material was subsequently presented again to several Reformed Baptist churches in the Northeast. As a result of that wrestling and interaction, intensified pressure was brought to bear on Trinity Baptist Church to recognize what other brethren felt was a stewardship God was giving Trinity to do something substantial in training men for the ministry.

From 1971 to 1975, the Trinity elders sought to engage a full-time resident scholar to assist them in providing the kind of ministerial training they envisioned. In each instance, it was clear to all concerned that the time was not yet ripe to move ahead in this endeavor. Meanwhile, pressure continued to come from some theological students themselves, including those from the Westminster and Reformed Episcopal seminaries who were attending Trinity, to provide instruction in certain aspects of practical theology, which would supplement what they were receiving in their seminary instruction. They wanted to learn more about experimental Calvinism and its relation to the work of the ministry. The Trinity elders responded by asking Pastor Martin to hold a monthly Sunday afternoon class geared to these men from the seminaries and from the Bible college who were regularly attending the assembly. It was in those monthly classes that Pastor Martin first brought a series of messages entitled *What is a Biblical Call to the Christian Ministry?* Those seminal materials now form the substance of the first unit of *Pastoral Theology Lectures* on the call to the pastoral office. Those monthly classes were held from 1973 through 1975 and the response to this meager effort was so encouraging that it served only to intensify the desire of the church to do something far more extensive, thus paving the way for the establishment of the Trinity Ministerial Academy.

Trinity Ministerial Academy (TMA)

Early in 1976, it was felt that the time had come for the church to initiate a program of specific theological training for young men in the church in Essex Fells. Pastor Robert Fisher, a graduate of Westminster Theological Seminary and one of Pastor Martin's fellow-elders, taught weekly courses in systematic and biblical theology on Saturday mornings. These classes began at the beginning of February 1976 and continued until the end of May. They were resumed again in October and continued until the opening months of 1977. The blessing of God on this endeavor encouraged the church to pray about expanding this into a full-time training program. By early 1977 it had become clear that God had provided Trinity with the personnel and vision to begin such a program in September of that year.

At a congregational meeting held on January 9, 1977, Trinity endorsed the proposal of its elders that the Trinity Ministerial Academy be opened in the fall of that year. The verse that they placed on the front cover of the TMA Prospectus was, "What you have heard from me in the presence of many witnesses entrust to faithful men who will be able to teach others also" (2 Tim. 2:2). The pastors who recommended men for admission to the Academy did so in accordance with the teaching of this passage, and examined each potential student to determine whether God had given him some measure of the gift of utterance, some ability to engage in concentrated biblical and theological study, and that he had attained a measure of consistent spiritual maturity as required by 1 Timothy 3:1–7.

Over the twenty years of the operation of TMA, the school was blessed with a godly and gifted faculty. They also had some of the finest young men in the program who were commended by established sister churches. Not a few of these men have developed into competent preachers, missionaries, theologians, and shepherds. Some of them have maintained lengthy and fruitful pastoral relationships with their congregations, both here in our country and in other countries as well. Some have continued to teach in seminaries in our country, and engage in modular instruction internationally.

It was never believed that the TMA model was the only valid expression of biblical precepts and precedents for ministerial training. There were times when the pastors and instructors at TMA encouraged men to attend one of the existing biblical and Reformed seminaries. In some cases, they encouraged men to pursue a hybrid form of ministerial preparation where certain disciplines could be acquired in one training setting, and other disciplines in another setting. With our entrance into the digital age, this model increased exponentially and many seminaries were (and still are) offering excellent online biblical and theological courses to men who can remain in their home churches for spiritual oversight and instruction from their own pastors.

TMA was a church-based Academy, specifically designed to train men for the gospel ministry.

> Trinity Ministerial Academy only accepts as students men who have given the overseers of their respective local churches reason to believe that they have been given by the Head of the Church certain basic gifts which, if developed, will make them "profitable for the ministry." Moreover, students who come to the Academy must commit themselves to pursuing the following goals: 1.) The student will immerse himself in the task of discovering and embracing those biblical perspectives and principles (both doctrinal and practical) which form the basis and substance of a valid biblical ministry; 2.) The student will endeavor to mature in those specific graces of Christian character which are essential to a valid biblical ministry; 3.) The student will seek to cultivate his gifts of teaching, preaching, and governing which are essential to discharging the major duties of a valid biblical ministry; 4.) The student

will give himself to getting well-started in those academic disciplines, the pursuit of which is normally necessary for effectively carrying on the work of a valid biblical ministry.[23]

Although gifts for the ministry are God-given, nevertheless they must also be cultivated diligently; therefore, Trinity Ministerial Academy requires strenuous academic discipline of all its students. Each man is expected to acquire a knowledge of the contents, the message, and the interrelation of the Scriptures of the Old and New Testaments, a working acquaintance with the biblical languages, and a theoretical and practical understanding of systematic theology, biblical theology, and historical theology. The student must also apply himself diligently to the experimental and practical aspects of the ministry. Principles of effective preaching and the many aspects of pastoral theology which touch upon the life and work of the church are emphasized in the course of study.[24]

Pastors' Conferences

With the expanding distribution of the Trinity Pulpit recorded sermons, the number of letters and phone calls Pastor Martin was receiving from Christians and pastors was increasing. With the load of correspondence Pastor Martin had been sustaining, his fellow-elders suggested that the time had come to consider having an annual pastors' conference. In such a conference, the men who were writing to him could gather both for a biblical ministry and workshop sessions in which he could address the practical concerns which would often arise in conjunction with the letter writing and telephone ministry. The men reasoned that in this way Pastor Martin might be more effective. Also, in the early stages of planning the startup of a pastors' conference, the elders suggested that he should consider taking segments out of the pastoral theology lectures to deliver them at the conference. The elders felt that they would be taking the Academy to men, rather than expecting men to come to the Academy. These considerations began when the Academy had been in operation for six years.

Closure of TMA

From the very beginning Trinity Baptist Church had determined that they would not establish a self-perpetuating entity for ministerial training within

---

23. *Trinity Ministerial Academy Prospectus, 5th Edition*, 3, 4.
24. *Trinity Ministerial Academy Prospectus, 5th Edition*, 6.

the framework of the life and ministry of Trinity Baptist Church. Several times over the two decades of the Academy's existence, the church leaders wrestled with the question of whether they ought to lay down that steward-ship, funded and supported primarily by Trinity.

Although the Academy closed in May of 1998, the church continued the annual pastors' conferences, even after health and other considerations led to Pastor Martin's retirement from the pastoral ministry at Trinity Baptist Church in June 2008.

Marilyn's Death and Marriage to Dorothy

In 1998 Pastor Martin's wife, Marilyn, was diagnosed with cancer. This diag-nosis led to a six-year battle with that disease, during which time Marilyn underwent multiple regimens of chemotherapy, a series of radiation treat-ments, as well as surgery. That battle ended on September 20, 2004 when she breathed her last and was at home with the Lord whom she dearly loved and served.

Prior to her homegoing, knowing that her days on earth were numbered, and with her mental faculties still fully operative, Marilyn clearly expressed to her husband three very distinct perspectives concerning his future. First of all, she was dogmatic in conveying to Albert her conviction that when the Lord took her home he should remarry. Then she charged her husband to ignore any man-made timeframe for when it would be appropriate for him to marry again. Third, after affirming her confidence that Albert would assess any potential spouse by the standards of Scripture, she made it very plain that she did not want him to marry someone simply because she met the biblical standards for a suitable wife. She stated that she wanted Albert to experience "falling madly in love again." He testifies that some months after Marilyn's death he was made acutely aware that Marilyn's first assertion was true, namely, that it is indeed "not good that man should be alone." He prayed that God would graciously intervene and grant him another "helper, answering to his need."

He was under his doctor's orders to be relieved of all pastoral responsi-bilities for an entire month to recuperate from some of the lingering physical and emotional effects of being Marilyn's primary caregiver. An unusual combination of providential factors worked together resulting in Albert being introduced to a godly widow, Mrs. Dorothy Chanski, of Grand Rapids, Michigan. That introduction led to their seeking godly counsel, and enter-ing into a serious 10-month courtship which culminated in their marriage on March 4, 2006. Many witnesses have testified that there was no question that Marilyn's third desire for Albert that "he fall madly in love again," was unmistakably fulfilled!

New Sphere of Ministry

Pastor Martin has not yet retired. His primary ministries at this time of his life are to his wife and family,[25] his local church, writing, and counseling and encouraging pastors around the world. To date he has written a book on the ministry of the Spirit in preaching entitled *Preaching in the Holy Spirit*,[26] a book entitled *Grieving, Hope and Solace: When a Loved One Dies In Christ*,[27] *Encouragements for Pastor's Wives*,[28] a book on ministerial burnout entitled *You Lift Me Up*,[29] a book on the fear of God entitled *The Forgotten Fear*,[30] and a book on the Christian's stewardship of the body entitled *Glorifying God in Your Body*.[31] In addition, The Banner of Truth Trust has published several of his books, such as *What's Wrong With Preaching Today?*, *The Practical Implications of Calvinism*, *A Life of Principled Obedience*, and *Living the Christian Life*.[32]

Though Albert Martin was used by God as a mighty preacher of the Word, and though he will always be remembered by many as a prince of preachers, he was, more than anything else in the church of Christ, a pastor. Though he had international recognition, his heart beat for the local church of which he was a pastor. A long-time member of Trinity Baptist Church, Katharine Birkett, wrote,

> Pastor Martin is known around the world, and yet has abhorred any kind of cult of personality, any kind of "great man sweeping through" attitude. Many times I heard him confess specific sins to us as a

---

25. As of March, 2017, including Dorothy's family, Pastor and Dorothy have 8 children, 30 grandchildren, and a growing number of great-grandchildren.

26. *Preaching in the Holy Spirit* (Grand Rapids: Reformation Heritage Books, 2011).

27. *Grieving, Hope, and Solace: When a Loved One Dies in Christ* (Adelphi, MD: Cruciform Press, 2011).

28. *Encouragements for Pastor's Wives* (Pensacola, FL: Chapel Library, 2013).

29. *You Lift Me Up, Overcoming Ministry Challenges* (Ross-Shire, U.K.: Christian Focus Publications, 2013).

30. *The Forgotten Fear, Where Have all the Godfearers Gone?* (Grand Rapids: Reformation Heritage Books, 2015).

31. *Glorifying God in Your Body: Your Body—Whose is it—Yours or His?* (Montville, NJ: Trinity Pulpit Press, 2017).

32. https://banneroftruth.org/us/store/theauthor/martin-a-n/

congregation, sins we might not have noticed or expected anyone to confess. His conscience would not let him do anything else. He is ready to praise and to commend faithfulness in others, and it is the things he has seen in Scripture, and not himself, that he has always wanted to be at the center of attention. He wanted us to have a Berean spirit; he never wanted us to believe something just because he held it. In fact, he wanted us to challenge the preacher if anyone rose up to preach contrary to the gospel, even if it were ever he, and he did not want to be our pastor if he ceased to hold our consciences with his life. He refused to bind our consciences beyond the Scriptures.[33]

Shehzad Khan wrote,

It was under the ministry of Pastor Martin that I was often convicted of my sins as an unbelieving teenager. His pointed applications and searching questions often made me feel like my secret sins had been uncovered and that all my efforts to hide them had been in vain. It was under his ministry that the Lord eventually saved me in my late teens, giving me freedom from the power of my shameful sins, and began shaping my life in the likeness of Christ. While I thank God for the privilege of hearing the many Spirit-blessed sermons of Pastor Martin, I believe his private counsels also testify of this sincere fatherly care.[34]

Pastoral Theology Lectures

In addition to painting a biographical sketch of the life and ministry of Pastor Albert N. Martin in this introductory biography, we have also seen how the *Pastoral Theology Lectures* developed over decades of his pastoral ministry to men aspiring to the ministry as well as existing pastors. Hear his own reflections on this development.

Little did I know when I began preaching at age seventeen that a time would come when I would be placed in the position of having to subject the activity of preaching to the kind of thorough and critical analysis essential to the composition of a series of lectures on this subject—lectures which would mold the thinking and practice of fledgling pastor-preachers. However, in 1977 I was placed in that very

---

33. *A Tribute to Pastor A.N. Martin: Eightieth Birthday Celebration*, Chet Jelinski, ed. (Self-published: Whiting, NJ, 08759), 94, 95.

34. *A Tribute to Pastor A.N. Martin: Eightieth Birthday Celebration*, Chet Jelinski, ed. (Self-published: Whiting, NJ, 08759), 156.

position with the opening of the Trinity Ministerial Academy and my responsibility to teach the courses in pastoral theology.

As I approached this daunting task I did so with two deeply rooted convictions as to the sources that should determine my formulations. The first of these convictions was that of the absolute authority and sufficiency of the scriptures as the primary source for any sound theology of preaching and pastoral work. The second conviction was that of the necessity for the constant "quality control" of historical theology over all my tentative conclusions with respect to my emerging understanding of the teaching of scripture on these issues.

Since I taught the entire course, first of all, in a three-year cycle, and then in a four-year cycle, I was constrained to subject the lectures to various degrees of serious revision and editing every three to four years.[35]

At the time he wrote this, there was a question in his own mind concerning the future of these lectures as published materials. He wrote further,

I have received continuing pressure from many to put my pastoral theology lectures into print. Until such time as this is done (if ever) I commend Dr. Borgman for capturing and stating in his way the heart of what I attempted to say in these lectures and what I would say if I were to commit them to writing.[36]

"If ever?" Now the time is here, and it is our prayer that much good will come to the church of Christ and her pastor-preachers from the study of these volumes.

I conclude this biographical sketch with a deeply rooted sense of gratitude to God for allowing me to know Pastor Martin for four decades and be shaped by the truths and principles found in these *Lectures*. Men, like me, who have looked up to Pastor Martin as a faithful pastor and mighty preacher have prayed, as Elisha said to Elijah, "Please, let a double portion of your spirit be upon me" (2 Kings 2:9)!

—John Reuther, Lumberton, NJ, 2018

---

35. Brian Borgman, *My Heart For Thy Cause* (Ross-Shire, U.K.: Christian Focus Publications, 2002), i. The last paragraph was slightly refined by Pastor Martin for the publication of the volume you are holding.

36. Brian Borgman, *My Heart For Thy Cause* (Ross-Shire, U.K.: Christian Focus Publications, 2002), iii.

UNIT ONE

The Call of the Man of God

CHAPTER 1

Introduction to Pastoral Theology

I am conscious of my accountability to God in discharging my stewardship of this instruction in pastoral theology. The apostle James says that not many should be teachers because teachers will receive stricter judgment (Jas. 3:1). James' warning implies an intensified accountability and judgment for the man who would be a teacher of teachers, since he molds the thinking of those who guide the thinking and shape the lives of many others. I feel the weight of that stewardship, and one of my comforts is that I have not taken this responsibility upon myself but have heeded the urging of many of God's servants over the years. Students of church history will know that Farel threatened Calvin with a divine curse if Calvin did not remain in Geneva to aid the work of the Reformation. Over the years I have felt something close to that Farel-like pressure from respected colleagues and friends if I did not leave behind this material in printed form as a helpful legacy to God's servants after I am gone to a better place.

As we take up the study of pastoral theology, our first concern is to consider the call of the man of God to the Christian ministry. Often this matter is taken up under the title of a call to preach or a call to the ministry, but, as I will subsequently explain, I have chosen this way to designate our subject for what I believe are good, wise, and essentially biblical reasons. So, our subject is *The Call of the Man of God to the Pastoral Office*. I will explain in the second chapter why I have chosen this designation and what it means, but let us now first consider some introductory perspectives concerning the theological disciplines of which our subject is a part.

Theological Disciplines Undergirding Pastoral Theology

You are probably aware that the formal study of Christian theology—the doctrine of God as He has revealed Himself in Scripture—has been subdivided into major categories which are often referred to as theological disciplines. These disciplines consist of exegetical theology, biblical theology, historical theology, systematic theology, and pastoral theology. Each of these makes valuable contributions to our understanding of God's nature, attributes, works, and ways.

The first theological discipline is *exegetical* theology.

This discipline is devoted to the issue of how to arrive at the precise, God-intended meaning of the words of Scripture. It will often bring within its scope such things as *canonics*, the study of the question of what books are to be regarded as part of God's revelation; *textual criticism*, which addresses the question of what is the purest text in which we may recognize the very words of God; *philology*, ascertaining the meaning of words; and *hermeneutics*, the science of accurate interpretation. Furthermore, the words of God come to us in various linguistic forms, genres of literature, and in the structures of grammar. There is a whole spectrum of concerns that comes within the field of hermeneutics, and hermeneutics itself should be viewed under the larger heading of *exegetical theology*.

The second theological discipline is *biblical* theology.

In its purest form, this discipline is devoted to the *history* of special revelation. It seeks to grasp what God is saying in each epoch of revelation to His people. Building upon and using the disciplines of exegetical theology, biblical theology seeks to discover what God is saying at any given point in the history of redemption, and to show the organic development between that revelatory data and what precedes it.

Geerhardus Vos defines it this way in his magisterial work on biblical theology:

> It is that branch of exegetical theology which deals with the process of the self-revelation of God deposited in the Bible.[1]

The third theological discipline is *historical* theology.

This discipline is devoted to discovering what the church has understood to be the truth of God, as deposited in the scriptures. This truth has often, of necessity, been articulated in the crucible of controversy and conflict. This particular discipline is often called the history of dogma or the

---

1. Geerhardus Vos, *Biblical Theology Old and New Testaments* (Edinburgh: The Banner of Truth Trust, 2000), 5.

history of Christian doctrine. Some classic examples of books committed to this discipline are William Cunningham's two-volume work called *Histori-cal Theology*, Louis Berkhof's standard work entitled *A History of Christian Doctrines*, and William G. T. Shedd's two-volume set labeled *A History of Christian Doctrine*. These are the best of the older works; there are some fine newer volumes available today as well.

The fourth theological discipline is *systematic* theology.

The peculiar concern of systematics is to ascertain the total witness of Scripture on any given subject to which the Scripture bears witness. It brings to its task all of the other theological disciplines: exegetical, biblical, and historical theology. It has often been rightly called the queen of the theological disciplines.

Professor Murray defined systematic theology this way:

It coordinates and synthesizes the whole witness of Scripture on the various topics with which it deals.[2]

B. B. Warfield wrote:

Professor Flint...took occasion to warn his students of what he spoke of as an imminent danger. This was a growing tendency to "deem it of prime importance that they should enter upon their ministry accomplished preachers, and of only secondary importance that they should be scholars, thinkers, theologians." "It is not so," he is reported as saying, "that great or even good preachers are formed. They form themselves before they form their style of preaching. Substance with them precedes appearance, instead of appearance being a substitute for substance. They learn to know the truth before they think of pre-senting it.... They acquire a solid basis for the manifestation of their love of souls through a loving, comprehensive, absorbing study of the truth which saves souls." In these winged words is outlined the case for the indispensableness of Systematic Theology for the preacher. It is summed up in the propositions that it is through the truth that souls are saved, that it is accordingly the prime business of the preacher to present this truth to men, and that it is consequently his fundamental duty to become himself possessed of this truth, that he may present it to men and so save their souls. It would not be easy to overstate, of course,

---

2. John Murray, *The Collected Writings of John Murray*, vol. 4 (Edinburgh: The Banner of Truth Trust, 1982), 19.

the importance to a preacher of those gifts and graces which qualify him to present this truth to men in a winning way—of all, in a word, that goes to make him an "accomplished preacher." But it is obviously even more important to him that he should have a clear apprehension and firm grasp of that truth which he is to commend to men by means of these gifts and graces. For this clear apprehension and firm grasp of the truth its systematic study would seem certainly to be indispensable. And Systematic Theology is nothing other than the saving truth of God presented in systematic form.[3]

Therefore, there ought to be in us a passion to be good systematic theologians in the truest sense, and I make this assertion even in light of what I am about to say in the next section regarding pastoral theology. It will be clear to the student that a healthy balance is necessary to be a good theologian and a faithful pastor.

Now we come to *pastoral* theology.

While it is not the queen of the theological disciplines, pastoral theology is the ultimate issue of these other theological disciplines. Pastoral theology has often been called practical theology. Whatever we call it, this discipline has as its concern the witness of Scripture to the actual work of shepherding the flock of God. In the other disciplines the pastoral or shepherding elements are more or less *latent*, but in pastoral theology they are *patent*. Pastoral matters are more or less *implicit* in the other theological disciplines, but in the discipline of pastoral theology they are *explicit*.

One of the great ends for which God has given us the scriptures is to make us pastoral theologians, "All Scripture is breathed out by God and profitable for teaching, for reproof, for correction, and for training in righteousness, that the man of God may be complete, equipped for every good work" (2 Tim. 3:16, 17). This great text does not say that the purpose of Scripture is to make us great theologians, although God has made many to be such by His design and blessing, but "for teaching, reproof, for correction, and for training in righteousness." What is the end of that? It is not that the people of God *generically* may be perfect or complete, but that "the man of God may be complete, equipped for every good work." In a very real sense then, Paul is telling Timothy that his manual of pastoral theology is his

---

3. Benjamin B. Warfield, *Selected Shorter Writings,* vol. 2 (Phillipsburg, NJ: P & R, 2001), 280, 281.

Bible: "Timothy, your Bible is your manual so that you may be an effective man of God equipped to use the scriptures for every good work."

Professor Morton Smith wrote:

> Practical theology has been defined as "the science and art of the various functions of the Christian ministry for the preservation and propagation of the Christian religion at home and abroad." Schaff goes on to say "it is the crowning consummation of sacred learning to which all other departments look and by which they become useful for the upbuilding of the kingdom of God in the world." He goes on to divide the various branches of practical theology as follows:

> I. Theory of the Christian Ministry
> II. Ecclesiology – Church Polity
> III. Liturgics – Worship
> IV. Homiletics – Preaching
> V. Catechetics – Teaching
> VI. Poimenics – Pastoral Work
> VII. Evangelistic – Evangelism and Missions[4]

Characteristics of *Pastoral Theology Lectures*[5]

The first characteristic that will be evident is that these lectures are *topical in their form and structure.*

They are topical, but based on exegetical theology, and therefore similar to what I will call in the section on preaching a topical-expository sermon. One could conceivably make an effort to expound the major passages from Genesis to Revelation which address some aspect of the work of the ministry. The end result would be the composition of a course in pastoral theology that would be thoroughly exegetical and expository, following the contours of biblical theology. However, it is my judgment that such a method would leave much to be desired in terms of comprehensiveness and practicality. Although this course will be topical in form and structure, the major segments of the biblical witness with respect to the work of the ministry will be

---

4. Morton H. Smith, *Systematic Theology,* vol. 1 (Greenville, SC: Greenville Seminary Press, 1994), 18. Smith gives the reference to the Schaff quote inside his as: Philip S. Schaff, *Theological Propaedeutic* (New York: Charles Scribner's Sons, 1909), 448.

5. Pastor Brian Borgman wrote a Doctor of Ministry thesis for Westminster Theological Seminary of California which was published in 2002, with a foreword by John MacArthur, entitled, *My Heart for Thy Cause: Albert N. Martin's Theology of Preaching* (Ross-shire, U.K.: Mentor, 2002).

identified, opened up, applied, and brought to bear on whatever issue we will
wrestle with along the way.

A second characteristic of these lectures is that they are *purposely selective in
their points of emphasis.*

I believe it would be impossible to be totally exhaustive or completely
comprehensive in treating this subject, to be either as deep or as broad as
the subject requires. I have sought to be selective in terms of three basic
guidelines.

First, I have employed the principle of selectivity by trying to be sensitive about where the Bible places its *primary emphases* regarding the work
of a man serving Christ and His people while occupying the pastoral office.

Second, I have tried to be sensitive to *common denominators* found in
the written works of godly men of previous generations, as well as those
from contemporary authors. Most of the men from previous generations
who wrote books dealing with pastoral theology wrote those books after
having spent years studying their Bibles, laboring in the work of the ministry, and seeking to discern the ways of God in dealing with them and with
fellow-pastors in their ministerial labors.

I remember one of the benefits I recognized when I first entered into
that rich vein of many of the old writers whose work saw only one edition. It
was interesting to see that though they approached many aspects of the work
of the ministry in a different way—such as what constitutes a call to the
ministry—when one read long enough and broad enough, there were certain fundamental common denominators that kept coming through as these
men observed, studied their Bibles, labored, and sought to discern the ways
of God in dealing with them. I have sought to be sensitive to those common
denominators and to give them due emphasis in the course of these lectures.

The third guideline for selectivity has been to *choose proven areas of
needful instruction and exhortation* in the work of the ministry. In other
words, issues that I faced over the course of more than five decades of pastoral ministry identified for me many of the subjects subsequently addressed
in these lectures.

The third characteristic of these lectures is that they are *enriched and illus-
trated with quotations and illustrations.*

Others have gone before us in these things. I hope to pass on much
of that legacy, even as Charles Bridges has done in his classic work, *The*

Christian Ministry.[6] I will never forget the first time that book came into my possession and I felt I had stepped into a marvelous legacy of thinking from the past. Bridges has many quotes and illustrations from other men in the text of the book. This feature is deliberate. It is so that we will realize that we are not the first people in the history of the church to study these matters. Others have gone before us, and God intends that we should benefit from the legacy they have left us in their writings.

When I read the Sermon on the Mount and remember the fact that the multitudes were amazed at our Lord's teaching because He spoke as one having authority and not like the scribes—constantly quoting Rabbi Ben so and so, and Rabbi Ben so and so—I say, "Lord, am I going to be like a scribe, quoting this one and quoting that one?" Well, there is a fundamental difference. I am very concerned not to be like a scribe, quoting this one and that one. However, the curse on the teaching of the scribes and Pharisees was that the quotes of the rabbis became a barrier between the masses and the plain teaching of Scripture. The men whom I will be quoting are men whose minds were in constant touch with Scripture. As they wrestled with the work of the ministry and what to say about that work in the light of their commitment to the absolute authority of Scripture, they speak with insights and freshness that take us into our Bibles and do not become a barrier between us and our Bibles. I am seeking to quote men whose insights will bring us into a greater affinity with and understanding of our Bibles.

Thomas Murphy speaks of the benefit of heeding the masters of the past. In dealing with the sources of materials for pastoral theology, Murphy presents this as one of a number of sources:

> *The accumulated experience of other workers in the same general field* is a vast storehouse from which the pastor can draw instruction in reference to all his duties. Indeed, this experience, classified and framed in accordance with the teachings of the Scriptures, is itself a system of pastoral theology. Men of sound and discerning minds, men full of the spirit of Christ, men whose lives have been spent in the most unwearied activity, have filled the office of the gospel ministry. They have given earnest attention to every department of their beloved calling. Whatever plans were likely to give success to their work they have tried. It would probably be very difficult to conceive of any scriptural method of building up the kingdom of Christ on which they have

---

6. Charles Bridges, *The Christian Ministry* (Edinburgh: The Banner of Truth Trust, 1976). There have been further reprintings of this volume by Banner of Truth.

not experimented. Long lives of thought, of wisdom and of toil have been spent in striving to make the ministry more effective. What one man or generation of men has attained to has been made the starting-point from which others have gone on in efforts to improve in doing the Lord's work. Even mistakes and failures in devising and executing methods have proved of great value in adding to the general store of knowledge on the subject. All this experience, whether written or unwritten, has accumulated into an invaluable fund for the ministry. When it is sifted, and tested by the sure precepts of God's inspiring, and classified, it forms a system of rules by which the workman in the ministry may safely be guided. No wise pastor will neglect this help of experience derived from all those who have gone before him. He can no more neglect it than the artist or the mechanic can neglect those rules which the skill of centuries has wrought out for his assistance.[7]

The genius of most of the older writers in this branch of theology, in contrast to some who teach pastoral theology today, is that often they were the bright lights in their denominations or ecclesiastical framework who were known to be men of unusual godliness, of great power and effectiveness in the ministry, and often they would be drafted to teach in their denominational seminaries. And then, after years of teaching, they would embalm in printers' ink the fruit of all of that ministerial and teaching experience. We have the cream of the thinking of those men of God. In addition, we have their excellent example for teaching pastoral theology today.

Pastoral theology should be taught by pastors. The exclusive pursuit of academic theological degrees, while a good thing in itself, is not sufficient for understanding or teaching on this subject. I am confident to speak and write on pastoral theology from my near fifty years of experience in the study of and service in the pastoral ministry, teaching pastoral theology for twenty years as an active pastor along the way. Many of the illustrations which I will use in setting forth the work of the ministry are going to come out of the crucible of my own experience—not that I will attempt to build principles upon that experience, but I trust you will not be offended when I illustrate principles from that experience.

---

7. Thomas Murphy, *Pastoral Theology* (Philadelphia, PA: Presbyterian Board of Publication, 1884), 20, 21.

The Formative Presuppositions of Pastoral Theology

I know that a presupposition can simply be a prejudice or a personal preference imposed on a subject. I am very conscious that I am vulnerable to that. However, a presupposition can also be a specific expression of a biblical reality rooted in the witness of the Word of God which we are determined will act like a grid as we take up a subject and then attempt to present it to others. I have had certain presuppositions in forming this course in pastoral theology, and I will now set forth five that appear crucial to me.

The first presupposition concerns *the primacy of preaching among the public duties of the ministry.*

In terms of how much time is given to each facet of the work of the ministry, I am presupposing the primacy of preaching among the public duties of the ministry. There are, as we shall see, both private and public duties connected with the office of an elder set apart to labor in the Word and in doctrine (1 Tim. 5:17), but among the public ministries and responsibilities, such as counseling the distressed, giving oversight, calling on the sick and evangelizing, none is so vital as that of the stated seasons of public preaching and teaching.

The simple reason for this is that in the wisdom and purpose of God, the primary means ordained by Him for gathering out His elect and edifying His people is the preaching and teaching of the Word of God. We all know Paul's conviction of this, "For since, in the wisdom of God, the world did not know God through wisdom, it pleased God through the folly of what we preach to save those who believe" (1 Cor. 1:21). What Paul preached is the *kerygma*, the thing preached, the content of the preaching, the message of the gospel as the opening up of the whole counsel of God. The *kerygma* is the thing preached as a herald in the name of the King, and God has ordained to bring His saving grace to men by this means. Paul speaks thus of preaching,

> For "everyone who calls on the name of the Lord will be saved." How then will they call on him in whom they have not believed? And how are they to believe in him of whom they have never heard? And how are they to hear without someone preaching? And how are they to preach unless they are sent? As it is written, "How beautiful are the feet of those who preach the good news!" (Rom. 10:13–15).

We pick up that emphasis again and again when we read the pastoral epistles and see how Paul envisions Timothy's functions, which are as close to standing pastoral functions as anything we will find in the scriptures. He tells Timothy, "Preach the word; be ready in season and out of season; reprove, rebuke, and exhort, with complete patience and teaching" (2 Tim. 4:2). This is another affirmation of the primacy of preaching in pastoral labor. Isaiah wrote of the beauty of preaching in prophetic overtones of this New Testament age: "How beautiful upon the mountains are the feet of him who brings good news, who publishes peace, who brings good news of happiness, who publishes salvation, who says to Zion, 'Your God reigns'" (Isa. 52:7). The description of overseers in Hebrews 13:7 contains this truth as well: "Remember your leaders, those who spoke to you the word of God. Consider the outcome of their way of life, and imitate their faith." Many things could be said about them, but the writer to the Hebrews underscores that, among the public responsibilities, there is a primacy of speaking the Word of God. It is the agreed testimony of Scripture and of church history that the pulpit is, in the words of Spurgeon, "the Thermopylæ of Christendom," that was the mountain pass in which the Persians destroyed the Spartans and turned the tide.

This is what Spurgeon said:

> Often have I said to my brethren that the pulpit is the Thermopylæ of Christendom: there the fight will be lost or won. To us ministers the maintenance of our power in the pulpit should be our great concern, we must occupy that spiritual watch-tower with our hearts and minds awake and in full vigour. It will not avail us to be laborious pastors if we are not earnest preachers. We shall be forgiven a great many sins in the matter of pastoral visitation if the people's souls are really fed on the Sabbath-day; but fed they must be, and nothing else will make up for it. The failures of most ministers who drift down the stream may be traced to inefficiency in the pulpit.
>
> The chief business of a captain is to know how to handle his vessel. Nothing can compensate for deficiency there, and so our pulpits must be our main care, or all will go awry. Dogs often fight because the supply of bones is scanty, and congregations frequently quarrel because they do not get sufficient spiritual meat to keep them happy and peaceful.... Men, like all other animals, know when they are fed, and they usually feel good-tempered after a meal; and so when our hearers come to the house of God, and obtain "food convenient for them," they forget a great many grievances in the joy of the festival, but if we send

them away hungry they will be in as irritable a mood as a bear robbed of her whelps.[8]

I personally believe that it has been the erosion of conviction on this point which in great measure has led to the shoddiness in preaching, the paralysis of godly ambition to excel in pulpit usefulness, and the inadequacies of formal ministerial training in this vital area.

Broadus made this accurate statement:

> The great appointed means of spreading the good tidings of salvation through Christ is preaching—words spoken whether to the individual, or to the assembly. And this, nothing can supersede. *Printing* has become a mighty agency for good and for evil; and Christians should employ it, with the utmost diligence and in every possible way, for the spread of truth. But printing can never take the place of the living word. When a man who is apt in teaching, whose soul is on fire with the truth which he trusts has saved him and hopes will save others, speaks to his fellow-men, face to face, eye to eye, and electric sympathies flash to and fro between him and his hearers, till they lift each other up, higher and higher, into the intensest thought, and the most impassioned emotion—higher and yet higher, till they are borne as on chariots of fire above the world,—there is a power to move men, to influence character, life, destiny, such as no printed page can ever possess.... It follows that preaching must always be a necessity, and good preaching a mighty power. In every age of Christianity, since John the Baptist drew crowds into the desert, there has been no great religious movement, no restoration of Scripture truth, and reanimation of genuine piety, without new power in preaching, both as cause and as effect.[9]

People sensitive to the voice of church history are forced to say a hearty *amen* to these sentiments![10]

---

8. C.H. Spurgeon, *Lectures to My Students* (Edinburgh: The Banner of Truth Trust, 2008), 375.

9. John A. Broadus, *A Treatise on the Preparation and Delivery of Sermons* (Birmingham, AL: Solid Ground Christian Books, 2005), 2, 3.

10. As I close this section on the primacy of preaching, I recommend that students read over William G. Blaikie, *For the Work of the Ministry: A Manual of Homiletical and Pastoral Theology* (London: Strahan and Co., 1873), 39–52. You can access this resource on Google Books. This excellent volume has been reprinted: William G. Blaikie, *For the Work of the Ministry: A Manual of Homiletical and Pastoral Theology* (Birmingham, AL: Solid Ground Christian Books, 1896, reprinted 2005), 26–36.

The second presupposition is *the vital place of biblical church order as the supportive context of effective preaching.*

As this course unfolds we will confront lectures dealing with the worship of the church, the constitution of a biblically qualified eldership, church discipline—matters which all relate to the passion of seeing a well-ordered, biblically framed church as the context in which the primacy of preaching is carried on. Now why such concerns? It is because of the apostolic truths which Paul expressed in 1 Timothy 3:14, 15 concerning the church as the household of God and our behavior in it. Although the apostle had labored longer in Ephesus than in any other place in all three of his missionary journeys, and though it was a well-established church and from its base the gospel penetrated into all of Asia, he parts with his dear spiritual son and companion Timothy and has him remain there in Ephesus for many reasons. Central are the reasons expressed in 1 Timothy 3:14, 15: "I hope to come to you soon, but I am writing these things to you so that, if I delay, you may know how one ought to behave in the household of God, which is the church of the living God, a pillar and buttress of the truth." You cannot read the pastoral epistles and take the latitudinarian attitude: "Well, as long as you have a gathering of people that in some way or another are attached to Christ, who love Jesus and want to please Him, why be concerned about really taking seriously biblical standards for ethics in the life of the people of God?" All of the practical issues with which Paul deals in the pastoral epistles, and in his other letters, of course, are about proper behavior in the house of God which is the support of the truth, particularly the *preaching* of the truth which we are presently considering.

He wants Timothy to carry on his preaching ministry of the truth in a context where the truth is fleshed out and biblical church order is the supportive context for that preaching. Let me put it this way: Under the blessing of God, when preaching is what it ought to be in content, form, spiritual energy, and comprehensiveness, then a vigorous, healthy, biblically ordered church will become both its fruit and its validation. Paul could say, despite all of the problems at Corinth, "You yourselves are our letter of recommendation" (2 Cor. 3:2). Better yet, he could say of the Thessalonians, "And you became imitators of us and of the Lord, for you received the word in much affliction, with the joy of the Holy Spirit" (1 Thess. 1:6).

The third presupposition is *the conviction that a life of vital godliness is the indispensable prerequisite for all ministerial efficiency.*

It is an old and oft-repeated saying, because it is true, that "a man's life is the life of his ministry." As it will be demonstrated in specific details, there is no aspect of pastoral duty which does not have its roots in the state of the pastor's own inner life before God. Proverbs 4:23 commands, "Keep your heart with all vigilance, for from it flow the springs of life." Every stream flowing out of a man into the various dimensions of ministerial labor can be traced back to the state of his heart.

According to 1 Timothy 3:2, the first requisite for anyone who has sanctified aspiration for the office of overseer is that he manifests a life of blamelessness: "Therefore an overseer must be above reproach." Here again, I found that the old writers outstrip contemporary writers in their constant emphasis of this fundamental presupposition which undergirds this course on pastoral theology.

I give you the words of James Stalker as an example:

Perhaps of all the causes of ministerial failure the commonest lies here; and of all ministerial qualifications this, although the simplest, is the most trying. Either we have never had a spiritual experience deep and thorough enough to lay bare to us the mysteries of the soul; or our experience is too old, and we have repeated it so often that it has become stale to ourselves; or we have made reading a substitute for thinking; or we have allowed the number and the pressure of the duties of our office to curtail our prayers and shut us out of our studies; or we have learned the professional tone in which things ought to be said, and we can fall into it without present feeling. Power for work like ours is only to be acquired in secret; it is only the man who has a large, varied and original life with God who can go on speaking about the things of God with fresh interest; but a thousand things happen to interfere with such a prayerful and meditative life.[11]

He writes later on in his book:

We are so constituted that what we hear depends very much for its effect on how we are disposed to him who speaks. The regular hearers of a minister gradually form in their minds, almost unawares, an image of what he is, into which they put everything which they themselves remember about him and everything which they have heard of his record; and, when he rises on Sunday in the pulpit, it is not the man

---

11. James Stalker, *The Preacher and His Models* (New York: A. C. Armstrong & Son, 1891), 54, 55.

visible there at the moment that they listen to, but this image, which stands behind him and determines the precise weight and effect of every sentence which he utters.[12]

Is this not true to your experience? It is psychologically, morally, and spiritually impossible simply to isolate and cocoon the words and separate them from the instrument that conveys the words. God did not make us that way. God does not intend that we be and function that way. Hence, I assert this foundational presupposition. It was said of an old divine, "He fed you with his doctrine, and edified you by his example. He wooed for Christ in his preaching, and he allured you to Christ by his walking." It would be a cause of great praise to God if we go to our graves and have people say this about us!

The fourth presupposition is that *there is a constant and delicate confluence and interaction of the divine and the human elements in every aspect of the work of the ministry.*

A confluence is a flowing together, as when two rivers merge into one. The constant and delicate confluence and interaction between the divine and human elements in every aspect of the work of the ministry is a crucial biblical reality.

As a relatively young Christian and an inexperienced preacher, I was constantly troubled with this question: "Where does God's work end and my work begin?" On the one hand, I did not want to grieve or quench the Holy Spirit in terms of deciding what and how to preach. I desperately desired and earnestly prayed for God's enablement and direct action upon my mind when wrestling with such questions. On the other hand, I did not want to neglect my responsibilities in sermonic selection, preparation, and delivery, and thereby be guilty of tempting God, waiting for Him to do something that He expected me to do. When God was pleased to open to me the truth of His Word concerning this dilemma, I saw very clearly that, in the majority of ministerial responsibilities and activities, there is indeed a confluence of the divine and human activities. For me, coming to some understanding of this vital principle became a wonderful means of personal liberation. This truth is a very precious reality to me, and I believe it is rooted in one of the most fundamental strands of biblical revelation. Christ Himself brought

---

12. James Stalker, *The Preacher and His Models* (New York: A. C. Armstrong & Son, 1891), 167.

these two confluent realities together in His discourse on the vine and the branches, as recorded in John 15:4, 5. In this passage, it is clear that our Lord Jesus commits Himself to abide in us, while at the same time He directs us consciously to abide in Him.

John Newton is known for his terse words: "None but he who made the world can make a minister of the gospel." There is a sense in which that is absolutely true. It is Paul who speaks of God as He "who has made us competent to be ministers of a new covenant" (2 Cor. 3:6). Who is sufficient? We are sufficient. How are we sufficient? God has made us sufficient as ministers of the New Covenant. Yet, this same Paul is the one who speaks to Timothy, his son in the faith, in this way,

> Let no one despise you for your youth, but set the believers an example in speech, in conduct, in love, in faith, in purity. Until I come, devote yourself to the public reading of Scripture, to exhortation, to teaching. Do not neglect the gift you have, which was given you by prophecy when the council of elders laid their hands on you (1 Tim. 4:12–14).

There were unusual, supernatural elements attending Timothy as God clearly gifted him for his task. The gift he was given was indeed a divine donation. Yet Timothy is exhorted not to neglect it. There is to be a confluence of God's stewardship over His gift to Timothy, and Timothy's stewardship over that gift. Paul also said to him, "For this reason I remind you to fan into flame the gift of God, which is in you through the laying on of my hands, for God gave us a spirit not of fear but of power and love and self-control" (2 Tim. 1:6, 7). "God gave, but with the thing God gave, Timothy, you are to take the poker of conscious effort and diligence and stir it into flame." Paul also said, "Do your best to present yourself to God as one approved, a worker who has no need to be ashamed, rightly handling the word of truth" (2 Tim. 2:15). Paul here uses the Greek imperative of *spudazo*. Do not float upon some expectation of the divine influence to make you this kind of a workman. You must bend all of your faculties and all of your powers to pursue it with passion. I love 2 Timothy 2:7, "Think over what I say, for the Lord will give you understanding in everything." In this chapter Paul is using metaphors to describe the work of the ministry, and then tells Timothy to bend his mental faculties in a concentrated way on what Paul is saying to him, because the Lord will give him understanding. Well, does the Lord give me understanding, or do I give myself understanding? Here is the confluence at work.

It is my persuasion that everyone of us by nature, temperament, previous and present relationships and influences, is either going to tend naturally toward a kind of overly mystical approach to the work of the ministry and pray for things that he ought to be consciously pursuing, or he will be overly practical and say, "Well, I am going to be practical; yes, I know God will do this, but I must do this," and neglect the conscious and constant awareness of our utter dependence upon the working of God.

Philippians 2:12, 13 is the watershed text that establishes this presupposition, and we will come back to it again and again in the course of these lectures. Paul says, "Therefore, my beloved, as you have always obeyed, so now, not only as in my presence but much more in my absence, work out your own salvation with fear and trembling, for it is God who works in you, both to will and to work for his good pleasure." Engage your whole being in the most concentrated, sober and serious way to this business of working out your salvation in an ongoing life of obedience to the revealed will of God. The incentive to do this is that God is working in us. God's working and my working are confluent realities in constant interaction. He does not work without us or against us, but with us and in us, so that His working comes to light in the blessing upon my working, and my working is blessed as He works in me to will and to work for His good pleasure.

The fifth presupposition is *the necessity of subjecting this field of Christian endeavor to specific critical analysis and structured presentation.*

It is true that much can be learned by example if we have an observant eye, but I am presupposing that this subject of pastoral theology ought not to be left to any less-focused analysis and structured presentation than any other theological discipline. That is the only reason I could, with good conscience, amidst the pressures of constant pastoral responsibilities over the years, throw myself into the kind of reading and thinking that was necessary to structure and compose these lectures in the first place.

Murphy underscores what I am saying in this final presupposition, and this quote will conclude this first chapter:

> Pastoral theology comes to the help of the young minister, and spreads
> out before him the teachings of Scripture, the accumulated experience
> of ages, and all other information that may have a bearing upon the
> successful pursuit of his calling. This knowledge it lays before him in
> a systematic form, so that he can easily find information on whatever
> point he chooses. In this way there is needful guidance furnished him

before he has had opportunity of making experiment for himself in the various branches of his work.... And when it is considered that the work of the minister is to cultivate the heart, to cultivate the head, to preach, to lecture, to visit the sick and sorrowing, to attend to the aged and the young, to assist in ecclesiastical affairs, to be busy outside and inside of his church, and to discharge many other duties, then it will be seen how important it is to use all means to make his time go as far as possible. He should have every help in a work so complicated and so momentous.[13]

---

13. Thomas Murphy, *Pastoral Theology* (Audubon, NJ: Old Paths Publications, 1996), 22–24.

CHAPTER 2

The Call of the Man of God
to the Pastoral Office

As we begin the journey of discovering what Scripture teaches about the call to the pastoral office, it will be good for us to see the route we will be taking. Not surprisingly, we begin with some introductory matters. After looking at these briefly, we will be devoting ourselves in this entire unit to considering *foundational principles, fundamental errors, unbiblical reasons for pursuing the pastoral office,* and *four major elements of a biblical call.* The subject is not complex, but it is deep enough to require our very careful attention to the issues which I purpose to cover.

Introductory Terminology

I have chosen the term *man of God,* because it is a biblical phrase rich in both its Old and New Testament usage. This is the designation used of Moses in Deuteronomy 33:1 and Joshua 14:6. He is called "Moses, the man of God." We find it appearing in 1 Kings 17:18 with respect to the prophets, and among them Elijah, whom the widow woman addressed in this way, "O man of God." Paul says to Timothy, "But as for you, O man of God, flee these things" (1 Tim. 6:11). He speaks generally about ministers of the gospel when he says, "that the man of God may be competent, equipped for every good work" (2 Tim. 3:17). The term *man of God* is a good term to use for a man fashioned by God into a minister of the New Covenant and recognized in the church as a gift of the ascended Christ. I have also chosen to use this term because of the constant emphasis that I will be giving to the fact that it is the man that makes the minister and not the minister who makes the man.

It is obvious that I have chosen to bypass the ordinary terminology of a call to preach or a call to the ministry. Rather, I have chosen the words, *The Call of the Man of God to the Pastoral Office.* Permit me to explain why I have done this.

I am not seeking to be novel. I have a great respect for the old verbal coinage of the people of God; I do not lightly throw it away or exchange it for freshly minted verbal coinage. However, ideas are captured, shaped, and conveyed by words, and it is my judgment that much of the confusion and imprecision concerning what constitutes a legitimate call to the pastoral office is perpetuated by the older and more common terminology of a call to preach or a call to the ministry. The terminology I prefer reflects a sensitivity to the words of 1 Timothy 3:1, "If anyone aspires to the office of overseer, he desires a noble task." As Fairbairn suggests, we might render the words more literally, if anyone *desires or reaches out after overseership*.[1] In other words, in that most relevant passage which gives the requirements for one who has reason to believe he is being fashioned into a gift of Christ to the church, the designation of his function is not just *preaching* or *ministry*, but is locked into the concepts of *overseer, shepherd,* and *elder* in Christ's church.

John Brown says:

> It is comparatively a modern, at any rate it is not a New Testament usage, to apply the term "pastor" exclusively to those teaching elders; that term naturally expressing the whole work of the Christian eldership, and, like the kindred term, "bishop," being given in the New Testament to Christian elders indiscriminately. But that such a distinction as that between elders who taught and ruled, and elders who only ruled, existed from the beginning, is made probable by the reasonableness and almost necessity of the arrangement, and its obvious tendency to secure the gaining in the best way and in the greatest degree the ends of the Christian eldership; and appears to me proved by the passage in the First Epistle to Timothy v. 17, of which, after all that has been said for the purpose of reconciling it to the episcopal or independent order of church polity, I am disposed to say, with Dr. Owen, that "on the first proposal of this text, that 'the elders who rule well are worthy of double honours, especially those who labour in word and doctrine,' a rational man who is unprejudiced, who never heard of the controversy about ruling elders, can hardly avoid an apprehension that there are two sorts of elders; some of whom labour in word and doctrine, and some who do not do so."[2]

---

1. Patrick Fairbairn, *The Pastoral Epistles* (Minneapolis, MN: Klock & Klock Christian Publishers, 1980), 134f.

2. John Brown, *Expository Discourses on 1 Peter,* vol. 2 (Edinburgh: The Banner of Truth Trust, 1975), 188, 189.

To speak in terms of *a call to preach*, or even of *feeling a call to preach*, treats preaching as though it were the beginning, middle, and end of the responsibility of the pastoral office. Yet it is not. I have already sought to demonstrate that preaching is primarily a public function. In fact, it is central to the public functions. Yet preaching is only one function. The words *call to preach* do not capture the entire spectrum of what it is to be a gift of the ascended Christ to the church, which is why I say that it can easily lead to imprecise thinking, and likely, practice. The Bible uses the terms *poimén* for shepherd, *epískopos* for overseer, and *presbúteros* for elder, to identify, in terms of his office, a man whose gifts are such as to capture more accurately that strand of biblical emphasis. So I trust that you will now be able to join with me in asserting that the proper terminology for the call of which we are speaking is *the call of the man of God to the pastoral office.*

The Biblical Warrant for Addressing the Subject

I set before you three arguments.

The first is that *it is the clear responsibility of every individual man in the church to think soberly regarding the identity and measure of his giftedness.*

You will remember that in the first eleven chapters of Romans the apostle systematically set forth the whole scope of God's great saving acts in Jesus Christ as contained in the gospel, which is the power of God unto salvation. Then, in light of these truths, he calls all believers to present themselves as living sacrifices to God. This involves a commitment, on the one hand, not to be fashioned according to this age, but on the other hand, to be continually "transformed by the renewal of your mind, that by testing you may discern what is the will of God, what is good and acceptable and perfect" (Rom. 12:1, 2).

Then, in Romans 12:3, Paul says, "For by the grace given to me I say to everyone among you not to think of himself more highly than he ought to think, but to think with sober judgment, each according to the measure of faith that God has assigned." In the context of the church, in this disposition of glad response to the saving mercies of God in Christ, every member of the church is called to this exercise of sober self-assessment with respect to the measure of giftedness with which God has endowed him. It is to be a *sober* assessment. It is interesting that, though some may underestimate the identity and measure of their giftedness, Paul does not believe that underestimation is the primary practical danger. So he says that none is to think of himself *more highly*, but to think *with sober judgment*. In other words, his assessment of himself is to answer to what he is in himself by the giftedness of God. He is to know his true state in terms of giftedness. That is a responsibility, and if that is a responsibility laid upon every man in the body of Christ, then there must be biblical materials that will help a man to make that sober assessment regarding his giftedness, and how it fits in the purpose of God.

Professor John Murray comments:

> One of the ways in which the design contemplated by the apostle is frustrated is by the sin of pride. Pride consists in coveting or exercising a prerogative that does not belong to us. The negative is here again to be noted and the liability to indulgence is marked by the necessity of directing the exhortation to all—"to every one that is among you." No one is immune to exaggerated self-esteem. In Meyer's words, "He, therefore, who covets a higher or another standpoint and sphere of activity in the community, and is not contented with that which corresponds to the measure of faith bestowed on him, evinces a wilful self-exaltation, which is without measure and not of God."
>
> But that which is commended must be observed no less than that which is forbidden. We are to "think so as to think soberly." Thus humble and sober assessment of what each person is by the grace of God is enjoined. If we consider ourselves to possess gifts we do not have, then we have an inflated notion of our place and function; we sin by esteeming ourselves beyond what we are. But if we underestimate, then we are refusing to acknowledge God's grace and we fail to exercise that which God has dispensed for our own sanctification and that of others. The positive injunction is the reproof of a false humility which equally with over self-esteem fails to assess the grace of God and the vocation which distinguishing distribution of grace assigns to each.[3]

The second reason why it is incumbent upon us to wrestle with this issue of what constitutes a call to the pastoral office is *the sober warnings to anyone contemplating any public teaching office, including the pastoral office.*

The warning is found most succinctly and pointedly in James 3:1, "Not many of you should become teachers, my brothers, for you know that we who teach will be judged with greater strictness."

---

3. John Murray, *The Epistle to the Romans*, vol. 2 (Grand Rapids: Wm. B. Eerdmans Publishing Co, 1968), 117, 118.

Lenski's comments are most helpful:

The participle states the reason that many should not want to avail them-selves of this privilege: "since you know that we shall receive greater judgment." James says that "we shall receive"; he includes himself. He is teaching in this epistle and is a teaching elder in the congregation at Jerusalem. He shows that he feels the weight of responsibility or rather his accountability because of this teaching.

Everyone of us who assumes to teach, whether he is in office or not, shall receive greater or heavier (R. V.) judgment, namely from God. God will hold us the more answerable. This, of course, means in case we are faulty or wrong in what we teach or in the manner of our teaching. The claim that "to receive judgment" means "to receive condemnation" (A. V.) goes too far. James did not expect condemna-tion for his teaching, nor does he intend to say that all teachers will be condemned. *Kríma* is and remains a *vox media*. God will look more closely at all teachers when he judges them. Teachers undertake to con-vey God's Word in the way in which God wants it conveyed; God will judge them on that score. Those who do not teach will, of course, not be judged in this way.[4]

The damage that wrong teaching may cause, whether it be in substance or in manner, is indicated by what James later says about the tongue. Untold damage may result; we see it everywhere to this day. This text about the judgment that teachers shall receive cannot be impressed too deeply upon all who teach today, whether they do it officially, occupying an office in the church, or not. Hebrews 13:17 voices the warning, "Obey your leaders and submit to them, for they are keeping watch over your souls, as those who will have to give an account." Surely, with this warning before us, we want to be absolutely certain that we have not intruded into the pastoral office, which is fundamentally a teaching office, when, as an elder, we are set apart to labor in the Word and in teaching.

The third reason why it is incumbent upon us to wrestle with this issue of what constitutes a call to the pastoral office is that *we are given an encourage-ment, coupled with a God-given standard.*

This encouragement comes at the front end of the list of qualifications for an elder in 1 Timothy 3:1–7, where Paul says, "The saying is trustworthy."

---

4. Richard C. H. Lenski, *The Interpretation of the Epistles of the Hebrews and the Epistle of James* (Minneapolis, MN: Augsburg Publishing House, 1966), 599, 600.

This was one of those five sanctified clichés present among the churches by the time the pastoral epistles were written. One of the faithful sayings is that "if anyone aspires to the office of overseer, he desires a noble task" (1 Tim. 3:1). Here is the encouragement. *The task is noble and the saying concerning pursuing that task is trustworthy.* When desire for the office is conceived in a man's heart, he is not immediately to be met with words of discouragement. He himself has this faithful saying, so that he can have a sense of openness to nurturing this desire even though the requirements are demanding and sobering. This standard constitutes a warrant for addressing the subject which is, "How can a man know for certain that he is called to this office and function? How shall we counsel and guide a man who is encouraged to aspire to the office of elder?" A man would be sinning if he proceeded to move forward without the confidence that it was the right thing to do (Rom. 14:23). When men approach pastors with the desire for the office of elder, we ought to take their desire seriously. After all, we are motivated by 2 Timothy 2:2, "and what you have heard from me in the presence of many witnesses entrust to faithful men who will be able to teach others also." We are looking for such men.

This encouragement is joined to the standard, the means by which we may know what constitutes a man a trustworthy man, to whom the church can begin to give its concentrated counsel, energy, and monetary support, and even further ministerial training. If we do not know what a faithful man is, then we are on the sea of subjectivism or sentimentalism. The issue is not simple but complex, and my fear is that I should personally promote in others a perspective that encourages men, where they ought not to be encouraged, and discourages men where they ought not to be discouraged.

Spurgeon wrote:

> When I think upon the all but infinite mischief which may result from a mistake as to our vocation for the Christian pastorate, I feel overwhelmed with fear lest any of us should be slack in examining our credentials; and I had rather that we stood too much in doubt, and examined too frequently, than that we should become cumberers of the ground. There are not lacking many exact methods by which a man may test his call to the ministry if he earnestly desires to do so. It is imperative upon him not to enter the ministry until he has made solemn quest and trial of himself as to this point. His own personal salvation being secure, he must investigate as to the further matter of his call to office; the first is vital to himself as a Christian, the second equally vital to him

as a pastor. As well be a professor without conversion, as a pastor without calling. In both cases there is a name and nothing more.[5]

Encouraging those who should be discouraged or discouraging those who should be encouraged was one of the marks of the false prophets in Ezekiel 13:22, "Because you have disheartened the righteous falsely, although I have not grieved him, and you have encouraged the wicked, that he should not turn from his evil way to save his life." Here, the false prophets were, contrary to God's will, discouraging the righteous and encouraging the wicked.

Spurgeon obviously felt the pressure of this responsibility when he wrote:

How may a young man know whether he is called or not? That is a weighty enquiry, and I desire to treat it most solemnly. O for divine guidance in so doing! That hundreds have missed their way, and stumbled against a pulpit is sorrowfully evident from the fruitless ministries and decaying churches which surround us. It is a fearful calamity to a man to miss his calling, and to the church upon whom he imposes himself, his mistake involves an affliction of the most grievous kind. It would be a curious and painful subject for reflection—the frequency with which men in the possession of reason mistake the end of their existence, and aim at objects which they were never intended to pursue.[6]

Here I want to interact with Spurgeon's question: "How may a *young* man know whether he is called or not?" I know that often, if someone is going to acquire the disciplines essential to be a competent man to labor in preaching and teaching, those acquisitions ought to be made while yet a relatively young man. However, we ought not limit this question to the young man's call, nor neglect men of years and greater maturity and how they may know whether they are called. I agree wholeheartedly with James Henley Thornwell who demolishes the notion that we only think in terms of *young* men when we talk about the divine call. God may lay hold of men in the ripeness of their years who have mature minds without need for the discipline of a formal theological education. Even these can be greatly used.

Thornwell writes:

It is a popular error, proceeding from defective views of a call to the ministry, and indicated in our prayers and our whole theory of

---

5. Charles Spurgeon, *Lectures to My Students* (Edinburgh: The Banner of Truth Trust, 2008), 24.

6. Charles Spurgeon, *Lectures to My Students* (Edinburgh: The Banner of Truth Trust, 2008), 23. I prefer to say "any man" rather than "young man" as Spurgeon did.

ministerial training, that we must look principally to *young* men as the persons whom God shall select to become the Pastors and Rulers of his people.... We expect them to be called *early*, that they may go through the discipline which we conceive to be necessary, and hence we limit our prayers to this class of persons. But if the call be Divine, it must be sovereign; and it must impart a peculiar fitness, an unction of the Holy Ghost, which alone can adequately qualify for the duties of the office. If it be sovereign, it may extend to all classes and ages, to young and old, to rich and poor; to all professions and pursuits, to publicans at the receipt of custom, lawyers at the bar, merchants at the desk and physicians in their shops. We are not authorized to limit God's Spirit in this more than in any other department of His operations. He can call whom He pleases, and we should pray for an increase of labourers, without respect to the classes from which they are to spring.[7]

With those introductory concerns behind us and beneath us, we now come to wrestle with what I am calling *the foundational principles which must regulate our thinking and our actions regarding a call to the pastoral office.*

Foundational Principles of the Call to the Pastoral Office

The first foundational principle is that *we must approach the subject fully aware that we are considering the call of an ordinary, as opposed to an extraordinary, office in the church.*

The offices of an apostle and prophet, and possibly evangelist, are confirmed in an extraordinary manner by vision, divine voice, or, in the case of Timothy, his unique giftedness and function was validated with accompanying prophecy and the laying on of the hands of an apostle (2 Tim. 1:6). However, the office of the *presbúteros* (elder), the *poimén*, (shepherd), the *epískopos*, (overseer), who functions as one who teaches and rules in Christ's church, is of a fundamentally different nature. This is critical as we think through what constitutes a call to the pastoral office. We must not revert to principles operative in a framework when direct and special revelation were being given.

Dr. Edmund Clowney wrote:

God's call came suddenly to Elisha; he was plowing a field when Elijah cast the prophet's mantle on him. Levi was in a toll booth, and Peter held

---

7. James Henley Thornwell, "The Call of the Minister," in *Collected Writings*, vol. 4 (Richmond: Presbyterian Committee of Publication, 1873), 27.

a fishing net when Jesus called them. But how does the Lord call today? You have not been blinded by a heavenly light on the road to Damascus, but you are ready to say with Saul of Tarsus, "Lord, what wouldst thou have me to do?" How does the Lord answer that question?[8]

In seeking the Lord's will, therefore, you are not in the position of Gideon who sought the sign of the fleece (Judges 6:36–40) or of David who consulted the oracular ephod of the high priest (1 Sam. 23:6–12), or even of Paul who was guided at times by prophetic messages given to others or to him directly (Acts 16:6–10; 21:10–11). All these things have been written for our sakes… (Rom. 15:4; 1 Cor. 10:11). God does not give us either Urim and Thummim or new prophecies, for the simple reason that we do not need them. The fullness of revelation has come through Christ.[9]

In his Word he reveals the principles of his will—indeed, he reveals himself. Through his Spirit he quickens your understanding of his will and your living fellowship with himself.[10]

James Garretson writes:

In his lecture notes Alexander distinguishes between two kinds of calls: the first he describes as 'ordinary'; the second as 'extraordinary.' When discussing the subject of an extraordinary call to the ministry, he is careful to observe that this is no longer the way in which men receive a call to the ministry. Extraordinary calls were often the result of direct inspiration; on other occasions they came in some miraculous manner. Believing that the period of extraordinary miracles and revelation had ceased, he argued that the circumstantial aspects of extraordinary calls are no longer relevant for our time. Therefore, it is with the ordinary call that we must concern ourselves.[11]

This point is critical. If someone comes to you with a faraway, saintly look in his eyes, anxious to tell you how he had an amazing and overwhelming impression upon his soul in prayer the day before, convincing him that without doubt he is called to the pastoral ministry, do not be overly

---

8. Edmund P. Clowney, *Called to the Ministry* (Phillipsburg, NJ: Presbyterian and Reformed Publishing Company, 1964), v.

9. Edmund P. Clowney, *Called to the Ministry* (Phillipsburg, NJ: Presbyterian and Reformed Publishing Company, 1964), 70.

10. Edmund P. Clowney, *Called to the Ministry* (Phillipsburg, NJ: Presbyterian and Reformed Publishing Company, 1964), 71, 72.

11. James M. Garretson, *Princeton and Preaching: Archibald Alexander and the Christian Ministry* (Edinburgh: The Banner of Truth Trust, 2005), 35.

impressed by his testimony. You may say, "My friend, I am so glad that you had a wonderful, warm, apparently precious time with the Lord, but you should not view that as a validation that the Head of the church is fashioning you into one who should labor in the Word and in doctrine." People are often intimidated and very reticent to challenge someone who claims to have experienced something that borders on a claim to direct revelatory experience. Such reticence should yield to the pressure of the clear directive given to us in 1 Thessalonians 5:21, "but test everything; hold fast what is good." If we are persuaded that the call to the pastoral office is a call to an ordinary, and not an extraordinary office, we will be prepared graciously and lovingly, yet boldly and forthrightly, to challenge what we believe to be a fundamental misconception of precisely how God calls men into the pastoral office and function. We will then seek to persuade such men that the call to the pastoral office is a call to an ordinary office, for which there is an ordinary, orderly, biblically grounded call to function in that office.[12]

Though it is an *ordinary* call, I am not denying that it is a *divine* call to this office. Acts 20:28 assures us of that: "Pay careful attention to yourselves and to all the flock, in which the Holy Spirit has made you overseers, to care for the church of God, which he obtained with his own blood." Here is the divine action. Ephesians 4:8, 11 refers to the ordinary call when Paul speaks of apostles, prophets, evangelists, pastors and teachers. They are a gift from the ascended Christ and from the Holy Spirit who is the executor of the will of Christ on earth. He constitutes men overseers. What is the medium of the activity of the Holy Spirit in constituting men overseers? What is the medium of the activity of the ascended Christ giving gifts to men? Different men respond to this question in different ways.

Whenever I say anything critical of Spurgeon, I almost feel profane, but on this point I think Spurgeon's overly mystical view comes into play. I believe that it is a view which can do much harm if embraced as normative. He said:

> In the present dispensation, the priesthood is common to all the saints; but to prophesy, or what is analogous thereto, namely, to be moved by the Holy Ghost to give oneself up wholly to the proclamation of the gospel, is, as a matter of fact, the gift and calling of only a comparatively

---

12. For an extensive, detailed treatment of extraordinary offices and extraordinary spiritual gifts in the New Testament, as well as the origin, duration, use, and end of such gifts, I commend to you *The Works of John Owen*, vol. 4, pages 438–486, followed by a treatment of the ordinary gifts of the Spirit in connection with the ministry on pages 486–520.

small number; and surely these need to be as sure of the rightfulness of their position as were the prophets; and yet how can they justify their office, except by a similar call?[13]

If he had said, "except by *as certain* a call, *issued in totally dissimilar ways*," I would have no reluctance in issuing a hearty amen, but notice the language he uses instead is, "except by a similar call." There is all the difference in the world between these two things. To me, the call of which he speaks is a call that puts it above and beyond the commitment that we only know the will of God from the scriptures, being enlightened and applied under the guidance and ministry of the Holy Spirit.

The second foundational principle is that *we think of the call to the ministry primarily in terms of the biblical teaching concerning an elder who labors "in preaching and teaching"* (1 Tim. 5:17).

It is necessary for me to explain this principle. If the office is an ordinary one, then the primary directives for recognition for that office are to be found in passages like 1 Timothy 3, Titus 1, Acts 20, and 1 Peter 5. Since these passages deal explicitly with the office and functions of an elder, surely they are the passages which must have preeminence in our thinking as we wrestle with the issue of what constitutes a call to the pastoral office. A failure to deal with the subject from this perspective has brought untold tragedy to the church of Christ.

In the early days of my ministry, there was no ordination council in which I participated that gave prominence to these passages which I just identified. Rather, I have known and been a part of ordination councils composed of pastors and theological instructors, charged with the responsibility of assessing a man's fitness for the pastoral office, who have carried out their responsibilities in this capacity and never once opened their Bibles to 1 Timothy 3 or Titus 1. Hours were given to a careful examination of a man's doctrinal convictions, his competence to teach and preach the Word of God, and to other matters deemed relevant in seeking to make an objective assessment of this man's fitness for the office and functions of a pastor. I do not remember ever sitting in one of these eclectic ordination councils in which there was an agenda which at least approximated the following pattern.

---

13. Charles Spurgeon, *Lectures to My Students* (Edinburgh: The Banner of Truth Trust, 2008), 21.

Each man sitting in the council, along with the man who is being examined, is asked to open his Bible to 1 Timothy 3:1–7. Then, with that passage open before all who are present, the men on the council begin to ask the ministerial candidate questions based upon the actual words of that passage: "Do you stretch out for this office? Do you have a holy desire for this work which this office entails?" If the man sitting before them answers such initial questions in the affirmative, they make it plain to him that the Word of God has placed before him a Spirit-inspired standard of what he must be in terms of his Christian character, and what he must manifestly possess in the way of a pastoral disposition and gifts, if he is to be recognized as a gift of the ascended Christ to His church. They then inform the candidate that they are committed to working down through those previously mentioned passages, seeking to discern with Judgment Day honesty whether or not the man sitting before them manifests at least a discernible measure of the graces and gifts identified in those passages.

Whatever the particular steps of any church or denomination may be in recognizing approved aspirants to the office and function of pastor, surely the above-mentioned passages ought to be central to the established protocol. Yet, where, when, and by whom are these crucial portions of the Word of God given the predominant place which they ought to hold in the proceedings of any group of men charged with assessing and validating or invalidating a man's sense of call to the Christian ministry? Often these passages are not even read, let alone expounded or impressed upon the conscience of the aspiring preacher-pastor who sits before them.

Can you imagine either Timothy or Titus, both of whom were responsible to help the churches in Ephesus and Crete to assess and ordain elders, going about that task without taking out Paul's letter and using it as the basis for evaluating the fitness of any potential or aspiring elders, including those men who are being considered as so-called "lay elders" or "non-vocational elders?" I say again, the failure to take these passages seriously in the process of discerning whether or not a man ought to enter the pastoral office has brought untold tragedy to the church of Christ.

Dabney is helpful to us here. In discussing what a call to the ministry is, he said:

> This leads us to add another important class of texts by which the Holy Spirit will inform the judgment, both of the candidate and his brethren, as to his call. It is that class in which God defines the qualifications of a minister of the gospel. Let every reader consult, as the fullest

specimens, 1 Timothy 3:1–7; Titus 1:6–9. The inquirer is to study these passages, seeking the light of God's Spirit to purge his mind from all clouds of vanity, self-love, prejudice, in order to see whether he has or can possibly acquire the qualifications here set down. And his brethren, under the influence of the same Spirit, must candidly decide by the same standard whether they shall call him to preach or not.[14]

I believe Dabney has identified a crucial issue. Seek to follow very closely now, as I use what I trust will prove to be a helpful illustration. Imagine with me an army sergeant who had been given orders by his superior officer to conscript six men from his platoon of soldiers who would be qualified to perform an unusually dangerous and demanding military operation. The sergeant was told by his superior officer that all six of the men he was to choose must meet all ten of the specific requirements included in his commander's orders. Those ten specific requirements would include matters related to physical characteristics, skill in the use of specific weapons, an ability to follow orders carefully and conscientiously, and other objectively verifiable qualifications.

What would the superior officer think of this sergeant, if the sergeant were to come back to him with six men, three of whom met all ten requirements, one of whom met six, one of whom met nine, and the remaining one only three? How would the sergeant be regarded by his superior officer in the face of such a blatant dereliction of duty? In the light of the clear commands he had been given by his superior officer, and the detailed description of the ten qualifications which were mandated to be present in any man chosen for this special mission, what excuse could he present to his superior officer for his willful failure to follow his orders? Would the sergeant escape a severe reprimand, if not a harsher military penalty, for manifesting such indifference to the clear orders that had been given to him? Would the sergeant be excused, if he sought to justify his delinquency of duty, by saying something along these lines? "But sir, I thought that it was not reasonable to expect that I would find all six men meeting all ten requirements, and that it would be acceptable if the requirements were met by fifty percent of the men brought back and presented to you for this strategic mission."

I trust that the point of this illustration is clear to every reader. As we shall see in the 1 Timothy 3 and Titus 1 passages, the apostle Paul uses the

---

14. Robert Lewis Dabney, "*What is a Call to the Ministry?*" in *Discussions: Evangelical and Theological*, vol. 2 (Edinburgh: The Banner of Truth Trust, 1967), 29.

little imperative particle *deî*: *it is necessary*, in conjunction with setting forth the qualifications of graces and gifts required of any man who aspires to the pastoral office and function. The church is given executive authority to carry into practice the orders of King Jesus (Matt. 28:20). However, she is not given legislative powers to reduce or expand those orders as they relate to a man's fitness for the pastoral office and ministry.

The third foundational principle is that *we must be conscious that we are in the realm of experimental divinity or the theology of Christian experience.*

Granted, all theology has an experiential or practical implication. If we trace every revealed truth out far enough, it should end up in doxology and practical Christian experience. However, some aspects of God's revealed will in Scripture are more precise and objective, while others are subjective and less precise.

For example, when we are seeking to define the biblical doctrine of justification by faith through the imputation of the righteousness of Jesus Christ, there is a wealth of objective biblical material by which to state and frame this doctrine. However, when we take up the question of how the Spirit of God brings a man or woman to justifying faith, we are in a slightly different area because there must be a personal sense of one's need and conviction of sin, but how much conviction? Conviction focusing upon original sin, the guilt of sin, or sin as pollution? Considerations arise concerning the place of the law, by which comes the knowledge of sin. What place should the law have? How should it operate? When we come to understand that saving faith is the fruit of regeneration, we realize that there will likely be differences in the ways which the Spirit works, for our Lord said, "The wind blows where it wishes, and you hear its sound, but you do not know where it comes from or where it goes. So it is with everyone who is born of the Spirit" (John 3:8).

This is the realm of experimental divinity, and we do not have the same precision as with objective theological propositions and subjects. Because of this fact, two things are clear.

First of all, our thinking, and the thinking of others, is likely to be influenced more by temperament, personal experience, and by ecclesiastical association and environment, than with respect to other issues. If we are in the realm of the subjective and the experiential, our own temperaments, personal experience, church associations and context will more likely influence our thinking on matters of experiential divinity.

The second thing that is clear is that this accounts for the tremendous diversity of perspective on this subject among very good and godly men. If you read Dabney on justification in his systematic theology, and then read sermons of Spurgeon where he preaches on justification, Dabney and Spurgeon are found standing on the same ground, speaking with one voice. However, as you read Dabney and Spurgeon on the call to the ministry, you will find two extremes of a permissible perspective on the subject. As I tried to reduce them to their irreducible minimum, Spurgeon says, *if you can possibly do anything else, do not preach, do not go into the ministry.*

> "Do not enter the ministry *if you can help it*," was the deeply sage advice of a divine to one who sought his judgment. If any student in this room could be content to be a newspaper editor, or a grocer, or a farmer, or a doctor, or a lawyer, or a senator, or a king, in the name of heaven and earth let him go his way.[15]

Dabney says, *if you can at all preach, do not, you dare not, do anything else.*

> If, therefore, the young Christian does not feel this scriptural desire to glorify God by saving souls, so that he would be glad to do it by *preaching* if he might, he ought not, indeed to thrust himself into the ministry like a slave going to a hated task. But he ought immediately to suspect himself of some most unchristian influence, of selfishness, indolence, vanity, ambition or avarice; he ought immediately to crucify these base feelings at the foot of his Saviour's cross; he ought never to rest till his heart is in such a frame that the desire to do good, in any way God may point out, is his ruling passion, and he ought to do all this wholly irrespective of his finding his way into the ministry or not.[16]

We greatly esteem both of these men of God, but to whom do we listen? Dabney says that unless the impediments are so clear and the obstacles so evidently from God, and prayer, pains, effort, and faith cannot overcome them, do not assume that you should not preach or pursue the Christian ministry. If you can at all meet the biblical standard to aspire to the office, then you should not dare do anything else. Spurgeon says, if you can do anything else and maintain a good conscience, invest your life in any other calling but that of the Christian ministry.

---

15. Charles Spurgeon, *Lectures to My Students* (Edinburgh: The Banner of Truth Trust, 2008), 24.

16. Robert L. Dabney, *Discussions: Evangelical,* vol. 2 (Harrisonburg, VA: Sprinkle Publications, 1982), 34, 35.

Because of the fact that this is the realm of experiential divinity, I want to give some practical counsel.

The first counsel is, *do not yield your mind to any one man's counsel on this subject, including this author.*

I obviously have convictions about this matter of the call to the pastoral office. I know that these perspectives have not been formed hastily or irresponsibly, but do not yield your mind to any one man's counsel on this subject. As you read Spurgeon, do not accept him as the guru, as fully balanced and the final word, otherwise you may give up on this study of pastoral theology immediately! On the other hand, if you take Dabney as the final word, there are some of you that may feel you ought to move beyond your present sphere of usefulness in the church of Christ and aspire to the pastoral office without sufficient internal and external warrant to do that.

My second counsel is to *remember important biblical directives* such as 1 Thessalonians 5:21, "but test everything; hold fast what is good."

We might say that what we are to put to the test, in this regard, are the differing views on this experiential matter. Consider also Acts 17:11, "Now these Jews were more noble than those in Thessalonica; they received the word with all eagerness, examining the Scriptures daily to see if these things were so." Remember, we begin with the conviction that the inspired, inscripturated, revelatory data is sufficient to make the man of God competent for every good work (2 Tim. 3:16, 17); and, if the Scripture cannot clear up a man's call to the office and function of a pastor, where shall we go?

I do appreciate Dabney's comments at this point:

> What, then, is the call to the gospel ministry? Before the answer to this question is attempted, let us protest against the vague, mystical and fanatical notions of a call which prevail in many minds, fostered, we are sorry to admit, by not a little unscriptural teaching from Christians. People seem to imagine that some voice is to be heard, or some impression to be felt, or some impulse to be given to the soul, they hardly know what or whence, which is to force the man into the ministry without rational or scriptural deliberation. And if this fantastic notion is not realized—as it is not like to be, except among those persons of feverish imagination who of all men have least business in the pulpit—the young Christian is encouraged to conclude that he is exempt. Let the pious young man ask himself this plain question, Is there any other expression of God's will given to us except the Bible?

Where else does God authorize us to look for information as to any duty? The call to the ministry, then, is to be found, like the call of every other duty, in the teachings of God's revealed word. The Holy Spirit has ceased to give direct revelations. He speaks to no rational adult now through any other medium than his word, applied by his gracious light to the understanding and conscience. To look for anything else from him is superstition. While the call of prophets and apostles was by *special* revelation, that of the gospel minister may be termed a *scriptural call.*[17]

As with any area of the Christian life and the need for guidance based on the Word of God, we recognize the strategic place of godly counsel. This applies no less in the consideration of the call to the pastoral office. "Where there is no guidance, a people falls, but in an abundance of counselors there is safety" (Prov. 11:14). "Without counsel plans fail, but with many advisers they succeed" (Prov. 15:22). "Whoever isolates himself seeks his own desire; he breaks out against all sound judgment" (Prov. 18:1). These perspectives and admonitions from the wisdom of Proverbs dovetail with the point I have been making in this third foundational principle, that we are in the realm of experimental divinity when considering the call to the pastoral office.

---

17. Robert Lewis Dabney, "*What is a Call to the Ministry?*" in *Discussions: Evangelical and Theological,* vol. 2 (Edinburgh: The Banner of Truth Trust, 1967), 26, 27.

CHAPTER 3

Fundamental Errors Regarding a Call to the Pastoral Office

The purpose of this lecture is to attempt to collate into several categories the errors or unbiblical perspectives which have existed, and yet exist, with respect to what constitutes a biblical and orderly call to the pastoral office. Others have addressed this very thing in the history of the church.

I give you the writings of James Henley Thornwell as a prominent example. In this quote, he is assessing some sermons of one of his contemporaries who was addressing this issue:

> All pretensions which are not founded upon a real call of God, properly authenticated according to the provisions of His Word, must either claim to be extraordinary, and then extraordinary evidence should be produced; or, they rest upon a perpetual succession which has transmitted the rights and properties of the office from Christ the Head through an unbroken line of office-bearers to the present incumbent, and then the succession becomes a question of fact to be proved by testimony, and the validity of the title founded upon it a doctrine to be established by Scripture; or, they rest upon the conviction and belief of the individual himself, unsupported by any proof but his own extravagance or enthusiasm.[1]

The three things enumerated here are, and I state them in more simple language, 1) the fanatical claim to special revelation in receiving a call to the ministry, 2) the belief in apostolic succession, warranting that a man be placed in the office, and 3) the claim of crass individualism.

Instead of using the three headings drawn from Thornwell's analysis, I will present four categories of my own. Under these four can be subsumed the vast majority of errors with respect to what constitutes the substance of a biblical and orderly call to the pastoral office. My list is based upon the

---

1. *The Collected Writings of James Henley Thornwell,* vol. 4 (Richmond, VA: Presbyterian Committee of Publication, 1873), 23.

observations and critical analysis of others, as well as my own observations and interaction with men over the course of many years of ministry.

Unbiblical Perspectives Pertaining to a Call to the Pastoral Office

First, there are men who assume that they are called to the pastoral office, called to preach, or called to the ministry, because of an *uninstructed ignorance and zeal.*

Paul speaks of this kind of zeal, "For I bear them witness that they have a zeal for God, but not according to knowledge" (Rom. 10:2). It is indeed possible to be zealous in pursuit of something that in itself is a noble thing, but to pursue it in ignorance and uninstructed zeal, just as some were doing with respect to how sinful men are to obtain a righteous standing before God.

A man who has been genuinely converted will manifest, to some degree, the fundamental fruits of true conversion: a passionate love for Christ, a love for the souls of men, a desire to serve Christ, and a desire to communicate the truth of Christ to others. Passion and zeal, in themselves good gifts and graces from Christ, can be improperly channeled so that zeal becomes the predominant force, not knowledge. The uninstructed zeal may be the zeal of the man who is intent on preaching or entering into the ministry, or the zeal of others who encourage a man to do it. In either case, zeal without instruction, knowledge, and a sober understanding of what is required in a minister of the gospel and in the ministry to which God calls men, is not pleasing to God nor conducive for the growth and establishment of the church.

A short survey of select passages will suffice to establish this point that zeal must not be uninformed. Titus 1:9 says, "He must hold firm to the trustworthy word as taught, so that he may be able to give instruction in sound doctrine and also to rebuke those who contradict it." Second Timothy 2:15 says, "Do your best to present yourself to God as one approved, a worker who has no need to be ashamed, rightly handling the word of truth." Acts 20:28 points to the solemnity of the Spirit's own appointment, "Pay careful attention to yourselves and to all the flock, in which the Holy Spirit has made you overseers, to care for the church of God, which he obtained with his own blood."

It may be easy to think, "You can't argue with zeal!" Yet zeal, as crucial as it is, can be a mere shell of emptiness. Biblical substance and the indwelling Spirit must be at the core of zeal, otherwise that zeal stands condemned, just as Paul faulted his own countrymen. Zeal is often passionate in new converts, and often new converts feel convinced that they have a call from God to enter the Christian ministry. Paul deals with this when he states one of the most crucial requirements for the office, "He must not be a recent convert, or he may become puffed up with conceit and fall into the condemnation of the devil" (1 Tim. 3:6).

Second, *fanaticism or mystical piety* is another erroneous basis for a call to the pastoral office.

There are people who claim to have had a series of signs or a string of providences which they believe they have infallibly interpreted as God's finger pointing them in the direction of pursuing or actually assuming the pastoral office. The following rather humorous example which I first heard many years ago may be fictional, although I believe it could have happened. It is reported that a young farmer, having been recently converted, while plowing his fields happened to look up into the sky and saw an unusual formation of clouds that seemed to form three letters: *G, P,* and *C.* He interpreted this as a sign from God telling him to "Go Preach Christ." Later, an older man with a little more discernment, hearing this story asked, "Son, could it be that God was telling you to "Go Pick Corn?" This kind of "leading" would be humorous if it were not so tragic in real life. Even if this is a fictional story, it is this kind of fanaticism that rules in the minds of some.

In the same category is the case of a man who breaks one of his legs in a bizarre accident, loses his job, and suffers the death of a child, and then assumes that God is chastening him because he is a "Jonah," running away from the call. I have frequently heard men say something like this: "I ran away from the call and God did this to me, and finally, I capitulated to the call to the ministry and these dark providences ended." Yet, in all this testimony which I have described there is nothing of obeying the mandate for sober self-assessment (Rom. 12:3). Neither is there any careful self-evaluating for graces and gifts according to the biblical standard of 1 Timothy 3:1–7, or the quality control of the church perceiving and validating the man as one with the gifts and graces clearly required by the scriptures.

Here we can also include cases of people becoming convinced that the voice of God was calling them into the ministry because a particular text of Scripture in some way or another related to the ministry once seemed to jump out and overpower them.

A third faulty basis for a call is *privatism or isolated decision making*.

This is the carnal individualism of a "Lone Ranger." It includes men who have sought to make personal judgments concerning their call to the pastoral office based on the Word of God, but they have done so with an illicit measure of isolation from the input and counsel of the body of Christ. Specifically, they lack input from the church of which they are a member.

To their credit, some men guilty of this error have taken Romans 12:3 seriously. They have recognized that they have a personal responsibility to make a sober assessment of their giftedness. However, there are men who engage in sober self-assessment who forget that the context of the imperative to personal self-evaluation is one of the richest passages demonstrating that the church is constituted as a body and is intended to function as a body. Men like this should keep reading in Romans 12, starting at verse four, and see that we are members of the body, the church. Therefore everything we think about ourselves and do as members of the church must be conditioned by *union*, not in *isolation*.

A rather fanciful illustration may help to reinforce this reality of the necessity and benefits of such quality control in conjunction with our own self-assessment. I have been fascinated with airplanes and aviation for many years. This fascination began during World War II which took place when I was seven to eleven years old. During that time, I memorized the identity and the particular function of all the fighter planes and bombers in the US Air Force. During many years of my adult life I entertained a secret wish that I might be able to take flying lessons and obtain a bona fide pilot's license. Now suppose that I were to purchase flight simulation software which would enable me to learn to fly an airplane while sitting at my computer. Such software does exist. Assume with me that I went through the entire program and was actually given a certificate, validating that I had completed the computer training as a first step to further licensing. Imagine me standing in the aisle the next time I take a commercial airline trip and saying, "Fellow travelers, I want to inform you that I recently completed a computer simulation program for flying this type of aircraft. I would like all of you passengers to confirm that you support me in my desire to enter the cockpit and fly this aircraft to its destination." Needless to say there would either be spontaneous laughter, or they would usher me off of that plane.

In a similar way, God intends that the self-assessment of our pastoral gifts and graces should be undertaken in the context of our attachment to and active involvement in a local church indwelt by the Spirit of God, all holding to the same standard of requirement for the office of elder and preaching. Proverbs contains this warning, "Whoever isolates himself seeks his own desire; he breaks out against all sound judgment" (Prov. 18:1). In fact, there are some men who have been examined by the church and have been judged to be patently unqualified for the ministry, and yet they have pursued the ministry anyway. Unshaken in their own personal conviction about their fitness, they go from church to church, seeking people who will be undiscerning enough to agree with their inordinately individualistic perspective concerning their fitness for, and call to, the pastoral office and its manifold functions.

Even the apostle Paul did not trust his own independent judgment with regard to a relatively younger man named Timothy.

> Paul came also to Derbe and to Lystra. A disciple was there, named Timothy, the son of a Jewish woman who was a believer, but his father was a Greek. He was well spoken of by the brothers at Lystra and Iconium. Paul wanted Timothy to accompany him, and he took him and circumcised him because of the Jews who were in those places, for they all knew that his father was a Greek (Acts 16:1–3).

Paul clearly saw things in Timothy that greatly impressed him, but he took time to find out whether or not his perspectives lined up with the perspectives of those who had known Timothy more intimately for a longer period of time, and in greater depth and breadth. In the case of Timothy, at least two churches concurred with Paul's initial assessment of Timothy's fitness for the work of the ministry.

Fourth, some err by *pragmatism or a rationalistic ecclesiology.*

In this case, the whole issue of determining good candidates for the ministry as a lifelong occupation is dealt with as though the church were merely a commercial business or corporation. In a secular corporation, those who are in the upper echelons of leadership generally think of encouraging men to aspire for future leadership with the following perspective:

> Fix your eye on the sharp young man that seems to have the charisma of leadership. Fix your eye on the young man that has the gift of gab and that unique ability to motivate others with his words. Then condition and encourage that man to think that, if he continues in his present career track, he could possibly become the future CEO of that corporation.

In other words, where this worldly corporation mentality prevails, a young man will regard the corporation as existing to promote his career. With such a mindset, the young man is lured into making a commitment of himself to that corporation, not in terms of being a servant to the corporation and its goals, but viewing the corporation as his servant to promote his career and his well-being. When this mentality carries over into any aspect of our thinking concerning the work of the ministry, it stands in diametric opposition to the perspective which our Lord articulated:

> And Jesus called them to him and said to them, "You know that those who are considered rulers of the Gentiles lord it over them, and their great ones exercise authority over them. But it shall not be so among you. But whoever would be great among you must be your servant, and whoever would be first among you must be slave of all. For even the Son of Man came not to be served but to serve, and to give his life as a ransom for many" (Mark 10:42–45).

No one should consider himself called of God to the work of the ministry who has the mindset that the church exists to promote the man and his gifts. Rather, a man equipped by Christ and truly called to the work of the ministry will recognize that he exists to promote the advancement of Christ's Kingdom in and through His church, being a bondservant to all, as Christ was to us.

Furthermore, this worldly ecclesiology greatly contributes to the shameful brevity of the tenure of many evangelical pastors. It amazes me that, in most cases, when men declare that they "feel led to move on to another sphere of ministry," that *moving on* is generally accompanied by a *moving up* in terms of a higher profile with greater personal perks and material benefits. When pragmatism or carnal ecclesiology dictates who should or should not believe himself called to the pastoral office, there is very little thought given to discern whether or not Christ is furnishing men with the gifts and graces required by Scripture. Before any man can be given to the church as a gift of the ascended Christ, that same Christ must furnish the man with at least a discernible measure of the very graces and gifts which He Himself has specified in His Word. It would be far better for a church to live with the burden of a vacant pulpit, receiving ministry from sister churches, while crying to the Lord of the harvest that He would fill the pulpit with someone whom Christ has endowed with the necessary gifts and graces, than to push a man into the pulpit who has the gift of gab and the charisma of a charming personality but who would not fare well under the searching light of 1 Timothy 3:1–7 and Titus 1:5–9.

I want to identify one other way in which carnal ecclesiology rears its ugly head. It is when it is assumed that a measure of proven competence in a specific occupation or profession will automatically indicate great potential usefulness in the work of the ministry. What are the results of believing this notion? It may strongly suggest to men who have known success to think they are being called to the ministry and will be equally successful in it. Within this framework of thinking, which I have designated as pragmatic or carnal ecclesiology, there is a fundamental assumption that competence in another profession forms a legitimate foundation for competence in the ministry. Some think that if a man shows competence as a physician, an athlete, a politician, or an educator, then he will automatically be a competent pastor. This conclusion is certainly not warranted by the Word of God.

Granted, a man may learn certain disciplines on the football field, in business, or in the practice of medicine or law, which may be part of what God has woven into the fabric of his life to make him more competent as an elder. However, the clearly revealed biblical context for proving the graces and gifts of any man is a healthy local church, a church composed of discerning leaders and well-instructed members who have been trained to think and act biblically in assessing a man's fitness for the work of the ministry.

I urge you, brethren, you who are in places of spiritual leadership, to think through these issues, not only with regard to your own calling, but with regard to the influence God may be pleased to give you as you work with others who are seeking to settle their own thinking regarding their call to the pastoral office.

Unbiblical Reasons or Improper Motivations for Pursuing the Pastoral Office

Often accompanying these four fundamental categories of unbiblical thinking regarding what constitutes a call to the pastoral office are improper motivations for pursuing the ministry. Over the course of many years I have observed, discussed, read, and mentally wrestled with this question of what are the proper and righteous motivations to pursue the ministry. At the same time, and by the same means, I have sought to observe and take note of those things which should be designated as improper or even sinful motivations to pursue the office and its functions. It appears to me that there are at least seven categories which comprise the full spectrum of unbiblical, unrighteous, and wrong reasons why men either aspire to this office, or actually believe themselves called to it.

As we come to the identification and consideration of these unbiblical motivations, I urge any reader wrestling with the great question of his call to the pastoral office to pray earnestly using the words of Psalm 139:23, "Search me, O God, and know my heart! Try me and know my thoughts!" Any of these factors which we will now consider may be lurking in our hearts. If they are, pray that God would uncover them by the teaching of His Word and the ministry of His Spirit. Pray not only with the disposition of David's prayer, but with the attitude of the apostles, "And they prayed and said, 'You, Lord, who know the hearts of all, show which one of these two you have chosen to take the place in this ministry and apostleship from which Judas turned aside to go to his own place'" (Acts 1:24, 25).

There is overlap and interpenetration in the things that follow, so I have resisted seeking to put them into categories such as those rooted in the heart, the head, ignorance, bad teaching, and so forth. I lay them out with no specific significance in the order in which they are addressed.

First, do not pursue pastoral ministry from *a falsely instructed conscience*.

The men who sat under my ministry at the Trinity Academy know that one of the major emphases in my instruction had to do with the maintenance of a good conscience toward God and men. I will attempt to explain why this was so. Doing this will demand that we delve a bit into the biblical doctrine concerning the function of our consciences. Our consciences are the eyelash of God upon the eye of the soul with respect to our moral choices and moral actions. When the apostle Paul was giving specific instructions to Timothy concerning his responsibility to maintain doctrinal purity in the church at Ephesus, he reinforced his charge to Timothy with these words, "The aim of our charge is love that issues from a pure heart and a good conscience and a sincere faith" (1 Tim. 1:5). Then, later on in the chapter, he said,

> This charge I entrust to you, Timothy, my child, in accordance with the prophecies previously made about you, that by them you may wage the good warfare, holding faith and a good conscience. By rejecting this, some have made shipwreck of their faith, among whom are Hymenaeus and Alexander, whom I have handed over to Satan that they may learn not to blaspheme (1 Tim. 1:18–20).

Paul could say, in light of the coming Day of Judgment, "So I always take pains to have a clear conscience toward both God and man" (Acts 24:16).

According to Scripture, conscience has a very critical place in healthy, ethical Christian living. Yet, the same Bible makes it clear that sin has so affected the totality of what we are, both when sin *reigned* before our conversion and as sin *remains* in us as believers, that there is no department of our redeemed humanity which is not affected by remaining sin, including our consciences. Although the claims of conscience are always supreme and magisterial, and we must never violate them, they are not infallible nor perfectly sanctified. We read of the weak conscience, "Thus, sinning against your brothers and wounding their conscience when it is weak, you sin against Christ" (1 Cor. 8:12).

However, even when conscience is speaking falsely, its voice must never be stifled or disregarded, "For whatever does not proceed from faith is sin" (Rom. 14:23). The context of this verse shows that whatever is not done with a good conscience is sin. In other words, to maintain a good conscience, we must be convinced that the action contemplated or performed is well-pleasing to God, otherwise our consciences will condemn us.

I believe that there are men aspiring to the ministry, and actually in the ministry, because they have yielded themselves to the pressure and dictates of a falsely instructed conscience. Let me explain. When they were young believers, sincere and godly preachers conditioned their consciences to believe that, if they were truly "sold out" to Christ, they would aspire, first of all, to be missionaries, second to be pastors, and third to be devoted laymen, getting married and rearing children to be pastors or missionaries in their place. They have been falsely told that otherwise, if you have permitted yourself to be just an ordinary Christian, you would be lying down on a bed of spiritual mediocrity and becoming settled with God's "second best." You would merely go to church, sing the hymns, pay your tithe, listen to preaching and live a decent life as a good family man, a good churchman, and a good witness to Christ and the truth of the gospel.

The scenario I have drawn is not theoretical for me. In my early days as a Christian my thinking was greatly influenced by the kind of teaching I have just described. It took a long while for my conscience to be properly instructed with regard to these matters. So, when dealing with such people, we must seek, lovingly and patiently, to instruct their consciences with the light of God's truth. As you will remember, the apostle Paul could say in Acts 26:9, 10 that he thought he was pleasing to God when he was aggressively ripping mothers and fathers away from their children, putting them in prison, and even handing some of them over to death. He was under the compulsion of a falsely instructed conscience. Jesus said, "They will put you out of the synagogues. Indeed, the hour is coming when whoever kills you will think he is offering service to God" (John 16:2).

This is how skewed in its dictates one's conscience can be. In the light of this reality, we need, lovingly and tenderly, to sit down with brothers who feel that they are "called to the ministry," or are inclined to pursue training for the ministry, and make sure that they are not doing so under the pressure of a wrongly instructed conscience pressuring them to pursue the ministry because they assume that this is the only way to be "sold out" to Christ. Such teaching undercuts the biblical doctrine of the sacredness of every calling when it is pursued according to the precepts and principles of Scripture.

Second, *the unwise and unsanctified ambitions of others* are no good reason to pursue pastoral ministry.

I have known of situations where mothers and fathers could not get to the mission field themselves, and thus felt that they had missed "God's best." In order to deal with this, they decided to rear future missionaries, conditioning the consciences of their children very early in life that, if *they* desired "God's best" for *their* lives they should seek to be missionaries, or, if they were boys, preachers. The result of this scenario is that there are people who come to adulthood under the pressure of a conscience wrongly conditioned to make them think that they should become preachers, missionaries, or some kind of "full-time" Christian worker. In one sense their desires are noble. However, such desires are no proof of a divine call, because the driving force behind those desires is a poorly or wrongly instructed conscience.

Samuel Miller wrote:

> And here I cannot help bearing testimony against what appears to me a dangerous mistake which, though it may not be common, yet sometimes occurs among parents and guardians of the more serious class. I mean the mistake of *destining* young persons to the gospel ministry from a very early period of life, before they can be supposed, from any enlightened view of the subject, to concur in the choice themselves; and before they give any satisfactory evidence of vital piety. Brethren, I venerate the parent who desires, and daily prays, that it may please God to prepare and dispose his child to serve him in "the ministry of reconciliation" (2 Cor. 5:18). Nay, I think that parent worthy of the thanks

of every friend to religion, who solemnly devotes his child, even from the earliest period of his life, to the service of the church, and avowedly conducts every part of his education with a view to this great object; provided the original consecration, and every subsequent arrangement, is made on the condition, carefully and frequently *expressed*, as well as *implied*, that God shall be pleased to sanction and accept the offering, by imparting his grace, and giving a heart to love and desire the sacred work. But there is a wide difference between this, and resolving that a particular son shall be a minister in the same manner, and on the same principles, as another is devoted to the medical profession, or to the bar, as a respectable employment in life without recognizing vital piety, and the deliberate choice of the ministry, from religious motives, as indispensable qualifications. This kind of destination to the sacred office is as dangerous as it is unwarranted.[2]

I cannot improve on these sagacious words of Samuel Miller. In the light of the issues just addressed, if you are given the privilege and responsibility to help men discern whether or not they are called to the pastoral office, do all within your power to make sure that, in considering this call, they are not acting under the pressure of the unwise and unsanctified ambitions and desires of others. Sometimes the pressure comes from pastors, who can say with feigned humility that "there are no fewer than four men who sat under my ministry who are now in seminary preparing for the ministry." The real question is "Why are they there?" If it is because the pastor put unwise and unsanctified pressure on them so that they began to subtly feel that this is what they must do to please an earthly spiritual father, then this is not good. Although Paul wrote with reference to his unique calling as an apostle, in principle, every man who enters the Christian ministry should be able to say with him of his calling that it is "not from men nor through man, but through Jesus Christ and God the Father, who raised him from the dead" (Gal. 1:1).

Third, beware of *unbalanced and unbiblical concepts of spirituality.*

Spirituality refers to life in the Spirit. Some relate usefulness in the Christian ministry or the exercise of spiritual gifts as the major indicator of spirituality. It is easy to subtly assume that wider public usefulness is the way to a higher level of spirituality, or that public usefulness is automatically an expression of a higher level of spirituality. Yet this understanding is not

---

2. Samuel Miller, *An Able and Faithful Ministry* (Dallas, TX: Presbyterian Heritage Publications, 1984), 5, 6.

supported by the Word of God. It is true, and church members recognize, that those who exercise public gifts have a place of more extensive influence to promote the glory of God and advance the Kingdom of God. Still, spirituality is not to be associated primarily with the exercise of spiritual gifts, but with the fruit of the Spirit.

R. C. Sproul says:

> It is no accident that the fruit of the Spirit is not elevated in our ranks as the highest test of righteousness. There abides so much flesh in us that we prefer another standard. The fruit test is too high; we cannot attain to it. So within our Christian subcultures we prefer to elevate some lesser test by which we can measure ourselves with more success.[3]

Furthermore, according to Paul's presentation of spiritual gifts in Romans 12, it is clear that we are to assess our giftedness in conjunction with the total functioning of the body of Christ (Rom. 12:4–8). There is no indication in the entirety of this section on spiritual gifts (Rom. 12:1–8) that the identity of a specific gift somehow puts a person higher or lower on a scale of spirituality. Moreover, in Ephesians 5:18–6:9, when the people of God generically are urged to continue to be filled with the Spirit, it is assumed by the apostle that being filled with the Spirit will be expressed primarily in terms of faithfulness to the design and roles of wives, husbands, children, fathers, bondservants, and masters.

True spirituality is measured, not in terms of great giftedness in public ministry, but in practical Christlikeness, manifested in the horizontal relationships where God has sovereignly placed us. If this perspective is the prevailing emphasis of the Word of God, we must not create a climate in which those under our ministry assume that spiritual vitality and stature are necessarily related to specific gifts or offices. In fact, sometimes it is just the opposite, as our Lord indicated in that sobering passage in the Sermon on the Mount, where He indicated that, "On that day many will say to me, 'Lord, Lord, did we not prophesy in your name, and cast out demons in your name, and do many mighty works in your name?'" (Matt. 7:22). Essentially, the Lord Jesus is saying that they had ministerial gifts and outstanding ministerial success but no transforming grace making them holy men. Since He calls them "workers of lawlessness," we know that they were engaging in acts of secret sin while parading their "gifts." Clearly, this is demonic activity parading as spiritual light and gift. When Paul closes the section of

---

3. R.C. Sproul, *The Mystery of the Holy Spirit* (Wheaton, IL: Tyndale, 1990), 165.

qualifications he says, "Moreover, he must be well thought of by outsiders, so that he may not fall into disgrace, into a snare of the devil" (1 Tim. 3:7). We leave the door wide open for men to fall into that snare of the devil if we give the impression that public profile in ministry means a higher level of spirituality.

Fourth, be careful about *an inaccurate self-assessment.*

Attaining accuracy here is not an easy spiritual task. In taking up this subject, the apostle Paul is careful to underscore the necessity for sober thinking (Rom. 12:3). In a literal sense, sober thinking is the product of a man who is not drunk, whose mental activity is not altered or skewed by the influence of alcohol in his brain, but who is in possession of all of his rational faculties. Hence, when he looks at something, his brain accurately conveys what that object really is. A sober man does not look at a tree and say that he sees a pink elephant.

However, sober thinking with regard to the nature and measure of our spiritual gifts is not so easy a task as it might seem. Our remaining sin can be manifested in the subtle and deceitful actings of pride. Paul assumed that pride would be the great enemy of accurate self-assessment (Rom. 12:3). Pride would be the spiritual alcohol that makes our spiritual judgment distorted. Although sober thinking includes the need to avoid thinking too lowly of oneself, the majority of people are not inclined to this error, but are inclined to think more highly of themselves than they should. Pride operates on my self-assessment in a way similar to that in which a distorted funhouse mirror operates on my appearance. If you have ever looked into one of these, you know what happens. You recognize enough of your distinctive features that you know you are looking at a reflection of yourself, but you might appear to be four feet wide and ten feet tall, and shaped like the letter S. You recognize yourself in the image, but you are not seeing yourself as you really are. You are seeing yourself as the mirror distorts your image. This is what pride does to our self-assessment.

Jeremiah said, "the heart is deceitful above all things, and desperately sick; who can understand it?" (Jer. 17:9). This is clearly a description of the wretched state of the unregenerate heart. After the heart has been regenerated and the Spirit dwells within what the Bible calls the "new heart," that desperate condition changes. However, remaining sin, just as in any area of sin, still operates at the level of deception and pride. Believers are commanded to put these sins to death (Rom. 6:6–12; 8:13; Col. 3:5).

Because of natural pride and the deceitfulness of our hearts, we can have a distorted and inaccurate assessment of who we are and what gifts and graces we actually possess. Added to this, there can be ignorance of what a Christ-equipped pastor looks like. Because so little real preaching and wise, responsible oversight is exercised in our day, men are often surrounded by a low standard against which to measure themselves. With nothing around them to expose the fact that they are far from competent for the pastoral office, men can easily and mistakenly assume that they do meet the biblical standards. We must cry to God to remove our deceitful pride and ignorance. Then too, we must humbly and graciously seek the help of others.

Listen to Spurgeon as he addresses this issue:

> We must, however, do much more than put it to our own conscience and judgment, for we are poor judges. A certain class of brethren have a great facility for discovering that they have been very wonderfully and divinely helped in their declamations; I should envy them their glorious liberty and self-complacency if there were any ground for it; for alas! I very frequently have to bemoan and mourn over my non-success and shortcomings as a speaker. There is not much dependence to be placed upon our own opinion, but much may be learned from judicious, spiritually-minded persons. It is by no means a law which ought to bind all persons, but still it is a good old custom in many of our country churches for the young man who aspires to the ministry to preach before the church. It can hardly ever be a very pleasant ordeal for the youthful aspirant, and, in many cases, it will scarcely be a very edifying exercise for the people; but still it may prove a most salutary piece of discipline, and save the public exposure of rampant ignorance.[4]

Fifth, some err by *craving for personal identity.*

A man who is unsure of who he is might seek a level of acceptance and recognition based on what he does. Recognizing that there are many people who admire what ministers do, such a man might seek the position and office of an overseer in order to acquire some measure of a sense of self-worth. Similarly, some men might seek to be given a platform to express their views in order to gain some sense of identity in connection with what they regard as their own distinctive contribution to people's understanding of the truth.

---

4. Charles Spurgeon, *Lectures to My Students* (Edinburgh: The Banner of Truth Trust, 2008), 27, 28.

Brethren, the pastorate is no place in which to seek what can only be found in coming to grips with the fundamental issues which are bound up in the biblical doctrines of man and salvation. In other words, the answer to an unmet sense of need for personal identity and worth will not be found in ecclesiology, but in biblical anthropology and soteriology. You must first understand the biblical doctrine of who you are as a fallen image-bearer of God, and the doctrine of who and what you are as a renewed and transformed image-bearer in Christ. Once your understanding of those issues is firmly established, then you will know who you are. You will have a sense of personal identity. You do not need the ministry to define, nor to secure, your identity.

Sixth, a common mistake is to enter the ministry because one *underestimates pastoral responsibilities.*

Pastoral responsibilities are what these lectures on pastoral theology are all about; they are not just lectures on preaching or the call to preach, though we will address preaching extensively. These lectures constitute a call to assume the pastoral office, understanding something of the broad spectrum and full extent of its responsibilities. Therefore, an underestimation of pastoral responsibilities becomes a seriously flawed motivation for seeking the office and its activities.

In many ways it is impossible for a young man and woman to understand and possess an adequate view of the breadth or responsibilities connected with marriage. Before their wedding day, they may read several excellent books that set forth a biblically based, comprehensive view of what is entailed in saying the words "I do." However, it is only when they are actually married that they begin to truly understand all that they have taken upon themselves by making their lifetime covenantal commitment to one another, "till death do us part." In a similar way, no man can fully understand and appreciate the breadth of responsibilities connected with the pastoral office and functions until he actually begins to make a conscientious effort to fulfill those manifold responsibilities in relation to the flock of God among which he finds himself an undershepherd.

While the things I have just asserted are unquestionably true, every man who aspires to the pastoral office should do all within his power to acquire a biblically based, comprehensive, and accurate understanding of what will be involved in his assuming this office. If simply becoming a disciple of Christ mandates our "counting the cost" (Luke 14:28), how much more should there be a sober consideration of what will be involved in taking on an office with its functions in the church for which we must give an account to the Head of the church on the last day (Heb. 13:17). It is for this very reason that Paul charges Timothy, "Do not be hasty in the laying on of hands, nor take part in the sins of others" (1 Tim. 5:22).

Seventh, a most despicable motive is the *unmortified lust for personal gain*.

The pastoral office can become a source of authority, attention, influence, and in some cases, a position of monetary gain. An unmortified lust for such personal benefits in connection with the pastoral office is condemned in Scripture. We see this in the Pharisees, "And they love the place of honor at feasts and the best seats in the synagogues and greetings in the marketplaces and being called rabbi by others" (Matt. 23:6). This is the very thing which Peter says must not motivate elders,

> So I exhort the elders among you, as a fellow elder and a witness of the sufferings of Christ, as well as a partaker in the glory that is going to be revealed: shepherd the flock of God that is among you, exercising oversight, not under compulsion, but willingly, as God would have you; not for shameful gain, but eagerly; not domineering over those in your charge, but being examples to the flock (1 Pet. 5:1–3).

The compulsion of others, be they parents or pastors, shameful gain or the love of money, domineering or lording it over the people of God, a lust for authority—these are base and ungodly motives for taking on the solemn responsibilities of becoming an overseer.

May God grant, whenever we are given the opportunity to exert any influence upon men aspiring to the ministry, that we will do all within our power to encourage them to search their hearts, to make sure that they are not being moved toward this office by any unmortified lust for authority, attention, influence, and monetary gain often connected with it. I have set before the reader seven improper or even sinful motives which can find their way into one's aspirations for the pastoral office, as well as one's claim to having received a divine call to it. If the Spirit of God has uncovered in the heart of any man one or more of these motives, I urge such a man to acknowledge his error or sin and flee to the fountain open for sin and uncleanness.

CHAPTER 4

Aspiration to the Pastoral Office

We come now to address those things which comprise a biblical and orderly call to the pastoral office. My present understanding of the Word of God leads me to assert that there are four elements which comprise this call. Reducing them to a minimum of words, they are *aspiration, qualification, confirmation,* and *recognition.*

As we stand on the threshold of taking up this very serious question, we do well to listen again to the words of Isaiah who said, "To the teaching and to the testimony! If they will not speak according to this word, it is because they have no dawn" (Isa. 8:20). I am not denying that God can and does sovereignly ordain, permit, and overrule abnormalities, irregularities, and gross deficiencies when leading some men into the pastoral office. We know from the Word of God that God can and does work in ways that do not follow the norms prescribed in His Word, as in the way He used the disobedient prophet Jonah. We must understand, however, that what God may do is His business. What we ought to do is our business, and we ought to attend to our business with our minds and wills tethered to our Bibles.

Because I was initially ordained to the ministry in a deficient manner, I was prepared, after being in the ministry for a number of years, to have my calling and fitness reassessed in a more vigorously biblical framework. As my understanding of the biblical teaching concerning what constitutes an orderly call to the pastoral office grew, I became increasingly convinced that I needed to backtrack and reconsider the legitimacy of my initial ordination. Thankfully, at that time, I was in an ecclesiastical framework which made this possible. No doubt some would have regarded this proposed course of action as unnecessary. However, I needed this if I were to maintain a good conscience before God and be comfortable every time I read 1 Timothy 3:1–7 and Titus 1:5–9. I also gained the strong conviction that my own life and calling had to be consistent with my instruction of others on this subject. The ensuing years never found me doubting that I did the right thing.

We must take the biblical norms seriously and seek to follow them, even while remembering that God may, in some cases, sovereignly bring a man into the pastoral ministry where those norms have not been understood or conscientiously followed. Lucid teaching and clear thinking on any subject demand that the issues considered be presented in well-structured and logically connected units of thought. For this reason, I have already indicated that I will identify four specific categories of concern in answer to the question concerning what constitutes a biblical and orderly call to the pastoral office. However, I do not mean to suggest that everything must necessarily be experienced in this order, in each and every case, of a man whom God brings into the office of a teaching and ruling elder in His church.

This first element of a biblical call is *an enlightened and sanctified desire for the pastoral office.*

It is critical that we understand what is meant by the choice of these words. I am using the word *enlightened* to underscore the fact that, in a valid call, the desire does not flow out of ignorance, error, superstition, or romantic notions. Rather, an enlightened desire for the work is one that has been born of a biblical and realistic understanding of the fundamental nature and demands of the work involved in the pastoral office.

It is an unenlightened desire which Dabney attacks with withering sarcasm when he writes:

> Away with the notion that the young man is not called to preach unless he hath *fallen in love* with this special work, in some senseless and unaccountable manner, as though pierced with the invisible arrow of some spiritual Eros, or Cupid! It is nonsense, it is wickedness. The Holy Spirit is a rational being, the Bible is a rational book, and every Christian emotion which he produces in the human soul by applying Bible truth is produced according to the laws of the human understanding; it is a reasonable emotion prompted by reasonable and intelligent views of truth.[1]

I deliberately repeat these words for emphasis. This desire is not an unenlightened, ignorant, superstitious, romantic desire and aspiration, but a desire enlightened by the Word of God.

Furthermore, it is a *sanctified* desire.

---

1. Robert Lewis Dabney, "*What is a Call to the Ministry?*" in *Discussions: Evangelical and Theological,* vol. *2* (Edinburgh: The Banner of Truth Trust, 1967), 34.

I use this word to describe a desire that emerges under the purifying influence of the Holy Spirit, in direct contrast to a desire that emerges under the impulses and actings of unmortified remaining sin of one kind or another. A sanctified desire will be found in a heart in which the Spirit of God has in great measure negated the intoxicating influences of pride, of carnal ambition, of a distorted view of one's own importance, or of an inaccurate assessment of the nature and measure of one's gifts and graces. This enlightened and sanctified desire will be distinguished by four characteristics, namely, the *necessity* and *legitimacy* of the desire, the *focus* of the desire, the *assumed context* of the desire, and the *ideal disclosure* of the desire.

The Necessity and Legitimacy of the Desire for the Office

According to 1 Timothy 3:1, the desire ordinarily precedes and attends recognition to function in the work of the ministry. It is therefore, first, *a legitimate desire*. A man *aspires* to the office of overseer, and thus *desires* a noble task. This desire is to be strong and prevailing, as opposed to weak and intermittent. The two Greek words used are present indicatives. The first, *oregomai*, means to be eager for, and the second, *epithumeo*, means to lust after or desire strongly. Used in the present tense, these two verbs underscore the reality that the desire is not only to be present, it is also to be sustained. It is not a desire that occasionally and obliquely touches the heart and mind of a man, but a strong, continual desire that may grow into a kind of holy obsession.

Second, it is *a noble desire*, buttressed by the identity in 1 Timothy 3:1 of the faithful saying.

This is not a saying of which we ought to be ashamed. Rather, it is a saying identifying something that is noble and desirable when it is found in a man's heart.

Fairbairn's comments are worthy of note:

> The sentiment here expressed, then, is, that one who seeks (*oregetai*, stretches forth towards, longs after) the pastoral office, desires to be engaged in what is emphatically a good work. It is not merely a post of honour, or a position of influence; not that primarily at least, or in its more direct aspect, but a work of active service, and one that from its very nature brings one into living fellowship with the pure and good. The seeking here intended, therefore, after such an office, must be of the proper kind, not the prompting of a carnal ambition, but the aspiration of a heart which has itself experienced the grace of God, and

which longs to see others coming to participate in the heavenly gift. Other objects of a subordinate or collateral kind may not be unlawful, and may justly enough be allowed a certain share in the motives which draw men to the pastoral office; but if the heart is right with God, and takes anything like a correct estimate of the work of the ministry, it will be that work itself, considered with respect to its own excellent nature, and the blessed fruits that may be expected to spring from it, which ought more especially to awaken the desire and determine the choice. Hence the prominence given in the directions that follow to qualifications of a spiritual and moral kind, in order to its efficient discharge; introduced also by an *oun, therefore,* as much as to say: The work being so good, there is of necessity required in him who would enter on its functions a corresponding character of goodness.[2]

The emphasis of 1 Timothy 3:1 is that passionate desire for the ministry must precede and attend the work. Furthermore, how can a man fulfill the mandate of 1 Peter 5:2 without it? There Peter says, "Shepherd the flock of God that is among you, exercising oversight, not under compulsion, but willingly, as God would have you; not for shameful gain, but eagerly." Serving with willingness and eagerness is the fruit of passionate desire for the work. The additional words of this text emphasize that the man called by God does not regard himself as one who has been drafted or conscripted against his will. He has eagerly and joyfully volunteered for the task.

The Focus of the Desire for the Office

The focus is the office of overseer itself (1 Tim. 3:1). It is the entire work or task of the overseer that is to be the focus of a man's desire, not just teaching and preaching. This fact brings me back to underscore once more why I do not feel comfortable with the terminology couched in the words, *I am called to preach,* or *I desire to preach.* Many a man loves the sound of his own voice but does not want to take the towel and the basin and wash feet. Yet, much of true pastoral oversight and ministry is a form of spiritual foot-washing labor carried on in the humble spirit manifested by our Lord Jesus Christ when He literally washed the feet of His disciples (John 13:1–11). The desire is to focus upon *the work,* not on any apparent glory and prominence attached to one aspect of the work such as preaching, which is usually most associated with the ministry. The work is specifically taking care of the church of God

---

2. Patrick Fairbairn, *The Pastoral Epistles* (Edinburgh: T. & T. Clark, 1874), 136, 137.

(1 Tim. 3:5). I set before you three strands of concern which ought to mark a sanctified desire for taking care of the church of God.

The first strand of desire for taking care of the church of God is *the edification of God's people.*

It is a longing to be used in self-denying service to edify, build up, advance, and promote the ongoing sanctification of the people of God. This first strand is beautifully captured in the inspired words of the apostle Paul when he wrote to the Colossian church, "Him we proclaim, warning everyone and teaching everyone with all wisdom, that we may present everyone mature in Christ. For this I toil, struggling with all his energy that he powerfully works within me" (Col. 1:28, 29). Paul gave the reason why pastors and teachers are given to the church by the ascended Christ, in Ephesians 4:11–13,

> And he gave the apostles, the prophets, the evangelists, the shepherds and teachers, to equip the saints for the work of ministry, for building up the body of Christ, until we all attain to the unity of the faith and of the knowledge of the Son of God, to mature manhood, to the measure of the stature of the fullness of Christ.

The writer to the Hebrews indicates that the shepherd's work is for "keeping watch over your souls" (Heb. 13:17). These are the facets in the prism of light that shine in the care which the Great Shepherd gives through His undershepherds.

The second strand of desire for taking care of the church of God is *the calling out of God's elect.*

The book of Acts shows that most recorded instances of the church's growth through conversions is found in connection, not with the generic witness of the individual saints of God or the corporate witness of the church functioning as light and salt, but with the proclamation of the Word by the appointed servants of God. Paul expressed this perspective when he said, "Therefore I endure everything for the sake of the elect, that they also may obtain the salvation that is in Christ Jesus with eternal glory" (2 Tim. 2:10).

The New Testament oozes with evangelistic passion, especially in the hearts of the ministers of the gospel. After our Lord Jesus, Paul is the great and predominant model for us, and he said, "for though I am free from all, I have made myself a servant to all, that I might win more of them" (1 Cor. 9:19). He then went on to give examples of how he became as a Jew to win the Jews, and as one outside the law to win them, and as weak to win them. In summary, he became all things to all people, "that by all means I might save some" (1 Cor. 9:22).

Paul shows the necessity which God has imposed upon the church to preach in order to further the calling out of His elect,

> For "everyone who calls on the name of the Lord will be saved." How then will they call on him in whom they have not believed? And how are they to believe in him of whom they have never heard? And how are they to hear without someone preaching? And how are they to preach unless they are sent? As it is written, "How beautiful are the feet of those who preach the good news!" (Rom. 10:13–15).

Luke also records the fact that the lifestyle of the people of God, in general, validated the gospel as it was being preached, and the corporate life of the church formed the context of that preaching. This combination of powerful preaching in the context of godly church life was the open secret of the effectiveness of the preaching of the Word of God in the early days of the Jerusalem church (Acts 4:32–35). Yes, there is a proper emphasis to be placed upon the duty of every believer to seize every opportunity, according to his gifts and other circumstances, to speak of Christ and the salvation procured by His Person and work. I neither doubt nor deny this fact. Yet, neither can we deny that the text of Scripture leads us to believe that God chooses to call out His elect primarily through the sent ones, as they proclaim the message of salvation in the power of the Holy Spirit. Paul commanded Timothy to "do the work of an evangelist" (2 Tim. 4:5). Therefore, if part of the pastoral office and function is the privilege of standing as a commissioned herald to speak forth the truth of the gospel, then surely a desire for that office should manifest itself, not only in a longing to be used in self-denying service to edify the people of God, but in a longing to be used in Spirit-filled ministry to call out the elect of God.

Here Spurgeon speaks passionately:

> It is a marvel to me how men continue at ease in preaching year after year without conversions. Have they no bowels of compassion for others? no sense of responsibility upon themselves? Dare they, by a vain misrepresentation of divine sovereignty, cast the blame on their Master? Or is it their belief that Paul plants and Apollos waters, and that God gives no increase? Vain are their talents, their philosophy, their rhetoric, and even their orthodoxy, without the signs following. How are they sent of God who bring no men to God? Prophets whose words

are powerless, sowers whose seed all withers, fishers who take no fish, soldiers who give no wounds—are these God's men? Surely it were better to be a mud-raker, or a chimney-sweep, than to stand in the ministry as an utterly barren tree.[3]

The yearning must at least be present. Notice I am not saying that one must have a constant evidence of being used to convert sinners, but that there ought to be a longing to be so used. I find it very disturbing, when attending evangelical and even Reformed churches where there is a robust commitment to confessional biblical orthodoxy and expository preaching, and yet preachers find no avenue out of the text or subject to address the unconverted passionately and plead with them to be reconciled to God. Do they really believe that everyone to whom they preach is in a state of grace? Surely they do not. Yet, if there are indeed lost men and women and boys and girls sitting before them, and they believe that we do not know what a day may bring forth, and that some could pass into hell before the following Monday, how can they go through Lord's Day after Lord's Day with no impassioned entreaty to the lost? One has to question why men like that are in the ministry. Did they ever have a desire to be used in calling out God's elect?

The third strand of desire for taking care of the church of God is *the longing to discharge a growing sense of God-given stewardship.*

I address this aspect of a sanctified desire particularly to those who have not yet entered the office. Paul speaks of our stewardship in two important passages. The first is, "I am still entrusted with a stewardship" (1 Cor. 9:17). The other is, "This is how one should regard us, as servants of Christ and stewards of the mysteries of God" (1 Cor. 4:1). I do not believe that the mysteries of God referred to in this context are the sacraments of baptism and the Lord's Supper. Rather, the mysteries of God are the revealed truths of the gospel, truths concerning the Person and work of the Lord Jesus, and the spiritual blessings offered to sinners in the proclamation of that gospel.

In bringing to a conclusion my treatment of this aspect of a sanctified desire as an essential element in a legitimate call to the pastoral office, I can do no better than recommend the words of Charles Bridges. I will quote portions to whet your appetite for this excellent section in Bridges, and recommend that you read further in the pages I reference in the footnote:

---

3. Charles Spurgeon, *Lectures to My Students* (Edinburgh: The Banner of Truth Trust, 2008), 31.

The desire of the work was a prominent feature in the Ministerial character and qualifications of Christ.... The Apostle strongly marks *a constraining desire* as a primary Ministerial qualification; something far beyond the general Christian desire to promote the glory of God.... It should also be a *considerate desire*—the result of matured calculation of the cost. This, we fear, has been sometimes lost sight of, in the exchange of secular profession.... Waiting time is of the utmost moment to scrutinize the real principles of the heart, which have dictated an abandonment of the calling originally, (as it was presumed) suggested by the Providence of God; and in which ordinarily it is the will of God that we should "abide."... It must also be a *disinterested* desire. Pure intention is indispensable to the meanest service in the Lord's work.... One of the most certain marks of the Divine call is, where it is the purpose of a man's heart *to live, to labour, and to possess nothing*, but for Jesus Christ and his Church.... God implants a love in the heart for the service to which he calls; and better would it have been for you to have felt, that it was not the Ministry for which you were intended, than that you should possess a want of inclination for the performance of its duties. *It is not necessary*, that a voice from heaven should say to you in secret—"The Lord hath not sent you." Your judgment, enforced by the dictates of your conscience, tells you so.[4]

The Assumed Context of the Desire for the Office

The all-important 1 Timothy 3 passage, with its presentation of the desire for office as a noble pursuit, and the sobering qualifications for the office-bearer, comes in the context of an already healthy, biblically functioning church. Paul referred to this when he said, "I hope to come to you soon, but I am writing these things to you so that, if I delay, you may know how one ought to behave in the household of God, which is the church of the living God, a pillar and buttress of the truth" (1 Tim. 3:14, 15). You remember the history of the church in Ephesus. That church was birthed through the labors of Paul and his companions during Paul's second missionary journey. He left Timothy at Ephesus some years later while he went on to Macedonia. So when the apostle repeated this faithful saying to Timothy concerning church officers, it was not a saying coined by naïve theorists. It was a saying approved by an apostle and given in the context of a church already graced with qualified

---

4. Charles Bridges, *The Christian Ministry* (Edinburgh: The Banner of Truth Trust, 1976), 94–98. Be sure to read the excellent footnotes as well in this section of Bridges.

men who were actively engaged in pastoral labors in the church at Ephesus (Acts 20:17–31).

Therefore, when any man began to desire the office and labor of an overseer, he should have before his eyes what that labor involved, as he saw it fleshed out in the lives and the labors of the existing eldership. It was these very men whom Paul gathered together at Miletus toward the end of his third missionary journey, charging them with their ongoing pastoral responsibilities to the flock of God in which the Holy Spirit had made them overseers. The context in which this desire for overseership was to be regarded as a noble thing, and in which this desire would grow in the heart of a man, was the context of a functioning, well-ordered church, a church in which the counsel of mature men and women could be sought, and in which there would be all of the privileges, as well as the checks and balances, of that context.

The Ideal Disclosure of the Desire for the Office

If, by God's grace, a man is beginning to experience the kind of enlightened and sanctified desire for the work of the ministry of the pastoral office as I have described in the previous pages, to whom should he make that desire known? Suppose he is persuaded it is necessary to possess that desire. Suppose the focus of his desire is increasingly characterized by a longing to be used in self-denying service to edify God's people, as well as to be used in exercising a Spirit-filled ministry of calling out the elect. Suppose he has a growing sense of burden which might be expressed in words like these: "I believe increasingly that God may be bestowing a stewardship upon me. I did not seek it or ask for it; I believe that it is being laid upon me. In the context of the church I want to know if this desire should be pursued." In such a case, to whom should a man express this sense of possibly being called to the office and ministry of an overseer? I suggest four legitimate recipients of the man's disclosure of this desire.

First and foremost, he should express his growing desire *to God Himself.*

Many of us can remember that, as young Christians, one of the first verses we memorized was Proverbs 3:5, 6, "Trust in the Lord with all your heart, and do not lean on your own understanding. In all your ways acknowledge him, and he will make straight your paths." As this desire begins to be birthed in a man's heart, encourage him to lay it out before God in the confidence warranted by this promise. Encourage him to ask God to search his heart and to intensify the desire, if it is being divinely kindled. Encourage men who may seek your counsel concerning this matter to consider when this desire is most intense and most consciously throbbing in their hearts. Encourage them to ask themselves if this desire is most active in the times when they are closest to the Lord, when they are most consistent in their devotional life, and most conscious of growing in grace. Desires birthed and nurtured in the context of a healthy devotional walk with God are the desires that are most likely rooted in the working of the Holy Spirit.

Second, if he is a married man, he should express his growing desire *to his wife.*

First Timothy 3:4 tells us that an elder "must manage his own household well." No little part of this management is found in a husband's ability to incorporate his wife's perspectives on matters that will involve a major impact upon their life together. In light of this text, it is my persuasion that if a man desires to be recognized as a gift of Christ to His church in an orderly and biblical manner, his wife should concur with him that indeed the requisite gifts and graces are becoming more and more evident in his life. Her husband, if recognized as an elder, will be her pastor, or one of her pastors. If that thought is utterly incongruous to her, inclining her to say, "You, my pastor? Forget it!" then he had better say to himself, "Wait a minute, this desire may be premature, or even illegitimate."

Encourage men to bare their hearts to their wives and to ask their wives very frank questions, pleading with them to give honest answers as they work through 1 Timothy 3:1–7 and Titus 1:5–9 together. "Dear, be as honest with me as God will be on the Day of Judgment. The issues at stake are too great to allow any indulgence of carnal sentiment or fear of hurting me by telling me the truth." Some already in the work of eldership may be reading these pages who might be afraid to do what I am suggesting even now, because you know the shortcomings to which your wife would point.

My personal testimony may be helpful here. One of the most salutary periods in my life was a period after our adult children were out of our home. One of our church members had a cottage near the New Jersey shore. My wife and I would get away there for seven to ten days once a year, and part of that time was called our annual Judgment Day, in which my wife was asked, "Dear, please tell me honestly what changes you would make in me to make me more like Christ, no matter what those changes would be." The ground rules were that I was permitted to make no defense, no excuses, and to speak only when I needed clarification. I agreed to place invisible duct tape on my mouth and just listen. Then, the next day, she put the duct tape on her mouth and just listened. Of course, those initial mutual disclosures would lead to further amplification, explanation, and helpful interaction. By God's grace, this practice proved to be helpful in promoting our individual sanctification, as by this means we were able to identify areas where we needed to grow in grace.

The issues my wife identified in the sessions were not matters that were so crassly contrary to the Word of God that I should have disqualified myself in light of 1 Timothy 3 and Titus 1. Yet, they certainly were areas that I needed to work on if my wife were to sit under my ministry and from the depths of her being continue to embrace me as her shepherd. She needed to see me growing in grace, if I were to keep a hold on her conscience with an iron grip, when she sat as one of my sheep and listened to me preach.

If a man's growing desire for the office and labor as an overseer is of God, then surely his wife with whom he is one flesh will share with him his own personal growing conviction that he should continue to pursue the office. If she does not grow in her conviction that our aspirations are just and righteous, then we will have to ask questions like these: "Is it the will of God for me to pursue this matter at the price of threatening our marital oneness?" "If we are not agreed regarding my calling, can we together be an example of what a God-honoring Christian marriage looks like?"

Third, he should express his growing desire *to his pastors*.

If you are in a place of leadership in the church, encourage men in the church who may begin to feel this desire to bare their hearts to their pastors, and to ask probing questions: "Have you seen the emergence of graces, and the emergence, at least in some seed form, of gifts that have caused you, as one of my pastors, to wonder whether it could be that Christ is forming me into a gift to give to His church?" "Can you, at this time, encourage me to continue nurturing my growing desire for the eldership, or should I simply put it on the shelf and give myself to my other stewardships like my job, my family, and my other roles in the church?"

Those of you who are in places of spiritual responsibility should encourage men who come with such questions and concerns to remember that they are coming for counsel which may not conform to their present inclinations. They should understand this, and not have the attitude that, if your counsel does not agree with their desires, they will jump ship and seek to find

some other church leaders in another place who will rubber-stamp their
own independent decision concerning this issue. You should make it very
plain to them that they should listen to your responses, prayerfully weigh
your counsel, and be ready to embrace it, insofar as it has been rooted in
the teaching of the Word of God and conditioned by an accurate knowledge
of you.

> Obey your leaders and submit to them, for they are keeping watch over
> your souls, as those who will have to give an account. Let them do this
> with joy and not with groaning, for that would be of no advantage to
> you (Heb. 13:17).

This exhortation should exert its proper influence on how we respond to
the counsel we have sought from our legitimate overseers.

Fourth, he should express his growing desire *to mature, trusted, spiritually minded friends and counselors*, especially if among them are men and
women who are older than he is.

It can be very helpful for him to bare his heart to those who know him
best, love him most, know God and His Word, and love the man enough to
be honest with him concerning his aspirations to the pastoral office.

Concurring with me in this counsel, Spurgeon wrote:

> Considerable weight is to be given to the judgment of men and women
> who live near to God, and in most instances their verdict will not be a
> mistaken one. Yet this appeal is not final nor infallible, and is only to
> be estimated in proportion to the intelligence and piety of those con-
> sulted. I remember well how earnestly I was dissuaded from preaching
> by as godly a Christian matron as ever breathed; I endeavored to esti-
> mate, with candour and patience, the value of her opinion; but it was
> outweighed by the judgment of persons of wider experience. Young
> men in doubt will do well to take with them their wisest friends when
> next they go out to the country chapel or village meeting-room and
> essay to deliver the Word. I have noted—and our venerable friend, Mr.
> Rogers, has observed the same—that you, gentlemen, students, as a
> body, in your judgment of one another, are seldom if ever wrong. There
> has hardly ever been an instance, take the whole house through, where
> the general opinion of the entire college concerning a brother has been

erroneous. Men are not quite so unable to form an opinion of each other as they are sometimes supposed to be.[5]

When the Trinity Ministerial Academy was in existence, we took that observation from Spurgeon seriously. For a period of time, we used to have an annual season of peer evaluation. As elders and instructors, we prepared a brief list of the things concerning which the men were to evaluate one another. We prepared a list of all the men enrolled so that each student could evaluate each of his brethren. The students understood that their evaluation was to be based on their exposure to one another's graces and gifts of utterance in their regular opportunities to preach to one another at the Academy chapel times. Their time in the classroom together afforded ample opportunity to observe the measure of their biblically required graces of Christian character.

The elders and instructors would meet with each student, having taken careful notes of the various comments concerning one another. After all of that material was collated, we would meet with each man privately, asking him, "Do you want to know what you look like in the eyes of your brethren? Here is a summary and distillation of their assessment." With no names mentioned, we would summarize positive and negative qualities. For example, in giving a man his peer evaluation, we might say to the brother something along these lines:

> Your brethren in the Academy perceive in you some evident leadership qualities. They have seen you taking the initiative in numerous situations, where your initiative was very evident and commendable. On the other hand, they see in you a streak of stubbornness. When it comes to matters that are not matters of principle, you are ready to stand your ground just because it is your ground and you are not willing to yield your position, even though the issues are not black-and-white biblical issues, but matters of judgment.

This gave us a wonderful opportunity to identify and give exhortations concerning areas of character that needed to be shored up, as well as give commendation concerning aspects of character that were commendable. One of the most searching questions we asked toward the conclusion of each interview was this: "If [student's name] continues to grow in the graces and

5. Charles Spurgeon, *Lectures to My Students* (Edinburgh: The Banner of Truth Trust, 2008), 29.

gifts required for an overseer, in five years' time could you with good conscience picture yourself embracing him as your pastor or fellow-elder?"

In addressing this vital issue of what constitutes a biblical and orderly call to the pastoral office, I have asserted that the first of four components of such a call is an enlightened and sanctified desire for the work of the pastoral office. I trust that what I have laid out concerning these matters is true to the Word of God, and that the reader will find it helpful as we seek to evaluate our own calling, and as we give counsel to others who aspire to the office of an overseer.

CHAPTER 5

Qualifications of Christian Character

Having looked at aspiration for the Christian ministry, we now devote ourselves to understanding what the Scripture says concerning qualification or fitness for the pastoral office. We will consider the relevant biblical material concerning qualifications under three headings: *Christian character, Christian experience,* and *pastoral gifts.* I begin first, as I often do, with words of encouragement and of caution.

In dealing with the matters of fitness for the pastoral office, I am seeking to expound the biblical standard which must be attained by the time a man is formally proposed to the church for recognition as a gift of Christ to His church. Therefore, I urge any man with some degree of desire for the work of the ministry not to be discouraged and assume that he must not be called because he discovers that he is presently lacking one or more of these scripturally mandated graces or gifts. These requisite graces or gifts for pastoral labor are not acquired automatically. Do not assume, that if any of them are lacking, that they will simply appear and fall into place with the passing of time. Do not expect them to suddenly show up on their own or on the day of your formal scrutiny for official recognition. If you see, or others see, specific deficiencies in any of these areas of your character, experience, or gifts, you must do what Peter says all believers must do, "Make every effort to supplement your faith" (2 Pet. 1:5). With the blessing of God on your diligent efforts, you and other discerning people may see these deficiencies in graces or gifts wonderfully and powerfully overcome by the grace of God.

Dabney is especially helpful here:

> Our definition of the call to preach asserted that God would make known his will to the candidate and to his brethren, not only through the medium of the Scriptures, but also of outward circumstances and qualifications viewed in the light of Scripture truth. Much has been said by Christians concerning "the leadings of providence," touching the duty of preaching and many other duties. And not a little nonsense,

with perhaps some profanity, has been uttered on this subject. It is true that everything which befalls us is determined by God's special providence, for which reason we justly conclude that, in many cases, an occurrence, after it has happened, is a real expression to us of God's will. But there is another truth, that the designs of God's special providence are chiefly reserved among the awful secrets of his own fathomless wisdom. He forbids us to attempt to surmise his secret purpose from the apparent tendencies of his sovereign dealings, and pointedly remands us "to the law and the testimony" for our practical guidance. The light which "providences" cast upon the question of God's will as to our conduct is chiefly cast backward on the past, not forward on the future. The man who attempts to frame the "leadings of providence" into an indication of duty, instead of resorting to his revealed will, is often in danger of wickedly intruding into those secrets which belong to the Lord our God, and of profanely foisting the selfish leanings of his own inclination upon the Holy One as the teaching of his acts.

There are, indeed, certain dispensations of providence which, in the light of the word, do clearly reveal God's will. If he has deprived any man of the health, the voice, or the knowledge, without which he cannot possibly preach, and has made it absolutely impossible to acquire or regain them, or if he has surrounded a man with clear, unavoidable duties which cannot possibly be postponed or delegated, and which are clearly incompatible with the ministry, here is indeed a sure expression of the divine will that he may not preach. But it has often been said, in well-meant treatises on the call to the ministry, that a Christian may know whether God designs him to preach by the providential facilities which open, or hindrances which seem to bar, the entrance into the sacred office. This rule is to be accepted with many "grains of allowance." If God has facilitated the acquisition of the suitable learning and the other means for preaching, it does indeed present a probable evidence that the person may be called. But the converse is not true. If circumstances have hedged up the young Christian's access to the ministry with obstacles, difficulties, hardships, we freely admit that all these are determined by God's special purpose and providence. But we do not know what God means by them. He has not told that young Christian whether he means to tell him thereby that he must not preach, or whether he means it for "the trial of his faith, that being much more precious than gold that perisheth, it may be found unto praise, and honor, and glory at the appearing of Jesus Christ." Let that man, therefore, take heed how he presumptuously misinterprets a providence which God has not authorized him to read at all; let him turn to the Bible and to prayer. How plausibly might the great apostle have argued after the modern fashion when he met shipwreck, scourgings, prisons, stoning, wanderings, neglect, poverty in the prosecution of his ministry, that "the leadings of providence clearly indicated he was not called to a foreign mission!" But he argued no such thing; he knew better. He said, "None of these things move me; neither count I my life dear, so that I might finish my course with joy, and the ministry which I received from the Lord Jesus." Does the reader object that Paul had a revealed call, but we common mortals must judge by just these providential events, which he properly disregarded? Let us take then the case of Dr. Wm. Carey, the great Baptist missionary to Hindostan. When he first began to seek his duty, a poor shoemaker with a growing family already upon his hands, without classical learning, without money, without patronage, with the power of the East India Company so arrayed against the gospel that it was forbidden to all their ships even to carry a missionary across the ocean, might not he have plausibly concluded, according to this argument, that "the leadings of providence" were against him? But who can now doubt that he was called of God, first to become a preacher of the gospel, and then to begin the Serampore mission? By this cowardly argument Washington would have judged the "leadings of providence" to be against the cause of his country. But why mention the ten thousand cases in which history shows us the noblest enterprises were conducted to success, with the final blessing of providence, as no one now doubts, only by braving obstacles almost insuperable? If, then, the young Christian is surrounded with outward hindrances, it is his duty to ask: "Is it possible for me lawfully to conquer them by the most strenuous exertions of my best faculties, nerved by deathless love for Christ?" If it is, then it may be his duty to preach.[1]

Having issued that word of encouragement, the word of caution I offer is this. While the emphasis in these next few chapters will fall on the presence and manifestation of those graces and gifts becoming evident prior to and upon one's entrance into the pastoral office, you and I must never forget that the maintenance and increase of these graces and gifts is a biblical responsibility laid upon every overseer. We must never become like the college professor who begins to breathe more easily once he obtains academic tenure. He may never study as he did before, may never read as widely and deeply as before, and may only occasionally dabble in a non-challenging

---

1. Robert Lewis Dabney, "*What is a Call to the Ministry?*" in *Discussions: Evangelical and Theological*, vol. 2 (Harrisonburg, VA: Sprinkle Publications, 1982), 29–31.

writing project here or there. In other words, once made secure by the attainment of his tenured professorship, he may never again do the things that brought him to the position of a tenured professor. Once safely nestled, he may begin and continue to coast.

Similarly, a young man who aspires to get his officially recognized law enforcement officer's badge in a very prestigious law enforcement agency may do everything to pass the mental acumen test, the strength and endurance test, and the weapons proficiency test. However, once he has earned his badge, he may become slovenly, out of shape, and generally unfit to perform the tasks for which he was formerly recognized and for which he was given his badge.

First Timothy 4:12–16 epitomizes the thrust of the teaching of God's Word at this point:

> Let no one despise you for your youth, but set the believers an example in speech, in conduct, in love, in faith, in purity. Until I come, devote yourself to the public reading of Scripture, to exhortation, to teaching. Do not neglect the gift you have, which was given you by prophecy when the council of elders laid their hands on you. Practice these things, immerse yourself in them, so that all may see your progress. Keep a close watch on yourself and on the teaching. Persist in this, for by so doing you will save both yourself and your hearers.

Paul does not tell Timothy to do these things until he is forty years old, or until he is well established as a mature and well-respected minister. No, Timothy was to render obedience to this solemn charge from the apostle until the end of his days. He used a present imperative verb when he directed him to keep a close watch on himself. He used another present imperative when he directed him to persist in these things.

When those in leadership fall short of being and doing what is so plainly revealed in Scripture, so that this is plain even to the man sitting in the pew with his Bible on his lap, it can do untold harm to the people of God. In your functions as a pastor, you are continually calling on others to conform their lives to the standards of Scripture. How grievous, then, should your hearers read in their Bibles what the overseer *must be*, and yet see in you things which contradict that standard, and areas in which you have fallen short! How could they receive the Word of God from you and believe that you are really sincere? Beware of calling them to obedience from a posture of patent disobedience, when one or more of the required graces and gifts which God says must be present in an elder are notably absent in the pattern of your life and ministry.

How dare we traffic in the things that are calculated to cause our people to grow up into conformity to Christ, to grow in love for Christ, and in zeal for the Kingdom of Christ, while we ourselves are not making observable progress in those very things? How can we persuade our people that the truths which we declare in our public ministries are indeed effectual to produce those ends mentioned in the previous paragraph, if they are not evidently producing them in those of us who traffic in those realities with our words, but are not manifesting them in our lives? May that old proverbial statement never legitimately be spoken of us: "What that preacher is and does speaks so loudly that I cannot hear a word of what he says."

By the word of encouragement given earlier, I have aimed to immunize some of you against an unwarranted discouragement, if areas of personal deficiency are identified, as we work through these specific biblical requirements which constitute a man's fitness for the office of overseer. By means of my word of caution, I hope that some of my readers who already occupy the sacred office are stirred up to a new level of diligence by this fresh reminder that you have no right to coast or to assume that you can just allow things to go on as they have for years in your life and ministry.

There are three categories of qualification for the office: qualifications of *Christian character*, *Christian experience*, and *spiritual gifts*. I now take up the first of the three categories which make up this second aspect of the call.

Christian Character

God requires, of all who aspire to the pastoral office, the manifested graces indicative of a genuine, matured, balanced, and proven Christian character.

There are key words here to which we do well to pay attention. The first is the word *character*. By this I mean what a man is in his moral constitution, not what he says he is or possesses, but what he actually is. In describing character as *Christian*, I have in mind character that has its source in the grace of God in Jesus Christ and the operations of the Holy Spirit. Christian character is what a man is as Christ lives in him (Gal. 2:20), or as Christ is formed in him by the power of the Holy Spirit (Gal. 4:19). We certainly expect that a man aspiring to the pastoral office, or a man already in the pastoral office, will be a man in whom the Spirit of Christ is *powerfully* working. Do you not wholeheartedly agree with this? Is not this what you expect from your pastor? Of course, unless you are out of touch with the gospel! Conformity to the image of Christ (Rom. 8:29, 2 Cor. 3:18) and the fullness of the Spirit producing His fruit in the heart of a minister (Gal. 5:22–24) are *essential* and *expected*.

When I speak of *manifested graces*, I am referring to specific aspects of Christian character in all of its manifold components, as they are present and discerned in a man's life. If Christian character is the sun, then the manifested graces are the rays as they reach the earth with discernible light and heat. In fact, when Paul lists the specific graces in 1 Timothy 3 and Titus 1, he takes for granted that Timothy, Titus, and others will be able to recognize the presence or absence of those graces in a man's life by human observation, without any need for possessing or claiming either divine omniscience or divine infallibility.

The four final key words can be grouped together as adjectives describing the Christian character which must be manifested in a man qualified for the pastoral office. Those adjectives are *genuine, matured, balanced* or *symmetrical*, and *proven*.

It must be *genuine* Christian character.

Paul speaks to Timothy in a way that points to Paul's persuasion of Timothy's unfeigned, genuine, sincere faith, "I am reminded of your sincere faith, a faith that dwelt first in your grandmother Lois and your mother Eunice and now, I am sure, dwells in you as well" (2 Tim. 1:5). Christ condemns spiritual leaders who appear impressive on the outside but are something else inwardly, "Woe to you, scribes and Pharisees, hypocrites! For you are like whitewashed tombs, which outwardly appear beautiful, but within are full of dead people's bones and all uncleanness" (Matt. 23:27). The Christian character required of a man called to the pastoral office is not to be like a lump of lead overlaid with a thin layer of gold. Although such a lump may appear to be a solid gold nugget, if you were to cut off a slice, you would know very quickly that you have simply been looking at a ball of lead overlaid with a thin layer of gold leaf. I use the word *genuine* to indicate that the Christian character manifested in a man truly called to the pastoral office must indeed begin in his inner disposition and character. God wants us to be pure gold in our godliness, not lumps of gilded lead.

It must be *matured* Christian character.

By this word I am underscoring the fact that these graces of Christian character in a man for ministry must be more than the buds just sprouting on the tree of a recent convert, or a tree full of blossoms in the spring but not yet laden with mature fruit. A study of the words used in 1 Timothy 3 and Titus 1 describing the required Christian character reveals that those same words are used elsewhere in Scripture for character traits required of all the people of God without distinction. However, in the man of God who would take up the work of an overseer, these graces must be matured beyond the level of the rank and file of God's people. If not, he will be unable to fulfill one of the major aspects of an elder's job description, that of being an example to the flock,

> Shepherd the flock of God that is among you, exercising oversight, not under compulsion, but willingly, as God would have you; not for shameful gain, but eagerly; not domineering over those in your charge, but being examples to the flock (1 Pet. 5:2, 3).

Paul said, "Be imitators of me, as I am of Christ" (1 Cor. 11:1). Paul exhorted Timothy, "Let no one despise you for your youth, but set the believers an example in speech, in conduct, in love, in faith, in purity" (1 Tim. 4:12). A similar charge was laid upon the conscience of Titus when Paul wrote to him, "Show yourself in all respects to be a model of good works, and in your teaching show integrity, dignity, and sound speech that cannot be condemned, so that an opponent may be put to shame, having nothing evil to say about us" (Titus 2:7, 8).

It must be *balanced* Christian character.

Symmetry refers to the interrelationship of parts to form a whole which is aesthetically pleasing to the eye. The dictionary definition of symmetry is, "beauty of form arising from balanced proportions." Balance refers to equal weight in the offsetting parts of an object. Using these words in the context of my concern to describe the kind of Christian character required in one aspiring to the eldership, I am seeking to underscore the necessity for taking seriously all of the specific graces identified by the apostle in 1 Timothy 3:1–7 and Titus 1:5–9. A man with great moral courage who obviously lacks sensitivity to people is a man whose character is out of balance. The same is true of a man who has great sensitivity to people, but who lacks moral courage. Both categories of men are lacking in a balanced or symmetrical Christian character, and are therefore unfit for the pastoral office and function, as long as that imbalance remains in any dominant manner.

It must be *proven* Christian character.

This points to the fact that a man has undergone sufficient time and experience to test the apparent genuineness of his graces and to ripen the quality of those graces. The apostle wrote, "we rejoice in our sufferings, knowing that suffering produces endurance, and endurance produces character, and character produces hope" (Rom. 5:3, 4). When tribulation or suffering comes upon us with its attendant pressures, this will be on display in us if we are the real thing. James begins his epistle with a reference to the relationship between tribulation and provenness when he says,

> Count it all joy, my brothers, when you meet trials of various kinds, for you know that the testing of your faith produces steadfastness. And let steadfastness have its full effect, that you may be perfect and complete, lacking in nothing (Jas. 1:2–4).

This relates to the diaconate as well, for Paul says that a man must first be tested or proven before he is formally recognized as a deacon (1 Tim. 3:10). How much more is this necessary for elders, who have the responsibility of spiritual leadership of the people of God? In addition, Paul indicates that this quality of provenness applies to the issue of how long a man has been in the faith, "He must not be a recent convert, or he may become puffed up with conceit and fall into the condemnation of the devil" (1 Tim. 3:6).

The first and most fundamental category of fitness for the office is manifested graces indicative of genuine, matured, balanced, and proven Christian character. This brings us back to the old adage, "It is the man that makes the minister, not the ministry that makes the man."

Particular Graces

We now come to review the specific graces which are presented to us as the standard of qualification for the pastoral office in 1 Timothy 3:1–7 and Titus 1:5–9. The first thing we will address are the differing circumstances of these two lists of qualifications. When we compare the two lists, it is obvious that they are not mirror images of one another. I am convinced that part of the answer to why these differences exist lies back of the peculiarities of the differing circumstances in Ephesus and in Crete.

Patrick Fairbairn emphasizes this in his commentary on 1 Timothy 3:6 (while focusing on the requirement found in Titus, not 1 Timothy):

A further qualification: *not a novice,* or *recent convert (neophuton,* literally, newly planted*).* Of course such a qualification must be understood relatively—in some a less, in others a longer period of probation being required, according to circumstances. In quite recently planted churches, such as those of Crete mentioned in Titus, it would not be possible to obtain persons for the presbyterate who had been long established in the Christian faith, though even there also differences in this respect would be found to exist. But in Ephesus, and various other churches in that locality, where for probably not less than twelve or fifteen years there had been Christian communities, there was ample room for the prescription in question; hence it has a place here, while quite naturally it is not found in the instructions given to Titus. And as at Ephesus there were not only numerous adversaries outside the church, but adherents of error also beginning to ply their wiles within, it was of the more importance that those invested with the oversight of the community should be persons of some experience in the divine life—men whose intelligence and solidity of character had been already proved, lest, amid the fermenting of false opinions and the craft of designing hypocrites, they might be betrayed into evil.[2]

Furthermore, I believe the two lists of requirements are not identical because of an undergirding principle. Each list is only broadly suggestive of the fundamental requirement of being *blameless,* or *above reproach.* Two different Greek words, basically synonymous, meaning *blameless,* are used in 1 Timothy 3:2 and Titus 1:7. In each case, what follows is, in a sense, a commentary with specific examples of what it means to be blameless. If each of these lists were to comprise the beginning, middle, and end of the requirements, then they would have to be the same, or we would have two different standards for the eldership, one that applied only in Crete, and another only in Ephesus. We know that would not be the mind of God for the simple reason that the office and functions of a pastor-teacher, elder, overseer, is one office, demanding the same qualifications that constitute fitness for that office in all places and at all times. Therefore, we should consider these two lists as specimens of some of the principal graces to be included in a description of blameless Christian character. By no means are either of these lists meant to be regarded as exhaustive. In comparing the two lists and trying to lay out in sequential form the specifics contained in them, I have sought to

2. Patrick Fairbairn, *The Pastoral Epistles* (Edinburgh: T. & T. Clark, 1874), 142, 143.

grasp the larger category, of which the specifics are illustrations or indications. I want to list the major concerns of the two statements combined.

The first is that in both passages there is a requirement that *this non-negotiable, uncompromising standard must be maintained.*

This is seen in the emphatic particle of necessity, *dei*, translated *must be*,
in 1 Timothy 3:2, and in Titus 1:7. This is the same particle of necessity that
our Lord used in Luke 24:26, "Was it not necessary that the Christ should
suffer these things and enter into his glory?" The very necessity which moved
our Lord to the cross stands before the standard required of the overseer and
elder. It is not only *good* that he possesses these gifts and graces, or simply
desirable that he possess them, but *essential*, a non-negotiable requirement
for the office-bearer.

Christ has given us the portrait of those whom He is giving as gifts to the
church, that we might look at the portrait and compare it to the spiritual face
and form of the one aspiring to the office. If the two do not match, that man
is not a gift of Christ. God has given us, in these passages, a heaven-drawn
portrait of those men whom Christ has prepared to give to His church as
pastors, teachers, and overseers. That this standard must become normative in the church is seriously underscored by the employment of that little
particle of necessity.

The second major concern of both passages is the requirement of *blamelessness.*

In both passages it is required that there be no just grounds to charge an
overseer with any pattern of inconsistency in godly character.

Lenski comments on these two key passages by saying:

> It has been remarked that all of these save the ability to teach and that
> of not being a novice or beginner in Christianity are requirements that
> apply to all Christians, which is quite true and shows that, as far as
> morals are concerned, the New Testament has only one standard for
> both clergy and laity and not two. Yet we may note that in the case of
> the members of the congregation faults may be borne with which can-
> not be tolerated in ministers, for they are to be examples of the flock
> (Phil. 3:17; II Thess. 3:9; I Pet. 5:3). A man who aspires to the ministry
> must be of proved character.[3]

---

3. Richard C. H. Lenski, *The Interpretation of St. Paul's Epistles to the Colossians, to the
Thessalonians, to Timothy, to Titus, and to Philemon* (Minneapolis, MN: Augsburg Publishing
House, 1937), 579, 580.

A third area found in the two passages is the *requirement of unquestioned sexual integrity.*

The sexual integrity required in 1 Timothy 3:2 is that the overseer must be, translated literally, a "one-woman man," *mias gunaikos andra.* The natural, on-the-surface meaning is that he must be attached to only one woman, not a polygamist, and by implication, only one woman in his eyes and heart and bed. This same requirement is stated in Titus 1:6, using the same phrase, *mias gunaikos aner.* A man who aspires to or occupies the pastoral office must be patently, not marginally or barely acceptably, a one-woman man. This reality must be abundantly evident in his general demeanor in relating to women, and in his observable interaction with his own wife. He must be a man who has one woman in his heart, in his eyes, in his arms, in his bed, and in his desires. There must be unquestioned sexual purity and marital fidelity, so much so that one would have to be wicked and slanderous even to raise the slightest suggestion that there is any other woman in his heart or in his arms other than his wife.

I passionately plead with every reader of these pages, do not be naïve concerning this aspect of the biblical qualifications for an elder. Massive amounts of reproach have been heaped upon the name of Christ in our generation as high-profile Christian leaders have fallen prey to the sin of adultery. Indulgence in pornography has risen to epidemic proportions, not only among the rank and file of men in evangelical churches, but in men who are entering into, and who remain actively engaged in pastoral ministry. Responsible evangelical organizations have conducted surveys which reveal that an alarming number of evangelical pastors are indulging in the frequent viewing of pornographic sites on the Internet. Such men are not one-woman men. They are finding delight in the sight of other women's bodies.

When Solomon is instructing his son to avoid immorality, he charges him in this language:

> Let your fountain be blessed, and rejoice in the wife of your youth, a lovely deer, a graceful doe. Let her breasts fill you at all times with delight; be intoxicated always in her love. Why should you be intoxicated, my son, with a forbidden woman and embrace the bosom of an adulteress? (Prov. 5:18–20).

Men who view pornography, as they fantasize having sexual intimacy with the nameless naked bodies paraded on the screen before them, are indulging in mental adultery. Our Lord solemnly warned,

You have heard that it was said, "You shall not commit adultery." But I say to you that everyone who looks at a woman with lustful intent has already committed adultery with her in his heart. If your right eye causes you to sin, tear it out and throw it away. For it is better that you lose one of your members than that your whole body be thrown into hell. And if your right hand causes you to sin, cut it off and throw it away. For it is better that you lose one of your members than that your whole body go into hell (Matt. 5:27–30).

For many, this sinful indulgence is carried on in the privacy of their studies. Late at night, early in the morning, an unsuspecting wife thinks she has a devoted husband and a dedicated pastor who is diligently studying, while much of the time he is ogling the filthy and vile images that come over the Internet. If you are a pastor, press the issue of sexual purity with any man, married or single, that you are responsibly shepherding, and especially with any man aspiring to the ministry. Graciously charge them to be honest with you as they will have to be with our Lord in the Day of Judgment, perhaps using questions such as these: "What are you doing with your computer? Are you bringing up images that are defiling your mind? How frequently are you indulging in this sinful behavior? Do you have an Internet filter or account-ability software that blocks questionable Internet content? Or do you have a trusted friend to check on what you are watching on your computer, tablet, or smartphone? What practical steps are you taking to deal with this pattern of sin with gospel motives, provisions, and power?"

If you are in the category of someone frequently falling in this area, blow the whistle on yourself. Deal with yourself, your heart and your spirit, before God, with relentless steps and resolves to put this degrading, defiling, and disqualifying sin to death (Rom. 6:11; 8:13; Col. 3:5). Go to your pastor, your fellow-elders, or a trusted brother, and come clean with them about your need for deliverance from this pattern of sinfulness. Be prepared, if necessary, to embrace some form of church discipline as a means of grace and aid to your deliverance.

If the words which I have written have been like arrows that have found their mark in you, remember two texts of Scripture. The first is Numbers 32:23, "But if you will not do so, behold, you have sinned against the LORD, and be sure your sin will find you out." The other is Proverbs 28:13, "Whoever conceals his transgressions will not prosper, but he who confesses and forsakes them will obtain mercy." Obedience to the clear command of James may never be more needed than in conjunction with dealing with this sin,

"Therefore, confess your sins to one another and pray for one another, that you may be healed. The prayer of a righteous person has great power as it is working" (Jas. 5:16).

A man called to the pastoral office must be a one-woman man. This must be a reality in his heart, and unquestionably in his conduct. And not only with regard to the negative and sinful issues which we have just considered, but in the manifestly positive expressions of love and tender care which a godly husband and lover shows to his beloved wife. A man may be *clean* with respect to the sins of immorality, but *cold* or *callous* toward her whom the Scripture declares is his companion and wife by covenant (Mal. 2:14). Think about what this expression, a one-woman man, is really saying about the exclusive love which a man is to have for his own wife. It is similar to the first commandment, which requires us to worship God *alone* and have Him as the *sole* object of our worship. We are not to worship our wives, but we do adore our wives with an exclusive, God-honoring and passionate love. This pleases God and does not violate our love for Him. Paul described this love as love which reflects Christ's love for His bride the church (Eph. 5:25).

In our exegesis of the phrase *a one-woman man*, we have only spoken of the faithfulness and devotion of a man to his wife, but does the text say more? Does it say anything about his marital status, whether he is divorced or a widower? Clearly, the text does not say anything explicit about either of these subjects, leaving us to the teaching of other passages on divorce to determine what the Bible says about it. Some hold the position that a man divorced under any circumstances is disqualified from the pursuit of, or for continuing in, the pastoral office. I do not hold this position, for I believe that there are two biblical exceptions to the stringent divorce law of Christ and Paul, namely adultery (Matt. 5:32; 19:9) and desertion (1 Cor. 7:15). And it is difficult to imagine that a widower would be disqualified, based on the principle stated in Romans 7:2, 3.

Lenski comments on these issues:

> Paul had a reason for beginning with "*one* wife's husband." In those days mature men were chosen for the eldership, who, as a rule, were married and had families; there were no seminary graduates who were awaiting calls. The bulk of the membership from which the elders had to be chosen had come from paganism. What this means as to sexual vices is written large in the New Testament and in the moral records of the day. Even the early apostolic conference in Jerusalem warns against "fornication" and uses this wide term to cover all the prevalent pagan sexual

excesses (Acts 15:29). The epistles fairly din the word into their readers'
ears. There was the regular institution of the *hierodouloi*, pagan temple
prostitutes; the common custom of having *hetaerae* ("companions,"
see Liddell and Scott *etairos*), girls from non-citizen families who were
used by unmarried and married men; and thus, besides these standard
practices, all the rest of the vileness that formed the soil from which
these grew. Converts to the gospel did not at once step into perfect
sexual purity. Hence this proviso regarding the "overseers": to begin
with, a man who is not strictly faithful to his one wife is debarred.[4]

A fourth requirement is *exemplary domestic piety*.

First Timothy 3:4, 5 describes the overseer as one who "must manage
his own household well, with all dignity keeping his children submissive,
for if someone does not know how to manage his own household, how will
he care for God's church?" Titus 1:6, 7 says, "If anyone is above reproach,
the husband of one wife, and his children are believers and not open to the
charge of debauchery or insubordination. For an overseer, as God's steward,
must be above reproach." If you go into a man's home and spend an evening
with his family, you should, at the end of that evening, be forced to conclude,
"This man knows how to manage his family. He knows how to use authority with clout and with gentleness, with grace and with dignity. He governs
his family with a steel hand covered with a velvet glove. It is evident that he
knows how to manage them with the dynamics of grace working in his own
heart, as the steward of his own home."

While he still has governance over his children, there must be no just
accusation that they are guilty of a pattern of riotous or unruly living as a
result of his negligence as a father and as the appointed head of his household. This requirement for domestic competence does not speak to the state
of his children when they leave home, and if they choose to reject the God of
their mother and father. I have no sympathy for the position that, if a man's
children ultimately prove to be unconverted and throw off all of their early
training, this disqualifies a man from the pastoral office. This position is not
sustainable by a responsible exegesis of these two foundation passages in
1 Timothy 3 and Titus 1, nor the overall teaching of Scripture, particularly

---

4. R. C. H. Lenski, *The Interpretation of St. Paul's Epistles to the Colossians, to the Thessalonians, to Timothy, to Titus, and to Philemon* (Columbus, OH: Lutheran Book Concern,
1937), 580, 581. For an extended treatment of the words, *a one-woman man*, see Patrick Fairbairn, *The Pastoral Epistles* (Edinburgh: T. & T. Clark, 1874), 418–432.

the book of Proverbs. In fact, God, the perfect Father, declares, "Children have I reared and brought up, but they have rebelled against me. The ox knows its owner, and the donkey its master's crib, but Israel does not know, my people do not understand" (Isa. 1:2, 3). Would anyone be prepared to charge God with parental failure because His children rebelled against Him?

My former wife and I experienced the sadness of having two grown children, both of whom were professing Christians and baptized members of TBC, whose lives became inconsistent with being in a state of grace. This reality eventually led to both of them being disciplined by the church. When our children turned away from their profession of discipleship, I solemnly charged my fellow-elders to make a judgment concerning whether or not they believed that the actions of my adult children disqualified me from retaining my position as an elder in the church. The following contains the gist of what I said to them on that occasion:

> Brethren, you must make me a faceless man. You must not allow your love and respect for me to prejudice your honest judgment. If you believe that the state of my adult children is the fruit of my failures and delinquency as the God-appointed ruler in my home, you must honestly convey that conclusion to me and to the congregation. You have seen the patterns of my life as a father over decades. Based on what you have seen, you are responsible to judge whether or not the present spiritual condition of these children is the result of patent failures in the way I ruled my own house. If their state is not in any way demonstrably attributable to my failures, then I believe you ought to announce this judgment to the people of God, so that I may continue to preach to them, while holding their consciences respecting my integrity as a servant of Christ.[5]

I am not writing about these things in a theoretical framework. I am saying them out of deep wrestlings of heart, touching my own fitness for the pastoral office. There must be exemplary domestic piety in any man who would serve Christ in the pastoral office.

A fifth requirement is the *graces essential in a pattern of self-control*.

First Timothy 3:2 uses the word *nephalios*, meaning *sober, temperate, self-controlled*. It speaks of a man's self-restraint, and of a man who acts in

---

5. Thankfully, one of these dear children, at the age of fifty-six, has professed conversion and is manifesting many hopeful indications of possessing new life in Christ.

a restrained manner, as if he has a halter on himself,[6] as the overall pattern of his life. Titus 1:8 says, "but hospitable, a lover of good, self-controlled, upright, holy, and disciplined." The ESV renders the word self-controlled as *disciplined*. This is an appropriate translation. As we so often see, one English word does not always capture every nuance of a Greek word.

Lack of self-control and discipline can be present in ways not obvious to the world. However, when an individual does not have self-control over his eating, others will know that such a man lacks self-control with regard to his appetite and consumption of food. Now I realize that I am going "from preaching to meddling." I do not write this to be insulting or to unnecessarily offend anyone who is grossly overweight who is reading these pages. You are faceless and nameless to me. Yet, the fact is that you cannot preach with conscience-gripping power those truths of God's Word which call God's people to a life of self-denial, self-control, and moderation, when your paunch is hanging over the pulpit, and jiggling jowls declare your lack of discipline. You cannot do it, my brother. Furthermore, your obesity precludes rendering that obedience to that clear command originally given to Titus, but applicable to every servant of God, to "show yourself in all respects to be a model of good works, and in your teaching show integrity, dignity" (Titus 2:7).

As a general rule, and except where there is a distinct physical pathology of one kind or another, a simple formula explains reality for most of us. Here is the formula: *What goes into our mouths when we eat, minus what goes out in bodily elimination, and what is burned up by metabolism and physical exercise, stays on.* So, if more and more is staying on, then you need either to intensify what gets burned up, or lower the amount of what goes in. Better yet, in most cases, do both. This is where the issue of self-control confronts many of us. I know what foods enable me to stay within the range of a healthy caloric intake. When I lived in North Jersey there were many times when I would drive by a local *Dunkin' Donuts* establishment, and I had to learn to say to myself times without number, "Albert, you don't have time for an extra half hour on the treadmill. What goes in with that *Dunkin' Donuts* doughnut will eventually give *you* a doughnut on your midsection." I had to learn to apply the truth spoken by Paul, "I discipline my body and keep it under control, lest after preaching to others I myself should be disqualified" (1 Cor. 9:27).[7]

---

6. Louw, J. P., & Nida, E. A., *Greek-English Lexicon of the New Testament: Based on Semantic Domains* (New York: United Bible Societies, 1996), reference #88.87.

7. See also Deuteronomy 21:20 and Proverbs 23:21 where God places the glutton (the one who overeats as a pattern of life) alongside the drunkard.

With respect to my disciplines of exercise, I know what kind of exercise I have to do so that I maintain a healthy weight, sustain a healthy cardiovascular system, and preserve reasonably healthy bones and muscular mass and strength in my eighty-two-year-old body (as I write). If I am to preach and write concerning these things with a good conscience, a "couch-potato" pattern of living will not cut it. Furthermore, to allow myself to go to pot would undermine my credibility with those of you reading this book.[8]

I am not unsympathetic to those who struggle with the temptation to gluttony. I love food. I am not addressing this specific aspect of self-control as someone who is indifferent to, or utterly detached from, the difficulties and frustrations involved in exercising discipline and self-control with respect to my own eating habits. I have entertained preachers in my home that would sit at my table and eat three times as much food as I ate. Yet, looking at them, you would think that they had been fasting for forty days. In some sense, it is not self-evident that all men are created equal! Robert Murray M'Cheyne rightly said, "The man who loves you the most is the one who tells you the most truth about yourself." Although I may not know you personally, I love you enough to tell you the truth about yourself. If you have a problem in this area, you need to stop saying, "Well, I know I need to do something about it." Rather, you need to begin to do something about it. Do what you must to obtain and maintain a good conscience in these matters. Often, in matters of this nature, it is a helpful means of grace to choose an accountability partner, a mature brother in Christ to whom you report on a regular basis regarding your progress.

If you are counseling any man, young or old, who is seeking to discern if he is called to the pastoral office and ministry who obviously is overweight, you should lovingly but firmly instruct him that you could not consent to laying hands on him until it was evident that he had attained a good measure of self-control with regard to his struggle with weight issues. Remember, self-control and discipline are mentioned as one of the *must be* character traits of a man who aspires to the office of an elder.

---

8. For an extensive treatment of this issue, see Albert N. Martin, *You Lift Me Up: Overcoming Ministry Challenges* (Ross-shire, U.K.: Mentor, Christian Focus Publications, 2013). Also, see my book, *Glorifying God in Your Body–Whose is it–Yours or His?* (Montville, NJ: Trinity Pulpit Press, 2017).

The sixth requirement is for graces indicative of *sound judgment*.

The Greek adjective *sophron* points in this direction. It means *sober-minded, self-controlled, sensible, prudent*. This adjective appears both in 1 Timothy 3:2 and Titus 1:8. In both passages the ESV translates it *self-controlled*. The control envisioned in the word is the control of the thoughts, which in turn controls the man. It is the opposite of a forgetful or scatter-brained person who cannot hold things together in a way that work can be done adequately, stewardships can be carried out faithfully, and plans can be made prudently. The end result envisioned by the word is responsible action. Here we place the requirement that the man not be "a drunkard" (ESV), or, "addicted to much wine" (NASB). This specific requirement is attached to self-control and sound judgment, but with respect to the moderate use of wine. Wine alone is mentioned, as it is in many places in the Bible, as a good gift of God (Ps. 104:15; Prov. 3:10), while the excessive use or abuse of wine is identified in Scripture as the sin of drunkenness.

A seventh area is the requirement of *graces essential to good relationships with people.*

We can call it *amiability*, and it is expressed in three of the four words found in 1 Timothy 3:3, "not a drunkard, not violent but gentle, not quarrel-some, not a lover of money." The word translated *violent* is the Greek word *plektes*. It refers to a *pugnacious* person, a *bully*, a *striker*. It is also used in Titus 1:7. Physical striking is probably not in view, though that can happen, but rather, to a man who hurts with words. The word translated *gentle* is the Greek word *epiekes* which means "not insisting on every right of letter of law or custom, *yielding, gentle, kind, courteous, tolerant*."[9] The word translated *not quarrelsome* in the ESV is the Greek word *amakos*. A form of the root word *makos* in Greek means to *quarrel* or *fight*. So the alpha privative negates the idea, rendering the word *amakos* as *not quarrelsome* (ESV), or, *peaceable* (NASB). The ASV renders it *not contentious*. Each of these translations is good, but it is best to keep all three in mind because the word includes both aspects, positive (peaceable) and negative (not quarrelsome or contentious).

It is easy to see that these words speak of our relations to others in the thick and thin of life. These qualities are essential for relating to people in

---

9. Frederick William Danker, et al., *A Greek-English Lexicon of the New Testament and Other Early Christian Literature, Third Edition* (Chicago: University of Chicago Press, 2000), 371.

a way that reflects the power of the gospel in the heart, life, emotions, and even in the general social graces of the man of God.

The eighth requirement is that a man *not be a lover of money.*

Both 1 Timothy 3:3 and Titus 1:7 require that the aspiring elder have pure, non-mercenary motives for desiring the office. He must not be *a lover of money* (1 Tim. 3:3) or *greedy for gain* (Titus 1:7). I like the ASV translation of Titus 1:8, *not greedy of filthy lucre.* It makes the mercenary motive out to be what it in reality is, *filthy!*

Here again I express my growing concern as I become more aware of men who pursue the ministry as if they are on a career track in the corporate world. They seem to be unashamed and very forward about their baseline salary, extra benefits, paid vacations, and other monetary perks. Such a mindset is at odds with Paul's exemplary disposition and perspective,

> I coveted no one's silver or gold or apparel. You yourselves know that these hands ministered to my necessities and to those who were with me. In all things I have shown you that by working hard in this way we must help the weak and remember the words of the Lord Jesus, how he himself said, "It is more blessed to give than to receive" (Acts 20:33–35).

The Bible clearly teaches that the gospel worker is entitled to have his living from the gospel (Matt. 10:10; Luke 10:7; 1 Cor. 9:14; 1 Tim. 5:18). It teaches that a minister should, all things considered in each situation, receive an honorable recompense for his labor (1 Tim. 5:17). But Paul did not always use this right, as he explained. "If others share this rightful claim on you, do not we even more? Nevertheless, we have not made use of this right, but we endure anything rather than put an obstacle in the way of the gospel of Christ" (1 Cor. 9:12). This reveals Paul's heart in the matter of money. He understands, believes, and teaches the people of God that they have a divine duty to take care of their ministers, but he is sensitive to his situation and willing to work to teach others how to work (2 Thess. 3:8, 9), and to forego the right of compensation to give the false apostles no ground to accuse him of being mercenary. Paul was able to "present the gospel free of charge" (1 Cor. 9:18).

I well remember the words I stated to the official board of the first church I pastored in North Jersey: "It is my conviction that, if God is bringing me to this church, He will provide for me, and if He does not choose to provide for all I need through your hands, He will have His ravens to provide whatever is lacking for me and my family."

The ninth requirement is for *graces indicative of an aggressive love of people.*

Both 1 Timothy 3:2 and Titus 1:8 use the Greek word *philoxenos* which means *lover of strangers.* It is often rendered *hospitable* in English versions. There were no motels, as we now know them; travelers depended on hospitality. The same word is used in 1 Peter 4:9, "Show hospitality to one another without grumbling." Here we have a clearer sense of the nature of the requirement. The requirement that an elder be a man who shows a genuine love to people does not apply simply to strangers who may come among the congregation from some distance, but to the household of God. As is true with all generic Christian duties, those in the pastoral office are to show themselves "examples to the flock" (1 Pet. 5:3). The biblical teaching on hospitality, applied to the aspiring and the existing elder, points to what I am calling an aggressive love of people. We do, and we should, expect this of a man whose work is to shepherd souls.

The tenth requirement is for *graces essential for effective leadership of others.*

This, and the final two areas of requirement, are peculiar to 1 Timothy 3. They are not found in the Titus 1 passage. "If someone does not know how to manage his own household, how will he care for God's church?" (1 Tim. 3:5). Here the important word *epimeleomai* is used. We will look deeply into this subject in Unit 6, but may it suffice now to say that this is one of the major terms which define the nature of the pastoral office. The pastor-elder *takes care of* the church of God. He considers all the needs and determines how those needs are to be met, and he sets out to meet them or see that others meet them. It is the word used of the Samaritan in the parable of Luke 10:34. He "took care of" the man in need.

The eleventh requirement is for *graces essential for maintaining a good testimony before the unconverted.*

Paul says, "Moreover, he must be well thought of by outsiders, so that he may not fall into disgrace, into a snare of the devil" (1 Tim. 3:7). Whoever is responsible for recognizing a man as a gift of Christ to the church for the pastoral office must make specific efforts to find out whether he does indeed have a credible testimony with the non-Christians in his neighborhood, his place of work, and in the other settings of interaction with "outsiders." I will also discuss this requirement in more detail in Unit 6.

The twelfth and final requirement is for *graces issuing from tried experience which in some measure will neutralize vulnerability to pride.*

This requirement is found in the words of 1 Timothy 3:6, "He must not be a recent convert, or he may become puffed up with conceit and fall into the condemnation of the devil." This is a reference to mature Christian experience which will diminish pride to some extent.

Fairbairn's comments are especially perceptive:

> The verb (from *tuphos*, smoke, mist, cloud) denotes not simply the self-elating spirit which would raise one as to the clouds, but also the senseless, stupid character of such a spirit; its confusing, mystifying tendency acting like a lure to the emotions, and a cloud to the reason. What the apostle feared was, that the too sudden elevation to office might carry the individual off his feet, as it were, and render him an easy prey to the arts of plausible and designing men. The very probable result he expressed by a reference to the fall of the great adversary, as if this in such a case would be repeated afresh; for there can be little doubt that the condemnation spoken of—judgment in the sense of condemnation—is the genitive of object: the judgment passed upon the devil. The supposed neophyte, through his inexperience and undue elation of spirit, first falls into the sin of the old aspiring apostate, and then shares in his condemnation, passing from the sphere of a minister of light into the doomed condition of an instrument of darkness. The lesson, with its attendant warning, is for all times. It tells the church, that as there are temptations and perils peculiar to the ministerial office, so men should not be in haste to enter it, nor should others seek to push them prematurely forward. At the same time, the matter is wisely left in a certain indefiniteness; no precise age or specific term of probation is fixed in Scripture.[10]

In summary, I say that this is only a cursory overview of those graces which are indicative of genuine, balanced, proven Christian character. Fairbairn again:

> Thus ends the apostle's list of qualifications, which he desired to see meeting in every one who might be placed in the responsible position of an overseer of Christ's flock. They are, as already stated, predominantly moral, and consist of attributes of character rather than of gifts and endowments of mind. The latter also to some extent are included, in so far especially as they might be required to form clear perceptions

---

10. Patrick Fairbairn, *The Pastoral Epistles* (Edinburgh: T. & T. Clark, 1874), 143, 144.

of truth and duty, to distinguish between things that differ, and in difficult or perplexing circumstances to discern the right, and know how to maintain and vindicate it. Yet, withal, it is the characteristics which go to constitute the living, practical Christian, which together make the man of God, that in this delineation of pastoral equipments are alone brought prominently into view. And whatever else the church may, in the changeful circumstances of her position and history, find it necessary to add to the number, in order to render her responsible heads fit for the varied work and service to which they are called, the grand moral characteristics here specified must still be regarded as the primary and more essential elements in the qualifications of a true spiritual overseer.[11]

Above all, dear reader, if you presently occupy the pastoral office, I urge you to periodically read through and pray over these passages, remembering that you dare not attempt merely to coast. If God has enabled you to experience a measure of development and maturity in these graces, I urge you to pray that they may increase and abound yet more and more, so that your growth in grace may be evident to all.

With regard to a man's fitness for the office, at the head of the list are not gifts, but the graces of true godliness. Our primary area of concern should be one of seeking to assess a man's character, looking for symmetry and balance in those graces which are wrought in the heart and life by the Holy Spirit. If, indeed, as we have seen, the primary emphasis in the two basic passages which set forth the requirements for any man aspiring to the office of overseer is the matter of a man's graces, we ought to place our primary emphasis on the same area that the Spirit of God has underscored in 1 Timothy 3 and Titus 1.

---

11. Patrick Fairbairn, *The Pastoral Epistles* (Edinburgh: T. & T. Clark, 1874), 145, 146.

CHAPTER 6

Qualifications of Christian Experience (1)

We resume our consideration of qualifications for the pastoral office. I stated that there are three areas of qualification: *Christian character, Christian experience,* and *pastoral gifts.* We are coming now to the area of divine requirements for the pastoral ministry in terms of a man's Christian experience, which I describe simply as *clear indications of an enlarged, balanced, and tested Christian experience.*

First, let me explain the meaning of the key words of this description. By *Christian experience,* I do not mean some specific individual experience. Rather, I have in mind the totality of a man's personal, experiential acquaintance with those things that form the very essence of the life of God in the soul of a man. An able minister of the New Covenant must minister to the broad spectrum of the real spiritual needs of the flock of God. Such a man must have more than a theoretical acquaintance with the spiritual realities that are set forth in Scripture as normative. I am referring to realities as manifested and confirmed in the lives of God's people recorded in Scripture and confirmed in Christian biography and church history, those things which pertain to the actual outworking of the dynamics of grace in the soul of a redeemed man or woman.

I fully acknowledge that we cannot read men's hearts. This text often comes to mind in this regard, "For the LORD sees not as man sees: man looks on the outward appearance, but the LORD looks on the heart" (1 Sam. 16:7). However, since the church through its appropriate channels must make a judgment regarding a man's fitness for the pastoral office, then there must be some clearly visible and discernible indications of these things in the realm of Christian experience. I am referring to indications concerning which the church and discerning men not only ought to, but can and must make judgments. What those clear indications are, and how we perceive them, will differ in the case of each man under consideration as a potential pastor.

In some cases, these dimensions of Christian experience will come to light in the way a man prays. Unless he is a downright hypocrite who simply echoes the language of experimental divinity, the prayers of such a man will reflect that he knows something of soul-wrestling in a true believer's experience. In other cases, as a man is given opportunities for public ministry, there will be nuances and emphases in his preaching and teaching which clearly manifest his understanding of Christian experience. Whatever age he may be, as you sit under his ministry, you say to yourself, "that man understands something of the struggles of sin and grace in the life of a true believer; he knows something of the reality of the highs and the lows of normal Christian experience." Or it may be evident that people begin to be drawn to a specific man for his counsel in practical matters. As you keep your ear to the ground, you will find different people in the assembly beginning to testify how they were helped by this man, who, during a time of fellowship with them after a worship service was able to give them just the precise application of a biblical truth that they needed to hear. In these differing ways, as we seek to assess men who have aspirations to the ministry, we will begin to discern whether or not they do indeed manifest and give clear evidence of an enlarged, balanced, and tested Christian experience.

I use the word *enlarged* to describe that measure of Christian experience which is beyond that of a babe in Christ, a novice in the things of God. We see this distinction in our Bibles. As John wrote his first epistle, he was very conscious that, among those who would read it, or to whom it would be read, there were saints in various stages of spiritual development. For example,

> I am writing to you, little children, because your sins are forgiven for his name's sake. I am writing to you, fathers, because you know him who is from the beginning. I am writing to you, young men, because you have overcome the evil one. I write to you, children, because you know the Father. I write to you, fathers, because you know him who is from the beginning. I write to you, young men, because you are strong, and the word of God abides in you, and you have overcome the evil one (1 John 2:12–14).

See how he begins with a generic description of those whom he was addressing, and then descends to the specific groups among them.

Robert Candlish writes:

> As such, as little children, he first addresses them all, and appeals to them all collectively. But then, secondly, he separates them into two

classes,—"fathers" and "young men,"—old and spiritually exercised Christians on the one hand, and on the other hand, those who are in the fresh and vigorous prime of recent but yet manly Christian experience. All alike are "little children;" but some are "fathers," ripe for glory; others are "young men," strong for work. Such, as I apprehend, is the real primary meaning of this threefold appeal of John.[1]

You will remember how the writer to the Hebrews addresses his readers,

For though by this time you ought to be teachers, you need someone to teach you again the basic principles of the oracles of God. You need milk, not solid food, for everyone who lives on milk is unskilled in the word of righteousness, since he is a child. But solid food is for the mature, for those who have their powers of discernment trained by constant practice to distinguish good from evil (Heb. 5:12–14).

They become mature not primarily by stuffing their heads with theology, but by becoming casuists in Christian living, keeping a good conscience before God and man, and constantly bringing their consciences to the touchstone of Scripture. *Casuistry* in Christian living is the ability (to which the writer referred in these verses) to discern good and evil by constant practice. This is what I am referring to when I speak of enlarged Christian experience. Those who aspire to be overseers must not be babes who are ignorant of the fundamental struggles of the Christian life and of the provisions of grace available to us in Christ by His Spirit. There must be a measure of *enlarged*, as opposed to *minimal*, Christian experience.

I use the word *balanced* in the same way I used it with respect to Christian character. It is an obvious fact of pastoral interaction with people, and in the reading of Christian biography, that a man's experience can in great measure color his whole view of God's truth in its various operations in the life of God's people. When I use the word *balanced*, therefore, I mean a man whose Christian experience is not overloaded in one direction, so as to distort both his understanding and representation of the truth, as it impinges upon the experience of the lives of God's people.

An example may help. I remember years ago there was a preacher in the southern part of our country who for years had been an unconverted preacher. God brought him into the crucible of a Bunyan-like experience of deep, disruptive, and lengthy conviction of sin. On the other side of it,

---

1. Robert S. Candlish, *I John* (Edinburgh: The Banner of Truth Trust, 1973), 151.

he came out a thoroughly converted man. However, his ministry to God's people became imbalanced because he took his experience as the paradigm for everyone else. He assumed that, in any given church, the majority of the people were deceived as he was for years, and that they had to go through the same experience in order to be true believers. When this man preached on certain themes, he preached with tremendous power and insight. Yet, to sit under his ministry for any length of time would be to have either a totally distorted view of the biblical doctrine of conversion, or to be brought into unnecessary and crippling bondage, because his own Christian experience was imbalanced.

Then there are some people who seem to be constantly living in the sunshine of such texts as Romans 5:1–5 and the peace and glorious hope of which Paul so eloquently writes, even when they are passing through sufferings. Such a person knows an almost perpetual experience of the sunshine of felt communion with God and joy in the Holy Spirit. He has not known periods of struggle—what the old writers called a "dark night of the soul"—a period of struggle with indwelling sin that has thrown them into a paroxysm of uncertainty and doubt, causing them to question whether or not they are even truly in a state of grace. If the Christian experience of such a man consistently full of hope, peace, and joy is not in some measure brought to a more balanced state, he will be unable to enter into, empathize with, and give proper counsel to a child of God who may come to him in a prolonged state of spiritual depression.

Conversely, there are some who seem to live, morning, noon, and night, January through December, in the last half of Romans 7. It seems that, every time one of these brethren opens his mouth, we hear him say, "Wretched man that I am!" (v. 24). Such people live under the dark shadow of the struggle with remaining and indwelling sin, and they hardly know a day of cloudless joy. A man in the ministry like this will most likely have his whole view of the Christian life colored by this experience, when he preaches, when he counsels, and when he interacts with the people of God.

What I am saying is that such a man should never enter the pastoral office. He may not be disqualified to be a member in good standing of a well-ordered gospel church. He may even have great usefulness in Christ's church. However, if he does not experience a greater measure of balanced Christian experience, he will not be able to minister adequately to the people of God who will come under his ministry and pastoral care.

I use the word *tested*, based on the requirements that are given for the office of deacon. "And let them also be tested first" (1 Tim. 3:10). The Greek word *dokimazo* means to prove by putting to the test, or, we might say, put to the proof. If this qualification is required of a serving office, how much more of a pastoral office? There must be more than the passion and the enthusiasm of the neophyte. The indication that a man may possess these requisite graces must take some time. God has to bring the rod of discipline on a man and scour him a bit, bringing him into days of great joy, and then days of great struggle with various forms of spiritual trials, in order to test the reality of his Christian experience. Paul alludes to this as one of the reasons why a new convert should not be put into the pastoral office. He has not had enough testing with respect to the sin of pride, and he may fall prey to the very same sin that was the downfall of the devil, "He must not be a recent convert, or he may become puffed up with conceit and fall into the condemnation of the devil" (1 Tim. 3:6). We also see the place of affliction in testing in the parable of the soils (Matt. 13:20, 21; Mark 4:16, 17; Luke 8:13), and from the teaching of Scripture in James 1:2–4 and Romans 5:3–5. Pressure and affliction test the reality of our profession, as well as serving as an instrument of God to conform us more to the image of Christ.

So, this is what I mean when I say that in addition to the manifest graces indicative of a genuine, matured, balanced, exemplary, proven Christian character, fitness for this office demands clear indications that a man possesses an *enlarged, balanced, and tested Christian experience.*

The Major Aspects of Christian Experience

We come now to an identification of some of the major aspects of such Christian experience. As I focus on these things, I confess that I have a fear of the personal bias and imbalance of my own experience as a Christian for over six decades. Therefore, I have leaned heavily upon the quality control and insights of others who have addressed this issue.[2] We will be looking at four major aspects in this chapter and the next, namely, *love for Christ, faith*

---

2. In all of the things I have read over the years, none can compare to John Owen in focusing on those things that are the major aspects of this Christian experience that equip a man to be a shepherd after God's own heart, who will feed His people with knowledge and with understanding. In the area of experimental (or, experiential) religion, especially with respect to its place in the life of a man aspiring to, and competent for, the pastoral office, I consider Dr. Owen to be the doctor of doctors.

in the great unseen realities, acquaintance with the dynamics of sin and grace, and *humility and self-distrust.*

Love for Christ

A proven love for, and devoted attachment to, the person of Christ Himself heads the list of these four major aspects of Christian experience which are necessary qualifications comprising fitness for the pastoral office. I say this without any fear of contradictions from my Bible or from the confirming voices of the past. Our Lord, in dealing with the Twelve, and in preparing them for their distinctive function as apostles, made it clear right from the outset that attachment to Him in faith, love, and obedience was to be the soil out of which their ministerial usefulness would grow.

You will remember that the Lord called Simon with his brother Andrew, and James and John, the sons of Zebedee, away from their nets to Himself, saying, "Follow me, and I will make you become fishers of men" (Mark 1:17). He was saying that it would be in their individual attachment to Him in faith, love, and obedience that they would be formed into men who would "fish" for other men to follow Christ even as they were learning to follow Him. Attachment to Christ is the central idea and governing principle of discipleship according to this strategic discipleship statement, when Christ "appointed twelve (whom he also named apostles) so that they might be with him and he might send them out to preach and have authority to cast out demons" (Mark 3:14, 15). Do not reverse the order! "With Him" comes before "send them out to preach." They were disciples before they were preachers, and their ministry of preaching and healing is out of, in the light of, and under the dynamics of, their attachment to Him.

This great principle is wonderfully and patently underscored subsequent to our Lord's resurrection from the dead in His very poignant dealings with Peter. There by the Sea of Galilee, after the disciples shared breakfast with their risen Lord, Jesus singled out Peter in order to have special dealings with him. Peter had denied three times that he even knew the Lord at His trial. Peter's lips had spoken oaths of self-malediction in his repudiation of Jesus. That makes Jesus' response all the more striking,

> When they had finished breakfast, Jesus said to Simon Peter, "Simon, son of John, do you love me more than these?" He said to him, "Yes, Lord; you know that I love you." He said to him, "Feed my lambs." He said to him a second time, "Simon, son of John, do you love me?" He said to him, "Yes, Lord; you know that I love you." He said to him, "Tend my

sheep." He said to him the third time, "Simon, son of John, do you love me?" Peter was grieved because he said to him the third time, "Do you love me?" and he said to him, "Lord, you know everything; you know that I love you." Jesus said to him, "Feed my sheep" (John 21:15–17).

It is not my purpose to exegete this important portion, nor to comment on the two Greek words which the Lord used, *bosko*, to *feed*, and *poimaino*, to *shepherd*. I would simply establish the point that the key to fulfilling the stewardship tasks of ministry is our attachment to Christ in love. The Lord is telling Peter that if Peter truly loves Him, then fulfilling this task which He has assigned will be the manifestation of that love.

The apostle Paul described himself as "a servant of Christ Jesus, called to be an apostle, set apart for the gospel of God" (Rom. 1:1), and, with Timothy, "servants of Christ Jesus" (Phil. 1:1). In both cases, the Greek word *doulos*, meaning *slave* or *bondslave*, is an indication of Paul's love for and attachment to the Person of Christ. What lay beneath the apostolic call? It was Paul's attachment to Christ in faith, love, and obedience. This was very clearly established from the outset, as we read the account of his conversion. Consider the significance of Acts 26:14 which says, "And when we had all fallen to the ground, I heard a voice saying to me in the Hebrew language, 'Saul, Saul, why are you persecuting me?'" The Lord Jesus was binding His bondslave to Himself, and out of that relationship would grow Paul's mighty ministry. Paul's testimony confirms this, "But when he who had set me apart before I was born, and who called me by his grace, was pleased to reveal his Son to me, in order that I might preach him among the Gentiles, I did not immediately consult with anyone" (Gal. 1:15, 16). Paul carried out his ministry with that revelation of Christ still in his heart, so that, as a man coming near the end of his days, he could say that he still had one great passion, "that I may know him" (Phil. 3:10).

We might object and say that Paul knew Jesus by direct revelation, and that he later spoke of being caught up to the third heaven (2 Cor. 12:2–4). How could he desire to know Him more than that? He certainly would tell us that he wanted to know Him as much as any man can know Him until he sees Him face to face. Paul's love for Christ and unrelenting desires for Christ—extraordinary experiences notwithstanding—are expressed in the strongest devotional language in the book of Philippians. Consider just a few of them now: "Christ will be honored in my body, whether by life or by death" (Phil. 1:20); "For me to live is Christ, and to die is gain" (Phil. 1:21); "My desire is to depart and be with Christ, for that is far better" (Phil. 1:23;

cf. 2 Cor. 5:8); "I count everything as loss because of the surpassing worth of knowing Christ Jesus my Lord…that I may gain Christ and be found in him…that I may know him…because Christ Jesus has made me his own" (excerpts from Phil. 3:8–12).

Surely these strands of biblical evidence point to the fact that if we are to be the true servants of Christ, with this proven, tested, matured, balanced Christian experience, lying at the foundation of it will be this proven faith in, love for, and devoted attachment to the Person of our wonderful and precious Lord Jesus Christ. As Peter says, "though you have not seen him, you love him. Though you do not now see him, you believe in him and rejoice with joy that is inexpressible and filled with glory" (1 Pet. 1:8).

If there is any group of men that must make it evident that they are willing to do anything short of sinning to maintain their first love, it must be the servants of Christ, so that after we have sought to present Him to others, He will not have to say to us, as He did to the Ephesian church,

> "I know your works, your toil and your patient endurance, and how you cannot bear with those who are evil, but have tested those who call themselves apostles and are not, and found them to be false. I know you are enduring patiently and bearing up for my name's sake, and you have not grown weary. But I have this against you, that you have abandoned the love you had at first" (Rev. 2:2–4).

This "first love" is the love we had for Christ when we knew so much less but felt so much more of the wonder of being forgiven, cleansed, justified, and adopted into the family of God. It is the love for Christ that inclined us never to leave the house without making sure that there were a few gospel tracts in our shirt pocket. It is the love for Christ that caused our consciences to smite us if we succumbed to some silly excuse to skip our normal devotional exercises of prayer and meditation in the Bible. We may know much more about Christ theologically as we should, and we may have experienced much more of the ongoing saving work of Christ in us, but do we have that love for Christ Himself which we had at first?

Anyone aspiring to the pastoral office ought to have evidence that he is a man who is passionate about seeking to maintain his first love. He has to acknowledge with the best saints, "I have not fully attained. I am conscious that there are areas of coldness and deadness," but he must be able to say honestly, "I have not resigned myself to accept the status quo. I am passionately committed to the rekindling of my love for Him." The heart and soul of New Covenant ministry is the proclamation of Christ publicly and privately. Yet, how can this be done effectively, and with the blessing of God, if there is no present, manifest, experiential, contagious love and devotion to the Person of Christ? Concerning his ministry Paul could say, "Him we proclaim, warning everyone and teaching everyone with all wisdom, that we may present everyone mature in Christ" (Col. 1:28).

> Alexander Whyte, describing his Saturday walks and talks with Marcus Dods, declared: "Whatever we started off with in our conversations, we soon made across country, somehow, to Jesus of Nazareth, to His death, and His resurrection, and His indwelling; and unless our sermons make for the same goal, and arrive at the same mark, they are simply beating the air." It was a favourite dictum of the preachers of a bygone day that, just as from every village in Britain there was a road which, linking on to other roads, would bring you to London at last, so from every text in the Bible, even the remotest and least likely, there was a road to Christ. Possibly there were occasions when strange turns of exegesis and dubious allegorizings were pressed into service for the making of that road; but the instinct was entirely sound which declared that no preaching which failed to exalt Christ was worthy to be called Christian preaching. This is our great master-theme. In the expressive, forthright language of John Donne: "All knowledge that begins not, and ends not with His glory, is but a giddy, but a vertiginous circle, but an elaborate and exquisite ignorance."[3]

There are times when, reading devotional books such as Spurgeon's *Morning and Evening*, James Smith's *Daily Remembrancer*, or Oswald Chambers, *My Utmost for His Highest*, you may be saying to yourself, "the author really forced Christ into that passage, before he could ever draw Christ out of the passage, in the way that he did in that devotional meditation." Whenever I find myself thinking this way, I am reproved by my own lack of love to the Person of Christ, and I find myself praying,

> O God, give me the same exegetical and homiletical 'affliction' that Spurgeon, Chambers, and Smith had, the 'affliction' of a white-hot and passionate love for Christ that would tempt me to find Christ in a portion of Scripture even where God has not placed Him.

Yes, we can sit back, and with a cold and calculating smugness, criticize some of the older writers who at times allowed their burning love for Christ

---

3. James S. Stewart, *Preaching* (London: The English Universities Press, 1955), 54, 55.

to lead them to indulge in some exegetical excesses and irregularities, but would it not be wonderful to be so presently and passionately in love with Him, that we were even tempted to indulge in this aberration as they did? It was justly proverbial among the people of my own congregation in the months of courting my present wife, Dorothy, that there was hardly a sermon, a counseling session, a conversation, but that Dorothy leaped into or leaped out of what I was saying. Yet I never once had to plan my "Dorothy" references in my sermons or counseling sessions. God was turning my night of weeping as a widower into a morning of joy, at the prospect of receiving another helper answering to my need (Gen. 2:18). Dorothy filled my heart's vision, and therefore Dorothy was constantly in my speech. As Matthew 12:34 indicates, "For out of the abundance of the heart the mouth speaks." Our mouths are the echo chamber of our hearts and the sounding board of our deepest thoughts. If Christ does not fill our hearts in our times alone with Him, in our walking with Him, so that for us to live is Christ, speaking about Him with glowing hearts will not be natural for us. We dare not attempt to artificially and insincerely insert Him into our sermons in an effort to hide our loveless hearts.

That contagion of our own present, living, vibrant attachment to our Lord Jesus in faith, love, growing knowledge, and obedience to Him, will naturally flow into our sermons and into all of our pastoral work. This element of Christian experience is not only a vital prerequisite in assessing a man's qualification for the pastoral office, it is indispensable for us to cultivate this obsession with Christ if we are to do justice to the ongoing functions of our office.[4]

Faith in the Great Unseen Realities

A measure of sustained and vigorous faith in the great realities of the unseen world is another aspect of matured, balanced, tested Christian experience that must be richly evident in one who aspires to and assumes the pastoral office. Referring to the difficulties that he and his fellow servants faced, Paul could say these very significant words:

---

4. I highly recommend volume 1 of John Owen's works in seeking to cultivate a deeper and richer love for the Lord Jesus. Also helpful in gaining a deeper and richer understanding of our distinct communion with the three Persons of the Godhead, I recommend volume 2 of Owen. For gaining a deeper experiential acquaintance with the danger of apostasy and the cultivation of spiritual mindedness, volume 7 of Owen is unsurpassed.

So we do not lose heart. Though our outer self is wasting away, our inner self is being renewed day by day. For this light momentary affliction is preparing for us an eternal weight of glory beyond all comparison, as we look not to the things that are seen but to the things that are unseen. For the things that are seen are transient, but the things that are unseen are eternal (2 Cor. 4:16–18).

Notice that there are two categories of "things" or realities. There are things that are seen, and these are substantial realities. Then there are substantial realities that are not seen. It is not a contrast between things that are seeable, touchable, dispensable, disposable, and things that are wispy non-entities, mere notions that float by concerning some vague ideas out there that have no real existence. There are substantial, real, unseen things that fill the gaze of the apostle's soul, and ours. We are given a clue as to how this relates to faith in one of the closest things to a formal definition or description of faith found in the Bible, "Now faith is the assurance of things hoped for, the conviction of things not seen" (Heb. 11:1).

My fellow-pastors, and you who aspire to become pastors, we traffic in that unseen world of the things of the Spirit, especially the things of heaven and of hell—eternal life in the presence of God in the new heavens and the new earth, or eternal death in the lake of fire, in the company of the devil and his angels. You will be struck, as I have been, in the degree to which our Lord spoke of the unseen world as one who lived in its realities. Vivid references to that unseen world oozed out in His preaching and teaching again and again.

Jesus gives us a powerful motivation for radical mortification of our sins: "It is better for you to enter life crippled or lame than with two hands or two feet to be thrown into the eternal fire" (Matt. 18:8). In the Sermon on the Mount (Matt. 5–7), our Lord begins by describing the character traits of the sons and daughters of the Kingdom. He asserts that people with such character traits constitute both the salt and the light of an ungodly world. He then describes how the true sons and daughters of the Kingdom are to live in relationship to the moral and ethical standards established in the law of God. He further instructs them concerning the righteous motives which must characterize all their religious exercises of giving, praying, and fasting. From there, He goes on to describe how the subjects of the Kingdom must relate to this present world of housing, food, and clothing, trusting God to provide what they need, while they continually seek first the Kingdom of God and His righteousness.

Having gone through that broad spectrum of addressing vital issues regarding Kingdom living, He then issues some sober warnings, encouragements regarding prayer, and the unforgettable Golden Rule for deciding ethical issues. Not satisfied that He has merely given all of this rich instruction concerning Kingdom living in a fallen world, our Lord proceeds to give His appeal, with words of regal grace, urging His hearers to enter the Kingdom, "Enter by the narrow gate. For the gate is wide and the way is easy that leads to destruction, and those who enter by it are many" (Matt. 7:13). Matthew records the Greek word *enter*, but Luke, in the parallel passage uses the word *agonizomai*, meaning to *struggle* and *strive* to enter (Luke 13:24), again, because the broad way leads to destruction. That reality must arrest and hold us in its grip as it did with our blessed Lord.

When our Lord is seeking to get inside the consciences of mere nominal adherents of the Kingdom, He warns,

> Not everyone who says to me, "Lord, Lord," will enter the kingdom of heaven, but the one who does the will of my Father who is in heaven. On that day many will say to me, "Lord, Lord, did we not prophesy in your name, and cast out demons in your name, and do many mighty works in your name?" And then will I declare to them, "I never knew you; depart from me, you workers of lawlessness" (Matt. 7:21–23).

He warns of outer darkness with weeping and gnashing of teeth (Matt. 8:11, 12). He gives sober warnings to the cities of Chorazin and Bethsaida concerning the Day of Judgment (Matt. 11:21, 22). This brief survey of the early chapters of the gospel of Matthew validates my statement that the vision of eternal realities does indeed constantly ooze out of our Lord's preaching. He knew that world as none of us knows it. I do not mean to be flippant, but whatever hell is, as prepared for the devil and his angels, Jesus the Creator of all things made it. He knows the horror of it that awaits the unbelieving and impenitent.

Fellow pastor, we feed our souls on those unseen realities too infrequently! No man should enter the ministry who does not have some measure of sustained and vigorous faith in these great realities of that unseen world.

Charles Bridges dedicated a whole chapter to the lack of faith as one of the major causes of ministerial fruitlessness. After dealing generally with the place of faith in the life of a minister, he wrote:

> We remark also the supreme importance of the *Ministerial exercise of faith in its own character and office*, as substantiating unseen realities

to the mind. The grand subjects of our commission have an immediate connection with the eternal world. The soul derives its value from its relation to eternity. The gift of the Saviour opens and assures to the Christian a blissful prospect of eternity. The sufferings of this present time are supported by an habitual contemplation of "things not seen," and by an estimate of the preponderating "glory that shall be revealed in us." We realize the vanity of this transitory scene only by an accurate comparison with the enduring character of the heavenly state. Daily experience reminds us of the extreme difficulty of maintaining spiritual perceptions of eternal things. The surrounding objects of time and sense spread a thick film over the organs of spiritual vision, and the indistinct haziness, in which they often appear, is as if they were not. Now a vivid apprehension of truth is the spring of a "full assurance of faith," such as will infuse a tenderness, seriousness, and dignity into our discourses, far beyond the power of the highest unassisted talents. "Faith is the master-spring of a Minister." Hell is before me, and thousands of souls are shut up there in everlasting agonies. Jesus Christ stands forth to save men from rushing into this bottomless abyss. He sends me to proclaim his ability and his love. I want no fourth idea! Every fourth idea is contemptible. Every fourth idea is a grand impertinence.

We must also remark the *personal assurance of faith* as a spring of our effectiveness. "We are confident" (says the Apostle); "*wherefore* we labour." The assured "knowledge" of Him, "whom he had believed," was at once his support under sufferings, and his principle of perseverance. The persuasion "whose he was"—enabled him to confess with greater confidence—"Whom I serve." And who does not find, that "the joy of the Lord"—the joy of pardon, of acceptance, of communion, and of expectation—"is our strength" for our work in simple, affectionate, and devoted faith? The "spirit of adoption" converts toil into pleasure. What to a slave would be drudgery, to a child is privilege. Instead of being goaded by conscience, he is acted upon by faith, and constrained by love. "*Labor ipse voluptas.*" Thus faith is the principle, love is the enjoyment, and active devotedness is the habit of the work.[5]

I do not know how any man can satisfy himself that he is called to be a special instrument of Christ and a gift of Christ to His church, with these great issues as the substructure of all that he does, if there is not some measure of sustained and vigorous faith in the great realities of the unseen world.

---

5. Charles Bridges, *The Christian Ministry* (Edinburgh: The Banner of Truth Trust, 1976), 179–181.

May God grant that those of us who are in this office will be given fresh measures of the Spirit's ministry, constraining us to love and to labor under the felt pressure of the weighty realities of the age to come.

It costs to live, think, pray, preach, counsel, as men who believe that, although we are here now, in a few ticks of the clock we will be gone, along with those to whom we minister. A few more ticks of the clock for both the minister and those to whom he ministers, and each will be in his eternal state, ultimately either in the unspeakable glory and delights of the new heavens and the new earth, or in the indescribable agonies of body and soul in hell, in the sordid company of the devil and his angels. Am I being called and fashioned to be a minister of the New Covenant? May God grant that, by His grace, any reader wrestling with this question will weigh these issues soberly before God, seeking honestly to discern whether or not these graces of love to Christ and faith in unseen realities are working deeply in his soul.

CHAPTER 7

Qualifications of Christian Experience (2)

In the last chapter, we considered two of the four qualifications for the pastoral office that relate to a man's Christian experience. They were *love for Christ* and *faith in the great unseen realities*. Needless to say, these two aspects of Christian experience are woven together tightly. We move on to two more qualifications of Christian experience for the pastoral office, namely, *acquaintance with the dynamics of sin and grace*, and *humility and self-distrust*. These two are also tightly woven together.

The Major Aspects of Christian Experience

Acquaintance with the Dynamics of Sin and Grace

Among the indispensable aspects of proven Christian experience, not only must there be a proven love for and devoted attachment to the Person of Christ with a living faith in the great unseen realities, but there must also be evidence that the man aspiring to the eldership has obtained a personal and perceptive acquaintance with the fundamental workings of sin and grace in the soul of a true believer.

The framework of the apostolic witness was in many ways unique. The apostles were eyewitnesses of Christ, and God validated their witness with signs and wonders. This is emphasized in Hebrews,

> How shall we escape if we neglect such a great salvation? It was declared at first by the Lord, and it was attested to us by those who heard, while God also bore witness by signs and wonders and various miracles and by gifts of the Holy Spirit distributed according to his will (Heb. 2:3, 4).

However, there are some principles operative in the apostles' ministries which also apply to the ordinary office of a pastor. For example, consider John's statement,

That which was from the beginning, which we have heard, which we have seen with our eyes, which we looked upon and have touched with our hands, concerning the word of life—the life was made manifest, and we have seen it, and testify to it and proclaim to you the eternal life, which was with the Father and was made manifest to us—that which we have seen and heard we proclaim also to you, so that you too may have fellowship with us; and indeed our fellowship is with the Father and with his Son Jesus Christ (1 John 1:1–3).

John wants his readers to know that he is writing with apostolic credentials. We do not write or speak with those credentials. We will not see and hear apostles either, but surely, if we are to speak with conviction and persuasiveness, without becoming the grossest of hypocrites, we must be able to speak to our people concerning areas of Christian experience as those who have seen and handled and touched and felt these realities.

Confirming this is a striking verse in Acts, "Now when they saw the boldness of Peter and John, and perceived that they were uneducated, common men, they were astonished. And they recognized that they had been with Jesus" (Acts 4:13). The apostles are the ones who had been in Christ's company. Something of the effect of that fact was seen in their boldness, so that when they were solemnly charged by the religious leaders not to speak any more, they responded to those leaders by saying, "we cannot but speak of what we have seen and heard" (Acts 4:20).

These words highlight a crucial principle. God's people, His true sheep, are seeking to be holy men and women, living their lives in the midst of a crooked and perverse generation. They are seeking to grow in grace while constantly harassed by the impediment of their own remaining sin. They are seeking to walk with integrity and uprightness, having to resist the enticements of a wily devil who prowls about as a roaring lion, seeking whom he may devour. If we are to be true shepherds to these sheep seeking to live Christ-exalting lives in the context of the world, the flesh, and the devil, they need to be able to say the following about us as their pastors:

That man instructing us is in touch with the spiritual realities which are the stuff of my life as a child of God. He does not simply quote something to us that he has read from the Puritans; he is a modern-day Puritan. He is committed to cultivating in himself, and conveying to us, an experiential acquaintance with God as our Father, Christ as our Savior, and the Holy Spirit as our Sanctifier. Like the Puritans, he is not content to open up texts with good exegesis and arrange his thoughts and be a great preacher, without showing us the uses of those texts as the Puritans did.

Now I realize that they may not use all of these words, but I say them in this form to give you an idea of the kind of thoughts that they may have about our own experience of the realities that they deal with every day. We may not use this Puritan format in our sermonic structures, but surely, we need to follow their pattern of constantly moving from responsible and accurate exposition to clear, searching, convicting, and comforting application in all of our preaching. We must never forget why God gave us His Spirit-inspired Word in the Old and New Testaments (Ps. 19:11; 1 Cor. 10:6–13; 2 Tim. 3:16, 17).

To buttress these assertions which I am making concerning this matter, I will give thoughts from the old masters which I trust will persuade you, as they have persuaded me, that an experiential acquaintance with the realities that constitute genuine Christian experience must to some degree be present in any man who is set apart to the work of the ministry.

As we ought not to be Ministers at all, however, if we be not Christians, regenerated men, so, assuming this, I believe that one of our chief sins, and the parent of all other evils in the really Christian Ministry together, is to be found in the low state of godliness, of the life of God, in our own souls. I am aware that this statement is liable to be misunderstood; and all I can afford time to say, to obviate misapprehension, is just this, that I am not here comparing us with our former selves. In this view, perhaps, we may have made some happy progress; and this, that we are not quite so far off as before, may just be the secret of our seeing more distinctly today our fearful distance from the mark. I am comparing our spiritual state with such words, such notes of a lively and prosperous Christian as the following: "Our conversation is in heaven—Thy word was found of me and I did eat it; and it was to me the joy and the rejoicing of my heart—To me to live is Christ—Enoch walked with God—I press towards the mark—My soul thirsteth for God, for the living God; when shall I come and appear before God?"

Now let me try if I can bring out, in a sentence or two, the vital connection between this state of soul, and the discharge of the whole work of the Ministry. See it, for instance, in that word of Paul, (2 Tim. 1:12), "I suffer these things; nevertheless I am not ashamed, *for*"—mark the secret of his heroic bearing; we talk of the magnanimity, the heroism of Paul; but observe the secret of all his labours, and toils and sufferings,— "for I know," says he, "whom I have believed, and am persuaded that he is able to keep that which I have committed unto him against that day." Ah! that is what will make a man go through the flames for Christ, that element deep and strong in his soul, "I know whom I have believed, and am persuaded that he is able to keep that which I have committed to him." Or, see the same in the words of David we were just singing, "Restore unto me the joy of thy salvation, and uphold me with thy free Spirit; *then* will I teach transgressors thy ways, and sinners shall be converted unto thee"; *then*,—Lord, how shall I teach thy ways, unless I am seeking to walk close and straight in them myself,—unless, restored and upheld by thy good Spirit, I am both discovering and loathing my own ways, and carefully and constantly seeking to tread in thine. Or, take it thus. Our themes, fathers and brethren, the hinges of the Ministry, are Sin and Christ. Well; how shall a man discover the sins of others, solidly and tenderly, not harshly, but tenderly and lovingly, who is not seeing and weeping in secret places over his own iniquities? And as for Christ, the very idea of the Christ, the Beloved of the Father, his "elect, in whom his soul delighteth," is one of the heart and soul. It is not to be taken up by mere intellectual apprehension. "The love of Christ constraineth us," says Paul, giving the spring of his whole labours. "Lovest thou me," Peter? then "feed my lambs," "feed my sheep,"—thou can'st never feed them otherwise. "That which we have seen and heard declare we unto you." "Out of the abundance of the heart the mouth speaketh."[1]

With regard to the dynamics of sin and grace in the soul, I recommend John Owen's works, especially volume 6, which includes his treatises on the mortification of sin, temptation, and indwelling sin, followed by a detailed but marvelous, heart-warming exposition of Psalm 130.[2]

Psalm 130 was profoundly significant in Owen's own spiritual experience. His exposition of that psalm drips with the honey of experiential application of the comforts of the gospel, aimed especially at ministering to troubled souls who are finding it difficult to embrace God's promises of free and full forgiveness in the gospel. It is also a spiritual gold mine concerning how the Spirit and the Word function in bringing sinners from deep conviction of sin into the joy and peace of forgiveness.

The first time I picked up volume 6 and began to read his treatise on the mortification of sin, I found the experience unnerving. The only way I can describe it is to say that I felt, time after time, as I read four or five pages

---

1. Charles J. Brown, "Ministerial Guilt," *The Banner of Truth Magazine*, Issue 25 (May, 1962), 6.

2. These portions have been republished as individual volumes in recent years.

each morning and prayed over them, that God had resurrected John Owen and placed a miniature Owen in my heart with a magnifying glass, notebook, pen, and flashlight, and said to him, "Write what you see." It seemed as though John Owen had gotten inside of me. He was describing me in ways that no one else had ever described me, except for certain portions of the Word of God that had searched me through and through on previous occasions. The bats and the ugly vermin of remaining sin which had found a safe refuge in the dark caverns of my heart were exposed for what they really are. Then, when the flashlight had accomplished this work of exposing my sin, Owen tenderly and vigorously set forth the only gospel remedy by which to mortify and put to death my sins, that is, by the fresh appropriation of the virtue of the cross of Christ and of the power of the Holy Spirit. The two subsequent treatises on temptation and indwelling sin were also profoundly biblical, searching, and most helpful in enabling me to crystallize my thinking concerning many of the basic issues involved in living the Christian life as God intends that we should live it.

There is something universal and timeless about the insights of John Owen. When the Trinity Ministerial Academy was in full swing, we took two weeks to study Owen, volume 6, during one of our break sessions between semesters. If you aspire to the pastoral ministry, or if you are engaged in pastoral ministry, I urge you, if you have not prayerfully read this volume from beginning to end, that you make it a top priority for your reading, apart from and in addition to the Word of God. Then periodically reread it, even as I continue to do to this day for the good of my own soul.

There are others whose testimony I highly recommend to you. Charles Bridges is one of those confirming voices:

> It is evident, however, that this Ministerial standard presupposes a deep tone of experimental and devotional character—habitually exercised in self-denial, prominently marked by love to the Saviour, and to the souls of sinners; and practically exhibited in a blameless consistency of conduct. The Apostle justly pronounces "a novice" to be disqualified for this holy work. The bare existence of religion provides but slender materials for this important function. A babe in grace and knowledge is palpably incompetent to become "a teacher of babes," much more a guide of the fathers. The school of adversity, of discipline, and of experience, united with study and heavenly influence, can alone give "the tongue of the learned." Some measure of eminence and an habitual aim towards greater eminence are indispensable for Ministerial completeness; nor

will they fail to be acquired in the diligent use of the means of Divine appointment—the word of God and prayer.[3]

Returning to Owen, here are several passages offered as a confirming witness. In volume 16 of his works, he lists several things necessary for pastoral preaching:

Experience of the power of the truth which they preach in and upon their own souls. Without this they will themselves be lifeless and heartless in their own work, and their labour for the most part will be unprofitable towards others. It is, to such men, attended unto as a task for their advantage, or as that which carries some satisfaction in it from ostentation and supposed reputation wherewith it is accompanied. But a man preacheth that sermon only well unto others which preacheth itself in his own soul. And he that doth not feed on and thrive in the digestion of the food which he provides for others will scarce make it savoury unto them; yea, he knows not but the food he hath provided may be poison, unless he have really tasted of it himself. If the word do not dwell with power *in* us, it will not pass with power *from* us. And no man lives in a more woful condition than those who really believe not themselves what they persuade others to believe continually. The want of this experience of the power of gospel truth on their own souls is that which gives us so many lifeless, sapless orations, quaint in words and dead as to power, instead of preaching the gospel in the demonstration of the Spirit. And let any say what they please, it is evident that some men's preaching, as well as others' not preaching, hath lost the credit of their ministry.[4]

He says something similar in another place:

Another thing required hereunto is, *experience* of the power of the things we preach to others. I think, truly, *that no man preaches that sermon well to others that doth not first preach it to his own heart.* He who doth not feed on, and digest, and thrive by, what he prepares for his people, he may give them poison, as far as he knows; for, unless he finds the power of it in his own heart, he cannot have any ground of confidence that it will have power in the hearts of others. *It is an easier thing to bring our heads to preach than our hearts to preach.* To bring

3. Charles Bridges, *The Christian Ministry* (Edinburgh: The Banner of Truth Trust, 1976), 27, 28.
4. John Owen, *The Works of John Owen*, vol. 16 (Edinburgh: The Banner of Truth Trust, 1968), 76.

our heads to preach, is but to fill our minds and memories with some notions of truth, of our own or other men, and speak them out to give satisfaction to ourselves and others: this is very easy. But to bring our hearts to preach, is to be transformed into the power of these truths; or to find the power of them, both before, in fashioning our minds and hearts, and in delivering of them, that we may have benefit; and to be acted with zeal for God and compassion to the souls of men. A man may preach every day in the week, and not have his heart engaged once. This hath lost us powerful preaching in the world, and set up, instead of it, quaint orations; for such men never seek after experience in their own hearts: and so it is come to pass, that some men's preaching, and some men's not preaching, have lost us the power of what we call the ministry; that though there be twenty or thirty thousand in orders, yet the nation perishes for want of knowledge, and is overwhelmed in all manner of sins, and not delivered from them unto this day.[5]

To those who would assume the pastoral office, Owen says:

It belongs unto them, on the account of their pastoral office, to be *ready, willing, and able, to comfort, relieve, and refresh, those that are tempted,* tossed, wearied with fears and grounds of disconsolation, in times of trial and desertion. "The tongue of the learned" is required in them, "that they should know how to speak a word in season to him that is weary." One excellent qualification of our Lord Jesus Christ, in the discharge of his priestly office now in heaven, is, that he is touched with a sense of our infirmities, and knows how to succour them that are tempted. His whole flock in this world are a company of tempted ones; his own life on the earth he calls "the time of his temptation"; and those who have the charge of his flock under him ought to have a sense of their infirmities, and endeavour in an especial manner to suc-cour them that are tempted. But amongst them there are some always that are cast under darkness and disconsolations in a peculiar manner: some at the entrance of their conversion unto God, whilst they have a deep sense of the terror of the Lord, the sharpness of conviction, and the uncertainty of their condition; some are relapsed into sin or omis-sions of duties; some under great, sore, and lasting afflictions; some upon pressing, urgent, particular *occasions;* some on sovereign, divine *desertions;* some through the *buffetings of Satan* and the injection of

---

5. John Owen, *The Works of John Owen*, vol. 9 (Edinburgh: The Banner of Truth Trust, 1968), 455.

blasphemous thoughts into their minds, with many other occasions of an alike nature.[6]

Owen says that if we are to be competent pastors, we must attain some degree of skill, born out of experience in ministering to this broad spectrum of the needs of God's people:

> The proper ways whereby pastors and teachers must obtain this skill and understanding are, by diligent study of the Scriptures, meditation thereon, fervent prayer, experience of spiritual things, and temptations in their own souls, with a prudent observation of the manner of God's dealing with others, and the ways of the opposition made to the work of his grace in them. Without these things, all pretences unto this ability and duty of the pastoral office are vain; whence it is that the whole work of it is much neglected.[7]

We can receive help in many of these things pertaining to individual pastoral care from such sources as Richard Baxter's *Christian Directory*, and the many books, booklets, and recorded materials now available, addressing various aspects of biblical counseling. However, unless to some degree these things pass through the crucible of our own experience, and are to some measure covered with our own fingerprints, and have picked up the scent of our unique spiritual "odor," they will lack authority and persuasiveness.

James Stewart is a more contemporary source whose penetrating words confirm these perspectives:

> It is one of the mightiest safeguards of a man's ministry—to be aware of that hungry demand for reality breaking inarticulately from the hearts of those to whom he ministers. For that cry puts everything shoddy, second-hand or artificial utterly to shame. You do not need to be eloquent, or clever, or sensational, or skilled in dialectic: you *must* be real. To fail there is to fail abysmally and tragically. It is to damage incalculably the cause you represent. Anything savoring of unreality in the pulpit is a double offense. Let me urge upon you two considerations. On the one hand, you will be preaching to people who have been grappling all the week with stern realities. Behind a congregation assembling for worship there are stories of heavy anxiety and fierce

---

6. John Owen, *The Works of John Owen*, vol. 16 (Edinburgh: The Banner of Truth Trust, 1968), 85.

7. John Owen, *The Works of John Owen*, vol. 16 (Edinburgh: The Banner of Truth Trust, 1968), 86.

temptation, of loneliness and heroism, of overwork and lack of work, of physical strain and mental wear and tear. We wrong them and we mock their struggles if we preach our Gospel in abstraction from the hard facts of their experience. It is not only that they can detect at once the hollowness of such a performance, though that is true; there is also this—that to offer pedantic theorizings and academic irrelevances to souls wrestling in the dark is to sin against the Lord who died for them and yearns for their redeeming.

But there is a further indictment of unreality in preaching. This is rooted not so much in the hard problems men and women are facing—what Whittier called this "maddening maze of things"—as in the very nature of the Christian faith itself. The Gospel is quite shattering in its realism. It shirks nothing. It never seeks to gloss over the dark perplexities of fate, frustration, sin and death, or to gild unpalatable facts with a coating of pious verbiage or facile consolation. It never sidetracks uncomfortable questions with some naïve and cheerful cliché about providence or progress. It gazes open-eyed at the most menacing and savage circumstance that life can show. It is utterly courageous. Its strength is the complete absence of utopian illusions. It thrusts Golgotha upon men's vision and bids them look at that. The very last charge which can be brought against the Gospel is that of sentimentality, of blinking [overlooking] the facts. It is devastating in its veracity, and its realism is a consuming fire.[8]

We also glean some choice words from Samuel Miller:

How can a man who knows only the theory of religion, undertake to be a practical guide in spiritual things? How can he adapt his instructions to all the varieties of Christian experience? How can he direct the awakened, the inquiring, the tempted, and the doubting? How can he feed the sheep and the lambs of Christ? How can he sympathize with mourners in Zion? How can he comfort others with those consolations wherewith he himself has never been comforted of God? He cannot possibly perform, as he ought, any of these duties, and yet they are the most precious and interesting parts of the ministerial work. However gigantic his intellectual powers; however deep, and various, and accurate his learning, he is not able, in relation to any of these points, to teach others, seeing he is not taught himself. If he make the attempt,

---

8. James Stewart, *Preaching* (London: The English Universities Press, 1955), 29, 30.

it will be the blind leading the blind; and of this, unerring wisdom has told us the consequence.[9]

Permit me to give a word of caution, lest some younger man reading these pages come into unnecessary bondage. When I was in my early twenties I remember reading the biographies of well-known preachers from previous generations. Seeing the graces that were manifested in these matured, tested, tried, experienced preachers, I found myself praying along these lines: "O God, give me the kind of clear-headed grasp of Your Word, the warmhearted engagement with people, the consuming passion for Your glory evidenced in these men of whom I have read." I was striving to possess at age twenty-five the spiritual experience, and the subsequent ministerial fitness drawn from that experience that some of these men experienced at ages forty, fifty, and sixty. At that time I did not understand that there are certain aspects of this experiential walk with God and the cultivation of our graces in the midst of the various situations of our lives and ministries, which only time and the varied circumstances of life can supply.

We cannot bring into the soul of someone in his twenties the cumulative experience of someone who has walked closely with God for decades. Granted, there are some notable exceptions to this general principle of God's dealings with us. Among them are men like Robert Murray M'Cheyne, David Brainerd, George Whitefield, and Charles H. Spurgeon. Notwithstanding this necessary qualifying word of caution, if we have been genuinely converted and are indwelt by the Holy Spirit and thereby united to Christ, we will be introduced quite early in our pilgrimage to the basic issues that touch the greatest struggles, joys, disappointments, and perplexities of the Christian life.

Let me paraphrase Paul: "Timothy, let no one think lightly of you because you are a relatively young man; but, as a relatively young man, be an example of the believers in speech, in conduct, in love, in faith, in purity" (1 Tim. 4:12). Obviously, Paul did not expect Timothy to manifest these graces to the same degree to which they would be manifested in a much older man who had walked with God for many years. Yet, this verse reveals Paul's confident expectation that the broad spectrum of Christian graces indicative of a balanced and matured Christian character would not only be present in young Timothy, but would be sufficiently developed for Timothy

---

9. Samuel Miller, *The Sermon, Delivered at the Inauguration of the Rev. Archibald Alexander* (New York: Whiting and Watson, 1812), 13, 14.

to become a viable model for those to whom he ministered, regardless of their age and experience.

Paul was not talking to matured saints when, coming back through the areas of his missionary labors, he spoke to the members of these young churches, "strengthening the souls of the disciples, encouraging them to continue in the faith, and saying that through many tribulations we must enter the kingdom of God" (Acts 14:22). He assumed that God would test and prove the reality or lack of the reality of their faith. So, if you are having real dealings with God in the realm of the operations of His grace in the "already-but-not-yet" of your experience of God's grace, you will know what it is to struggle with certain pockets of your remaining sin that seem to be particularly stubborn and resistant to the sanctifying influences of the Holy Spirit.

God took my beloved first wife at the time of His appointment. I can now, in my eighties, minister tenderly and empathetically to those who must nurse a spouse to the grave, and then return to the haunting silence of an empty house, having experienced those realities in my early seventies. I could not wish this on myself as a younger man so that I could accelerate my growth or usefulness. All of this is by divine design and appointment. We cannot accelerate the things God has wisely woven into the unique plan of His dealing with each of His children. Nevertheless, I insist that, even in the case of a younger man, there must be some degree of personal and perceptive acquaintance with the fundamental workings of sin and grace in the soul if we are to be true shepherds, feeding and shepherding God's sheep and His lambs.

John Erskine agreed:

> But, above all, inward piety assists in understanding and explaining experimental religion. Those can best unveil the pangs of the new birth, and the nature of union and communion with Christ, and describe conversion, progressive sanctification, a life of faith, the struggles of the flesh and spirit, and such like subjects, who can speak of them from their own experience. Those are best suited to speak a word in season to weary souls, who can comfort them, in their spiritual distresses, with those consolations wherewith they themselves have been comforted of God. Their experience of the influence of truths which have been most useful to their own souls, leads them to insist much upon these in their public ministrations, and determines them to know nothing in comparison of Christ, and him crucified.[10]

---

10. John Erskine, *Discourses Preached on Several Occasions* (Edinburgh: D. Willison, 1801), 14.

Humility and Self-Distrust

The last of the four qualifications I will address in the area of Christian experience is that *the man of God must be characterized by a chastened disposition of humility and self-distrust*. If a man is indeed biblically qualified for the work of the ministry and if he is to be useful in that work, he must, by God's own personal disciplines, be brought to the place where, in facing the task, he cries out from the deepest recesses of his heart, "Who is sufficient for these things?" (2 Cor. 2:16). This was Paul's cry when, by the unique inspiration of the Spirit, he wrote about the nature, the privileges, and the responsibilities of New Covenant ministry.

He wrote further:

> Such is the confidence that we have through Christ toward God. Not that we are sufficient in ourselves to claim anything as coming from us, but our sufficiency is from God, who has made us competent to be ministers of a new covenant, not of the letter but of the Spirit. For the letter kills, but the Spirit gives life (2 Cor. 3:4–6).

When we think of the things that are needed for the task, he said, in effect, "we do not look for any one of those things as having its root in the soil of what we are by nature." Rather, he recognized that one's sufficiency is from God. If we are to be qualified to assume the office and functions of an overseer, we must have some measure of a fundamental, personal, experiential consciousness of who and what we are by nature that causes us to cry out this way concerning our felt lack of sufficiency.

This is in direct contrast to the notion entertained by some men as they are about to enter the pastoral office. They whisper to themselves inwardly, if not audibly, "I am delighted that the Lord and His people have finally come around to realizing what a wonderful commodity has been patiently waiting in the wings, to be thrust upon the church, to be as greatly used of God as I believe I will be." I always get a queasy feeling when young men counsel with me and tell me, "Well, you know, Pastor Martin, I just have a growing sense that God has something very special for me to do in the work of the ministry." I am tempted to say,

> My friend, if that is an accurate expression of where you are in your thinking, let me be a prophet and tell you something. I do not know what God may purpose to do through you should you enter the Christian ministry. However, what you have just said makes me bold to predict that, if God indeed has some special things to do in you and

with you, it will be seen in His work to humble you and to bring you to the place where you sense in the very core of your being the truth that you are nothing, and if God ever does anything with you, it will be all of His grace and His power.

Some think it is spiritual to want to be greatly used by God in some unusual and special way so that their names will appear in some book of church history describing God's work in our generation. This is a subtle error. Jesus said, "I am the vine; you are the branches. Whoever abides in me and I in him, he it is that bears much fruit, for apart from me you can do nothing" (John 15:5). The Lord Jesus made plain His purpose to use Peter as a very special instrument in His hands for the advancement of His cause on earth. Peter was going to be the instrument of God to open the door of the Kingdom to the Gentiles. He was marked out by God to be greatly and especially used.

Yet, you remember how Christ gave Peter the sobering news that the flock would be scattered when the Shepherd was stricken according to prophecy (Matt. 26:31, 32). Peter assumed that his own rock-like resolve would carry him through the coming ordeal with flying colors, and that the other weaklings would be scattered. Christ responded to his protestations by saying to him, "Simon, Simon, behold, Satan demanded to have you, that he might sift you like wheat, but I have prayed for you that your faith may not fail" (Luke 22:31, 32). The pronoun *you* is plural in verse 31. In verse 32, the pronoun is singular, showing that the Lord's prayer was focused on Peter and the maintenance of his faith in particular. Peter did not realize how vulnerable he truly was, how immature he was, how proud he was. He was not yet humbled. How did God produce a chastened spirit of humility in Peter's heart and life, before using him to strengthen his brethren? He overruled the devil's desires, as well as answering the prayer of the Lord Jesus, working everything together according to His wise plan and good purposes.

One of the greatest evidences that our Lord's prophecy about Peter was fulfilled is the existence of 1 Peter. There, he wrote to the suffering saints of Asia Minor and underscored the unique place of humility in the Christian life, "Likewise, you who are younger, be subject to the elders. Clothe yourselves, all of you, with humility toward one another, for 'God opposes the proud but gives grace to the humble.' Humble yourselves, therefore, under the mighty hand of God so that at the proper time he may exalt you" (1 Pet. 5:5, 6). This is the reality I seek to capture when I say that one of the qualities of tested, proven, Christian experience is this chastened disposition of humility and self-distrust.

It is clear from Paul's experience that even he had to be brought back, again and again, to acknowledge the crucial importance of maintaining this disposition. The classic statement of this fact is when he speaks of having a "thorn in the flesh," a "messenger of Satan" to buffet him (2 Cor. 12:7–10). Whatever the thorn was, Paul was persuaded that it was incompatible with his usefulness in gospel labor. So he engaged in three seasons of concentrated prayer, pleading with God to remove the thorn from him. This prayer was not focused on pursuing his personal convenience or comfort, but on the removal of this seeming impediment to his usefulness. Then the Lord said, in essence,

> Paul, you are missing a fundamental element. I will tell you what it is. You have been a very special chosen vessel in My hands. In the course of My dealings with you, I have given you the privilege to see and hear things that very few are privileged to see and hear. I know that your remaining sin could greatly betray you, causing you to be swollen with pride in the light of these great privileges. So, to keep you from being too elated by the greatness of the revelations given to you, I have given you this thorn to keep you consciously weak, so that you may be constantly reminded that your strength to serve Me acceptably lies outside of yourself. Furthermore, I want you to know that your present assumption is defective. You think that your maximum usefulness and your troubling thorn are incompatible. In reality though, your maximum usefulness will be experienced only as the thorn is My instrument to keep you in the posture of chastened humility and self-distrust. The thorn will be My instrument to keep you constantly aware of the fact that, while I can empower and enable a humble and weak man, I cannot and will not empower a proud man, for I Myself have said that "I resist the proud and give grace to the humble." In the light of these things that you know, embrace from the heart this truth that "My grace is sufficient for you, for my power is made perfect in weakness."

Scripture reveals that sometimes God's power is manifested by removing weakness. We read of some

> who through faith conquered kingdoms, enforced justice, obtained promises, stopped the mouths of lions, quenched the power of fire, escaped the edge of the sword, were made strong out of weakness, became mighty in war, put foreign armies to flight (Heb. 11:33, 34).

In this instance, however, God's power was made perfect *in* weakness! Paul understood, and said,

> Therefore I will boast all the more gladly of my weaknesses, so that the power of Christ may rest upon me. For the sake of Christ, then, I am content with weaknesses, insults, hardships, persecutions, and calamities. For when I am weak, then I am strong (2 Cor. 12:9, 10).

If we wish to have the Spirit of God resting upon us in power, we must have this chastened spirit of humility and of self-distrust. This spirit must be evident to some degree in any man before we encourage him to enter the ministry. Those of us who are in the ministry must also embrace the reality that God will be determined to cultivate, enlarge, and deepen this grace in us in order that the power of Christ may rest on us in ever greater measures, "God opposes the proud, but gives grace to the humble" (Jas. 4:6). What a contradiction it is to be a proud minister of the gospel, especially when we consider that the Christ in whose name we minister is "gentle and lowly in heart" (Matt. 11:29), and we are to *reflect* Him as we *preach* Him.

This concludes my presentation on the qualifications related to Christian experience which must be found in the man aspiring to or presently in the pastoral ministry. Surely not one of us would have any argument with any of the four qualifications that I have presented: *love for Christ, faith in the great unseen realities, acquaintance with the dynamics of sin and grace,* and *humility and self-distrust.* The first two look outside of ourselves, the latter two look inward.

May the Spirit of God search our hearts through the application of His Word with respect to each of these areas. May we discern in ourselves growing measures of these four aspects of Christian experience. Further, may we seek to discern whether or not these elements of Christian experience are present in those whom we encourage to pursue the office and functions of an elder in the church of Christ.

> Our Father, we pray that our love to Your Beloved Son may be rekindled and deepened into a white-hot passion. We pray that, by the operations of your Holy Spirit, we may go deeper in our understanding and experience of the ways of Your grace in our hearts and in the hearts of Your people. Help us that we may be determined to go deeper in our experience of the dynamics of Your grace, in making us holy men in an unholy world. We ask as well that we may grow in the graces of self-distrust and genuine humility. We pray that we will become more heavenly minded. God, together we acknowledge that the tender plant

of passionate, pure, unsullied love for and attachment to Your Son so often withers because of the influences that we allow to distill upon our hearts. Forgive us, we pray. We ask for a rekindling of a deep and ever-growing love for Your Beloved Son, so that, as we minister in His Name, He may not have to say to us, "I have this against you, that you have left your first love." May we press ever toward the mark of the prize of the upward calling You have given us in Christ, and may we go from strength to strength. Seal Your Word to our hearts, we plead in Jesus' name. Amen.

CHAPTER 8

Qualifications of Mental Gifts

The second category of qualifications which indicate a biblical call to this office and ministry is the presence of the gifts essential for fulfilling the purposes and functions for which Christ Himself has instituted this office. I use the word essential to describe the gifts which indicate fitness for the office and to emphasize the fact that these gifts are not optional, but absolutely necessary. If Christ does not furnish a man with these gifts, then it is clear that Christ is not fashioning that man into one whom He will give to the church as a gift. As we take up this aspect of our subject, I begin with two qualifications.

The first qualification is that *I am not saying that either the order in which I present these things, or the precise terminology which I use, has divine sanction.*

Having spent decades studying, teaching, and revising these lectures, I doubt that further study and reflection will lead me to make any major changes in the substance of my thinking. In my present judgment, then, I am prepared to assert that, whatever terminology I may use, and in whatever order that terminology is presented, I believe that what I am about to present will identify those gifts which, according to the scriptures, are essential to fulfilling the purposes and functions of the pastoral office. Without possessing these gifts in some measure, there is no legitimate entrance into, or remaining in, the pastoral office.

The second qualification is that *I am conscious that some of my readers may be men for whom the question of their call to this office is not yet fully resolved in their minds or in the minds of others to whom they are accountable.*

I recognize that, in this period of indecision regarding your call, you may be seeking to cultivate these gifts, looking to others for counsel and assessment as to whether they see the emergence of these gifts in you. I am not saying that these gifts must all, right now, be as clearly seen in your life as the sun is seen at noon on a cloudless day. What I am insisting is that, when it comes time for you to formally present yourself as a candidate for this office, by whatever process your ecclesiastical setting may require, if these gifts are not evident in you to some degree and you continue to seek formal ordination, you will be seeking to intrude yourself into an office for which you have not been equipped by Christ. Furthermore, you will be tempting others to violate the clear mandate given to Timothy by the apostle Paul when he wrote, "Do not be hasty in the laying on of hands, nor take part in the sins of others; keep yourself pure" (1 Tim. 5:22).

There is nothing shameful about coming to the conclusion that one does not possess the requisite gifts for the work of the ministry, and that they will most likely never be acquired by prayer, wise and godly mentoring, and arduous effort. However, it is shameful and ultimately tragic to acknowledge the absence of the requisite gifts and yet force one's way into the Christian ministry. To do this is to bring oneself under the indictment concerning the false prophets in Jeremiah's day, of whom the LORD said, "The prophets are prophesying lies in my name. I did not send them, nor did I command them or speak to them. They are prophesying to you a lying vision, worthless divination, and the deceit of their own minds" (Jer. 14:14).

In seeking to collate and present the precepts, principles, and precedents of the Word of God concerning the gifts which constitute the essential components of a call to the pastoral office, I will group them under two major headings. First, we will consider the *identity* of the requisite gifts for the pastoral office. Second, we will address the *source* or *origin* of these gifts.

The Identity of the Required Gifts for the Pastoral Office

As we now consider the identity of the specific gifts required for the pastoral office, we will do so under three categories of gifts which, to one degree or another, ought to be present and evident before any man should satisfy his conscience that he is indeed a shepherd-teacher to a specific flock of Christ. In identifying some of the specific gifts which make up these categories, we will also consider the biblical basis for insisting that they are a necessary evidence of a genuine call of God to the pastoral office.

Mental Gifts

I am describing the first of these three categories as *the gifts which find expression in the disposition, capabilities, and acquisitions of the mind.* By *disposition,* I am referring to a prevailing attitude or characteristic. We say of a certain woman, "She has a sweet or gracious disposition," or we may say of a man, "He has an energetic or courageous disposition." I hope it is never said of any of us, "He has an ugly, sour, and critical disposition." When we use the word *disposition* in that way, we are speaking of a prevailing characteristic of an individual. I am saying that there ought to be a discernible and prevailing disposition of the mind of any man whom Christ is gifting for the labor and office of an elder. The primary descriptive words that ought to characterize such a mind are humility and teachableness. By *capabilities*, I am speaking of one's natural God-given mental capacities. The scriptures and general revelation clearly teach us that one's mental capacities can be cultivated and to some degree enlarged. However, a modicum of God-given mental ability is essential in any man who is to acquire and exercise the mental disciplines that are essential to preach, teach, counsel, and shepherd the people of God. By *acquisitions*, I am referring to what our minds have taken on board by serious study, reflection, observation, instruction, and by our interaction with others. Track with me now as I seek to identify five characteristics of the kind of mind that is ordinarily essential as a prerequisite for the work of the pastoral office.

The first characteristic is *a mind which is reverently and lovingly submissive to the absolute authority of the scriptures as the inerrant Word of God.*

This quality heads the list. In Titus 1, Paul is guiding Titus with respect to those men whom he ought to mark out, and who ought to be recognized and installed as elders in the churches in Crete. An essential requirement is that, "he must hold firm to the trustworthy word as taught, so that he may be able to give instruction in sound doctrine and also to rebuke those who contradict it" (Titus 1:9). The Greek verb *antecho* means to hold on to something, that is, to cling tenaciously to something. The elder, then, is to be one who clearly clings tenaciously to the faithful Word, lining up with the apostolic teaching. Since the apostles regarded the entire Old Testament canon as existing revelatory data, it is right for us to extrapolate the following conclusion from Titus 1:9. Holding to the faithful Word, which is according to the teaching, involves clinging tenaciously to all of God's revelatory, inscripturated data which we now possess in the Old and the New Testaments of the Holy Scripture.

The apostle Paul was very conscious that he was speaking as the mouthpiece, or writing as the penman, of God. He gave what we would say were rather practical, mundane, but necessary directives for sorting out the charismatic free-for-all that was occurring in the public gatherings for wor-ship in the church at Corinth. Following those specific directives, he boldly wrote to them, "If anyone thinks that he is a prophet, or spiritual, he should acknowledge that the things I am writing to you are a command of the Lord" (1 Cor. 14:37).

Likewise, looking back to that earlier occasion when he had preached among the Thessalonians, he commended them and expressed gratitude for the work of God among them. There is a wonderful parallel between the way the Word of God has been given to us, and the delightful way in which one, effectually called by God, receives that Word, "When you received the word of God, which you heard from us, you accepted it not as the word of men but as what it really is, the word of God, which is at work in you believers" (1 Thess. 2:13). God's Word is "the mystery hidden for ages and generations but now revealed to his saints" (Col. 1:26), showing us how the Word was given. In a parallel passage, Paul says more, "When you read this, you can perceive my insight into the mystery of Christ, which was not made known to the sons of men in other generations as it has now been revealed to his holy apostles and prophets by the Spirit" (Eph. 3:4, 5). Paul also wrote,

> Now we have received not the spirit of the world, but the Spirit who is from God, that we might understand the things freely given us by God. And we impart this in words not taught by human wisdom but taught by the Spirit, interpreting spiritual truths to those who are spiritual (1 Cor. 2:12, 13).

Although it is difficult to know what is the best translation for the last part of verse 13, the point is clear.[1] The apostle was conscious that he was an instrument through which God was giving revelation to the church. Furthermore, he was conscious that the revelation was expressed in Spirit-directed words, not just general thoughts, leaving to the apostle the choice of the words. Although the apostle's mental faculties were fully engaged, he was conscious that the very words which captured and expressed the thoughts of God were words chosen by the direct and supernatural agency of the Holy Spirit.

In His high priestly prayer, Jesus Himself made reference to the manner in which the apostles received His Word, "For I have given them the words

---

1. The NASB translates 1 Corinthians 2:13 as, "which things we also speak, not in words taught by human wisdom, but in those taught by the Spirit, combining spiritual *thoughts* with spiritual *words.*" This may be the main point Paul is making here.

that you gave me, and they have received them and have come to know in truth that I came from you; and they have believed that you sent me" (John 17:8). Our blessed Lord was conscious that, in His role as the obedient servant, He did not speak the thoughts of God in His own words but in God's words.

Therefore, one called by God to the pastoral office is given in a heightened way that which God gives to all of His people to some degree. He gives a mind gripped in this grace of reverent submission to the absolute authority of the Word of the living God. It follows that everyone whom God is fashioning into an able minister of the New Covenant can say with the prophet Jeremiah, "Your words were found, and I ate them, and your words became to me a joy and the delight of my heart" (Jer. 15:16). Jeremiah did not say, "Your Words were found, and I picked over them to separate the wheat from the chaff and then ate the finest of the wheat." No, they were all the best of food. Since it is the whole of Scripture which is "God-breathed" and thoroughly able to furnish the man of God, the gift of a mind reverently submissive and receptive to the whole of Scripture is an essential aspect of the divine call. Without that mind, no man has any right to intrude himself into this office.

Our posture before the Word of God is to be one of total receptivity. Paul shows his concern about the transfer of truth from Timothy to faithful men, "And what you have heard from me in the presence of many witnesses entrust to faithful men who will be able to teach others also" (2 Tim. 2:2). Even they must be wholly receptive to the truth, and in this way the truth passes on from man to man, place to place, and generation to generation. This is the apostolic deposit, the transferable deposit. When Paul writes, "if you put these things before the brothers, you will be a good servant of Christ Jesus, being trained in the words of the faith and of the good doctrine that you have followed" (1 Tim. 4:6), he is referring to the things that he himself has been addressing, concerning aspects of behavior in the house of God in all of their meticulous detail. Timothy, who is in a sense the passive receptor of this divine legacy, is to pass this on without any addition, dilution, or extraction.

One passage in particular is Paul's holy "swan song" to his spiritual son Timothy. Knowing that shortly his head will drop into a basket somewhere in the execution area of a Roman prison, he wrote,

> I charge you in the presence of God and of Christ Jesus, who is to judge the living and the dead, and by his appearing and his kingdom: preach

the word; be ready in season and out of season; reprove, rebuke, and exhort, with complete patience and teaching (2 Tim. 4:1, 2).

Here Paul is charging Timothy to "Take the role of a herald who has a message from the King. Do not tamper with the King's message; just herald it as one who has received it."

I mention another passage which has always been to me a transforming reality in connection with this disposition of mind concerning the Word of God,

> Thus says the LORD: "Heaven is my throne, and the earth is my footstool; what is the house that you would build for me, and what is the place of my rest? All these things my hand has made, and so all these things came to be, declares the LORD. But this is the one to whom I will look: he who is humble and contrite in spirit and trembles at my word" (Isa. 66:1, 2).

Humility of spirit is what we feel in the presence of God when we own our creatureliness with all of the limitations of our created minds. Contrition is what we feel in the presence of God when we own our sinfulness which has darkened and twisted our minds. Yet God says through the prophet that He will look to the person who owns, from the heart, his limitations as a creature, who owns that he is a sinner, and who, when God speaks, trembles in the hearing of the Word of the majestic God of holiness speaking from heaven. We do not set ourselves up as the critics of His Word to evaluate its merits or reshape it; we tremble in the receptive posture of humble, redeemed sinners.

On many occasions, when I have seen people struggling intellectually with certain aspects of revealed truth that in their judgment just do not seem to fit together, I have said something like this to myself, "Would I not be a fool, if I were to make a trip to the New Jersey shore, take a tea cup, fill it to the brim with Atlantic Ocean water, and then stand up and announce to the world that I had the ocean in my cup?" We can never contain all that God is and does in the teacup of our little sin-darkened brains.

When our thoughts of who God is and of what we are as creatures and sinners raise us up to experience breathless wonder in worship, we will then be the man of Isaiah 66:2, who, owning the limitations of the creature and the humbling realities of the sinner, trembles before the Word that God has given. All who enter a pulpit, or sit in a counseling situation, or stand in a congregational meeting to give biblical directions to the people of God, and who, in the slightest way, have listened to and entertained the whispers of the devil first spoken in Eden, "Did God actually say?" need to have deep dealings with God until those devilish questions concerning the veracity of God's Word give way to holy trembling before that same Word. Such whispers may only be a temporary or fleeting assault of the enemy, quickly vanquished by raising the shield of faith. However, if this temptation to doubt the absolute veracity of the Word of God should ever become a prevailing disposition of the mind, the man who has yielded to such a temptation ought to leave, or never enter, the ministry. The mental disposition of a true man of God will always be one of total receptivity before the words of God deposited in the inerrant words of Holy Scripture.

The second characteristic is *a mind furnished with a grasp upon the basic contents of Scripture.*

By that I mean that a man must have a general familiarity with the contents of the Bible in his own native language. For me, that is my English Bible in a good, reliable, formal-equivalence translation, in which the translators do not engage in excessive dynamic-equivalence translation, making the version more interpretive than literal.[2] This knowledge should also be sought by those who have no aspiration or aptitude to be found laboring in teaching and preaching as their life's calling. The requirement for every elder, however, is firm. He must be "able to teach" (1 Tim. 3:2), "able to give instruction in sound doctrine," and also able "to rebuke those who contradict it" (Titus 1:9).

Obviously, this requirement is increased in degree in the case of those elders who will labor in preaching and teaching. However, all elders must have a mind furnished with a grasp upon the basic contents of Scripture, including a clear understanding of the basic plot line of the Bible.

When Paul taught Timothy that all Scripture is God-breathed and useful for his thorough equipping (2 Tim. 3:16, 17), it follows that one who is not acquainted with the broad content of that inscripturated revelation is not complete as a man of God, that is, as a minister of that Word. Our minds instinctively turn back to this passage,

And he humbled you and let you hunger and fed you with manna, which you did not know, nor did your fathers know, that he might make

---

2. A very helpful summary of the various approaches to Bible translation is found at *http://www.esvbible.org/resources/esv-global-study-bible/preface-to-the-english-standard-version/.*

you know that man does not live by bread alone, but man lives by every word that comes from the mouth of the LORD (Deut. 8:3; Matt. 4:4).

Since Scripture is its own infallible interpreter, how can a man be a safe guide in handling any one of the individual parts without being familiar with the quality-control of the whole? Paul takes it to a higher level in his instruction to Timothy, "Do your best to present yourself to God as one approved, a worker who has no need to be ashamed, rightly handling the word of truth" (2 Tim. 2:15). Paul uses an interesting Greek word in this verse, *orthotomeo*, which means to *cut a path in a straight direction*. We have the word *orthodontics* which means to make the teeth straight. The meaning of *orthotomeo* is to guide the Word of truth along a straight path, that is, a path that is straight-forward, without rabbit trails, confusing twists and turns, potholes, and other impediments which would keep people from understanding its clear meaning. Contrast this with the Pharisees, who came under the condemnation of Christ when He said to them, "You are wrong, because you know neither the Scriptures nor the power of God" (Matt. 22:29).

Surely, whether we are in a counseling situation, assessing what to do in a congregational crisis, or seeking to guide the church in matters of discipline as shepherd-teachers of Christ's church, we must have an acquaintance with the basic contents of the whole Bible. We dare not blunder with imbalanced and imprecise statements in public ministry. We cannot give inept, unwise, unreasonable, or unjust judgment in congregational difficulties. Careful reflection reveals that the inept guidance of the Pharisees was due to a fundamental ignorance concerning issues that are clearly addressed in Scripture, which they missed, purposely obscured, and negated by their man-made traditions.

Considering that the mind furnished with a grasp of the basic contents of Scripture is an essential requirement of the pastoral office, should this not cause us to understand why chronological age is relatively meaningless in determining a man's fitness for this office? Chronological age does not in itself give a man such an acquaintance with the contents of the Bible. I have seen young men in their late twenties who knew more of the general content of their English Bibles than some men who had been in the ministry for thirty years. Remember what is said of Timothy, "From childhood you have been acquainted with the sacred writings, which are able to make you wise for salvation through faith in Christ Jesus" (2 Tim. 3:15). From a nursing babe, a *bréphos*, Timothy began to know Holy Scripture. He got Bible with his mother's breast.

Timothy was a relatively young man by the time Paul encountered him on his second missionary journey (Acts 16:1, 2). However, Timothy was already manifesting a maturity of perspective and understanding beyond his years. Paul could discern this after a relatively short time. Apparently, the brethren in Lystra and Iconium could also. Luke informs us that Timothy "was well spoken of by the brothers at Lystra and Iconium" (Acts 16:2). There was a universal testimony that this young man possessed a mind that was saturated with a broad acquaintance with the Old Testament scriptures which in turn resulted in his above-average maturity and unquestioned fitness for a place of spiritual leadership. How did Timothy get such knowledge? The answer is that God was putting Scripture into the mind of Timothy from the time he was nursed at his mother's breast. I have known young men who, having had similar privileges of biblical instruction from their childhood, are already gifted with an expansive knowledge of the contents of their Bibles. This becomes evident when one listens to their prayers and hears them preach.

In order to increase your gift of a mind increasingly furnished with a grasp upon the basic contents of Scripture, you must determine to commit yourself to some program of systematic assimilation of the whole of your Bible for the whole of your life. Conscientiously establish a Bible reading program whereby, in a structured and orderly way, you are continually reading through the entirety of your Bible at least every one or two years. Several such Bible reading programs are readily available. Whatever suggested pattern you may use, you must choose one and stick to it. There is no substitute for reading through the whole of the scriptures, again and again, in a prayerful and seriously reflective way. After several years with one program, you may wish to use a different one, for the sake of the freshness of variety. Over the years, I have found a pattern that works best for me, but I have to change it occasionally because I get into a rut. To keep freshness, I find it necessary to alter my Bible reading plan from time to time.

Generally, the suggestion I give people is to read various sections of their Bibles concurrently. I do not recommend that you start in Genesis and go straight through to the book of Revelation. If you follow that pattern, it will not be long before you get bogged down in some of those sections of the Old Testament that seem at first to yield so little devotional fruitfulness, that your spirit can begin to feel shriveled. Instead, I recommend working through the Old and New Testament sequentially and concurrently. For me, this has ordinarily meant a chapter of the New Testament every day for six days a week. This takes me through the New Testament approximately once a year. Reading two chapters from the Old Testament daily gets me through the Old Testament once every two years. To these readings in the Old and New Testaments, I add a daily reading of one of the psalms, in order. This pattern takes me through the book of Psalms approximately once every six to nine months. For a number of years, I added a chapter in Proverbs, which took me through Proverbs once a month. My passion was, and still is, that I might absorb the content of my English Bible, so that the whole of my Bible is constantly conditioning my thinking as I seek to grow in my knowledge of God, as I seek to live my life before the face of God, as I seek to prepare edifying sermons, and as I seek to be helpful to those sheep of God who seek my counsel and advice.

Years ago, someone suggested to me a very helpful prayer when approaching our time of personal Bible reading. I have found it a very salutary spiritual exercise to pray this prayer. It goes like this: "O God, as I am about to read and meditate upon Your Word, where I am ignorant, please teach me. Where I am wrong, please correct me. And where I am right, please confirm me in my understanding of Your truth."

Several decades ago I was looking over the many books in my library that I had never read. I came to the conclusion that I would not live long enough to read them all. However, that reflection created in me a fresh desire to know the one book whose content is indispensable to my spiritual well-being, and to my usefulness in the work of the ministry—my Bible. In the light of this experience, I began to make it a practice, commensurate with and parallel to my Old and New Testament readings, to obtain, or to take from my bookshelves, a good, solid, popular commentary. It does not need to be intensively technical, but it must be exegetically responsible and devotionally warm and practical. I have made it my habit to read such a commentary from beginning to end, keeping pace with my regular Bible reading. Among the best ones for this purpose are many in the series published by InterVarsity Press, entitled *The Bible Speaks Today*, or those from the series entitled *Let's Study the Bible*, published by the Banner of Truth Trust. Then, we must never forget the timeless usefulness of Matthew Henry's unabridged *Commentary on the Whole Bible*, and Bishop Ryle's *Expository Thoughts on the Gospels*, in this category of devotional commentaries. Charles Bridges's commentary on *Psalm 119* and his commentary on the book of *Proverbs* have proven very helpful in this discipline.

I must confess that, if I could turn back the clock of my life thirty or forty years, I would set a personal goal to read all of Calvin's commentaries in conjunction with my own personal Bible study. I now read these commentaries with no conscious thought of sermon preparation. It is just Albert N. Martin, sitting in his prayer-and-reading chair, wanting to know his Bible, with the disposition expressed in the following words, "Lord, there are many things in many books that it would be good and helpful to know. However, there is only one book that I desperately need to know as thoroughly as is humanly possible, and that book is my Bible." It is amazing to me how many commentaries I have read through from beginning to end, some of them as much as four or five times. Each time I come back to one of those commentaries in conjunction with my regular Bible reading, I find myself confessing, "O God, forgive me, that I have forgotten so much."

When our children left our home, my former wife (with the Lord since 2004) and I began a similar practice in our family worship. My present wife, Dorothy, and I began this practice during our courtship, and we continue in it to this day. The mental leakage seems to increase with the passing of the years, but I am not giving up. I want to go to my grave still pressing after a deeper, richer, and more extensive knowledge of my Bible.

Spurgeon spoke of this matter of having a mind saturated with Scripture in a sermon containing a well-known quotation about John Bunyan:

> Oh, that, you and I might get into the very heart of the Word of God, and get that Word into ourselves! As I have seen the silkworm eat into the leaf, and consume it, so ought we to do with the Word of the Lord; not crawl over its surface, but eat right into it till we have taken it into our inmost parts. It is idle merely to let the eye glance over the words, or to recollect the poetical expressions, or the historic facts; but it is blessed to eat into the very soul of the Bible until, at last, you come to talk in Scriptural language, and your very style is fashioned upon Scripture models, and, what is better still, your spirit is flavoured with the words of the Lord. I would quote John Bunyan as an instance of what I mean. Read anything of his, and you will see that it is almost like reading the Bible itself. He had studied our Authorized Version, which will never be bettered, as I judge, till Christ shall come; he had read it till his very soul was saturated with Scripture; and, though his writings are charmingly full of poetry, yet he cannot give us his *Pilgrim's Progress*—that sweetest of all prose poems—without continually making us feel and say, "Why, this man is a living Bible!" Prick him anywhere; his blood is Bibline, the very essence of the Bible flows from him. He cannot speak

without quoting a text, for his very soul is full of the Word of God. I commend his example to you, beloved, and, still more, the example of our Lord Jesus. If the Spirit of God be in you, he will make you love the Word of God; and, if any of you imagine that the Spirit of God will lead you to dispense with the Bible, you are under the influence of another spirit which is not the Spirit of God at all. I trust that the Holy Spirit will endear to you every page of this Divine Record, so that you will feed upon it yourselves, and afterwards speak it out to others. I think it is well worthy of your constant remembrance that, even in death, our blessed Master showed the ruling passion of his spirit, so that his last words were a quotation from Scripture.[3]

To me, Spurgeon's words are the greatest thing that was ever said about Bunyan. He knew his English Bible through and through. He thought in biblical categories: its history, poetry, praises, precepts, promises, and above all, its constant setting forth of our Lord Jesus Christ and His grace as our only hope for life and salvation.

I say this to my brethren in the pastoral office, and to those who aspire to that office. If we are to have ministries that are ministries of the Word, if we are to be a gift of Christ in His hands who equips the saints and enables them to become mature and stable and useful in Christ, then we must be men who know our Bibles. In order to be such a man, you must determine to commit yourself to some program of systematic assimilation of the whole of your Bible. You also must jealously guard the use of your time in relationship to what I would call diversionary or recreational mental activities. For you the newspaper may be a diversional, recreational mental activity. You may like certain magazines related to special interests that you have. You may like browsing the Internet simply searching for general information. With all the stuff that is aggressively seeking an entrance into our minds through the eye-gate, we need to resolve this. I can only know so much in this life about anything. With respect to any sphere or subject of inquiry, I must confess with Paul, "we know in part and we prophesy in part" (1 Cor. 13:9).

Some men face a peculiar temptation from books, to become carnally fascinated with and proud of them. When they are together with their peers, they can easily drift into conversations that constitute a kind of intellectual one-upmanship. When we are interacting with other men in the ministry, the conversation can so easily drift into the following kind of exchange: "My

---

3. Charles Haddon Spurgeon, *The Metropolitan Tabernacle Pulpit*, vol. 45 (Pasadena, TX: Pilgrim Publications, 1977), 495.

brother, what are you reading these days? Oh, yes, I have heard of that particular book, and that it is considered a very perceptive treatise, but have you read this other one?" Resist that temptation. Say to yourself:

> I am determined to learn what is in my Bible. What is in my Bible I want to get into my head, and the Bible that is in my head I want to be in my heart. I want those biblical truths that find a lodging place in my heart to shape all of my thinking concerning every facet of my life and my pastoral labors.

Cultivate the ambition so that it could justly be said of you what was said of Apollos, that he was "an eloquent man, and mighty in the scriptures" (Acts 18:24 KJV).[4] Make it your life's ambition to be *mighty* in the scriptures. Years ago, I was part of an ordination council gathered by an independent church in which the ministerial candidate could not even name all the books of the Bible in order from Genesis to Revelation! The mind properly furnished by Christ and fitted for the pastoral office is not only a mind which is reverently submissive to Scripture, but also a mind furnished with a grasp upon the basic contents of the Bible in one's primary or native language.

The third characteristic is *a mind furnished with a basic understanding of and love for the true meaning, interrelatedness, and self-consistency of Scripture.*

"The ignorant and unstable twist to their own destruction, as they do the other Scriptures" (2 Pet. 3:16). The language here is very graphic, portraying their "work" as twisting or putting the Scripture on a torture rack. We, as ministers of the New Covenant, are commanded to "follow the pattern of sound words" (2 Tim. 1:13). In concrete terms this means that we must have a firm grasp on disciplines which I will shortly identify. I am not saying that a man must have studied these disciplines under their formal name and identification. Neither am I saying that he necessarily would be able, if interrogated concerning those categories, to pass a formal, seminary-level written test. He may have attained his understanding of and love for the meaning, interrelatedness, and self-consistency of Scripture informally, while sitting for years under a preaching and teaching ministry which had these qualities, by formal instruction in a seminary or similar setting, or by

---

4. The ESV says, "competent in the Scriptures." The Greek word is *dunamis*, so "mighty" is best, and a literal translation. From this we derive the interpretation that he was strong in his understanding of Scripture and competent in handling it, because the Scripture filled his mind and heart.

a combination of both, as he has sought to absorb the message of the Word of God, and as the Spirit of God has taught and nurtured his understanding. What I am saying is that this understanding will involve elements which have been identified under the categories which we will now consider.

First, the man aspiring to the pastoral office must have some understanding of *biblical theology*, which I explained at the beginning of this unit.

He will know, for example, that some of the historical events[5] that are recorded in the apostolic history in the book of Acts are not *paradigmatic*[6] for the church in all ages. I am referring, for example, to the casting of lots for the apostolic replacement of Judas (Acts 1:24–26). In addition, the selling of property and having all things in common (Acts 2:44, 45) is not a requirement placed upon the churches in all ages and places. The apostolic signs and wonders are also not part of the unchanging design of church ministry or evangelism. These are not *paradigmatic*, but *programmatic*,[7] unfolding the history of redemption in which God was endorsing the ministry of the apostles by the signs and wonders that validated their claim to be the unique, God-appointed, representatives of the risen and exalted Christ. It was necessary for the apostles to be unmistakably identified as those unique foundation stones (Eph. 2:19, 20; 2 Cor. 12:12) in the New Covenant temple that was being constructed by their labors (Heb. 2:3, 4).

Similarly, a man must understand why we do not lift up out of the Mosaic economy the directives for clothing and food and impose those directives upon the people of God in the New Covenant. A competent shepherd must understand that God is working in the epochs of redemptive history, consistent with Himself and His overall purposes, but not in a wooden or flattened way.

Second, the man aspiring to the pastoral office must have some understanding of *systematic theology*.

He cannot hope to attain to some worthy grasp of this theological discipline after he is recognized for the office. He must possess it beforehand, as John Owen wrote:

> 4. It is incumbent on them *to preserve the truth or doctrine of the gospel* received and professed in the church, and to defend it against all

---

5. Theologians distinguish between the *historia salutis* (historical events which form the basis of salvation and are unrepeatable) and the *ordo salutis* (the application of salvation to individuals in all ages).

6. A God-intended pattern to be applied to all subsequent situations.

7. Related to God's program for a specific time.

opposition. This is one principal end of the ministry, one principal means of the preservation of the faith once delivered unto the saints. This is committed in an especial manner unto the pastors of the churches, as the apostle frequently and emphatically repeats the charge of it unto Timothy, and in him unto all to whom the dispensation of the word is committed, 1 Epist. i. 3, 4, iv. 6, 7, 16, vi. 20; 2 Epist. i.14, ii. 25, iii. 14–17. The same he giveth in charge unto the elders of the church of Ephesus, Acts 20:28–31. What he says of himself, that the "glorious gospel of the blessed God was committed unto his trust," 1 Tim. 1:11, is true of all pastors of churches, according to their measure and call; and they should all aim at the account which he gives of his ministry herein: "I have fought a good fight, I have finished my course, I have kept the faith," 2 Tim. 4:7. The church is the "pillar and ground of the truth;" and it is so principally in its ministry. And the sinful neglect of this duty is that which was the cause of most of the pernicious heresies and errors that have infested and ruined the church. Those whose duty it was to preserve the doctrine of the gospel entire in the public profession of it have, many of them, "spoken perverse things, to draw away disciples after them." Bishops, presbyters, public teachers, have been the ringleaders in heresies. Wherefore this duty, especially at this time, when the fundamental truths of the gospel are on all sides impugned, from all sorts of adversaries, is in an especial manner to be attended unto. Sundry things are required hereunto; as,—(1.) *A clear, sound, comprehensive knowledge of the entire doctrine of the gospel*, attained by all means useful and commonly prescribed unto that end, especially by diligent study of the Scripture, with fervent prayer for illumination and understanding. Men cannot preserve that for others which they are ignorant of themselves. Truth may be lost by weakness as well as by wickedness. And the defect herein, in many, is deplorable. (2.) *Love of the truth* which they have so learned and comprehended. Unless we look on truth as a pearl, as that which is valued at any rate, bought with any price, as that which is better than all the world, we shall not endeavour its preservation with that diligence which is required. Some are ready to part with truth at an easy rate, or to grow indifferent about it; whereof we have multitudes of examples in the days wherein we live. It were easy to give instances of sundry important evangelical truths, which our fore fathers in the faith contended for with all earnestness, and were ready to seal with their blood, which are now utterly disregarded and opposed, by some who pretend to succeed them in their profession. If ministers have not a sense of that power of truth in their own souls, and a taste of its goodness, the discharge of this duty is not to be expected from them.[8]

Third, the man aspiring to the pastoral office must have some understanding of *historical theology.*

Remember that pastors shepherd the people of God in their understanding of the truth, their spiritual food, and this requires an awareness of how the conflict between truth and error developed, and how the church responded to it, in defense of the faith.

Here I commend to you the following sagacious words of Dabney:

> If we knew nothing of the transactions of past ages, we should only know those phases of man's nature, and should only have an experimental acquaintance with those affairs which fall under our own limited observation. What a mere patch is this in the great field of life! He who knows but this, must be a man of most narrow mind. And again: that experience which comes from our own observation is only obtained in any completeness after the observation is finished; that is, after our race is run, and experience is too late to help us. It is the knowledge of the past which gives to the young man the experience of age. While yet he retains the energy and enterprise of youth, and it is not too late for action, history guides his activity with the prudence and wisdom of venerable infirmity. It is hers to unite the attributes of both seasons in one person. In private and personal affairs, the force of these observations may not be so distinctly illustrated, because the field is limited, the results of steps taken are near at hand, and the agent himself is the person most concerned. Here the narrow but increasing experience of the young man, united with caution, may protect him from all ruinous errors. But public institutions or influences, whose operations are far-reaching, whose right conduct involves the welfare of many passive persons subject to them, should never be committed to any man who has not gained a wide experimental knowledge of similar institutions in all former times. *The man who undertakes to teach, to legislate, or to govern, either in church or state, without historical wisdom, is a reckless tyro* (emphasis mine). His wicked folly is like that of the quack who should venture upon the responsibilities of the physician without having either seen or read practice. For a series of human generations constitute but one lifetime of a political or ecclesiastical

---

8. John Owen, *The Works of John Owen*, vol. 16 (Edinburgh: The Banner of Truth Trust, 1968), 81, 82.

institution. The incidents of one human lifetime, or one era, constitute but a single "case," a single turn of the diseases of society. And no man has experience of those diseases who has not studied the symptoms and results through many generations.[9]

Acquaintance with biblical, systematic, and historical theology is the vital means by which a man may meet the biblical requirements of holding firm to the trustworthy Word (Titus 1:9) and rightly handling the Word of truth (2 Tim. 2:15). Do you see the rationale for the standard seminary curriculum? Some of us were not privileged to acquire these disciplines by means of a classical seminary curriculum. Consequently, we have had to direct our studies to acquire some of these disciplines along the way, in sufficient measure, in order to satisfy our consciences that we would be safe guides to God's people.

In the past several decades there have been many reprints of the Puritans, those masters of the theology of the Christian life and of the heart. Moreover, there has been an increasing availability of the reprints of time-tested orthodox theologians, as well as sound theological works by modern authors whose labors are captured not only in standard written books, but in the manifold digital technologies.[10] If you occupy the office and function of a teaching, preaching elder, do not stop studying theology. Do not give up those mental disciplines by which Christ will continue to furnish your mind to be an able minister of the New Covenant.

The fourth essential characteristic is *a mind furnished with the necessary tools and spiritual dexterity to discover and make plain to others the meaning and application of Scripture.*

Surely, if Christ is giving a man as a shepherd-teacher, He is going to provide him with these tools and with this ability. It is interesting that Paul compares the work of the ministry to the work of the soldier, athlete, and farmer (2 Tim. 2:3–6). Then he tells Timothy to "think over what I say, for

---

9. Robert L. Dabney, *Discussions: Evangelical and Theological,* vol. 2 (Edinburgh: The Banner of Truth Trust, 1967), 12, 13.

10. At the time of writing this book, the Logos Digital Library System is the most comprehensive available. Base packages and upgrades are available, so that, over time, a pastor may build an extensive library. Even if you prefer "real books," this library has invaluable search capabilities, as well as the ability to copy and paste for preparing sermon notes (https://www.logos.com). This software can be used, not only on the computer, by also on an iPad or tablet using their apps. The computer search capabilities are the most sophisticated.

the Lord will give you understanding in everything" (2 Tim. 2:7). Timothy must have the necessary tools and spiritual dexterity to discover, and then by inference, to make plain to others, the meaning and application of Scripture.

The story is told of a young preacher who made an appointment with a famous preacher, seeking an answer to the question of why his own preaching was ineffective. The older man asked the young man to preach the very sermon he had preached to his congregation on the previous Lord's Day. At the end of the exercise, the famous preacher said to the young man, "Young man, you have spent the past twenty minutes trying to get something out of your head, rather than putting something into mine." At least at that point in his ministry, the young man lacked "a mind furnished with the necessary tools and spiritual dexterity to discover and make plain to others the meaning and application of Scripture."

The fifth essential mental characteristic is *a mind disposed to, and furnished with, sound practical judgment.*

In informal language, some of us might call this a good measure of plain old "horse-sense." This characteristic is sometimes hard to pin down, but when you are in the presence of it, you know it. You also know all too well when someone lacks it and comes up with a "solution" to a problem that is totally off-base.

Samuel Miller describes this characteristic in some depth:

Another essential requisite to form the character of such a minister is, TALENTS. By which I mean, not that every minister must, of necessity, be a *man of genius*; but that he must be a man of *good sense*, of *native discernment* and *discretion*—in other words, of a *sound respectable natural understanding.*

When our blessed Lord was about to send forth his first ministers, he said to them, "Be ye wise as serpents," as well as "harmless as doves." And truly, there is no employment under heaven in which wisdom, practical wisdom, is so important, or rather, so imperiously and indispensably demanded, as in the "ministry of reconciliation." A man of a weak and childish mind, though he were as pious as Gabriel, can never make an able minister; and he ought never to be invested with the office at all. For with respect to a large portion of its duties, he is utterly unqualified to perform them; and he is in constant danger of rendering both himself and his office contemptible.

No reasonable man would require proof to convince him that good sense is essential to form an able physician, an able advocate at the bar, or an able ambassador at a foreign court. Nor would any prudent man entrust his property, his life, or the interests of his country, to one who did not bear this character. And can it be necessary to employ arguments to show that interests, in comparison with which, worldly property, the health of the body, and even the temporal prosperity of nations, are all little things, ought not to be committed to any other than a man of sound and respectable understanding? Alas, if ecclesiastical judicatories had not frequently acted as if this were far from being a settled point, it is almost an insult to my audience to speak of it as a subject admitting of a question.

Though a minister concentrated in himself all the piety and all the learning of the Christian church, yet if he had not at least a *decent stock of good sense*, for directing and applying his other qualifications, he would be worse than useless. Upon good sense depends all that is dignified, prudent, conciliatory, and respectable in private deportment; and all that is judicious, seasonable, and calculated to edify, in public ministration. The methods to be employed for *winning souls* are so many and various, according to the taste, prejudices, habits, and stations of men: a constant regard to time, place, circumstances, and character, is so essential, if we desire to profit those whom we address. And some tolerable medium of deportment, between moroseness and levity, reserve and tattling, bigotry and latitudinarianism, lukewarmness and enthusiasm, is so indispensable to public usefulness, that the man who lacks a respectable share of discernment and prudence had better, far better, be in any other profession than that of a minister. An *able* minister he cannot possibly be. Neither will anything short of sound judgment, a native perception of what is fit and proper (or otherwise), preserve any man who is set to teach and rule in the Church, without a miracle, from those perversions of scripture; those ludicrous absurdities; and those effusions of drivelling childishness, which are calculated to bring the ministry and the Bible into contempt.[11]

There is a good summary of this matter in John Owen as well:

But there belongeth more unto this wisdom, knowledge, and understanding, than most men are aware of. Were the nature of it duly considered, and withal the necessity of it unto the ministry of the gospel, probably some would not so rush on that work as they do, which they have no provision of ability for the performance of. It is, in brief,

---

11. Samuel Miller, *An Able and Faithful Ministry* (Dallas, TX: Presbyterian Heritage Publications, 1984), 7–9.

such a comprehension of the scope and end of the Scripture, of the revelation of God therein; such an acquaintance with the systems of particular doctrinal truths, in their rise, tendency, and use; such a habit of mind in judging of spiritual things, and comparing them one with another; such a distinct insight into the springs and course of the mystery of the love, grace, and will of God in Christ,—as enables them in whom it is to declare the counsel of God, to make known the way of life, of faith and obedience, unto others, and to instruct them in their whole duty to God and man thereon.[12]

These are the indispensable indications of a mind furnished by Christ for this sacred and marvelous work. I do not believe that these requisitions are setting the bar too high. Rather, this is minimalist pastoral theology 101! Would you want to have as your pastor-shepherd a man who lacked any of these five things related to the prevailing disposition of his mind? Would you want a man who had doubts about the plenary verbal inspiration of the Bible? Would you want a man who did not possess a grasp on the basic contents of the Bible so that you did not feel safe that he was constantly under the pressure of the quality control of the whole Bible, whenever he dealt with any one of its parts? Would you want to have a pastor who did not see the interrelatedness and integration of biblical truth throughout the various epochs in which God dealt with His people in differing words? Could you entrust the well-being of your soul to a man who was ignorant of the basic conflicts between truth and error that have marked the history of God's people? Would you want a pastor who did not understand the beautiful symmetry of divine truth as captured in a sound systematic theology? Would you be comfortable having a pastor who constantly manifested an absence of sound judgment? I am certain you would not; be certain that you are not such to God's people.

---

12. John Owen, *The Works of John Owen*, vol. 4 (Edinburgh: The Banner of Truth Trust, 1968), 509.

CHAPTER 9

Qualifications of Spiritual Gifts:
Speaking Gifts

The second category of gifts required for those who enter into and occupy the pastoral office are speaking gifts or gifts of utterance.

These are gifts which are manifested in the act of sanctified utterance. Our first task will be to demonstrate the biblical basis for asserting the necessity of such gifts. Here we will find both implicit and explicit testimony from Scripture. The *explicit* testimony is set before us in those passages which give us the watershed of biblical requirements for those aspiring to the office and function of an elder, especially one who labors in preaching and teaching the Word (1 Tim. 5:17). As I stated earlier, Paul uses the particle of necessity, *dei*, in 1 Timothy 3:2. As the first word in the Greek text of this verse, *dei* applies to each of the characteristics in that verse. Just as the one who aspires to the office of overseer *must* of *necessity* be blameless, he *must also* of *necessity* have an aptitude to teach.

The Greek word *didaktikos*, able to teach, refers not merely to a disposition and inclination to help others by instruction, but one who is skillful in teaching. This is the standard lexical definition. Everything that contributes to a proven ability to teach must be present to some degree in every man who aspires to the office of overseer, even though the measure of that gift of teaching may not warrant his having a primary role in the public instruction of the gathered church. Now, if this gift is required of all elders, regardless of their particular function in the shepherding of the flock of God, how much more in one who is to labor in preaching and teaching?

Another pivotal text shows Paul identifying the gifts and graces that Titus must find in any man who will be appointed as a church elder on the isle of Crete, "He must hold firm to the trustworthy word as taught, so that he may be able to give instruction in sound doctrine and also to rebuke those who contradict it" (Titus 1:9). This verse first emphasizes that to which the elder must hold firm: the faithful and trustworthy Word according to the teaching. The apostle is underscoring the fact that any man qualified to be an elder will be unmistakably characterized as a man whose mind and heart are submissive to revealed truth. He must be a man who clings to the revealed truth of God with a death-grip of faith and love.

Paul says further that the two ends for which such a man is to use that faithful Word are to exhort in sound teaching and to reprove or convict those speaking against it. The elder must be submissive to the truth himself, have proven ability to communicate that truth to the people of God, and convict those who oppose the truth. Titus 1:9 therefore presents a double-sided requirement. One side relates to the positive work of edification and building up the church of God. The other side concerns the response to those who speak against it. This work of defending the truth is a requirement for all elders. How much more for "those who labor in preaching and teaching" (1 Tim. 5:17).

Another foundational text gives us the rationale for specialized ministerial training, "What you have heard from me in the presence of many witnesses entrust to faithful men, who will be able to teach others also" (2 Tim. 2:2). Notice first that the primary emphasis falls on the character of the men who should be the recipients of special training. They are to be faithful, trustworthy men. However, Paul does not stop with his usual emphasis on the primacy of godly character, but adds that they must be able to teach others also. Thus, those who are to be trained must show some ability in the area of sanctified utterance. The word *hikanos* in this verse means *fit, sufficient, competent, qualified*, meeting adequate standards for a purpose. Timothy was not at liberty to expend extra time and energy to entrust apostolic doctrine to men whom he hoped might possibly, eventually, in some way or another, begin to manifest some small measure of a gift of utterance. Rather, he had this apostolic mandate to invest his time and energy passing on the truth to faithful men who manifest at least a nascent ability to teach others. The testimony of Scripture is clear and unequivocal.

Spurgeon strongly emphasized this point:

> Still, a man must not consider that he is called to preach until he has proved that he can speak. God certainly has not created behemoth to fly; and should leviathan have a strong desire to ascend with the lark, it would evidently be an unwise aspiration, since he is not furnished with wings. If a man be called to preach, he will be endowed with a degree of speaking ability, which he will cultivate and increase. If the gift of

utterance be not there in a measure at the first, it is not likely that it will ever be developed.[1]

It may be a proper application of 2 Timothy 2:2, in some situations, to give special training to some who have no particular gift of utterance, but who show a facility in writing or in some other means of communication. One example would be those who have skill to communicate in sign language. Nevertheless, the norm of Scripture is that if someone aspires to this office, it must be evident that the Head of the church has endowed him with those faculties that are essential for sanctified utterance.

Two more passages should be added to this list:

> Having gifts that differ according to the grace given to us, let us use them: if prophecy, in proportion to our faith; if service, in our serving; the one who teaches, in his teaching; the one who exhorts, in his exhortation; the one who contributes, in generosity; the one who leads, with zeal; the one who does acts of mercy, with cheerfulness (Rom. 12:6–8).

> As each has received a gift, use it to serve one another, as good stewards of God's varied grace: whoever speaks, as one who speaks oracles of God; whoever serves, as one who serves by the strength that God supplies—in order that in everything God may be glorified through Jesus Christ. To him belong glory and dominion forever and ever. Amen (1 Pet. 4:10, 11).

Both of these texts confirm the testimony of the Word of God that none should enter this office who do not evidently possess some measure of gift which I have been describing as the gift of sanctified utterance.

Now then, let us look at the *implicit* testimony of the Word of God, and that under three categories: 1) *the apostolic model of pastoral labor*, 2) *the apostolic injunctions concerning pastoral labor*, and 3) *the apostolic description of one who is sent or duly commissioned by Christ*.

First, consider *the apostolic model of pastoral labor*.

Paul can look the Ephesian elders in the face and say that, in his labors among them, there existed not only things unique to him as an apostle, but things that were the pattern for ordinary elders, "In all things I have shown you that by working hard in this way we must help the weak and remember the words of the Lord Jesus, how he himself said, 'It is more blessed to give

---

1. C. H. Spurgeon, *Lectures to My Students* (Edinburgh: The Banner of Truth Trust, 2008), 27.

than to receive'" (Acts 20:35). Although the specific point of the context is the example of his willingness to labor with his hands to provide for others, surely it would be truncating the passage to say that the *all things* is limited to that particular focus. Indeed, he had stated earlier in the address that, "I did not shrink from declaring to you anything that was profitable, and teaching you in public and from house to house, testifying both to Jews and to Greeks of repentance toward God and of faith in our Lord Jesus Christ" (Acts 20:20, 21). The three words which he used, *declaring, teaching,* and *testifying,* all have to do with nuances of public utterance of the Word of God: the *heralding* aspect, the *teaching* aspect, and the *witnessing* aspect.

Paul importantly states the scope, intent, and focus of his apostolic ministry here:

> To them God chose to make known how great among the Gentiles are the riches of the glory of this mystery, which is Christ in you, the hope of glory. Him we proclaim, warning everyone and teaching everyone with all wisdom, that we may present everyone mature in Christ. For this I toil, struggling with all his energy that he powerfully works within me (Col. 1:27–29).

This is a rich passage and reveals the ultimate aim and goal of Christian ministry, which is to present redeemed sinners perfect in Christ. This perfection obviously refers, not to justification, but to sanctification. Perfection in Scripture refers to wholeness, integrity, and blamelessness. The ultimate perfection envisioned is glorification, but the Christian ministry is preparation for that glorification in the here and now. The means which God has ordained to pursue this goal are identified by the words *proclaim, warning,* and *teaching,* all of which are accomplished by verbal communication.

Paul's apostolic labor had a fatherly aspect as well, "For you know how, like a father with his children, we exhorted each one of you and encouraged you and charged you to walk in a manner worthy of God, who calls you into his own kingdom and glory" (1 Thess. 2:11, 12). The words used, *exhorted, encouraged, charged,* are all expressions of sanctified utterance which were instrumental in the spiritual health and well-being of the Thessalonians.

Second, there are *the apostolic injunctions concerning pastoral labor.*

I recognize that Timothy and Titus, technically speaking, were not pastors or ordinary elders and overseers. They were apostolic representatives. Some would say they embody what is meant by the gift of the ascended Christ of an evangelist. I am not about to discuss that point because in this discussion it is irrelevant. While they did have unique authority as apostolic representatives, they were not apostles with unique apostolic gifts. There is wisdom in the fact that apostolic letters to those men have been called the pastoral epistles. By collating all of the other data of the New Testament, it is evident that what Timothy and Titus are called upon to be and to do among the existing churches in Ephesus and the island of Crete most closely approximates what we learn to be the responsibilities of the ordinary office of a pastor-teacher. Hence, the apostolic injunctions concerning the labors of these men do surely give a powerful, though we might say *implicit*, testimony to what our functions and responsibilities are in conjunction with the pastoral office and function. A brief survey of the pastoral epistles yields a wealth of texts. The emphasis in all of them is upon the things that are to be taught, conveyed, and how the apostolic representatives are to do it, with authority, patience, and love. I will demonstrate this by simply listing a string of texts.

"As I urged you when I was going to Macedonia, remain at Ephesus so that you may charge certain persons not to teach any different doctrine, nor to devote themselves to myths and endless genealogies, which promote speculations rather than the stewardship from God that is by faith" (1 Tim. 1:3, 4).

"Command and teach these things" (1 Tim. 4:11).

"Until I come, devote yourself to the public reading of Scripture, to exhortation, to teaching" (1 Tim. 4:13).

"Keep a close watch on yourself and on the teaching. Persist in this, for by so doing you will save both yourself and your hearers" (1 Tim. 4:16).

"Do not rebuke an older man but encourage him as you would a father, younger men as brothers, older women as mothers, younger women as sisters, in all purity" (1 Tim. 5:1, 2).

"As for the rich in this present age, charge them not to be haughty, nor to set their hopes on the uncertainty of riches, but on God, who richly provides us with everything to enjoy" (1 Tim. 6:17).

"And what you have heard from me in the presence of many witnesses entrust to faithful men who will be able to teach others also" (2 Tim. 2:2).

"Do your best to present yourself to God as one approved, a worker who has no need to be ashamed, rightly handling the word of truth. But avoid irreverent babble, for it will lead people into more and more ungodliness" (2 Tim. 2:15, 16).

"And the Lord's servant must not be quarrelsome but kind to everyone, able to teach, patiently enduring evil, correcting his opponents with gentleness. God may perhaps grant them repentance leading to a knowledge of the truth" (2 Tim. 2:24, 25).

"Preach the word; be ready in season and out of season; reprove, rebuke, and exhort, with complete patience and teaching" (2 Tim. 4:2).

"This testimony is true. Therefore rebuke them sharply, that they may be sound in the faith" (Titus 1:13).

"And sound speech that cannot be condemned, so that an opponent may be put to shame, having nothing evil to say about us" (Titus 2:8).

"Declare these things; exhort and rebuke with all authority. Let no one disregard you" (Titus 2:15).

Surely, no one can read this litany of texts without gaining the conviction that if Timothy or Titus did not have some measure of the gift of sanctified utterance, none of these injunctions could have been obeyed. The implication is that Christ had given to both Timothy and Titus sufficient gifts of sanctified utterance to fulfill these manifold directives among the churches in Ephesus and on the island of Crete.

Third, consider the implicit testimony of God's Word in *the apostolic description of one commissioned by Christ.*

Consider this magnificent description of the call of the preacher, "How then will they call on him in whom they have not believed? And how are they to believe in him of whom they have never heard? And how are they to hear without someone preaching?" (Rom. 10:14). This "chain" includes the *call* of the preacher to the task, the *sending* of the preacher to those in need of hearing, and the *faith* of those who hear the message preached. So the sent one is sent to preach, to be a herald, to proclaim the message and to be, in the process, the very mouthpiece of Christ.

We find the same emphasis where the Lord Jesus says, "And I have other sheep that are not of this fold. I must bring them also, and they will listen to my voice. So there will be one flock, one shepherd" (John 10:16). How do the other sheep of the Gentile hordes hear the voice of Christ? I answer, He lays His hand upon men whom He sets apart, with the character and graces which warrant them being His mouthpiece, and, in the power of His Spirit anointing those preachers, Christ calls His sheep. Peter was one of the first in this long line of preachers, "Brothers, you know that in the early days God made a choice among you, that by my mouth the Gentiles should hear the word of the gospel and believe" (Acts 15:7). I love the way he said "by my mouth." He did not just say "by me."

Paul said,

> In Christ God was reconciling the world to himself, not counting their trespasses against them, and entrusting to us the message of reconciliation. Therefore, we are ambassadors for Christ, God making his appeal through us. We implore you on behalf of Christ, be reconciled to God (2 Cor. 5:19, 20).

I do not believe he is giving a generic description of all believers here. He is specifically referring to the recognized, duly-sent servants of Christ. A careful reading of the text indicates that Paul and his companions are the ambassadors carrying the message of their king, and those who are implored to be reconciled to God are the recipients of the letter, that is, the church at Corinth. Similar in this respect is this statement, "For Christ did not send me to baptize but to preach the gospel, and not with words of eloquent wisdom, lest the cross of Christ be emptied of its power" (1 Cor. 1:17).

Finally, Paul's sense of stewardship is revealed here,

> For if I preach the gospel, that gives me no ground for boasting. For necessity is laid upon me. Woe to me if I do not preach the gospel! For if I do this of my own will, I have a reward, but if not of my own will, I am still entrusted with a stewardship (1 Cor. 9:16, 17).

In summary, the testimony of Scripture is manifold and conclusive on this point. If a man is being given to the church as a gift of Christ to function as a pastor-teacher, surely there will be undeniable evidence that he has been furnished with all of the things necessary to give him a gift of sanctified utterance. There is a world of difference between a merely natural "gift of gab" and a supernaturally imparted gift of sanctified and Spirit-empowered utterance.

I commend to you the confirming comments of John Owen, tinged with rare humor and withering sarcasm:

> *Ability of speech* in time and season is an especial gift of God, and that eminently with respect unto the spiritual things of the gospel; but a *profluency of speech*, venting itself on all occasions and on no occasions, making men open their mouths wide when indeed they should shut them and open their ears, and to pour out all that they know and what they do not know, making them angry if they are not heard and

impatient if they are contradicted, is an unconquerable fortification against all true spiritual wisdom.[2]

The Basic Elements Which Comprise the Gift of Utterance

The first element is *a natural, acquired, and cultivated ability to speak so as to secure the listening ear of the average person.*

I have labored in conjunction with the choice of my words, because once again we are confronting the delicate confluence and interaction of nature and grace. There are things God may give a man in his mother's womb, in his development from infancy to manhood, and then by direct divine donation, by an immediate operation of the Holy Spirit upon everything that is brought within the compass of speaking. I am not prepared even to attempt to identify all the things that are brought within the compass of that which I am calling *sanctified utterance.*

In identifying this first element of what is involved in sanctified utterance, I am not saying that one must demonstrate such an advanced ability to speak, or to have a measure of the gift of utterance, that would make him vie with Ezekiel in terms of sanctified eloquence in preaching and teaching. Permit me to explain this. Ezekiel lived in a time when people did not hunger for the Word of God, yet what happened when Ezekiel preached? God states His assessment,

> And they come to you as people come, and they sit before you as my people, and they hear what you say but they will not do it; for with lustful talk in their mouths they act; their heart is set on their gain. And behold, you are to them like one who sings lustful songs with a beautiful voice and plays well on an instrument, for they hear what you say, but they will not do it (Ezek. 33:31, 32).

Ezekiel had such a gift of utterance, that even people who had no intention to receive his preaching with the disposition of obedience loved to run and hear him preach. With a little imagination, one can think of the following exchange between two of Ezekiel's contemporaries: "Ezekiel's preaching? Oh, it's like going to a concert. He's like Paganini on his violin; he's like Pavarotti singing—wonderful! What did he say? I don't know, but it sounded so good! It was beautiful!"

---

2. John Owen, *The Works of John Owen*, vol. 4 (Edinburgh: The Banner of Truth Trust, 1968), 459.

Now, I am not saying that one must manifest Ezekiel-like, captivating, crowd-pleasing eloquence. On the other hand, a man whose faculties of speech, in spite of all that surgery and disciplined effort and prayer can produce, can only be listened to by the most devoted, highly motivated, patient, enduring people—such a man is not called to labor in preaching and in teaching.

Dabney stated this principle in a most balanced way:

Once more, the incurable stammerer, the man of totally diseased throat, the man who cannot acquire the capacity of speaking in public without a slowness, rudeness, confusion or hesitation painful to the hearers, is not called to preach. Public speaking is the most prominent function of the pastor. But there is scarcely any qualification about which young Christians are more apt to reason delusively. The promise of fluency in early manhood is no sufficient proof of fitness for the pulpit, and the lack of it at that season is no evidence whatever of unfitness. Experience shows that many who early win the reputation of "the college orator" in actual life sink into obscurity, and many who go through college without a particle of reputation for fluency become afterwards famous as effective speakers. And let the reader remember, that a minister may be effective without being melodious, polished or graceful. No young man whose vocal organs are not fatally maimed is entitled to conclude, because he is now unskilled, that he cannot learn to speak to edification. On the contrary, he should conclude that he *can learn* to speak, no matter what his difficulty, if only he will endeavor and persevere. Such is the emphatic testimony of Lord Chesterfield to his son, and he declares that his own eloquence (of no mean fame in his day) was wholly the result of his perseverance. There was a candidate for the ministry in the Presbyterian Church who, even after he commenced his seminary course, stammered painfully. But he resolved, by God's help, to conquer the obstacle, and he is now a most fluent and impressive extempore preacher. There is a most mischievous mistake as to the nature of good speaking. It is but unaffected, serious, perspicuous *talking*. That which is simplest is best. That language which presents the idea with the most transparent naturalness is in the best style. Who is there in his senses that cannot talk when he is interested? The man of plain good sense, whose mind is thoroughly informed with divine truth, and whose heart is instinct with divine love, will not fail to find words and utterance.[3]

Similar sentiments are expressed very strongly by Spurgeon:

Physical infirmities raise a question about the call of some excellent men. I would not, like Eusthenes, judge men by their features, but their general physique is no small criterion. That narrow chest does not indicate a man formed for public speech. You may think it odd, but still I feel very well assured, that when a man has a contracted chest, with no distance between his shoulders, the all-wise Creator did not intend him habitually to preach. If he had meant him to speak he would have given him in some measure breadth of chest, sufficient to yield a reasonable amount of lung force. When the Lord means a creature to run, he gives it nimble legs, and if he means another creature to preach, he will give it suitable lungs. A brother who has to pause in the middle of a sentence and work his air-pump, should ask himself whether there is not some other occupation for which he is better adapted. A man who can scarcely get through a sentence without pain, can hardly be called to 'Cry aloud and spare not.' There may be exceptions, but is there not weight in the general rule? Brethren with defective mouths and imperfect articulation are not usually called to preach the gospel. The same applies to brethren with no palate, or an imperfect one.

Application was received some short time ago from a young man who had a sort of rotary action of his jaw of the most painful sort to the beholder. His pastor commended him as a very holy young man, who had been the means of bringing some to Christ, and he expressed the hope that I would receive him, but I could not see the propriety of it. I could not have looked at him while preaching without laughter if all the gold of Tarshish had been my reward, and in all probability nine out of ten of his hearers would have been more sensitive than myself. A man with a big tongue which filled up his mouth and caused indistinctness, another without teeth, another who stammered, another who could not pronounce all the alphabet, I have had the pain of declining on the ground that God had not given them those physical appliances, which are as the prayer-book would put it, "generally necessary."[4]

3. Robert L. Dabney, *Discussions: Evangelical and Theological*, vol. 2 (Edinburgh: The Banner of Truth Trust, 1967), 37.

4. C. H. Spurgeon, *Lectures to My Students* (Edinburgh: The Banner of Truth Trust, 2008), 36, 37.

So, brethren, when I say, with regard to the gift of utterance, that there must be a natural, acquired, cultivated ability to speak to secure the listening ear of the average person, this is what I am talking about. I am not saying that, unless from the womb you manifested unusual facility in expressing your thoughts, you or others should conclude that you are not called. What I am saying is that a man must not allow himself to enter into that office, if at the time of his entrance he does not have this God-given gift of sanctified utterance, which will involve an ability (whether given, acquired, nurtured, or possibly helped by surgery) to be listened to by the average person with some degree of comfort.

Second, *sanctified utterance involves possessing a natural, acquired, and cultivated ability to express one's thoughts clearly and convincingly to the average person.* Notice that the words *a natural, acquired, and cultivated ability* relate to the confluence of the divine and the human, involving both the deposit in the womb, and the nurture and cultivation of training, education, and of specific disciplines.

It was said of our Lord, "And the great throng heard him gladly" (Mark 12:37). There are potential hearers on both ends of the spectrum. At one end are those who have such a highly refined, cultivated sense of appreciation for eloquence, that only someone who speaks with perfect diction and an impeccable syntactical structure would be acceptable to them. At the other end are people who, as long as you give them the truth, you can mumble in ghetto language and they will love and appreciate you, almost as though you were second cousin to the angel Gabriel. In saying the *average person*, I have in mind not those on either end of the spectrum, but the middle block of the people of God. You cannot make the discerning people of God believe you are a gift of Christ given for their edification if there is not this natural, acquired, and cultivated ability to express your thoughts clearly and convincingly. Whatever combination of these things may be present, one called by God to labor in the Word and in doctrine must be able to speak out his thoughts in such a way as to be understood, and carry the judgment of the average listener, that what is being asserted and demonstrated and proven from the Word of God is being asserted because it is in the Word.

Without this element, how can a man be called an *apt* or a *competent* teacher? How can he comfort God's people, incite them to action, and motivate them to godliness? How can he exhort them in the sound doctrine? How can he bring the heretic and his heresy to the bar of the judgment of men and leave him convicted and condemned, with his sophistry stripped away? God promises His people, "I will give you shepherds after my own heart, who will feed you with knowledge and understanding" (Jer. 3:15). The assumption is that when these shepherds take their sheep into the pasture of public instruction, the sheep see the rich pasture and are able to feed upon it, digest and assimilate it, and make it a vital part of their spiritual nourishment. If people cannot do that under our teaching and preaching, we are not shepherds after God's own heart. Brethren, I have sat and listened to some men whose preaching and teaching has forced me to say to myself, "Everybody has an occasional off day, but I doubt that someone could have so off an off day, and yet have this indispensable manifestation of the giftedness of Christ in the area of sanctified utterance."

Third, sanctified utterance is *a natural and conferred ability to be received as a messenger of God without torturing the discernment of the true people of God.*

When an elder laboring in the Word stands to speak, he does so in the context of the words of Jesus, "Whoever receives you receives me, and whoever receives me receives him who sent me" (Matt. 10:40). Now, where Christ sends His men, His people hear His voice speaking through His servants, and this happens: "We also thank God constantly for this, that when you received the word of God, which you heard from us, you accepted it not as the word of men but as what it really is, the word of God, which is at work in you believers" (1 Thess. 2:13). Without equating our comments and interpretation with apostolic infallibility (yet bearing in mind the principle of Matthew 10:40), we see that if men cannot receive the messenger as credible, they do not receive the divine message.

What are the things which are discerned in the utterance of one called and equipped by God to be a shepherd and teacher of the people of God? I will set before you two very elementary things.

The first thing that the hearer discerns is *spiritual authority.*

The scribes could quote and quote, and quote more of their rabbinical traditions. Into such a situation our Lord came saying, "But I say to you" (Matt. 5:22, 28, 32, 34, 39, 44). His discourse on the mountain was received with astonishment because "he was teaching them as one who had authority, and not as their scribes" (Matt. 7:29). His teaching was attended with the power and presence of the Spirit of God giving weight and authority to what our Lord uttered.

In a similar, albeit not an identical way, a man who has been given the gift of sanctified utterance will so speak that men will recognize that note of authority and penetrating power which attend his words, as he expounds and applies the words of Scripture. It is this reality to which the apostle Paul referred when he wrote, "my speech and my message were not in plausible words of wisdom, but in demonstration of the Spirit and of power" (1 Cor. 2:4). If we are to be received as the messengers of God, there must be a note of authority in what we say.

The second thing that the hearer discerns is *spiritual edification*.

People are built up and nourished by that word which comes to them from the man of God. They recognize that Christ has given to His servant the gift of sanctified utterance. Receiving that man whom Christ has fashioned into an able minister of the New Covenant, the true people of God are built up and edified, and in them the purpose for which Christ gives such gifts to His church is realized (Eph. 4:11–14).

John Owen spoke to this issue:

Hereunto, also, belongs that authority which accompanieth the delivery of the word, when preached in demonstration of these spiritual abilities. For all these things are necessary that the hearers may receive the word, "not as the word of man, but, as it is in truth, the word of God."[5]

Ideally, these are the things which should, to some degree, be evident to the discerning people of God in the congregation where someone aspiring to the eldership is given opportunities to teach and to preach in settings appropriate to his maturity of knowledge, grace, and gift. I would further assert that before a man is sent off to a seminary to receive specialized training for pastoral labor, there should be some discernible evidence that he is being given the gift of sanctified utterance. When such a man is given opportunities to discern whether or not he is being given such a gift of utterance, the leaders of the congregation should poll[6] a cross-section of those who have been exposed to the man's ministry in order to discern whether people are being edified when he speaks. Before sending a man off to seminary for specialized training, the leadership of the church should be persuaded that

---

5. John Owen, *The Works of John Owen*, vol. 4 (Edinburgh: The Banner of Truth Trust, 1968), 513.

6. To *poll* is simply to ask a number of people a question or series of questions in order to gain an idea of what most people think about something.

a man is manifesting more than a minimal measure of both the graces and gifts which God mandates must be present in a man who is qualified for the pastoral office.

If there is a man who seems to have potential for the ministry, then responsible spiritual oversight should surround that man with appropriate counsel, and with the structure within which those gifts can begin to be exercised and tested. In this way, there would be some emergence of the gift of sanctified utterance, at least in seed form, before someone is shipped off to seminary, and assumed after his graduation to be called by God to the ministry simply because he attended seminary. When seminaries spend thousands of dollars for full-page ads in Christian magazines, seeking men to enroll as ministerial candidates, they are not likely to tell such applicants, as Spurgeon did, "You cannot come to this college, because you do not have the gift of utterance; you have had no seals upon your ministry." He would ask men, "What souls have been won to Christ through you? What believers have been strengthened? What old saints have you visited and nurtured and nourished?"[7]

Fourth, sanctified utterance is *a special endowment of the Holy Spirit, enabling one to speak with divine unction.*

This is the most elusive, but at the same time the most vital aspect of what constitutes sanctified utterance. On the one hand, I believe that it is clearly taught in Scripture that this special endowment of the Spirit is essential to a call to labor in the Word. On the other hand, how does one ascertain this for himself, apart from some unusual experience, such as God has given to some of His servants?

Some Christians can trace their conversion to a date, a place, and the surrounding circumstances. In a similar way, there are some men who have been set apart by God and greatly used of Him who could identify the place, the time, and the circumstances, in which they received a special endowment of the Holy Spirit. They testify that this experience was critical to forcing them into the ministry and was the secret of their usefulness for many years. I am aware of this reality, both in biblical data and in Christian biography. Humanly speaking, I might want to state it and run away from any further attempt to comment upon it, but that would be irresponsible.

---

7. C.H. Spurgeon, *CH Spurgeon Autobiography: 1 The Early Years* (Edinburgh: The Banner of Truth Trust, 1976), 386.

There is clear indication in the scriptures that this endowment of the Holy Spirit, issuing in sanctified utterance, is an essential thing. We trace it to our Lord Jesus Himself, in whom the prophecy of the obedient Servant is fulfilled (Isa. 61:1–3). The Spirit of God came upon our blessed Lord in the Jordan River in a distinct and definitive way, marking Him out as the representative Head of His people. As He identifies with the people He came to save in a sinner's ordinance, and officially, formally, and publicly becomes a representative sinner, the Spirit comes upon Him, setting Him apart, marking Him, and endowing Him with the necessary equipment for His messianic role.

When He stands for the first time in His "home church" (His home synagogue in Nazareth), and the scroll is handed to Him, He reads the passage,

> The Spirit of the Lord GOD is upon me, because the LORD has anointed me to bring good news to the poor; he has sent me to bind up the brokenhearted, to proclaim liberty to the captives, and the opening of the prison to those who are bound; to proclaim the year of the LORD's favor, and the day of vengeance of our God; to comfort all who mourn; to grant to those who mourn in Zion—to give them a beautiful headdress instead of ashes, the oil of gladness instead of mourning, the garment of praise instead of a faint spirit; that they may be called oaks of righteousness, the planting of the LORD, that he may be glorified (Isa. 61:1–3).

Then He says, "Today this Scripture has been fulfilled in your hearing" (Luke 4:21).

We see this in the case of the apostles in a passage like this:

> Such is the confidence that we have through Christ toward God. Not that we are sufficient in ourselves to claim anything as coming from us, but our sufficiency is from God, who has made us competent to be ministers of a new covenant, not of the letter but of the Spirit. For the letter kills, but the Spirit gives life (2 Cor. 3:4–6).

The ministry of the New Covenant is empowered by the same Holy Spirit who gives us spiritual life, regeneration, and sanctification. All Christians are baptized in and sealed by the Spirit (1 Cor. 12:13; Eph. 1:13; 4:30). If a man does not have the Spirit of God through regeneration, that man does not belong to God (Rom. 8:9). Paul knew that the Thessalonians were true believers "because our gospel came to you not only in word, but also in power and in the Holy Spirit and with full conviction" (1 Thess. 1:5).

James Thornwell wrote:

Then, again, as to their training, the old adage is certainly true: "Whom God appoints He anoints." The characteristic qualification for the ministry, the unction from on high, is the immediate gift of the Holy Ghost, and cannot be imparted by any agency of man. Human learning is necessary—the more, the better; but human learning cannot, of itself, make a preacher. Discipline is necessary, but discipline is not Divine power, and is only an incidental help. The whole routine of theological education supposes a previous fitness in this subject, which it may aid but cannot impart. Hence this training becomes necessary only among novices—among those whose faculties have not been developed and expanded by previous pursuits and previous studies. But in cases in which men of cultivated minds are called from other walks of life, it is absurd to suppose that they cannot be efficient preachers unless they have been graduated in a Theological Seminary. There is no charm in such institutions: they only burnish the weapons which the Minister is to use, but they do not supply him with his armour. Men may be able Ministers of the New Testament without being trained to it as a mere profession; and although human learning is indispensable, yet human learning is not of the essence of a call.[8]

Spurgeon wrote:

We will now come to the core of our subject. To us, as ministers, the Holy Spirit is absolutely essential. Without him our office is a mere name. We claim no priesthood over and above that which belongs to every child of God; but we are the successors of those who, in olden times, were moved of God to declare his word, to testify against transgression, and to plead his cause. Unless we have the spirit of the prophets resting upon us, the mantle which we wear is nothing but a rough garment to deceive. We ought to be driven forth with abhorrence from the society of honest men for daring to speak in the name of the Lord if the Spirit of God rests not upon us. We believe ourselves to be spokesmen for Jesus Christ, appointed to continue his witness upon earth; but upon him and his testimony the Spirit of God always rested, and if it does not rest upon us, we are evidently not sent forth into the world as he was. At Pentecost the commencement of the great work of converting the world was with flaming tongues and a rushing mighty

---

8. James Henley Thornwell, *Collected Writings*, vol. 4 (Richmond: Presbyterian Committee of Publication, 1873), 27.

wind, symbols of the presence of the Spirit; if, therefore, we think to succeed without the Spirit, we are not after the Pentecostal order. If we have not the Spirit which Jesus promised, we cannot perform the commission which Jesus gave.[9]

John Owen also spoke to this issue:

Authority is required. What is authority in a preaching ministry? It is a consequent of unction, and not of office. The scribes had an outward call to teach in the church; but they had no unction, no anointing, that could evidence they had the Holy Ghost in his gifts and graces. Christ had no outward call; but he had an unction,—he had a full unction of the Holy Ghost in his gifts and graces, for the preaching of the gospel. Hereon there was a controversy about his authority. The scribes say unto him, Mark 11:28, "By what authority doest thou these things? and who gave thee this authority?" The Holy Ghost determines the matter, Matt. 7:29, "He preached as one having authority, and not as the scribes." They had the authority of office, but not of unction; Christ only had that. And preaching in the demonstration of the Spirit, which men quarrel so much about, is nothing less than the evidence in preaching of unction, in the communication of gifts and grace unto them, for the discharge of their office: for it is a vain thing for men to assume and personate authority. So much evidence as they have of unction from God in gifts and grace, so much authority they have, and no more, in preaching: and let every one, then, keep within his bounds.[10]

Now, a word of caution is in order. This unction has nothing necessarily to do with animation, nor with what we might call elevated eloquence. It has nothing necessarily to do with volume, unusual pace, or fluency of utterance.

I offer this true incident. Many years ago I was preaching as a guest preacher in a place long forgotten. When I was finished preaching, a man came down the aisle walking at a brisk pace heading straight toward me. I sensed from the look in his eyes that he was coming to me to make what he believed was a very important observation. Observing this, I said to myself, "I believe this man's desire to get to me spells trouble." He took me aside and whispered in my ear, "Brother Martin, I *know* the Holy Spirit was upon you today." I said, "Oh, you do?" "Oh, yes, the Holy Spirit was upon you." I said,

---

9. C. H. Spurgeon, *Lectures to My Students* (Edinburgh: The Banner of Truth Trust, 2008), 225.

10. John Owen, *The Works of John Owen*, vol. 9 (Edinburgh: The Banner of Truth Trust, 1968), 455.

"Oh, how did you know that?" He answered, "Because I watched your feet."
I said, "My feet?" "Ah, yes, Brother Martin. I have noticed that any man who
is full of the Holy Ghost when he preaches, his feet are always moving." He
was dead serious.

Now, in some circles, being full of the Spirit is thought to consist in
having a certain fluctuating tone in the use of one's voice. In other places, it
is the holy grunt. I have heard and seen it all! This unction of the Spirit has
nothing necessarily to do with any of these things. In fact, some of them may
be evidence that the Holy Spirit is totally absent.

Yet, at the end of the day, in order to preach the Word as we ought, we
must experience a supernatural endowment of the Holy Spirit, enabling us
to speak with divine unction. Some of the specific manifestations of that
endowment are a heightened sense of the spiritual realities in which we
are trafficking as we preach; unfettered liberty and a heightened facility of
utterance; an enlarged heart, suffused with increased measures of selfless
love that yearns to do our hearers good by means of our preaching; and a
heightened sense of the absolute authority, sufficiency, and trustworthiness
of the scriptures. I discussed these manifestations in my book *Preaching in
the Holy Spirit*.[11] This book grew out of two pastors' conference sermons
which were the fruit of a lifetime of wrestling with the issue of the immediate
agency and operation of the Holy Spirit in and upon the preacher in the
act of preaching.

Now, I want to make a final, clear disclaimer. I am not saying that we
must seek, obtain, and be able to bear witness to, a distinct, memorable
post-conversion experience in the Holy Spirit that some would call a "fresh
baptism of the Spirit." I have no sympathy with that teaching. I do not know
how to state the matter more plainly. Yet, I am saying that when a man stands
to minister the Word of God, it must be evident to the discerning people of
God that he is giving them something more than the cumulative effect of
what he has been given by nature and what he has acquired by discipline and
practice. As in conversion, the ways of the Spirit are like the wind; God can
and does come upon His servants in various circumstances and ways. The
way a man may have acquired this unction is all in God's hands, but it will
be evident that there is something in his preaching and teaching that has no
explanation but the presence, power, and activity of the living God.

---

11. Albert N. Martin, *Preaching in the Holy Spirit* (Grand Rapids: Reformation Heritage
Books, 2011).

With regard to the unction of the Holy Spirit, we do recognize that there are fanatics who have cut themselves loose from responsible, historic, biblical Christianity. Yet we must never, never allow this fact to cause us to yield the field. We must hold to the biblical necessity for a supernatural endowment of the Holy Spirit, enabling a man to preach with divine unction.

CHAPTER 10

Qualifications of Leadership Gifts

We come now to the third category or component of gifts, namely, those gifts which come to expression in a proven ability to oversee, guide, and govern the people of God with sanctified leadership. So far we have seen the necessity for a sanctified mind and sanctified utterance. These are followed naturally by the requirement of proven sanctified leadership skills. In opening up this third category of spiritual gifts, I will do so under two major headings. The first is the *biblical basis* for asserting the necessity of such gifts of sanctified leadership. Here we will consider both the *explicit* and the *implicit* testimony of Scripture. The second will point out the *fundamental components*.

At the outset of considering this matter, I will seek to establish the biblical basis for asserting that any man who aspires to the office of pastoral ministry must exhibit some measure of this gift of sanctified leadership. In seeking to demonstrate the biblical basis for that assertion, we will look, first of all, at the *explicit* testimony of the Word of God.

The Explicit Testimony

This point further subdivides into two, the *unequivocal requirements* and the *unmistakable assertion*.

Consider first the *unequivocal requirements*.

The apostle addresses the matter of an aptitude and proven ability to govern lovingly, wisely, and reasonably in 1 Timothy 3:4, 5. He says that the overseer must have proven gifts to rule and govern with dignity and stateliness. On the one hand, he must not govern with carnal sternness. He must not act with a passive, wimpish indifference to the responsibilities and the authority which come with the office. He is assertively and lovingly to *take care* of the church of God. Therefore, before being given that responsibility, he must manifest some measure of a God-given gift to qualify for it.

For most men, the sphere in which a God-given ability to rule and govern in Christ's church is manifested by the manner and effectiveness of a man's rule and government of his own family. It is interesting to note that, of all the specific character requirements in 1 Timothy 3:1–7, the only one which Paul amplifies concerns how a man manages his own household. He clearly asserts that a pattern of domestic failure and incompetence should bar a man from assuming the office and function of an overseer in the house of God, "He must manage his own household well, with all dignity keeping his children submissive, for if someone does not know how to manage his own household, how will he care for God's church?" (1 Tim. 3:4, 5). The basic issue addressed is not that a man must be a married man with children or be banned from the pastoral office. Rather, it is that a man must not enter the pastoral office unless he has manifested a measure of competence and gift to govern well in that position of responsibility. Ordinarily, a man old enough and mature enough to meet the other requirements of gifts and graces would be a married man with a family. Thus, the ordinary proving-ground for such a gift of leadership would be manifested in a man's relationship to his wife and to his children. Paul fleshes out this generic requirement in this specific way. Rather than stating a principle in the abstract, it embodies the principle in concrete, specific examples.

In speaking of a man managing his own house, the apostle uses the word *proístemi*, which means, *to be over, care for, give attention to, rule, govern*. In arguing from the lesser to the greater, the apostle is saying that if a man does not know how to rule well or govern his own house, that is, if he is incompetent in that smaller sphere in which a man is to exercise responsible leadership, how shall he take care of, *epimeléomai*, the larger family with its greater spectrum of need, greater pressures and demands for grace, wisdom, boldness, authority, and all the other things that go into the wise government of the house of God? It is the concept of taking care of the church of God that is analogous to the family. Here is an unequivocal requirement for those aspiring to overseership.

Now, while the Word of God is crystal clear on this issue, one can only marvel that this requirement for a proven gift of leadership is either ignored or willfully violated. I will say more about this in Unit 6 with some personal illustrations from my own experience. There must be proven gifts of sanctified leadership; this is a non-negotiable. If a man is not married, or is married and does not have children, it is incumbent upon those responsible for examining that man's fitness for the pastoral office to see what relationships God has providentially put in place in this man's life where he has legitimate authority, and to see how he exercises that authority. The question will be in those other relationships, does he manifest those gifts of sanctified rule and government?

We come now to *the unmistakable assertion* that there are special gifts of rule and government given to members of the body of Christ. We find this in two particular passages. The first is Romans 12:3, "For by the grace given to me I say to everyone among you not to think of himself more highly than he ought to think, but to think with sober judgment, each according to the measure of faith that God has assigned." He then goes on to list many of those gifts. Prophecy, teaching, and exhorting are *word* or *speaking* gifts. Serving, contributing, and doing acts of mercy are *service* gifts. The reference to *one who leads*, or *rules, proistámenos*, indicates that some men will have a discernible gift to exercise rule, government, leadership.

This much is clear from this passage: *Paul is assuming that some will have word gifts who may not have the gift to rule.* One of the problems is that, in many churches, if a man has evident *word* gifts, an assumption is made that he is thereby qualified for the office of elder, though he has no patent, manifested provenness of a gift to *rule*. There must be this combination of word and leadership gifts. The reverse sometimes is true. If a man has some evident gift of government, it is assumed that he will have a modicum of a word gift; yet he is given an office that demands both. Although not all elders labor in the Word and in doctrine, all elders cannot truly shepherd if they have no aptitude to teach, if they cannot sit down with one of the sheep and open the Word of God to comfort, instruct, and reprove. If there is an incipient heretical tendency, he must be able to speak and address that skewed thinking and bring the Word of God to bear upon it.

The second passage which asserts unambiguously that there are special gifts of rule and government given to members of the body of Christ is 1 Corinthians 12 which deals with the *variety* of gifts given by the Spirit. Paul lists these various gifts, including gifts *of administration* (ESV), or *governments* (KJV, ASV), the plural indicating proofs of ability to hold a position of leadership in the church. The Greek word *kubernéseis* is used only in 1 Corinthians 12:28. In Acts 27:11 and Revelation 18:17, a word related to the same root is used which refers to piloting and steering a ship. So, bound up in that concept of gifts of government is that thought of the gift of giving direction to the church as a steersman does with the ship, knowing where the people of God ought to go, and how best to get there, seeking to keep them on course in their journey.

John Owen explains:

> From these things it may appear what is the nature, in general, of that skill in the rule of the church which we assert to be a peculiar gift of the Holy Ghost. If it were only an ability or skill in the canon or civil law, or rules of men; if only an acquaintance with the nature and course of some courts, proceeding litigiously, by citations, processes, legal pleadings, issuing in pecuniary mulcts, outward coercions, or imprisonments,—I should willingly acknowledge that there is no peculiar gift of the Spirit of God required thereunto. But the nature of it being as we have declared, it is impossible it should be exercised aright without especial assistance of the Holy Ghost. Is any man of himself sufficient for these things? Will any man undertake of himself to know the mind of Christ in all the occasions of the church, and to administer the power of Christ in them and about them? Wherefore the apostle, in many places, teacheth that wisdom, skill, and understanding to administer the authority of Christ in the church unto its edification, with faithfulness and diligence, are an especial gift of the Holy Ghost, Rom. 12:6, 8; 1 Cor. 12:28. It is the Holy Ghost which makes the elders of the church its bishops or overseers, by calling them to their office, Acts 20:28; and what he calls any man unto, that he furnisheth him with abilities for the discharge of.[1]

Where there is no gift in the area of rule, there is no gift of Christ to the church of a shepherd. This constitutes the explicit testimony of the Word of God. Added to this evidence, there is also an implicit testimony.

The Implicit Testimony

In seeking to show the biblical basis for the assertion of the necessity for gifts of rule and government, we come now to the implicit testimony of the Word of God. Under this heading I want to trace out two lines of thought, the *titles* of the pastoral office (the nouns), and the *tasks* of the office (the verbs).

We begin with the nouns which describe the *titles* of the office. The first is *epískopos*, from *skopéo, to look*, joined to *epí, upon* or *over.* He is a *looker-over.*

---

1. John Owen, *The Works of John Owen*, vol. 4 (Edinburgh: The Banner of Truth Trust, 1968), 515, 516.

A pastor is an *epískopos,* an *overseer.* He is also *presbúteros,* an *older man,* an *elder.* The assumption is that with age ought to come the wisdom drawn from knowledge and experience. You may remember what Elihu said of Job,

> And Elihu the son of Barachel the Buzite answered and said: "I am young in years, and you are aged; therefore I was timid and afraid to declare my opinion to you. I said, 'Let days speak, and many years teach wisdom.' But it is the spirit in man, the breath of the Almighty, that makes him understand. It is not the old who are wise, nor the aged who understand what is right. Therefore I say, 'Listen to me; let me also declare my opinion.' Behold, I waited for your words, I listened for your wise sayings, while you searched out what to say. I gave you my attention, and, behold, there was none among you who refuted Job or who answered his words. Beware lest you say, 'We have found wisdom; God may vanquish him, not a man.' He has not directed his words against me, and I will not answer him with your speeches. They are dismayed; they answer no more; they have not a word to say. And shall I wait, because they do not speak, because they stand there, and answer no more? I also will answer with my share; I also will declare my opinion" (Job 32:6–17).

In effect, he said:

> I kept my mouth shut; you old men were talking and I assumed that wisdom was going to come from your gray heads. I have listened long enough, however, and there is nothing but nonsense coming out of your mouths, so I am going to go contrary to the normal order of things and I am going to open my youthful mouth and call upon you old men to listen to me.

We might call that a loose dynamic equivalent and paraphrase of the text, but that is the essence. Elihu recognized that normally it is the old who are wise. This is why, in the Jewish system of the synagogue, the leaders were elders. This traces all the way back to the counsel of Jethro to Moses and the appointment of the seventy assistants, who could give wise guidance in matters of casuistry within the covenant community.

Finally, he is a *poimén,* a *shepherd* or *pastor.* Christ "gave the apostles, the prophets, the evangelists, the shepherds and teachers" (Eph. 4:11). Christ gave shepherds and teachers, or shepherd-teachers.

Now, I ask you, what has become of the significance of these Spirit-inspired nouns used as titles for the office, if they are given to a man who has no ability to oversee the lives of the people of God corporately? What do these nouns mean if they are applied to a man who has tunnel vision and cannot back off and see the broad picture—where the church has been, where it is, where it ought to move under the blessing of God in the days to come—who has no ability to back off and see trends emerging among the people of God?

No, the very title *epískopos*, an *overseer*, assumes some divinely given gift of ability to look over the flock of God, accurately perceiving their particular needs and concerns. What is the name *elder*, if one does not have the wisdom of an older man in order to give wise counsel, in order to see what needs to be done? You will remember that it is said of the men of Issachar that they were "men who had understanding of the times, to know what Israel ought to do" (1 Chron. 12:32). What is a *shepherd* who looks upon the sheep, but has no eyes to discriminate between a sick and a healthy sheep, to recognize a sheep that looks like it has the mange, or that has some kind of infectious disease in its system that has the potential to infect the whole flock? What is a shepherd who has no ability to see a wolf prowling around the perimeter of the sheep pen, or one who, having seen the wolf, has no moral courage of leadership to go out and confront it?

When David was assuring Saul that he was competent in God's strength to go forth and encounter the giant Goliath, he said to Saul,

> Your servant used to keep sheep for his father. And when there came a lion, or a bear, and took a lamb from the flock, I went after him and struck him and delivered it out of his mouth. And if he arose against me, I caught him by his beard and struck him and killed him. Your servant has struck down both lions and bears, and this uncircumcised Philistine shall be like one of them, for he has defied the armies of the living God (1 Sam. 17:34–36).

David was saying, in essence, that his life was expendable, not the life of his sheep. As Christ declared,

> I am the good shepherd. The good shepherd lays down his life for the sheep. He who is a hired hand and not a shepherd, who does not own the sheep, sees the wolf coming and leaves the sheep and flees, and the wolf snatches them and scatters them. He flees because he is a hired hand and cares nothing for the sheep (John 10:11–13).

Now we come to the *tasks* involved in the office. The *titles* just considered demand that we think of the office in terms of proven gifts of leadership.

The same is true of the *tasks* associated with the office. Now we will look at the verbs.

First is the verb *poimaíno, to act the part and fulfill the functions of a shepherd*. We find this verb in Acts 20:28, translated *to care for* (ESV), or *to feed* (KJV, ASV). This verb is found again in Peter's first epistle (1 Pet. 5:2). Now, what is a shepherd? He is not someone who simply sits in a comfortable spot on the side of a hill composing clever little tunes about the beautiful clouds floating by him in the sky and the verdant pastoral landscape. Further, a true shepherd is not someone who happens to be sitting with a staff resting on his shoulder, a rod lying next to him, while the sheep graze, while he occasionally glances in the direction of his flock. That is not the life of a faithful shepherd. No! To fulfill the functions of a shepherd is a manifold, often a dangerous, and always an arduous task. Yes, it means to feed the sheep by leading them to rich pastures. As a spiritual shepherd, he must have gifts of utterance, but much more. Shepherding involves the additional responsibilities of faithfully protecting and guiding the flock of God as a whole, as well as skillfully detecting and alleviating the diseases and wounds of individual sheep in particular.

First Thessalonians 5:12 uses the verb *proístemi, to lead, be at the head of, direct, manage*. We find the verb *egéomai* in Matthew 2:6 citing the messianic prophecy, "But you, O Bethlehem Ephrathah, who are too little to be among the clans of Judah, from you shall come forth for me one who is to be ruler in Israel, whose coming forth is from of old, from ancient days" (Mic. 5:2). It appears in the present participle form in Greek, often translated into English as the noun *ruler*, or *governor*. The same verb is used in Hebrews 13:7, 17, 24, in this present participial form, translated into the noun form, *leader(s)*.

Then we have the verb *episkopéo, to oversee or care for*, used in 1 Peter 5:2, "Shepherd the flock of God that is among you, exercising oversight, not under compulsion, but willingly, as God would have you; not for shameful gain, but eagerly." We find the verb *epimeléomai* in 1 Timothy 3:5, "for if someone does not know how to manage his own household, how will he care for God's church?" This is the word used with respect to the Samaritan's treatment of the man who fell among thieves: he "took care of him" (Luke 10:34). This aspect of pastoral service is indispensable. We must be wise and compassionate caregivers of God's church. It is true that the Lord Jesus Himself continues to nourish and cherish His church (Eph. 5:29). However, no little part of that ministry of Christ is mediated through the under-shepherds whom He gives to His church. If the men who assume pastoral office have no divinely imparted gifts for the kind of sanctified leadership bound up in these various verbs which we have just examined, the door is left wide open to confusion, schism, discord, and to disorderliness within the church.

Toward the end of Paul's third missionary journey, he gathered the Ephesian elders together at a place called Miletus. Anticipating that he would not see these men again, he reviewed the substance and manner of his several years of labor among them, reminding them that his own life and labors constituted a pattern for all faithful servants of God. Then he charged them, laying upon their consciences their pastoral responsibilities to the flock of God at Ephesus with these words,

> Pay careful attention to yourselves and to all the flock, in which the Holy Spirit has made you overseers, to care for the church of God, which he obtained with his own blood. I know that after my departure fierce wolves will come in among you, not sparing the flock; and from among your own selves will arise men speaking twisted things, to draw away the disciples after them. Therefore be alert, remembering that for three years I did not cease night or day to admonish everyone with tears (Acts 20:28–31).

Now what are those other gifts which are unmistakably inferred from Paul's charge to these elders? By using the verbal form of the noun *shepherd*, Paul is charging these elders to perform, in a spiritual way, the functions which a shepherd performs towards his flock in a literal and physical way. In so doing, he assumes that these men have been gifted by God to perform those functions. Shepherding the flock would involve leading the sheep to nourishing spiritual pastures, guiding them to refreshing spiritual streams of water, protecting them from the spiritual wolves from without that will seek to intrude upon the safety and well-being of the sheep, and protecting the people of God from perverse men who will rise up from among themselves who would make a calculated effort to draw disciples to themselves.

Some of the most basic tasks of the pastoral office are clearly delineated in this charge. As good and efficient shepherds, they are responsible to feed the sheep, guide the sheep, and protect them from dangers—dangers arising from within and from outside the church. Surely then, before a man assumes the office of a spiritual shepherd, it ought to be unmistakably evident that he possesses the gifts essential to fulfilling a shepherd's responsibilities.

Ephesians 4:8–11 teaches that the risen and exalted Christ gave gifts to men, and among them are shepherd-teachers. To what end did He do this, and does He continue to give such gifts to men? The answer to this question is in Ephesians 4:12–14 where we are told that such men are given to the church by the exalted Lord of the church. A man must have the gifts essential for instructing the people of God and equipping them for service, so that, with the blessing of God, he can bring them from spiritual infancy to a place of spiritual stability and maturity.

We would not expect God to command these tasks and functions of pastors while withholding the gifts essential to perform such tasks and functions. God is not like the Egyptian taskmasters who said, "No straw is given to your servants, yet they say to us, 'Make bricks!' And behold, your servants are beaten; but the fault is in your own people" (Exod. 5:16). We have sufficiency in or from God as ministers of the New Covenant (2 Cor. 3:5, 6).

I rest my case for asserting that any man aspiring to the pastoral office should manifest a good measure of the God-given gifts of sanctified leadership, that is, the ability to oversee, guide, govern, shepherd, lead, and take care of the people of God. According to 1 Timothy 3:4, 5, these God-given gifts will ordinarily become evident in a man's domestic competence.

Brethren, we cannot be too insistent here. It is not enough that a man show some facility with words. Is he manifesting, at least to some discernible degree, those gifts requisite for the task of shepherding God's precious sheep? Is he showing a love and sensitivity to God's people, without having yet entered into the office? If not, what makes us think that giving him the title of *Reverend*, or calling him *Pastor*, is suddenly going to suffuse his heart with a passion to love, care for, and minister to God's people? Does he show good sense in dealing with people? Does he manifest the gifts of wise, gentle, but firm government in his own home, with his own wife and his own children? It is vital but not enough that a man pass his theological examination and show that he is well grounded in a biblical, historic, creedal, orthodox, Reformed theology. It is not enough if he does not manifest the gifts essential to the functions of the office.

The Fundamental Components

Having laid out the biblical case for the necessity of gifts of sanctified leadership, we now come to the fundamental components of those leadership gifts. There are five components, and each one required in a more than ordinary degree: *spiritual wisdom, spiritual discernment, spiritual and moral courage, the spiritual disposition consistent with the unique nature of rule in Christ's church,* and *spiritual force of character.*

The first component of those leadership gifts is *a more than ordinary measure of spiritual wisdom.* This is the commodity which Solomon asked of God:

> And now, O LORD my God, you have made your servant king in place of David my father, although I am but a little child. I do not know how to go out or come in. And your servant is in the midst of your people whom you have chosen, a great people, too many to be numbered or counted for multitude. Give your servant therefore an understanding mind to govern your people, that I may discern between good and evil, for who is able to govern this your great people?" It pleased the Lord that Solomon had asked this. And God said to him, "Because you have asked this, and have not asked for yourself long life or riches or the life of your enemies, but have asked for yourself understanding to discern what is right, behold, I now do according to your word. Behold, I give you a wise and discerning mind, so that none like you has been before you and none like you shall arise after you" (1 Kings 3:7–12).

J. I. Packer defines wisdom as "the power to see, and the inclination to choose, the best and highest goal, together with the surest means of attaining it."[2] We desperately need wisdom to fulfill the manifold responsibilities of the pastoral office effectively. The Lord gives wisdom to us just as He did to Solomon in answer to his prayer. Like His anointed servant Jesus, we will be able to say, "The Lord GOD has given me the tongue of those who are taught, that I may know how to sustain with a word him who is weary. Morning by morning he awakens; he awakens my ear to hear as those who are taught" (Isa. 50:4).

Men aspiring to the office of overseer, and men in the ministry, should immerse themselves in the wisdom literature of the Bible, particularly Proverbs and Ecclesiastes. Elders ought to be at home in the book of Proverbs because it contains those sententious statements which bring into sharp focus issues that continually pass before us in our work.

It would be foolish to attempt killing a mosquito with a baseball bat or driving away a pit bull with a flyswatter. Yet I have seen pastors who dealt with some of Christ's sheep in ways just as unwise. These pastors saw a situation that had to be addressed, which was, in reality, like a mosquito on the

---

2. J.I. Packer, *Knowing God* (Wheaton, IL: IVP, 1973), 80.

forehead, and it was not in the best interest of the person to whom they took the spiritual baseball bat. I have seen other instances where the pit bull was coming after one of the sheep, but the pastor went after it with a flyswatter because of the fear that he and his fellow elders would be criticized as "heavy-handed shepherds." There is a place to be "heavy-handed" as Paul teaches,

> But I will come to you soon, if the Lord wills, and I will find out not the talk of these arrogant people but their power. For the kingdom of God does not consist in talk but in power. What do you wish? Shall I come to you with a rod, or with love in a spirit of gentleness? (1 Cor. 4:19–21).

Wisdom comes not simply from immersion in the wisdom literature of the Old Testament, but, more importantly, and built on that foundation, from the wisdom of the One "greater than Solomon" (Luke 11:31), and His Spirit, "the Spirit of wisdom" (Acts 6:3, 10; 1 Cor. 2:4; Eph. 1:17). Furthermore, we need a growing stock of that wisdom which comes from an increasingly familiar acquaintance with the ethical portions of the New Testament epistles and the Sermon on the Mount. The ethical norms in these portions of Scripture are overlaid with, and take their contours from, the dynamics and motivations derived from God's redemptive activity in the Person and work of our Lord Jesus, and in the gift of the Holy Spirit.

The second component of those leadership gifts is *a more than ordinary degree of spiritual discernment.*

Discernment is a feature of wisdom, a more specific application of the broad gift and facility of wisdom.[3] The crowning benefit of New Covenant privilege secured by the death of Christ and His ascension is the anointing of the Spirit, "But the anointing that you received from him abides in you, and

---

3. Proverbs 1:1–7 shows the full spectrum of wisdom in the use of an impressive number of Hebrew words and their English renderings: "instruction" (*musar*, 1:2), "discernment" (*binah*, 1:2), "prudence" (*haskel*, 1:3), "righteousness, justice, equity" (1:3), "shrewd" (*aramah*, 1:4), "knowledge" (*daat*, 1:4), "discretion" (*mizmah*, 1:5), "learning" (*lekah*, 1:5), "counsel" (*hebel*, 1:5). Instruction is formative discipline with correction as needed. Discernment is the faculty of perception between two things or choices. Prudence is pondering a matter with careful attention so that a keen grasp is attained, leading to proper action and success. Shrewdness is linked to the skill of the serpent in Eden and his ability to accomplish his sinister purpose (Gen. 3:1). Knowledge is revealed truth which is always the foundation for our wisdom choices or decisions. Discretion is the power of planning as image-bearers of God. Learning means to seize or snatch, to capture. The word translated counsel signifies, literally, the "ropes" which set the sails and move the ship to the port. Counsel steers the ship. Finally, Proverbs 1:7 is the all-important statement that "the fear of the LORD is the beginning of knowledge."

you have no need that anyone should teach you. But as his anointing teaches you about everything, and is true, and is no lie—just as it has taught you, abide in him" (1 John 2:27). This is the anointing that constitutes us *spiritual* men in contrast to *natural* men (1 Cor. 2:14, 15). Every true believer has a measure of spiritual discernment. However, in those who are responsible to lead and care for the people of God there must be more than an ordinary degree of spiritual discernment. Spiritual discernment is the ability to distinguish things that differ in the realm of the spirit. For example, the parent who is unable to tell the difference between the cry of pain and the cry of petulance in a child is not a discerning parent. To discipline for a cry of pain is cruelty and real child abuse. To fail to correct a cry of petulance is wickedness (Prov. 23:13, 14).

The third component is *a more than ordinary degree of spiritual and moral courage.*

You and I may possess a natural temperament that is more akin to a Jeremiah or a Timothy than to an Amos or a Peter. If so, God is able to impart to us a good measure of spiritual and moral courage, as He did to those servants of His. Remember the story of Jeremiah,

> Now the word of the LORD came to me, saying, "Before I formed you in the womb I knew you, and before you were born I consecrated you; I appointed you a prophet to the nations." Then I said, "Ah, Lord GOD! Behold, I do not know how to speak, for I am only a youth." But the Lord said to me, "Do not say, 'I am only a youth'; for to all to whom I send you, you shall go, and whatever I command you, you shall speak. Do not be afraid of them, for I am with you to deliver you, declares the LORD." Then the LORD put out his hand and touched my mouth. And the LORD said to me, "Behold, I have put my words in your mouth. See, I have set you this day over nations and over kingdoms, to pluck up and to break down, to destroy and to overthrow, to build and to plant" (Jer. 1:4–10).

Then, God spoke further to him,

> But you, dress yourself for work; arise, and say to them everything that I command you. Do not be dismayed by them, lest I dismay you before them. And I, behold, I make you this day a fortified city, an iron pillar, and bronze walls, against the whole land, against the kings of Judah, its officials, its priests, and the people of the land. They will fight against

you, but they shall not prevail against you, for I am with you, declares the LORD, to deliver you (Jer. 1:17–19).

Paul said to Timothy, "For this reason I remind you to fan into flame the gift of God, which is in you through the laying on of my hands, for God gave us a spirit not of fear but of power and love and self-control" (2 Tim. 1:6, 7). If this element of moral courage is lacking, there will be an aversion to confrontation and dealing with the unpleasant. You will cave in when people begin to frown or threaten you, and you will become to your spiritual children what Eli was to his physical children, an unprincipled and sinfully indulgent parent (1 Sam. 3:13). He loved them with a saccharine, unprincipled, mousy kind of love. I have seen this again and again in the course of my years in the ministry. So, if we are to govern wisely, lead justly, and honorably care for the flock of God, we must have a more than ordinary degree of moral courage.

The fourth component of the gift of sanctified leadership consists in *a more than ordinary degree of the spiritual disposition consistent with the unique nature of rule in Christ's church.*

Here I want us to give attention to Matthew 20:25–28,

> But Jesus called them to him and said, "You know that the rulers of the Gentiles lord it over them, and their great ones exercise authority over them. It shall not be so among you. But whoever would be great among you must be your servant, and whoever would be first among you must be your slave, even as the Son of Man came not to be served but to serve, and to give his life as a ransom for many."

Two important Greek words are used in this incident: *katakurieo, lord it over,* and *katexousiaszo, exercise authority over.* These rulers of the Gentiles stand over others and press them down beneath their authority to their own advantage. Christ illustrates for His disciples a glaring example of the abuse of power in the Gentile perversion of authority, but neither the apostles nor us, in the ministry to the flocks of Christ in every age and in every place, are allowed to do that. Whoever aspires to become great in this sense of rule and lordship must live and minister as a table-waiter, and whoever wishes to be first must be the professed bondservant. Jesus forcefully prohibited our finding a paradigm for church leadership in the worldly exercise of authority, whether found in corporate or military or political structures.

Now, is the Lord saying that there is to be no legitimate authority structure? Of course not! We would have to rip out one passage after another to support such a foolish and unscriptural notion. Take the example of Hebrews 13:17 where the people of God are commanded to obey their leaders. The Lord is not neutralizing the reality of a divinely instituted order of authority in which some rule and others are ruled, in which some lead and others follow. Rather, He is going after the disposition with which we exercise that God-given sphere of authority and rule. We must do this in a way that reflects the manner of the One who has all authority in heaven and on earth (Matt. 28:19). He to whom all authority has been given as the God-Man, is the One who came not to be served but to serve (Matt. 20:28). He is the Christ of the towel and the basin (John 13:1–11). When no one else in the upper room was willing to grab that basin and towel and do what an in-house servant would have ordinarily done, the Lord Jesus shames them all by laying aside His outer garment, taking the towel and the basin, kneeling, and washing and drying the disciples' feet. At that time, He was exercising His Lordship while taking the role of the servant (Phil. 2:7, 8).

With this very same spirit, we must carry out our responsibilities and functions of legitimate rule, government, and leadership in the church of Christ. There cannot be a legitimate accusation of "heavy-handed shepherding" if the prevailing spirit of our shepherding is service to the people of God. Now I am not saying that we will never be accused of "heavy-handed shepherding." In an egalitarian society such as ours, in which there is little or no delight in the structures of strong leadership, and most people believe that each individual has as much right as anyone else to do, say, and throw his weight around as anyone else, that accusation may very likely come. Give absolutely no basis for it. Make sure that those in the church of Christ whom you govern from the posture of a servant's heart know in their conscience that it is not a fair characterization of your character and conduct.

You will be given many opportunities to show true humility when you are not even conscious that your people are observing you. For example, they may see you walking across the foyer to pick up the gum wrapper ignored by everyone else. Perhaps a young mother may be coming through the front door of the church, seven months pregnant, a diaper bag in her left hand, her right hand holding a two-year-old clutching her skirt, while her husband is off fellowshipping somewhere, and then you are the one who instinctively goes over and helps her remove her coat and take her diaper bag to the nursery.

In acts such as these you will show the disposition of a servant. You are not trying to impress anybody; that is just who you are, their servant for Christ's sake. This disposition is seen when you take the initiative to go to them in their times of distress and felt need, with a disposition of preparedness to open up your heart, to feel their anguish, and to weep with those who weep. They also see it when your heart is broken and you somehow manage to rejoice sincerely with them in their rejoicing. Sometimes it is much harder to rejoice with those who rejoice when you have a broken heart, than it is to weep with those who weep when you have a happy heart. In both we must exhibit a servant's heart. When that disposition, by the Spirit of God, begins to percolate through the stuff of our inner being, there are untold ways in which our souls, deeply and truly humbled by the grace and power of God, will be known by others. We must have that disposition of Christlike servanthood in our relationship to our people.

The apostle Paul could say to the Corinthians, "I will most gladly spend and be spent for your souls. If I love you more, am I to be loved less?" (2 Cor. 12:15). The first verb is *dapanáo, to spend*; the second time, he uses the compound word *ekdapanáo*, from *dapanáo, to spend*, and *ek, out of*—literally, *to spend out*, or *expend*. This is why any of us are Christians in the first place. Christ expended Himself for sinners. We spurned Him, but though we did not love Him, He continued to love us and track us down. So there must be more than an ordinary degree of this spiritual disposition, consistent with the unique nature of rule in Christ's church.

Here again I commend to you the good Dr. Owen who alludes to the very incident with which we began the consideration of this fourth component:

> When our Saviour forbade all rule unto his disciples after the manner of the Gentiles, who then possessed all sovereign power in the world, and told them that it should not be so with them, that some should be great and exercise dominion over others, but that they should serve one another in love, the greatest condescension unto service being required of them who are otherwise most eminent, he did not intend to take from them or divest them of that spiritual power and authority in the government of the church which he intended to commit unto them. His design, therefore, was to declare what that authority was not, and how it should not be exercised. A lordly or despotical power it was not to be; nor was it to be exercised by penal laws, courts, and coercive jurisdiction, which was the way of the administration of all power among the Gentiles. And if that kind of power and rule in the church which is for the most part exercised in the world be not forbidden

by our Saviour, no man living can tell what is so; for as to meekness, moderation, patience, equity, righteousness, they were more easy to be found in the legal administrations of power among the Gentiles than in those used in many churches. But such a rule is signified unto them, the authority whereof, from whence it proceedeth, was spiritual; its object the minds and souls of men only; and the way of whose administration was to consist in a humble, holy, spiritual application of the word of God or rules of the gospel unto them.[4]

Spiritual-mindedness is essential in one's concept of rule. Humility and servanthood should be the posture of our rule.

The fifth component of a Spirit-imparted gift to rule and govern in Christ's church I have chosen to describe as *a more than ordinary degree of spiritual force of character*. What goes into this force of character?

First, *an unmistakably masculine demeanor*.

I am fully aware that many in our day believe that God did not create distinctively masculine and feminine demeanors. They hold that such notions are nothing more than arbitrary social constructs imposed upon us by those who wield the most power over us. However, the scriptures clearly assert that since God made them in the beginning male and female, He intends that maleness and femaleness be unashamedly owned and manifested by all His male and female creatures.

Now in asserting that godly leadership in the man will mean that he manifests unmistakably masculine demeanor, I do not suggest that we all must begin to pump iron and attempt to look like professional body-builders. By a masculine demeanor, I mean that the way we carry ourselves, the way we speak, the way we act and react, should be distinctively masculine. I am trying to capture what Paul meant when he said, "Be watchful, stand firm in the faith, act like men, be strong" (1 Cor. 16:13). Paul was not a misogynist; he understood that there are distinctively masculine characteristics that are different from the distinctively feminine characteristics. He does not say, "acquit yourselves like noble persons," but "like *men*." Be distinctively masculine in the expression of your Christian manhood. The verb he uses is an imperative of *andrízomai*, closely related to the noun *anér*, *man* or *husband*,

---

4. John Owen, *The Works of John Owen*, vol. 4 (Edinburgh: The Banner of Truth Trust, 1968), 514, 515.

not the generic word for mankind. When I speak of *force of character*, it involves this unmistakably masculine demeanor.

Second, force of character involves *soundness of judgment*, not a mind that flits here and there like a child, but as a grown-up responsible man.

You are not a waffler, for whom today's *yes* is tomorrow's *no* and yesterday's *no* is today's *yes*. Rather, you must be a man of resolute purpose. Once your way is clear, you are committed to it. Sound judgment manifests likeness to the Lord Jesus, of whom Luke writes, "When the days drew near for him to be taken up, he set his face to go to Jerusalem" (Luke 9:51). Martin Luther showed this worthy trait when he said, "Here I stand, so help me God, I can do no other."

Third, force of character necessitates *seriousness of demeanor*.

Paul says, "When I was a child, I spoke like a child, I thought like a child, I reasoned like a child. When I became a man, I gave up childish ways" (1 Cor. 13:11). This does not require that you maintain a somber or stern demeanor in some kind of an artificial way. People should know that laughter was not invented by the devil. It is God's gift to us, and they should see you as a whole man and know that you are a happy man and that you enjoy life. Yet, in all of that, even in what we may call your lightest, most jocular moments, there should be a bearing, a seriousness of demeanor, so that people know they can entrust guidance and direction and oversight to men who are men and not foolish boys or irresponsible teenagers.

I close this attempt to explain "spiritual force of character" by quoting from Dabney as he addressed this matter:

> The Scriptures which define the necessary qualifications of the minister may be digested in substance into the following particulars: He must have *a hearty and healthy piety, a fair reputation for holiness of life, a respectable force of character, some Christian experience and aptness to teach*.[5]
>
> The three qualifications next mentioned, a fair reputation for sanctity of life, a respectable moral force of character, and some degree of Christian experience, may be grouped together. The man whose Christian character does not command confidence and respect would, as a minister, only dishonor God and his cause. Yet it is every man's duty to reform those inconsistencies by which he has forfeited the respect of mankind, whether he is to preach or not. And having thoroughly

---

5. Robert L. Dabney, *Discussions: Evangelical and Theological*, vol. 2 (Edinburgh: The Banner of Truth Trust, 1967), 31.

reformed them, he may find his way open into the pulpit. The minister must have some force of character. The feeble, undecided, shuffling man, who cannot rule his own family, nor impress and govern his inferiors by his moral force, had better not preach.[6]

This captures my intention. Granted, seeking to give it precise definition and description is like attempting to trap a little ball of quicksilver under your thumb. It is a rather elusive thing, but I think that any man reading these pages will know what I am talking about. You know when you are in the presence of men who embody, to one degree or another, those qualities that together constitute force of character.

These then are the five fundamental components of the leadership gifts required for the office of overseer: a more than ordinary degree of spiritual wisdom, discernment, spiritual and moral courage, the spiritual disposition consistent with the unique nature of rule in Christ's church, and spiritual force of character. May God in His grace and by His Spirit grant these to men aspiring to the work of the ministry and men laboring in the ministry.

---

6. Robert L. Dabney, *Discussions: Evangelical and Theological*, vol. 2 (Edinburgh: The Banner of Truth Trust, 1967), 35.

CHAPTER 11

The Source of Spiritual Giftedness

I trust I have persuaded you, or confirmed you in your previous persuasion, regarding the *necessity for* and the *identity of* the gifts which must be evident in one who is called and equipped by God for the pastoral office and function. We now move on to address the issue of the *source* or the *origin* of these gifts. I want to break down this heading under two subheadings, the *ultimate or immediate* source of the gifts, and then the *secondary or mediate* sources of the gifts.

The Ultimate or Immediate Source of the Gifts

The scriptures teach that the ultimate source of all spiritual gifts is God Himself in the full engagement of His triune Being. In Paul's first letter to the church at Corinth, he stated that he did not want them to be uninformed concerning spiritual gifts (1 Cor. 12:1). The detailed instruction concerning this subject refers explicitly to the Holy Spirit, to the Lord Jesus Christ, and to God the Father.

> Now concerning spiritual gifts, brothers, I do not want you to be uninformed. You know that when you were pagans you were led astray to mute idols, however you were led. Therefore I want you to understand that no one speaking in the Spirit of God ever says "Jesus is accursed!" and no one can say "Jesus is Lord" except in the Holy Spirit. Now there are varieties of gifts, but the same Spirit; and there are varieties of service, but the same Lord; and there are varieties of activities, but it is the same God who empowers them all in everyone (1 Cor. 12:1–6).

This passage proves that God, in the entire engagement of His triune Being, is the ultimate source of all spiritual gifts given to His Church: *the same Spirit, the same Lord (Jesus), the same God (Father).*

While urging each man to soberly assess what his gifts may be, Paul declares that it is God who deals, assigns, or divides to each man a measure of faith, "For by the grace given to me I say to everyone among you not to think of himself more highly than he ought to think, but to think with sober judgment, each according to the measure of faith that God has assigned" (Rom. 12:3).

William Hendriksen helpfully observed:

> The term *faith* is here used in the more usual sense of the trust in God by means of which an individual lays hold on God's promises. In the present context, however, the apostle is not thinking in quantitative terms (a large or a small amount of faith). He is thinking rather of the various ways in which each distinct individual is able to be a blessing to others and to the church in general by using the particular gift with which, *in association with faith*, God has endowed him or her.[1]

This ought to be a tremendous encouragement to us. I have heard my friend, Pastor Achille Blaize, bellow out with his resonant, inimitable West Indian-English accent: *"It takes the whole Trinity to save one sinner!"* Similarly, where these essential pastoral gifts emerge in men, and we see them functioning in the church, we recognize that it takes the whole Trinity to impart one true spiritual gift.

However, it is also right to recognize, as in all the other dimensions of redemptive activity, that one or more of the Persons of the Godhead take a prominent role. In 1 Corinthians 12:7–9, the emphasis moves from the activity of the entire triune Godhead to the work of the Spirit. So, while we recognize that the entire engagement of the triune God is present in granting gifts to the church, it is predominantly a ministry of God the Holy Spirit to impart spiritual gifts. The Holy Spirit is specifically designated five times in the space of these three verses.

There are other passages in Scripture which support the concept of spiritual gifts being given by God. For example, Solomon prayed for wisdom and received it from God, "Behold, I now do according to your word. Behold, I give you a wise and discerning mind, so that none like you has been before you and none like you shall arise after you" (1 Kings 3:12).

Paul is explicit regarding the ministerial gift in both of his letters to Timothy, "Do not neglect the gift you have, which was given you by prophecy when the council of elders laid their hands on you" (1 Tim. 4:14). He also says, "For this reason I remind you to fan into flame the gift of God, which is

---

1. William Hendriksen, *New Testament Commentary: Romans Chapters 9–16* (Grand Rapids: Baker, 1981), 407, 408.

in you through the laying on of my hands" (2 Tim. 1:6). Even when considering the secondary or mediate sources of spiritual gifts, we must recognize that the ultimate source is God Himself, "Every good gift and every perfect gift is from above, coming down from the Father of lights with whom there is no variation or shadow due to change" (Jas. 1:17).

As we will see below, some of the secondary or mediate sources of gifts are rooted in what God has made us to be by nature when He knit us together in our mothers' wombs. The psalmist prayed, "For you formed my inward parts; you knitted me together in my mother's womb" (Ps. 139:13). The coming together of the various genetic strains that would determine precisely who and what you are in many facets of your native humanity was not a chance occurrence. Furthermore, there are certain dimensions of what God fashioned you to be that become the substructure or the platform of your giftedness for the work of the ministry. We are not naturalists; we do not have a mechanistic view of life. This whole process of development is ultimately traced back to the wisdom and the sovereign activity of our gracious God. In spite of the clear teaching of Scripture, the direct action of the Spirit of God in imparting spiritual gifts was apparently denied by some in John Owen's day, so he addresses that subject in his writings:

> There is this disadvantage in preaching upon a particular occasion, especially for one who hath no more strength than I, that either we must omit insisting on the particular explication of the text, or be prevented in that which we aim at particularly from it. Both cannot be done; therefore I shall only give you the substance of the words, in that proposition which I intend to insist upon; namely,—
>
> That it is the work of the Spirit of God, in all ages of the church, to communicate spiritual gifts and abilities to those who are called according unto his mind to the ministry of the church, to enable them unto all evangelical administrations, to his glory, and the edification of the church.
>
> Had I time, I would inquire into these two things:—1. Whether the Holy Ghost doth indeed continue to communicate *spiritual gifts*, distinct from *natural* endowments and *acquired* abilities, to the discharge of the work of the ministry, to his glory, and the edification of the church. And, 2. Whether these spiritual gifts and abilities, so communicated, be not the material call to the work of the ministry, antecedently required to the formal call thereunto.
>
> As to the first, it is opposed by them who say that these spiritual gifts we talk of are nothing, indeed, but men's natural and acquired

abilities, with an ordinary blessing of God upon their ministry; and for other spiritual gifts there are none.[2]

I keep insisting that it is not to be presumed that these ministerial gifts will automatically come with the conferral of the office; rather, they must be evidently manifested to some degree before the conferral of the office. As I make this bold assertion, I have Owen at my side in hearty approval again and again. Owen insists that there are gifts that go beyond mere natural endowments and acquired abilities, gifts that are distinct from these things. He asserts that God gives what men do not have by nature and He gives such things supernaturally and efficaciously by His own immediate action upon the mind and the spirit in the exercise of a particular gift. God gives gifts that are not necessarily organically related to natural endowments or acquired abilities. Owen says, in essence, that though there are those who deny this reality, he is committed to believing and teaching it since he sees it taught in the Word of God. After refuting those who affirm that there is no such thing as spiritual gifts which are supernatural in their essence, origin, and conferral, Owen goes on to say:

> As to the second, it is denied that there is, or ought to be, an outward way and order for calling men to the office of the ministry; and that a compliance therewith makes their call good, valuable, and lawful, whether they have of these gifts we talk of or no. And in these two lie all the contests about church order and worship that we have in the world.
>
> But I shall only speak in the general unto the above proposition,— namely, that it is the work of the Holy Spirit, in providing of an able ministry of the New Testament, for the use of the church to the end of the world, to communicate to them who are called according to his mind spiritual gifts and abilities, to enable them to the discharge of their duty in the administration of all ordinances, to the glory of Christ and the edification of the church. The proving of this one proposition, in which is the life of all gospel order, is all I shall do at this time.[3]

---

2. John Owen, *The Works of John Owen*, vol. 9 (Edinburgh: The Banner of Truth Trust, 1968), 442. The opening words of this quote indicate that he was passing through a particular season of unusual physical weakness or disability, a disability which he felt made it impossible for him to give himself to his normal painstaking exegetical method in preaching, and that there were time constraints upon him given the fact that this material was being preached at an ordination service.

3. John Owen, *The Works of John Owen*, vol. 9 (Edinburgh: The Banner of Truth Trust, 1968), 442.

Then he proceeds to do just that, in the form of eight observations, principles, and deductions, occupying about as many pages. I urgently encourage any man who is seeking to discern whether or not he is being equipped by Christ to become a pastor to prayerfully read and ponder these pages in Owen. Furthermore, I would also urge the same beneficial exercise for any man who has any ecclesiastical position and responsibility in conjunction with formally recognizing men as gifts of Christ.[4]

The Secondary or Mediate Source of the Gifts

Some gifts which are essential to the functions of the pastoral office are imparted in their raw materials at our conception. One example would be possessing a mind with sufficient mental strength and acuity to be able to understand the Word of God, and to acquire and wisely use the tools necessary for a responsible handling of the Word. The word Paul used for this mental gift is *orthomounta*, right-cutting, or *cutting a straight course* in the Word of truth (2 Tim. 2:15). Another such gift would be sufficiently normal hearing and speaking faculties, which things are essential to fulfilling pastoral duties, both publicly and privately. An example of a gift being withheld by a mediate or secondary source would be a man to whom God has not given the faculty of clear speech, such as an uncorrectable stutter or a very distracting and pronounced lisp—when that condition is irremediable by speech therapy or surgery. In such a case, God is making it plain that He is not calling such a man to speak forth His Word to the edification of His people. In one of the chapters in which Paul is addressing the subject of spiritual gifts he says, "So with yourselves, if with your tongue you utter speech that is not intelligible, how will anyone know what is said? For you will be speaking into the air" (1 Cor. 14:9).

Nevertheless, as a believer endowed with other gifts, such a man may have many situations where he can be very useful, particularly in a more private setting, as he gains the confidence of people who become accustomed to his abnormal speech patterns, perhaps to the point where they hardly notice the abnormality.

Many years ago I met a dear brother in Christ who was afflicted with a serious neurological disease. God had given him a good mind, much understanding of Scripture, and spiritual discernment, but because of that particular

---

4. John Owen, *The Works of John Owen*, vol. 9 (Edinburgh: The Banner of Truth Trust, 1968), 442–451.

disease his speech was very inarticulate. However, for several years, he led a
Bible study in a dormitory of the college he attended and was used of God
in the lives of many. But such a man would be unable to carry out the functions of the pastoral office and therefore would not be qualified to be an elder
laboring in preaching and teaching.

Then there are those gifts given or withheld from us in a secondary or
mediate way in our years of maturation, such as a decent education that has
helped us to think clearly and perhaps to express ourselves succinctly and
with clarity, and parental training that modeled for us what was involved in
exercising a wise, loving, patient, but firm government over others. Many
of us are exceedingly thankful that God was laying up in our souls what
it meant to be godly, caring shepherds in the way we were nurtured under
the godly domestic government of our Christian parents. When the apostle
Paul recounted his pastoral dealings with the Thessalonians, he was able to
say to them, "For you know how, like a father with his children, we exhorted
each one of you and encouraged you and charged you to walk in a manner
worthy of God, who calls you into his own kingdom and glory" (1 Thess.
2:11, 12). Little did some of us know that God was cultivating in us a gift for
godly spiritual fatherhood by the mediate and secondary means of the kind
of exemplary domestic government under which we were reared.

Other gifts essential for pastoral ministry begin to manifest themselves
in seed form as the normal fruit of regeneration and true conversion. When
God creates us anew in Christ Jesus and gives us the gift of the Holy Spirit, He
begins to produce in us the nine-fold fruit of the Holy Spirit: love, joy, peace,
patience, kindness, goodness, faithfulness, gentleness, self-control (Gal. 5:22,
23). That love which is the fruit of the Spirit inclines us to begin to reach
out to others with a view to being of spiritual help to them. As we become
incorporated into the life, fellowship, and ministry of a biblically ordered
church, some graces of the Holy Spirit may begin to give birth to seedling
gifts of ministry. For example, as a man begins to lead in prayer in the prayer
meetings of the church, others may begin to recognize a special gift of edification as he becomes the mouthpiece of the congregation when leading in
prayer. As that same man takes his place in a Sunday school class or in a
small group gathering, his love for the truth and his growing insight into the
scriptures may begin to be evident to those around him. He may be asked, or
may volunteer to be a substitute Sunday school teacher. The children who sit
in the class report to their parents that, whenever that particular young man
teaches, they find his teaching particularly helpful.

Furthermore, as this man seeks to fulfill more and more of the approximately thirty "one-anothering" directives of the New Testament, it becomes evident that he has a more than ordinary facility of being able to "rejoice with those who rejoice, weep with those who weep" (Rom. 12:15). Also, it becomes evident that, when he is among his peers, they look instinctively to him for initiative in group activities and for help when they need personal counsel. As this particular man periodically reviews his life and his place of service in the Kingdom of God, he and others around him begin to wonder whether or not this beautiful little garden of growing spiritual seedlings is indeed pointing him in the direction of beginning to aspire to the work of an overseer among God's people.

When we think of the source of the gifts essential for the pastoral office, all of them ultimately come from God, yet some more directly, and some of them secondarily by mediate sources. However, whether the gifts are from an immediate or mediate source, they are to be recognized, consciously cultivated, and nurtured to their optimum measure of potential usefulness to the glory of God and to the good of others. Furthermore, these gifts must be evident, at least in fundamental seed form, before a man is set apart to the work of the ministry.

Many questions may arise in our minds as we seriously consider what I have attempted to lay before the reader, in terms of the necessity, identity, and the source or origin of those gifts which are essential to the pastoral office and function. "What is seed form?" "How much gift is needed in this or that area?" God has not given us a detailed manual with an alphabetical index for finding answers to our many questions. However, we come back to one of our fundamental presuppositions: the sufficiency and perspicuity of the written Word of God. Paul told Timothy that the God-breathed scriptures were sufficient to equip him for every good work (2 Tim. 3:16, 17), even that of guiding men and churches into God's way of bringing men into the pastoral office. In addition to a sufficient Bible, God has given us this wonderful and expansive promise:

> If any of you lacks wisdom, let him ask God, who gives generously to all without reproach, and it will be given him. But let him ask in faith, with no doubting, for the one who doubts is like a wave of the sea that is driven and tossed by the wind. For that person must not suppose that he will receive anything from the Lord; he is a double-minded man, unstable in all his ways (Jas. 1:5–8).

Still, we must start with a deep persuasion with regard to ourselves and with regard to our counsel and influence with others. If a man is being fashioned by Christ to be a gift to His church as a pastor-teacher, one of the indispensable evidences will be, not only the graces of Christian character and matured Christian experience, but the presence of those gifts which are essential to the function of the office: speaking gifts, serving gifts, and leadership gifts. As Owen insisted again and again, if a man does not possess all the necessary gifts from Christ, he is not a gift of Christ to His church—*no gifts, no gift*!

Christ nourishes and cherishes His church (Eph. 5:29), and a major expression of this ministry of His in the church is giving her gifted men (Eph. 4:11). It would not be an act of tender loving nourishment to give as a gift to any church a man who lacks gifts essential to fulfilling the functions of the pastoral office. Without gifts, you are no gift to Christ's church. You may be an intruder into that office with sincere motives. You may have come into it because of the shoddy, unbiblical thinking of others. Yet, you can never regard yourself as a gift of Christ to His church unless Christ has first of all granted you the gifts necessary to function in that office for the purposes for which Christ Himself has instituted that office.

In concluding this section of our study, I believe that it is important to underscore the fact that some of the graces, and especially the gifts, will have a peculiar and concentrated application to those elders who will be set apart to labor in preaching and teaching, as Paul distinguishes between elders in 1 Timothy 5:17, "Let the elders who rule well be considered worthy of double honor, especially those who labor in preaching and teaching." Nevertheless, I would insist that the standard for graces, and at least a discernible measure of gifts of utterance and government, do apply even to those who may be described by some as *ruling elders*. This designation is used to describe those whose primary function in the pastoral office is found in shepherding, governing, and taking care of the flock of God, and not public preaching and teaching. While it is obvious that 1 Timothy 5:17 envisions a division of labor among the elders, neither that nor any other passage suggests that there is another distinct office, or a different set of requirements for ruling elders, and elders who rule as well as teach and preach. It is clear from 1 Timothy 5:17 that any elder who rules well is worthy of double honor, and most agree that this involves financial remuneration. It is also clear that this double honor should be especially given to those elders who labor in preaching and teaching.

However, the first part of the verse clearly prescribes that if the level of a man's gifts and the church's financial ability warrants it, a so-called ruling elder who is particularly gifted in his functions is worthy of the financial support of the church. If we dismiss the authority of the *must be* of 1 Timothy 3:1–7 and Titus 1:5–9 as applicable to all elders regardless of the division of labor, we give up a clear standard of the biblical requirements for anyone holding the office designated as overseer in the household of God. God does not set before us a double standard for elders based on their diversity of gift or primary focus of function. I insist that it is not possible to establish genuine parity of ecclesiastical function and authority among the elders in any congregation unless there is a strict parity in holding every man to the same biblical standard of graces and gifts required of those who aspire to the office and function of an overseer.[5]

The clear demands of the most relevant texts of Scripture demonstrate the necessity for and importance of the requisite gifts for the pastoral office. These texts, to which frequent reference has been made, are 1 Timothy 3:1–7 and Titus 1:5–9, together with other portions in the pastoral epistles. There are unmistakable and non-negotiable demands in these passages that certain graces and gifts be evident in any man who continues to aspire to or is recognized for the function of the pastoral office.

Consider carefully John Owen's thought on the parable of the talents in Matthew 25:14–30:

> And they are abilities which Christ, as the king and head of his church, giveth unto men in an especial manner, as they are employed under him in the service of his house and work of the gospel. The servants mentioned are such as are called, appointed, and employed in the service of the house of Christ; that is, all ministers of the gospel, from first to last. And their talents are the gifts which he endows them withal, by his own immediate power and authority, for their work. And hence these three things follow:—1. That wherever there is a ministry that the Lord Christ setteth up, appointeth, or owneth, he furnisheth all those whom he employs therein with gifts and abilities suitable to their work; which he doth by the Holy Spirit. He will never fail to own his institutions, with gracious supplies, to render them effectual. 2. That where any have not received talents to trade withal, it is the highest

---

5. I strongly urge you to read John Murray, *Collected Writings of John Murray, 2: Systematic Theology* (Edinburgh: The Banner of Truth Trust, 1977), chapters 28–30, pp. 345–365, on parity and term eldership. I would make these required reading for my students.

presumption in them, and casts the greatest dishonour on the Lord Christ, as though he requires work where he gave no strength, or trade where he gave no stock, for any one to undertake the work of the ministry. Where the Lord Christ gives no gifts, he hath no work to do. He will require of none any especial duty where he doth not give an especial ability; and for any to think themselves meet for this work and service in the strength of their own natural parts and endowments, however acquired; is to despise both his authority and his work. 3. For those who have received of these talents, either not to trade at all, or to pretend the managing of their trade on another stock,—that is, either not sedulously and duly to exercise their ministerial gifts, or to discharge their ministry by other helps and means,—is to set up their own wisdom in opposition unto his, and his authority. In brief, that which the whole parable teacheth is, that wherever there is a ministry in the church that Christ owneth or regardeth, as used and employed by him, there persons are furnished with spiritual gifts from Christ by the Spirit, enabling them unto the discharge of that ministry; and where there are no such spiritual gifts dispensed by him, there is no ministry that he either accepteth or approveth.[6]

Why do I insist on the necessity and the importance of requisite graces and gifts in any biblical and orderly call to the ministry? As I have demonstrated in the course of describing the various requisite gifts, it is because of the explicit and implicit testimony of the Word of God. In conclusion, I would like to reinforce the urgency of this matter by a consideration of the inescapable connection between the pastoral office and the intention of Christ who gives men to fill that office. Again, it is at this point that John Owen is at his perceptive best. Owen makes this point concerning the necessity for spiritual gifts, not only convincingly, but repeatedly, in several of his writings. Most of that material is found in volumes four and nine of his collected works, and is included in sermons preached at various ordination services. It is helpful to see that Owen repeated himself, saying in one church essentially the same thing that he said in a different church. Reading such sermons reveals Owen's common denominators of passion in this area and enables the reader to appreciate the degree to which Owen himself felt the weight of this concern. The essence of what he repeats is that when Christ confers no gifts essential to the function of the pastoral office, He intends no

6. John Owen, *The Works of John Owen*, vol. 4 (Edinburgh: The Banner of Truth Trust, 1968), 504, 505.

assumption of that office. Where He gives no gifts to a man, He is not giving that man as a gift to any church.

There is another testimony given to this (to name one or two among many), in Rom. 12:4–8, "For as we have many members in one body, and all members have not the same office; so we, being many, are one body in Christ, and every one members one of another. Having then gifts, differing according to the grace that is given to us, whether prophecy, let us prophesy according to the proportion of faith; or ministry, let us wait on our ministering; or he that teacheth, on teaching; or he that exhorteth, on exhortation," etc. It is not to my present concern whether offices or duties are intended in this place; but three things are plain to me in this text:—1. That this discourse and direction doth concern the ordinary state of the church in all ages. I profess to you I had rather a thousand times be of their opinion, bad as it is, who say that all church-state is ceased, than that there may be a church-state when these gifts and graces are not. If I did not see these graces and gifts continued to some, to keep up the ordinances of the church in some measure, I should believe it had ceased. 2. That gifts are the foundation of all church work, whether it be in office or out of office. "Having therefore gifts, let us," saith the apostle, do so and so. If there be no spiritual gifts, there is no spiritual work. Spiritual gifts are the foundation of office, which is the foundation of work in the church, and of all gospel administrations in a special manner, according to the gifts received. Truly, it may be you may think it lost labour to prove this; but there is nothing more despised or reproached in this world than this one apprehension, that there are spiritual gifts given unto persons, to enable them to perform all gospel administrations. 3. That not only the discharge of duty and work depends on the administration of gifts, but the measure of work depends upon the measure of gifts; it is according to the measure every one hath received: and there are many *measures*. As long as there is any measure of spiritual gifts, let it not be despised among you. The gifts of the Holy Ghost are not only for work, but, I say, for the measure of work, Eph. 4:8–13. All these spiritual gifts the Holy Ghost doth bestow, to enable persons to perform their work.[7]

As *spiritual gifts* are bestowed unto this end, so they are *necessary* for it. There can be no gospel administration without spiritual gifts; the ministration of the gospel being the ministration of the Spirit, and all gospel ministrations are spiritual ministrations. The truth is, one

---

7. John Owen, *The Works of John Owen*, vol. 9 (Edinburgh: The Banner of Truth Trust, 1968), 448, 449.

reason why they are called so, and are so, is, because they are no way to be administered to the glory of Christ but by the aid and help of these spiritual gifts. If the Lord Jesus Christ had appointed carnal ordinances, such as are suited to the reason and strength of a man, there had been no need for him to promise the assistance of the Spirit. The spirit of a man knows the things of a man, 1 Cor. 2:11. All the things within the compass of a man, the spirit of a man will find them out, and give strength for the performance of them. Saith Christ, John 6:63, "My words, they are spirit, and all my offices and ordinances are spiritual;"—and thus there is a necessity of spiritual gifts for their administration: so that *spiritual gifts and spiritual administrations live and die together.* And the way whereby the world lost the spiritual ministrations of the gospel, was by the neglect and contempt of spiritual gifts; whereby alone they can be performed.[8]

Owen also raises the question: How does Christ continue to give ministers to His church? Owen answers that He does it by

"the giving spiritual gifts" unto men, whereby they may be enabled unto the discharge of the office of the ministry, as to the edification of the church in all the ends of it. *Gifts make no man a minister; but all the world cannot make a minister of Christ without gifts.* If the Lord Jesus Christ should cease to give out spiritual gifts unto men for the work of the ministry, he need do no more to take away the ministry itself; it must cease also: and it is the very way the ministry ceases in apostatising churches,—Christ no more giving out unto them of the gifts of his Spirit; and all their outward forms and order, which they can continue, are of no signification in his sight.

Thirdly. Christ doth it by giving power unto his church to call persons to that office, by him appointed and prepared by the gifts He bestows. And you may observe three things concerning this power:—

1. That this power in the church is not despotical, lordly, and absolute. It is not from any authority of their own; but it consists in an absolute compliance with the command of Christ: it is but the doing what Christ hath commanded; and that gives virtue, efficacy, and power unto it, "Look not upon us as though, by our power and our virtue," may the church say, "we have made this man a minister this day. It is in the name and authority of Jesus Christ alone, by which we act; in obedience unto that, he is so constituted and appointed.

---

8. John Owen, *The Works of John Owen*, vol. 9 (Edinburgh: The Banner of Truth Trust, 1968), 449.

2. There is no power in any church to choose any one whom Christ hath not chosen before; that is, no church can make a man *formally* a minister, that Christ hath not made so *materially*, if I may so say. If Christ hath not pre-instructed and prefurnished him with gifts, it is not in the power of the church to choose or call him. And where these two things are,—where the law of Christ is the foundation, and where the gifts of Christ are the preparative,—thereupon the church calls, and persons are constituted elders by the Holy Ghost, and overseers of the flock; as in Acts 20:28. Because he gave the law of the office, and because he gave these gifts to the officers, therefore are they constituted by the Holy Ghost. They were the ordinary elders of the church of Ephesus to whom the apostle gives in charge "to feed the flock of God, over which the Holy Ghost had made them overseers."[9]

The same is manifest from the nature of the gift itself; for this gift consisteth in gifts: "He gave gifts," Eph. 4:8. There is an active giving expressed, "He gave;" and the thing given, that is, "gifts." Wherefore the ministry is a gift of Christ, not only because freely and bountifully given by him to the church, but also because spiritual gifts do essentially belong unto it, are indeed its life, and inseparable from its being. A ministry without gifts is no ministry of Christ's giving, nor is of any other use in the church but to deceive the souls of men. To set up such a ministry is both to despise Christ and utterly to frustrate the ends of the ministry, those for which Christ gave it, and which are here expressed; for,—(1.) Ministerial gifts and graces are the great evidence that the Lord Christ takes care of his church and provides for it, as called into the order and unto the duties of a church. To set up a ministry which may be continued by outward forms and orders of men only, without any communication of gifts from Christ, is to despise his authority and care. Neither is it his mind that any church should continue in order any longer or otherwise than as he bestows these gifts for the ministry. (2.) That these gifts are the only means and instruments whereby the work of the ministry may be performed, and the ends of the ministry attained, shall be farther declared immediately. The ends of the ministry here mentioned, called its "work," are, the "perfecting of the saints, and the edifying of the body of Christ, until we all come unto a perfect man." Hereof nothing at all can be done without these spiritual gifts;

---

9. John Owen, *The Works of John Owen*, vol. 9 (Edinburgh: The Banner of Truth Trust, 1968), 433.

and therefore a ministry devoid of them is a mock ministry, and no ordinance of Christ.[10]

This is strong language, but the logic involved in it is inescapable. There is an intimate connection between the purpose for which Christ gives pastors and teachers, and the necessity of the gifts for that function.

Owen asserts further:

> All I shall say at present is, that spiritual gifts of themselves make no man actually a minister; yet no man can be made a minister according to the mind of Christ who is not partaker of them. Wherefore, supposing the continuance of the law and institution mentioned, if the Lord Christ do at any time, or in any place, cease to give out spiritual gifts unto men, enabling them in some good measure unto the discharge of the ministry, then and in that place the ministry itself must cease and come to an end. To erect a ministry by virtue of outward order, rites, and ceremonies, without gifts for the edification of the church, is but to hew a block with axes, and smooth it with planes, and set it up for an image to be adored. To make a man a minister who can do nothing of the proper peculiar work of the ministry, nothing towards the only end of it in the church, is to set up a dead carcass, fastening it to a post, and expecting it should do you work and service.[11]

Owen again sounds these basic notes with unmistakable clarity and conviction when he writes:

> The church hath no power to call any unto the office of the ministry, where the Lord Christ hath not gone before it in the designation of him by an endowment with spiritual gifts; for if the whole authority of the ministry be from Christ, and if he never give it but where he bestows these gifts with it for its discharge, as in Eph. 4:7, 8, etc., then to call any to the ministry whom he hath not so previously gifted is to set him aside, and to act in our own name and authority.[12]

Paul told Timothy to give himself wholly to the cultivation of his gifts and graces so that all would see his progress, "Practice these things, immerse

---

10. John Owen, *The Works of John Owen*, vol. 4 (Edinburgh: The Banner of Truth Trust, 1968), 491.

11. John Owen, *The Works of John Owen*, vol. 4 (Edinburgh: The Banner of Truth Trust, 1968), 494.

12. John Owen, *The Works of John Owen*, vol. 4 (Edinburgh: The Banner of Truth Trust, 1968), 495.

yourself in them, so that all may see your progress" (1 Tim. 4:15). Brethren, this ought to be true of us by the grace and the enabling power of the Holy Spirit. Imagine Paul returning to Ephesus and saying to the people, "How is my spiritual son Timothy doing?" What a thrill it would be to the heart of the apostle to have the people respond, "Oh, Paul, do you remember how, when you left him here at Ephesus, he evidenced tangible graces and gifts? You will be surprised at what you see now. He is growing before our eyes, both in the graces of Christlike character and in the measure of his pastoral gifts."

CHAPTER 12

Confirmation to the Pastoral Office

We come now to the third element of a biblical and orderly call to the Christian ministry, which is the *confirmation* of a man's call to the pastoral office and function. I want to state an axiom and then seek to open and demonstrate the scriptural roots of this axiom.

The axiom is that *while sober self-assessment of our desires, graces, and gifts is a personal responsibility which no man can righteously evade, an external confirmation of that assessment by a cross-section of spiritually minded people is essential to a valid call to the pastoral office.*

Now, what proof do I offer for this axiom? What scriptural precepts, precedents, and principles do I set forth to demonstrate that such an axiom is rooted in the scriptures? I have repeatedly emphasized, from passages such as Romans 12:3 and 1 Peter 4:10, 11, the responsibility of personal, sober, self-assessment. Every man has a moral obligation to engage in sober self-assessment. Peter assumes in this latter passage that none are brought into the body of Christ whom Christ does not gift in some way for mutual service to the body. The assumption is that if we are to exercise whatever gift or gifts have been given to us, we must identify that gift or those gifts, in part, by sober self-assessment. God has not left us to the mercy of our own resources in giving this responsibility to us. According to 1 John 2:27, He has given His Spirit to everyone in the body, and we can therefore understand that these Spirit-anointed believers will have an important part in the assessment of our gifts. Every member of the New Covenant community has received the gift of the Holy Spirit.

Self-assessment alone is neither safe nor biblical. To demonstrate this, consider the immediate context of the passage, "For by the grace given to me I say to everyone among you not to think of himself more highly than he ought to think, but to think with sober judgment, each according to the measure of faith that God has assigned" (Rom. 12:3). Here we have a directive to assess ourselves as individuals planted within the body of the church.

In its context, Paul speaks of one body with a diversity of gifts (Rom. 12:4–6), and it is in the assumed context of the life, ministry, discernment, and assessment by the body that the individual engages in this assessment.

It is likewise with Peter's letter to the suffering saints in Asia Minor and surrounding provinces. We must not assume that there were individuals who had no vital attachment to the church and had received a copy of Peter's letter in order to have something to read in their personal devotions. Peter is speaking in 1 Peter 4:10, 11, to those who are members of the various churches throughout Asia Minor and also who are subject to the elders God gave to those churches (1 Pet. 5:1–4).

Now, for someone like myself, from a background devoid of any solid biblical ecclesiology, that was something new to me. I will never forget the day when it dawned on me that these letters which I was reading in my devotions were not written primarily to me as an individual believer. Rather, they were written to churches. Some of them were written to individuals, but even the individuals like Timothy, Titus, and Philemon who received their letters, received them in the context of their churches, where they would fulfill the directives written in them. For me, this realization was nothing short of a spiritual Copernican revolution. Suddenly I found that there was something that was the center of the universe of God's communication in the New Covenant documents other than the individual. At the center was the church, and it is assumed in these letters that the individual believer is embedded in and deeply involved in the life and ministry of the church.

One man beautifully expressed this truth by saying that when we come to the Lord Jesus in saving faith, we find that He has a bride on His arm. If we take Him to be our Savior and Lord, we take His bride with Him as we become members of His church. This fact has great implications with regard to the validation of our sense of call to the pastoral office.

Robert Breckenridge wrote:

> It cannot be denied that we are liable to be deceived in this matter, as well as in that of our personal interest in Christ, and indeed in every other which concerns our inward state and exercises; and that we are so is precisely one chief reason why the testimony of our conscience cannot be sufficient evidence to others, and why it needs to be enforced, even to ourselves, by other and concurring proofs. The human heart is not only desperately wicked, but is deceitful above all things, and the most difficult part of knowledge is to know ourselves; and sin itself is not only infinitely deceitful but is also most deceivable, and therefore to

the extent that it reigns in us it subjects us to the risk of being deceived and of deceiving ourselves. What I have before said, plainly shows that the danger of being deceived by others into a conviction that we ought to preach the Gospel—is by no means imaginary; and all those have endeavored to fathom the wiles of Satan, and who have wrestled earnestly with the plague of their own hearts, will know that the danger of self delusion is real and constant.[1]

It is clear from Scripture that earned credibility by a cross-section of spiritually minded people is crucial. By *cross-section* I mean presently recognized leaders in the church whatever our ecclesiastical framework may be, and also non-office-bearers of proven discernment and wisdom. The richest deposit of wisdom and discernment is not necessarily found in the eldership alone, or in the presbytery alone, or in a called council of Baptist pastors or independent pastors alone. Sometimes, a little, elderly, half-blind, half-deaf, wizened, shriveled-up old lady may have more spiritual discernment about a man's fitness for the ministry than five or six preachers together who may have some personal interest in encouraging Johnny to become a "Reverend." It is true, brethren, and we must recognize that fact.

What other scriptures point in the direction of the necessity of this external, objective validation of our personal, subjective, individual self-assessment? Consider this one, "You then, my child, be strengthened by the grace that is in Christ Jesus, and what you have heard from me in the presence of many witnesses entrust to faithful men who will be able to teach others also" (2 Tim. 2:1, 2). Who makes the final assessment that a man is a faithful man? Does Timothy stand up in the next gathering of the church at Ephesus and make an announcement:

> I have a letter from the apostle Paul who tells me that I am solemnly charged by his apostolic authority to commit to faithful men the apostolic body of truth with a view to these men becoming competent to be the teachers of others. Therefore, all of you who assess yourselves to be faithful men and able to teach, show up next Saturday morning, when I will begin the first class in which I propose to commit the apostolic tradition to you.

---

1. Robert J. Breckenridge, "The Christian Pastor, One of Christ's Ascension Gifts," in *The Southern Presbyterian Review* 35:3 (July 1884), 470–472. Archived at http:/www.pcahistory .org/periodicals/spr/v35/35-3-5.pdf.

No, Timothy was responsible to make that assessment! The personal self-assessment of the men in Ephesus that they were faithful men who would be able to teach others was not enough. Timothy was responsible to make a judgment concerning this. Though there is no explicit account that he did so, most likely Timothy would have engaged in some kind of polling of the mature saints at Ephesus regarding any man who presented himself as a candidate to receive the special training. How did Timothy come into the orbit of his tremendous sphere of influence as Paul's spiritual son, as the one whom Paul tutored? Paul himself testified, "For I have no one like him, who will be genuinely concerned for your welfare. For they all seek their own interests, not those of Jesus Christ" (Phil. 2:20, 21). Imagine how the other "self-seeking" men would feel when they heard these words of commendation for Timothy.

Here is Luke's account of Paul's initial assessment of Timothy,

Paul came also to Derbe and to Lystra. A disciple was there, named Timothy, the son of a Jewish woman who was a believer, but his father was a Greek. He was well spoken of by the brothers at Lystra and Iconium. Paul wanted Timothy to accompany him, and he took him and circumcised him because of the Jews who were in those places, for they all knew that his father was a Greek (Acts 16:1–3).

This is written of Paul's assessment of Timothy, but also note that Paul did not trust his own assessment exclusively. He took time to go around to the believers in those places where Timothy had more extensive interaction to discover what he could, and he found that Timothy was well reported of by the brethren. So Paul took Timothy as his companion. The Holy Spirit moved Luke to record these details as a clear precedent for us to follow.

Now, going a step further, Paul wrote, "Do not neglect the gift you have, which was given you by prophecy when the council of elders laid their hands on you" (1 Tim. 4:14). This council of elders surely was a group of recognized discerning leaders who, by laying their hands upon Timothy, were outwardly validating that as duly-recognized leaders in Christ's church, they were convinced that God had given to Timothy the necessary graces and gifts essential to his calling as an apostolic representative.

Paul wrote, "For this reason I remind you to fan into flame the gift of God, which is in you through the laying on of my hands" (2 Tim. 1:6). Now, whether that was an event where Paul joined with the presbyters or council of elders does not materially alter the point that there was an extensive external validation of Timothy's call by many of the rank and file of the people of God, as well as by the official leaders of God's people, all the way up to an apostle. Then and only then is Timothy set apart, not for his pastoral office, but for that unique function, whether he is a classic evangelist or whether he is an apostolic representative. Again, that issue is moot in this discussion, but the principles are very clear with respect to Timothy's entrance upon an official function in Christ's church. He was not sitting home, praying, having his devotions, assessing his fitness alone. The people of God, all the way up to the evaluation of the apostle himself, had their input.

A situation arose in Acts 15 as to whether or not Paul and Barnabas were to take John Mark with them on the second missionary journey,

> Now Barnabas wanted to take with them John called Mark. But Paul thought best not to take with them one who had withdrawn from them in Pamphylia and had not gone with them to the work. And there arose a sharp disagreement, so that they separated from each other. Barnabas took Mark with him and sailed away to Cyprus, but Paul chose Silas and departed, having been commended by the brothers to the grace of the Lord (Acts 15:37–40).

They had a verbal fuss over this. It does not mean that they were cursing at one another or had their jugular veins standing out on their necks while shaking their fists. Nevertheless, a sharp disagreement is more than a minor one where they might have sat there sipping Coke, and saying, "Well, we do not quite see eye-to-eye on this, but let us just talk it through." It was a *sharp* disagreement and they separated from each other. The church again affirms its support for Paul and Silas, but the Scripture is silent as to whether or not the church placed its approbation and blessing on Barnabas and Mark.

I am fully aware of the fact that one must "exegete some of the white spaces" in order to build a strong case from this passage. However, the Holy Spirit has chosen to record the fact that it was Paul and Silas who left with the unmistakable blessing of the church and its corporate confirmation of the legitimacy of their new mission and the men who were fit to perform it. Was it that the church shared Paul's reservations concerning John Mark's fitness for the next missionary journey? Apparently it did, for Luke does not record that Barnabas and Mark were sent out with its blessing, whereas Paul and Silas were. John Mark had previously gained the approbation of the church relative to his fitness to be one of Paul's companions in ministry. However, while the scriptures do not give us any details as to why he left Paul and returned home from that first missionary journey, Paul believed that

Mark's action revealed a character weakness which disqualified him to be Paul's companion in the next missionary journey. Apparently, the apostle's judgment was something like this, "Until he proves over time that he has overcome whatever character weakness precipitated his desertion, he will not have my approbation for further missionary endeavors." Over time John Mark did prove himself, as we see when Paul wrote to Timothy, "Luke alone is with me. Get Mark and bring him with you, for he is very useful to me for ministry" (2 Tim. 4:11). Bless God!

John Mark obviously regained the approbation of the apostle, and, we can assume indirectly, of the rank and file of God's people. These passages surely point in the direction of underscoring the necessity of the external validation of our internal personal self-assessment.

Over the years, I have had interactions with men who were a bit restive, and even resentful, while having to wait for the external validation of their call. Their thinking went something like this, "Look, I know God has called me, and I have these gifts. Why must I wait for other people to validate this reality?" They are unwilling to wait for the approbation and the encouragement of the external call. Proverbs 18:1 is a key text which I have used many times with such men, "Whoever isolates himself seeks his own desire; he breaks out against all sound judgment."

Keil and Delitzsch provide us with a helpful exegesis of the meaning and nuances of the Hebrew words in this particular text:

> Instead of seeking to conform himself to the law and ordinance of the community, he seeks to carry out a separate view, and to accomplish some darling plan.... Thus putting his subjectivity in the room of the common weal, he shows his teeth, places himself in fanatical opposition against all that is useful and profitable in the principles and aims, the praxis of the community from which he separates himself. The figure is true to nature: the polemic of the schismatic and the sectary against the existing state of things, is for the most part measureless and hostile.[2]

Here is the picture of the man who says, "I am so certain that I am called. I do not care whether or not others validate my self-assessment." Scripture says that it is a man who, having separated himself, evidences that he is seeking his own desire and is raging against all sound wisdom. He is flying in

---

2. C.F. Keil, & F. Delitzsch, *Commentary on the Old Testament*, vol. 6 (Peabody, MA: Hendrickson, 1996), 268.

the face of those generic instructions and comments of Proverbs about the safety found in the multitude of counselors (11:14; 15:22; 24:6).

Here again, Owen speaks perceptively:

> And this may at present suffice, as unto the call of meet persons unto the pastoral office; and, consequently, any other office in the church. The things following are essentially necessary unto it, so as that authority and right to feed and rule in the church in the name of Christ, as an officer of his house, may be given unto any one there by, by virtue of his law and the charter granted by him unto the church itself. The first is, That antecedently unto any actings of the church towards such a person with respect unto office, he be furnished by the Lord Christ himself with *graces*, and *gifts*, and *abilities*, for the discharge of the office whereunto he is to be called. This divine designation of the person to be called rests on the kingly office and care of Christ towards his church. Where this is wholly wanting, it is not in the power of any church under heaven, by virtue of any outward order or act, to communicate pastoral or ministerial power unto any person whatever. Secondly, there is to be *an exploration or trial of those gifts* and abilities as unto their accommodation unto the edification of that church whereunto any person is to be ordained a pastor or minister. But although the right of judging herein doth belong unto and reside in the church itself (for who else is able to judge for them, or is intrusted so to do?), yet is it their wisdom and duty to desire the assistance and guidance of those who are approved in the discharge of their office in other churches.[3]

Owen was an ecclesiastical independent (lower case *i*). Trinity Baptist is an independent church (lower case *i*), but we have deep, meaningful, active relationships with other churches and to their office-bearers. Over the years I have had many a Presbyterian say to me: "Al, you have real Presbyterianism that really works, in the relationships you and your people sustain to other churches and their overseers. We have the name and the framework of such relationships, but not the actual substance." These are pastors who have been my mentors and counselors, and pastors to whom I was both mentor and counselor.

What a delight it is, in this matter of assessing whether or not a man is a "Timothy," and "well reported of among the churches," to have a pastoral aspirant minister at one of our sister-churches, and then to receive the frank

---

3. John Owen, *The Works of John Owen*, vol. 16 (Edinburgh: The Banner of Truth Trust, 1968), 73, 74.

input of the pastors and elders of that church subsequent to such a visit. It is helpful to have the input of different eyes and ears regarding a man's demeanor, how he relates to people, whether or not his teaching and preaching was clear and accompanied by the unction of the Holy Spirit. In this way, the confirming voice of God's people is being heard relative to a man's sense of his call to the pastoral office.

By way of application, I am constrained to say the following. In a day of crass individualism and existential subjectivism, to insist on the quality control of this external validation of the church is to go against the whole prevailing mood of the hour. Crass individualism is part of the zeitgeist of our present society, in and out of the church. Added to this nasty reality is the prevalence of skewed thinking concerning how God calls men to the pastoral office at this point in redemptive history. By erroneously using the paradigm of how God called men to the extraordinary offices and functions of a prophet, of an apostle, or of a king, rather than that of the ordinary office of elder and overseer, men's understanding of the necessity for the confirming voice of the church is diminished even more.

We do well to listen to Edmund Clowney. As he opens up the subject of a call to the ministry, he first seeks to address how a man may biblically, and in a balanced way, make a self-assessment of his calling from the Lord; what we recognize to be the internal call. Then, he comes to the external call:

> Nothing can concern you more personally or intimately than your own calling of Christ. He has called you by name—not by number or by classification, for no selective service draft is so selective as Christ's. Your own new name is written on that white stone in his hand; he knows it and one day he will show it to you alone (Rev. 2:17).
>
> Can your calling, then, be the business of anyone else? When you are assured of the Lord's call, doesn't that settle the matter? Why not present yourself to a church of your choice and inform the congregation that the Lord has called you to be their pastor?[4]

Then he demonstrates from the life of the apostle Paul, called into grace by a direct revelatory act of the ascended and glorified Christ, commissioned in the midst of that calling out of darkness into light, that even in his life there was an external and corporate dimension in sealing his call. He is told that he is going to be a mouthpiece and a messenger of this exalted

---

4. Edmund P. Clowney, *Called to the Ministry* (Phillipsburg, New Jersey: Presbyterian and Reformed Publishing, 1964), 84.

and glorified Christ. Yet, when he subsequently travels to Jerusalem, what is the first thing he attempts to do? He attempts to become a church member! However, in the light of his previous "well-earned" reputation as a persecutor of Christians, some of the members of the church in Jerusalem are doubtful and frightened at the prospect of receiving him into their membership. We can just imagine the thoughts that were going through their minds! But God placed Barnabas there to encourage and assure the church in Jerusalem that Paul was indeed a true child of God. Luke records this incident,

> And when he had come to Jerusalem, he attempted to join the disciples. And they were all afraid of him, for they did not believe that he was a disciple. But Barnabas took him and brought him to the apostles and declared to them how on the road he had seen the Lord, who spoke to him, and how at Damascus he had preached boldly in the name of Jesus (Acts 9:26, 27).

Thus Paul became a member of the church at Jerusalem, "So he went in and out among them at Jerusalem, preaching boldly in the name of the Lord" (Acts 9:28). Paul did not say, "Who needs the church? Jesus spoke to me from heaven." So clearly, you need the church.

Then, in a subsequent visit to Jerusalem, Paul wants everyone to know that the gospel that he preaches among the Gentiles is the same gospel that Peter and James and the other Jerusalem apostles are preaching among the Jews,

> And when James and Cephas and John, who seemed to be pillars, perceived the grace that was given to me, they gave the right hand of fellowship to Barnabas and me, that we should go to the Gentiles and they to the circumcised (Gal. 2:9).

Clowney demonstrates that, even in the case of these eminent servants of God with an extraordinary office, there is a sensitivity to the external call given by established and recognized leaders in Christ's church:

> Christ's calling draws us to our brethren as well as to our Saviour. We are to exercise our calling in the fellowship of the church; we must find it there too. Take the towel and basin and discover your calling at your brother's feet; go with him to visit the prisoner and find your calling at his side. You may be convinced of your calling to the ministry long before others mark your gifts, but if you are diligent in the fellowship of the gospel your profiting will appear to all; Christ's calling will be acknowledged by Christ's church. Or it may be that your first inkling

of the call of Christ came from the lips of a fellow Christian who saw the evidences of the Lord's blessing on your life. Whether your calling was first apparent to you or to your brethren is not of decisive importance. Christ's gospel is preached today by hundreds who yearned for the ministry from childhood and hundreds more who fought their calling with a rising panic while their friends prayed. What is important is that your own awareness of Christ's gifts should be joined with the perception of the church.[5]

I trust that every man who is reading these pages does so as someone who is deeply involved in and thoroughly committed to his own local church in the totality of its life and ministry. However, those words may not describe you. You may be in seminary, and are not even a member of a biblically functioning local church, let alone deeply embedded in the life of that church and looking to God that, through that church, you will receive an external validation of your personal conviction concerning your calling to the pastoral office and ministry. I urge you, then, to find a place where you can become a loyal, submissive member of the church, a place with discerning leaders and Spirit-indwelt, discerning people—a real church—not a church in name only. I did not say to find a perfect church, but a real church, a healthy church, a church where people are determined to follow the scriptures when it comes to the matter of a call to the ministry.

When you become a covenant member of such a church, I also urge you to ask for a meeting with your overseers, and say something like this:

> Brethren, I want the standard of the Word of God to be applied to me as a faceless man. I do not care how many of you love me and think I am a nice guy; that is irrelevant. The issue is this: Is Christ forming me to be a gift to His church? I want you to look at the portrait of what God says one of His gifts will look like, as found in 1 Timothy 3, Titus 1, Acts 20, and 1 Peter 5, and in deductions from other passages regarding the pattern of Jesus as the True and Great Shepherd of His people. I want you to continually compare me to that portrait. If what you discern me to be, in graces and gifts, does not match the portrait, please have the spiritual integrity to tell me, so that I may find a sphere of honorable employment by which I can provide for myself and my family, glorify God in that calling, support the work of the church, and find my sphere of usefulness in the body of Christ.

---

5. Edmund P. Clowney, *Called to the Ministry* (Phillipsburg, New Jersey: Presbyterian and Reformed Publishing, 1964), 88.

This matter of the validation of the people of God is essential to a biblical and orderly call to the ministry.

Now, for those of you who are being nurtured in a well-ordered church, this external confirmation of fitness will generally come naturally and gradually, but, as in all other experiential or experimental divinity, there are times when this confirmation may come rather dramatically over a short period of time. The issues of the time and the details of the manner of that confirmation are irrelevant. What counts is that you do not run into the pastoral office unsent and unconfirmed in your call by the confirming voice of the church. If you are even further back along the line, in terms of whether or not you should even pursue acquiring those tools that generally are necessary to make a man an able teacher and preacher and a safe guide in the scriptures, then wait for the confirmation of discerning people, primarily and hopefully your own spiritual overseers, and a cross-section of spiritually minded, discerning, mature saints of the Lord found in the assembly to which you have attached yourself.

I say to you, my brethren in the ministry who may be reading these pages, may God use what you are reading to bring you to the place where you become committed in heart to seek to dismantle this wretched system, in which a man's subjective sense of call, based upon his own personal assessment alone, puts him in the pipeline to be a pastor.

May God so work in us a burning biblical conviction relative to these concerns, so that when objective truth demands it, we will be able to say to any man who will not wait for the quality-control of the voice of the church in conjunction with his call to the ministry:

> My dear brother, thus far and no further! Young man, middle aged man, old man, where did you get the notion that you can simply look in the mirror of self-evaluation, and come away saying "Christ is fashioning me into a gift to His church. I need no confirming voice of the people of God"?

It may be that some who are reading these pages are thinking to themselves, "If we take all these directives seriously, we will have far fewer men preparing for the ministry in our churches and in our seminaries."

In his magisterial book entitled *The Christian Ministry,* Charles Bridges responds to this very objection by quoting and elaborating upon a comment by a Mr. Ostervald:

"It will not fail to be objected,"—remarks, Mr. Ostervald—"that if none were to be omitted into holy orders, except those who are possessed of every necessary qualification, there could not possibly be procured a sufficient number of Pastors for the supply of our Churches." To which I answer, "that a small number of chosen Pastors is preferable to a multitude of unqualified teachers." At all hazards we must adhere to the command of God, and leave the event to Providences. But in reality the dearth of pastors is not so generally apprehended. To reject those candidates for holy orders, whose labours in the Church would be wholly fruitless, is undoubtedly a work of piety. Others, on the contrary, who are qualified to fulfill the duties of the sacred office, would take encouragements from this exactness and severity; and the Ministry would every day be rendered more respectable in the world.[6]

It is my personal conviction that the reason many men cannot preach with manifest authority in calling their congregations to biblical obedience is the basic fact that they stand behind the pulpits from which their words go forth having shaved off the right angles of what Scripture says every elder must be in grace and gift. May no reader of these pages join the swollen ranks of men who carry on their ministries with little authority and even less unction of the Holy Spirit.

---

6. Charles Bridges, *The Christian Ministry* (Edinburgh: The Banner of Truth Trust, 1976), 31.

CHAPTER 13

Recognition and Ordination to the Pastoral Office

Once a man has been biblically and ecclesiastically confirmed in his internal call by the external call of the church, the church is now prepared to formally recognize or ordain that man to the pastoral office. I have chosen to express this reality of recognition in the next paragraph.

No man should undertake to assume the pastoral office unless he is assured that he is indeed a gift of Christ to His church. This persuasion will come when his aspiration has been thoroughly examined, his qualifications with reference to graces and gifts unmistakably established, and the recognition of his home church (presbytery, consistory, denominational ministerial credentials committee, etc.), has been firmly secured. Then, when God providentially opens the door for pastoral labors in a specific congregation that expresses, by its suffrage, the conviction that this man is indeed Christ's gracious gift to them in particular as a pastor-teacher and overseer, the formal process of recognition or ordination may begin.

I would insist that these perspectives must not be looked upon as something unique to what has generally been designated as congregationalism or independency of church government. If these four elements are, as I firmly believe, rooted in biblical precepts, principles, and precedents, then any ecclesiastical regulations, practices, or traditions standing in the way of their implementation should be challenged. In anything other than an independent church, those challenges should work their way through the church courts, until the established process of assessing a man's call to the pastoral office is more thoroughly shaped by these scriptural directives. If we refuse biblical reformation in this way simply because "we have never done it this way before," we bring ourselves under the indictment of our Lord Jesus, who, when speaking of the religious leaders of His day said, "You leave the commandment of God and hold to the tradition of men" (Mark 7:8).

When one reads the thinking, convictions, and the passionate concerns of such Presbyterians as Breckenridge, Thornwell, Dabney, and others, it

becomes obvious that this matter of seeking to implement a biblical pattern of recognition and installation is wider and deeper than any particular
ecclesiastical tradition.

First of all, in seeking to establish the biblical basis for this perspective
on the recognition of a man of God, we might look into the Old Testament
for some broad principles and precedents. There we find men who were
clearly set apart by God for a specific function in the will of God. Yet, in
some cases it was years before they were actually installed in that particular
office and function for which they had previously been marked out by God.
David's anointing by Samuel with the years during which he waited until he
became king over all Israel is certainly an example of this principle. Moses
constitutes another example. God's appointment of Moses to be the human
leader of the exodus was given when God revealed Himself to Moses in the
burning bush. However, considerable time passed before Moses was actually recognized and began to function as the God-appointed leader of the
children of Israel.

In the New Testament we find the apostle Paul. In conjunction with
his call into grace on the Damascus road, he was dramatically called to the
apostolic office and was given clear directions that the ultimate sphere of
his labor would be to take the gospel to the Gentiles (Acts 9:15, 16). Years
passed before the events of Acts 13, when the Spirit of God said the time
had come for Paul and his companion Barnabas to engage in the Gentile
ministry. According to Acts 13:3, the hands of the existing leadership were
laid on Saul and Barnabas, indicating that the church at Antioch recognized
God's calling of these two men to go forth on their first missionary journey.
We see some principles and precedents that point in the direction of what I
have designated as *recognition* and *installation*.

I will now state an axiom with regard to *recognition,* and it is that *the
crowning validation of a man's call to the pastoral office is effected when a specific congregation, objectively assessing a man's graces and gifts, and acting by
the authority of Christ, does by its corporate suffrage, acknowledge that man
as a gift of Christ to them, leading to his formal ordination and installation to
that office in that specific congregation.*

Church history teaches us that men have literally spilled blood for the
truth that Christ does not impose spiritual guides upon a flock of Christ
from without, but that each congregation of Christ by its own suffrage
recognizes and receives with gratitude Christ's gifts to them. However, if this
is to be a valid call, then it must be a congregation that thinks and acts by the

authority and rule of Christ, as contained in the Word of Christ. Whatever the details of the process of securing the mind and will of the congregation may be with respect to exercising its suffrage in the calling of a man to a specific office, that activity must be undertaken in a prayerful disposition. According to Acts 1:14–26, a dominant activity of the one-hundred-twenty in conjunction with the appointment of a replacement for Judas was the activity of corporate prayer. According to Acts 13:1–3, it is while those five teachers and prophets mentioned are ministering to the Lord, praying and fasting, that God speaks His more definitive word concerning Paul and Barnabas going forth to their mission among the Gentiles.

Further, this recognition must be by a church acting in conscious dependence upon Christ and His Spirit, a church submissive to the Word of Christ, not being pressured in its actions primarily by its ecclesiastical tradition, nor by sentiment, nor by the wealthy men and women in the church who may seek to use financial influence in order to "get their man" into the office.

A man's calling begins, perhaps, with some very nebulous pressures on his spirit, in which he begins to ask himself, "Could it be that God would have me invest my life in pastoral labor?" Over a process of years and along specific paths, God has brought him to fulfill the elementary biblical requirements. However, his calling comes to its crowning validation when a flock of Christ, prayerfully and submissively to the Word, judging by the standard of the Word, sees in that man Christ's gift to them. They receive him as such and conduct a public service in which that man is formally installed as an undershepherd in that particular assembly. He can now have that assurance, as much assurance as a man can have short of divine revelation, that Jesus Christ Himself has endowed him with the necessary gifts and graces to serve in the pastoral office, and has brought him to assume that office in a biblical and orderly manner.

Now we come to consider the biblical principles, precepts and precedents that frame our axiom. I commend most highly the thought of John Owen on this matter as it is found in his works, especially in volume 16, from which I have already frequently quoted in this unit. He gives a thorough and convincing biblical and historical defense of the principles which I have articulated in the main axiom of this lecture on recognition. We will also discuss this matter and Owen's treatment in unit seven when we address the establishment of a biblical eldership in the churches.

Now I want to capture some of the major biblical emphases which Owen includes and amplifies in his treatment.[1] We will proceed to look at the major passages in the New Testament which contain principles for recognizing a man for the pastoral office.

Principles from Acts 1:12–26

We begin with the filling of the vacant space in the apostolic circle left by the defection of Judas from the faith and his subsequent suicide. Even though there are elements peculiar to the matter of seeking out an apostle, there was also an obvious involvement of the one-hundred-twenty disciples in the decision which led to his replacement. Now to the biblical text,

> In those days Peter stood up among the brothers (the company of persons was in all about 120) and said, "Brothers, the Scripture had to be fulfilled, which the Holy Spirit spoke beforehand by the mouth of David concerning Judas, who became a guide to those who arrested Jesus. For he was numbered among us and was allotted his share in this ministry." (Now this man acquired a field with the reward of his wickedness, and falling headlong he burst open in the middle and all his bowels gushed out. And it became known to all the inhabitants of Jerusalem, so that the field was called in their own language Akeldama, that is, Field of Blood.) "For it is written in the Book of Psalms, 'May his camp become desolate, and let there be no one to dwell in it'; and 'Let another take his office'" (Acts 1:15–20).

Then Peter gives the non-negotiable requirements for any man who would be appointed as Judas's successor,

> "So one of the men who have accompanied us during all the time that the Lord Jesus went in and out among us, beginning from the baptism of John until the day when he was taken up from us—one of these men must become with us a witness to his resurrection." And they put forward two, Joseph called Barsabbas, who was also called Justus, and Matthias. And they prayed and said, "You, Lord, who know the hearts of all, show which one of these two you have chosen to take the place in this ministry and apostleship from which Judas turned aside to go to

---

1. The section of Owen to which I am referring is John Owen, *The Works of John Owen*, vol. 16 (Edinburgh: The Banner of Truth Trust, 1968), 51–74. You will see this again in Unit 7 in the last of my three lectures on the eldership.

his own place." And they cast lots for them, and the lot fell on Matthias, and he was numbered with the eleven apostles (Acts 1:21–26).

Who are the "they" putting forward these two men? I think, contextually, that they are the one-hundred-twenty disciples. By some process they came to a consensus that there were two men who met the non-negotiable biblical standard for an apostle. We read that "they prayed" (Acts 1:24). They had the objective standard articulated by Peter as the basis for praying for this confirmation. Surely there are principles embedded in this passage that point to this whole concept of congregational recognition. Even here the congregation was involved in the process of recognizing in an orderly way God's gift for this vacancy among the apostles.

Principles from Acts 6:1–6

We also find very helpful precedents regarding this matter in Acts 6. The chapter begins with the account of God's blessing in the multiplication of the number of the disciples which apparently included a considerable number of widows. Some of those were Greek-speaking Jews who alleged that they were being neglected in the daily ministry of service to the widows. So the apostles "summoned the full number of the disciples" (Acts 6:2). To see hundreds of women with differing linguistic and cultural biases being completely united is one of the most marvelous indications of a Spirit-filled church.

You have probably been present in meetings where the leaders have laid out a solution for a problem, together with the logic and rationale behind their recommended solution, only to be met with hesitation and objections. There was none of that here. Luke tells us that "the statement found approval with the whole congregation" (Acts 6:5). Nobody rose up with "a better idea." The congregation looked for those men who met the standard set by the apostles. The apostles, as Christ's appointed agents, set this standard as they were led by the Spirit for building the church in those early years. The multitude selected seven men whom they set before the apostles for the final validation of their choice. The apostles then prayed and laid their hands on these men.

Are we far from truth to say that this action of the apostles and laying on of the hands of the apostles did not confer any special grace? No, but they undoubtedly prayed that these men would be equipped to fulfill their efforts to meet the need of the widows, thus preserving the God-given priority of preaching. Here again we have some precedents that begin to give us the biblical data concerning this whole idea of congregational involvement in the activity of recognizing men for specific office and function within and on behalf of the church.

Principles from Acts 14:19–23

Three cities where Paul and Barnabas preached were Lystra, Iconium, and Pisidian Antioch. Before returning to Syrian Antioch and the mother church, they passed through those cities to encourage and strengthen the disciples in those places. This passage also says that they *appointed* (v. 23) elders in every church before taking leave of those churches. They prayed with fasting and commended the churches to the Lord. How much can we ascertain concerning the relationship between Paul's part as an official apostle and the involvement of the congregation? Were they just "appointed" or did the congregation appoint, approve, or "vote" for these elders?

In support of the idea that the congregation was involved in this process is the use of the Greek verb *cheirotonéo*, which has the possible meaning: to *choose*, to *elect by raising the hands*, to *vote by stretching out the hand*; or, with the loss of the notion of extending the hand: to *elect*, *appoint*. See the standard lexicons of *Bauer, Arndt, and Gingrich*, and also *Thayer's Greek Lexicon*. The *Greek-English Lexicon of the New Testament Based on Semantic Domains* by Louw and Nida gives the sense as to "choose or select, presumably by a group and possibly by the actual raising of the hand—'to choose, to elect, to select.'" The Greek word is a compound word made up of "hand" and "stretch." The question is whether the word itself and its etymology support this idea of raising the hand. The same word is used in 2 Corinthians 8:19, "and not only that, but he has been appointed by the churches to travel with us as we carry out this act of grace that is being ministered by us, for the glory of the Lord himself and to show our good will." This text is related to Acts 14:23 by virtue of their similar contexts, namely, appointing men either to the office of elder or to a specified function as in the administration of the offering for the poor. These are the only two uses of the word *cheirotonéo* in the New Testament.[2]

John Owen lists five reasons why he believes that the word *cheirotonéo* does not refer to an authoritative imposition of hands on the part of the

---

2. Acts 10:41 is a compound word used in a different context.

apostle but to a recognition on the part of the entire body.[3] In the first place, he says the word literally means to lift up the hands. In the second place, he argues for the Greek practice of people choosing their officers and magistrates by common suffrage. In the third place, he makes the point that 2 Corinthians 8:19 plainly states that a specific man "has been appointed by the churches to travel with us." He draws from this same passage, in the fourth place, that the word later came to be used, we might say, by *extension*, to refer to the act of choosing or appointing, without reference to the way in which the choice was made. However, he makes a convincing case that it would be inconsistent to insert this less than natural meaning into Acts 14:23 because it is inconsistent with the apostles' practice in other instances. Finally, he answers a claim that Acts 14:23, in denoting the act of Paul and Barnabas in appointing, cannot denote an act of the people.

I think that Owen has the most compelling philological treatment of the use of that verb along with the analogy of Scripture to support his case, but the fundamental issue is this. There was, with respect to the men who were placed in that office, an obvious recognition by the church, and the recognition by the men themselves, that they were indeed set apart to this task. This action was from within the churches themselves. Paul did not have a college of pre-approved, pre-hands-laid-on elders, which he deposited in the churches. He had the right as an apostle to do that with Timothy and Titus. That is why I say their office and function is difficult to identify precisely. Paul can say to Timothy, "As I urged you when I was going to Macedonia, remain at Ephesus so that you may charge certain persons not to teach any different doctrine" (1 Tim. 1:3). He can say to Titus, "This is why I left you in Crete, so that you might put what remained into order, and appoint elders in every town as I directed you" (Titus 1:5). However, the Acts 14:23 situation is within the churches themselves. The clear assumption of the text is that those elders appointed for the church were appointed as they were raised up from within the church. It is for this very reason that Paul gives the specific qualifications for the evaluation and recognition of men to be elders in the churches.

Here I want to include another excerpt from the section in John Owen which I earlier recommended:

---

3. John Owen, *The Works of John Owen*, vol. 16 (Edinburgh: The Banner of Truth Trust, 1968), 60–63. I have inserted a lengthy part of his treatment in Unit 7 on the eldership, in the last of the three chapters on eldership.

The call of persons unto the pastoral office in the church consists of two parts,—first, *Election;* secondly, *Ordination,* as it is commonly called, or sacred separation by fasting and prayer. As unto the former, four things must be inquired into:—I. What is *previous* unto it, or preparatory for it; II. *Wherein* it doth consist; III. Its *necessity,* or the demonstration of its truth and institution; IV. What influence it hath into *the communication of pastoral office-power* unto a pastor so chosen.

I. That which is previous unto it is the *meetness* of the person for his office and work that is to be chosen. It can never be the duty of the church to call or choose an unmeet, an unqualified, an unprepared person unto this office. No pretended necessity, no outward motives, can enable or warrant it so to do; nor can it by any outward act, whatever the rule or solemnity of it be, communicate ministerial authority unto persons utterly unqualified for and incapable of the discharge of the pastoral office according to the rule of the Scripture. And this has been one great means of debasing the ministry and of almost ruining the church itself, either by the neglect of those who suppose themselves intrusted with the whole power of ordination, or by impositions on them by secular power and patrons of livings, as they are called, with the stated regulation of their proceedings herein by a defective law, whence there hath not been a due regard unto the antecedent preparatory qualifications of those who are called unto the ministry.

Two ways is the meetness of any one made known and to be judged of:—1. By *an evidence* given of the qualifications in him before mentioned. The church is not to call or choose any one to office who is not known unto them, of whose frame of spirit and walking they have not had some experience; not a novice, or one lately come unto them.[4]

What would Owen think of men coming to "candidate" preaching two trial sermons, having two meetings with the elders, the session, or the consistory, and then calling a congregational meeting in order to discern if a certain percentage of the members desire to extend to this man a call to become their pastor? Surely he would throw up his hands and say, "I cannot believe it, that a people would submit themselves to the spiritual guidance and oversight and shepherding of a man so little known!"

He must be one who by his ways and walking hath obtained a good report, even among them that are without, so far as he is known, unless

---

4. John Owen, *The Works of John Owen,* vol. 16 (Edinburgh: The Banner of Truth Trust, 1968), 54.

they be enemies or scoffers; and one that hath in some good measure evidenced his faith, love, and obedience unto Jesus Christ in the church. This is the chief trust that the Lord Christ hath committed unto his churches; and if they are negligent herein, or if at all adventures they will impose an officer in his house upon him without satisfaction of his meetness upon due inquiry, it is a great dishonour unto him and provocation of him. Herein principally are churches made the overseers of their own purity and edification. To deny them an ability of a right judgment herein, or a liberty for the use and exercise of it, is error and tyranny. But that flock which Christ purchased and purified with his own blood is thought by some to be little better than a herd of brute beasts. Where there is a defect of this personal knowledge, from want of opportunity, it may be supplied by testimonies of unquestionable authority. 2. By *a trial of his gifts for edification.* These are those spiritual endowments which the Lord Christ grants and the Holy Spirit works in the minds of men, for this very end that the church may be profited by them, 1 Cor. 12:7–11. And we must at present take it for granted that every true church of Christ, that is so in the matter and form of it, is able to judge in some competent measure what gifts of men are suited unto their own edification. But yet, in making a judgment hereof, one *directive means* is the advice of other elders and churches; which they are obliged to make use of by virtue of the communion of churches, and for the avoidance of offence in their walk in that communion.[5]

What he is saying is that you may not have the opportunity to have months or years of exposure to an aspiring elder. However, you ought to seek and obtain the testimony of those who are discerning and have had that exposure. There was a practice among biblical apostolic churches of composing letters of commendation, not only for ordinary believers, but apparently for itinerant ministers as well. So, Paul asks, "Are we beginning to commend ourselves again? Or do we need, as some do, letters of recommendation to you, or from you?" (2 Cor. 3:1). The assumption is that some do need such letters, and they ought to be sought and be given weight in a congregational assessment of a man's graces and gifts. Owen is recognizing the fact that a given church may be able to acquire an understanding and knowledge of a man as to his gifts and graces in some other way besides a lengthy personal exposure.

---

5. John Owen, *The Works of John Owen*, vol. 16 (Edinburgh: The Banner of Truth Trust, 1968), 55.

Unquestionably, two well-preached sermons do not provide enough evidence that a man would be a competent pastor. I can remember some young men who were what I called "four-sermon wonders." The first time such a man preached you would think that God had raised up Whitefield, Spurgeon, and a little bit of Edwards and rolled them all up into one. Upon his first effort, the hearers said, "This seems too good to be true." The second time also, and maybe a third time—but after the fourth time it became obvious that there was not much left to be able to feed the flock of God, week in and week out, and year in and year out, for the foreseeable future. The practice of having a man preach a few trial sermons without some other knowledge of his gifts and his character is dangerous business, not only to the church, but to the man himself. He may have a totally distorted view of who he is, and how well he is or is not suited to be a gift of Christ to a church, until there is some sufficient interaction for the church to make a valid judgment about his gifts and graces. We could go on and quote much more from Owen but I trust that you will carefully read volume sixteen.[6]

I return to making my case for this concept that the crowning validation of a man's call to the pastoral office comes when there is a recognition and installation by a specific congregation.

Principles from Acts 20:13–38

In Acts 20 we have the record of Paul gathering together the elders of the church at Ephesus. He reviews the manner of his own labors among them from the first day he set his foot in their midst, and then he charges them with these solemn words, "Pay careful attention to yourselves and to all the flock, in which the Holy Spirit has made you overseers, to care for the church of God, which he obtained with his own blood" (Acts 20:28). Here Paul is emphasizing that they are overseers in particular churches. We see the same emphasis in Titus 1:5, "This is why I left you in Crete, so that you might put what remained into order, and appoint elders in every town as I directed you." Where there is an assembly of God's people in a given city or town, there, in that place and context, elders are to be appointed.

Now, this has some very crucial implications. I was struck the first time I came across an article by Robert J. Breckenridge in which it became very evident that he was greatly discouraged. In his time there were apparently

---

6. John Owen, *The Works of John Owen*, vol. 16 (Edinburgh: The Banner of Truth Trust, 1968), 51–74.

a considerable number of "Reverends" around in the Southern Presbyterian Church who were not shepherds of specific flocks, and this greatly disturbed him:

> There is a very great difficulty in proving that any *ordinary* office bearer in the church of Christ can be lawfully or even validly ordained at all—without he [sic] is ordained in a determinate office; and the only ground upon which the ordination of Evangelists can be justified, is that their office is an *extraordinary* one—But it is clear that the getting of this office as *extraordinary*, and then using it not at all, but in place of it using the *ordinary* office of a Minister of the word—is either a piece of rash and inconsiderate ignorance, or else is mere fraud and covenant breaking—and so is both void in law, and punishable besides as an immorality.[7]

Apparently there was a system in which a man that was not called to a specific church, but passed some elementary test of competence, was named an "evangelist," so that he could become an officially recognized minister. Breckenridge looked around with concern. We have all these "evangelists" around that are undermining the biblical concept of what it is to be a shepherd recognized by a specific congregation. He added:

> As to the validity of ordination to the ordinary office of Bishop, Pastor, or Minister of the word, without designations to any particular church: consider (1) That the thing is utterly unwarranted by precept or example, in the Word of God—and is contrary to the constant practice of the Apostles (Acts xiv. 23, xx. 28, Titus i. 5, Rev. ii. 3). (2) It was absolutely forbidden in the ancient church: the Council of Chalcedon pronounced all such ordinations invalid; and the Council of Ephesus even decreed that a real Bishop could be considered entitled to the name, title, and honor of one only by courtesy—but not at all to any office power, except as he stood related to some particular charge. (3) The election of the people is an absolute and indispensable element, of collation to office power; and therefore, without this an ordination to such power, is strictly invalid. (4) Every term, Bishop, Pastor, Elder—by which the ordained person is designated, is a relative term—and therefore to use them of one who has no church, people, or flock, implies, as *John Owen* well notes, as real a contradiction and impossibility, as

---

7. Robert J. Breckenridge, "The Christian Pastor, One of Christ's Ascension Gifts," in *The Southern Presbyterian Review* 35:3 (July 1884), 470–472. Accessed 13 Feb 2017 at www.pcahistory.org/HCLibrary/periodicals/spr/v35/35-3-5.pdf.

to make him a father who has no child, or him a husband who has no wife. (5) It is wholly inconsistent with the whole office, duty, and work of the ordinary ministry of the word—every part of which, and especially the whole power of rule—supposes a state of case the opposite of that supposed when a man is ordained *sine titulo* and at large, without any to rule over or amongst—or to care for, feed, and edify: especially is the thing absurd and unscriptural of such as are thus ordained in the immediate view and intention of secular offices and employments—agencies, professorships, etc.—which one could perform as well without as with ordination, and which he cannot perform and at the same time discharge his proper work, to any particular flock. The whole thing is manifestly repugnant to the fundamental principles of Presbyterian church order; and is in a high degree dangerous to the church.[8]

So I say that this is not just a persuasion of people of independent ecclesiology. It is a matter of whether or not the Scripture in its total witness allows us to think, "Once a pastor, always a pastor."

Early in the history of what is now Trinity Baptist Church of Montville, New Jersey, Mr. Don Dickson and I were recognized as gifts of Christ to the church. For thirty years Don Dickson served with me in the eldership. He was a noble man, a man of great discretion and wisdom, the model of what some would call a "lay elder," or as is more popular in our day, a "non-vocational" elder. He was a few years my senior in age. Providentially, he developed serious health problems. For a number of reasons, he became persuaded he could no longer do the work of a pastor and so he relinquished his office. The day he relinquished his office, out of respect for his person and his age, people referred to him as Pastor or Mr. Dickson. However, it was made clear to the congregation that the title Pastor was now being used without any notion that he still retained the office and function of an overseer in Trinity Baptist Church. There was no longer a flock of sheep for whom he had God-given, specific, solemn responsibilities and distinct pastoral responsibilities.

He continued to be an ideal church member, ministering one-on-one as a brother to needy brothers and sisters. He never caused the remaining pastors one millisecond of a headache by intruding his opinions as though

---

8. Robert J. Breckenridge, "The Christian Pastor, One of Christ's Ascension Gifts," in *The Southern Presbyterian Review* 35:3 (July 1884), 470–472. Archived at http:/www.pcahistory.org/periodicals/spr/v35/35-3-5.pdf.

he were still a functioning elder. If ever we needed to tap in to the pool of his wisdom, and his knowledge of the life of the church from its inception, he was more than willing to sit down with us, and to let us pick his brain, to get his insights, but he had relinquished the office before God. In his spirit, and in all of his actions, he was graciously functioning as an ordinary member of the church.

I relinquished my office as an elder in Trinity Baptist Church on June 15, 2008 after serving forty-six years in that capacity. Since then I have sought to follow the good example set for me by my fellow-elder, Don. Since grace does not war with nature, it would have been unnatural to force people to whom I had been one of their pastors for decades to address me in any other way than as Pastor Martin. However, the church has recognized that I do not retain the responsibilities or privileges of being one of their elders. Occasionally, the present elders in Trinity Baptist Church may refer someone in the congregation to seek my counsel on a specific issue. However, the elders and I worked out a very simple formula prior to my leaving for my present home in western Michigan. The formula, simply stated, is this: In relinquishing my office as an elder in the church, I was relinquishing all right of access to the internal workings of the church. The leadership of the church had an unqualified right of access to seek my counsel and input whenever they deemed such counsel would be helpful to them. Eight years have now passed since that major transition in my life, during which time there has not been a moment of tension or misunderstanding in the relationship between me and the existing leadership of the church in New Jersey. They still invite me to have a part in the annual Trinity Pastors' Conference. By their choice, the leadership and the members still address me as Pastor Martin while fully understanding that I sustain no official pastoral relationship to them.

If indeed this axiom is true, that the crowning validation of a man's call to the pastoral office is effected when a specific congregation, objectively assessing a man's graces and gifts and acting by the authority of Christ, does by its suffrage acknowledge that man as a gift of Christ to them, leading to his formal ordination and installation to that office in that specific congregation, then we must not think in terms of the perpetuation of the office apart from a specific congregation. Shepherds are shepherds to specific flocks of God. This principle is clearly underscored by Acts 20:28, in which it is the elders of the church in Ephesus who are charged to take care of the flock in which they were made overseers. A similar emphasis is highlighted by Peter's

words to the elders in the churches of Asia Minor, in which he charges them
to shepherd the flock of God which is among them (1 Pet. 5:2).

Another implication of this axiom is that a man with all the other necessary prerequisite qualifications must still wait upon God for the open door
for this crowning and final validation of his call.

Thornwell obviously shared this conviction. In his review of the sermon
by Dr. Breckenridge, he writes:

> The testimony of conscience, however, is not final and conclusive. We
> may deceive ourselves as well as be deceived by others; and to fortify
> our hearts and diminish the dangers of deception, God has appointed
> the approbation of His own people and the concurrence of the courts
> of His house as additional links in the chain of evidence, which, in all
> ordinary cases, is to authenticate a call from Him.
>
> But beyond all controversy, the saints are the best of all judges
> whether the ministrations on which they wait fructify them or not....
> He who cannot, in the work of the ministry, edify the body of Christ,
> cannot be called of God to that ministry. But, surely, the Church must
> define for itself whether or not it is edified by the ministrations offered
> to it. Its decision, therefore, is conclusive, so far as the case depends on
> its call.[9]

There is a wonderful example of the outworking of this axiom in the history of John Newton, the converted slave trader. He was asked by someone
about this issue of a call to the ministry and how a man could know whether
or not God was calling him. In answering this man, Newton set before him
three principles. Here is the last principle:

> That which finally evidences a proper call is a correspondent opening
> in Providence, by a gradual train of circumstances pointing out the
> means, the time, the place, of actually entering upon the work. And till
> this coincidence arrives, you must not expect to be always clear from
> hesitation in your own mind. The principal caution on this head is, not
> to be too hasty in catching at first appearances. If it be the Lord's will
> to bring you into his ministry, he has already appointed your place and
> service; and though you know it not at present, you shall at a proper
> time. If you had the talents of an angel, you should do no good with

---

9. James Henley Thornwell, *Collected Writings*, vol. 4 (Richmond: Presbyterian Committee of Publication, 1873), 35. Thornwell then distills his argument in this pungent sentence:
"The ordinary form in which the approbation of the Christian people is to be manifested is
through the call of some particular congregation" (p. 36).

them till his hour is come, and till he leads you to the people whom he has determined to bless by your means. It is very difficult to restrain ourselves within the bounds of prudence here, when our zeal is warm, a sense of the love of Christ upon our hearts, and a tender compassion for poor sinners is ready to prompt us to break out too soon:—but he that believeth shall not make haste. I was about five years under this constraint: sometimes I thought I must preach, though it was in the streets. I listened to everything that seemed plausible, and to many things that were not so. But the Lord graciously, and as it were insensibly, hedged up my way with thorns; otherwise, if I had been left to my own spirit, I would have put it quite out of my power to have been brought into such a sphere of usefulness, as he in his good time has been pleased to lead me to. And I can now see clearly, that at the time I would first have gone out, though my intention was, I hope, good in the main, yet I over-rated myself, and had not that spiritual judgement and experience which are requisite for so great a service. I wish you therefore to take time; and if you have a desire to enter into the Established Church, endeavour to keep your zeal within moderate bounds, and avoid everything that might unnecessarily clog your admission with difficulties. I would not have you hide your profession, or to be backward to speak for God; but avoid what looks like preaching, and be content with being a learner in the school of Christ for some years. The delay will not be lost time; you will be so much the more acquainted with the Gospel, with your own heart, and with human nature; the last is a necessary branch of a minister's knowledge, and can only be acquired by comparing what passes within us, and around us, with what we read in the word of God.[10]

During the years that I spent in an itinerant ministry, I saw more and more how far evangelical churches were from respecting and implementing the norms of Scripture in many things, from the clear qualifications for church officers, to the nature of God-honoring worship. More and more, a vision was being born in my heart of what the church ought to be, and what it could be with the blessing of God. However, when I would share these issues with experienced pastors in mainline evangelical churches, they would treat me like a Joseph with his naughty dreams. In some cases, I could not persuade pastors to set aside time to pray with me for their people while I was among them to minister to those people. When those who did meet with me began to open their hearts, often they would complain, "Oh brother,

---

10. John Newton, *Select Letters of John Newton* (Edinburgh: The Banner of Truth Trust, 1960), 55, 56.

my deacons' meetings!" Most of those churches had the traditional Baptist or independent structure of one pastor with deacons who, in some cases functioned more or less as elders. Others were Presbyterian churches with elders who often function more like deacons or trustees. Pastors would say things like, "Oh brother, what a headache! If you ever get to the pastorate, I tell you, you will find out soon enough. Brother, your biggest headaches will come from your deacons, your board members, and your elders." When I read the scriptures I thought "Lord, this should not be. If men meet the biblical standard for these offices, meeting regularly with such men in order to pray, discuss, and engage in the many activities of the work ought to be the most blessed time of the week." When I would try to share this vision with these men, they would look at me cynically and say, "You'll find out." Few, if any men encouraged me, nor do I remember any man that made an honest attempt to show me that I was misunderstanding my Bible. So this burden began to deepen in me more and more. By His grace and in His good providence, He led me along wonderful paths to blaze a biblical trail in North Caldwell, New Jersey, and the beginning of what would later become Trinity Baptist Church of Montville, New Jersey.[11]

I give you this personal testimony to underscore that this fourth axiom has been so clearly validated in my own experience. I urge you who are this far in the pipeline of believing that perhaps God's hand is upon you for pastoral ministry, do not force your way into a situation that seems to be desirable and resort to saying "I simply cannot hold back any longer." Wait for God's appointment. Either He is going to put you in a place where you will be duly commissioned as a church planter with a view to possibly becoming its biblically recognized elder, or He will put you in a church that is already established. Christ knows those who will be your sheep by name, for they are His sheep, and He is preparing and suiting you to shepherd that individual flock which He has purchased with His own blood.

As I bring this first unit of our study to a close, I leave you, the reader, with this final exhortation and earnest entreaty. May God grant, that in your thinking through this matter of what constitutes a biblical and orderly call to the pastoral office and function, you will be determined that you will not intrude yourself into the pastoral office. Rather, make a solemn covenant with God that you will not enter upon the pastoral office until your

---

11. You can read the rest of this story in the introductory biographical sketch at the front of this book.

conscience bears witness that you are moved to the task by *sanctified aspirations*, by the *possession of the requisite graces and gifts*, by the *validation of your ecclesiastical associations*, and the *congregational call* of a specific congregation of God's people.

If this is the path you follow in entering upon the pastoral office and ministry, then when you face the inevitable trials, pressures, and discouragements which are part and parcel of all biblical and Spirit-empowered pastoral ministry, you will be able to say, "O Lord Jesus, I did not put myself here. You put me here. This is not a demand on my frail humanity, but a demand on Your grace." He who did not spare His own Son will indeed freely give you all things (Rom. 8:32) necessary to persevere in your pastoral labors, remembering that precious promise given by Christ to faithful pastors through the apostle Peter, "and when the chief Shepherd appears, you will receive the unfading crown of glory (1 Pet. 5:4).

> Our Father, we gather up all the strands of the things we have thought and felt in these days together and thank You for answering our prayers and doing exceeding abundantly above what we could have asked or thought. Thank You for each of the men whom You have gathered for these lectures. Thank You for the sense of Your help and presence as we have wrestled with the call to the pastoral office. We pray that Your blessing would rest on men who will read these chapters in the future. We pray that more and more our thinking, our practice, our personal assessment and decisions, will be hammered out on the anvil of Your Word, and that You, by Your Spirit, will equip us then to run in the way of Your commandments, and fulfill our ministries according to Your design. May not one of us become wreckage along the road, but may we persevere by Your grace and be found at last standing before our Lord Jesus and hearing the words, "*Well done, good and faithful servant*." We ask in His name, and to the praise of the glory of His grace. Amen.

UNIT TWO

The Life of the Man of God

CHAPTER 1

The Life of the Man of God in the Pastoral Office

In Unit 1 I addressed the subject of *the call of the man of God to the pastoral office*. We are now assuming that a man has satisfied his and his church's conscience that he has a biblical and orderly call to the pastoral office. Now in this second unit, we will focus our attention on *the life of the man of God in the pastoral office*.

Our fundamental assertion is that *sustained effectiveness in pastoral ministry is generally realized in proportion to the health and vigor of the pastor in his relationship to God, the church, himself, the management of his time and manifold responsibilities, and his family.*

The Foundational Axiom Stated

There is a foundational axiom to all that we should think and say about the life of the man of God. It is that *a sustained effectiveness in pastoral ministry will generally be realized in direct proportion to the health and vigor of the redeemed humanity of the man of God.*

I am not referring simply to his spiritual health, nor to his intellectual or physical vigor, but to the health and vigor of the whole of his redeemed humanity. I offer the following four lines of thought to explain and give biblical support for this axiom.

In the first place, I am referring to a *sustained effectiveness*.

I use the word *effectiveness* to describe a ministry through which God's sovereign purposes are accomplished, a ministry framed by the Word of God and anointed by the Spirit of God. Note well that I am not using the words *success* or *successful*. In our day those words are associated with the secular market where mere human abilities and numbers are praised and rewarded. Paul, however, assigns a servant role to human instruments who are guided by God's sovereign hand and will.

What then is Apollos? What is Paul? Servants through whom you believed, as the Lord assigned to each. I planted, Apollos watered, but God gave the growth. So neither he who plants nor he who waters is anything, but only God who gives the growth (1 Cor. 3:5–7).

This assumes the truth of the words of our Lord, "The wind blows where it wishes, and you hear its sound, but you do not know where it comes from or where it goes. So it is with everyone who is born of the Spirit" (John 3:8).

Note also my use of the word *sustained*. The ministry that is framed by the Word of God and empowered by the Spirit of God should have a constancy and longevity, rather than only a sporadic and truncated usefulness.

In the second place, I have qualified this axiom by use of the word *generally*.

It is usually true that a man's sustained usefulness is directly connected to the health and vigor of his entire redeemed humanity. Observe the care that God shows for Elijah's entire redeemed humanity. After Elijah had faced down hundreds of false prophets and an apostate king, he panics and runs like a scared child from the threats of an idolatrous, painted woman named Jezebel. What was Elijah's need in that crisis? He did not need a rebuke or a kick in his spiritual pants. He needed sleep and food. God wisely and graciously provided those basic human needs, thereby renewing the entirety of Elijah's redeemed humanity for further usefulness in ministry (1 Kings 19).

Scripture and church history make clear, however, that there are exceptions to this general pattern. God sometimes used men who were devoid of saving grace to accomplish His saving purposes in the lives of others. These blatant hypocrites were eventually exposed even though they were very useful and appeared to be successful ministers of the Word.

On the eve of our Lord's death, there was no suspicion that Judas was a betrayer among the other disciples. When our Lord said, "One of you will betray Me," none of the eleven said, "Ah, I knew that Judas was a fraud. He has not had the same power in casting out demons as the rest of us." There is no indication that Judas lacked the gifts or effectiveness that had been evident in those other close followers of the Lord Jesus. To that example of Judas, we can add the familiar words of Jesus,

> Not everyone who says to me, "Lord, Lord," will enter the kingdom of heaven, but the one who does the will of my Father who is in heaven. On that day many will say to me, "Lord, Lord, did we not prophesy in your name, and cast out demons in your name, and do many mighty

works in your name?" And then will I declare to them, "I never knew you; depart from me, you workers of lawlessness" (Matt. 7:21, 22).

Among those who are ultimately banished to eternal perdition are men who have enjoyed successful ministries. All of the sobering exceptions recorded in the New Testament are prefigured in the Old Testament by the disobedience and madness of a prophet to whom God spoke by the mouth of a donkey. The tragic history of Balaam is recorded in Numbers 22–24.

The biblical exceptions to this maxim are confirmed in the experience of any man who has functioned in the pastoral ministry for an extended time. Most pastors will be quick to acknowledge that there are times, despite physical exhaustion or emotional burn-out, or even in spite of being spiritually dried out, that God has sovereignly and graciously used us in some extraordinary manner. All of these are indeed exceptions and thus only underscore the validity of the general principle being asserted.

In the third place, my general axiom is confirmed by scripture's broad assertion that *there should be no disparity between the man of God as a thorough-going Christian and the man of God in his pastoral labors.*

This is the truth that Paul is driving home to Timothy in his first letter to his son in the faith. In the midst of that litany of pastoral responsibilities given to his younger associate, Paul turns to Timothy and says, "Let no one despise you for your youth, but set the believers an example in speech, in conduct, in love, in faith, in purity" (1 Tim. 4:12). Was Timothy to avoid the ordinary liabilities of his relative youthfulness by the use of a forced ministerial bombast? Was he to put on an artificial, authoritarian demeanor, attempting to appear as a man in his sixties when he was probably in his thirties? No. Paul exhorts Timothy to overcome the potential liabilities of his youthfulness by being an example "in speech, in conduct, in love, in faith, in purity." Potential pastoral liabilities should be overcome or neutralized by obvious undeniable Christian character.

Paul gives similar exhortations to Titus in facing the peculiar challenges of church ministry in Crete. In the midst of specific directives given to Titus concerning the church's various gender and age groups, Paul says to him, "Show yourself in all respects to be a model of good works, and in your teaching show integrity, dignity, and sound speech that cannot be condemned, so that an opponent may be put to shame, having nothing evil to say about us" (Titus 2:7, 8).

Paul's foundational demand for elders is that they must be "above reproach" (Titus 1:6). The accompanying specific qualifications then serve as explanations of what is involved in this requirement. Where this divinely mandated congruity of life and message is lacking, we are driven to face the withering words of our Lord regarding religious professionals who "preach, but do not practice" (Matt. 23:3). Jesus acknowledged that the scribes and Pharisees often taught what God had said to Moses, and that when they did this, their teaching was to be obeyed. However, our Lord urges that men must never follow the actual conduct of such teachers.

In the fourth place, my central axiom is supported by *a cause and effect relationship between what a pastor is as a man* and what he *accomplishes as a minister of the Word.*

One of the clearest examples of this cause and effect relationship is reflected in Paul's first letter to the nascent, persecuted church in Thessalonica. Paul is bold to register his confidence that these believers have been chosen by God, not because God had allowed Paul to peek into the roll of the elect hidden away in a distant heavenly vault, but rather because of the manner in which the gospel had come to these people. It came "in power and in the Holy Spirit and with full conviction" (1 Thess. 1:5).

Within this dense combination of theological and pastoral analysis, there is an emphatic statement of this cause and effect relationship between a man's way of life and the effectiveness of his ministry. Paul also wrote in the same verse, "You know what kind of men we proved to be among you" (1 Thess. 1:5). He then connects his manner of life to the initial success of the gospel in Thessalonica and also to their subsequent spiritual progress. He adds, "And you became imitators of us and of the Lord, for you received the word in much affliction, with the joy of the Holy Spirit, so that you became an example to all the believers in Macedonia and in Achaia" (1 Thess. 1:6, 7). Paul makes no effort to explain the mysteries of how the fixed, electing purposes of God are blended with the personal piety of the human communicators of the gospel, but he is clearly asserting that God makes such a connection in accomplishing His saving purposes.

This same intimate connection is made again by Paul when he said,

> You are witnesses, and God also, how holy and righteous and blameless was our conduct toward you believers. For you know how, like a father with his children, we exhorted each one of you and encouraged you

and charged you to walk in a manner worthy of God, who calls you into his own kingdom and glory (1 Thess. 2:10–12).

There are some who read these words of Paul and say, "Well, this borders on a dangerous self-praise. Does not the book of Proverbs tell us to let someone else praise us instead of praising ourselves (Prov. 27:2)? But Paul's language puts his testimony far above self-serving praise. He says that God Himself is witness to "how holy and righteous and blameless was our conduct toward you believers" (1 Thess. 2:10).

Every true servant of God should be able to testify as Paul did in these passages. Furthermore, this living, organic connection between the personal life of a pastor and the fruit of his ministry is profoundly made in a text that has exerted a powerful influence on my own conscience for more than sixty years of ministry. Paul writes to his son in the ministry, "Keep a close watch on yourself and on the teaching. Persist in this, for by so doing you will save both yourself and your hearers" (1 Tim. 4:16). Paul could not lay before Timothy more emphatically this cause and effect relationship between what the servant of God accomplishes in his ministry and the kind of man that he is. Paul is saying, "Timothy, your first and most basic responsibility in ministry is to pay constant, close, and careful attention to the ongoing health and vigor of your own redeemed humanity. God's saving purpose toward you and toward others has a direct connection to this incessant spiritual watchfulness."

Are we to conclude that God's saving purposes are contingent and that they might ultimately fail? Never! But we must conclude that God's certain, saving purposes are linked to His saving work accomplished in the hearts and lives of the men He chooses to use as instruments in that saving purpose. This vital connection which God makes between a man's personal life and the fruit of his ministry is underscored in two passages in Acts, and I wish to conclude the evidence for our major axiom with these texts.

The first text tells us how Barnabas was chosen by the church in Jerusalem to go and make an assessment of God's work in Antioch. Luke writes,

> The report of this came to the ears of the church in Jerusalem, and they sent Barnabas to Antioch. When he came and saw the grace of God, he was glad, and he exhorted them all to remain faithful to the Lord with steadfast purpose, for he was a good man, full of the Holy Spirit and of faith. And a great many people were added to the Lord (Acts 11:22–24).

What Barnabas observed of the work of God and whatever personal contribution he made to the work of God in Antioch are directly connected to his character and experience as a man of God, which is described as good, since he was full of the Holy Spirit and of faith.

The other major passage in which Luke highlights this intimate connection between life and ministry is found in his account of Paul's eloquent address to the Ephesian elders. After describing the substance and manner of his own ministry among the Ephesians, Paul gives the following charge to the elders, "Pay careful attention to yourselves and to all the flock, in which the Holy Spirit has made you overseers, to care for the church of God, which he obtained with his own blood" (Acts 20:28). The order of the two imperatives is significant. These men must first give careful attention to themselves, and only after such proper self-attention can they care for the church of God. A man's life molds his ministry, and the health of his own soul leads to lasting fruit in his ministry.

I trust that each reader of these pages will give careful attention to words of Spurgeon which buttress this axiom. He lectured each Friday to the men who were training for pastoral ministry at the Metropolitan Tabernacle in London. His first lecture, "The Minister's Self-Watch," based on 1 Timothy 4:16, begins:

> EVERY workman knows the necessity of keeping his tools in a good state of repair, for "if the iron be blunt, and he do not whet the edge, then must he put to more strength." If the workman lose the edge from his adze, he knows that there will be a greater draught upon his energies, or his work will be badly done. Michael Angelo, the elect of the fine arts, understood so well the importance of his tools, that he always made his own brushes with his own hands, and in this he gives us an illustration of the God of grace, who with special care fashions for himself all true ministers. It is true that the Lord, like Quintin Matsys in the story of the Antwerp well-cover, can work with the faultiest kind of instrumentality, as he does when he occasionally makes very foolish preaching to be useful in conversion; and he can even work without agents, as he does when he saves men without a preacher at all, applying the Word directly by his Holy Spirit; but we cannot regard God's absolutely sovereign acts as a rule for our action. He may, in his own absoluteness, do as pleases him best, but we must act as his plainer dispensations instruct us; and one of the facts which is clear enough is this, that the Lord usually adapts means to ends, from which the plain lesson is, that we shall be likely to accomplish most when we are in the best spiritual condition; or in other words, we shall usually do our Lord's work best when our gifts and graces are in good order, and we

shall do worst when they are most out of trim. This is a practical truth for our guidance, when the Lord makes exceptions, they do but prove the rule.

We are, in a certain sense, our own tools, and therefore must keep ourselves in order. If I want to preach the gospel, I can only use my own voice; therefore, I must train my vocal powers. I can only think with my own brains, and feel with my own heart, and therefore I must educate my intellectual and emotional faculties. I can only weep and agonize for souls in my own renewed nature, therefore must I watchfully maintain the tenderness which was in Christ Jesus. It will be in vain for me to stock my library, or organize societies, or project schemes, if I neglect the culture of myself; for books, and agencies, and systems, are only remotely the instruments of my holy calling; my own spirit, soul, and body, are my nearest machinery for sacred service; my spiritual faculties, and my inner life, are my battle axe and weapons of war. M'Cheyne, writing to a ministerial friend, who was travelling with a view to perfecting himself in the German tongue, used language identical with our own:—"I know you will apply hard to German, but do not forget the culture of the inner man—I mean of the heart. How diligently the cavalry officer keeps his sabre clean and sharp; every stain he rubs off with the greatest care. Remember you are God's sword, his instrument—I trust, a chosen vessel unto him to bear his name. In great measure, according to the purity and perfection of the instrument, will be the success. It is not great talents God blesses so much as likeness to Jesus. A holy minister is an awful weapon in the hand of God."[1]

In the light of things that many of us have experienced in our own lifetime, we can add to M'Cheyne's statement its converse: *An unholy minister is a tragic weapon in the hand of the devil!*

My brethren, the health and usefulness of your ministry will ordinarily be realized in direct proportion to the health and vigor of your entire redeemed humanity. There are no shortcuts to this spiritual health and pastoral usefulness. The world, and even voices within the church, will seek to offer shorter, more convenient paths to success, but it is what we are before God that determines the character and usefulness of our ministries.

Our Father, we bow before You, the living God who knows us altogether, for Your Word tells us that all are naked and exposed to the eyes

---

1. C. H. Spurgeon, *Lectures to My Students* (Edinburgh: The Banner of Truth Trust, 2008), 1, 2.

of Him to whom we must give account. We know that out of Your perfect knowledge of us You are able to help us to know ourselves. We pray, as we begin to work out this foundational principle that Your Spirit will help us to come to a new and humbling knowledge of ourselves. Above all, we ask that we may be driven to our blessed Lord Jesus, the only perfect Pastor of His sheep. We want to be found fixing our gaze upon Christ, and experiencing what it is to be transformed more and more into His likeness. Seal to our hearts the principles of Your Word. Hear our cry, in the name of our Lord Jesus Christ. Amen.

CHAPTER 2

His Relationship to God Spiritually (1)

We come in this lecture to begin to address the first of five major subdivisions of our subject, namely, *the life of the man of God in relationship to God Himself.* As I introduce this aspect of our study, I want you to consider with me several texts of Scripture that place this concept into sharp relief, convincing us that fundamental to all that we are as men of God in the work of pastoral labor is that which we are as men before our God.

The first is the familiar text wherein Paul exhorts Timothy, "Do your best to present yourself to God as one approved, a worker who has no need to be ashamed, rightly handling the word of truth" (2 Tim. 2:15). By the use of the aorist imperative of that vigorous verb *spoudázo*, which carries in its arms the ideas of giving diligence and making conscious, concentrated endeavor in a given course of action, Paul tells Timothy, with divine authority, to give diligence specifically to presenting himself approved to God. That is to say, the object of his endeavor is that Timothy may present himself as one who has been tried, tested, and approved by God Himself. Now, while the primary emphasis falls in the latter part of the verse upon that approval in conjunction with the public handling of the Word of God, nonetheless, the foundational principle is to touch every facet of Timothy's life. Above all else, he is to be a man who is giving diligent effort to present himself as a minister whom God approves.

In the next passage, we find the apostle giving his testimony about his ministry, "For we are not, like so many, peddlers of God's word, but as men of sincerity, as commissioned by God, in the sight of God we speak in Christ" (2 Cor. 2:17). The immediate context is the act of preaching, but one cannot know that specific dimension of this God-centered perspective in the ministry of the Word of God unless it is the foundational principle of one's life. Paul also says,

> This is how one should regard us, as servants of Christ and stewards of the mysteries of God. Moreover, it is required of stewards that they

be found trustworthy. But with me it is a very small thing that I should be judged by you or by any human court. In fact, I do not even judge myself. For I am not aware of anything against myself, but I am not thereby acquitted. It is the Lord who judges me. Therefore do not pronounce judgment before the time, before the Lord comes, who will bring to light the things now hidden in darkness and will disclose the purposes of the heart. Then each one will receive his commendation from God (1 Cor. 4:1–5).

Here the apostle is exhorting the Corinthians to think rightly about those who claim to be apostles and true messengers of God. No matter what judgment people may render, this passage stresses that the judgment of the Lord is the only judgment that matters in the end. In this context, Paul has a relative indifference to how people view him. What is of supreme and central importance to him is what God knows him to be, not what men judge him to be or even what he judges himself to be. Even though he had no conscious unresolved controversy with God when he wrote to the Corinthians ("I am not aware of anything against myself"), his ultimate concern was what God knew about him. So, as we think of the man of God in his life and relationship to, and before the face of his God, we need to break down this area of our study into these categories: first, what we are as men before God *spiritually,* second, *intellectually,* and third, *physically* and *emotionally.*

As a Man Before God Spiritually

With respect to this first division of what we are before God spiritually, I purpose to set forth the principle or axiom that *we must strive to maintain a real, expanding, varied, and original acquaintance with God and His ways.*

This terminology is not original with me. I came across these words of James Stalker some years ago:

Perhaps of all causes of ministerial failure the commonest lies here; and of all ministerial qualifications, this, although the simplest, is the most trying. Either we have never had a spiritual experience deep and thorough enough to lay bare to us the mysteries of the soul; or our experience is too old, and we have repeated it so often that it has become stale to ourselves; or we have made reading a substitute for thinking; or we have allowed the number and the pressure of the duties of our office to curtail our prayers and shut us out of our studies; or we have learned the professional tone in which things ought to be said, and we can fall into it without present feeling. Power for work like ours is only to be acquired in secret; it is only the man who has a large, varied, and original life with God who can go on speaking about the things of God with fresh interest; but a thousand things happen to interfere with such a prayerful and meditative life. It is not because our arguments for religion are not strong enough that we fail to convince, but because the argument is wanting which never fails to tell; and this is religion itself. People everywhere can appreciate this, and nothing can supply the lack of it. The hearers may not know why their minister, with all his gifts, does not make a religious impression on them; but it is because he is not himself a spiritual power.[1]

Exegeting the Axiom

Let me explain and define the ideas which I have sought to capture in this axiom. I began by using the words *we must strive to maintain*. I am attempting to express two things. I am indicating that we are considering a standard or a goal that is to be set before us consciously and deliberately, and second that the attainment of that standard does not come automatically or easily.

In pursuit of this goal there is an element of the kind of spiritual agony to which Paul makes reference when he compares his own spiritual walk and ministry to the Grecian games. He says,

> Do you not know that in a race all the runners run, but only one receives the prize? So run that you may obtain it. Every athlete exercises self-control in all things. They do it to receive a perishable wreath, but we an imperishable. So I do not run aimlessly; I do not box as one beating the air. But I discipline my body and keep it under control, lest after preaching to others I myself should be disqualified (1 Cor. 9:24–27).

By the terminology *we must strive to maintain*, I am pointing toward a goal or a standard and insisting that it is going to cost us conscious, arduous effort as we pursue that standard.

I also use the words *acquaintance with God and His ways*. The word *acquaintance* is defined as knowledge gotten by personal experience or study of a person or a subject. We read, "Now acquaint yourself with Him, and be at peace; Thereby good will come to you" (Job 22:21 NKJV). The Hebrew word for *acquaint* is exactly the same word as David used when he said, "You search out my path and my lying down and are acquainted with all my ways"

---

1. James Stalker, *The Preacher and His Models* (New York: Hodder and Stoughton, 1891), 54, 55.

(Ps. 139:3). This is knowledge that grows out of God's omniscience, but it is real knowledge of the real man or woman. I am insisting that if we would be the men that we ought to be before God, we must seek this acquaintance with and knowledge of God that grows out of the reality of true dealings with Him. It is knowledge of the living God Himself, Father, Son, and Holy Spirit. It is a knowledge of God that is essentially Trinitarian, not only in its objective theological convictions and confession, but in its actual experience. We are not Deists or Unitarians. We are privileged to experience a distinctive communion with the Father as the Father, a distinctive communion with the Son as the Son, and a distinctive communion with the Holy Spirit as the Holy Spirit—the one God in the mystery and reality of His triune Being.

I have used the word *real* concerning our acquaintance with God and His ways. By this word I mean an acquaintance with God that captures this principle uttered by our Lord, "And this is eternal life, that they know you the only true God, and Jesus Christ whom you have sent" (John 17:3). The opening words of John's first epistle are based on this prayer and support the point I am making. John said,

> That which was from the beginning, which we have heard, which we have seen with our eyes, which we looked upon and have touched with our hands, concerning the word of life—the life was made manifest, and we have seen it, and testify to it and proclaim to you the eternal life, which was with the Father and was made manifest to us—that which we have seen and heard we proclaim also to you, so that you too may have fellowship with us; and indeed our fellowship is with the Father and with his Son Jesus Christ (1 John 1:1–3).

John is speaking here as an apostle, but he wants his readers to know that he is not trafficking in an abstract, barren, notional religion. He and his fellow-apostles had seen Christ, not in passing appearances, but in prolonged observation, with intimate fellowship as real disciples. Their proclamation and ministry flowed from this intimate relationship with Him. I am seeking to underscore that this acquaintance with God is to be real. It is to be one that grows out of touching God with the fingers of the soul, hearing God with the ears of faith, and not in feigned reality or formal and professional ecclesiastical activities and duties.

I love to think of the prophet Elijah who burst onto the stage of decadent Israel with this declaration, "As the LORD, the God of Israel, lives, before whom I stand, there shall be neither dew nor rain these years, except by my word" (1 Kings 17:1). The statement, "As the LORD, the God of Israel, lives," expresses an accurate and objective theological understanding. But when the man of God says, "before whom I stand," these are words of experimental and applied theology. He has a sound theology of God as the LORD God, Yahweh, God of the Covenant, the Almighty One, but He is not only the God about whom the prophet speaks with accurate theological language. He is also the God before whom the prophet stands. With these words, Elijah is asserting that he lives as one conscious of the presence of the God whom he knows, and with whom he experiences an ever-expanding acquaintance.

As glorious and memorable, or as undramatic and almost imperceptible, were our original saving dealings with God and His ways, these dealings will not suffice to sustain a ministry that is marked by the unction of the Spirit of God in a life of growing intimacy and expanding acquaintance with the triune God of the Bible. Let the concept be prominent in your desire for Him. Our expanding acquaintance with God and His ways must not be static and wooden. Paul could write, "And we all, with unveiled face, beholding the glory of the Lord, are being transformed into the same image from one degree of glory to another. For this comes from the Lord who is the Spirit" (2 Cor. 3:18). It is said of our incarnate Lord that "Jesus increased in wisdom and in stature and in favor with God and man" (Luke 2:52). Likewise, as we grow into the likeness of Christ and in our knowledge of Him, there will be an ever-expanding quantity of wisdom, spiritual stature, and favor with God and man in us as well.

We must stand firmly on the things that God has already taught us without believing that we have pushed our knowledge of God to its utmost reaches. Paul's experience contains an excellent paradigm for us to adopt. Having revealed Himself to Saul of Tarsus, the risen Lord went on to say to him, "But rise and stand upon your feet, for I have appeared to you for this purpose, to appoint you as a servant and witness to the things in which you have seen me and to those in which I will appear to you" (Acts 26:16). What could be more glorious than to have the very voice of the risen Christ graciously and powerfully arrest, draw, and commission you in the blinding light of the Shekinah glory? Yet with all that, it is Christ Himself who makes Paul know that there is more to come. Saul will become His witness to the things wherein Christ has already appeared to him, but also to those things in which He will yet appear to him. No wonder then, that as an old man about to finish his course, Paul could say that his great passion was, "that I may know him and the power of his resurrection, and may share his sufferings, becoming like him in his death" (Phil. 3:10). "That you may know Him?

Paul, you were arrested by His voice on the road to Damascus. You already know Him!" Paul says, "Yes, that is true, but I am not satisfied unless my acquaintance with Him is expanding." Even though Paul had an extraordinary experience of being caught up to the third heaven (2 Cor. 12:1–4) where he heard inexpressible words, he still spoke as though he were a neophyte after decades of knowing Christ. What he came to know made him thirsty to know Him more. This is the biblical mindset that I am trying to capture when I speak of an *expanding* acquaintance with God and His ways.

I have added the word *varied* in speaking of our acquaintance with God and His ways. The scriptures clearly indicate that any real acquaintance with God in the midst of the real world of real men and real things, and in dealing with the real issues of sin, grace, a wily devil, and a seductive world, is indeed a varied experience. This is especially emphasized in the book of Psalms. As surely as our joys become more solid, so our griefs become more acute. Take Psalm 23 for example. The psalmist envisions the all-sufficiency of the supply of the Great Shepherd in the quiet waters, where his thirst will be quenched and satisfied. He has been fed and refreshed in the green pastures where he lies down, but he has also known the Shepherd's presence and protection in the dark valley of the shadow of death in the midst of enemies and foes. Within the compass of that very brief psalm, we see David's own statement that true, vital, experiential acquaintance with God is a varied experience.

Stalker captured this biblical truth in a very accurate and helpful way when he wrote:

> A ministry of growing power must be one of growing experience. The soul must be in touch with God and enjoy golden hours of fresh revelation. The truth must come to the minister as the satisfaction of his own needs and the answer to his perplexities; and he must be able to use the language of religion, not as the nearest equivalent he can find for that which he believes others to be passing through, but as the exact equivalent of that which he has passed through himself. There are many rules for praying in public, and a competent minister will not neglect them; but there is one rule worth all the rest put together, and it is this: Be a man of prayer yourself; and then the congregation will feel, as you open your lips to lead their devotions, that you are entering an accustomed presence and speaking to a well-known Friend. There are arts of study by which the contents of the Bible can be made available for the edification of others; but this is the best rule: Study God's Word diligently for your own edification; and then, when it has become more to you than your necessary food and sweeter than honey or the honey-comb,

it will be impossible for you to speak of it to others without a glow passing into your words which will betray the delight with which it has inspired yourself.[2]

The final modifier I have used is that it must be an *original* acquaintance with God and His ways. Remember, the truth that we presently have before us is that *we must strive to maintain a real, expanding, varied, and original acquaintance with God and His ways.* This original acquaintance of the individual of which I am speaking must be understood in the setting of the corporate people of God. The Word of God teaches community and solidarity in the human race. This means that we are individually part of the whole race or body of mankind. Because we live in a society which thrives on crass individualism, we do well to think more in terms of the biblical doctrines that underscore the facts of our solidarity in Adam, our solidarity in Christ, and our solidarity with the one body and church of Christ.

However, the same Bible sets before us a doctrine of the most noble individualism. It is that individualism which extends back to our conception as described in Psalm 139 where David likens his formation in his mother's womb to God's working in a subterranean cavern, ordering the selection in the gene pool and the entirety of the marvelous and mysterious work of prenatal development. It is I who was conceived and woven in my mother's womb (Ps. 139:13), and all of my days are marked out for me in the sovereign plan and purpose of God (Ps. 139:15, 16).

There is a precious individualism in the biblical doctrines of creation and providence. He created us as individuals and He takes care of us individually. There is great comfort in His individual knowledge of us as well. We read these precious words, "But even the hairs of your head are all numbered" (Matt. 10:30). Not only does He know us in this amazing way, but He calls us by name, "The sheep hear his voice, and he calls his own sheep by name and leads them out" (John 10:3). I can be in a crowd of a thousand, but if I hear my name, I understand that somebody knows *me* and is seeking *me*. I am not just one face in the blur of nine hundred ninety-nine other faces. So our acquaintance with God is individual, and therefore intimate, personal, and not *simply* corporate. Recognizing this, we must never lose sight of the corporate aspects of our relationship with God for all that it entails—and it entails much.

---

2. James Stalker, *The Preacher and His Models* (New York: Hodder and Stoughton, 1891), 53, 54.

By using the word *individual*, I do not mean to suggest that we are to seek a kind of experience that no one else has ever known or experienced before. Such desires and claims are the stuff of fanatics, heretics, and men drunk with the heady wine of their own self-importance. I am using the word to express the fact that, as surely as there is only one you and one me, our dealings with God and His ways are not to be a reproduction or a copy of someone else's experience in all of its nuances and in all of its details.

Stalker is once more a helpful teacher when he asserts this:

> The man who is to be God's messenger must himself draw near to God and abide in His secret, as they did. The word must detach itself from the book and become a living element of experience before it can profit even the reader himself; and much more is this the case, of course, before it can profit others. It is the truth which has become a personal conviction, and is burning in a man's heart so that he cannot be silent, which is his message. The number of such truths which a man has appropriated from the Bible and verified in his own experience is the measure of his power. There is all the difference in the world between the man who thus speaks what he knows from an inner impulse and the man whose sermon is simply a literary exercise on a Scripture theme, and who speaks only because Sunday has come round and the bell rung and he must do his duty.[3]

Murphy writes in harmony with Stalker:

> He is to be a leader in the spiritual host of God; must he not go before others in spiritual attainments? To draw men up to a more and more elevated standard of piety and devotedness is the appointment he holds from the great Head of the Church; surely he must himself rise still higher?
>
> It is beyond all question that this eminent piety is before everything else in preparation for the duties of the sacred office. It is before talents, or learning, or study, or favorable circumstances, or skill in working, or power in sermonizing. It is needed to give character and tone and strength to all these, and to every other part of the work. Without this elevated spirituality nothing else will be of much account in producing a permanent and satisfactory ministry. All else will be like erecting a building without a foundation. This is the true foundation upon which to build—the idea which is to give character to all the superstructure.

---

3. James Stalker, *The Preacher and His Models* (New York: Hodder and Stoughton, 1891), 109, 110.

Oh that at the very beginning this could be deeply impressed upon the hearts of young ministers! Oh that they would take and weigh well the testimony of the most devoted and successful of those who have served God in his gospel! A man with this high tone of piety is sure to be a good pastor; without it success in the holy office is not to be expected.

The first thing for the young minister to consider is how he may attain to this high degree of holiness in heart and life. How often do other things occupy the mind! How much more anxiety there generally is about other branches of preparation! But this should be before them all, and at the root of them all, and ever present to give character to them all. As all other believers do, the pastor should strive to be filled with the Holy Ghost, but in view of his holy office he should strive far more earnestly. The one thought should be ever before him: "This is no ordinary profession that I hold; it is something more sacred, more heavenly, more Christ-like than the common callings of men, and therefore I must be more holy." There is no part of the training for the gospel ministry which requires so earnest and constant attention as that which pertains to the personal piety of those who are called to its duties.

We dwell long and minutely upon this branch of our subject because of its superlative importance. There is no other point in the whole subject that needs to be so thoroughly impressed as this. It must not be overshadowed by the consideration of other things, even though they too are necessary in preparing for the practical duties of the minister. We would have it so conspicuous and so deeply impressed on the heart and conscience that it may give complexion to all our other studies on this subject. This self-culture—culture of personal piety—is a branch of pastoral theology, and a most important one. It is especially noticed among the inspired rules laid down for the conduct of the minister. "Take heed unto thyself" is definitely commanded. The pastor's own heart is the place in which the work must begin. His closet is the armory in which he must equip himself for the service that may require great hardness. It is the mount where he may tarry in the presence of God, and thence come down with glory beaming in his face. It is the upper room in which he may commune with Christ and obtain that burning love that will ever sweetly constrain. It is the mercy-seat, made so by the divine presence, where the Holy Spirit may overshadow him and imbue him with a wisdom and a might that will be irresistible. It is the secret place in which he may find his God, and then go out fortified to a work from which he might otherwise well shrink, saying, "Who is sufficient for these things?"[4]

Vital Means for Attaining this Acquaintance with God and His Ways

Our next task will be to focus our minds upon those means which God has ordained by which to seek this real, expanding, varied, and original acquaintance with God and His ways. Before we do this, I believe it is critical to consider several things concerning these means, and then, in the next lecture, to begin to identify those means individually.

First, the means are *integrated and interdependent.*

Although each discipline will of necessity be addressed separately, each one is a recognizable spiritual activity which differs from the others. If one of them is abandoned, the others will lose their usefulness, even if their form and activity are maintained. When we consider these three major means that I will shortly set before you (devotional assimilation of the Word of God, the habit and spirit of secret prayer, and the maintenance of a good conscience), each of them will be seen to be a separate, identifiable spiritual discipline. However, though we treat them individually and we experience them individually, they are integrated and interdependent.

There is a helpful analogy with good physical health. Barring deformity, terminal illness, or serious accident, the three keys to good health are diet, rest, and exercise. Each of the three is an identifiable entity. My diet is not my exercise; my rest is not my diet. However, they are so integrated, that letting one of them go will inevitably cause a debilitating effect upon the others. They are interrelated and integrated, and all are essential in the normal course of things for the maintenance of good health. If one is totally disregarded or carelessly managed, it can neutralize all the benefits of having our act together in the other two. It is likewise with the disciplines by which we maintain this varied, real, and expanding acquaintance with God and His ways.

Second, these means are all *basic and foundational.*

It has been accurately stated, in addressing some of these very issues, that the Christian walk is won or lost in the battle of the basics. The believer (and here I emphasize *the man of God*) is such that he succeeds or falls in the trenches of the fundamentals. Little did I think as a seventeen-year-old

---

4. Thomas Murphy, *Pastoral Theology* (Audubon, NJ: Old Paths Publications, 1996), 38–40.

kid just out of the womb spiritually, when my great battle was maintaining consistent devotional exercises in the face of many pressures, that more than sixty years later that same battle would be engaged every single morning of my life. That has been the reality however.

Third, these means are *ultimately useful only because of their divinely ordained function in enabling us to draw upon the fullness of life and grace that is in our Lord Jesus Christ.*

Paul knew this in his own experience because he regarded Christ as the very source and sustenance of his spiritual life. We read, "When Christ who is your life appears, then you also will appear with him in glory" (Col. 3:4). We also find, "I have been crucified with Christ. It is no longer I who live, but Christ who lives in me. And the life I now live in the flesh I live by faith in the Son of God, who loved me and gave himself for me" (Gal. 2:20).

The basis of Paul's experience is what Jesus said about Himself in two Johannine discourses. In that marvelous discourse of Christ as the Bread of Life, the Lord Jesus speaks in terms of present tense spiritual activity when He says,

> Truly, truly, I say to you, unless you eat the flesh of the Son of Man and drink his blood, you have no life in you. Whoever feeds on my flesh and drinks my blood has eternal life, and I will raise him up on the last day. For my flesh is true food, and my blood is true drink. Whoever feeds on my flesh and drinks my blood abides in me, and I in him. As the living Father sent me, and I live because of the Father, so whoever feeds on me, he also will live because of me. This is the bread that came down from heaven, not like the bread the fathers ate and died. Whoever feeds on this bread will live forever (John 6:53–58).

Our spiritual life exists by a constant feeding upon Christ and the life that is in Him, particularly as the Crucified One.

He taught the same truth by use of a different analogy when He said,

> I am the true vine, and my Father is the vinedresser. Every branch in me that does not bear fruit he takes away, and every branch that does bear fruit he prunes, that it may bear more fruit. Already you are clean because of the word that I have spoken to you. Abide in me, and I in you. As the branch cannot bear fruit by itself, unless it abides in the vine, neither can you, unless you abide in me. I am the vine; you are the branches. Whoever abides in me and I in him, he it is that bears much fruit, for apart from me you can do nothing (John 15:1–5).

Eating and abiding, the two basic analogies of these discourses, are used by our Lord to point us to the fullness of life and grace which are in Him.

Christ is our life, not the Bible detached from real communion with Christ Himself. All of the disciplines which I will shortly address are God's appointed conduits by which the very life that is in Christ is communicated to us by the Person and ministry of the Holy Spirit. To expect the sustaining of spiritual life without these means is to tempt God and to despise His wisdom. He has said that by these means He will communicate the life of His Son into our souls. However, to use these means without constantly tracing them up to their source of life in Christ, being earnestly prayerful that they may be effectual in the deepening and increased communion with Christ Himself, is to be guilty of idolatry and a form of sacramentalism. By this I refer to thinking that virtue is in the act itself and will automatically be conveyed to us through that act or discipline.

I have sought to demonstrate that these means are integrated, interdependent, basic, and foundational. They are means by which our communion with Christ Himself is to be nurtured and developed.

The ordinary context within which we cultivate this real, growing, expanding, original life with God, for God's people in general, and especially for God's servants in particular, is one of suffering, tribulation, affliction, temptation, and opposition.

Consider what Octavius Winslow says about this:

> We verily believe that no Christian is thoroughly versed in the evidences of the truth of the Bible, or is in a right position to understand its divine contents, until he is afflicted. Luther remarks that he never understood the Psalms until God afflicted him. Fly to the Word of God, then, in every sorrow. You will know more of the mind and heart of God than you, perhaps, ever learned in all the schools before. We must be *experimental* Christians, if Christians at all. A bare notionalist, a mere theorist, an empty professor of religion, is a fearful deception. Study to know God's Word from a heartfelt experience of its quickening, sanctifying, comforting power. Sit not at the feet of men, but at the feet of Jesus. His Word can alone instruct you in these sacred and precious truths. You must learn in Christ's school, and be taught by the Holy Spirit. And if you are truly converted, spiritually regenerated, a real believer in the Lord Jesus, think not that some strange thing has happened to you when the Lord causes you to pass under the rod of discipline, brings you into trial, and makes you to partake of what may seem to you a soul-diet anything but healthful and nutritious,—"the

bread of adversity, and the water of affliction." (Isa. xxx. 20.) But affliction is one of the Lord's moulds for shaping you into an *experimental* Christian. And to be an experimental Christian His word must be inwrought into our soul. What can we know of the promises, the succourings, the sympathy of God's Word,—its perfect adaptation to the crushed and sorrowful condition of our humanity,—but for trial? Thus, more than one-half of the Bible is a "garden inclosed, a spring shut up, a fountain sealed," until the Lord lays sorrow upon our hearts, and brings us into circumstances of adversity. *Then* this garden unveils its beauty, and this spring pours forth its refreshment, and this fountain overflows with its rich and varied supply. Oh, with what power, depth, and sweetness does the Word of God unfold to us then! It is as though a new book had been composed,—another constellation in the spiritual hemisphere had burst upon the telescope of faith,—another Arcadia had floated into view,—a new world had been discovered! "Blessed is the man whom Thou chastenest, O Lord, and teachest him out of Thy law." "Unless Thy law had been my delight, I should then have perished in my affliction." Draw then, O child of sorrow, your consolation from God's Word. Put it not away as if it were for others, and not for you.[5]

I close this lecture by setting before you a specimen of texts which give scriptural proof that, generically, it is in the context of affliction and difficulty that the people of God are on their way to heaven and to the Kingdom in its glorious consummate form. This is the context in which the servants of God will cultivate their knowledge of and acquaintance with God.

In the first text we read,

> When they had preached the gospel to that city and had made many disciples, they returned to Lystra and to Iconium and to Antioch, strengthening the souls of the disciples, encouraging them to continue in the faith, and saying that through many tribulations we must enter the kingdom of God (Acts 14:21, 22).

I never cease to be amazed every time I come to that portion in Acts where Paul, in his initial follow-up of the infant churches, having so much to teach the people of God, urged this truth upon these young converts, that through many tribulations they must enter the Kingdom of God. Where did Paul get this truth? Apostolic truth is based on the teachings of Christ.

---

5. Octavius Winslow, *The Precious Things of God* (Ligonier, PA: Soli Deo Gloria Publications, 1993), 270–273.

Jesus taught in the Sermon on the Mount that "blessed are those who are persecuted for righteousness' sake, for theirs is the kingdom of heaven" (Matt. 5:10). Just as our Lord assumes that all of the true subjects of the Kingdom will be marked by poverty of spirit, holy mourning, meekness, hunger and thirst, a peacemaking disposition, etc., so He assumes that this kind of Kingdom lifestyle in a wicked world is going to produce its pressure, opposition, and hostility. Just before His death, He taught His disciples that "In the world you will have tribulation" (John 16:33). He was talking about pressured circumstances that drive you out of yourself and into your God.

I have been struck by just how many verses in Psalm 119 celebrate the blessing of affliction in which the psalmist came to know his God in ways he never knew Him before. For example, "It is good for me that I was afflicted, that I might learn your statutes" (Ps. 119:71). The clear implication here is that many of the statutes are locked to us until the key of affliction unlocks them.

Another passage that has been my meat and drink in various afflictions is,

> "My son, do not regard lightly the discipline of the Lord, nor be weary when reproved by him. For the Lord disciplines the one he loves, and chastises every son whom he receives." It is for discipline that you have to endure. God is treating you as sons. For what son is there whom his father does not discipline? If you are left without discipline, in which all have participated, then you are illegitimate children and not sons (Heb. 12:5–8).

God's purpose in this filial discipline is a growing, expanding conformity to His Son increasingly manifested in us.

Paul writes to the Corinthians,

> For we do not want you to be ignorant, brothers, of the affliction we experienced in Asia. For we were so utterly burdened beyond our strength that we despaired of life itself. Indeed, we felt that we had received the sentence of death. But that was to make us rely not on ourselves but on God who raises the dead (2 Cor. 1:8, 9).

Paul was enabled to respond to these trials because his God is the God

> who comforts us in all our affliction, so that we may be able to comfort those who are in any affliction, with the comfort with which we ourselves are comforted by God. For as we share abundantly in Christ's sufferings, so through Christ we share abundantly in comfort too. If we are afflicted, it is for your comfort and salvation; and if we are

comforted, it is for your comfort, which you experience when you patiently endure the same sufferings that we suffer (2 Cor. 1:4–6).

God keeps us in the crucible of affliction and suffering so that we might experientially know dimensions of His grace, to the end that those new dimensions will flower out and touch others, leading to blessing for them as we minister to them. James echoes this theme, "Count it all joy, my brothers, when you meet trials of various kinds, for you know that the testing of your faith produces steadfastness. And let steadfastness have its full effect, that you may be perfect and complete, lacking in nothing" (Jas. 1:2–4).

Here is a text that is most humbling for me, "Although he was a son, he learned obedience through what he suffered. And being made perfect, he became the source of eternal salvation to all who obey him" (Heb. 5:8, 9). At the level of His felt experiential relationship to God His Father, the holy, sinless, guileless Son of God had to learn what obedience was as a principle of life, and this could only be learned in the midst of suffering. Since this is true, how do we think that we are going to learn it in any other way than in the same crucible?

As we think in the next lecture about the means by which this expanding, real, varied, original life with God is to be experienced, let us face the fact that the ordinary context for the fruitfulness of these means is indeed the context of affliction, suffering, opposition, tribulation, and temptation. My dear brother, do not expect that God will exempt you from this context. God purposes that you are to exercise a ministry that touches His people where they are. Why would you want any other kind of ministry? When you crave such a ministry with understanding about His ways of producing it, then you will be saying, "Bring it on Lord; bring it on!" When I hear men pray, "O God, I want an enlarged ministry," I almost want to say, "Quiet! You know not what you ask." Then I want to go on and tell them that if they ever will have a Spirit-empowered ministry, God is going to enlarge their capacity to feel and enter into treasures of God's Word that are only unlocked in fiery personal trials.

So my brothers, I am not trying to discourage you. I am encouraging you to believe, as God has laid His hand upon you and confirmed your calling to your office and function in your own conscience and the consciences of His people, that you are not going to be exempt from that ordinary context in which these God-ordained means become fruitful with God's blessing to our attaining this expanding, varied, original acquaintance with God and His ways. May God by His grace grant that it shall be true.

CHAPTER 3

His Relationship to God Spiritually (2)

So far, we have "exegeted" the axiom, which is that *you must strive to maintain a real, expanding, varied, and original acquaintance with God and His ways*. Now we come to the first of three means to attain that end.

The Devotional Assimilation of the Word of God

The first of these means is *the discipline of the devotional assimilation of the Word of God*.

It is not my purpose to prove by the careful exegesis of many texts that there does indeed exist a profound relationship between spiritual health and the assimilation of the scriptures. The opening words of the psalter alone would suffice to prove the point,

> Blessed is the man who walks not in the counsel of the wicked, nor stands in the way of sinners, nor sits in the seat of scoffers; but his delight is in the law of the LORD, and on his law he meditates day and night. He is like a tree planted by streams of water that yields its fruit in its season, and its leaf does not wither. In all that he does, he prospers (Ps. 1:1–3).

There is a summary statement by Thomas Murphy in his *Pastoral Theology* that states this issue in a most compelling way:

> This is a very important duty for every Christian. The word is the great instrument by which the Spirit increases holiness in the hearts of believers. It is by faith in that word that men are ordained to be sanctified. Christ teaches the necessity of the truth when, in his great intercessory prayer, he made sure of its efficacy by the petition, "Sanctify them through thy truth; thy Word is truth." The Spirit will honor his own truth, and will make it effectual. It is by Christ, the Bread of life, that the soul is to be nourished; and Christ is to be found chiefly in the Scriptures. From the Scriptures come light, and heat, and strength, and

impulse, all of which are important elements of true godliness in the soul. Not only to the young man, but to all who ask a similar question, "Wherewithal shall a young man cleanse his way?" comes the inspired answer, "By taking heed thereto according to thy word." Oh how the devout study and personal application of the Scriptures enrich the soul! A simple passage devoutly meditated upon makes the heart better. Then the growth in piety which is produced in this way is not ephemeral or spurious in any sense; it is healthy, and will be permanent in its results. All the books on personal piety that were ever written are not to be compared in wisdom, in authority, or in efficacy with the Bible.

Now there is special need for the devotional study of the Bible by the pastor. His piety should be of the most elevated type. His own spiritual wants, as well as those of the people to whom he ministers, demand that it should also be progressive—ever rising and expanding as his work becomes more solemn, and nothing will meet these requirements but a piety that is truly scriptural....

For the minister especially it is very important that his soul be put in direct contact with the word of the Lord. He should get just as near as it is possible to the mind of the Spirit. The very thoughts of that Spirit he should endeavor to think over in his own heart. The soul will generally become assimilated to Him whose inspired utterances are kept constantly and impressively before it.[1]

Then comes his pressing application:

Adopt some rule of systematic devotional reading, and let it not be intermitted for any trivial consideration. Let your study of the word be profound, so as to get down to its very marrow and sweetness. Let your meditations be constant, so that all day long you may have some Scripture before the mind. Let it be with you as his biographer says of McCheyne, that "he fed on the word, not in order to prepare himself for his people, but for personal edification. To do so was a fundamental rule with him." And let all this devotional study of the word be mingled with prayer, that the same Spirit who inspired it would give it life and power in the effects upon your own soul.[2]

Now I am not suggesting that your more technical and official interaction with the scriptures should not be carried out in anything less than a devotional disposition of mind and heart. In tracking down the meaning

---

1. Thomas Murphy, *Pastoral Theology* (Audubon, NJ: Old Paths Publications, 1996), 76–78.
2. Thomas Murphy, *Pastoral Theology* (Audubon, NJ: Old Paths Publications, 1996), 78, 79.

of a Greek or a Hebrew word or the historical background of a passage, we should always be doing our work in a spirit of utter dependence on the Holy Spirit and in the devotional consciousness that I am doing this work in the presence of the living God to whom I shall give an account for my labor. This is the devotional spirit that should mark all of our dealings with Scripture. Yet I am asserting that if you and I would experience a real, expanding, varied and original acquaintance with God and His ways, then we must have regular dealings with God and His Word, not for the preparation of feeding others, as the primary focus, but instead, for the nurture of our own souls in the presence of God. That is, we are not dealing with the Word of God while preparing to speak His Word to another, but dealing with His Word to have God speak to us about ourselves and about Him and His ways.

Now I want to say three specific things concerning this devotional assimilation of the Word of God.

The first thing to remember in the devotional assimilation of the Word of God is that *it ought to be structured and consistent.*

Murphy pointed out earlier that we should adopt some rule of systematic, devotional assimilation of Scripture. There must be time marked out for this discipline and that time must be assiduously guarded. Just as physical health is determined primarily by the ordinary as opposed to our extraordinary physical disciplines of diet, rest, and exercise, so it is with the health of our souls.

Listen to the words of Jeremy Taylor quoted by the saintly Robert Murray M'Cheyne. Bonar writes concerning his friend, M'Cheyne:

> His diary does not contain much of his feelings during his residence in Dundee. His incessant labours left him little time, except what he scrupulously spent in the direct exercises of devotion. But what we have seen of his manner of study and self-examination at Larbert [his previous sphere of labor], is sufficient to show in what a constant state of cultivation his soul was kept; and his habits in these respects continued with him to the last. Jeremy Taylor recommends: "If thou meanest to enlarge thy religion, do it rather by enlarging thine ordinary devotions than thy extraordinary." This advice describes very accurately the plan of spiritual life on which Mr. M'Cheyne acted. He did occasionally set apart seasons for special prayer and fasting, occupying the time so set apart exclusively in devotion. But the real secret of his soul's prosperity lay in the daily enlargement of his heart in fellowship with his God. And the river deepened as it flowed on to eternity; so that he at least

reached that feature of a holy pastor which Paul pointed out to Timothy (iv. 15): "His profiting did appear to all."

In his own house everything was fitted to make you feel that the service of God was a cheerful service, while he sought that every arrangement of the family should bear upon eternity. His morning hours were set apart for the nourishment of his own soul; not, however, with the view of laying up a stock of grace for the rest of the day,—for manna will corrupt if laid by—but rather with the view of "giving the eye the habit of looking upward all the day, and drawing down beams from the reconciled countenance." He was sparing in the hours devoted to sleep, and resolutely secured time for devotion before breakfast, although often wearied and exhausted when he laid himself to rest. "A soldier of the cross," was his remark, "must endure hardness." Often he sang a Psalm of praise, as soon as he arose, to stir up his soul. Three chapters of the word was his usual morning portion. This he thought little enough, for he delighted exceedingly in the Scriptures: they were better to him than thousands of gold or silver. "When you write," said he to a friend, "tell me the meaning of Scriptures." To another, in expressing his value for the word, he said, "One gem from that ocean is worth all the pebbles of earthly streams."[3]

The psalms hint at this structured devotional time repeatedly: "Day and night" (Ps. 1:2); "I have chosen the way of faithfulness; I set your rules before me" (Ps. 119:30); "At midnight I rise to praise you, because of your righteous rules" (Ps. 119:62); "Oh how I love your law! It is my meditation all the day" (Ps. 119:97); "My eyes are awake before the watches of the night, that I may meditate on your promise" (Ps. 119:148).

It is likewise in the New Testament: "Let the word of Christ dwell in you richly, teaching and admonishing one another in all wisdom, singing psalms and hymns and spiritual songs, with thankfulness in your hearts to God" (Col. 3:16). With a thousand things that clamor for the focused attention of our minds, there will be no day and night meditation in the Word, no resolution or prosecution, no sense of expectation and perseverance, apart from a commitment to a structured and consistent pattern for the devotional assimilation of the Word of God.

---

3. Andrew A. Bonar, *Memoir and Remains of Robert Murray M'Cheyne* (London: The Banner of Truth Trust, 1966), 54, 55.

The second thing to remember in the devotional assimilation of the Word of God is that it ought to be *systematic and comprehensive*.

We need the complete Bible to make us complete and competent men in our service to God. "All Scripture is breathed out by God and profitable for teaching, for reproof, for correction, and for training in righteousness, that the man of God may be competent, equipped for every good work" (2 Tim. 3:16, 17). Paul had reminded Timothy in the previous verse that Timothy had known the sacred writings which are able to make us wise unto salvation through faith which is in Christ Jesus, from the time he was just a nursing baby (2 Tim. 3:15). No doubt Timothy could reflect back on those portions of the sacred writings learned from his mother and his grandmother which became effectual to drive him out of Adam and into Christ by making him wise for salvation through faith in Christ. Then, and only then, does he say in his final charge, "Preach the word; be ready in season and out of season; reprove, rebuke, and exhort, with complete patience and teaching" (2 Tim. 4:2). What word? The Word that is continually making you more and more of a complete man, furnishing you for every good work, and not simply giving you the intellectual stuff that forms the substance of your preaching. This is the Word that enables you as a man of God, in a very real sense, to become your message.

The temptation of our Lord points in the same direction, "But he answered, 'It is written, Man shall not live by bread alone, but by every word that comes from the mouth of God'" (Matt. 4:4). God has deposited a broad range of spiritual vitamins, minerals, and nutrients in the full corpus of Scripture, and He knows that we need them all for our spiritual health. In His creative wisdom, God has deposited in certain plants, vegetables, fruits, and meats that He has given us to eat, the nourishment of vitamins, minerals, and nutrients. Truly, we need a balanced diet to be whole and healthy men physically. So it is spiritually. We need every word that proceeds from the mouth of God, to the end that we may have a vigorous Christian life and experience. I am urging you then, if you have not committed yourself to this, or if you have shrunk back from past commitments, to adopt some plan by which you will cover the full range of Scripture in a reasonable length of time. Many of you are familiar with M'Cheyne's daily Bible reading schedule which is readily available on the Internet.[4] Another most helpful tool in

---

4. http://mcheyne.info/calendar.pdf (accessed 16 May 2017).

making a commitment to this kind of principled consecutive reading is a Bible version that is so arranged to be read in one year.[5]

A simple pattern that I have found helpful over the years may work for you. Read two chapters in the Old Testament and one chapter in the New Testament, and you will go through the entirety of the Bible in approximately a year. I have also found it very edifying to my soul, in addition to this consecutive reading through the Old and New Testaments, to be reading consecutively each day through the psalms. I get through the entire psalter about once every six to nine months. I start in Psalm 1 and pray through a psalm a day unless I come to one of the larger psalms, in which case I break up the reading of such a psalm into two or three days. When I come to Psalm 119, I generally take one or two of the eight verse sections and pray them back to God. Then, for a number of years, the discipline of reading one chapter in Proverbs according to the corresponding day of the month was an added discipline for me. It is a good thing to be able to say, "By the grace of God, my commitment to get through my entire Bible in a reasonable timeframe once or twice a year has been met, not as a mere formality, but in a context in which I have cried to God that I might know an increasing measure of a real, varied, personal, original, and expanding acquaintance with my God."

The third thing to remember in the devotional assimilation of the Word of God is that it ought to be *prayerful and meditative*.

By *prayerful*, I mean that we ought, consciously and consistently, to bow our heads over our Bibles and cry out, "Open my eyes, that I may behold wondrous things out of your law" (Ps. 119:18). Another example of this type of prayer is, "Search me, O God, and know my heart! Try me and know my thoughts! And see if there be any grievous way in me, and lead me in the way everlasting!" (Ps. 139:23, 24). By *prayerful*, I mean taking Jeremiah's words and saying, "Your words were found, and I ate them, and your words became to me a joy and the delight of my heart, for I am called by your name, O Lord, God of hosts" (Jer. 15:16). Jeremiah does not say, "and I *exegeted* them, and Your words were the sum and substance of my ministry to others," but he could say that he *ate* them as his finest and most delightful food.

Do we know this reality, or have we lost the excitement that we had when God first saved us and our personal Bible reading, which before had

---

5. https://www.amazon.com/s/ref=nb_sb_noss_2?url=search-alias%3Dstripbooks&field-keywords=one+year+bible+tyndale, or https://www.amazon.com/Through-Bible-One-Year-Introduction/dp/1563220148 (accessed 16 May 2017).

been mere drudgery, suddenly became a passionate delight? I can remember that for years, before I was converted, in order to satisfy my conscience that perhaps my profession was real, I would say that I read at least one chapter of the Bible a day. I am ashamed of that, but it is true. Can you guess what chapter I read those many times? The two verses of Psalm 117. I read the shortest chapter in the Bible just so I could pillow my head and say, "But Lord, I read my Bible today; I read my chapter!"

But, oh! What a difference when God opened my eyes and brought me out of darkness into light. I was pedaling my bike for Western Union for thirty-five cents an hour, and the only bike I had was a girl's bike. It was one of my sister's bikes, an old blue balloon tire girl's bike. I saved the money I earned pedaling that bike. It was not long before I ordered a Thompson Chain–Reference Bible with a blue Moroccan–leather cover. When it was delivered to my home I tore open the cardboard box in which it came, and hugged it to my chest. In two to three years some pages of that Bible had more verses underlined and highlighted than verses that were left unmarked! This book came alive to me. Now I am rebuked when I sometimes feel it a drudgery to pick up my devotional Bible. At times like that I realize that I have lost the excitement and the thrill of having God speak to me.

We desperately need this prayerful, meditative engagement with the Word of God. By *prayerful* I also mean coming earnestly to and pleading with God, in the language of Paul, that He would give us "a spirit of wisdom and of revelation in the knowledge of him" (Eph. 1:17). By *meditative* I mean that we are not merely threading words through our eyes in order to meet our daily quota of chapters read, but pondering and reflecting on what we are reading. I often find it helpful to read a passage out loud and say, "Is this what the Lord said?" I will then read it out loud a second time changing the emphasis and speed with which I previously read the passage. I ask myself, "How did the Lord say it? Lord, speak it to me as You spoke it to them." You open your mind and heart to the nuances of the Word of God, reflecting upon what you have read. All the while you may be praying like this:

> What does this portion teach me about my God, about my Savior, about my privileges, about my duties, about my sin, and about my heart? What does it teach me about the ways of God with men and with things? What does it show me of His mercy or His judgment?

Charles Bridges quotes a man of God from a generation before his own:

(Mr. Scott remarks) "I have found it advantageous sometimes to read the Scriptures with such exactness, as to weigh every expression, and the connexion, as if I were about to preach upon every verse; and then to apply the result to my own case, character, experience, and conduct, as if it had been directly addressed to me—in short—to make the passages into a kind of sermon, as if about to preach to others, and then to turn the whole application on myself, as far as suited to my case. At other times I have read a passage more generally, and then selected two or three of the most important observations from it, and endeavoured to employ my mind in meditation on them, and consider how they bore on the state of my heart, or on my past life, or on those things which I heard or observed, in the world or the Church, and to compare them with the variety of sentiments, experiences, conduct, or prominent characters, with which we become gradually more and more acquainted."[6]

It is a frightening thing when our Bible becomes a kind of toy, so that we are like the little boy who had acquired a pocket mirror and loved to sit around throughout the day and catch the rays of the sun in such a way that he could flash the mirror in the eyes of others. He never used that mirror to see his own dirty face. We can be handling the Word of God that way thinking, "What can I flash on the face of others?" God says, "No, here is the mirror by which to see yourself," and at times, brethren, our faces are not attractive at all, and the hairs we missed when we shaved are ugly. This is what I mean by meditative reading of the scriptures.

Here again Bridges is a great help:

This difficulty springs out of the peculiar self-deception, by which we are apt to merge our personal in our professional character, and in the Minister to forget the Christian. But time must be found for the spiritual feeding upon Scriptural truths, as well as for a critical investigation of their meaning, or for a Ministerial application of their message. For if we should study the Bible more as Ministers than as Christians— more to find matter for the instruction of our people, than food for the nourishment of our own souls; we neglect to place ourselves at the feet of our Divine Teacher; our communion with him is cut off; and we become mere formalists in our sacred profession. Mr. Martyn seems to have been tenderly conscious of this temptation—"Every time" (he remarked) "that I open the Scriptures, my thoughts are about

6. Charles Bridges, *The Christian Ministry* (Edinburgh: The Banner of Truth Trust, 1976), 53.

a sermon or exposition; so that even in private I seem to be reading in public."[7] We cannot live by feeding others; or heal ourselves by the mere employment of healing our people; and therefore by this course of official service, our familiarity with the awful realities of death and eternity may be rather like the grave-digger, the physician, and the soldier, than the man of God, viewing eternity with deep seriousness and concern, and bringing to his people the profitable fruit of his contemplations. It has been well remarked—that, "when once a man begins to view religion not as of personal, but merely of professional importance, he has an obstacle in his course, with which a private Christian is unacquainted."[8]

Mark this well, my brethren, especially younger brethren. It is here in the battle of the basics, in these trenches of spiritual warfare, that the issues are won or lost. If God spares you, I am prepared to prophesy that probably the most telling thing about you ten, twenty, or thirty years from now will be this: "Did you win or lose the battle here, in this place of structured, systematic, principled commitment to the devotional assimilation of the Word of God?" It is here, I say, that the battle is most likely to be won or lost. George Whitefield said that he read Matthew Henry through innumerable times on his knees. That is where he learned his theology. That is where the passion for Christ and for the souls of men, and a balanced, experimental Calvinistic divinity got into the bloodstream of Whitefield.

So, when I talk about devotional reading of the scriptures, I am not talking about what some of us experienced, and perhaps to some measure got caught up in when we were young believers, where we were waiting for the divine light to jump out and smack us. No, you are coming with your mind engaged, not to feed others, but to feed your own soul. Granted, your personal devotional assimilation of the scriptures will eventually make its way into your public ministry of the Word. But the conscious, deliberate focus of your engagement with the scriptures must never become focused on feeding others, but on feeding your own soul.

---

7. This footnote is in the quotation: '*Let me be taught, that the first and great business on earth is the sanctification of my own soul; so shall I be rendered more capable also of performing the duties of the Ministry in a holy solemn manner.*' The author references this quotation from Martyn's Life, p. 60.

8. Charles Bridges, *The Christian Ministry* (Edinburgh: The Banner of Truth Trust, 1976), 162, 163.

So, I commend to you with all of my heart, never get weary of having someone press you that you must have your devotions. I used to be embarrassed to sound this note in pastors' conferences, until pastors began to get honest with me, and we began to talk about the struggles of the Christian life. Men of God who have been used by God for decades confessed that their greatest battle is the maintenance of this kind of devotional assimilation of the Word of God. It is where the battle was engaged with me in preparation for this lecture. I did not get to bed till somewhere around eleven last night. I set the alarm clock for relatively early, woke up before the alarm rang, and there the battle was engaged.

> Albert, are you going to have the nerve to stand and tell these men that they ought to be committed to a systematic, prayerful, regular assimilation of the Word of God for the feeding of their own souls? Are you going to do that and rationalize, "Well, you are lecturing three times today and you want to have your lecture all in hand, surely you can skimp a little on your devotional reading of Scripture?"

I hope there is more motivation than merely being able to stand and look you in the eye and say, "I have a good conscience." I had to fight with that as well and say, "Lord, my heart is so wayward that I could be coming to my devotions not to meet with You but to brag before the men." Yet, by the grace of God, He met me in the Word this morning. I can stand before you and say that before this Bible is held out and opened up and applied to you men, it has ripped into the heart and into the soul and refreshed and renewed the soul of this old man, and that is where the battle will be engaged tomorrow morning and the next and the next and the next. I have said, "Lord, it is going to be this way until I cross the river or until I hear the voice of the archangel and the trumpet of God." I have given up thinking that the battle is going to be engaged somewhere else. That realization is a great encouragement to us to press on in the disciplines connected with this principled and structured devotional assimilation of the Word of God.

Maintaining the Habit and Spirit of Secret Prayer

This is the second of five disciplines in the life of the man of God in his relationship to his God *spiritually*. I am not referring here to what I will later call pastoral intercessory prayer, a subject so crucial that I will seek to address it under a separate heading. I am concerned here to address the subject of secret prayer as it pertains to our needs as men of God; our need to be worshipers as Christian men and ministers; our need to be engaged in secret private praise, the confession of our own sins, and wrestling with our own perplexities and struggles. Here we will consider the man of God praying for the concerns of his own heart as a Christian man.

We begin by talking about the *habit* and *spirit* of secret prayer.

By *habit* I mean secret prayer that occurs because we have marked out specific times for this discipline. Jesus said, "They ought always to pray and not lose heart" (Luke 18:1). David said, "Give ear to my words, O LORD; consider my groaning. Give attention to the sound of my cry, my King and my God, for to you do I pray. O LORD, in the morning you hear my voice; in the morning I prepare a sacrifice for you and watch" (Ps. 5:1–3). While not denying what has commonly been called ejaculatory prayer, or living in the spirit and disposition of prayer, David speaks here of the specific time when God will hear his voice in prayer. Also consider this:

> Let death steal over them; let them go down to Sheol alive; for evil is in their dwelling place and in their heart. But I call to God, and the LORD will save me. Evening and morning and at noon I utter my complaint and moan, and he hears my voice" (Ps. 55:15–17).

Here is the form of the psalmist's renewed will to seek God at specific times for prayer. We have the example of our Lord, "And rising very early in the morning, while it was still dark, he departed and went out to a desolate place, and there he prayed" (Mark 1:35). He had marked out this time to seek the face of His Father. Finally,

> "And when you pray, you must not be like the hypocrites. For they love to stand and pray in the synagogues and at the street corners, that they may be seen by others. Truly, I say to you, they have received their reward. But when you pray, go into your room and shut the door and pray to your Father who is in secret" (Matt. 6:5, 6).

Surely, this is pointing to something beyond living in the spirit of prayer. It is speaking of set seasons of purposed time in order to engage in secret prayer.

Remember the example of Daniel,

> When Daniel knew that the document had been signed, he went to his house where he had windows in his upper chamber open toward Jerusalem. He got down on his knees three times a day and prayed and gave thanks before his God, as he had done previously (Dan. 6:10).

Notice here that Daniel does nothing new in a crisis. It was his pattern to have set times of prayer.

So when I speak of maintaining the *habit* and the spirit of prayer, I am talking about our commitment to mark out specific times in order to seek the face of God with respect to the needs of our hearts, the duties we have to pray and worship, confessing our sins, seeking the face of God for strength and grace for what we are to be as Christian men, and what we are called upon to do as Christian pastors.

Now by using the term *spirit* with regard to prayer, I mean prayer in which there is an engagement of the heart by the enabling grace and power of the Holy Spirit. It is not without reason that God designates the Holy Spirit as "a spirit of grace and pleas for mercy" (Zech. 12:10). The apostle tells us, "Likewise the Spirit helps us in our weakness. For we do not know what to pray for as we ought, but the Spirit himself intercedes for us with groanings too deep for words" (Rom. 8:26). Jude gives this exhortation, "But you, beloved, building yourselves up in your most holy faith and praying in the Holy Spirit" (Jude 20).

So when I use the term the *spirit* of secret prayer, I am speaking of prayer which, by the enabling power of the Spirit, engages the whole heart of the child of God so that he can say with the psalmist, "With my whole heart I seek you; let me not wander from your commandments!" (Ps. 119:10). He understands the meaning of the words of Jeremiah when he said, "You will seek me and find me, when you seek me with all your heart" (Jer. 29:13). Any one of us who has any experience in the things of God knows that in seeking and praising God there ought to be the engagement of the whole heart. We are equally conscious that without the enabling power of the Spirit the heart goes out in a hundred directions, or is a mass of dullness and distractedness. So by the *spirit* of prayer, I am referring to prayer in which there is the engagement of the heart by the enabling grace and power of the Holy Spirit. This discipline of the habit and spirit of secret prayer in the life of the man of God is a vital means to advance the work of grace in our souls. Let me offer five reasons why this is so.

The first reason that this discipline is necessary to advance the work of grace in our souls is that *it is in such prayer that our personal communion with our heavenly Father and our Savior is both renewed, nurtured, and increased.*

Jesus said, "Pray then like this: 'Our Father in heaven'" (Matt. 6:9). J. I. Packer indicates, in his chapter on adoption (chapter 19) in the modern classic *Knowing God,* that the whole thrust of the revelation of God in Christ is to bring into being a community who can address God intelligently, with a filial delight in Him as their Father who is in heaven. Peter indicates that it is the prevailing disposition of believers that they call upon Him as Father, "you call on him as Father" (1 Pet. 1:17). So it is in the engagement of our Father in secret prayer that our communion with and our enjoyment of this filial relationship is deepened, nurtured, and enhanced. It is interesting that when Paul describes the evidence of the Spirit's work in the hearts of those who have come into the blessing of adoption, he focuses upon the Spirit who enables us to cry "Abba! Father!" (Rom. 8:15), giving us a felt awareness of our legal status as sons of God who address God in the warmth and security of our relationship to Him as His sons.

Consider the emphasis of the book of Hebrews. One of its dominant motifs is found in the words, "let us draw near," or "drawing near" (Heb. 4:16; 7:19, 25; 10:1, 22; 11:6). Everything in the Old Covenant worship said, "Keep your distance; you may draw near only through the priest." The New Covenant announces that we may now draw near because Jesus our High Priest has accomplished His work. He has offered the once-for-all, acceptable sacrifice. The motif of drawing near is based upon the reality of an accomplished redemption in our Lord Jesus. Because we draw near through Christ our mediator, High Priest, advocate, and intercessor, our communion with Christ is likewise renewed, increased, and deepened in the context of secret prayer.

The yearning of the apostle was to know Him (Phil. 3:10). The great prayer of the apostle is that we might know the love of Christ that passes knowledge (Eph. 3:14–19). The exhortation of Peter is to grow in grace and in the knowledge of our Lord Jesus (2 Pet. 3:18). Surely, if the fragrance of Christ is to infuse our labors, if there is to be filial delight and liberty in our public and private pastoral prayers, then the scent of the closet must be upon us, and when it is not, these things will be hollow and empty and will not touch the hearts of our people. This makes the discipline of the *habit* and the *spirit* of secret prayer crucial for us because it is here that our communion with the Father and our Savior is intensified, nurtured, and expanded.

The second reason that this discipline is necessary to advance the work of grace in our souls is that *it is in this kind of prayer that our perspective of reality is kept in proper focus.*

There are a thousand things constantly pressing upon our consciousness that tie us to the things that are seen, felt, heard, and observed, and make it difficult for us to keep a proper perspective on the things that are not seen. The apostle could say as he reflected on his present trials, that they were light afflictions which are but for a moment (2 Cor. 4:18). "Light afflictions, Paul? These do not seem light to us at all: a day and a night in the deep, stripes at the hands of the Jews, imprisonment, stoning. Light afflictions?" Yes. And he adds that they are but *momentary* light afflictions,

> For this light momentary affliction is preparing for us an eternal weight of glory beyond all comparison, as we look not to the things that are seen but to the things that are unseen. For the things that are seen are transient, but the things that are unseen are eternal (2 Cor. 4:17, 18).

It is in the secret place that this proper perspective is kept in focus.

Psalm 73 is a wonderful example of this in the experience of a man of God. In that setting, Asaph was looking around him and seeing the wicked prosper in life. They seemed to have an easy life and an easy death. Then He looks at himself and the people of God and laments that they are afflicted with troubles that come in perpetual waves. To him this does not make sense. He is deeply troubled. He speaks of how he got to the place where he was almost like a beastly creature tied to the world of sense and stuff. Then spiritual reality hit him. He speaks of this in the triumphant conclusion of the psalm, "But when I thought how to understand this, it seemed to me a wearisome task, until I went into the sanctuary of God; then I discerned their end" (Ps. 73:16, 17). Everything came into focus in that setting where God is. Perspective was once again regained in the context of the secret place. How crucial it is for us not to carry about a mere theoretical and correct theology of where we are in our present experience. We desire and aim to have an existential, felt, visceral experience of those issues whereby all that transpires around us and all that God does within us is seen in a proper biblical perspective. No little part of maintaining that perspective is the habit and the spirit of secret prayer.

The third reason that this discipline is necessary to advance the work of grace in our souls is that *it is the kind of prayer in which our own sins are seen in their true light.*

There is a fascinating phrase from the prayer of Moses, the man of God, "You have set our iniquities before you, our secret sins in the light of your presence" (Ps. 90:8). We marvel that in drawing near to the throne of grace we are drawing near to One who is infinitely holy. His holiness has not in any way been diminished in the full revelation of His grace; it is just the opposite. Holiness shines more brilliantly through the prism of the cross, more than it ever did even in the destruction of the wicked cities of Sodom and Gomorrah, or the thunder and lightning of Mt. Sinai. It is when we see immolated, incarnate Deity, with the heavens shrouded in blackness, and hear the cry of dereliction, "My God, my God, why have you forsaken me?" (Matt. 27:46), that we see His blazing holiness. When cross words spoken to one's wife, the second look at that attractive body, and the spirit of jealousy over the gifts of another brother, are viewed in the light of the revelation of holiness in the cross of Christ, our sins are seen in a new and more accurate light, and we abhor them all the more.

Remember the exalting and humbling experience of Isaiah. He was no bum or derelict, and yet when he sees the Lord high and lifted up on His throne, and beholds those angelic creatures with two wings covering each face and two wings covering their feet and two wings holding them aloft while they cry one to another, "Holy, holy, holy" (Isa. 6:3), he sees what he really is as a son of Adam. Even though he is a true son of the covenant and a child of God, he yet cries out, "Woe is me." His sense of uncleanness is concentrated, not upon what his hands have touched that they should not, or places his feet have gone where they ought not, but upon his lips, "I am a man of unclean lips" (Isa. 6:5).

The fourth reason that this discipline is necessary to advance the work of grace in our souls is that *it becomes the kind of prayer in which our pardon and acceptance in the Beloved One are sealed afresh to our hearts.*

We experience the living truth, "If you, O LORD, should mark iniquities, O Lord, who could stand? But with you there is forgiveness, that you may be feared" (Ps. 130:3). We know the confirming voice of the New Testament, "But if we walk in the light, as he is in the light, we have fellowship with one another, and the blood of Jesus his Son cleanses us from all sin" (1 John 1:7). In the context of 1 John 1, the blood of Jesus Christ His Son goes on cleansing from all sin. This is why I have never given stock to people who say, "Well, I do not want a ministry that shows me my sin. I want a ministry that encourages me." Encourages you with what? What is more encouraging than understanding the depth of sin's inner working in my heart and acknowledging my sins before the Lord? By these acknowledgements alone can I have the comforting assurance of knowing that these sins are continually covered under the blood of Christ. I say, "Lord, where can I go but to the fountain opened for sin and uncleanness?" Christ becomes more precious as my sin becomes more odious. The more I see my need of His cleansing blood, the more precious becomes the One who shed that blood.

The fifth reason that this discipline is necessary to advance the work of grace in our souls is that *it is in the engagement of the habit and spirit of secret prayer that it becomes the kind of prayer in which grace for our work is sought and obtained.*

The work of the ministry has its "for better, for worse." The habit and spirit of secret prayer is a discipline and disposition which equips and strengthens us for the wide diversity of pastoral experiences which are our portion in His providence. In all of them we pour out our hearts to God, "O people; pour out your heart before him" (Ps. 62:8). I love that imagery. Your heart is a vessel full of all kinds of stuff and you sometimes cannot even sort out the ingredients. God says, "Just tip it over and let it all spill out to Me." God is never shocked. He never says, "Ooh, that is in him?" Yes, He knows it all the time. Now He says, "You pour it out." There is a tremendous spiritual benefit in the dimension of secret prayer which comes to receive and obtain. "Let us then with confidence draw near to the throne of grace, that we may receive mercy and find grace to help in time of need" (Heb. 4:16). Mercy is divine pity joined to action. He is a God who sees the pitiable and responds according to His grace and mercy. The wisdom, courage, boldness, mental and spiritual strength, and patience we need as pastors to bear with some of God's children is all found for us at His throne as wonderfully depicted for us here in Hebrews.

Our felt need is so often heightened as we deal with the difficulties of the ministry, particularly the weak and those who have unusual struggles. Bunyan had it right when he described this as just getting some of those saints down to the river with their crutches. In cases like these, we say, "Lord, I have done my job; I have done all I can for them." You do not come to this realization as a fatalist, but with sanctified and informed realism that there are some saints who will go down to the river hobbling, and we are thankful if we can simply get them to the river's edge and safely across into Immanuel's land.

I think of one of my fellow-elders who is dealing now with one of our sheep, whose history is such that we come right up to the border of saying, "Enough is enough. The time has come for us to start the process leading to corrective church discipline." Then we deal with him and he comes back saying, "I sinned. Will you pray for me? Will you help me?" And there you go, you cannot discipline him for he is still acting like a child of God. When his sin is pointed out he deals with it. Well, where can we get the grace to be faithful with sheep who have these kinds of struggles? The answer is, at the throne of grace, and in crying out to God, "Lord, I am not like You. You bear with me. How many times, Lord, have I done the same evil thing? And yet I come and You forgive me, cleanse me, wipe the blood off my nose, pick me up and put me on my way." It is at the throne of grace that we are kept from irritation toward such sheep, that we obtain the grace we need to bear patiently with the sheep. We rest again on the promise which is one of the first passages I remember memorizing as a young Christian,

> He gives power to the faint, and to him who has no might he increases strength. Even youths shall faint and be weary, and young men shall fall exhausted; but they who wait for the LORD shall renew their strength; they shall mount up with wings like eagles; they shall run and not be weary; they shall walk and not faint" (Isa. 40:29–31).

Brethren, we must, if we are to have this expanding, varied, real walk with our God, continue in the spirit and the habit of secret prayer.

> Luther long since has said—"Prayer, meditation, and temptation, make a Minister." No one will hesitate to admit the importance of the first of these qualifications, who has ever realized the weight of Ministerial responsibility, who has been led to know that his "sufficiency is of God," and that prayer is the appointed channel of heavenly communications. The student's conscious need of wisdom, humility and faith, to ascertain the pure simplicity of his purpose, his necessary qualifications, and his Divine call to the holy office—will bring him a daily suppliant to the throne of grace. In his General Studies, abstracted from this spirit of prayer, he will find a dryness—a want of power to draw his resources to this one centre of the Ministry—or perhaps a diversion from the main object into some track of self-indulgence. And even in this special duty of the Scriptures he will feel himself, (as Witsius says) "like a blind man contemplating the heavens,"—or as when the world in its original confusion "was without form and void, and darkness was upon the face of the deep." God must speak to his heart—"Let there be light;" and "for this he will be inquired of to do it unto him."[9]

---

9. Charles Bridges, *The Christian Ministry* (Edinburgh: The Banner of Truth Trust, 1976), 60, 61.

Bridges goes further:

The most effectual hindrances, therefore, to our work are those which impede our personal communion with the Lord. When the great enemy thus successfully intercepts our spiritual supplies, the work of God in our hearts, and connected with it, the work of God in our hands, languishes from the want of its accustomed and needful support. We have great need to watch, lest public activity should be considered to atone for neglect of private intercourse with God; and thus our profession should become a snare to ourselves, and divested of all spiritual savour to our flock. Henry Martyn had occasion to lament, that "want of private devotional reading and shortness of prayer, through incessant sermon-making, had produced much strangeness between God and his own soul." And in the review of the first year of his Ministry, "he judged, that he had dedicated *too much time to public Ministrations, and too little to private communion with God.*" Mr. Scott gives a most wholesome caution on this point—"The principle that made the Apostle determine not to 'serve tables,' though a good work in itself, should render Ministers in this day very careful not so to give their services, even to the most useful Societies, and to attending the meetings of them, as to *prevent their 'giving themselves continually to the word of God and prayer.'* A danger at present seems to arise on this side." The Writer would therefore wish to draw his own mind and his brethren habitually to this recollection, that nothing will enrich or console us in the neglect of intimate communion with God. We must "walk with God" *at any rate,* or our souls will die. Even Christian communion will form an empty substitute for this hallowed intercourse. The command is—"Enter into thy closet, and shut thy door." Shut out not only vanity and the world, but even *for a time* "the communion of Saints." The soul may lose its spiritual vigour in any company but that of God—in the best as well as in the worst—in the Church, as well as in the world—in the active engagements of the Ministry, as well as in secular employments.

It was said of Fletcher, that "his deepest and most sensible communications with God *were enjoyed in those hours, when the door of his closet was shut against human creatures, as well as human cares. His closet was his favourite retirement, to which he constantly retreated, whenever his public labours allowed him a season of leisure. His public labours (astonishing as they were) bore but little proportion to those internal exercises of prayer and supplication, to which he was wholly given in private. The former of necessity were frequently discontinued; but the latter were almost uninterruptedly maintained from hour to hour. He lived in the spirit of prayer." Was not this the secret of the extraordinary power that rested upon his ministrations? The out-pouring of the Spirit of supplication would revive our work, and enlarge our success. We know who hath said—"Ask me of things to come concerning my sons; and *concerning the work of my hands command ye me.*"[10]

How many times must the Lord say to us, "You do not have, because you do not ask" (Jas. 4:2)? All that we need to be able ministers of the New Covenant is there in the bank of heaven, stored up in the infinite fullness of our Lord Jesus, but we must come to the teller's window. That teller's window is called the throne of grace.[11]

One of the best ways to secure return from a period of spiritual barrenness is the maintenance of the structures that were in place in times of our spiritual fruitfulness. Maintain the disciplines and the habits even in a period of dryness, and as you do engage in those God-ordained means, God will come with fresh life and vigor to your soul.

---

10. Charles Bridges, *The Christian Ministry* (Edinburgh: The Banner of Truth Trust, 1976), 150, 151.

11. There are some excellent books on the discipline and the habit of secret prayer: *The Privy Key of Heaven* in *The Works of Thomas Brooks*, Volume 2; *A Discourse Touching Prayer* by John Bunyan; McIntyre's helpful book, *The Hidden Life of Prayer*; and many others. However, brethren, when all is said and done, we learn to pray *by praying*. Without praying we will not learn to pray, and without the discipline and the habit of secret prayer, it is likely that we will never make much progress in the matter of our praying.

CHAPTER 4

His Relationship to God Spiritually (3)

Maintaining a Good Conscience Toward God and Men

I now set out to identify three more disciplines which, under the blessing of the Holy Spirit, become means by which the fullness of grace which is in our Lord Jesus is poured into the heart and life of the man of God. This next one is *the discipline of maintaining a good conscience toward God and men.*

If we have any question about the importance of maintaining a good conscience, the sober words of Paul will settle it,

> This charge I entrust to you, Timothy, my child, in accordance with the prophecies previously made about you, that by them you may wage the good warfare, holding faith and a good conscience. By rejecting this, some have made shipwreck of their faith (1 Tim. 1:18, 19).

According to this text, the first step to apostasy is thrusting away a good conscience—not necessarily sound doctrine or good morals, but a good conscience. This is the concern of the subject before us, and it may become a frightening concern if we begin to take the matter lightly and live loosely. This is the negative, the warning side of the matter.

On the positive side, we have these words, "So I always take pains to have a clear conscience toward both God and man" (Acts 24:16). Here Paul was giving a defense before a pagan ruler. Felix himself had no concern to keep a good conscience, but Paul the man of God, did. His resolve to maintain a good conscience is rooted in his anticipation of the coming day of the resurrection of the just and the unjust and the accounting that will take place at that time. In light of this Paul was consciously engaging in the constant spiritual discipline of the maintenance of a clear conscience toward both God and man.

We have previously considered two other disciplines, the assimilation of the Word and the maintenance of the habit and the spirit of secret prayer. Unless these two are joined to the discipline of the maintenance of a good conscience, they can degenerate into a kind of mystical thumb-sucking which produce no nourishment, but rather a false comfort. It is not difficult to see how this is so. Devotional reading of Scripture and praying to God are the two-way channel of revelation from and communication with God in the heart of a redeemed sinner. Hunger for God, humility before His Word, and prayerful response to God are the great evidences of spiritual life. How is it possible that a man could engage in these life-giving spiritual disciplines and yet not be concerned to have, nor passionately pursue, the maintenance of a good conscience toward God? A good conscience has to do with righteous living, holiness of life, consistency of walk, and ultimately love to God and man. So, having established the necessity for the discipline of keeping a good conscience, we must now address the question, "What does it mean to take pains to have a clear conscience toward both God and man?"

First, it means that *we will resolve to retain no conscious controversy with God.*

I will mention several kinds of controversy which we will need to avoid. One controversy with God is created when *sin is committed but not confessed.* Unconfessed sin is antithetical to the primary purpose of the gospel, which is to grant us forgiveness of sins. A child of God is one who is continually confessing his or her sins. John addresses this issue in 1 John 1:5–10 where he opens up the theme of living and walking in the light and having fellowship with Him, because "God is light." Yet, if we do not practice the truth, we are liars. No, walking in the light means that we do confess our sins, and when we do, He is faithful and just to forgive us our sins. Although John does not mention the conscience here, it is evident that this is a description of maintaining a good conscience in our walk with God.

There may be areas of spiritual concern in your life of which you have not yet become aware as you progress in sanctification. These may be attitudes, perspectives, ways of responding to people, or any number of issues of which we may be unaware. Calvin somewhere said that God does not allow us to see the one-hundredth part of our sin, yet He deals with us graciously and lovingly as our heavenly Father in this path of sanctification. A father does not deal with a five-year-old son as though he were fifteen. He has expectations consistent with and tailored to the young child's present level of development. Yet it does mean that we should at all times be able to speak as Paul did, "For I am not aware of anything against myself, but I am not thereby acquitted. It is the Lord who judges me" (1 Cor. 4:4). At any given moment in my spiritual life I must be able to say that I have no conscious controversy with God. To have a clear conscience toward God at all times means that at any point I can say, "By the grace of God, there is no sin which I have committed and concerning which I have become convicted, but have refused to confess and obtain the forgiveness and cleansing in the blood of Christ promised to us in the gospel."

Another type of controversy may be *a duty made plain but not performed or determined to perform*. What would you say to a person who failed to perform a duty clearly mandated by God? It is disobedience. Remember that we are servants and stewards of God, the essence of which is performing the duties and fulfilling the design of our work. How could we consciously fail to perform any one of these duties and not have a guilty conscience? We read, "So whoever knows the right thing to do and fails to do it, for him it is sin" (Jas. 4:17). Does not familial love urge us to fulfill our duties with delight for the sake of those whom we love? This then is a major component of keeping a good conscience.

Yet another type of controversy we may have with God relates to *a truth to be believed but which we reject in unbelief*. We live by faith and we believe glorious truths which transcend our finite human capacities of understanding. Therefore, there must be no revealed truth on the tablet of my mind that I reject because it exceeds the capacity of my comprehension. Rather, if I am to have a clear conscience toward God, I must be content to live with and rejoice in the great mysteries of the faith which create in me a constant movement toward my worship of His glory and majesty. Our conscience should smite us if and when, through carnal intellectual pride, we are in any way unwilling to receive in faith any facet of God's truth, simply because we are unable to wrap the stubby fingers of our little brains around expansive and transcendent realities.

It seems to me, as I have wrestled with the particular ingredients of a clear conscience toward God, that these three things are at the heart of its meaning. So then, to have this clear conscience means that I will be having constant recourse to the blood of Christ for cleansing and to the grace and power of Christ for an upright walk. This way we can say with Paul, "For I am not aware of anything against myself" (1 Cor. 4:4). We can also say with the psalmist, "I hold back my feet from every evil way, in order to keep your word. I do not turn aside from your rules, for you have taught me" (Ps. 119:101, 102). Now that is not a claim to sinless perfection. Rather, it is a claim to walking with a clear conscience toward God. Where God says a sin is to be avoided, you will be able to say, "I have held back my feet from every evil way." That means when you go to a store, and you know where the magazine racks are, you do not walk down that aisle. That is what it means to refrain my feet. So I can walk out of that store and say, "Thank you, Lord, I held back my feet from that evil way. I knew it was there, I knew it was enticing and inviting me, but I held back my feet." You will not say, "Thank You, Holy Spirit, that You held them back." No, I did it by an act of the will after spiritual resolutions made in the fullness of the Spirit; yet I do it. "Lord, take Your hand off me and I would wallow in the garbage and filth that pollutes the pure soul. Lord, that is who I am, left to myself, but by Your grace I am determined to walk with a good conscience. I will hold back my feet from every evil way. I will hold back my fingers from clicking those links on the browser of my computer that will bring up images that I know will defile my mind. I will hold back my *fingers* from every evil way." You will be able to walk by your computer with a good conscience that you do not allow it to become an inlet for uncleanness or wasted time. No sin committed but not confessed; no duty known but not performed or determined to perform by the grace of God; no truth impinging on the mind but rejected in pride or unbelief. I believe that is what it means to have a clear conscience toward God.

Second, *Acts 24:16 means that you seek biblically to repair any fractured or damaged human relationship caused by your sin.*

Having a clear conscience toward *man* means that you live a life in which you seek to continually resolve in a biblical manner any horizontal relationships which have been disrupted or damaged by your sin. If you have caused hurt to your wife with angry or insensitive words, you do not just mumble in some half-hearted tone of voice, "Well, Dear, I am sorry, I blew it." No, you own your sin and you say, "Dear, I sinned against you with my hasty, curt, unkind words. Will you forgive me?" People sometimes tell me that I am just a stickler for words when I say that merely saying "I am sorry" does not mean you have confessed your sin. When I say to someone, "I am sorry," I am telling them how I feel. I tell my wife, "Dear, I am sorry I am going deaf." But I do not say, "Will you forgive me for going deaf?" Yet I am sorry; I feel bad that she must bear the burden of my half-deafness. When someone comes to me and says, "Pastor Martin, I am sorry about this or that thing that I said or did to you," I say, "Well, that is interesting. What do you want me to do?" Perhaps then they will say, "I am coming to you seeking your forgiveness for this or that particular way in which I sinned against you. Will you forgive me?" At that point, I often will say, "I am a sinner who is being continually forgiven by God, and I am delighted to assure you that I freely and fully extend forgiveness for the things you have acknowledged were sins against me. They are buried in the depths of the sea, and should never be raised again between us."

When the children of a fellow-pastor friend of mine would come to him and say, "Dad, I am sorry," he tried to teach them this lesson. He would say, "Well, that is interesting. I am hungry. You tell me you are sorry and you feel bad. I tell you I am hungry and I feel bad too. My bad feelings are here in my stomach and yours are there in your heart."

These practical situations, and the words that transpire in them, must be brought to the touchstone of Scripture, particularly the broad teaching of Scripture on the reality of repentance and the dynamics of forgiveness. Human situations must conform to the realities of divine forgiveness even in the *language* that people use with one another. Simply saying to God, "I am sorry," is not acceptable in our relationship with Him. When we have sinned against Him, we must "confess our sins" and beseech Him for His promised forgiveness, assured that He grants it to us and deals with our sins through the ongoing cleansing of Christ's blood and righteousness. John wrote of this, "If we confess our sins, he is faithful and just to forgive us our sins and to cleanse us from all unrighteousness" (1 John 1:9). What is true *vertically* in forgiveness with God is true *horizontally* in forgiveness among men. Jesus said, "If your brother sins against you, go and tell him his fault, between you and him alone. If he listens to you, you have gained your brother" (Matt. 18:15). To have a clear conscience toward man means that if we have caused hurt to wife, children, church members, or fellow officer-bearers, by angry, insensitive, or untruthful words, we must own our sin and seek their forgiveness according to the biblical design and patterns of repentance and forgiveness.

If we ask for forgiveness and the other person withholds it, then "the ball is in his court" so to speak. The minute I say, "Bill, I sinned against you, will you forgive me?" I have taken my sin, knocked it over the net, and put it at his feet. Now he must take the racket of a Christ-like disposition and say, "My brother, I forgive you." Then the racquets are thrown away and the balls are disposed of and the net is taken down and our relationship is restored. As we deal with God we say, "Oh, God, forgive me for this or that violation of Your law. Forgive me for this duty not done. Forgive me for this transgression. Lord, wash me, cleanse me in Your blood. You have said, 'If we confess our sins, You are faithful and righteous to forgive.'" Likewise, in order to have a clear conscience in our relationship to one another, we must be willing to right those wrongs with others who have been the recipients of our moral aberrations. If it is the neglect of a clear duty to others, own your sin and seek their forgiveness. Many times, as God has shown me things from the Word that have been there all along to which I have not been sensitive, He has had dealings with me. I have had to stand before the congregation and confess. I say to them, "I have asked God's forgiveness; I ask your forgiveness. Now let us together bring forth fruits fit for repentance."

How often in the act of preaching have I overstated something or stated something with an edge, and upon reflection, sometimes even in the closing prayer, my heart has smitten me like David when he cut off that square inch of Saul's robe. His heart struck him just for that (1 Sam. 24:4, 5)! I could not lead in the closing prayer without saying, "Brethren, at this part in the sermon I said thus and thus. There was an edge of carnality in the manner in which I spoke those particular words, but now I have asked God's forgiveness. Will you forgive me?" And I have had people come and say, "Oh, Pastor Martin, that must have been hard." I have often responded by saying, "No, no, that is not hard. The hard thing would be to go home with an accusing conscience and know that my God is displeased because I was unwilling to deal with my sin. The hard thing is not to do it again."

It is vital that we say with Paul, "So I always take pains to have a clear conscience toward both God and man" (Acts 24:16). A defiled and accusing conscience will take away your hunger for the Word. In the sinner, hatred of the light is the dominant disposition of his soul,

> And this is the judgment: the light has come into the world, and people loved the darkness rather than the light because their works were evil. For everyone who does wicked things hates the light and does not come to the light, lest his works should be exposed (John 3:19, 20).

Though the disposition of hating the light is dominant in the unconverted, we must remember the principle that remaining sin, though it does not dominate in the believer, is the same in *kind*, not in *degree*. So also, our remaining sin has an aversion to light.

When you have sinned and you are not coming into the light of God's countenance in the way of confession and repentance, that aversion will manifest itself by finding flimsy excuses to skip those spiritual disciplines by which we experience a special nearness with God. These may be in the area of skipping your devotional reading, bypassing secret prayer, and most often for us as ministers, fulfilling some "holy pastoral duty" like visiting or studying. In reality though, at the root of it is an aversion to close dealings with God in the scriptures and in prayer because of sin that has not been dealt with in a biblical way. If you are honest, you know that what I say is true. Brethren, we dare not allow anything to cut the nerve of our passion to draw near and meet with God. A defiled and accusing conscience will give you an aversion to the Word. If it does not drive you to the throne of grace for forgiveness, it will drive you away in a sulking aversion to any close dealings with God.

> "I am persuaded," says Owen, "there are very few that apostatize from a profession of any continuance, such as our days abound with, but their door of entrance into the folly of backsliding was either some great and notorious sin, that blooded their consciences, tainted their affections, and intercepted all delight of having anything more to do with God; or else it was a course of neglect in private duties, arising from a weariness of contending against that powerful aversion[1] which they found in themselves unto them. And this also, through the craft of Satan, hath been improved into many foolish and sensual opinions of living unto God without and above any duties of communion. And we find that after men have, for a while, choked and blinded their consciences with this pretence, cursed wickedness or sensuality hath been the end of their folly."

> Of all people on earth, ministers most need the constant impressions derived from closet piety. If once they listen to the flattering voice of their admirers, and think they are actually holy because others treat them as such; if they dream of going to heaven *ex officio*; if, weary of public exercises, they neglect those which are private; or if they acquire the destructive habit of preaching and praying about Christ without any faith or emotion; then their course is likely to be downward. Far short, however, a minister of Christ may be of so dreadful doom, and yet be almost useless. To prevent such declension, the best advice I know of, is to be much in secret devotion; including in this term the reflective reading of Scripture, meditation, self-examination, prayer and praise. And here you must not expect from me any *recipe* for the conduct of such exercises, or rules for the times, length, posture, place, and so forth; for I rejoice in it as the glory of the Church to which we both belong, that it is so little rubrical. How often you shall fast or sing

---

1. aversion

or pray, must be left to be settled between God and your conscience; only fix in mind and heart the necessity of much devotion.[2]

I urge you to give the most scrupulous attention to these critical matters, trusting that I have gotten hold of your conscience in the exposition of them here. The importance of a healthy conscience cannot be overemphasized. A defiled conscience will take away relish for the Word and cause estrangement from the throne of grace.[3]

Engaging in Periodic Seasons of Intense Self-Examination and Protracted Seasons of Prayer

We ought to consider *engaging in periodic seasons of intense self-examination and protracted seasons of prayer.*

This is the fourth in the category of means ordained by God for the cultivation of our acquaintance with God and His ways. Yet I say that we *ought* to consider it. I cannot bind my conscience or anyone else's conscience from Scripture and put this in the same category as the previously addressed disciplines of the devotional assimilation of the Word, the habit and spirit of secret prayer, and the maintenance of a good conscience. However, there surely is much in Scripture to nudge us into a serious consideration of whether or not it would indeed contribute to that real, varied, expanding and original life with God if we engaged in periodic seasons of intense self-examination and protracted seasons of prayer. Therefore, let me set before you two categories of reasons why I believe we ought at least to consider this as a discipline, if not an essential one, yet greatly contributing to our spiritual growth and vigor.

First, the scriptures record such instances of periodic seasons of protracted time with God.

Though there are things peculiar to his unique place as the mediator of the Old Covenant, Moses had seasons of extended and extraordinary

---

2. J. W. Alexander, *Thoughts on Preaching* (Edinburgh: The Banner of Truth Trust, 1975), 110, 111.

3. Charles Bridges, *Psalm 119* (Edinburgh: The Banner of Truth Trust, 1987), 165–172 has some of the finest material on this subject of maintaining a good, healthy, and well-instructed conscience in our walk with God. Also, my audio series on *Perseverance* contains 10 sermons on the conscience. The late Pastor Robert P. Martin of Emmanuel Reformed Baptist Church in SeaTac, Washington, also preached a series of sermons on *The Conscience* which are valuable. These all are available on Sermon Audio.

intimacy of communion with God. Daniel also set himself to seek the Lord by prayer and fasting (Dan. 9:3). The call of the prophet Joel was a call to the entire covenant community, even to bridegrooms on their wedding night to forget their bride and to give themselves to seeking the face of God (Joel 2:12–17). We also have the example of our Lord Jesus, particularly His night seasons of prayer before critical periods in His life and ministry (Luke 6:12). Also, the apostle Paul, with respect to his thorn in the flesh, sought the Lord three times (2 Cor. 12:8).

The Lord corrected the thinking of His disciples by contrasting their devotional exercises with the Pharisees. He not only corrects wrong thinking about almsgiving and prayer, but says, "And when you fast, do not look gloomy like the hypocrites, for they disfigure their faces that their fasting may be seen by others" (Matt. 6:16). The assumption is that, among the community of His followers, there would be seasons of voluntary relinquishment of the normal indulgence of physical appetites to the end that they might give themselves to prayer. Surely this bulk of scriptural data at least nudges us in the direction of considering whether or not we too ought to engage in periodic seasons of intense self-examination and protracted seasons of prayer, possibly accompanied by fasting.

Second, Christian biography underscores the benefit of such seasons of intense self-examination and seasons of prayer.[4]

One cannot read through many Christian biographies without finding that at certain points along the way these men and women of God engaged in such seasons. Is this not one of the many reasons why such biographies have been reprinted, generation after generation, and still bless the people of God in modern times? Almost without exception, these men and women were not strangers to these seasons periodically undertaken for seeking the face of God in a protracted way.

Third, such seasons are necessitated by the power of indwelling sin, the dulling influence of constant contact with holy things, and the draining influence of the manifold tasks and burdens of the ministry.

There is much to consider under this point, since we are talking about three issues: indwelling sin, the nature of the work of the ministry, and ministerial burnout. We will now look at these one by one.

---

4. I refer again to my sermons series on *Perseverance*, in which I also deal with the subject of Christian biography and saints of old who persevered in their faith.

Perhaps the most fundamental problem necessitating such seasons is *the frightening power of indwelling sin that can dull our spiritual sensitivities and lead us into what, to us, is an almost imperceptible state of spiritual dullness.* We must remember from where we have fallen, repent, and do the first works (Rev. 2:5). This surely requires a season of remembering where we once were. What were the patterns of our devotional life in those better days? What were the patterns of our ruthless dealing with sin in former times? What things did we once recoil from with horror which we can now tolerate without a twinge of conscience? Often, there is a creeping weakness and degeneration in the soul that does not come into focus in the ordinary course of our devotional disciplines, but a season of intense self-examination and protracted prayer with fasting can be the means that God uses to help us to face that insidious, frightful power of our indwelling sin more realistically.

There is *the dulling influence of constant contact with holy things.* Where once we spoke of them with present feeling we can now speak of them with consistency and accuracy, but no longer with present feeling. The soul becomes dulled by its constant contact with these things. We become stale and tend toward professionalism and develop a ministerial shell. We need to pause, remove ourselves from our ordinary rhythms of life, and reflect long and hard on what the work of the ministry has become to us, and what this will mean for the flock of God over which we have been constituted over-seers if we do not deal with this trend.

There is also *the draining influence of involvement in the manifold tasks and burdens of the ministry.* They can simply wear us down to the point where only a season of protracted waiting upon God can refresh our souls and quicken again those graces of the inner life. I like to think of the mainte-nance of the aircraft on which we fly. I think most of you are probably aware that there is a schedule of aircraft maintenance. Standard maintenance is enacted upon various parts of the aircraft every so many hours of flight, but every so many thousands of miles or hours in flight certain parts of the aircraft are stripped of their skin. The main spar undergoes careful x-ray and examination for any stress cracks. I do not want to fly in a plane with-out those radical examinations. The standard day-by-day, week-by-week maintenance is not enough to ensure that the aircraft is a safe means of transportation. So it is with our souls. The daily discipline of seeking God, reading and meditating upon the Word of God, is like the standard mainte-nance of an aircraft, but occasionally we need the skin stripped off. We need the x-ray upon the substructure of the soul to bring to light what may be some dangerous area of spiritual declension. The prophet calls us to search ourselves and to commit ourselves to such a discipline. He says, "Let us test and examine our ways, and return to the LORD!" (Lam. 3:40).

Regular Exposure to the Masters of the Inner Life

We now address the last of the five means or disciplines by which we are seeking to experience that large, real, and varied acquaintance with God and His ways. We read, "And he gave the apostles, the prophets, the evangelists, the shepherds and teachers, to equip the saints for the work of ministry, for building up the body of Christ" (Eph. 4:11, 12). Though we are God's spiritual gifts to the church, we are yet members of the body and we need the exercise of those gifts in and upon us.

I love the statement of the apostle, where Paul is seeking to cut the nerve of the carnal attachment to this or that preacher, and he says to the Corinthian believers, "For all things are yours, whether Paul or Apollos or Cephas or the world or life or death or the present or the future—all are yours, and you are Christ's, and Christ is God's" (1 Cor. 3:21–23). God has given to the church in past days and in our own day men whose ministries have been particularly owned as "masters of the inner life," as I like to call them. I am referring to those men to whom God has given unusual insights concerning the struggles of the soul, the windings of remaining sin, the wiles of the devil, and the things that will keep us fresh in our relationship to the Lord. Such men are God's gift to me, and I ought to prayerfully, wisely, and judiciously own and use them, not as masters of my faith, but as helpers to my faith.

When I speak of things written by masters of the inner life, I am referring to John Owen's volumes on the *The Glory of Christ* (vol. 1), *Communion with God* (vol. 2), *Indwelling Sin, Temptation and Mortification of Sin* (vol. 6), and *Spiritual-Mindedness* (vol. 7); John Flavel's treatise on *Keeping the Heart*; Thomas Brooks's *Precious Remedies Against Satan's Devices* and *The Secret Key to Heaven*; John Bunyan's treatise entitled *Prayer*; *The Works of Sibbes*; Baxter's *The Reformed Pastor*; Scudder on *The Christian's Daily Walk*; Octavius Winslow's works, *The Glory of the Redeemer* and *The Precious Things of God*. These are some of the books to which I am referring when I talk about masters of the inner life. I have found in my own experience that often these men are a help. I call them my pump-primers. I simply take four or five pages as part of my devotional exercises when the wheels of engaging God seem to be sunk in the mud. Four or five pages of one of these men often lift me out of that state and begin to move me upward and outward to engage God in a meaningful way.

In summary, and concluding my treatment of these means which God has given us for the development of our inner spiritual life, I urge you, give yourself diligently to these things. Determine, by the grace of God, that in the battle of the basics you will not flinch, you will not quit the battle, but maintain this discipline of devotional assimilation of the Word, the habit and spirit of secret prayer, maintaining a good conscience toward God and man, periodic seasons of intense self-examination and protracted seasons of prayer, and maintaining regular exposure to the masters of the inner life. If, in spite of all that, there is no freshness, expansion, or increase of spiritual life in you, it is most likely because you are spiritually dead and not converted, and there is no life to expand and increase. If this is true of you, my dear reader, give yourself and give God no rest until you know that you have been born of the Spirit of God, are truly united to Christ, and indwelt by the Holy Spirit. May God mercifully grant that none of you will appear before God on the last day as an unconverted pastor!

May God help us as we have addressed these five disciplines. It is by them that God has ordained that we, His servants, may experience this large, real, varied, expanding experience of God and His ways. May God help us, so that the years ahead will prove that we have laid to heart the things in which our convictions have been refreshed and reinforced. For those who have considered them for the first time, I trust that they will be implanted, germinate, and continue to bear fruit until we cross the river.

CHAPTER 5

——○————————————○——

His Relationship to God Intellectually

Having addressed a pastor's spiritual relationship to God, let us now consider his intellectual relationship. By *intellectual,* I simply mean that aspect which involves the use of his mind in relation to God's truth and in every facet of pastoral life and pursuit. I begin, as I usually do, with an axiom to crystallize our thoughts about our need in the ministry to use our minds, and how we should proceed to meet that need.

You must seek a maturing, spiritual perception of the truth of God, both in its objective essence and in its practical application to the world of men and things.
    I need to immediately sound a note of caution as we ease our way into this aspect of our study. We must not think of this isolation and division of the spiritual and intellectual as if they were iron-clad or air-tight compartments of reality and experience. It should be obvious to all of us that the intellectual faculties are vigorously at work in the disciplines essential to a real, expanding, varied and original life with God. The issues I addressed in the previous lectures are as far removed from mindless mysticism as night is removed from day. Since we are sanctified by the truth (John 17:17), the activity of our minds in relationship to the truth is vital in our spiritual development. Furthermore, if we come to an increasing experiential acquaintance with God's good, acceptable, and perfect will by the renewal of our minds (Rom. 12:2), then there can be no mindless spirituality.
    Now, having made this qualification, it is possible that a man of God may experience a good measure of a humble walk with God along with the necessary intellectual exercises involved in such a walk, and yet fall short of his maximum potential for usefulness because of intellectual sterility, laziness, or a lack of general intellectual discipline. There is a sense in which a man may indeed be determined in his heart to love God wholly, but who is not prepared with equal diligence to love God with all his mind. Therefore, while fully recognizing the areas of overlap and interpenetration, we must

consider the intellectual development of the man of God as a distinct category of concern.

I now proceed to the first of the two major divisions of the lecture materials, explaining this axiom and its importance.

Explanation of the Axiom

I have asserted that the man of God must seek a maturing, spiritual perception of the truth of God, both in its objective essence and in its application to the world of men and of things. Now let me break this statement down into its major components and seek to explain them.

First, *the fundamental area of concern is our intellectual development with respect to the truth of God.*

I refer to the unchanging verities revealed to us by God in the books of general and special revelation, but with peculiar concern for the special revelation of Scripture. The perception of these verities ought to be at the heart of our intellectual pursuits and activities. We should not be dabbling in theories or in error, but plunging into the substantial realities of truth.

Here we do well to listen to the sagacious counsel of J. W. Alexander:

> The mind must be allowed some periods of calm, uninterrupted reflection, in order to librate [oscillate] freely, and find the resting-point between conflicting views. That time is sometimes expended in learning, examining, and collating arguments of all kinds, on different sides of a given question, which might, by a much more compendious method, have served to discern and embrace positive truth, or to make deduction from acknowledged truth. No wise counsellor would proscribe the perusal of controversies. Yet he who reads on different sides, must necessarily read much that is erroneous; and all tampering with falsehood, however necessary, is, like dealing with poisons, full of danger. If we might have our choice, it is better to converse with truth than with error; with the rudest, homeliest truth, than with the most ingenious, decorated error; with the humblest truth, than with the most soaring, original and striking error. The sedulous perusal of great controversies is often a duty, and it may tend to acuminate [sharpen] the dialectical faculty; but none can deny that it keeps the thoughts long in contact with divers falsities, and their specious reasons. Now these same hours would be employed far more healthfully in contemplating truths which in their own nature are nourishing and

fruitful. To confirm this, let it be remembered, that truth is one, while error is manifold, if not infinite; hence the true economy of the faculties is, wherever it is possible, to commune with truth. Again, while error leads to error, truth leads to truth. Each truth is germinal and pregnant, containing other truths. Only upon this principle can we vindicate the productiveness of solitary meditation....

With no common earnestness of entreaty we would therefore exhort the enterprising student to devote his days and nights to the search of verity, rather than the discovery, or as a first object, even the confutation of error. Offences must needs come, and must needs be removed; the Church must still have its controvertists; but in regard to the actor in these scenes, unnecessary polemics do harm.[1]

Far better that the mind be thoroughly impregnated with truth than inordinately cluttered with errors. A person who is responsible to identify counterfeit bills that are produced by the Federal Reserve spends most of his time, not examining the counterfeits, but mastering the distinctive qualities of the real thing. That person, by virtue of this thorough acquaintance and feel for the real, can at a glance detect the counterfeit. The mind of the man of God must be so conversant with truth that when he confronts an aberration he is able to detect it, not because he has spent an inordinate amount of time dabbling in the aberration, but because he has marinated his mind and heart in the truth of the living God.

Second, we must *strive for a maturing perception of the truth of God.*

When something is mature, it has reached its full development or its native ideal. The mature tree has reached its full potential. A normal infant child has all the appendages it will have in adulthood, namely, two hands, two eyes, two ears, a mouth and internal organs. However, these faculties have not come to their full development. A maturing perception of the truth of God concerns those truths that are implanted in the soul in our initial encounter with the grace of God in Christ through the gospel. These develop and flower and come to an ever-growing fullness in our understanding. They encompass what it means to be a child of God, who Christ is, our privileges in a state of grace, an ever-growing understanding of our duties and responsibilities, an ever-growing perception of the wonderful integration of truth, and how truth not only begets truth but beautifully dovetails with truth.

---

1. J. W. Alexander, *Thoughts on Preaching* (Edinburgh: The Banner of Truth Trust, 1975), 172–175.

Third, *this is a spiritual perception.*

We must use the word *spiritual* in accordance with New Testament usage. The *spiritual* is that which is given to a regenerated individual by the Person and ministry of the Holy Spirit. To be spiritual means to be in possession of the Holy Spirit and growing in all of His personal ministries in our lives. In this regard, we instinctively turn to His ministry of illumination, without which we cannot understand and apply the Word of God to ourselves or others. He is the One who alone can enable us to grasp spiritual realities so as to behold them in their inherent beauty and to feel the impress of their weight upon our souls, so that we perceive their implications for thought and practice. So when I say *spiritual*, I am not talking about something that bypasses the cognitive and the intellectual, I am referring to an operation upon the intellectual faculties of the man of God by the Holy Spirit Himself.

Fourth, *it is a spiritual understanding of truth's objective essence and in its application to the world of men and things.*

I refer to what Paul impressed on Timothy, "Follow the pattern of the sound words that you have heard from me, in the faith and love that are in Christ Jesus" (2 Tim. 1:13). The pattern of sound words is a reference to the objective body of truth which has come to us by inspiration through Jesus and the apostles.

Our postmodern society denies the possibility of objective truth formulated in specific words. This opposes Scripture. Paul tells Timothy of realities that were conveyed to him in words, and the words have form and structure. We must hold on to them and pass them on to others as the apostolic tradition for each generation. That is truth in its objective essence. However, we must also grow in our understanding, not only of objective truth, but of its application to the world of men and things.

Years ago, a man in our church was an instructor in auto-mechanics. From nine to noon every day, he lectured on what makes an automobile engine work. What are its parts? What are the pistons? What are the valves, what is the distributor, and how do the points and plugs and all the rest work? After he had instructed his students concerning the objective essence of an automobile engine in the morning hours, from one to four they went into the shop and dismantled an engine. They had the parts in their hands, and then they put the engine back together again. In this afternoon hands-on activity working with that hunk of iron that sits under the hood, they saw the theory in its application to the real world.

Each of us by temperament tends either to gravitate to an imbalanced obsession with truth in its *objective* essence or in its *application* to the world of men and things. As I have wrestled for many years with these tendencies in my own heart, I have also seen it in other men.

Take the *Westminster Shorter Catechism* for example. It gives us some of the best theology in a most helpful and memorable form. It helps us to grasp doctrine in its objective essence with accuracy, and work it out in dealing with others who need to apply the truth to their lives. We ought to strive to express God's truth in the form of sound words, not only as these are deposited in the scriptures, but as the apostolic tradition has been expressed and formulated in the crucible of the perpetual warfare between truth and error in the history of the church. I refer here to the historic creeds, confessions of faith, and catechisms which were produced in that warfare and are given to us as a precious legacy. We must love these biblically rooted, meticulously articulated and delicately balanced statements of objective truth. For example, when we are seeking to articulate to our people who Christ really is, we should love to quote the following words from the *Westminster Shorter Catechism* which asks: "Who is the Redeemer of God's elect?" The answer given is: "The only Redeemer of God's elect is our Lord Jesus Christ, who, being the eternal Son of God, became man, and so was and continueth to be, God and man in two distinct natures, and one person, forever" (#21).

Are you one that has a predisposition to love theological precision? Then you will need to work and pray that God will help you to be equally concerned with how these things apply in the real world of men and of things. If you have a more practical bent and you always want to know the how of things, you may have to take yourself by the back of the neck and the seat of the pants and plunk yourself down behind your desk and say, "I am going to memorize one question and answer of the Shorter Catechism per week in the coming year." I urge you to commit the Shorter Catechism to memory early in your ministry.

The Importance of the Axiom

I point you to J. C. Ryle's observations, who, in the following quote, is referring to counsel that Wesley gave a young preacher:

> To one who neglected the duty of private reading and regular study, he wrote as follows:—"Hence your talent in preaching does not increase;

it is just the same as it was seven years ago. It is lively, but not deep; there is little variety; there is no compass of thought. Reading only can supply this, with daily meditation and daily prayer. You wrong yourself greatly by omitting this; you never can be a deep preacher without it, any more than a thorough Christian. Oh, begin! Fix some part of every day for private exercises. You may acquire the taste which you have not; what is tedious at first will afterwards be pleasant. Whether you like it or not, read and pray daily. It is for your life! There is no other way; else you will be a trifler all your days, and a pretty superficial preacher. Do justice to your own soul; give it time and means to grow: do not starve yourself any longer."[2]

Charles Bridges also stresses that this is important:

It is of great moment, that the habit of study should, as far as possible, be maintained through life. For the most part—the ground work only has been laid. Let our early attainments excite, not satisfy, our thirst for information—divert, not bound, our investigations. If useful habits are gained, they are probably far from being matured. St. Paul's instructions so often alluded to, were given (as we have hinted) to an elder of some years' standing in the Church. Mr. Scott to the last combined the student with the Minister. "If we live only on old stores," (as a beloved brother has observed) "we shall never enlarge our knowledge." It is allowed, that it is not easy diligently to pursue a course of persevering study. Our families and our daily duties must not be neglected. It requires fixed plans, vigorously followed up. Our natural indolence, and the love of society, must be broken through. Cecil says—"Every man, whatever be his natural disposition, who would urge his powers to the highest end, must be a man of solitary studies."[3]

I have looked for many things in observing men over many years, trying to make whatever assessment was legitimate for me to make concerning their fitness for the ministry. However, I will mention two of those things as they relate to our present consideration. The first was a question that I asked myself, "Is this man a lover of people or only a lover of books?" The second question was, "Is he exclusively a lover of people and not a lover of books?" I have seen both kinds. I have seen men who thought they were called to

2. J. C. Ryle, *Christian Leaders of the 18th Century* (Edinburgh: The Banner of Truth Trust, 1978), 102.

3. Charles Bridges, *The Christian Ministry* (Edinburgh: The Banner of Truth Trust, 1976), 48, 49.

the ministry yet showed no real love for people. They did not spontaneously and viscerally connect with people and love people as people, but as bodies to which to preach. They were not patently lovers of men. I have seen others who were great lovers of men but who could not sit longer than five minutes in their study chair and engage in serious, lengthy, and demanding study. Yet, they felt they were called to the ministry because they loved people and people loved them, and they connected well. So, I repeat, we must be men who are committed to seek a maturing spiritual perception of the truth of God both in its objective essence and in its practical application to the world of men and things.

Directives for Implementing the Axiom

Now the big question is, "How is this maturing spiritual perception of the truth of God to be obtained?" I answer with two concrete directives, eight categories for balanced pastoral reading, and three basic cautions.

The first directive is that *you must make time in your weekly schedule for general reading.*

I deliberately did not say that you must *find* time, but that you must *make* time in your weekly schedule for general reading. Real, deep, thorough sermon preparation will force you to read and will therefore contribute to your intellectual vibrancy and freshness. In sermon preparation, your mind is coming into direct contact, not only with the oracles of God, but with other devout minds, well-trained men who have likewise grappled with that portion of God's Word which you intend to preach to His people. However, I am making a plea for regular reading beyond that which is necessary for responsible sermon preparation. I am speaking of the kind of reading which the old masters placed in the category of general, rather than specific preparation. They used that terminology, and I like it.

I find it helpful to think that, as a preacher, I am like a professional boxer who is described as a "club-fighter." Often, a "club-fighter" would be called on short notice to engage in a four-round boxing match conducted prior to the main event which would involve a ten or twelve-round match. Since the "club-fighter" never knew when he might be called upon to fulfill his role on short notice, he subjected himself to a continuous regimen of physical conditioning. In a similar way, pastors need to be engaged in continual regimens of mental conditioning, continually stretching and disciplining our minds to think in areas in which our sermon preparation might never take us if we were to preach for another fifty years. The old writers saw the benefit of this discipline.

Consider what Alexander has to say concerning this matter:

> If our brethren are unanimous in anything, it is, in Luther's judgment, that sound and varied learning must be sustained, if we would preserve the Church.
>
> There is such a thing as maintaining a transient popularity, and having a little usefulness, without any deep study; but this fire of straw soon burns out, this cistern soon fails. The preacher who is constantly pouring out, and seldom pouring in, can pour but a little while. I need hardly caution you against the sententious maxim, prevalent among freshmen, concerning those great geniuses, who *read little, but think much*. They even cite, as of their party, one of the greatest readers who ever wrote, as every work of his goes to prove; to wit, Shakespeare! The greatest thinkers have been the greatest readers, though the converse is by no means true. In reading the writings of those most remarkable for originality and invention—and mark, it is in reference to these qualities only the reference is now made—we know not whether most to admire the adventurous flights of their own daring, or their extensive acquaintance with all that has been written before, on their chosen topics.... What theologians say of preparation for death, may be said of preparation for preaching; there is *habitual*, and there is *actual* preparation: the current of daily study, and the gathering of material for a given task....
>
> These are evils which can be prevented only by the resolute pursuit of general studies, irrespectively of special pulpit performance. Such habits will tend to keep a man always prepared; and instead of getting to the bottom of his barrel as he grows older, he will be more and more prepared, as long as his faculties last.[4]

My second directive is *that you must establish a balanced reading program.*

You must not only allocate time to read, but give thought to *what* you are going to read and in what proportions you are going to read the various things that you believe will make you a more effective servant of Christ.

---

4. J. W. Alexander, *Thoughts on Preaching* (Edinburgh: The Banner of Truth Trust, 1975), 127, 128.

Dr. Lloyd-Jones has an excellent section on this point of the general reading of the man of God in his book, *Preaching and Preachers*. The doctor writes:

> Before I go on to other types of reading I would emphasize strongly the all-importance of maintaining a balance in your reading. I cannot stress this too much. Because of our natural differences we all have our prejudices and preferences, so there is the type of man who spends the whole of his time reading theology, another reading philosophy, another psychology; they tend to read practically nothing else. This is really dangerous, and the way to counteract it is to prescribe balanced reading for yourself. What I mean is this. Read theology, as I say, but always balance it, not only with Church history but with biographies and the more devotional type of reading. Let me explain why this is so important. You are preparing yourself, remember, and the danger for the intellectual type of man, if he is only reading theology or philosophy, is to become puffed up. He persuades himself that he has a perfect system; there is no problem, there is no difficulty. But he will soon discover that there are problems and difficulties; and if he wants to avoid shipwreck, the best thing he can do when he feels that he knows all, and is elated and tempted to intellectual pride, is to pick up say the *Journals of George Whitefield*. There he will read of how that man was used of God in England, Wales, Scotland and America, and also of his experiences of the love of Christ; and if he does not soon feel that he is but a worm, well then I suggest that he has never been regenerated. We continually need to be humbled. That is why balanced reading is an absolute essential. If your heart is not as much engaged as your head in these matters, your theology is defective—apart from anything else. There is this real danger of becoming over-theoretical, over-academic, over-objective, over-intellectual. That will mean not only that you are in a dangerous spiritual state yourself, but also that to that extent, you will be a poor preacher and a poor pastor. You will not help your people and you will be failing at the task to which you are called.[5]

Now let me seek to distill the counsel of these men, mixed with my own observation and experience. In any balanced reading program, as part of your ongoing intellectual maturity, you should include the following

---

5. D. Martyn Lloyd-Jones, *Preaching and Preachers* (Grand Rapids: Zondervan, 1972), 178, 179. See the whole section from 174–179. I also commend to you the section in Bridges, *The Christian Ministry*, pages 33–50, an excellent section on this matter of establishing a balanced reading program.

categories of reading. Now, I am not saying that all eight of these categories ought to be included in any given morning or afternoon, or two days marked out for general reading in any given week. That would be downright foolish and unrealistic, but in the time of your weekly schedule that is ordinarily marked out for general reading over the course of a month or two, most of these categories should be included, at least to some limited degree, in the scope of your general reading.

When I say these things, remember that for forty-six years I was doing the work of a resident pastor, lecturer, conference speaker, with a few other things thrown in besides. So please realize that when I outline what, in my judgment, would constitute a balanced reading program, I am not taking the role of a Pharisee and seeking to bind burdens impossible to be borne and burdens which I myself would never bear.

Categories for Balanced Pastoral Reading

The first category for a balanced pastoral reading program is *devotional reading*.

By this I mean reading that is aimed primarily at the cultivation of your heart, conscience, life, communion with Christ, and of your sense of what it is to live before God as a man of God. I am not talking about shallow, banal and sentimental little devotional thoughts which occupy some daily devotional books. I am talking about the things that Lloyd-Jones addresses when he says:

> Next in order I would say is—and I cannot think of a better term though I do not like it in some ways because it has been so abused— "devotional reading." I do not mean by that what are called devotional commentaries. I abominate "devotional" commentaries. I do not want other people to do my devotions for me; yet I cannot think of a better term here. I am thinking of a type of reading which will help you in general to understand and enjoy the Scriptures, and to prepare you for the pulpit. This type of reading comes next to the Scriptures. What is it? I would not hesitate to put into this category the reading of the Puritans. That is precisely what they do for us. These men were preachers, they were practical, experimental preachers, who had a great pastoral interest and care for the people. So as you read them you find that they not only give knowledge and information, they at the same time do something to you. Again I would emphasize that it is most important that the preacher should know not only himself in general

but also his particular moods and states and conditions. The preacher should never be moody; but he will have varying moods. No man can tell what he will feel like tomorrow morning; you do not control that. Our business is to do something about these changing moods and not to allow ourselves to become victims of them. You are not exactly the same two days running, and you have to treat yourself according to your varying conditions. So you will have to discover what is the most appropriate reading for yourself in these varying states.[6]

Following this counsel, your knowledge of yourself and your people will grow in accuracy. For example, you may read John Bunyan's *Pilgrim's Progress* as an aid to your devotions. You may find, as I have found, that every time you read *Pilgrim's Progress,* you say, "How in the world did I miss that the fourth or the fifth time through?" Your own experience becomes the key to understanding Bunyan. In a previous reading, you slid over things because your own experience did not find an echo in what Bunyan wrote. You will find yourself dealing with one of your sheep and lo and behold you will say, "Oh my, Bunyan had those kinds of people in his congregation as well." This is what I am addressing when I speak of devotional reading.

Alexander's comments are most helpful here:

> I hope you will let no kind of reading keep you from looking daily—if only for five minutes—into a class of writers, who are not attractive in regard to letters, but who unite great talents, great Bible knowledge, and great unction. At the head of these stands Owen. My father used to say one should read "Owen's Spiritual Mindedness" once a year. I add, his "Forgiveness of Sin"; his "Indwelling Sin," and his "Mortification of Sin."[7]

You may find it helpful, as I have many times in my pilgrimage, to use such reading as a pump-primer to the whole time set apart for devotional exercises. You may find the works of J. C. Ryle helpful for devotional reading. I recommend as well the devotional works of B. B. Warfield, particularly his *Faith and Life,* which is a collection of sermons he preached in the chapel sessions at Princeton Seminary. Read Spurgeon's sermons to have your own heart and mind come into friction with a man whose obsession with the Person of Christ is, at times, discouraging as well as encouraging, but always

---

6. D. Martyn Lloyd-Jones, *Preaching and Preachers* (Grand Rapids: Zondervan, 1972), 174, 175.

7. J. W. Alexander, *Thoughts on Preaching* (Edinburgh: The Banner of Truth Trust, 1975), 92, 93.

a prod. I get discouraged at times only because I ask myself, "Will I ever begin to love Christ like Spurgeon loved him?" Yet, coming near the heat of Spurgeon's heart, some of that heat is then transferred to our own hearts.

The second category for a balanced pastoral reading program is *theological reading*.

I mean especially systematic theology, in which God's truth is stated and demonstrated in its inter-relatedness and then defended. It is broken down into its component parts in a systematic and orderly fashion.

Listen again to the sagacious counsel of Alexander:

> Besides all your sermon making, *Theology, as a system, must be your regular study.* Neglect this, and your pulpit theology will be one-sided; many topics will never have due consideration. It shall augur badly for your career, if you are found uninterested in great theological questions. Some established works should be daily in your hands; and of such works a few should be often re-perused. Find a clergyman who knows nothing of such pursuits, and you will observe his preaching to be unmethodical, and little fitted to awaken inquiry among deep thinkers in his flock. He will soon attain his acme, and will continue to dispense milk where he should give strong meat. The analogy of other professions will occur to you; the lawyer or physician who reads law or physics only for this or that case, can never take high rank.[8]

I urge you to read primarily, though not exclusively, the proven masters in this field of systematic theology. There are men who are a great rage for a while in their own generation, but their systematic theologies and their theological treatises will die with them never to be resurrected in a second printing or subsequent edition. Among those that ought to be the stuff of our reading are Calvin's *Institutes,* Owen in his denser theological treatises, Jonathan Edwards, William Cunningham, James Buchanan, George Smeaton, Patrick Fairbairn, W. G. T. Shedd, Charles Hodge, R. L. Dabney, J. H. Thornwell, John Dagg, James P. Boyce, B. B. Warfield, and John Murray. We have these men in our possession, men who are proven gifts of Christ as theologians and who have been given to the church for establishment in the truth against every wind of doctrine. Surely there are more recent excellent systematic theologies, particularly the works of Louis Berkhof, G. C. Berkouwer,

---

8. J. W. Alexander, *Thoughts on Preaching* (Edinburgh: The Banner of Truth Trust, 1975), 168.

Herman Bavinck, Robert Reymond, J. I. Packer, Michael Horton, John Frame, and Wayne Grudem. These men may very well take their place with the great lights of previous generations. I hasten to add the recent publication of the first of eight projected volumes on *Systematic Theology*, by Gregory G. Nichols, former professor at Trinity Ministerial Academy.

I also want to make mention of giants in the experimental Calvinistic theology of the Dutch tradition. In my earlier years, when I was voraciously reading the proven British and American theologians, there were very few works from men in the Dutch tradition available in English translations. However, that situation has drastically changed in the past twenty-five years, primarily through the influence and ministry of Dr. Joel Beeke. Many of these works have been translated and printed and are readily available from Reformation Heritage Books.[9]

We should seek not only to master some of these works, but to be mastered by them. As we read a devout theologian, one who "trembles at [God's] word" (Isa. 66:2), while holding it in his hands, and one who is deeply solicitous to present the mind of God accurately in a systematic and organized way, something of their spirit touches us. I find myself periodically reading Warfield's essay on "The Emotional Life of our Lord" and I am moved every time, as I see him—almost with trembling hands—gleaning the data out of the gospels in which we are given little windows into the emotional life of our Lord Jesus. That penetrating essay is void of the shallow, clap-trap indulged by so many modern writers who have concocted a quasi-theological perspective out of the stuff of pop psychology. Men who approach the Scripture this way go searching the Word to find a text that looks something like a first-cousin-twice-removed from the theory they are propounding. In contrast, when we are reading men like Calvin, Murray, and Warfield, we sense that men of stature are handling the Word of God with holy trembling and seeking to bring out of the text that which He has already deposited in it.

The third category for a balanced pastoral reading program is *biographical reading.*

Scripture commands us to mark those who walk after the pattern of the apostolic example. Paul said, "Brothers, join in imitating me, and keep your

---

9. Reformation Heritage Books, 2965 Leonard St. NE, Grand Rapids, Michigan 49525 (USA). A catalog of their books is available upon request (616-977-0889 or online at www. heritagebooks.org).

eyes on those who walk according to the example you have in us" (Phil. 3:17). We are commanded to imitate the faith of those with an exemplary pattern of life (Heb. 13:7). One of the best ways to fulfill those biblical injunctions is to read biographical material. Read such books in order to discern the common denominators of the godliness and usefulness of the men whose lives are there pointing us to greater holiness, to greater zeal in advancing the Kingdom of Christ, and to what God's grace can do with frail yet sinful human beings in advancing the work of God in and through them. We read biography not to parrot those whose lives we read, but to penetrate into the principles which made them what they were.

For example, when I first composed this lecture, I was reading the larger biography of John Peyton, missionary to the New Hebrides. As I was reading that fascinating biography, I cited specific instances where such practical pastoral issues were being helped in my own life by reading his biography: his commitment to thorough sermon preparation, principles of guidance, and wise parental perspectives. Just within that short compass, my own life was being helped, and in turn, I was being given the stuff by which to illustrate and to enforce biblical principles in my preaching to God's people. Read the lives of those who made a mark in their own generation, and who, at the same time, inspired others to leave a record of their lives for future generations. The biographies of John Calvin, John Knox, Martin Luther, George Whitefield, Charles Spurgeon, Robert Murray M'Cheyne, David Brainerd, William Carey, Edward Payson, Asahel Nettleton, Philip and Matthew Henry, Mary Slessor, Amy Carmichael, and a host of others, have challenged the lives and ministries of untold multitudes over the course of many generations. We can add to that minimally framed list, in the more recent history of the church, the biographies of Jim Elliott, John Murray, D. Martyn Lloyd-Jones, and others who, by the blessing of God, have left a legacy of godliness and usefulness. We need to get into contact with these men of God through those well-written biographies which highlight what the grace of God wrought in them and worked through them.

The fourth category for a balanced pastoral reading program is *church history.*

Solomon could say that there is nothing new under the sun, and it is true even with reference to books. As we read the history of the church and some of the details of the specific epochs of the ongoing spiritual conflict between truth and error, we are enabled to see that error, though dressed in new clothing, is still error. Its external shape and the fashion of its dress may differ, but it is the same in substance. One of the great benefits of studying church history is that it makes us sensitive to the approach of various aberrations from the truth. Hence, in addition to exerting a quality-control effect upon our own thinking, it also gives us wonderful illustrative material for our preaching. You should have access to Philip Schaff's multi-volume *History of the Christian Church*. I trust that none of us is bored with history, because history is *His story*. History shows the footprints of God walking through His world in the bracket of space and time, and tracing out His footprints ought to be a thrilling, as well as a helpful thing to us.

The fifth category for a balanced pastoral reading program is *pastoral and homiletical reading*.

I am referring to books geared to instruct us in some area of pastoral theology. I pointed out in the introduction to Unit 1 that these lectures which you are reading are suffused with quotations from the time-tested and proven masters of pastoral theology. Here I emphasize William Perkins, *The Art of Prophesying*; Thomas Murphy on *Pastoral Theology*; J. W. Alexander's *Thoughts on Preaching*; D. Martyn Lloyd-Jones on *Preaching and Preachers*; and those books that are in the category of pastoral and homiletical issues— those that will aid us in understanding and fulfilling those tasks. Along with these men of the past, I heartily commend Pierre Ch. Marcel's excellent little book *The Relevance of Preaching*, and James S. Stewart's work entitled *Heralds of God*.

When it comes to matters more homiletical, let me express my prejudice that we be discerning or even beware (in some cases) of modern writers. On homiletics, they have often been shaped and formed in a context totally devoid of classic rhetorical training. By contrast, the older writers on this subject such as R. L. Dabney, Gardiner Spring, and John Broadus were men whose thinking about preaching as an art form was shaped by classical, rhetorical perspectives. I regard the insights of rhetoric to be a facet of general revelation, insofar and only as far that they do not contradict the scriptures.[10] Preaching is a form of one human being communicating to other human beings, and someone can stand outside that communication process and observe what makes one man grip the ears and minds of a group of people more than another. That activity is open to general observation and critical analysis resulting in the codifying of those principles which contribute to or undermine effective communication. Therefore, it is my

---

10. I deal with the subject of sacred rhetoric in Unit 4, chapter 1.

settled persuasion that while homiletics is dealing with the communication of special revelation, we are neither to be ignorant of nor indifferent to that general revelation which God has given us concerning the most effective ways to communicate the raw materials of special revelation.

Apart from a Speech 101 course which I was required to take in college, I have had no formal training in rhetoric. However, as I have read and reread some of these older writers, I have found that they have greatly confirmed me in my own tentative conclusions, gained by personal observation and reflection, concerning some of the most fundamental elements of effective oral communication.

For example, you know as I do that it is far easier to listen to a man speak when he looks you straight in the eyes, and when he is free, in the totality of his humanity to communicate to you as a whole person. Contrast this with the man who stands with his hands clasped behind his back and his face glued to his paper. After about ten minutes it takes an exercise of Herculean discipline for you to continue to listen to him with any serious attention. He may have material that in the mouth and in the person of a Whitefield or a Spurgeon would have melted thousands to tears, but he will not even move a worm. Need I say more? I urge you, do not be indifferent to those things that will help you to become a better communicator of the Word of God.

The sixth category for a balanced pastoral reading program is *polemical reading*.

One of the tasks of an elder is that of refuting the gainsayers. Paul says, "He must hold firm to the trustworthy word as taught, so that he may be able to give instruction in sound doctrine and also to rebuke those who contradict it" (Titus 1:9). Paul further says, "They must be silenced, since they are upsetting whole families by teaching for shameful gain what they ought not to teach" (Titus 1:11). Although this may not be the most pleasant of your tasks, it is necessary, and so I urge you to include in your structure of general reading some place for occasionally grappling with general apologetics, critiques of both ancient and modern cults and the New Age Movement. It is our responsibility to examine these movements to some degree (in keeping with all of our other responsibilities) which sweep through the church and carry so many with it. Such movements as Theonomy, the distortions of classic, covenantal Calvinistic thought, the so-called New Covenant Calvinism, and others.[11] Though we may dislike it, we ought to include the polemical in our balanced reading.

The seventh category for a balanced pastoral reading program is *technical reading*.

It is good for us to keep abreast of issues of textual criticism and other studies which are so encouraging in validating our confidence in the Word of God.

The eighth and final category for a balanced pastoral reading program is *contemporary and secular reading*.

This is God's world and we need to be sensitive to what He is doing in our world at this time. We need to be able to grasp what some of the current writers call the *horizon* of the New Testament Greco-Roman world, the circumstances of the churches then, and how we are to bring it to the horizon of the present time and the present world. What are the things that are pressing in on our people and seeking to conform them to the manifestation of a devil-controlled world system in our own time? What is the rage in terms of current television or Internet obsession? How many of our people who have cable television are dabbling in some of the popular sitcoms? We need to have some opportunity, by structured reading, to be in touch with the contemporary secular world in which we are ministering, the world which impinges upon our people. So, I urge you, brethren, not to be those who stick their heads in the sand. I am not urging that you get a daily newspaper and spend an hour with it. I could not do that with a good conscience, but you must make time in your balanced reading program for some exposure to the world that is.

Closing Cautions

I close this lecture with some warnings.

First, *do not make reading a substitute for thinking*. The aim of your reading ought to be the acquisition of true knowledge. Some forget that the

---

11. *The New Calvinism Considered* by Jeremy Walker is a helpful resource. Another excellent resource is *Going Beyond the Five Points: Pursuing a More Comprehensive Reformation*, by Dr. Richard Barcellos, Dr. Sam Waldron, Earl M. Blackburn, and Dr. Robert P. Martin; Foreword by Dr. James R. White; Rob Ventura, general editor. Published in 2015, it is available at www.amazon.com.

purpose of a good book is to ignite the fires of intense thought and reflection upon a given subject.

Lloyd-Jones is helpful here:

> In a sense one should not go to books for ideas; the business of books is to make one think. We are not gramophone records, we are to think originally. What we preach is to be the result of our own thought. We do not merely transmit ideas. The preacher is not meant to be a mere channel through which water flows; he is to be more like a well. So the function of reading is to stimulate us in general, to stimulate us to think, to think for ourselves. Take all you read and masticate it thoroughly. Do not just repeat it as you have received it; deliver it in your own way, let it emerge as a part of yourself, with your stamp upon it. That is why I emphasize the general principle that that is the chief function of learning. It is tragic when men become mere gramophone records, or tape-recording machines with the same thing being churned out and repeated endlessly. Such a man will soon become barren; he will soon be in difficulties; and his people will have recognized it long before he does.[12]

Second, *do not make the amount of reading you do a status symbol.* One has rightly stated that every enlargement of intellectual knowledge has a natural tendency to self-exaltation. Never forget that you are never more like the devil than when you are puffed up with pride.

Third, *do not make reading a substitute for the other duties of the ministry.* One of the great skills in the Christian life is knowing what truth you need to preach to yourself at any given time. There will be a sheep that needs to be visited and right at that time the devil will bring to mind this course in which I exhorted you to commit yourself to a schedule of balanced reading. You will be tempted to say, "What? This is my reading time! I cannot go visit the sheep."

Heed the exhortations given by Bridges:

> The habit of study must be guarded, lest it should become an unsanc-tified indulgence; craving to be fed at the expense of conscience or propriety; employed in speculative enquiries, rather than in holy and practical knowledge; pre-occupying the time that belongs to imme-diate duties; or interfering with other avocations of equal or greater

---

12. D. Martyn Lloyd-Jones, *Preaching and Preachers* (Grand Rapids: Zondervan, 1971), 181.

moment. A sound judgment and a spiritual mind must be exercised, in directing these studies to the main end of the Ministry. Let none of them intrench upon those hours, that should be devoted to our study of the Bible, or our preparation for the pulpit. And wheresoever we find our inclination too much attached to any particular human science, let us set a guard upon ourselves, lest it rob us of Divine studies, and our best improvement. A Minister should remember, that himself with all his studies is consecrated to the service of the sanctuary. Let every thing be done therefore with a view to one great end; and let us pursue every part of science with a design to gain better qualifications thereby for our sacred work.[13]

As I close this lecture, I also urge you to carefully and periodically read this sobering exhortation given by Thomas Murphy with regard to the necessity of study:

The pastor must study, study, study, or he will not grow, or even live, as a true workman for Christ. The want of this is the cause of innumerable failures which are seen in the ministry. Here is a young man who enters upon the office with fine talents, a fair amount of preparation, an encouraging field of labor and every prospect of success. But the promise is not fulfilled. He does not come up to the expectations which were excited, and which he himself entertained. On the contrary, his preaching decreases in interest, his congregation falls away and his whole work declines. The reason is, he has not kept his mind polished up by constant study, or continued to replenish it with the rich stores of thought which he might have gathered from other sources.[14]

This, then, is my burden concerning the intellectual relationship of the man of God in the pastoral office to his God. May He grant us grace and wisdom as we seek to pursue and structure our lives and work to feed our minds so that we may feed our people.

---

13. Charles Bridges, *The Christian Ministry* (Edinburgh: The Banner of Truth Trust, 1967), 49.

14. Thomas Murphy, *Pastoral Theology* (Audubon, NJ: Old Paths Publications, 1996), 93.

CHAPTER 6

His Relationship to God Physically and Emotionally (1)

The subject matter that I purpose to address in this lecture will in some ways be very difficult, both to persuade you of its importance, and for you to implement. We move on now to consider the man of God in relationship to his physical and emotional health and vigor. We will follow the same basic outline which framed the previous lectures dealing with the spiritual and the intellectual aspects of the life of the man of God before his God as he labors in the pastoral office. I will state a major axiom, and then I will seek to support, explain, and apply it.

The axiom is that *you must seek to attain and maintain an accurate understanding of your present physical and emotional constitution, and engage in a regular but flexible discipline aimed at keeping these two aspects of your redeemed humanity in optimum health and vigor.*

The Necessity of the Central Concern of This Axiom

I begin with addressing the matter of the necessity and the inevitability of this concern for the pastor's physical and emotional health and vigor. I am fully aware that there are some who might question whether such issues should even be made a part of a course on pastoral theology. My answer to such doubts is that there are at least five basic categories of reality which not only make this concern legitimate, but actually demand that the subject be addressed by any responsible teacher of pastoral theology.

These things must be taken seriously by every man, one either preparing for, or one already engaged in pastoral labor. I will set forth five reasons for this necessity. The first four of these five reasons are taken from special revelation and the fifth from general revelation.

First, we ought to seek and attain an understanding of our present physical and emotional constitution, and the engagement in a regular and flexible discipline to maintain them in optimum health, *because the biblical doctrine of man demands it.*

Anthropology, a heading in systematic theology, asserts that man is not simply, or even essentially or primarily, a soul housed in a shell called a body, like the knife is housed in its sheath or a hand is placed in a glove. Rather, according to the scriptures, man as a living soul is a *psychosomatic* (soul-body) entity, and his essential identity cannot be understood, nor does it exist apart from this reality, as this foundational text declares, "Then the LORD God formed the man of dust from the ground and breathed into his nostrils the breath of life, and the man became a living creature" (Gen. 2:7). Having formed man's bodily dimensions out of the dust of the earth, God breathed into him the breath of life and man became a living creature. That psychosomatic entity is the *image of God,* not just his soul, not just the non-material dimension of man's created being. Here is the divine design at the pronouncement of man's creation,

> "Let us make man in our image, after our likeness. And let them have dominion over the fish of the sea and over the birds of the heavens and over the livestock and over all the earth and over every creeping thing that creeps on the earth." So God created man in his own image, in the image of God he created him; male and female he created them (Gen. 1:26, 27).

There is a clear distinction between the body (material) and the soul (non-material) in man's constitution. Jesus said, "And do not fear those who kill the body but cannot kill the soul. Rather fear him who can destroy both soul and body in hell" (Matt. 10:28). However, the Bible teaches that there is a powerful, delicate, and constant interplay between the body and the soul in man. We see it in the book of Proverbs, "Be not wise in your own eyes; fear the LORD, and turn away from evil. It will be healing to your flesh and refreshment to your bones" (Prov. 3:7, 8). As there is a compliance in terms of the mind and the spirit—not being wise in our own eyes, fearing the Lord and departing from evil—there will be a spillover into the physiology of the godly man in terms of the blessing of refreshment to the body. That idea appears again in this passage:

> My son, be attentive to my words; incline your ear to my sayings. Let them not escape from your sight; keep them within your heart. For they are life to those who find them, and healing to all their flesh. Keep

your heart with all vigilance, for from it flow the springs of life (Prov. 4:20–23).

Here, the proper nurture of the inner man spills over into the life and the health of the flesh. We see it yet again when the wise man wrote, "A joyful heart is good medicine, but a crushed spirit dries up the bones" (Prov. 17:22).

So here in these passages and throughout the scriptures, we see the health of the soul pumping life into the body. The converse is also true, the non-health of the soul pumping its negative influence into the body. God's Word gives us some graphic illustrations of this damaging interplay between the soul and the body. David's sin bloodied his conscience and cut him off from realized communion with God. We find the record of this in Psalms 6, 32, and 51. Read and see how many physical problems he speaks of in these portions. He talks of *crying* till he can cry no more. He speaks of the *roaring* of his bones. There was a tremendous impact upon the totality of David's humanity because of his sin. Elijah's depression reveals the physical, emotional, and spiritual complex of problems which he faced (1 Kings 19:2, 3).

One of the most touching illustrations of this outside of the Bible is from the life of Spurgeon. The first time I read it I wanted to resurrect Spurgeon and throw my arms around him and encourage him as my brother. Standing before his students who came back to the Metropolitan Tabernacle for an annual convocation, he said to them:

MY DEAR BRETHREN,—I greatly value your prayers, and I feel intensely grateful for that Benjamin's share in them which is ever my portion. I never consciously needed your intercessions more than I do just now, for I may say with the psalmist, "He weakened my strength in the way." After my severe illness, I am trembling like a child who is only just commencing to use his feet. It is with difficulty that I keep myself up; what can you expect from one who can scarcely stand? During the last six weeks, I have considered from day to day what to say to you, but nothing has come of my consideration. My meditations have been a failure. I have gone to the pits and found no water, and returned with my vessel empty. My brain has been so occupied with sympathy for the poor body that it has not been able to mount aloft with the eagle, nor even to plume its wings for the lower flight which I must needs attempt this morning. One thing, however, is clear,—I am in special communion with my subject, and can speak, as the good old people used to say, "experimentally." I cannot, however, draw much aid from that fact; but I cast myself upon the power Divine, which has so many times been displayed in weakness. "The Lord hath been mindful of us: He will bless us."[1]

Spurgeon then went on to preach from Paul's confession, "For the sake of Christ, then, I am content with weaknesses, insults, hardships, persecutions, and calamities. For when I am weak, then I am strong" (2 Cor. 12:10). Do you have to restrain weeping when you read of this mighty giant confessing that his brain was so occupied with sympathy for the poor body that it was not able to produce any sense of preparation for a particular ministry? I say that the biblical doctrine of man demands that we consider the place of the physical and emotional health of the man of God in the ministry. This principle of the interplay between the body and the soul is even more serious for the man who has been called and equipped for the work of the ministry.

We are not like the angels who are sent forth to minister to the heirs of salvation! Whatever we may be as new men in Christ and as men equipped by Christ, we are still human, by virtue of our distinct identity established by God in our creation. He who forgets this fact and acts as though it were not true does so to his own peril and harm, and often to the truncating of his optimum usefulness in the work of the ministry. God has made us with a nervous system that has sophisticated circuitry, and if you run too much current over that system for too long something is going to blow. We have a body that God likens to a clay vessel which, if pressed beyond reason, will crack and shatter. Granted, special grace will be given under special demands in the path of revealed duty. However, we must not tempt God. My understanding of what it means to tempt God, according to Matthew 4:7, is to place ourselves in a position of danger to which our duty has not brought us, but rather our own folly or presumption. The Tempter commanded Christ to cast Himself down and to put Himself in the place of danger, promoting the rationale that the angels would bear Him up. Our Lord would not put Himself in the place of danger of being splattered on the base of the temple. He would not tempt His God.

I know that some will take what I am saying and become ministerial sluggards and clerical parasites. Others will go to the extreme of the asceticism condemned in Colossians 2:20–23 and 1 Timothy 4:1–5. The solution is for you to accept the reality that you have a bodily existence and an emotional constitution. Furthermore, you must have a proper anthropology which looks

---

1. C. H. Spurgeon, *An All-Round Ministry* (Edinburgh: The Banner of Truth Trust, 1960), 198, 199.

that reality straight in the face and responsibly seeks to do what must be done to keep this psychosomatic entity in optimum strength, health and vigor.

The second reason for the necessity of this axiom is that *the law of God demands this conscious concern* for our physical and emotional health and vigor.

If you are not familiar with the Larger and Shorter Catechisms of the Westminster standards, I urge you to obtain them and make yourself familiar with them. I alluded to this in a previous lecture. Under our present subject look specifically at the sections on the moral law of God. The Shorter Catechism question #68 asks, "What is required in the sixth commandment?" The answer is, "The sixth commandment requires all lawful endeavors to preserve our own life, and the life of others." Then question #69 asks, "What is forbidden in the sixth commandment?" The answer is, "The sixth commandment forbiddeth the taking away of our own life, or the life of our neighbor unjustly, or whatsoever tendeth thereunto." This matter is critical; whatever tends to the taking away of life is condemned by the Sixth Commandment. So I say that the law of God demands that we be concerned about this issue as men of God seeking to live before the face of God with optimum usefulness in the work of God. There must be a concern for our physical and emotional health and vigor.

The third reason for the necessity of the axiom I have set forth is that *the biblical doctrine of salvation demands it.*

You and I must not hone our consciences by the pressures or expectations of men, but by the law of God. We must not allow ourselves to be bullied by the growing burdens of the ministry until we succumb to ministerial burnout. We must underscore and assert that the biblical doctrine of salvation demands this concern. As sin has radically altered, for the worse, the totality of our body-soul humanity, so God in grace has designed and provided a remedial and restorative power that touches the whole of our humanity.

The Word of God is plain in its teaching that God's saving purpose is to conform us to the image of Christ in His glorified bodily existence. It is not only to be conformed to Him in our nonmaterial existence when we will know, in the language of M'Cheyne, the blessedness of loving God with an unsinning heart and have spirits in which every last vestige of sin will be taken away. The Bible is just as clear that until these bodies are resplendent with the glorified body of our Lord Jesus, we have not come to the full inheritance of our salvation. Supporting texts are abundant (Rom. 8:23; Phil.

3:20, 21; 1 Thess. 4:14; 1 Cor. 15). We readily acknowledge that this physical deliverance awaits the return of Christ. Yet precisely because we are marked out for such a destiny, we must manifest our conviction about the dignity of the body which God has marked for resurrection at the practical level.

Yes, it is now the body of our humiliation. It is our outward tent that is getting torn and ripped and frayed (2 Cor. 5:1). The outward man is perishing (2 Cor. 4:16). Yet our service to God is to be rendered bodily, and in that service we are to mirror something of God's regard for the body. Romans 12:1 does not say, I beseech you by the mercies of God to present your *hearts* holy, undivided to God. No, it says,

> I appeal to you therefore, brothers, by the mercies of God, to present your bodies as a living sacrifice, holy and acceptable to God, which is your spiritual worship. Do not be conformed to this world, but be transformed by the renewal of your mind, that by testing you may discern what is the will of God, what is good and acceptable and perfect (Rom. 12:1, 2).

Paul says, "for you were bought with a price. So glorify God in your body" (1 Cor. 6:20). The bodies of the redeemed are purchased property. God thinks enough of them that He bought them at the price of the blood of His own Son, and they are marked for resurrection glory. Between now and the consummation, the concern for my bodily existence, as well as my nonmaterial subsistence, is to reflect God's concern for both of these aspects of my redeemed humanity.

Therefore, when the apostle is giving a litany of ministerial and personal duties to his spiritual son Timothy, he says to him, "Have nothing to do with irreverent, silly myths. Rather train yourself for godliness; for while bodily training is of some value, godliness is of value in every way, as it holds promise for the present life and also for the life to come" (1 Tim. 4:7, 8). Timothy was to commit himself to all the disciplines that are essential to growth in likeness to Christ. He was to exercise himself for the purpose of godliness in the vigor of the inner man. The reason for this is rooted in what Paul said to him, and I paraphrase Paul's directive to Timothy for emphasis, "Timothy, I am laying on your conscience the responsibility of exercising yourself to godliness. While bodily exercise is profitable for a little, godliness is profitable for all things, having promise of the life which now is and of that which is to come."[2] So, when we speak of *relative* importance, surely the disciplines essential to growth in godliness take precedence over the responsibilities of those disciplines called "profitable bodily exercise." Yet the disciplines of godliness do not negate the disciplines of the body, which are profitable. The relative importance of something does not negate the validity, necessity, or even urgency of the thing, and this is the case here. Bodily training or discipline is an essential physical necessity.

For what is bodily discipline profitable? I answer, it is profitable for the care of this *body* purchased by Christ and marked for resurrection glory. Furthermore, it is the only instrument in which I can serve God in this life. Paul has no scruples in saying to Timothy, "No longer drink only water, but use a little wine for the sake of your stomach and your frequent ailments" (1 Tim. 5:23). What is Paul doing? He is saying in effect, "Timothy, I am giving you a home remedy for your frequent infirmities. Do not be indifferent to the reality of your infirmities, and do not be reluctant to take the practical steps to alleviate them, in order that you may fulfill the responsibilities I have given to you more effectively." The text at least says that much, because as men of God our service is rendered in our bodily existence. The biblical doctrine of salvation demands a legitimate concern for our physical as well as our emotional health and vigor.

The fourth reason for the necessity of the axiom I have set forth is that *the biblical doctrine of preaching demands it.*

Preaching as God's Word describes and explains it implies the importance of the integration between the preacher's mind, heart, and body as the entire vehicle of communication. A man whose mind and heart are impregnated with God's truth and borne along by the power of God's Spirit seeks to convey to others through the totality of his redeemed humanity that which the Word and Spirit have put into his mind and heart. Just as surely as the most penetrating spiritual insights into the meaning of Scripture are not preaching until translated into speech, articulated by the lips of the preacher with the assistance of the larynx, the diaphragm, and the lungs, so there is no effective use of the lips without bringing into its service the whole physiology of the man of God.

---

2. First Timothy 4:8 is one of the most positive statements about concern for our physical well-being in all of Scripture, yet it is quoted to the opposite end for downplaying the importance of bodily disciplines.

Likewise, to speak convincingly and with earnestness requires one whose own emotions have felt the pressure of the truth conveyed. Therefore, the emotional energy of the truth in which the preacher traffics is channeled through his emotional constitution, which becomes the handmaiden of an impregnated mind and heart. If the emotions are overly strained and exhausted, then to some degree, he cannot be what he ought to be as a preacher, and the people of God are robbed. If I can state it bluntly, if you are not concerned to do something about your physical and emotional health, you have some dimension of indifference to the highest good of your people. Think about this. Will your preaching be more effective if you bring to it a well-tuned physiology and a healthy and vibrant emotional constitution? Then you owe that to your people. Just as you would not think of willfully, deliberately, or carelessly bringing to them the fruit of sloppy exegesis, then surely you do not want to bring to the act of preaching an emotional and physical constitution that robs your people of your best.

The words of Paul should be true for the preacher in his physical and emotional state in the act of preaching, "Whatever you do, work heartily, as for the Lord and not for men" (Col. 3:23). A man may have worked hard to develop a well-furnished mind, but through excessive and relentless use, this same man may come to the pulpit mentally exhausted, and because of this, his mind does not have enough alacrity to assist him in articulating that truth to his utmost capacities. Therefore, he either fumbles along, or is glued to his paper, which, in either case, negates the establishment and sustaining of that living current between him and his people.

The fifth and final reason for the necessity of the axiom I have set forth is that *the past and present experience of men of God demands this concern.*

It is sad to read John Owen's acknowledgement that irreparable damage was done in his earlier years because of failure to come to grips with the physical and emotional health that he ought to have sustained during those years.

Ebenezer Porter wrote:

> But the truth is, that my own *experience* is not less admonitory to young men, than my *precepts*; as a brief sketch of this experience will show. I entered College at the age of fifteen. Those active habits, which had previously sustained my health, were gradually diminished during two and a half years of severe study, often continued to a late hour at night. Without one admonition or apprehension of my danger, my strength imperceptibly declined, till a single cold threatened to destroy

my lungs. Six months' travelling enabled me to resume my studies. Thus admonished, I proceeded with more regularity and caution, till my health was confirmed by the saddle exercise [horseback riding], which I was called to take, as a candidate for the ministry. As a pastor, I soon became so involved in labors, that I gradually forgot the past, and presuming too much on the stock of strength I had acquired, devoted to my study every hour, that I dared to retrench from my exercise and parochial duties. Upon emergencies I often sat at my table [desk] from *twelve to fifteen* hours in a day; and not unfrequently read or wrote an hour or two after midnight.... Eight years after my ordination, during the accumulated labors and excitements, incident to a revival, in my congregation, my health failed, so that I was unable to preach for forty-six sabbaths. By resorting again to the saddle, to mechanical labor at the work bench, to wood-sawing, to gardening, and at last to holding the plough (*instar omnium*, in my case,) sufficient strength was gained to go on with my ministry; but it was only the strength of an invalid. Now, it was my *calamity* to have inherited a constitution predisposed to catarrh and dyspepay; but it was my *fault*, (and a grievous one,) that I invited disease, by indulging love of study, without a more settled *plan of daily exercise*. I bless God, that for the last twenty years, a thorough reformation has enabled me, not indeed to retrieve former mistakes, but to *live*; and by his gracious smiles on my imperfect labors, to live, as I hope, not wholly in vain.[3]

We also have Blaikie's testimony:

It now remains to say a few words on *physical* preparation for preaching. The present generation is much more disposed than some of its predecessors to believe in a certain connection between good health and good preaching, although to many persons it may seem that there is no such connection, while a smaller number may think that a preacher's delicate health actually aids a right impression. And no doubt there is a certain class of truths which are taught more impressively by a man who bears the seal of death on his wasted face; but, on the other hand, such a man's influence in other respects is feeble, if not injurious. "It is impossible," says Mr. Beecher, "for an invalid to sustain a cheerful and hopeful ministry among his people. An invalid looks with a sad eye on human life. He may be sympathetic, but it is almost always with the shadows that are in the world. He will give out moaning and drowsy

---

3. Ebenezer Porter, *Lectures on Homiletics and on Preaching and on Public Prayer and Lectures on Eloquence and Style* (Andover, MA: Gould and Newman, 1836), 510, 511.

hymns. He will make prayers that are almost all piteous. It may not be a minister's fault if he be afflicted and ill, and administers his duties in mourning and sadness, but it is a vast misfortune for his people."

The sad, sombre, melancholy look of the invalid preacher, and, indeed, a heavy, dull, dreary look in any preacher, has a specially repulsive effect on the young. It insensibly leads them to associate with church services the very opposite of those happy feelings which they so readily associate with their sports....

It is very certain that due attention to physical exercise is an essential condition of sustained vigorous preaching. The command to be "strong in the Lord" includes strength of body as well as strength of soul. A whole Saturday spent in the study, and particularly a whole Saturday night, is not favourable to that physical vigour which usually underlies good preaching. "The speakers that move the crowd," says Beecher, "men after the pattern of Whitfield, are usually men of very large physical development, men of very strong digestive powers, and whose lungs have great aerating capacity. They are men of great vitality and recuperative force.... They are catapults, and men go down before them."

Some men may affect to despise these things, but it is a foolish affectation. Subordinate though their place may be, it is a real place notwithstanding; at least in every case where "the bow *abides* in strength, and the *arms of the hands* are made strong by the hands of the mighty God of Jacob" (Gen. xlix. 24).[4]

Those testimonies ought to make us weep, and they ought to be like huge yellow caution lights blinking about a foot in front of our eyes. We need to listen to the old masters. They have something to teach us. I submit then, that these five lines of evidence should convince us of the necessity and the inevitability of being concerned about our physical and emotional health as men of God in the pastoral office.

This is not a matter of seeking to cultivate body worship. I have never been one that gets an endorphin "high" with my exercise regimen. I put my physical exercise in the category of praying—it is an activity in which to engage whether I feel like it or not. When it is time to pray, you go to pray; when it is time to read your Bible, you read your Bible; when it is time to put on your exercise clothing and footwear, you put them on and go down to your cellar and get on the treadmill or make your way to the local YMCA or health club, or off to the local park with its bike and walking trails. You

---

4. William G. Blaikie, *For the Work of the Ministry* (London: J. Nisbet & Co., n.d.), 83–85.

do it because you are persuaded you ought to do it. You do this because you are persuaded from the Word of God that it is your duty. You do not want to bloody your conscience by not doing it, since you believe the words of James who said, "So whoever knows the right thing to do and fails to do it, for him it is sin" (James 4:17).

Over the years, I have found great spiritual profit in using the central thought of Romans 12:1 as the basis of a prayer I pray when I am about to begin my exercise regimen. I say something to the Lord along the following lines:

> Gracious God, I come once more to offer up my body to You as a living sacrifice. Bless this regimen of exercise to contribute to my overall health and strength since this body, destined for the grave, is the only body in which I will serve You until the resurrection. I want to serve You as well as I can, with as much vigor and strength as I can, for as long as I can, and to this end I pray that You will bless this practical endeavor to attain that goal.

For a number of years, while on my treadmill, I listened to the recording of the scriptures done by Alexander Scourby. In recent years, I read spiritually edifying books, often one of Owen's works, loaded on my Kindle. Having prayed for God's blessing upon the cultivation of my physical wellbeing, I then plead with God for His blessing upon the material I will read. I can honestly say that this has often turned the space my treadmill occupies at the gym to become nothing less than a veritable Bethel, a house of God.

If God chooses to afflict me with some form of debilitating disease, it will be important to have a good conscience at that point and say, "Lord, I did not welcome this affliction, nor did I bring it on myself by my careless indifference to the necessity and benefits of physical exercise." I am quite certain that there are some men who will read these lines and seek to rationalize their refusal to yield to the truth they contain. They may desire to say to me something like, "Well Pastor Martin, over the years you have been careful about your diet, your weight, your exercise, and your vitamins, and look at all the surgeries you have had, and now you are going deaf, what good did it do you?" I respond:

> I tell you what good it did me. I am standing up here lecturing three times a day for two solid weeks while in my mid-to-late seventies. I am not puffing like an old horse ready to go to the glue factory. Furthermore, at the end of these two weeks, I can go home to a wife who is

attracted to me, not just because of what is on the inside, but because of what she puts her arms around on the outside. And I can stand in that pulpit behind me as I lecture, and from that sacred place call men to a life of discipline, self-control, manly bearing and demeanor, and know that I have on my side the conscience of those to whom I speak.

With regard to diet, when people ask me what I eat and I tell them, they say, "Well that is like living on a partial fast." I say, "Yes, it is, because that is the realistic assessment of where I am right now at my age and my metabolism." That is reality, and God, being the Lord of reality, calls me to live and function within that framework.

I am not sharing these personal things to set myself forth as a perfect example, but I do say these things with a good conscience, as the writer to the Hebrews could say, "for we are sure that we have a clear conscience, desiring to act honorably in all things" (Heb. 13:18). I trust and pray that your consciences will be persuaded that indeed these four lines of biblical argumentation and the fifth from general revelation are sufficient to incline you to embrace a legitimate concern for the well-being of our physical and emotional lives. If this persuasion is realized, then all of us should be prepared to seek, obtain, and maintain a realistic assessment of where we are physically and emotionally, and to commit ourselves to a lifestyle regimen that, with God's blessing, will keep us in optimum physical and emotional health, to the glory of God and to the good of our people.

> Our Father, help us to think biblically about who we are and where we are in our physical and emotional constitution, and to be good stewards of what You have entrusted to us, that we might serve You all the days of our lives, and then, when our task is done, to fall asleep in Jesus. Hear our prayers, and continue Your blessing upon us. We plead these mercies in Jesus' name. Amen.

CHAPTER 7

His Relationship to God Physically and Emotionally (2)

In this lecture, we again take up the axiom that you must seek to attain and maintain an accurate understanding of your present physical and emotional constitution, and engage in a regular, but flexible discipline aimed at keeping these two aspects of your redeemed humanity in optimum health and vigor.

In the previous lecture, I concentrated on the necessity and inevitability of this concern for the pastor's physical and emotional health and vigor. In this lecture, I will focus on the explanation and implementation of this principle.

If you have any acquaintance with the incessant workings of your own remaining sin, and I am assuming you do, then you know very well that there is always a fibrous strain of indisposition in our hearts toward our revealed duties. So, at the beginning of this lecture we need to pray with the psalmist, "Incline my heart to your testimonies, and not to selfish gain!" (Ps. 119:36). David was conscious that though he loved the testimonies of God, and though the prevailing disposition of his heart was obedience to those testimonies, there was always a disinclination in another direction. The apostle Paul captures the reality of these things when he writes, "So I find it to be a law that when I want to do right, evil lies close at hand" (Rom. 7:21).

Having set before you in the previous lecture the five reasons as to why this subject, in my judgment, ought to be included in any responsible course in pastoral theology, I want to explain the significant words in that axiom as stated, and then make a number of concrete applications by way of warnings and exhortations. Let me explain what I have in mind when I state that we must seek to attain and to maintain an accurate understanding of our present physical and emotional constitution.

Explanation of the Principle

The first area of concern is *attaining and maintaining an accurate assessment of who and what you are physically and emotionally.*

It is God who knit us together in our mothers' wombs. This is the comforting teaching of Psalm 139:13–16 and Job 10:8–12. He did not knit us all together in the same way. As a result of His creative wisdom, we each have a multitude of individual traits inherent in our genes. Our early training contributes to the differing constitutions which we all have. Some have naturally strong, vigorous constitutions, while others have naturally weak constitutions and are susceptible to all kinds of ills. Likewise, some have been knit together in their mothers' wombs and trained in their youthful development so that we can say of them that they have great emotional strength and resilience. Others are relatively weak emotionally, and it does not take much pressure for them to have their emotional strings unstrung.

This is reality, and God is the Lord of that reality. We need to face this continually because the various factors involved in this reality are not static but constantly changing. Paul's exhortation is a constant call to sober self-assessment of who and what and where we are at any point in life: "For by the grace given to me I say to everyone among you not to think of himself more highly than he ought to think, but to think with sober judgment, each according to the measure of faith that God has assigned" (Rom. 12:3). That is why I write of attaining and maintaining an accurate assessment of who and what we are both physically and emotionally. Paul reminds us that the "outer self is wasting away" (2 Cor. 4:16).

This means that the measure of physical and emotional resilience that one had at thirty is unlikely to be his at fifty and sixty. I eventually had to come to grips with this in my ministry at Trinity. I began to consider relinquishing the place of prominent leadership which I had for years at Trinity, not only because of the undeniable evidences of attrition and diminution of physical strength, but particularly my emotional strength. I found in my later years that when we as elders faced certain kinds of pastoral issues that exerted tremendous emotional pressure upon us, I would feel the same kind of weakness that I felt after the lengthy trial with my wife's illness and her ultimate death. I experienced lightheadedness and symptoms that I do not know how else to explain, as though someone had opened the petcock at the bottom of the radiator and all of the antifreeze and coolant has been drained. I realized that it was not right for the people of God to have a man in a position of key leadership who was not emotionally strong and resilient.

We find that incident with respect to David and his physical ability as a warrior, "There was war again between the Philistines and Israel, and David went down together with his servants and they fought against the Philistines.

And David grew weary" (2 Sam. 21:15). At least he had learned one lesson, that to stay back at Jerusalem while his troops went out to fight was to leave himself unnecessarily vulnerable to sin. However, we read that David's weariness nearly got him killed on the battlefield,

> And Ishbi-benob, one of the descendants of the giants, whose spear weighed three hundred shekels of bronze, and who was armed with a new sword, thought to kill David. But Abishai the son of Zeruiah came to his aid and attacked the Philistine and killed him. Then David's men swore to him, "You shall no longer go out with us to battle, lest you quench the lamp of Israel" (2 Sam. 21:16, 17).

Notice here that there came a time when David's sword got heavy too soon, when the millisecond of reflexive response in battle was critical. We need to realistically face, not by coddling ourselves, but in an honest, sober assessment, the present status of our physical and emotional strength.

The second area of concern has to do with *establishing a regular but flexible discipline of activities related to personal, domestic, and ministerial issues, which will sustain us at optimum physical and emotional levels of strength and vigor.* We pray:

> Our Father in heaven, hallowed be your name. Your kingdom come, your will be done, on earth as it is in heaven. Give us this day our daily bread, and forgive us our debts, as we also have forgiven our debtors. And lead us not into temptation, but deliver us from evil (Matt. 6:9–13).

If those petitions are sincere, then we will do all within our power to put ourselves in the way of their answer. We are praying hypocritically to be led not into temptation if we deliberately place our feet, hands, eyes, or ears, in a path of temptation. If, indeed, we are praying to be delivered from the evil one, then we will both watch, as well as pray; we will flee the occasions of sin. Likewise, when we are committed to serve God with optimum physical and emotional strength, then we will be prepared to do what we ought to do in establishing a structure of activities and relationships—personal, domestic and ministerial—that will contribute to that optimum strength and vigor, both physically and emotionally.

Granted, God calls us to submit to the unexplained and the unexpected intrusions that negatively affect our physical and emotional strength. Paul recounted one of these in his own life in that fascinating account in 2 Corinthians 12. God may use different means to bring us into a place of unexpected and undesired weakness. It may be a weakness like Paul's thorn, which we too may think is an impediment to our fulfilling the will of God for us. When Paul says, "Three times I pleaded with the Lord about this, that it should leave me" (2 Cor. 12:8), I have no question that his primary motive was not his own convenience or his own comfort. Paul was a man who had experienced so much in the way of physical and emotional discomfort in the cause of Christ, but he saw this thorn in the flesh as an impediment to fulfilling the purpose of God for him as an apostle. So, he prays that it might be removed, not expecting the Lord's wonderful, alternate response, "My grace is sufficient for you, for my power is made perfect in weakness" (2 Cor. 12:9). The Lord was saying to Paul, "There is another element in the equation, Paul, and the element is this. I can spread the power of My Son over you like a tent.[1] I can use a weak man by enveloping him with My power, but I will not use a proud man, because I resist the proud and give grace to the humble." Then, whether by a direct verbal revelation or by imparting spiritual understanding to Paul, the apostle came to recognize the divine design behind this trial. He expressed that insight when he wrote, "So to keep me from becoming conceited because of the surpassing greatness of the revelations, a thorn was given me in the flesh, a messenger of Satan to harass me, to keep me from becoming conceited" (2 Cor. 12:7). With this insight firmly embraced, Paul could go on to say,

> Therefore I will boast all the more gladly of my weaknesses, so that the power of Christ may rest upon me. For the sake of Christ, then, I am content with weaknesses, insults, hardships, persecutions, and calamities. For when I am weak, then I am strong (2 Cor. 12:9, 10).

The psalmist said, "He has broken my strength in midcourse; he has shortened my days" (Ps. 102:23). I am not ignorant, either from the scriptures or my own experience, that God does bring upon us unexplained, unexpected intrusions. These weaken us physically and utterly drain and enervate us emotionally. However, in the light of the overall teaching of the Word of God, we have a responsibility to seek to establish a structure of

---

1. Some commentators suggest that the verb translated "may rest" suggests that Paul may be using an analogy drawn from the Shekinah glory dwelling over and inhabiting the tabernacle. See the extended footnote in Philip E. Hughes, *The Second Epistle to the Corinthians* NICNT (Grand Rapids: Eerdmans Publishing Co., 1962), 452, 453. Also, see Charles Hodge, *1&2 Corinthians*, Geneva Series of Commentaries (Edinburgh: The Banner of Truth Trust, 2000), 662–664.

activity and relationships that will most likely, with God's blessing, contribute to our physical and emotional health and vigor.

The third and final area of concern focuses on *our redeemed humanity*.

It keeps in focus that you and I are redeemed sinners purchased by the blood of Christ and indwelt by the Spirit of God. Our entire being is the redemptive property of another, and that has profound implications for this matter of seeking optimum physical and emotional health and vigor. Paul said, "For you were bought with a price. So glorify God in your body" (1 Cor. 6:20). Since I am the property of another, I have a responsibility to conduct myself in all of the areas of my life on the basis of that relationship. I know of no truth that influences me more profoundly at the practical level of my own thinking and my practice, than the reality that I am blood-bought property. This body is the very temple and sanctuary of God, the Holy Spirit. I should seek to do all within my power to keep this temple in good order, that God may be glorified and that His purposes will be accomplished through me.

Having sought to demonstrate the necessity of this concern by means of the five lines of truth expounded in the previous lecture, and having asserted and given a brief explanation of the significance of the words of the axiom, we now come to the practical directives for the implementation of these concerns.

Practical Implementation of the Principle

I am conscious that there is some overlap and interpenetration between these two areas of concern, but I want to address this heading nonetheless in two basic subheadings—those directives pertaining to our physical health and those pertaining to our emotional health. I couch them both in the form of warnings. Keep in mind the importance of warning in the Bible, "Moreover, by them is your servant warned; in keeping them there is great reward" (Ps. 19:11). I trust that you have more sense than to be irritated by warnings, and that you are men who will welcome gracious warnings for your own well-being.

Our Physical Health

The first warning is to *beware of indulging a fundamental ignorance of or indifference to the basic facts of health and nutrition.*

Paul says, "So, whether you eat or drink, or whatever you do, do all to the glory of God" (1 Cor. 10:31). How can we consciously say, "Oh God, I am seeking to eat and drink to Your glory," though I am blissfully and willfully ignorant of what foods will do me good and nourish me, and what foods or drinks may harm me? You simply cannot do it, brethren. The preacher who loads his system with excessive salt, excessive amounts of caffeine, whether in his coffee, his tea, or his soft drinks, and then has high blood pressure, is setting himself up for a stroke; he is not eating and drinking to the glory of God. He is eating to the destruction and harm of a blood-bought temple of the Holy Spirit. Now that is blunt language, but I am not fearful that I can be challenged on scriptural or factual grounds. It is a *fact* that excessive imbibing of salt and caffeine in combination are great contributors to high blood pressure, and high blood pressure to other physical maladies, some of them deadly. Some say, "Well, I just do not read the articles." Willful ignorance does not exempt from culpability. I am not making a plea for body worship, nor am I making a plea for over-fastidious obsession in which someone reads the labels on everything, and after scrutinizing, finds one little ingredient that is not organic and readies himself to pronounce a curse on it. Let all things be done in moderation. I have no sympathy for that kind of nonsense. Go to the library if you cannot afford to get a couple of good, responsible books on what the body needs in the way of a balanced, nutritional diet and the things that contribute to the overall vigor and health of your body. Find out what things are least likely to contribute to setting yourself up for the diseases that ravage millions in our own country.

The second warning is to *beware of excessive weight accumulation.*
Although this exhortation could properly be ranged under the first, it is important enough to give this higher profile by a distinct heading. As a general rule, ministerial fat and maximum ministerial usefulness are incompatible. "Ah, but look at so-and-so; he was grossly overweight and used of God." Yes, he may have been, and to his own Master he stands or falls, but the sin of another is not the justification for my sin. How do we know what years some of the men of God of the past might have had of greater and longer usefulness had they been conscientious about the matter of their excessive weight?

Now, why does excessive weight accumulation ordinarily erode ministerial usefulness? I give three reasons.

The first reason is that *excessive weight produces sluggishness.*

There is a strain upon your heart to pump blood through that extra flesh. You will be unable to throw yourself into preaching without puffing and wheezing like an old pack mule. I have seen some men, who when they experienced a "holy fit" in preaching with something of the fire and the spiritual energy of their souls coming through, it had to break through so much fat that they almost undid what they were seeking to say.

The second reason is *the crippling effect of a guilty conscience.*

I have yet to meet a grossly overweight preacher, whom, if he is honest with me, does not tell me that his conscience smites him continually. I know it is not fair that a man can be secretly feeding his soul upon the foul, noxious, devilish filth of Internet pornography and nobody know but him and God, but if a man is feeding on too many calories, everybody knows. It is not fair, but that is reality, and it has a crippling effect upon a man because his conscience smites him. He cannot deny what he sees when he looks in the mirror or when he tightens his belt. If we are committed to maintaining a clear conscience toward God and man, one of the most sensitive areas in the maintenance of that conscience is what the scales tell us. I love the scales. They do not listen to my rationalization or my argumentation. They just look up at me and tell me the truth. The scale does not read, "You weigh somewhere in the range of so many pounds today." It gives the precise number. I do not say to it, "Oh, please just shave the truth a little bit for me because when you tell me the truth my conscience smites me."

The third reason is that *it breaks your grip on the consciences of others.*

How can we be blameless as self-controlled men (1 Tim. 3:2) when what we carry on our bellies and our jiggling jowls scream to our people, "I do not have control over my fingers at the table." How can we project blamelessness in the area of self-control if there is a continual visual declaration to our people that we do not have control over our physical appetite for food? We must be ruthless with ourselves. This is exactly what Paul was talking about when he said, "I discipline my body and keep it under control, lest after preaching to others I myself should be disqualified" (1 Cor. 9:27). He used the vigorous verb *hypōpiazō*, which means to *bruise* till black and blue. This is why the whole concept of mortification is at times grossly brutal and ugly, like cutting off the hand and plucking out the eye that offends (Matt. 5:30; 18:8).

It is a terrible thing to lose a grip on the consciences of your people. How can we say to our people, "Be imitators of me, as I am of Christ" (1 Cor. 11:1)? How can we say that we are seeking to be obedient to the injunction, "We put no obstacle in anyone's way, so that no fault may be found with our ministry" (2 Cor. 6:3)? My brothers, if you have a struggle in this area, you must do whatever is responsibly necessary to get a handle on this issue, to the glory of God. This is so that you might be optimally strong, vigorous, and energetic to serve Him, that you might have a clear conscience toward God, and that you might have a grip upon the consciences of others.

The third warning is to *beware of the no-planned physical exercise syndrome.*

Our technological age has made much of the normal, ordinary physical activity of a bygone day outmoded and obsolete. We read Porter in a previous lecture where he said that he went back to the plow, splitting wood, and horseback riding to regain his lost health and physical vigor. These are the things that an ordinary man might have done in the course of his ordinary life in those days. With our technology, we have produced a very sedentary lifestyle, and the nature of our pastoral work brings maximum mental and emotional strain with a minimum of vigorous physical activity. In light of this, ministers are prime candidates for the results of no-vigorous-cardiovascular exercise, exercise that makes the heart pump and causes the blood to surge through the entire circulatory system.

The evidence of the connection between planned exercise and optimum health is also clear. We are not talking about having to go out and pump iron and having to do something that is unusually vigorous. Just twenty minutes to a half an hour of a brisk walk every day at the end of the day is more of what I have in mind as a modicum of exercise. All that I read in my medical newsletters keeps coming back and emphasizing the same thing. If our society would give itself simply to that suggested measure of physical exercise five days a week, the degree of the declension of heart disease and all of the rest would lessen. I urge you, establish a plan and do it now, whether walking, jogging, swimming, or whatever it is, something in which you can consciously say, "Lord, you made the body in such a way that it functions best when it undergoes some element of stress upon the cardiovascular system, so I am seeking to respond to this conscientiously." Please, I beg of you, do not treat this as an Al Martin hobby horse. It is not. I believe it grows out of a biblical perspective of what our bodies are and what it means to glorify God in them.[2]

---

2. See my book, *Glorifying God in your Body: Your Body—Whose is it—Yours or His?* (Montville, NJ: Trinity Pulpit Press, 2017).

The fourth warning is to *beware of a pattern of cheating on a necessary measure of sleep.*

Now, I am aware that the Bible is unsparing in its castigation of the sleep-lover. We see an example of this in the words,

> Go to the ant, O sluggard; consider her ways, and be wise. Without having any chief, officer, or ruler, she prepares her bread in summer and gathers her food in harvest. How long will you lie there, O sluggard? When will you arise from your sleep? A little sleep, a little slumber, a little folding of the hands to rest, and poverty will come upon you like a robber, and want like an armed man (Prov. 6:6–11).

We may paraphrase and modernize Solomon's words as follows, "You lazy guy, push your sheets off and find a little ant hill somewhere and sit down with a notebook and learn from the ant and his industriousness."

Furthermore, the Bible has a doctrine of self-denial, and self-denial sometimes impinges upon the measure of our sleep. The Lord said to the three in the garden, "So, could you not watch with me one hour? Watch and pray that you may not enter into temptation. The spirit indeed is willing, but the flesh is weak" (Matt. 26:40, 41). It was late at night. It was ordinary sleep time, yet our Lord graciously castigates them that they were sleeping when they ought to have been watching with Him. This is why Paul spoke about "many a sleepless night" (2 Cor. 11:27). The biblical doctrine of self-denial calls us at times to yield up the ordinary measure of sleep for the higher interest of the Kingdom. However, the same Bible teaches us the truth, "It is in vain that you rise up early and go late to rest, eating the bread of anxious toil; for he gives to his beloved sleep" (Ps. 127:2). This is the picture of the man that is cheating on his sleep because he believes it is necessary for him in order to make provision for himself and his family.

God can give, while you are sleeping, the things that you think can only be attained when you are awake and cheating on your legitimate measure of sleep. While the Bible is silent on so many details of the earthly life of our Lord, it does give us an interesting detail when we compare Mark 4:35–38 with Luke 8:22, 23. Jesus unashamedly took a nap in the late afternoon and He did it in front of all of His disciples in a boat! I know some men who are reluctant to ever tell anyone that they take a nap, as if it were somehow like going to the local bar. No, for some of us an afternoon nap is a great means of grace for the restoration of our vigor, in order to live out the day and not quit at six or seven, but still be productive into the evening hours. The necessity for a realistic cycle of sleep and work is part of our creaturehood, not our sinnerhood. Day and night are not going to be part of the new creation, but they were part of the original creation.[3]

Think again of what God did for His servant Elijah (1 Kings 19), when the painted witch Jezebel sent notice that she was after him, and the prophet of God who had previously stood courageously before several hundred false prophets and wicked King Ahab was now reduced to a shaking leaf with a death wish. Elijah's Lord did not immediately take him out to a cave and begin to weight his conscience. Rather, the Lord said (in effect), "My servant is all messed up, has lost sleep, and there has been excessive heat going over the wires of his emotional constitution. I am going to feed him and put him to sleep." That does not sound very spiritual, but that is what God did. He put Elijah to sleep, fed him, woke him up, fed him some more, and then He began to help him realize that it was sleep that had refreshed him. Through rest the emotional wires had cooled down so that he began to think rationally. God showed him that his *perception* of reality was not the *measure* of reality: "You think you are the only one left? This is what I have done. I have reserved seven thousand who have not bowed the knee to Baal. Now you just get on your way; I have more work for you to do." What did he do then? He ran a marathon in the strength that the Lord gave him, clearly derived from the Lord's R&R and nourishment. So, beware of the cheat-sleep syndrome.

Spurgeon said:

> IN THE MIDST OF A LONG STRETCH OF UNBROKEN LABOUR, the same affliction may be looked for. The bow cannot be always bent without fear of breaking. Repose is as needful to the mind as sleep to the body. Our Sabbaths are our days of toil, and if we do not rest upon some other day we shall break down. Even the earth must lie fallow and have her Sabbaths, and so must we. Hence the wisdom and compassion of our Lord, when he said to his disciples, "Let us go into the desert and rest awhile." What! when the people are fainting? When the multitudes are like sheep upon the mountains without a shepherd? Does Jesus talk of rest? When Scribes and Pharisees, like grievous wolves, are rending the flock, does he take his followers on an excursion into a quiet resting place? Does some red-hot zealot denounce such atrocious forgetfulness

---

3. If you want a wonderful uninspired picture of what sleep was and what marital bliss was, read Milton's *Paradise Lost* in the section of the first night in Eden with Adam and Eve lying down to sleep together. It is a beautiful literary picture of the sanctity of the God-given blessing of sleep.

of present and pressing demands? Let him rave in his folly. The Master knows better than to exhaust his servants and quench the light of Israel. Rest time is not waste time. It is economy to gather fresh strength.

Look at the mower in the summer's day, with so much to cut down ere the sun sets. He pauses in his labour—is he a sluggard? He looks for his stone, and begins to draw it up and down his scythe, with "rink-a-tink—rink-a-tink—rink-a-tink." Is that idle music—is he wasting precious moments? How much he might have mown while he has been ringing out those notes on his scythe! But he is sharpening his tool, and he will do far more when once again he gives his strength to those long sweeps which lay the grass prostrate in rows before him. Even thus a little pause prepares the mind for greater service in the good cause. Fishermen must mend their nets, and we must every now and then repair our mental waste and set our machinery in order for future service. To tug the oar from day to day, like a galley-slave who knows no holidays, suits not mortal men. Mill-streams go on and on for ever, but we must have our pauses and our intervals. Who can help being out of breath when the race is continued without intermission? Even beasts of burden must be turned out to grass occasionally; the very sea pauses at ebb and flood; earth keeps the Sabbath of the wintry months; and man, even when exalted to be God's ambassador, must rest or faint; must trim his lamp or let it burn low; must recruit his vigour or grow prematurely old. It is wisdom to take occasional furlough.

In the long run, we shall do more by sometimes doing less. On, on, on for ever, without recreation, may suit spirits emancipated from this "heavy clay," but while we are in this tabernacle, we must every now and then cry halt, and serve the Lord by holy inaction and consecrated leisure. Let no tender conscience doubt the lawfulness of going out of harness for awhile, but learn from the experience of others the necessity and duty of taking timely rest.[4]

The fifth warning is to *beware of dependence upon or addiction to stimulants or depressants.*

Paul says, "for while bodily training is of some value, godliness is of value in every way, as it holds promise for the present life and also for the life to come" (1 Tim. 4:8). A man could have said fifty years ago, "There is no reason that I cannot enjoy my cigars or my cigarettes and inhale them; it is a liberty and God has given us all things richly to enjoy" (1 Tim. 6:17), but

---

4. C. H. Spurgeon, *Lectures to My Students* (Edinburgh: The Banner of Truth Trust, 2008), 186–188.

not today. You would find it a very fascinating essay if you read in Thorn-well's works of his love of expensive suits and high-class cigars. Spurgeon also smoked cigars. Yet, in the light of the medical data available to us, I do not believe that any man can say, "I can use tobacco with some degree of regularity and inhale it to the glory of God." The connection between tobacco and heart and lung disease is undeniable. It is therefore a violation of the Sixth Commandment. Now, if there is somebody who occasionally finds it relaxing to light up a cigar, and while not inhaling it to puff on it while reading a book on his back porch or deck, I am not ready to recommend his excommunication or make any attempt to deny him this liberty.

When the Bible says that everything created by God is good, and nothing is to be rejected (1 Tim. 4:4, 5), it is speaking of food and drinks, including drinks that have caffeine in them. Yes, I believe drinks with caffeine are a gift of God. If not, I have times, without number, sinfully thanked God for my morning cup of coffee. I remember the days when I could push back the blankets, put my feet on the floor, walk out into the hallway leading to the half-flight of stairs into my study, get on my knees with my Bible at my prayer chair and begin to read and pray. If I try to do that now, it would be a lost cause, since my aging brain needs the effect of the caffeine in my coffee if I am to profit from my Bible reading and remain focused in my prayers. So, I have learned to thank God for His good gift of the moderate use of caffeine and the good gift of bifocals. Between the effect of the caffeine on my brain and sitting to read instead of kneeling, I am still able to go to my prayer chair and profit from my time alone with God and His Word.

There may be times when you are passing through an intense crucible of emotional pressure, when a proven sleeping tablet or some melatonin may be a gift of God for you as you seek the blessing of a good night of rest. However, whether it is caffeine, a sleeping tablet, or some melatonin, beware of dependence upon or addiction to these gifts of God. Remember what Paul said,

> "All things are lawful for me," but not all things are helpful. "All things are lawful for me," but I will not be enslaved by anything. "Food is meant for the stomach and the stomach for food"—and God will destroy both one and the other (1 Cor. 6:12, 13).

Paul here reminds us that we are Christ's free men. Do not allow your-self to become a slave to any of His gifts. Further, the same Paul who urged Timothy to "use a little wine for the sake of your stomach and your frequent ailments" (1 Tim. 5:23) had previously made it plain to Timothy that addiction to wine would disqualify any man from spiritual leadership in the church of Christ (1 Tim. 3:3).

The sixth warning is to *beware of the no-day-off pattern of life.*
    Listen to the words of Murphy:

> We would earnestly recommend that Monday be observed as a day of mental and bodily rest. The minister must have his resting day as well as other men, or he will suffer the consequences. His physical constitution demands it. If it is denied, in time he will break down in health, as hundreds are doing. Nor must it be supposed that devoting one day of the week to absolute rest will be a loss of time in the end. No; the work of the other days will be more vigorous, the physical and mental tone will be kept up, and at the end of the year far more will be accomplished. One day of wakeful, energetic work is worth three or four spent in half dreaming and forcing one's self to unattractive tasks.[5]

We are called as New Covenant servants of God to labor on the appointed day of Sabbath rest. We do not have the physical, emotional rest of others on that day. We have rest in God and the worship of God, and we experience the invigoration of our souls as we lead our people in worship. These things take no little toll upon us, and if we try to live as though we are exempt from the principle of Sabbath rest as it touches physical and emotional refreshment, we will eventually suffer for it.

The seventh warning is to *beware of the no-planned vacation pattern of life.*
    I will not go into the details of it, but there was a time when I allowed myself to become a prisoner to the needs of others and the unusual opportunities that were coming my way to serve Christ. I believe that I not only cheated my family, but in some ways cheated my own well-being. Jesus said, "Come away by yourselves to a desolate place and rest a while" (Mark 6:31). Now, I know that it was shortly after pursuing this rest that multitudes began to follow. Jesus saw them and went out to minister to them. I understand that, but the principle is valid nonetheless. Jesus unashamedly indicated to His disciples that it is necessary to have periods of resting in between times of ministry.
    I am going to say something that I hope does not shock you, but there is something I believe we need to take into consideration as we think of Jesus

---

5. Thomas Murphy, *Pastoral Theology* (Audubon, NJ: Old Paths Publications, 1996), 104.

as our pattern. As a vigorous and strong thirty-year old man, He knew that He had but three years to accomplish His work. There is a sense in which He could push beyond limits that would be reasonable and right for us. Think about that. It was a number of years before I was willing to think along those lines, but I do believe it is something worthy of our consideration.

The eighth and final warning is to *beware of stubborn refusal to listen to others.*

I mean others who see the signs of our becoming frayed physically and emotionally and perhaps heading for a complete breakdown of our physical and emotional well-being.

The following document was drawn up by a pastor-friend of mine after his first heart attack. He entitled it the "Solemn Covenant of Kilbirnie Place."

> It is hereby declared most definitely, dogmatically, decidedly and determinately, that a certain mad preacher by the name of _____ — to be referred hereafter in this document as "the Turkey"—will submit to his wife's direction in matters medical. When the aforementioned wife tells him to phone the doctor, the aforementioned Turkey will do so without dispute, dissertation, deliberation or dissent. When the aforementioned wife states that a medical checkup, either at the doctor's office or the emergency department of the local hospital is indicated, the aforementioned Turkey will not denounce her with John Knox-like thunderings, oppose her with Calvinian logic, change her mind with Spurgeonic persuasion, or resist her with Athanasian obstinacy. He will, with that sweet reasonableness, indescribable meekness, and overpowering sweetness, with which he has now become possessed, simply answer her, "Whatever you say dear"; or it may be permitted for him to say, (at his wife's discretion of course) "Yes dear."
>
> To this non-negotiable, never-to-be-changed document, I hereby fix my signature, and agree on any occasion when the aforementioned wife deems it necessary, this document may be waving under my nose, or all else failing, stuffed down my throat![6]

---

6. This document was drawn up and signed by a man who is now in heaven. His wife was a nurse who saw signs that his heart problem was increasing, and that he ought to get to a doctor. He repeatedly refused his wife's entreaties to seek medical assessment and intervention until a heart attack landed him in the emergency room of a local hospital, after which he drew up this document. Some of it is obviously "tongue in cheek" but my friend's commitment to the "covenant" was serious and was blessed of God to give our brother significantly more years of useful service until a final heart attack was God's means to answer the prayer of our Lord Jesus recorded in John 17:24.

The spirit of that document contains much wisdom in its own light-hearted way.

Our Emotional Health

Our emotional health is also very important.

The first warning is to *beware of unnaturalness and ministerial stoicism.*

God has made us with emotional pores which act like the physical pores that keep our bodies ventilated and provide needed relief to our emotional constitution. I am thinking of such things as hearty laughter, vigorous discussion on a secular matter, playfulness with one's wife, and interaction with one's children or grandchildren. These are means by which our emotions can be channeled into legitimate expressions. Some men allow their role as pastor to clog those pores. They think that there is something unspiritual about letting it be evident that they are emotional creatures, so they are reluctant to weep unashamedly when it is appropriate to weep, to laugh from their gut when it is appropriate to laugh, or to pour out their complaints to God when appropriate. I love Psalms for this and many other reasons. There is no indication that God was upset when a psalmist would say, "Oh Lord, have You forgotten to be merciful? What is going on here? It does not make sense. You promised this and yet all looks like this." There is tremendous emotional health to be found in doing what the Scripture says in such words as, "pour out your heart before him" (Ps. 62:8). Unnatural stoicism chokes up frank dealings with God and honesty in our posture before the people of God. Our Lord wept openly and unashamedly. Our Lord "rejoiced in the Holy Spirit" (Luke 10:21). It radiated in His countenance. Our Lord showed anger, "He looked around at them with anger, grieved at their hardness of heart" (Mark 3:5). The full range of human emotions was wonderfully manifested in our blessed Lord. I urge you to read and ponder Warfield's essay on "The Emotional Life of Our Lord," even to read it periodically. Plead with God that in your ongoing conformity to the image of Christ, you may be given the ability to be like your Savior in the full, Spirit-controlled expression of all of your God-given emotions.

Gardiner Spring spoke with penetrating insights:

> We are no believers in an unsocial Christianity, nor do we desire to see its ministers unsocial and cheerless. This might be in keeping with the dark ages of Rome, but it has no alliance with the cheered spirit

of the Gospel. Cheerlessness is not piety; gloom and depression are
not piety. They are precisely that artful counterfeit of piety which the
devil imposes upon many a minister of the Gospel, for the purpose
of blasting those fruits of the Spirit, which are "not meat and drink,
but righteousness, and peace, and joy in the Holy Ghost." There is a
worldly joy, a joy that is found only in the world and from the world;
but it is "like the crackling of thorns under a pot." But there is too a
"joy of the Lord," which is the strength of God's ministers, as well as
the strength of his people; it is joy in God, and joy from God, through
Jesus Christ. Some of the best, and most devoted, and most successful
ministers I have ever known, have been distinguished for their attractive cheerfulness.

There are not wanting those who impugn the character of the
Christian ministry, because they do not carry the *solemnity* of the pulpit into all the scenes of social life. Many indeed are the scenes of social
life where the solemnity of the pulpit is called for; nor in any of them
are the dignity and proprieties of the ministerial character unfitting.
But as well might secular time be transformed into the Sabbath, and
the busy scenes of the world into the formal services of the sanctuary,
as the emotions of the pulpit pervade the uniform intercourse of a min-
ster, either with the people of God, or the men of the world. Levity and
worldliness are sufficiently out of place in him who is an ambassador of
God to guilty men; but affected solemnity is even worse. Ministers there
are who are so solemn that you never see a smile, or a pleasant expression upon their countenances; they are absolutely *fearful*. There is no
piety in this. Were an angel from heaven to dwell with men, his spirit
and example would be perpetual rebuke to such ministers. Christianity, though of divine origin, is not the religion of angels; it is ingrafted
on the human nature. Angels would delight to be its preachers; but the
treasure is committed to men; the whole arrangement is adapted to
what is human; and while its great object is to purify and elevate, it is
no part of its design to terrify. It is not a sort of personified apathy, nor
is it some ghostly messenger that lives only among the tombs; it moves
among men as the messenger of heaven's tenderest mercy; and though
wherever it goes, it rebukes iniquity, its footsteps are radiant with light
and love. It multiplies the joys of men, and only admonishes them that
they may not be sinful joys.[7]

---

7. Gardiner Spring, *The Power of the Pulpit* (Edinburgh: The Banner of Truth Trust,
1968), 158, 159.

The second warning is to *beware of social isolationism.*

God has made us social beings in creation. Many have the idea that in the ministry one should not cultivate and establish deep, intimate friendships. We are told that developing such relationships will provoke others to jealousy. This is nonsense. Jesus was unashamed to choose the Twelve out of a multitude of followers, and from the Twelve the three, and among the three, the one who leaned upon His bosom. Paul lets the whole Greco-Roman world know, wherever his letters circulated, that Timothy was his special spiritual son, "For I have no one like him, who will be genuinely concerned for your welfare. For they all seek their own interests, not those of Jesus Christ. But you know Timothy's proven worth, how as a son with a father he has served with me in the gospel" (Phil. 2:20–22). Paul obviously did not care if people said, "Timothy is Paul's favorite."

Then we have that beautiful example where Paul says,

> For even when we came into Macedonia, our bodies had no rest, but we were afflicted at every turn—fighting without and fear within. But God, who comforts the downcast, comforted us by the coming of Titus, and not only by his coming but also by the comfort with which he was comforted by you, as he told us of your longing, your mourning, your zeal for me, so that I rejoiced still more (2 Cor. 7:5–7).

God ordinarily comforts those that are cast down, not by sending an angel, not by a fresh infusion of the Spirit in His ministry as the Comforter and One called alongside to help. He comforted Paul by the coming of Titus. Paul was in the dumps one day. Sometime during that day there was a knock on the door where Paul was staying. Standing outside that door was Paul's intimate friend, Titus. Immediately, and in the subsequent hours of interaction between these two men, God poured oceans of consolation into Paul's downcast spirit which revived and rejuvenated him emotionally. Had Paul not previously cultivated a special friendship with Titus, he would not have known the preciousness of being comforted by his unexpected visit. Time invested in cultivating deep and long-term friendships is never lost time.

The third warning is to *beware of taking on excessive responsibilities. Do not let people determine the will of God for you.*

Cultivate a wholesome domestic climate. Your home should be an emotional catharsis where there is hearty laughter and open, transparent communication. I am so thankful to God that He has given me the privilege in my lifetime of having two women with whom I have been and currently am utterly uninhibited in the legitimate expressions of my emotions. God knows what a miserable wretch I would be to live with if I did not have the wives God was pleased to give me—one at a time, I assure you, one at a time.

The fourth warning is, *do not take yourself too seriously.*

People will take you so seriously that you will be tempted to look at yourself the way they do. If you succumb to this temptation, it will have profound negative effects upon your life and ministry. Always strive to think of yourself as God defines you. You are His creature, made in His image, utterly depraved in Adam, yet now a new creation in Christ, justified and adopted into the family of God and indwelt by the Person of the Holy Spirit. Furthermore, God has imparted to you specific gifts with which you are to serve Him in the sphere of His appointment. Regardless of the extent to which God may be using you as you fulfill your ministry, never forget that you are not indispensable to the advancement of God's Kingdom. If you should have a massive heart attack while reading this particular paragraph and be ushered into the presence of your Savior, the work of God's Kingdom would not skip a beat.

The final suggestion is to *cultivate a pattern of timely, wholesome, emotional diversions.*

Find the thing that helps to bleed off emotional pressure. For me, for many years, it was engaging in vigorous yard work throughout a Monday morning, and then after lunch, putting on my headphones and listening for several hours to a well-trained masculine voice, to an entire opera, or to various symphonic renderings while engaging in a thorough reading of a substantive newspaper. I love the operatic voice and the sounds of a disciplined symphony orchestra. Since undergoing profound sensory-neural hearing loss, I can no longer process music of any kind. I have had to seek legitimate substitutes for my emotional diversions. What works for one man will not work for another. Find those things that are an emotional catharsis for you. All things are yours. This is God's world and you are God's child, and His gifts are there to be used to keep us in a healthy emotional frame.

CHAPTER 8

His Relationship to His People (1)

The Pastor's Growing Measure of Unfeigned Love for His People

In this lecture, we proceed from the man of God in relation to his God to *the man of God in relation to his people.* This is a relationship that should be characterized by three dominant realities. First, *an increasing measure of unfeigned love for his people*; second, *an increasing measure of deliverance from a carnal fear of his people*; and third, *an increasing measure of the earned respect and confidence of his people.* I will elaborate a simple axiom, then demonstrate the crucial importance of the axiom in relation to pastoral ministry, and then offer some practical suggestions regarding the nurture, practice, and manifestation of a pastor's love for his people.

Elaboration of the Axiom

You and I must experience a growing measure of unfeigned love for our people.

Central to this axiom is the word *love.* While there are few words more familiar to us than love, few things are more elusive and difficult to define with any degree of precision. However, since the issue here is so crucial, we must make a modest attempt to define love. We will say something about the *quality* of love, the *measure* of love, and the *objects* of love.

It is clear from Scripture that love is much better understood in its working and manifestations than in terms of precise definitions. When seeking to grapple with what this love is which is commended to us, we should be careful not to try to make the answer to that question fit into philological or philosophical categories. First Corinthians 13 is the classic example of this fact. Love is set before us there in terms of what it does and does not do. It is not described in terms of a person's feelings, but attitudes and actions.

So it is with God's love. John says, "In this is love, not that we have loved God but that he loved us and sent his Son to be the propitiation for our sins" (1 John 4:10). He is the source and pattern of our love. John had stated earlier in his epistle, "By this we know love, that he laid down his life for us, and we ought to lay down our lives for the brothers" (1 John 3:16). Here we see the working out of the pattern of our love toward others in our lives. Our motivation in loving others is the same motivation as it is in His love toward us.

It is not inappropriate or unwise to seek to define love based on what the Bible says and shows us about love. For our purposes, I will attempt a working definition, or better, a working description of love.

Love is that gracious and principled disposition of goodwill which desires and practically seeks the good of its object, even at personal cost.

It is a *gracious* disposition. By this word I mean that it is the fruit of God's grace working in us, whether common grace, for many unbelievers have true love toward others, or in the case of the pastor, the activity of special grace. The fruit of the Spirit is love, and it is that grace that is implanted in us by the Holy Spirit which enables us to truly love.

I have also used the word *principled*. It operates not by whims and impulses but by fixed perspectives and commitments of the soul. Underneath true love in the heart of a man of God for his people is the pressure of the very law of God which commands us to love one's neighbor as oneself.

I also use the word *disposition*. A person's disposition is the normal or prevailing aspect of a person's nature. There are as many adjectives to describe different dispositions as there are kinds of people. Some are cheerful; others are gloomy. Some are outgoing; others are reserved. Some are loud; others are soft-spoken. Some are by nature critical; others are understanding. The disposition of love which is the fruit of the Spirit operates by the divine principle or impulse undergirded and nourished by the pressure of the law of God. This love may or may not grow into deep affection which always has a spontaneous affinity for its object. The older writers called this *a love of complacency,* that is, a love which delights in its object. Though pastoral love may struggle to be active toward some of the sheep, it is imperative that the man of God prayerfully seek to cultivate greater measures of this divine love toward each one.

Furthermore, the axiom speaks of *desiring and seeking the good of its object*. Love is the opposite of selfishness. Paul speaks of love in this way, "it does not insist on its own way" (1 Cor. 13:5). There is an echo of this in the words, "Love does no wrong to a neighbor; therefore love is the fulfilling of the law" (Rom. 13:10). The good towards its object which love seeks is the good defined by God, not the subjective understanding of man, and love is always prepared to do this at personal cost. God Himself is the supreme model of this, "'God so loved the world, that he gave his only Son'" (John 3:16). "Christ loved the church and gave himself up for her" (Eph. 5:25). John states the matter of self-denying love for others in a powerful way: "By this we know love, that he laid down his life for us, and we ought to lay down our lives for the brothers" (1 John 3:16). We are under solemn obligation to love in this way.

So, while I am not prepared to say that this is the most accurate, most fulsome, and the most precise definition of love, I do believe that it reflects some of the leading lines of biblical thought on the doctrine of love. So, when I say in the axiom that we must have a growing love for our people, I am speaking of love as that *gracious and principled disposition of goodwill which both desires and practically seeks the good of its objects, even at personal cost.*

First, we want to consider the *quality* of this love.

The key word in Scripture which defines its quality is the word *unfeigned*. The Greek word *anypokritos* means to be genuine, sincere, and without pretense. Peter uses this word, "Having purified your souls by your obedience to the truth for a sincere brotherly love, love one another earnestly from a pure heart" (1 Pet. 1:22). Peter is indicating that sincere or unfeigned love is the fruit of regenerating grace. Paul echoes this, "Let love be genuine. Abhor what is evil; hold fast to what is good" (Rom. 12:9). God's servants commend themselves "by purity, knowledge, patience, kindness, the Holy Spirit, genuine love" (2 Cor. 6:6). So, the quality of this love is to be genuine, sincere, and without pretense, not fake or false or put on. We are not merely to put on a show of love, but to possess love deeply in our hearts and manifest it in our lives, so that what people see is the reality of what is.

Remember the touching example of this in the life of our Lord when He went to the graveside of Lazarus. Though He knew that shortly after His arrival in Bethany He would raise His friend from the dead, He entered (instinctively, automatically, empathetically), into the climate of grief as was His prevailing disposition, and wept tears of love for His friend (John 11:35). Those who were looking on as our Lord wept said, "See how He loved him!" (John 11:36). No doubt, the whole situation, the death of Lazarus, the sadness and loss of Mary and Martha, the tragic consequences of sin in human life and love, affected Him deeply and drew forth His loving emotion through His tears. This was unfeigned love. Even His deity and His soon-to-come pronouncement that Lazarus would come forth from the tomb could not keep this kind of love back from an appropriate visible manifestation. The quality of our love as pastors is to be unfeigned in this precise way.

I want to say something about the *measure* of this love.

It is to be a growing measure of love, ever-increasing in its quantity, multiplying in its manifestations, and growing stronger and more resolute with every challenge to its existence and activity. Paul urged the Thessalonian believers to have this kind of growing love,

> Now concerning brotherly love you have no need for anyone to write to you, for you yourselves have been taught by God to love one another, for that indeed is what you are doing to all the brothers throughout Macedonia. But we urge you, brothers, to do this more and more (1 Thess. 4:9, 10).

The disposition was clearly planted in them by virtue of their conversion, so that Paul was able to say that he did not even need to write to them about this duty to love one another. In spite of this reality, he still exhorts them to cultivate growing measures of love.

We see this aspect of the growing measure of love in a pastoral setting in Paul, "I will most gladly spend and be spent for your souls. If I love you more, am I to be loved less?" (2 Cor. 12:15). He speaks not only of loving them, but of loving them more abundantly. That is the dimension of biblical truth I am seeking to capture in my axiom.

Now a word about the *objects* of pastoral love.

When I write in the axiom of *your people*, I am referring, first of all, to those who are members of the church in which you are a pastor, that is, those who are officially under your charge and for whom you have official ecclesiastical responsibility to shepherd. Of course, we love those who attend the church and who are not members. We are always deeply concerned about the non-membership of professing believers and seek to instruct them on this matter. However, we only have official responsibility toward those who have placed themselves under the oversight of our churches. When Paul speaks of his love for the people of God in the churches, he had in mind specifically those who were members of those churches, the people who were responsible to render obedience to the command, "Obey your leaders and submit to them, for they are keeping watch over your souls, as those who will have to give an account. Let them do this with joy and not with groaning, for that would be of no advantage to you" (Heb. 13:17). When we read the charges given to pastors in Hebrews 13:17, Acts 20:28, and 1 Peter 5:1-5, the assumption in these passages is that shepherds recognize who their sheep are. So when I speak of the growing measure of unfeigned love which we are to have for the people of God, I am thinking primarily of those who have been committed to our charge.

I am also thinking of the children of those who have been committed to our pastoral care, and visitors who providentially come within the orbit of our church life and ministry. Beyond these, our love should grow and reach out to all men in general. None of us will rise to the measure of love which Paul expresses in Romans 9:1-5, where he speaks of his passionate love for his fellow Jews who were still in their spiritual blindness and lost estate. When Paul said, "Therefore I endure everything for the sake of the elect, that they also may obtain the salvation that is in Christ Jesus with eternal glory" (2 Tim. 2:10), it should be clear to us that he did not know who the elect were. His love was broad and deep for all men, manifested in genuine sincerity and passion, with the ultimate goal of reaching the elect of God. Paul knows that through his sacrificial labors for all, God will call out the many upon whom He has set His love from all eternity.

In summary then, this is the axiom which embodies what you and I must experience as men of God among our people. We must experience a growing measure of unfeigned love for our people.

The Importance of Love in the Work of the Ministry

Now I want to demonstrate the importance of this axiom in conjunction with the work of pastoral ministry. The biblical material which demonstrates this importance is so vast that it is unwieldy. Yet I offer five lines of thought which I trust will persuade you with increasing conviction that, if you are to be the man God wants you to be in fulfilling the manifold tasks of the pastoral office, you must be able to say, "By the grace of God I have a growing measure of unfeigned love for my people."

The importance of love is seen, in the first place, in the *explicit teaching of 1 Corinthians 13.*

This chapter is nestled between his treatment of spiritual gifts. Paul obviously wants us to know that without the grace of love the exercise of all spiritual gifts is futile and failing. The "success," or the prosperity, of spiritual gifts comes only when the Spirit is filling us with the grace of love. The surrounding chapters of 1 Corinthians 12 and 14 emphasize, in keeping with this profound truth, that the purpose of gifts in the first place is the edification, or building up, of the body. Here is the selfless, other-centered motive. Paul said, if I do not have love,

> I am a noisy gong or a clanging cymbal. And if I have prophetic powers, and understand all mysteries and all knowledge, and if I have all faith, so as to remove mountains, but have not love, I am nothing. If I give away all I have, and if I deliver up my body to be burned, but have not love, I gain nothing (1 Cor. 13:1–3).

Without love, Paul's speaking would irritate and drive away, instead of console and comfort. His orthodoxy, taught in the form of the sound words which he utters, without love, would not strengthen the church.

The importance of love is seen in the second place, *in the general demand for evangelical law-keeping.*

Although there are specific duties and responsibilities laid upon us in connection with our office, none of the generic duties of a Christian man are suspended with respect to us as gospel ministers. That simple principle has been a great help to me over the years. When I have been tempted to trade off a generic Christian duty because of the pressures of a specific pastoral duty, God has yanked me by the back of the neck and by the seat of my pants, again and again, and helped me to see that He did not put me in the Christian ministry to negate what He has commanded me to be and do as a Christian man. You too must get hold of that principle if you have not already. It will save you from many a pitfall, and one of the generic duties of all Christians is evangelical law-keeping. Romans 13 tells us what evangelical law-keeping means. Paul says,

> Owe no one anything, except to love each other, for the one who loves another has fulfilled the law. For the commandments, "You shall not commit adultery, You shall not murder, You shall not steal, You shall not covet," and any other commandment, are summed up in this word: "You shall love your neighbor as yourself." Love does no wrong to a neighbor; therefore love is the fulfilling of the law (Rom. 13:8–10).

Insofar as I am loving my neighbor as myself and doing what love requires according to the standard of Scripture, I am fulfilling the law of God, and that is my duty. What greater love can I show to my neighbor in this duty than to seek his highest good by bringing him the Word of God and the gospel of Christ?

The importance of this axiom concerning love is seen, in the third place, *because of the specific nature of our office.*

We are constituted as undershepherds of the Chief Shepherd (1 Pet. 5:1–4). In this passage we have a play on words which indicates that as surely as we are to shepherd only by the Word of Christ, so we are always to manifest the Spirit of Christ in the act of shepherding. We are commanded to "shepherd (*poimanate*) the flock," but always remembering the One who is the Chief Shepherd (*archipoimenos*). Now, what is the dominant characteristic of the Great Shepherd in all of His dealings with the sheep? Jesus answers this question, "I am the good shepherd. The good shepherd lays down his life for the sheep" (John 10:11). This is the ultimate expression of love, and the greater includes the lesser; all expressions of love are seed forms of this greatest expression of love, laying down one's life for the beloved. Christ said, "Greater love has no one than this, that someone lay down his life for his friends" (John 15:13).

If there is not a growing measure of unfeigned love for our people, a love that they can read in our demeanor and perceive in our interaction with them in and out of the pulpit, we are impoverished and unfit to serve them as the servants of Christ. We also greatly misrepresent the Chief Shepherd without this increasing measure of love. With it we are a real and life-giving reflection of the disposition of the Savior and Shepherd of the sheep. What an exciting prospect this is for *us*—to reflect Him! And for the *sheep*—to receive Him!

We must have this growing measure of love, in the fourth place, because of *the constituted relationship between assured love and an open ear.*

Now these words may sound a little strange, so let me explain them. We must have the ears of our people if we are to do them any good in communicating the Word of God to them. They must be favorably inclined to listen to us and know that we love them. Without their ears, we cannot get to their hearts. Yet if we are to have their ears, they must have the confidence that we love them, and if that confidence is shaken, so will be the connection to their listening ears.

Listen to what Richard Baxter wrote:

The whole of our ministry must be carried on in tender love to our people. We must let them see that nothing pleaseth us but what profiteth them; and that what doeth them good doth us good; and that nothing troubleth us more than their hurt. We must feel toward our people, as a father toward his children: yea, the tenderest love of a mother must not surpass ours. We must even travail in birth, till Christ be formed in them. They should see that we care for no outward thing, neither wealth, nor liberty, nor honour, nor life, in comparison of their salvation; but could even be content, with Moses, to have our names blotted out of the book of life, i.e. to be removed from the number of the living: rather than they should not be found in the Lamb's book of life. Thus should we, as John saith, be ready to "lay down our lives for the brethren," and, with Paul, not count our lives dear to us, so we may but "finish our course with joy, and the ministry which we have received of the Lord Jesus." When the people see that you unfeignedly love them, they will hear any thing and bear any thing from you; as Augustine saith, "Love God, and do what you please." We ourselves will take all things well from one that we know doth entirely love us. We will put up with a blow that is given us in love, sooner than with a foul word that is spoken to us in malice or in anger. Most men judge of the counsel, as they judge of the affection of him that gives it: at least, so far as to give it a fair hearing. Oh, therefore, see that you feel a tender love to your people in your breasts, and let them perceive it in your speeches, and see it in your conduct. Let them see that you spend, and are spent, for their sakes; and that all you do is for them, and not for any private ends of your own.[1]

Charles Bridges adds:

We are not arguing, however, for that sensitive delicacy, which refrains to wound, when the patient shrinks. But we know not, why the most energetic tone of faithfulness should not be blended with that considerate treatment, which unquestionably, is best adapted to the exigency of the case. The brute creation may be driven: but rational creatures require to be drawn. The compulsion of love is the mighty lever of operation. Even the Heathen sophists insisted upon kindness in an orator as indispensable to his success; and doubtless none will open their hearts to the Christian orator except the tone of his instructions has impressed them with a sincere conviction of his love to their best

---

1. Richard Baxter, *The Reformed Pastor* (Edinburgh: The Banner of Truth Trust, 1974), 117, 118.

interests. Love is the life, power, soul, and spirit of pulpit eloquence; entreating rather than denouncing the character of our office; and it is the delivery of our Master's message with the looks and language of his own manifested tenderness, that attracts and triumphs over the hearts of a willing people.[2]

Calvin, writing on Philippians 1:8, "For God is my witness," said:

He now declares more explicitly his affection for them, and, with the view of giving proof of it, he makes use of an oath, and that on good grounds, because we know how dear in the sight of God is the edification of his Church. It was, too, more especially of advantage, that Paul's affection should be thoroughly made known to the Philippians. For it tends in no small degree to secure credit for the doctrine, when the people are persuaded that they are beloved by the teacher.[3]

A story is told of a man who was in the Salvation Army working among the outcasts in various cities of London. He came to the founder, General Booth, and poured out his heart to the General and said, "General Booth, I have tried this and I have tried that, and I cannot break through to these people." General Booth's counsel was simple. He said, "My brother, try tears." In other words, make known to these people that you truly love them.

We must experience this growing measure of love to our people, in the fifth place, because of *the specific ways in which love will influence your preaching, both in its preparation and in its delivery.*

Let me illustrate. Is effective preaching marked by its fidelity to the text of Scripture, by the conviction that only the truth of God is wholesome food? If so, the accurate handling of the truth is the means of demonstrating our love for our flock. This love for your people will accompany you at your desk, pressuring you to demonstrate the genuineness of your love by the accurate handling of the Word of God. It is this love for your people that will drive you to the arduous task of exegesis, and urge you to press on, by prayer and pains, when the passage is dark and murky. You will not just wing it because of these difficulties, or succumb to laziness and sloth, but press on in love for their souls. Love to God and love to the truth channels into love

---

2. Charles Bridges, *The Christian Ministry* (Edinburgh: The Banner of Truth Trust, 1967), 336–338.

3. John Calvin, "Commentary on the Epistle to the Philippians" in *Calvin's Commentaries*, vol. *XXI* (Grand Rapids: Baker Book House, 1979), 30.

for the people of God. When the pressure of the week is on and the Lord's Day is drawing near and Christ's sheep need to be fed with wholesome, rich pastures of the accurate exposition of His Word, it is love that will operate in your heart in the lonely place of the study.

Is effective preaching marked by its logical and transparent structure? Then, it is love to your people that will make you labor to pursue clarity in your preaching. If effective preaching is marked by the searching element that seeks to rivet the Word to the conscience of the hearer, what is it but love that will keep you working in the passage when it is not yielding its practical application as quickly as you would like? You are confident that there is not only a road from that passage to Christ and His saving work, but there is a road into the conscience, the moral awareness and ethical sensitivities, of your people, so that, having opened up the "what" of the passage, you do not leave your sheep wondering about the "So what."

It is love that will move you to labor even in the act of preaching. Every element of preaching is motivated and manifested by love. Listen to Martyn Lloyd-Jones:

> A special word must be given also, though in a sense we have been covering it, to the element of pathos. If I had to plead guilty of one thing more than any other I would have to confess that this perhaps is what has been most lacking in my own ministry. This should arise partly from a love for the people. Richard Cecil, an Anglican preacher in London towards the end of the eighteenth century and the beginning of the nineteenth said something which should make us all think. "To love to preach is one thing, to love those to whom we preach quite another." The trouble with some of us is that we love preaching, but we are not always careful to make sure that we love the people to whom we are actually preaching. If you lack this element of compassion for the people you will also lack the pathos which is a very vital element in all true preaching. Our Lord looked out upon the multitude and "saw them as sheep without a shepherd," and was "filled with compassion." And if you know nothing of this you should not be in a pulpit, for this is certain to come out in your preaching. We must not be purely intellectual or argumentative, this other element must be there.[4]

---

4. D. Martyn Lloyd-Jones, *Preaching and Preachers* (Grand Rapids: Zondervan, 1971), 92, 93.

Spurgeon adds his voice saying:

The class requiring logical argument is small compared with the number of those who need to be pleaded with, by way of *emotional persuasion*. They require not so much reasoning as heart-argument—which is logic set on fire. You must argue with them as a mother pleads with her boy that he will not grieve her, or as a fond sister entreats a brother to return to their father's home and seek reconciliation: argument must be quickened into persuasion by the living warmth of love. Cold logic has its force, but when made red hot with affection the power of tender argument is inconceivable. The power which one mind can gain over others is enormous, but it is often best developed when the leading mind has ceased to have power over itself. When passionate zeal has carried the man himself away, his speech becomes an irresistible torrent, sweeping all before it. A man known to be godly and devout, and felt to be large-hearted and self-sacrificing, has a power in his very person, and his advice and recommendation carry weight because of his character; but when he comes to plead and to persuade, even to tears, his influence is wonderful, and God the Holy Spirit yokes it into his service. Brethren, we must *plead*. Entreaties and beseechings must blend with our instructions. Any and every appeal which will reach the conscience and move men to fly to Jesus we must perpetually employ, if by any means we may save some. I have sometimes heard ministers blamed for speaking of themselves when they are pleading, but the censure need not be much regarded while we have such a precedent as the example of Paul. To a congregation who love you it is quite allowable to mention your grief that many of them are unsaved, and your vehement desire, and incessant prayer for their conversion. You are doing right when you mention your own experience of the goodness of God in Christ Jesus, and plead with men to come and taste the same. We must not be abstractions or mere officials to our people, but we must plead with them as real flesh and blood, if we would see them converted. When you can quote yourself as a living instance of what grace has done, the plea is too powerful to be withheld through fear of being charged with egotism.[5]

These are some of the ways in which this grace of holy love will mightily influence your preaching, as well as your other ministerial labors.

---

5. C. H. Spurgeon, *Lectures to My Students* (Edinburgh: The Banner of Truth Trust, 2008), 418, 419.

Practical Suggestions for the Nurture, Practice, and Manifestation of this Love

How are we to *nurture* this kind of extraordinary love? We must pray and cry out to God for it with urgency and dependence upon His gracious Spirit. Tell God in prayer, "Left to myself I am a mass of lovelessness; love does not come easily for me." Ask Him to give it to you. When we pray this way, we never need to append our prayer with the words, "if it be Your will." It is His will that we abound more and more in love. It is His promise to give us more and more of His Holy Spirit when we ask (Luke 11:13). We must deliberately and periodically meditate on those truths which are calculated to produce it, such as the worth of the people of God in the sight of God.

Baxter writes:

> Oh, then, let us hear these arguments of Christ, whenever we feel ourselves grow dull and careless: "Did I die for these souls, and wilt not thou look after them? Were they worth my blood, and are they not worth thy labour? Did I come down from heaven to earth, 'to seek and to save that which was lost'; and wilt thou not go to the next door, or street, or village, to seek them? How small is thy condescension and labour compared to mine! I debased myself to this, but it is thy honour to be so employed. Have I done and suffered so much for their salvation, and was I willing to make thee a fellow-worker with me, and wilt thou refuse to do that little which lies upon thy hands?" Every time we look upon our congregations, let us believingly remember that they are the purchase of Christ's blood, and therefore should be regarded by us with the deepest interest and the most tender affection. Oh, think what a confusion it will be to a negligent minister, at the last day, to have this blood of the Son of God pleaded against him; and for Christ to say, "It was the purchase of my blood of which thou didst make so light, and dost thou think to be saved by it thyself?" O brethren, seeing Christ will bring his blood to plead with us, let it plead us to our duty, lest it plead us to damnation.[6]

Calculate the worth of the human soul according to Jesus: "For what will it profit a man if he gains the whole world and forfeits his soul? Or what shall a man give in return for his soul?" (Matt. 16:26). Consider the agonies of Christ for sinners: "And being in agony he prayed more earnestly" (Luke 22:44). Reflect long on the true state and condition of men: "And they

---

6. Richard Baxter, *The Reformed Pastor* (Edinburgh: The Banner of Truth Trust, 1974), 131, 132.

may come to their senses and escape from the snare of the devil, after being captured by him to do his will" (2 Tim. 2:26).

What will the *manifestation* of this love look like? It will be manifested, simply, in *words* and in *deeds*. "Little children, let us not love in word or talk but in deed and in truth" (1 John 3:18). Love is communicated both non-verbally in deeds and verbally in our words. This is how we manifest love, in both words and deeds, by what we say and what we do. We speak out of a heart of love, and we show that love by tangible deeds and works.

I have been on a one-man campaign for many years to get men over the hang-up of not saying the words, "I love you" to anyone but their spouse or relatives. Can you say to your brother in Christ, "I love you"? Can you tell one of God's sheep, "I love you"? Why not? Are you afraid to tell another brother, "I love you," because of the perverted society in which we live? Paul unashamedly spoke of his love for the people of God, "So, being affectionately desirous of you, we were ready to share with you not only the gospel of God but also our own selves, because you had become very dear to us" (1 Thess. 2:8). The Lord Jesus spoke of His love to His own disciples, "I have loved you" (John 15:9, 10, 12).

When Pastor Brian Borgman was preparing to write *My Heart for Thy Cause*,[7] he interviewed one of the families of Trinity Church. I officiated at the wedding of the parents, so the children sat under my ministry for their entire lives up to that point. Pastor Borgman asked the children, all of whom by then were young adults, "Were you ever intimidated by Pastor Martin's powerful voice and preaching when you were young?" They laughed and said, "He's been our friend. He's been in our backyard and jumped in our pool with his clothes on!" When people see our affection for their children, we are coming into their own hearts through the back door. Some people are trying to shut the front door into their hearts, but love can open the back door.

So we must love in word and in deed. We must love the children. We must make those quick phone calls just to see how the sheep are doing. At times we send a real card, not an email, expressing our sympathy, or a real, old-fashioned letter when something significant has entered their lives. Through these and other simple expressions, we build up a tower of love by word and deed. May God help us to grow in this unfeigned love to our people, both in the reality of it in our hearts, and in the manifestation of it in word and deed.

---

7. Brian Borgman, *My Heart for Thy Cause: Albert N. Martin's Theology of Preaching* (Ross-shire, U.K.: Christian Focus Publications; Mentor, 2002).

CHAPTER 9

His Relationship to His People (2)

In this lecture, we turn our attention to the second major area of concern with respect to our relationship to our people, and it is that *we must experience an increasing liberation from the fear of man and we must grow in the grace of holy boldness.*

Increasing Liberation from the Fear of Man

We must begin by identifying one of the most fundamental facts of our created identity, which is that God has made us social beings. Genesis 2 is the zoom-lens perspective on God's creation of the man and the woman. Having created the man and having placed him in the garden with his assigned tasks, a divine assessment was then made: "Then the LORD God said, 'It is not good that the man should be alone; I will make him a helper fit for him'" (Gen. 2:18). Now the same created need which reaches out in us for its greatest fulfillment in the multifaceted intimacy of marriage is the need which reaches out, in lesser degrees, for other human relationships of intimacy and reciprocal acceptance. Hence, the desire in every one of us to be loved by another or others, accepted, cordially received, appreciated, and even esteemed, is native to our humanity. It is neither a manifestation of the old man in Adam or something distinct to the new man in Christ. This desire to be loved and accepted by others is simply part of what we are as human.

Yet, as all the other components of our complex humanness have been marred and perverted by the tragedy of the fall, so it is with this yearning for acceptance. Sometimes this yearning for acceptance collides with our duty to bring the light of truth to the minds and hearts of others. Because men by nature have an aversion to the truth, they do not always accept us when we speak the truth to them. They, in fact, suppress the truth, as Paul says, "For the wrath of God is revealed from heaven against all ungodliness and unrighteousness of men, who by their unrighteousness suppress the truth"

(Rom. 1:18). Again, "For the mind that is set on the flesh is hostile to God, for it does not submit to God's law; indeed, it cannot. Those who are in the flesh cannot please God" (Rom. 8:7, 8). Again, "And this is the judgment: the light has come into the world, and people loved the darkness rather than the light because their works were evil" (John 3:19).

What is one of the ways that men most frequently manifest this native antipathy to the truth? The answer of Scripture is clear. They do it by rejecting or attacking the messenger and his message. Inwardly they are attacking God, but they cannot see Him, nor get their hands on Him, nor lash Him with their tongues in some more direct way. As a result, their antipathy to the truth is directed toward the bearer of that truth. Our Lord very clearly identifies this reality in a passage such as John 15:18–27. I direct your attention to a specimen section of this passage,

> If the world hates you, know that it has hated me before it hated you. If you were of the world, the world would love you as its own; but because you are not of the world, but I chose you out of the world, therefore the world hates you (John 15:18, 19).

Christ goes on to say, "If I had not come and spoken to them, they would not have been guilty of sin, but now they have no excuse for their sin" (John 15:22). In these words, our Lord makes it clear that the speaking of His words has brought this antipathy against the truth to the surface.

This was the experience of the prophets of old. When God commissioned Jeremiah, He made it very plain that Jeremiah would meet with opposition to the message that he would bear:

> But you, dress yourself for work; arise, and say to them everything that I command you. Do not be dismayed by them, lest I dismay you before them. And I, behold, I make you this day a fortified city, an iron pillar, and bronze walls, against the whole land, against the kings of Judah, its officials, its priests, and the people of the land. They will fight against you, but they shall not prevail against you, for I am with you, declares the LORD, to deliver you (Jer. 1:17–19).

We find the same thing in the ministry of Amos who wrote, "They hate him who reproves in the gate, and they abhor him who speaks the truth" (Amos 5:10). Their hatred toward God and His truth terminated upon the instrument that conveyed His truth.

I have established the fact that God has made us social beings who natively long for the goodwill and acceptance of others. I would now like to demonstrate that as a result of the fall this very human characteristic has been twisted and marred. Because of the fact of sin, we are all born with a native antipathy to God's truth, and that antipathy will be manifested not only by hatred of the truth, but hatred toward those who convey that truth to us. This antipathy to the truth is radically dethroned in the heart of every regenerate man or woman. Yet, *remaining* sin acts in the same *way*, though not to the same *degree* as it did when it was *reigning* sin in the unconverted heart. For this reason, Paul had to say, "Have I then become your enemy by telling you the truth?" (Gal. 4:16). In his reasoning in Romans 9:14 and following, he anticipates that in the community of the believers who would hear the reading of his Roman letter, particularly chapters 9–11, there would be a native negative reaction from the remaining sin of the Roman Christians toward the absolute free sovereignty of God in His electing and reprobating rights.

Do you see why we must experience an increasing measure of liberation from the fear of men if we are to be faithful servants of the living God? Without that increasing liberation from the fear of men we will not be able to say as Paul said, "I did not shrink from declaring to you the whole counsel of God" (Acts 20:27). This is helpful to me as I view this struggle within me from a biblical perspective and realize that this is often the reason why I am held back from unfettered boldness in the proclamation of the truth. More than recognizing the struggle, I realize the need for the very axiom which I am setting forth here, that I must have a growing measure of liberation from the fear of the frowns of my people and grow in holy boldness.

Imagine that you are sitting across the desk or in the living room with one of your sheep, knowing that you need to bring the Word of God to bear upon some specific areas of sin. As you anticipate fulfilling this unpleasant responsibility, you know you may well provoke their frowns if you are to be faithful and able to say with Paul, "Him we proclaim, warning everyone and teaching everyone with all wisdom, that we may present everyone mature in Christ" (Col. 1:28). If we are to prove faithful to the souls of those entrusted to our care, we must have a growing measure of liberation from the fear of men coupled with an increasing measure of holy boldness.

The Biblical Basis for the Grace of Holy Boldness

Having sought to give this rather broad biblical overview of the subject, we now come to consider the biblical basis for seeking this increasing deliverance from the fear of man and growth in the grace of holy boldness. We will consider the example of Elihu, the example of the Lord Jesus, and the example of the apostle Paul.

The first line of evidence of the grace of holy boldness in Scripture is seen in *Elihu*.

Elihu was of special comfort to me when, as a teenager, God laid His hand upon me to preach, and I found myself in situations where everything in me said, "I ought not to be speaking." God was working powerfully in a few of us young men in Stamford, Connecticut, eventually giving us some unusual opportunities to preach the gospel in different settings. On one occasion, we found ourselves in a debate with the theologically liberal pastor of a local Methodist church, a man who had an earned doctorate from one of the liberal seminaries in New England. A relative of mine, who was present to witness that debate, and who looked back on that experience said to me, "Oh, Al, it was thrilling! That middle-aged liberal pastor was just waffling about as he sought to justify his liberal theology, while you young guys just kept flipping through your Bibles to identify more scriptural reasons for what you believed." Yet it was one of those situations where I questioned what we, a bunch of "kids," were doing engaged in a public debate with this learned man. It was in that context that I first became acquainted with the young man Elihu. He said to Job's friends,

> I also will answer with my share; I also will declare my opinion. For I am full of words; the spirit within me constrains me. Behold, my belly is like wine that has no vent; like new wineskins ready to burst. I must speak, that I may find relief; I must open my lips and answer. I will not show partiality to any man or use flattery toward any person. For I do not know how to flatter, else my Maker would soon take me away (Job 32:17–22).

Elihu was deeply conscious that he was answerable to his Maker for what he said, and the consciousness of that fact enabled him to speak without fear and with holy boldness. Paul, like Elihu many years later, did not shrink back from declaring anything that was profitable (Acts 20:20).

The second line of evidence of the grace of holy boldness in Scripture is seen, more importantly, in *the example of our Lord Jesus and the acknowledgement of this dimension of the total absence of the fear of man, even in the face of His bitterest enemies.*

Mark informs us that

> they sent to him some of the Pharisees and some of the Herodians, to trap him in his talk. And they came and said to him, "Teacher, we know that you are true and do not care about anyone's opinion. For you are not swayed by appearances, but truly teach the way of God. Is it lawful to pay taxes to Caesar, or not? Should we pay them, or should we not?" (Mark 12:13, 14).

This was insincere, fawning flattery, but they did at least recognize what marked the ministry of Jesus, namely, that He did not fear anyone, nor their opinions, or their opposition.

Lenski comments on this passage:

> The following clauses state how this is meant. "And carest for no one," οὐ μέλει σοι περὶ οὐδενός (idiomatic, "it is no care for thee," etc.), means that Jesus is swayed by no man's personal interests. He does not modify the truth in the least to further the opinions or plans of any man. In fact, "thou dost not look on man's countenance" like the partial judge to see who the person is before him and pronouncing a different sentence for a friend than for a stranger or for an enemy. It is all the same to Jesus who faces him, his verdicts are invariably the same. All this is made specific by adding the positive after the negative: "on the contrary (ἀλλά after negatives) thou dost teach the way of God on the basis of truth." This final phrase is emphatic. "The way of God" (Hebrew *derek*) is the way he marked out for every Israelite to follow. Jesus taught that way "on the basis of truth," ἐπ' ἀληθείας, on the ground of reality. He taught what was true about the way of God over against what was not true. He taught the solid facts, nothing else.[1]

The third line of evidence highlighting the grace of holy boldness is seen *as we observe how this grace was abundantly manifested in the great apostle Paul.*

We see it clearly in his letter to the Galatians. Conscious that he had some very severe things to say to the Galatians, he first expressed to them his ultimate allegiance to God in the face of any potential recoil from them, "For am I now seeking the approval of man, or of God? Or am I trying to please man? If I were still trying to please man, I would not be a servant of Christ" (Gal. 1:10). We see from this passage that Paul was very conscious of the

---

1. R. C. H. Lenski, *The Interpretation of St. Mark's Gospel* (Minneapolis, MN: Augsburg Publishing House, 1961), 517, 518.

working of this disposition of desiring to be accepted by and pleasing to men, a disposition that is native to us all as human beings even in our regenerate state. So, these opening words of the letter to the Galatians reveal that Paul was determined that he would not allow this carnal fear to dominate him to the point of being unfaithful to their souls. He is saying, "If I do, I would negate my fundamental identity as the bondslave of Christ."

The same emphasis appears in Paul's dealings with the Thessalonian church,

> For our appeal does not spring from error or impurity or any attempt to deceive, but just as we have been approved by God to be entrusted with the gospel, so we speak, not to please man, but to please God who tests our hearts. For we never came with words of flattery, as you know, nor with a pretext for greed—God is witness. Nor did we seek glory from people, whether from you or from others, though we could have made demands as apostles of Christ (1 Thess. 2:3–6).

Paul could say, "When we ministered among you, we were not men-pleasers, but we were passionate God-pleasers, and it is this that enabled us to speak the truth with unfettered boldness and fidelity."

Consider how this dynamic was at work in Paul's relationship with the Ephesian church. He begins to close his letter to them by exhorting them to be a praying people. First, he exhorts them to pray at all times in the Spirit (Eph. 6:18). Then he urges them to pray perseveringly for one another. Finally, he urges them to pray for him as he preaches the gospel, "and also for me, that words may be given to me in opening my mouth boldly to proclaim the mystery of the gospel, for which I am an ambassador in chains, that I may declare it boldly, as I ought to speak" (Eph. 6:19, 20). Here is a man who has already been marked by fidelity to Christ in situation after situation that has brought upon him suffering, affliction, beatings, and even imprisonment. Yet he is conscious that he has not incorporated into the stuff of his soul an abundant stock of the boldness that will enable him to continue to be faithful. Rather, he asks for prayer. Because God did answer their prayers, and because God gave him that unfettered boldness which was not in any way impeded or restrained by the fear of men, Paul could say to the Ephesian elders, "I did not shrink from declaring to you anything that was profitable" (Acts 20:20). Paul knew that there were elements in his message which could possibly prove to be unpalatable to them, but knowing that those truths were profitable to the Ephesians, he did not shrink from declaring his message to them.

We see in the apostle Paul a staggering breadth of sympathetic feeling joined to courageous boldness. To the Thessalonians he compared himself in his pastoral dealings to a nursing mother (1 Thess. 2:7) and a loving, nurturing, hands-on father (1 Thess. 2:9, 10). To the Ephesian elders he spoke of his fearless commitment to telling them everything that was profitable for their souls, even if those truths had the potential of alienating them. In the life and ministry of the great apostle, the absence of the fear of man was intertwined with the tenderest compassion, so that Paul could also say to the same elders that his ministry among them was carried on "night or day with tears" (Acts 20:31).

The fourth line of biblical evidence to undergird the necessity for an increasing measure of deliverance from the fear of man is found *in the general teaching of Scripture.*

Nathan fearlessly confronted his king. Elijah confronted wicked King Ahab, his equally wicked spouse, and the entire nation with its hordes of false prophets. Noah confronted a whole generation for a hundred twenty years. All these and others have faithfully delivered God's message. They were men marked by liberation from the fear of men's faces. The ministry of a true man of God will manifest the working of the Spirit of God in his heart so that he is no longer in bondage to the fear of man.

The Vital Necessity of the Grace of Holy Boldness

Why is it essential that, along with a growing love for our people, we also experience an increasing measure of liberation from the fear of our people? The answer is, in part, the fact that as we get to know our people more intimately and accurately, we become more and more conscious of the defining issues of their lives and the perspectives in their thinking that need to be addressed by the Word of God.

What usually happens is this. You find yourself working through a portion of Scripture for teaching or preaching, or you have settled on a subject which you believe needs to have the collation of the total witness of Scripture. Then, lo and behold, you come to a given passage in your sermon preparation, and as you do you say, "Man oh man, this text has the name of John Smith written all over it." Growing out of your dealings with John and his family last week in a pastoral visit, you have come to realize that this is the very issue that needs to be addressed with John. You begin to think,

"What will John think if I make powerful application of this matter knowing it so directly applies to him?" What are you going to do? Are you going to have a homiletical burp and just preach over and around the text or the issue? Or are you committed to expound that passage faithfully and press it into the consciences of your dear flock even though you know John Smith will most likely be present and will possibly turn red with embarrassment or resentment as the arrows of truth find their mark in his conscience?

The more you know your people and the patterns of their lives and their thinking, the more vulnerable you will become to the temptation to draw back from addressing certain issues. On any given Lord's Day, as you are preparing your message, you think to yourself, "This sermon is going to be an arrow to John Smith's conscience, and this is going to be an arrow to Henry Jones and to Mary Clark." As the stock of your knowledge of your people grows, so the tendency to draw back here and there will also grow. Unless you are experiencing an increasing measure of deliverance from the fear of man, there will be a decreasing measure of fidelity to the Word of God and to the faithful shepherding of the souls of your people in the public and private ministry of the preaching and teaching of the Word of God.

Furthermore, if you are not increasingly liberated from the fear of their faces, how will you know when your words of comfort and encouragement are mere flattery, calculated to secure their smiles? How will you know when your gentleness is the meekness and gentleness of Christ or when it is a sickening and effeminate moral weakness? How will you know that your bold denunciations of sin are not always calculated to be denunciation of the sins "out there," outside the congregation—issues like the wickedness of Marxist materialism, the irrationality of evolutionary thought, the obsession with digital technology—while being strangely silent about American materialism and about the materialism you see among your own people? Are you unwilling to do what Paul said Timothy was to do? I marvel at the way Paul expects timid Timothy to do some of the things he asked him to do. For example, he told Timothy, "As for the rich in this present age, charge them not to be haughty, nor to set their hopes on the uncertainty of riches, but on God" (1 Tim. 6:17). This is holy boldness!

Solomon linked this whole matter of holy boldness and liberation from the fear of man to wisdom. Solomon says, "The fear of man lays a snare, but whoever trusts in the LORD is safe" (Prov. 29:25). The fear of man will ensnare your mind in the process of your preparation, as I have already intimated, when the text is taking you in a direction that you know is going to plop the truth in the lap of this or that sheep in the flock; your mind will be snared from going there if the fear of man is crippling its activities. The fear of man will ensnare your spirit and your tongue in the act of preaching. I find this so often in preaching to the people of God and to ministers of the gospel. I simply pray, "Lord, set me loose." If you can be made to hold back truth by the pressure of the frowns or the anticipation of the smiles of your people, you will never be a faithful man of God. If ever we are to reflect the image of God, should it not be when we are imparting His Word privately or publicly?

This issue is related to and rooted in the doctrine of God, His nature and attributes. What is our God like? The Old Testament lays the foundation, "Now then, let the fear of the LORD be upon you. Be careful what you do, for there is no injustice with the LORD our God, or partiality or taking bribes" (2 Chron. 19:7). The Scripture tells us, "Masters, do the same to them, and stop your threatening, knowing that he who is both their Master and yours is in heaven, and that there is no partiality with him" (Eph. 6:9), or, "there is no respect of persons with him" (ASV). Paul also says, "For God shows no partiality" (Rom. 2:11). Peter says, "And if you call on him as Father who judges impartially according to each one's deeds, conduct yourselves with fear throughout the time of your exile" (1 Pet. 1:17).

Suggestions for Cultivating the Grace of Holy Boldness

How do we increase in the grace of holy boldness? How do we experience increasing liberation from the fear of man? I believe that this grace is imparted in regeneration when God takes away our heart of stone and gives us a heart of flesh. In the language of Jeremiah 32, He puts His fear into our hearts, and then the fear of God, the desire to be well-pleasing to God and to have the approbation of God, becomes a dominant disposition of the soul. That is why Jesus can say, "So everyone who acknowledges me before men, I also will acknowledge before my Father who is in heaven, but whoever denies me before men, I also will deny before my Father who is in heaven" (Matt. 10:32, 33). No matter what our native temperament may be, in the grace of regeneration there is implanted within the soul of every child of God a fundamental disposition of the fear of God that prevails over the fundamental disposition of the fear of man. This is why Paul said,

> If you confess with your mouth that Jesus is Lord and believe in your heart that God raised him from the dead, you will be saved. For with

the heart one believes and is justified, and with the mouth one confesses and is saved (Rom. 10:9, 10).

God enables every regenerate person to subdue the dominant crippling effect of the fear of man.

Many other factors enter into the outworking of Christian growth. However, as with so many other aspects of Christian experience, we must consciously cultivate that virtue implanted by the Spirit of God and by the grace of our Lord Jesus. So, let me suggest two categories within which we ought to cultivate this godly character trait of increasing liberation from the fear of man and the grace of holy boldness.

Our Walk Before God as Christian Men

First, I offer some suggestions that pertain to *our walk before God as Christian men.*

I urge you *to maintain a good conscience before both God and men.*

A good conscience is the taproot of holy boldness in the work of the ministry. You will remember Paul in those instances of his standing before pagans who, humanly speaking, held the destiny of his life in their hands, "And looking intently at the council, Paul said, 'Brothers, I have lived my life before God in all good conscience up to this day'" (Acts 23:1). He is effectively saying, "I have lived before the eye of my God, so I can look you straight in the eyes and not be intimidated." He says, "So I always take pains to have a clear conscience toward both God and man" (Acts 24:16). As he stands there on trial he can say that, in the light of the coming day of judgment, he has exercised himself always to have a good conscience before God and men. And that is why we read, "The wicked flee when no one pursues, but the righteous are bold as a lion" (Prov. 28:1). This boldness is not fundamentally a matter of temperament or a lack of sensitivity. It is rooted in being a righteous man with a perfect and imputed righteousness which imparts a joyful consciousness that the court of heaven has no controversy with us. However, that *imputed* righteousness, based on our union with the Lord Jesus, is always accompanied by an *imparted* or *infused* righteousness, the necessary fruit of regeneration.

Now if a good conscience is the taproot of holy boldness, our justification in Christ is the taproot of a good conscience. I will never forget when the truth and reality of justification first broke in upon me and these words gripped me, "There is therefore now no condemnation for those who are in Christ Jesus" (Rom. 8:1). With regard to the penal dealings of God with my sin, Judgment Day has come and passed. There is therefore *now*, in the present moment, no condemnation to me. So, the man who has no legal controversy with God, and no present issues of conscience before God or man, is as bold as a lion (Prov. 28:1). He walks in integrity before God and has boldness in the work of the ministry, and this delivers him from the crippling fear of men. So, unless you would put yourself on the low road to apostasy, you will not have unfettered boldness in all the facets of your labor as a man of God unless you maintain a good conscience. To maintain boldness with a bloodied conscience is the low road to apostasy!

Then, as Christian men before God, we ought not only to maintain a good conscience before God and men, but to *keep good models before us.*

This is what Paul was doing in his letter to the Philippian church. He first set himself before them in chapter one, describing his perspectives on the imprisonment he was experiencing at the time of writing and his response to it. Then he set Christ before them in chapter two. Then he set Timothy and Epaphroditus before them (Phil. 2:19–30). Then he says, "Brothers, join in imitating me, and keep your eyes on those who walk according to the example you have in us" (Phil. 3:17). He says to Timothy,

> You, however, have followed my teaching, my conduct, my aim in life, my faith, my patience, my love, my steadfastness, my persecutions and sufferings that happened to me at Antioch, at Iconium, and at Lystra— which persecutions I endured; yet from them all the Lord rescued me (2 Tim. 3:10, 11).

Here is timid Timothy, with his natively unhealthy physical constitution; yet in the midst of all of that Paul can say these words, "You saw me Timothy, with holy boldness delivered from the fear of man. Timothy, follow my example."

Look for examples like this as you read the scriptures. See Elijah daring to confront the king and the nation, standing firm in delivering the Word of God. See Peter and John before the Sanhedrin as men marvel at their boldness and take note of them that they have been with Jesus. In reading good biographies, who cannot help but get the goose bumps when he envisions Luther standing at the Diet of Worms, uttering those famous words into the ears of those who had the power to put him to death as a heretic, "Here I stand; so help me God. I can do no other."

Here is a portion of the interview of John Knox before Queen Mary in 1561:

> Queen Mary: "Yea, but ye are not the Kirk [Church] that I will nourish. I will defend the Kirk of Rome, for it is, I think, the true Kirk of God."

> John Knox: "Your will, Madam, is no reason; neither doth your thought make that Roman harlot to be the true and immaculate spouse of Jesus Christ. Wonder not, Madam, that I call Rome an harlot; for that Church is altogether polluted with all kind of spiritual fornication, as well in doctrine as in manners. Yea, Madam, I offer myself to prove, that the Church of the Jews which crucified Christ Jesus, was not so far degenerate from the ordinances which God gave by Moses and Aaron unto His people, when they manifestly denied the Son of God, as the Church of Rome is declined, and more than five hundred years hath declined, from the purity of that religion which the Apostles taught and planted."

> Queen Mary: "My conscience is not so."

> John Knox: "Conscience, Madam, requireth knowledge; and I fear that right knowledge ye have none."[2]

There is also a lovely anecdote shared by Gardiner Spring. After stating that deliverance from the fear of man is vital, and citing some biblical allusions to it, he recalls this incident:

> That distinguished American preacher, Samuel Davies, then the President of the College of New Jersey, when on a visit to England, in behalf of the College, was invited to preach before King George III. His youthful queen was sitting by his side; and so enchanted were they by the preacher's eloquence, that the king expressed his admiration in no measured terms, and so audibly and rudely as to draw the attention of the audience, and interrupt the service. The preacher made a sudden and solemn pause in his discourse, looked around upon the audience, and fixing his piercing eye upon England's noisy monarch said, "When the lion roars the beasts of the forest tremble; when Jehovah speaks, let the kings of the earth keep silence before Him!" He was God's

---

2. You can read the transcript of John Knox before Queen Mary at http://www.reformation.org/john-knox-interview.html

messenger; he feared not man, who is a worm. It is not God's ministers who tremble amid such scenes.[3]

I wish I could have been there and seen the look on the king's face. We commend very highly the courage of bold Mr. Davies.

Another thing that we can do in seeking to cultivate this grace of holy boldness as Christian men is to *listen to bold preaching by recordings* if you cannot physically sit under a preacher whose ministry has this quality.

Among the many things I love about John MacArthur is his utter fearlessness in addressing whatever unbiblical movement is making its way through the evangelical church, diluting or weakening its vigorous and unashamed declaration of the whole counsel of God. When you hear someone with this kind of gracious but holy boldness, it becomes contagious and you find yourself praying, "God, give me that boldness! Lord, increase such in me that I will tremble before no mere earthly creature."

Our Walk Before God as Christian Ministers

Second, I offer some suggestions concerning how to increase our boldness, suggestions that pertain to *our walk before God as Christian ministers.*

The first suggestion is that *you must remind yourself again and again that you have taken up the responsibilities of the pastoral office in a scriptural and orderly way.*

You must constantly remind yourself that the ascended Christ is the Lord who has given you as a gift to His church. You must be able to say, "I did not appoint nor send myself; God, by His Word and His Spirit, through His church, without any direct revelation, but through His ordained means, has placed me here." Then and only then has your identity been established and the path of holy boldness been marked out for you. On this basis, you need not fear man.

Paul's unique apostleship was his fundamental identity. He stated it at the beginning of many of his letters to the churches (e. g., Rom. 1:1, 5; 1 Cor. 1:1; 2 Cor. 1:1; Eph. 1:1; Col. 1:1; Acts 20:28). Though the gift and office of apostle no longer exists, we have similar boldness by virtue of our biblical calling to the office of an elder, overseer, and shepherd. The Third Person of

---

3. Gardiner Spring, *The Power of the Pulpit* (Edinburgh: The Banner of Truth Trust, 1986), 72.

the Trinity has constituted you overseers (Acts 20:28). Constantly feed your minds upon that reality. Remind yourself often:

> I am not here because a group of men laid their hands upon me. I am not here because I had some consciousness of inclination to the ministry. I have soberly assessed my desires and fitness for this office. Other mature and discerning Christians have validated my assessment that I have been endowed with the requisite graces and gifts to serve in the church of Christ as an undershepherd. Therefore, I am here by the will of God. That is it. God Himself has called me to the task.

The second suggestion for increasing your boldness as a Christian minister is to *tell yourself that the eye of God is upon you when you are preaching and teaching the Word of God.*

Paul said, "For we are not, like so many, peddlers of God's word, but as men of sincerity, as commissioned by God, in the sight of God we speak in Christ" (2 Cor. 2:17). He charged Timothy,

> I charge you in the presence of God and of Christ Jesus, who is to judge the living and the dead, and by his appearing and his kingdom: preach the word; be ready in season and out of season; reprove, rebuke, and exhort, with complete patience and teaching (2 Tim. 4:1, 2).

Again, "In the presence of God and of Christ Jesus and of the elect angels I charge you to keep these rules without prejudging, doing nothing from partiality" (1 Tim. 5:21). "Timothy, ever keep before you the fact that you preach under the eye of God who is the appointed judge of the world."

> The pulpit is a place where the fear of God must be paramount. I once asked a preacher if he was intimidated by the presence of a national celebrity in his congregation. He said, "No, why should I be? I speak in front of God every Sunday morning."[4]

The sentiment may be simple, but it is devastatingly true. If we were to take seriously the attendance of God at our services, our passion for accuracy in truth would surely be augmented, and I would add to that, our liberation from the fear of men's faces would be increased.

"What!" said John Welch (a fervent Scottish Minister, son-in-law to the celebrated John Knox,) "that I should regard or fear the face of any

---

4. R. C. Sproul, "The Whole Man," in *The Preacher and Preaching*, ed. Samuel T. Logan, Jr. (Phillipsburg, NJ: P & R Publishing, 1986), 122.

man, when I remember and assure myself that I am standing before that sacred and Glorious Majesty, whose word, in his very sight, I am preaching to his servants and creatures! Believe me, when this thought enters my mind, I could not pay any regard to the face of any man, even if I wished ever so much to do so."[5]

The third suggestion with respect to cultivating holy boldness as a Christian minister is the recognition that *the living God will judge you for your faithfulness in fulfilling the responsibilities of your office.*

Consider the following texts:

Cursed is he who does the work of the LORD with slackness, and cursed is he who keeps back his sword from bloodshed (Jer. 48:10).

"Son of man, I have made you a watchman for the house of Israel. Whenever you hear a word from my mouth, you shall give them warning from me. If I say to the wicked, 'You shall surely die,' and you give him no warning, nor speak to warn the wicked from his wicked way, in order to save his life, that wicked person shall die for his iniquity, but his blood I will require at your hand. But if you warn the wicked, and he does not turn from his wickedness, or from his wicked way, he shall die for his iniquity, but you will have delivered your soul. Again, if a righteous person turns from his righteousness and commits injustice, and I lay a stumbling block before him, he shall die. Because you have not warned him, he shall die for his sin, and his righteous deeds that he has done shall not be remembered, but his blood I will require at your hand. But if you warn the righteous person not to sin, and he does not sin, he shall surely live, because he took warning, and you will have delivered your soul" (Ezek. 3:17–21).

So whether we are at home or away, we make it our aim to please him. For we must all appear before the judgment seat of Christ, so that each one may receive what is due for what he has done in the body, whether good or evil (2 Cor. 5:9, 10).

And when the chief Shepherd appears, you will receive the unfading crown of glory (1 Pet. 5:4).

The gist of every one of those texts is that the living God will judge me.

John Brown writes eloquently to this point:

---

5. Charles Bridges, *The Christian Ministry* (Edinburgh: The Banner of Truth Trust, 1976), 124.

It is a minister's duty to use every proper means to stand well in the estimation of those to whom he ministers, and it argues not magnanimity, but stupidity and ingratitude, to be insensible to the pleasure which the successful use of these means is calculated to excite. But he is a fool who makes the attainment of what is usually called popularity a leading object—he is worse than a fool who, in order to secure or retain it, conceals or modifies, in the slightest degree, his conscientious convictions, either as to faith or duty. The present approbation of conscience, and the anticipated approbation of his Lord, these are the objects the Christian minister should continually keep in view. When popularity is gained along with these, it is really valuable, for it insures the probability of usefulness; but the hosannas of the crowd are dearly purchased at the expense of one pang of conscience—one frown from the Saviour.[6]

Common Objections to the Grace of Holy Boldness

The first objection is that *holy boldness will make preachers hard, caustic, pugnacious and insensitive.*

I answer that it is not so in the biblical examples cited. The apostle Paul, who is a paragon of deliverance from the fear of men, is also the great example of tenderness, love, compassion, tears, and deep solicitude for the well-being of the people of God (Acts 20:20, 31; 1 Cor. 16:13; 2 Cor. 2:1–4; 2 Cor. 7:2–4, 8; Gal. 1:10, 11; Gal. 4:19; 1 Thess. 2:7, 8, 11). I answer as well that it is impossible in the economy of God's grace. Love is the fruit of the Spirit, and boldness is also the fruit and the result of the operation of the Holy Spirit liberating us from the fear of men's faces. Spirit-wrought boldness is joined with love.

The second objection is that *holy boldness will alienate some people.*

Well, yes, it may alienate the enemies of the truth. Paul says, "If I love you more, am I to be loved less?" (2 Cor. 12:15). Why did they love him less? Because he was being faithful to their souls. Yes, the enemies of truth may indeed love us less by our boldness, but so what? God never promised that we were going to be everybody's hail-fellow-well-met. In one of the last sermons that Tozer preached he said, "These soft-handed preachers, with the saintly flush on their cheek, trying to get along with everybody. Quit

---

6. John Brown, *An Exposition of the Epistle of Paul the Apostle to the Galatians* (Edinburgh: The Banner of Truth Trust, 2001), 217, 218.

it, Reverend, quit it! It won't do you any good. In seeking to get along with everybody, you'll eventually get along with nobody." He went on to say, "If you lose the capacity to hate, then when you say you love, it means nothing." This anecdote is from my personal recollection.

Yes, the enemies of truth may not love us, but that is alright. That is part of the turf upon which a faithful man of God walks and works. However, some may temporarily dislike us, but eventually they will be ready to spill their blood for us. Scripture encourages us with this hope, "Whoever rebukes a man will afterward find more favor than he who flatters with his tongue" (Prov. 28:23). They are the ones who say with the psalmist, "Let a righteous man strike me—it is a kindness; let him rebuke me—it is oil for my head; let my head not refuse it" (Ps. 141:5). When my pastor lays the Word of God upon me in a way that stings and bites and burns, I love him because I know that what he is doing is for my good.

Finally, *unbelievers will be awed and angered.*

Remember Stephen, "Now when they heard these things they were enraged, and they ground their teeth at him. But he, full of the Holy Spirit, gazed into heaven and saw the glory of God, and Jesus standing at the right hand of God" (Acts 7:54, 55). When we have breathed our last, my brothers, the only thing that will matter to us will be to hear our blessed Lord say to us by His grace, "Well done."

> Our Father, we are in Your presence. We pray earnestly that the consciousness of that reality will grip us more and more, and that we will be increasingly delivered from every trace of our fear of men's faces. Wash us in the blood of Your Son. Baptize us afresh with the consciousness that You have called us. We preach before Your face, and we will stand before You in the last day. Fill our hearts with Your Spirit, that Spirit who will enable us to speak with unfettered boldness. Hear our cry and answer us we plead in Jesus' name. Amen.

CHAPTER 10

His Relationship to His People (3)

In this lecture, we come to a third and equally crucial aspect of our consideration of the man of God in relationship to his people. I will state it as an axiom in this way. *You must earn and thereby experience the increasing respect and confidence of your people.*

It is necessary for me to give a justification for this axiom, as well as a qualification for stating it this way.

Earning and Experiencing the Increasing Respect and Confidence of Your People

The world of grace in which the Christian lives may make one feel uncomfortable with this language of *earning* confidence. Therefore, I need to justify my use of this language. Earning confidence seems foreign to God's whole scheme of restorative and redemptive purpose towards the sons of men which is pervasively a system of grace. This sphere of God's grace is beautifully expressed by Paul, "For by grace you have been saved through faith. And this is not your own doing; it is the gift of God, not a result of works, so that no one may boast" (Eph. 2:8, 9). I have used the words *earning confidence* because it is a simple fact, both of biblical revelation and observable human experience, that the commodities of respect and confidence are, of necessity, earned commodities. They cannot be conferred gratuitously or as a matter of grace. We have an example of this in the parable of the talents,

> But his master answered him, "You wicked and slothful servant! You knew that I reap where I have not sown and gather where I scattered no seed? Then you ought to have invested my money with the bankers, and at my coming I should have received what was my own with interest. So take the talent from him and give it to him who has the ten talents. For to everyone who has will more be given, and he will have

an abundance. But from the one who has not, even what he has will be taken away" (Matt. 25:26–29).

Here we see an instance where one man has earned trust from the master while another has not, and the master deals with each one according to what has been earned. We see this emphasis in Proverbs, "A servant who deals wisely has the king's favor, but his wrath falls on one who acts shamefully" (Prov. 14:35); "A servant who deals wisely will rule over a son who acts shamefully and will share the inheritance as one of the brothers" (Prov. 17:2).

Now it is true that any man who righteously earned the respect and confidence of his people, and increasingly earns a stock of additional measures of them, will gladly acknowledge with the apostle, "By the grace of God I am what I am" (1 Cor. 15:10). Also, feeling the humbling reality of his own sins and failures, he will freely confess that if people really knew the depths of his secret struggles with sin, and if they could read his thoughts, they would perhaps have a different opinion of him. Yet, by the grace of God he has so walked before his people that he has earned their respect and confidence. As God enables us to walk with integrity and not indulge the temptations that we wrestle with at the level of our thoughts, we do indeed earn an increasing measure of their respect and confidence. The apostle Paul was obviously conscious of this principle when he wrote these words to the Thessalonians: "You are witnesses, and God also, how holy and righteous and blameless was our conduct toward you believers" (1 Thess. 2:10).

I also need to give a *qualification*. If a man has received concentrated ministerial education before being called to a specific pastoral charge, he ought to have received that training because mature people of God in the church judged him to be a man who fits Paul's description, "And what you have heard from me in the presence of many witnesses entrust to faithful men who will be able to teach others also" (2 Tim. 2:2). So the church ought to make a judgment about a man's earned respect and confidence *before* they ever commend him as a candidate for the ministry and urge him to receive concentrated, structured ministerial education. Furthermore, if he has undergone a realistic and biblical scrutiny before actually being recognized as a gift of Christ to a specific church in which he will labor as a pastor-teacher, he will have secured an affirmation of God's people in the area of confidence and respect. Unless a man shuffles from one pastorate to the other every few years, which sadly happens in many evangelical churches, it is assumed that confidence and respect will accrue to the man who is faithful and trustworthy in one place over the course of many years.

In addition, when new people come into the church, they are under obligation to recognize the existing stock of confidence and respect that the men in spiritual leadership have already gained while living and laboring in that congregation. Frankly, it is disconcerting when people come into a church as newcomers and think that it is their right to view the existing leaders as though they had no previously earned respect and confidence. They think that those leaders therefore must go back to square one in their judgment, even though they are newcomers. That is simply not the biblical perspective. When newcomers come into an assembly where there are proven men of God in places of leadership, it is the responsibility of those newcomers not to join the church until they have sensed from the members in that church that the leaders are greatly respected. We read, "Paul came also to Derbe and to Lystra. A disciple was there, named Timothy, the son of a Jewish woman who was a believer, but his father was a Greek. He was well spoken of by the brothers at Lystra and Iconium" (Acts 16:1, 2). Timothy had an earned stock of respect and confidence by the brethren in at least two cities and their respective congregations. Paul recognized the existing stock of respect and confidence which Timothy had earned, and on that basis desired to take him with them as a companion in ministry.

However, some years later, lest Timothy at any time would think he could afford the luxury of coasting or drawing upon the previously earned confidence and respect of those to whom he ministered, Paul solemnly charged him with these words,

> Let no one despise you for your youth, but set the believers an example in speech, in conduct, in love, in faith, in purity. Until I come, devote yourself to the public reading of Scripture, to exhortation, to teaching. Do not neglect the gift you have, which was given you by prophecy when the council of elders laid their hands on you. Practice these things, immerse yourself in them, so that all may see your progress (1 Tim. 4:12–15).

These things must be taught and imparted to your people. However, unless we would revert to Romish superstition and sacerdotalism, and reconstruct the mindless awe of the clergy so rife in medieval spiritual darkness, the bulk of the stock of our respect and confidence must be earned by the kind of life we live and the patterns of our ministry which our people observe over the long haul.

There is an illustration of this principle from the way in which stalactites and stalagmites are formed. What happens in the formation of those massive cave structures is that water rich in lime deposits drips down, and when the water evaporates and the lime remains bit by bit, those massive structures are built upward or hang downward from the ceiling of the cave. Well, in the same way, the lives that we live among our people must be leaving a continual deposit of increasing confidence and respectability, and all of those things that go into being a man of God in truth.

Now, with this introduction behind us, let me address the subject under three headings. First, *the biblical basis* for this axiom. Second, the *areas of crucial concern* with reference to this matter of earning ongoing respect and confidence. Third, some *concluding observations and exhortations*.

The Biblical Basis for This Axiom

I propose to set forth a demonstration of the scriptural basis for this principle regarding this matter of earning and increasing our stock of the respect and confidence of our people. Regarding this issue, we must have our thinking hammered out on the anvil of Scripture. The foundation for this concern is clearly laid in the nature of the biblical requirements for one who would assume an official position of leadership among God's people. The Spirit-inspired standards of ministerial qualifications set forth in 1 Timothy 3:1–7 and Titus 1:5–9 are comprised of the non-negotiable character traits of everyone whom Christ is forming as a gift to His church. If our task is to shepherd the flock of God by leading them into maturity, then we must have their respect and confidence as those who, in some measure, exemplify that to which we trust our ministry will take them. To point the people of God in a direction which we ourselves are not pursuing would be utter hypocrisy and would bring us under the indictment of our Lord to those consummate hypocrites, the scribes and the Pharisees. It was of them that our Lord spoke when He said, "For they preach, but do not practice" (Matt. 23:3).

The basic respect and confidence expressed when you are initially recognized as an elder must grow and increase as you live and walk and fulfill your office among your people. Time will either confirm the initial respect and confidence they placed in you when they received you as a gift of Christ, or time will, by degrees, push you out of that place in their estimation and cut the nerve of your usefulness in their lives. The scriptures connect the necessity for the minister to be an example of growth before the people of God and their obligation to regard their ministers.

A number of important statements are found in the pastoral letters regarding this: "Let no one despise you for your youth, but set the believers an example in speech, in conduct, in love, in faith, in purity" (1 Tim. 4:12); "Practice these things, immerse yourself in them, so that all may see your progress" (1 Tim. 4:15); "Declare these things; exhort and rebuke with all authority. Let no one disregard you" (Titus 2:15). We could paraphrase Paul's words in this way:

> Timothy, when I return to Ephesus and enter into conversation with the people at Ephesus concerning your ministry, there ought to be a spontaneous expression from the people. I anticipate that they will say, "Oh, Paul, I know you were impressed the last time you heard Timothy preach, but you should hear him now! His exposition is much clearer. His organization is more helpful. His applications are much more penetrating. Paul, his progress is evident to all of us!"

This, therefore, is not a secondary or optional issue in the maintenance of effective pastoral ministry.

One of the most perceptive and searching statements of this principle that I have ever encountered is what I found in Stalker many years ago:

> We are so constituted that what we hear depends very much for its effect on how we are disposed towards him who speaks. The regular hearers of a minister gradually form in their minds, almost unawares, an image of what he is, into which they put everything which they themselves remember about him and everything which they have heard of his record; and, when he rises on Sunday in the pulpit, it is not the man visible there at the moment that they listen to, but this image, which stands behind him and determines the precise weight and effect of every sentence which he utters.[1]

I am sure that you say "Amen!" to those words. It simply happens in keeping with the way God has put us together. You know that is true and you do not have to think about it.

John Brown writes:

> MAN is a being endowed with affections as well as intellect, and these different parts of his mental constitution mutually influence each other. While, on the one hand, you cannot obtain a secure hold of the

---

1. James Stalker, *The Preacher and His Models* (New York: Hodder and Stoughton, 1891), 167.

affections without first bringing the understanding over to your side; on the other, the having the affections on your side makes it a comparatively easy work to obtain the suffrage of the intellect.[2]

Brown then demonstrates that Paul understood how crucial this was in his relationship to the Galatians. The Judaizers sought to turn the affections of the people against the apostle in order that they might rip out of the minds and hearts of the people of God the perceptions of truth imparted to them by the apostle.

Brown further writes:

Hence the importance of a teacher of Christian truth standing well in the affections of those whom he instructs. If a teacher of Christianity be generally viewed as a man altogether destitute of, or greatly deficient in, integrity and piety, anxious to promote his own interest and reputation, but careless of the spiritual interest of those to whom he ministers— however able and eloquent may be his discourses, however clear his statements of truth and powerful his enforcements of duty—it is not at all likely that his labours will either be very acceptable or very useful.[3]

Brown then goes on to state the contrasting principle and how it applied in Paul's dealings with the Galatians in the attempt of the Judaizers to undermine Paul's ministry. We also must grasp this principle. We must be convinced that in our relationship to our people, we must earn an increasing measure of respect and confidence if we would effectively minister to them in the full range of our pastoral relationships to them.

Now I move to articulate the areas of concern with reference to this assertion.

Areas of Crucial Concern

In one sense, any sin and any lack of grace will erode respect and confidence in the long haul of ministry, but I want to focus on some specific areas. If you ask what guided me in my selection of these areas of concern, I would say three things: my pastoral involvement with men for over fifty years of ministry, my exposure to the proven guides who have written on their concerns in

---

2. John Brown, *An Exposition of the Epistle of Paul to the Galatians* (Edinburgh: The Banner of Truth Trust, 2001), 204.

3. John Brown, *An Exposition of the Epistle of Paul to the Galatians* (Edinburgh: The Banner of Truth Trust, 2001), 204, 205.

this matter, and the input of the people of God and their reaction to men in the church. I am not selecting these seven things arbitrarily or in an imbalanced way. They grow out of that threefold exposure. I call these *killers of respect and confidence.*

The first killer is when your people have solid reasons to suspect you of *laziness or sloth.*

Sloth is defined as a disinclination to work or to exert oneself. You and I are supported by the gifts of God's people in order to do what Paul directs, "Let the elders who rule well be considered worthy of double honor, especially those who labor in preaching and teaching" (1 Tim. 5:17). The Greek word for *labor* is a form of *kopiōntes* which is used of hard and painstaking toil. When elders are set apart to labor in teaching and preaching, that labor is antithetical to laziness. Toil and labor are the standard of ministerial output. Therefore, if our people have legitimate grounds to suspect us of laziness, their confidence in and respect for us will be eroded. Laziness in general is resented by the people because it makes the ministry appear as an ecclesiastical relief program. Paul and his companions in ministerial labor, in contrast to this kind of ministerial sloth that is often seen in men, set themselves forth to the church at Thessalonica as examples of men who worked hard. Paul said,

> For you yourselves know how you ought to imitate us, because we were not idle when we were with you, nor did we eat anyone's bread without paying for it, but with toil and labor we worked night and day, that we might not be a burden to any of you. It was not because we do not have that right, but to give you in ourselves an example to imitate (2 Thess. 3:7–9).

Paul was exhorting the people at Thessalonica to be diligent in their legitimate labors, and he was able, with a good conscience, to press this duty on their consciences. His industry was not only in distinctive ministerial labors, but in what we might call secular labors, undertaken to provide for himself and his companions.

If men cheat in diligence in the labor required on their secular jobs, sooner or later it catches up with them either in their paycheck or in periodic evaluations for a potential raise or advancement in positions of responsibility. Men in the world cannot generally get away with that kind of laziness for long. Now just because we do not answer to anyone with a punched time card, or we are not having someone scrutinize how we invest our powers, we can fall into patterns of ministerial laziness. That laziness can take the form of addiction to TV, or the Internet, or social media, sports, the daily newspaper, even to puttering around the house and other diversions. Sooner or later that is going to leak out and be evident in the quality of our work. Our people are not fools. They are going to notice signs of laziness along the way, and when they do, there will be an erosion of their respect and confidence in us. We will not be able to say with the apostle Paul that we are an example of diligence (Acts 20:34, 35; 1 Thess. 2:8, 9). He was able to say this everywhere he labored because he set an example of diligence in his commitment to labor, not only in the proclamation of the Word, but in secular employment, and thereby he did commend the gospel.

Think about the caustic castigation by Ezekiel of the false prophets who fed themselves and not the flock,

> Thus says the Lord GOD, Behold, I am against the shepherds, and I will require my sheep at their hand and put a stop to their feeding the sheep. No longer shall the shepherds feed themselves. I will rescue my sheep from their mouths, that they may not be food for them (Ezek. 34:10).

Ralph Turnbull advises pastors about this:

> A Turkish proverb has it, "A busy man is troubled with but one devil; the idle man with a thousand." And a Spanish proverb, "Men are usually tempted by the devil, but the idle man positively tempts the devil." In a holy life there must be control of time. We must discipline the hours and bend them to God's purpose. The late James M. Gray, president of The Moody Bible Institute, was wont to say, "Push your work." The slippered life does not befit the minister of Jesus Christ, who ought to be always on the alert, always about his Master's business, ready to put himself at the disposal of the Holy Spirit. If the hours are frittered away by secondary interests and calls, we are succumbing to the vice of sloth. Laziness through religious fussing about with trifles is an idleness for which God will bring us into judgment.
>
> Out of his ripe experience, the late J. H. Jowett counseled ministers to be as systematic and as businesslike as the businessman. He said: "Enter your study at an appointed hour, and let that hour be as early as the earliest of your businessmen goes to his office. I remember, in my earlier days, how I used to hear the factory operatives passing my house on the way to the mills, where work began at six o'clock.... The sound of clogs fetched me out of bed and took me to my work.... Shall the

minister be behind them in his quest of the Bread of life? In off-setting sloth there must be a wise conservation of the hours."[4]

I want to address laziness *in sermon preparation* in particular.

As we shall see in subsequent units in this course of study, the production of exegetically sound, theologically balanced, homiletically clean, and rhetorically convincing sermons week after week and year after year is just plain hard work. Whatever your native abilities may be, whatever seasons there are when you cannot believe that you are "getting paid to do this," sermon preparation is just plain hard *work*. Whatever we judge our measure of native gifts to be, the difference between mediocrity and excellence is work.

I am dating myself, but I will mention the famous golfer Jack Nicklaus. Think of him at the top of his game, going out between tournaments and hitting golf balls until his hands actually bled. I remember a concert pianist in our congregation, who, in preparing for a particular concert, sat at the piano twenty hours in the space of two days, ten hours at a stretch! When he came out onto the platform and raised his hands over the keyboard, it was as though he owned that piano. It all looked so simple, easy, and natural.

I am not talking about the preacher who travels around the world preaching the same sermons over and over again, but about the man who labors for decade after decade, rooted in one place, with a very patient people. If there is going to be any consistent quality of excellence in our preaching, it means that we must know how to deal with the demon of laziness. The edification of our people depends on our giving them rich fare. How can we gain their respect, and maintain and increase the acquisition of their respect, if we are lazy in our sermon preparation?

Listen to Baxter:

> O brethren! do you not shrink and tremble under the sense of all this work? Will a common measure of holy skill and ability, of prudence and other qualifications, serve for such a task as this? I know necessity may cause the Church to tolerate the weak; but woe to us, if we tolerate and indulge our own weakness! Do not reason and conscience tell

---

4. Ralph G. Turnbull, *A Minister's Obstacles* (Westwood, NJ: Fleming H. Revell Company, 1966), 20. While it may have been a proper exercise in personal discipline for Mr. Jowett to determine to be at his desk earlier than any of his church members were in their factories or offices, we cannot set that framework as the law for others. The fundamental issue is, are we being good stewards of the hours given to us to fulfill our God-given calling and responsibilities?

you, that if you dare venture on so high a work as this, you should spare no pains to be qualified for the performance of it? It is not now and then an idle snatch or taste of studies that will serve to make an able and sound divine. I know that laziness hath learned to allege the vanity of all our studies, and how entirely the Spirit must qualify us for, and assist us in our work; as if God commanded us the use of means, and then warranted us to neglect them; as if it were his way to cause us to thrive in a course of idleness, and to bring us to knowledge by dreams when we are asleep, or to take us up into heaven, and show us his counsels, while we think of no such matter, but are idling away our time on earth! O that men should dare, by their laziness, to "quench the Spirit," and then pretend the Spirit for the doing of it! "O outrageous, shameful and unnatural deed!" God hath required us, that we be "not slothful in business," but "fervent in spirit, serving the Lord." Such we must provoke our hearers to be, and such we must be ourselves. O, therefore, brethren, lose no time! Study, and pray, and confer, and practise; for in these four ways your abilities must be increased. Take heed to yourselves, lest you are weak through your own negligence, and lest you mar the work of God by your weakness.[5]

Turnbull writes further:

Thomas Shepard, Pilgrim father and founder of Harvard University, worked hard early in the week at his sermons, and on Saturday he prepared himself. Read his word: "God will surely curse that minister who lumbers up and down the world all the week, and then thinks to prepare for his pulpit by a hurried hour or two on Saturday night. God knows, Saturday night were little enough time in which to weep and pray and to get his sinful soul into a fit frame for the approaching day."[6]

Now I want to touch on *laziness and reluctance in necessary diaconal duties*.

The general sphere of our work is laboring in preaching and teaching (1 Tim. 5:17), in prayer and in the ministry of the Word (Acts 6:4). Yet often, especially in pioneer or church-planting ministries that are not yet furnished with a broad range of men and giftedness for the distribution of labor, it will be our responsibility from time to time to engage in labors that ordinarily would be classified as diaconal and taken up by those called to that office.

---

5. Richard Baxter, *The Reformed Pastor* (Edinburgh: The Banner of Truth Trust, 1974), 71.
6. Ralph G. Turnbull, *A Minister's Obstacles* (Westwood, NJ: Fleming H. Revell Company, 1966), 22, 23.

We have the examples of Christ and the apostle Paul to establish for us that, notwithstanding the office of deacon in the church, pastors are to be engaged in and prepared for necessary diaconal duties in many circumstances. Christ took the towel and basin to wash the disciples' feet. Paul, though he had the right not to work (1 Cor. 9:1–14), engaged in "tent-making" work to teach many in the churches to work hard (2 Thess. 3:7–12) and to send a message to the false apostles that he was one who offered the gospel without charge (1 Cor. 9:15–18). If you are to gain the confidence and respect of your people in those circumstances where such labors are necessary, you must not shrink from them.

In the early days of Trinity Baptist Church, I was called upon to become involved in going to the local board of education in pursuit of a meeting-place for the congregation. The men of the church at that time were at work and not available to go to meetings during normal business hours. The people appreciated and respected this involvement, although it was a labor ordinarily classified as diaconal. It was a delight to be able to throw myself into those tasks. My main purpose was not to gain the respect and confidence of the people. It was that we could have a place to meet so I could have a pulpit behind which to preach! Then, when we renovated "The Cracker Box,"[7] it was again a delight, though at times demanding, to give myself to as many of the physical labors as I could and still be able to preach to the congregation on the Lord's Day. During that time, many other concerns had to be placed on hold. The renovation project required nightly work that resulted in a wonderful bonding among the men committed to the task. So, I urge you, where it is necessary for you to show diligence in necessary diaconal work, do not be reluctant to do it. It helps in cementing relationships of respect and confidence.

The second killer of respect and confidence is when your people detect in you a *prevailing spirit of self-defense and excuse-making with reference to your known deficiencies.*

Which one of us claims not to have them and know them? When there is occasion for them to be mentioned and you show a prickly self-defensiveness, you are going to erode respect and confidence. We are told to be examples of the believers in everything, and the ordinary believer has his deficiencies and sins with which he struggles. We preach that *he* needs to be

---

7. See the Introductory Biography in Volume 1 for the history of "The Cracker Box."

honest, "But exhort one another every day, as long as it is called 'today,' that none of you may be hardened by the deceitfulness of sin" (Heb. 3:13). So *we* must be honest too.

What happens when people exhort us? What happens when people meet us at the door and say, "You know, Pastor, you said thus and thus was such and such from this text, but in the light of this passage, does that really wash?" Lo and behold, when they show you, you realize you made a careless judgment about the text, and had you considered a parallel text which they showed you, you would not have made it. What will you do? Will you waffle and try to cover your tracks, or will you say, "You know John, you are right. I should have seen that. I was wrong." Then you get up that same Lord's Day in the evening service and say,

> When I said thus and thus this morning based on such and such a text, one of the brothers came to me and helped me to see that was not accurate. I retract it. Forgive me for the carelessness in my handling of that portion of the Word of God.

In this way you deal with it righteously and honestly. You will not defend that you are the perfect know-it-all, next-to-infallible exegete of the Word of God. Do not be self-defensive. Do not rationalize. Do not resent exposure of your weaknesses. Do not be inflexible.

Now here is one of the great benefits of establishing a biblical elder-ship with men who are truly your pastors, who feel free to correct you and point out your faults and weaknesses and then encourage and help you to grow in grace. In any case, if you would grow in the confidence and respect of your people, do not be the fool by being guilty of a prevailing pattern of self-defense and excuse-making in the light of your evident faults. The book of Proverbs asserts this: "The way of a fool is right in his own eyes, but a wise man listens to advice" (Prov. 12:15); "The ear that listens to life-giving reproof will dwell among the wise. Whoever ignores instruction despises himself, but he who listens to reproof gains intelligence" (Prov. 15:31, 32).

The third assertion I make is that respect and confidence will be eroded or even shattered if your people discern in you *a spirit of selfishness and grasping after material things.*

This is covetousness. One of the requirements for those who aspire to the office is that he be "not a lover of money" (1 Tim. 3:3). The traditional

English rendering is "not greedy of filthy lucre" (KJV), capturing its depravity. Paul instructed Timothy in detail about this,

> But those who desire to be rich fall into temptation, into a snare, into many senseless and harmful desires that plunge people into ruin and destruction. For the love of money is a root of all kinds of evils. It is through this craving that some have wandered away from the faith and pierced themselves with many pangs. But as for you, O man of God, flee these things. Pursue righteousness, godliness, faith, love, steadfastness, gentleness (1 Tim. 6:9–11).

How can we call our people to biblical perspectives if we do not reflect them ourselves? If God's Word is clear on anything, it is that the people of God are not to "lay up for yourselves treasures on earth, where moth and rust destroy and where thieves break in and steal" (Matt. 6:19). We are all exhorted, "Set your minds on things that are above, not on things that are on earth" (Col. 3:2). I therefore urge you, do not give your people any grounds to suspect you of selfishness and grasping after material gain. Do not be guilty of covetousness.

To be more specific, do not become a fashion-hound with your clothes. Do not become addicted to new cars. Do not always talk about the wonderful salary and perks and benefits that this or that preacher has, or you may have by the congregation's generosity. If you are in a parsonage, do not complain about it. When the time comes for you to conclude your ministry, you want to be able to say, in your very different circumstances, in essence what Samuel said,

> "I am old and gray; and behold, my sons are with you. I have walked before you from my youth until this day. Here I am; testify against me before the LORD and before his anointed. Whose ox have I taken? Or whose donkey have I taken? Or whom have I defrauded? Whom have I oppressed? Or from whose hand have I taken a bribe to blind my eyes with it? Testify against me and I will restore it to you." They said, "You have not defrauded us or oppressed us or taken anything from any man's hand." And he said to them, "The LORD is witness against you, and his anointed is witness this day, that you have not found anything in my hand." And they said, "He is witness" (1 Sam. 12:2–5).

There was silence when he was finished.

Paul spoke similarly,

"I coveted no one's silver or gold or apparel. You yourselves know that these hands ministered to my necessities and to those who were with me. In all things I have shown you that by working hard in this way we must help the weak and remember the words of the Lord Jesus, how he himself said, 'It is more blessed to give than to receive'" (Acts 20:33–35).

It is a wonderful thing to be able to look God's people in the eyes and say, "for I seek not what is yours but you" (2 Cor. 12:14). May God grant that each of us will have this blessing at the end of our days.

The fourth thing that will sweep away the respect and confidence of your beloved people are any *just grounds to question your moral integrity with those of the opposite sex.*

Here we are looking beyond the entrance requirements of blamelessness and being unquestionably a one-woman man. We are looking at the tragic erosion or loss of trust which comes about by moral failures with the opposite sex. Proverbs warns,

> Do not desire her beauty in your heart, and do not let her capture you with her eyelashes; for the price of a prostitute is only a loaf of bread, but a married woman hunts down a precious life. Can a man carry fire next to his chest and his clothes not be burned? Or can one walk on hot coals and his feet not be scorched? (Prov. 6:25–28).

The adulteress hunts for the precious life, and God's captains and lieutenants and generals are the peculiar objects of the attacks of the devil through her. I believe that in his stratagems the devil assigns some of the imps of hell to bring down God's servants that he might, as in the case of David, cause the enemies of God to blaspheme the name of God. Why are pastors peculiarly susceptible to this sin? I believe that it is related to the access that we have to our people's homes, to their affections, and to their burdens at the deepest level in which we must, of necessity, open our hearts to them and they to us.

I urge you to be careful to do everything you can to prevent a fall in this area in order to maintain the respect and the confidence of your people. Maintain good spiritual health in general. Watch and pray that you enter not into temptation. Maintain a wholesome intimacy with your wife. Nurture everything that true marital intimacy is to be emotionally, psychologically, and verbally, and do that at the level of your sexual life, as well. The scriptures are clear that one way God keeps us in the way of sexual purity is by our drinking water only from our own well (Prov. 5:15–20).

Commit yourself also to necessary preventive disciplines such as not going to a home when a woman is alone, not counseling a woman alone in the church building, being circumspect in every situation with a woman, along with keeping your hands off, and other necessary resolutions that you soberly determine to put in place. Load your conscience with the warnings of the Word of God. When the scriptures say that the reproach of the adulterer shall never be wiped away (Prov. 6:33), believe it! You will go to your grave with a scarlet "A" on your forehead. Look at the fine print when sexually tempted.

Whenever there is any proposal to your flesh of uncleanness with a woman, go back and read the chapters that always make us weep. I dread it when, in my regular consecutive reading through the Old Testament, I know I am coming to 2 Samuel 11. I say, "God, how could it be? But this is what happened to the man after God's own heart." May God help us, brethren.

The fifth killer of increasing respect is *a just suspicion of an erosion of domestic competence.*

Domestic competence is a fundamental requirement to enter the office with the approbation of God and with the suffrage of a discerning, Bible-instructed people. Few things are more critical to maintain credibility in the office than this. Since a man's ability to care for his own family is so closely allied to shepherding care, the erosion of this competence in the home is a dark omen to the people of God of your future in the ministry on their behalf.

The sixth potential erosion of respect comes if they discover that we are *living by a double standard, calling people to be something that we ourselves are not seeking to be, and where we are not open and willing and honest in our confession of the same.*

"Let no one despise you for your youth, but set the believers an example in speech, in conduct, in love, in faith, in purity" (1 Tim. 4:12).

Charles Bridges writes:

> But is not also the lax, indulgent approximation to the spirit of the world—either in our general habit and appearance—or in our intercourse with the world—a leading, though not always a tangible, cause of failure? Even the faithful exhibition of the cross must be materially weakened by a want of the corresponding exhibition of its power, in

crucifying its Ministers to the lusts and affections of the world. A connexion with the world beyond the point of clear duty, (or even within
these narrow bounds, without a heavenly temper) must bring us into a
worldly atmosphere, which deadens the vigorous actings of a spiritual
life, till, like the torpedo, we benumb every thing we touch. Conscience in a tender and susceptible state, might almost determine the
question—What is the effect of such connexions upon the spiritual
frame? Has there not been in this atmosphere a closer communion
with the world than with God? Has not the spirit of prayer been well
nigh extinguished, and delight in *the more spiritual exercises* of our
work fearfully lost? And does not our Ministry thus become (perhaps
unconsciously to ourselves) weak, general, and indefinite upon the
main point of separation from the world? Or, even if our exhortations
reach the scriptural standard of decision, must not their power be
wholly counteracted by this compromising spirit?

Accurate and earnest statements of truth, combined with sociable
conformity to the world, will give no offence, and bring no conviction.
Cowper's line—"If parsons fiddle, why may'nt laymen dance?"—has at
least as much truth as wit in it. If we go one step into the world, our flock
will take the sanction to go two; the third will be still more easy, and the
atmosphere more enticing, till at last it proves, "as a bird hasteth to the
snare, and knoweth not that it is for his life." "The Minister, therefore,
who would not have his people give in to worldly conformity such as he
disapproves, must keep at a considerable distance himself. If he walks
near the brink, others will fall down the precipice." "A preacher who
enjoys the smiles of the world, can hope for little success from God";
but "a Minister of the Church, who is entirely disengaged from the love
of earthly things, is a great treasure, and a great 'consolation' to her."[8]

The seventh observation is that respect and confidence will erode *if you are
odd, artificial, or slovenly in your appearance and demeanor.*

One of the characteristics and requirements of love is that it is "not rude"
(1 Cor. 13:5 ESV). This phrase has also been translated as "does not act unbe-
comingly" (NASB), "does not behave itself unseemly" (ASV), and, "does not
act improperly" (CSB). The verb *aschēmonei* indicates that love does not
behave itself against the scheme of things, and there is an acceptable scheme

8. Charles Bridges, *The Christian Ministry* (Edinburgh: The Banner of Truth Trust, 1967),
120, 121. See this whole section from pages 112–137, entitled "Conformity to the World." For
further reading see C. H. Spurgeon, *Lectures to My Students* (Edinburgh: The Banner of Truth
Trust, 2008), "The Minister's Ordinary Conversation," 193–203.

of things in terms of behavior that is bizarre as opposed to that which is seemly, appropriate, and acceptable. There is an unwritten canon of what is acceptable in the way we present ourselves in our dress, our grooming, our laughter, in general manners, and in general social graces. I urge you, brethren, do not allow the respect and confidence of your people to erode because you are boorish in your manners or slovenly in your dress, so that they are reluctant to introduce you to people in some settings because of the way you appear, or the way you react, and the way you interact with those to whom they may introduce you.

R. C. Sproul writes:

While teaching a graduate course in seminary to eighteen ministers, I performed a simple experiment. At the beginning of the course, before the men had the opportunity to get to know each other or form opinions of each one's talents and gifts, I posed a hypothetical situation in which the seminary had submitted a proposal to a large charitable foundation for a grant of two hundred thousand dollars. The seminary wanted this class to select three of its members to visit the board of the foundation to make a presentation of the seminary's request. I then asked the class to select by secret ballot three of their members to present the proposal.

Before the vote was taken I wrote the names of three class members on a piece of paper and concealed it from their view. When the balloting was over, I dramatically produced the three names I had written and astonished the class by showing my list matched exactly the three men who had just been elected. The response of the class was one of wonder: "How did you know?" I felt like a magician who had pulled a rabbit out of his hat. But it was not magic; it was not done by mirrors. All I did was choose the three men in the room who were dressed in the uniform of leadership. Before I revealed my "magic" method to the class, I bounced the question back to them: "Why did you select these three men?" They stammered a bit until the consensus emerged that they really had no idea why they voted the way they did. When I explained my procedure, they groaned at the simplicity of it and were suddenly open to a discussion on the impact of clothes on first impressions of credibility.

The point is not that clothes make the man. The point is that clothes are a part of the complex process of communication. Clothes affect both the speaker and the listener. The effect can intensify when we probe deeper to the dynamic of reciprocity of exchange between the speaker and hearer. When an individual listener or a congregation responds to us by positive signals ranging from warm applause to the tilting of an eyebrow, our confidence is increased and our freedom of expression is enhanced.

The wise preacher considers the message of his clothes when he speaks. He must avoid the hypocrisy of sending a false message, as well as avoiding those forms of dress which are offensive to the hearts of recalcitrant sinners. It is not our call to *add* to the offense by placing unnecessary barriers to communication before our hearers.

Finally we must be conscious that every article of clothing we wear communicates a nonverbal message. The preacher can gain ground in his communication by carefully answering two questions: What do his clothes communicate? What does he want his clothes to communicate? If the answers to these questions are not the same, then change is in order.[9]

May we walk before God as men who are concerned about every detail of our lives so that we give no reproach in anything, and do nothing to undermine a growing measure of respect and confidence. We must be great with the same ambition which gripped the great apostle when he said, "We put no obstacle in anyone's way, so that no fault may be found with our ministry, but as servants of God we commend ourselves in every way" (2 Cor. 6:3, 4).

Concluding Observations and Exhortations

It is possible to be respected where you are not loved.

This was the experience of John the Baptist and our Lord. There may be those who oppose you in your ministry. They may not love you, but you can have an iron-like grip on their consciences by the way you live and relate to them. They will be compelled to respect you by your undeniable manner of life and integrity. Ultimately, in the end, integrity always commands respect.

It takes longer to earn the respect and confidence of some fellow-believers than of others.

For example, the person who has been burnt by ministerial betrayal or pastoral abuse in another church, who then comes within the orbit of your life and ministry, may be somewhat suspicious of you. It may take such a

---

9. R. C. Sproul, "The Whole Man," in *The Preacher and Preaching*, ed. Samuel T. Logan, Jr. (Phillipsburg, NJ: P& R Publishing, 1986), 110–112. Also, look at "The Body in the Pulpit" by Gwyn Walters, in this volume.

person a long while to give you what you deserve and what he or she ought to give you. Just hang in there and patiently love them. Live and walk before them as a consistent, growing, godly man and eventually you will earn their respect and confidence, if indeed the Spirit of God dwells in them.

Do not make the earning of respect and confidence your primary aim.

Your primary aim is to be well-pleasing to your Master and Lord, "so whether we are at home or away, we make it our aim to please him" (2 Cor. 5:9). Live before the eyes of your God, then, as one of the blessings of the vertical patterns of your life, you will have the horizontal blessings of respect and confidence.

The respect and confidence earned over many years can be lost in a day.

Respect and confidence go into the bank a nickel and a dime at a time, week in, week out, month in, month out, year in, year out. One foolish act and the bank is empty, the bottom is pushed out, and you are in a debit mode. That is reality. You say, "That is not fair!" Fair or not, it is reality. David, the classic example, is a blinding, flashing, warning light to us all, that, by the grace of God, the measure of respect and confidence which we have earned will not all be sent down the tubes by one foolish, irresponsible indulgence of our flesh. However, by the grace of God and the power of the Holy Spirit, may we so conduct ourselves in the midst of our people, that when we come to the end of our days, there will be a massive stock of earned respect and confidence. Whatever else we leave as a legacy, that is the legacy which we should desire to leave to our loved ones and our people, so that they will be able to say of us, "Amidst all of the sham, phonyism, disappointment and disgrace of men who bring shame to Christ, *there* was a man who walked with his God until he breathed his last."

May God grant that it will be true of us, by His grace and by His power. Take encouragement from those bracing words with which, after issuing sober warnings concerning the danger of apostasy, Jude closes his brief letter:

Now to him who is able to keep you from stumbling and to present you blameless before the presence of his glory with great joy, to the only God, our Savior, through Jesus Christ our Lord, be glory, majesty, dominion, and authority, before all time and now and forever. Amen (Jude 24, 25).

CHAPTER 11

The Man of God in Relation to Himself

As we begin this new consideration in the life of the man of God in the pastoral office, we will do so once again with an axiom in which I seek to embody the heart of the issue at hand. We will then proceed to demonstrate the significance of the words of that axiom, the biblical concerns embodied in it, and then issue some practical suggestions and admonitions in light of the truths we will have considered together.

Explanation of the Axiom

The axiom is that *you must seek to gain and maintain an increasingly realistic understanding and acceptance of your own unique and present identity as a man and as a servant of God.*

We will now set out to examine each part of this axiom.

I use the terms *gain* and *maintain*. You must do this no matter what your present status is in the ministry, whether preparing for the ministry or already called to the ministry. We must seek to gain this understanding of ourselves during the process of the call, and then go on to maintain it throughout our ministries. The assessment made prior to, or upon entrance into the ministry, must not be accepted as having been set in concrete. It must be maintained.

Then I have used the words, *an increasingly realistic understanding of your unique identity*. I am using the word *realistic* as opposed to visionary. A visionary understanding is an inaccurate sense of your identity, a distorted picture of reality. I use the word *unique* identity to underscore that as a man of God you are one of a kind, both as a man and as a servant of God. We all have a responsibility not to force ourselves into some artificial, precast mold of what we think we should be as men or servants of God, but to find the precise identity that God intends us to be both as men and servants of God.

You and I are men first and pastors second. Whatever God intends us to be and do as pastors is not intended to neutralize who and what we are as men. The labor of the ministry is overlaid upon the identity of the man, and it is what we are as men that is brought into and lies at the foundation of what we are and do as servants of God.

I am also referring to our *present* unique identity. Here I am underscoring the fact to which I have already alluded, that what we are as men and what we are as servants of God is not static. The things that constitute our unique manhood and identity as servants of God are not petrified at age twenty-five, thirty, forty, or even at age seventy. They are in a constant state of flux. Some fundamental issues are not subject to change, but many things are. For example, there is the constant development and enrichment of our giftedness, our understanding of what we are in relation to our people in terms of how they view us and their comfort level in relating to us.

Remember the incident from the life of David to which we alluded in a previous lecture, where David goes out to battle with the hosts but almost loses his life (2 Sam. 21:15). He grows faint and his fainting state became obvious to his fellow-soldiers. They understood that David was going to lose his head if he continued to go out to battle. David needed a realistic assessment of who and what he was as a man growing old, losing some of the quickness with his sword in his reaction to battle situations. David had to face realistically who and what he was as a man at that point in his life and factor that in with his responsibilities as king in Israel.

On the other hand, we have that interesting record of Caleb. I do not think it is an unrealistic kind of masochism or boasting on the part of Caleb, that he is able to say with realism,

> "And now, behold, the LORD has kept me alive, just as he said, these forty-five years since the time that the LORD spoke this word to Moses, while Israel walked in the wilderness. And now, behold, I am this day eighty-five years old. I am still as strong today as I was in the day that Moses sent me; my strength now is as my strength was then, for war and for going and coming. So now give me this hill country of which the LORD spoke on that day, for you heard on that day how the Anakim were there, with great fortified cities. It may be that the LORD will be with me, and I shall drive them out just as the LORD said" (Josh. 14:10–12).

Caleb said that at a time when most men are ready to kick up their feet and get into their easy chair and retire! Caleb was making an honest assessment at age eighty-five and he saw indications that he was then as he was at forty-five. God had sustained his strength. He was still ready for battle. When he went out to take a mountain, he did not come back defeated.

We have the analogies in 1 John 2:12–14, where John is comparing certain spiritual states to what is true in the natural state. He speaks of young men who are strong and older men who are established in their understanding of the ways of God.

We must continually come to grips with this realistic assessment of who and what we are in the present, both as men and as servants of God. I would be a fool to attempt to do now what I could do when I was between my thirties and forties. I look back to those times when I left home to engage in a special conference, and not infrequently preach at nine-thirty in the morning, preach again at eleven, preach again at two in the afternoon, and once again preach at seven in the evening. There are times when I did that three or four times during the week, then came back and preached twice on the Lord's Day. My fellow-elders assessed who and what I was as a man, and the unusual measure of native strength that God was pleased to give me both by the genes He chose to form my physical constitution, and by the disciplines of my life. But my fellow-elders would not permit me, unless they had lost their common sense and judgment, to do that if it were not right for me in those years. Even if I were foolish enough to attempt such a schedule at this stage in my life, my elders would undoubtedly do for me what David's men did for him when they called him away from the battlefield.

This also has reference to the way I relate to the people of God. I relate to many of them now as a father or as a grandfather, and there is flavor and color to the manner in which I relate to them now that would have been ludicrous or even cheeky when I was in the first five or ten years of my ministry among them. Ministry in one place over the long haul brings lasting influence into the second and third generations of a church family.

The Biblical Basis for this Axiom

Romans 12 is a pivotal text which establishes the biblical basis for what I am asserting. The chapter begins with Paul's impassioned entreaty and summons to progressive sanctification. Paul first gives the *motivation* for this sanctification, "I appeal to you therefore, brothers, by the mercies of God" (Rom. 12:1). Then he gives the *means* of that sanctification, "Be transformed by the renewal of your mind" (Rom. 12:2). Finally, he gives the *essence* or *end* in view, "That by testing you may discern what is the will of God, what is good and acceptable and perfect" (Rom. 12:2). Paul then gives the practical *implementation*, "For by the grace given to me I say to everyone among you not to think of himself more highly than he ought to think, but to think with sober judgment, each according to the measure of faith that God has assigned" (Rom. 12:3).

The apostle lays this responsibility upon those whose hearts have responded in gratitude to God for His mercies, and who take the posture of recognizing that they are not their own, but that the totality of their humanity belongs to Him. It is they who long to glorify Him by this ever-growing conformity to His will. It is to them that he directs this command to sober thinking. Since pride and ambition are native to the human heart, it is all too possible that the believers think too highly of themselves with regard to their spiritual gifts. Realism is skewed by pride and ambition. This command also implies that we might think too lowly of ourselves. He warns against any assessment that is not sober.

Professor Murray's comments are most helpful:

> One of the ways in which the design contemplated by the apostle is frustrated is by the sin of pride. Pride consists in coveting or exercising a prerogative that does not belong to us. The negative is here again to be noted and the liability to indulgence is marked by the necessity of directing the exhortation to all—"to every one that is among you." No one is immune to exaggerated self-esteem. In Meyer's words, "He, therefore, who covets a higher or another standpoint and sphere of activity in the community, and is not contented with that which corresponds to the measure of faith bestowed on him, evinces a willful self-exaltation, which is without measure and not of God."
>
> But that which is commended must be observed no less than that which is forbidden. We are to "think so as to think soberly." Thus humble and sober assessment of what each person is by the grace of God is enjoined. If we consider ourselves to possess gifts we do not have, then we have an inflated notion of our place and function; we sin by esteeming ourselves beyond what we are. But if we underestimate, then we are refusing to acknowledge God's grace and we fail to exercise that which God has dispensed for our own sanctification and that of others. The positive injunction is the reproof of a false humility which equally with over self-esteem fails to assess the grace of God and the vocation which distinguishing distribution of grace assigns to each.[1]

---

1. John Murray, *The Epistle to the Romans* (Grand Rapids: William B. Eerdmans, 1997), 117, 118.

There are a number of supporting texts. The first comes in a parable of Jesus:

> For it will be like a man going on a journey, who called his servants and entrusted to them his property. To one he gave five talents, to another two, to another one, to each according to his ability. Then he went away (Matt. 25:14, 15).

When the master returned, he dealt with each one in terms of what had been deposited with each one individually as a trust from the master. Whatever we identify these talents to be, in the day of reckoning, each man is dealt with in terms of the reality of what abilities and opportunities were given to him individually, and the way he used them. He was not cruelly treated by a master who was expecting the same returns from the man who received two talents as he expected from the man who received five.

Hence, my brothers, this confirms the necessity for a realistic understanding and acceptance of our own identity as men and as servants of God. Included in that is surely the measure of gift, along with a host of other factors.

Arnot writes:

> It is necessary at the outset to indicate the relation which subsists between this parable and that of the talents, (Matt. xxv). Although in many of their features they are the same, in others there is a decisive difference. Both show that the Lord bestows privileges on His servants, and demands faithfulness in return; and both show that the diligent are rewarded and the unprofitable condemned. But the one supposes a case, in which all the servants receive equal privileges, and shows that even those of them who are faithful, may be unequal as to the amount of their success; the other supposes a case in which unequal privileges are bestowed upon the servants, and shows that when unequal gifts are employed with equal diligence, the approval is equal in the day of account. Both alike exhibit the grand cardinal distinction between the faithful and the faithless; but in pointing out also the diversities that obtain among true disciples, they view the subject from opposite sides, each presenting that aspect of it which the other omits. The parable of the talents teaches that Christians differ from each other in the amount of gifts which they receive; and the parable of the pounds teaches that they differ from each other in the diligence which they display.[2]

---

2. William Arnot, *Parables of our Lord* (Grand Rapids: Kregel Publications, 1981), 520, 521. He says in the footnote, "The man who cannot perceive, or will not own that these are

Surely this parable underscores the necessity of seeking to discern whether the Master has deposited five talents with me, or two, or only one. If I do not assess correctly, and I assume that He has given me but one when He has given two, to some degree I am an unfaithful servant. If I assume I have five when I have only two, I will either be inflated with the heady wine of pride or be continually on a guilt trip that I do not seem to be able to produce what a five-talent man ought to produce.

I have had people in my ministry who have read a biography of Spurgeon or some other exceptionally great man, who came to me and said, "Pastor Martin, Spurgeon did this, why do you not do this?" On more than one occasion I have said, "Would you please spell Spurgeon for me?" And they looked at me and spelled S-p-u-r-g-e-o-n. I said, "Lovely. Now would you please spell Martin." By then they got the message that I have a responsibility not to conform to what Spurgeon may have done as a fifteen or twenty-talent man, but by an accurate assessment of what God has deposited in me.

Another supporting text is Psalm 139:13–17 where we read of David worshiping and praising God for the fact that he was knit together in his mothers' womb. He used the metaphor of a subterranean cavern called "the depths of the earth." You and I need to come to grips with the reality of what God put together in our mothers' wombs when each of us was created as a truly unique creation.

I recall another marvelous text that I have used many times in trying to govern my own life before God while seeking the counsel of others, "Like a bird that strays from its nest is a man who strays from his home" (Prov. 27:8).

Bridges comments aptly:

> Instinct teaches *the bird*, that *the nest* is the only place of safety or repose. Here God has provided her special cover. (Deut. xxii. 6, 7.) Nothing therefore but danger awaits her in her *wanderings*. And seldom does she return without some injury to herself or her nestlings. Perhaps *her nest* is cold and inconvenient. But her *wanderings* make her more restless and dissatisfied. She is safe and happy only while she keeps *her nest*.
>
> Not less senseless and dangerous is it lightly to leave the place, society, or calling, which Divine Providence has marked out. Here man is 'in God's precincts, and so under God's protection;' and if he will be content to remain in *his place*, God will bless him with the rich

---

two different cases, charged with different, though cognate lessons, is not fit to be an expositor of any writing, either sacred or profane."

gain of "godly contentment." (1 Tim. vi. 6.) But *the man wandering from his place* is 'the rolling stone, that gathers no moss.' 'He is always restless, as if he had a wind-mill in his head. Every new crotchet puts him into a new course.' His want of fixed principles and employment exposes him to perpetual temptation. (Chap. xxi. 16.) Always wanting to be something or somewhere different to what and where he is, he only changes imaginary for real troubles. Full of wisdom is to know and keep our place. The soul, the body, the family, society—all have a claim upon us. This feverish excitement of idleness is the symptom of disease, wholly opposed to religion, the bane both of our comfort and usefulness.

The plain rule cannot ordinarily be broken without sin—"Let every man, wherein he is called, therein abide with God." (1 Cor. vii. 24.) Would we then abide in fellowship with God? We must "abide in our calling." Every step of departure, *without a clear Scriptural warrant*, is departure from God. We are safe in following Providence. But to go before it; much more to break away from its guidance (Jonah, i. 1–4)—*a man thus wanders from his place* to his own cost. Never can we put our foot out of God's ways, but we shall tread the path back with a cross.[3]

Major Qualifications Conditioning our Understanding of this Axiom

I now make some major qualifications or bring some additional perspectives to condition our understanding of this axiom. I believe that the axiom is solid and represents a clear reflection of biblical principles. However, without the added insights of these qualifying perspectives, that axiom in its application might lead us to some imbalance.

The first qualification is that *there exists, in the wisdom and sovereignty of God, a great diversity of legitimate preaching styles and patterns of effective pastoral ministry.*

Paul's teaching on the diversity of spiritual gifts certainly applies here (1 Cor. 12:4–7). The diversity relates not only to the *nature* of the gifts but the *manner* and extent in which those gifts are exercised. An earlier chapter in 1 Corinthians points us in the same direction,

---

3. Charles Bridges, *The Christian Ministry* (Edinburgh: The Banner of Truth Trust, 1968), 507, 508.

For when one says, "I follow Paul," and another, "I follow Apollos," are you not being merely human? What then is Apollos? What is Paul? Servants through whom you believed, as the Lord assigned to each. I planted, Apollos watered, but God gave the growth. So neither he who plants nor he who waters is anything, but only God who gives the growth (1 Cor. 3:4–7).

The nature—may I be so bold as to say the *style*—of their giftedness is a matter of divine conferral with respect to what God implanted in the womb of their mothers. Providential influences have shaped a man, as well as what God has brought to light by the endowment of the Spirit and the cultivation of those gifts. There is great diversity of legitimate style in effective preaching, as well as in effective pastoral ministry, and this is to be traced to the inscrutable wisdom and the unrestricted sovereignty of God.

Now we may ask the question, "Who was the ideal preacher in the New Covenant, Peter or Paul?" I answer, "Neither of them, and both of them." God marked out Peter for a distinctive ministry to the circumcision. He marked out Paul for a distinctive ministry to the Gentiles. From their mothers' wombs, in their development and training, and in all of His individual dealings with them, He perfectly suited them for their respective spheres of labor. As a result of all these factors there was diversity of style, both in their preaching, and in the manner in which they dealt with others at the pastoral level.

"Who was more effective as a preacher in the Old Covenant, Amos or Isaiah?" I answer, "Neither of them, and both of them." "Who was more successful, Jeremiah who preached the nation into captivity, or Haggai and Zechariah who helped preach them out of captivity and into the land of Israel?" We must think biblically, and not have in our minds that this or that man in the past or present is *the* ideal preacher, and that if I am to be all I ought to be as a preacher I must become like him more and more.

This qualification has some very serious implications for us to consider. It requires a warning concerning our encounter with men of God in the past whom we come to admire in our reading and study. We can be tempted, when our minds and hearts are ravished with a sense of wonder and thankfulness to God for this or that servant of God to think, "Oh if only I could be like him!" But one has wisely said, our faithfulness to the fathers of our faith is not in *copying* them but in *comprehending* them, that is, understanding what are the changeless, timeless principles transcending culture that were clothed with their particular humanity and their particular giftedness in their particular sphere of service. We can dig beneath these things and lay hold of those principles, pray them in, but then we must dress them up in our own cut of cloth and in our own God-given identity as men of God. Let oaks be oaks, cedars be cedars, and weeping willows be weeping willows. Let larks sing like larks, nightingales like nightingales, and let crows crow like crows. God made them all, and it is the design of the bird to have a song commensurate with its distinct identity.

> From our own poor pedestrian level let us look up at the mighty preachers of the past—the Bossuets, Whitefields, Wesleys, Chalmerses, and Masons, and own that God accomplishes his gracious ends not only by a variety of instruments, but in a variety of ways. If there is any maxim which you might inscribe on your seal-ring and your pen, it is this, *Be yourself.* As Kant says, every man has his own way of preserving health, so we may assert that every true servant of the gospel has his own way of being a preacher; and I pray that you may never fall among a people so untutored or so straitened as to be willing to receive the truth only by one sort of conduit. Every genuine preacher becomes such, under God, in a way of his own, and by a secret discipline. But after having reached a certain measure of success, it will require much humility, much knowledge of the world, and much liberality of judgment, to preserve him from erecting his own methods into a standard for even all the world.[4]

Do not get all your formative influences as preacher and pastor from one source. Remember again what Paul said to the Corinthians, "So let no one boast in men. For all things are yours, whether Paul or Apollos or Cephas or the world or life or death or the present or the future—all are yours, and you are Christ's, and Christ is God's" (1 Cor. 3:21–23). This text has been a great benefit to me over the years. All of the living preachers who love God and His Word and who have the oil of God upon their forehead are mine, not only to benefit me from the content of their preaching, but that I might learn what it is that makes them effective.

I rarely went anywhere without somebody preaching by tape or CD in my car, and I find over the years that there are certain preachers I love to listen to again and again. They are very diverse in the manner of their preaching. As I listen, I seek to discern what it is that makes a man's preaching

---

4. James W. Alexander, *Thoughts on Preaching* (Edinburgh: The Banner of Truth Trust, 1975), 160.

so endearing, attractive, penetrating, and gripping. Then I pray, "Oh, Lord, help me to grasp that principle and then let me cover it with Albert Martin's fingerprints."

All preachers are yours. Do not, consciously or unconsciously, set up someone as your ideal model and attempt to fit into that frame and shape in all of its details. Christ is the only perfect model as a man and a preacher. All merely human and sinful models reflect only certain dimensions or facets of the perfection of our Lord. Fasten on those and emulate them but do not seek to pattern yourself after any man so that people will say you are simply aping that preacher.

The second major principle conditioning our axiom is that *the Holy Spirit is not the author or the owner of the unnatural and the affected.*

He is called the Spirit of Truth, who works by and with the truth in a context of truth. Christ has set me free (John 8:32). I am free to be God's bondservant in who I am, stripped of what is sinful and enhanced and empowered by the Holy Spirit. When the Holy Spirit came upon the authors of Scripture, what they penned were and are the very words of God (1 Cor. 2:12). "Men spoke from God as they were carried along by the Holy Spirit" (2 Pet. 1:21). Yet any neophyte in the Greek language knows when he picks up his Greek New Testament, that Paul writes like Paul, Peter writes like Peter, and John writes like John. In that highest ministry of the Spirit, when He was most in control of a man's mind and thought processes, down to the actual words chosen, it is evident that the Spirit's operation clothes itself with Peter's mind and Peter's vocabulary and Peter's syntax and, in the same way, Paul's and John's. Here is, I believe, the most powerful argument for this principle, that we, in seeking a realistic assessment of our own particular giftedness and identity as men and servants of God, must never allow ourselves to drift into the artificial, the unnatural, and the affected. Rather, everything about us in ministry, preaching, and pastoral labors, should indeed, as I alluded earlier, be covered with our fingerprints, and that without shame.

MacPherson writes:

> You are to carry Christ to the people. Through you, as through Mary of old, God is to come omnipotently into his world.
>
> To say that is not to imply anything merely automatic or mechanical in the process. The preacher's personality is not to be thought of as no more than a kind of conduit by means of which the Word is conveyed like water through a pipe: rather may he be likened to the trunk of a

living tree with the sap seeping through every fiber. When the Word was born of Mary, he did not, so to speak, transmit himself magically, without partaking of her nature or assimilating her substance. The old tree speaks of the substance of Mary. On the contrary, he laid hold of her very flesh and blood, brought into vital concentrated action every part of her dedicated being. So with the minister and his message. When, in true preaching, the Word is livingly communicated, the personality of the preacher is not dormant or passive. Far from it. Only when his every power and faculty are brought into full, harmonious, and vigorous display can the Word be properly conveyed at all.[5]

God made some of us intense, passionate people. He did that in our mothers' wombs and before we were converted. Everything we did on the ball-field, on the acting-stage, whatever it was, we did with every fiber of our being. That is who God made us as men. Now, should that all be neutralized when God makes such a man into a preacher? No! Accept who and what you are as a man and expect that your distinctive manhood will be expressed in the way you preach. He put some of us together so that we cannot think without close, logical, sequential thought, but he put some people together with the mind and soul of the musician and the poet. One of my favorite preachers does not preach with close argument and logical progression, but he is an effective, powerful preacher and I love to listen to him preach. He never fails to bless my soul. And there are other preachers that draw you in by their rather laid back, less than passionate temperament, but in whom there is a sweet fragrance of the meekness and the gentleness of Christ that dominates in their whole pulpit demeanor.

It is wrong to think that if you are as full of the Spirit as the preacher you want to emulate that you will be like that man. No, if you are full of the Holy Spirit you will be like the man that you look at in the mirror when you comb your hair in the morning. Nobody else. The Holy Spirit does not work in the context of the artificial and the affected.

In concluding this lecture, I offer some qualifying perspectives about this second observation.

The first is that *I am not implying that we should accept our weaknesses and our limitations fatalistically and make no conscious effort to overcome them.*

---

5. Ian MacPherson, *The Burden of the Lord* (New York: Abingdon Press, 1955), 16, 17.

A man may naturally have bad diction with an indistinct enunciation. He may never have been taught that proper speech does not terminate at the back of the throat but with the lips and the tongue and the teeth. The classic teachers in rhetoric recognize that teeth and tongue, along with larynx, throat, and diaphragm, are all part of the speaking mechanism, and therefore, if through training and upbringing and associations your enunciation is indistinct, and your pronunciation is often incorrect, is it artificial for you to work on those things? No. You will simply be obeying what the Scripture says, "Do your best to present yourself to God as one approved, a worker who has no need to be ashamed, rightly handling the word of truth" (2 Tim. 2:15). "Practice these things, immerse yourself in them, so that all may see your progress" (1 Tim. 4:15). Never forget Demosthenes, the great orator who overcame his speech impediments by filling his mouth with pebbles, standing by the roaring seashore until his voice could be heard distinctly above the roaring of the waves—so he might become a mighty orator.

So, I urge you, my brothers, remember that principle. Though the Holy Spirit does not work in the context of the artificial and the unnatural, this does not mean that out of the pulpit we should not work on overcoming limitations and impediments to effective speaking.

The second qualification is that *this does not imply that we will not be influenced by the unconscious imitative element in true preaching.*

There is an unconscious influence of imitation, and that is why Paul says, "Do not be deceived: 'Bad company ruins good morals'" (1 Cor. 15:33). Proverbs teaches the same, "Whoever walks with the wise becomes wise, but the companion of fools will suffer harm" (Prov. 13:20). As we expose our whole being to effective preaching across a broad range of differing styles of preaching, without even thinking of it we are absorbing such things as attitudes, perspectives, exegetical and homiletical devices, and a host of other things. That is perfectly legitimate, because as we absorb them they become ours, and then as we express them, they are covered with our fingerprints.

The third qualification is that *I am not implying that we should not consciously imitate both biblical principles and sound rhetorical principles embodied in other men.*

The Bible has a doctrine of conscious imitation. Paul says, "Brothers, join in imitating me, and keep your eyes on those who walk according to the example you have in us" (Phil. 3:17). "What you have learned and received and heard and seen in me—practice these things, and the God of peace will be with you" (Phil. 4:9). "Be imitators of me, as I am of Christ" (1 Cor. 11:1). When we see and hear things such as vivid simplicity or striking illustrative devices being used by other preachers, then we need to cry to God, "Lord, help me to incorporate those things into my preaching."

I remind you that discerning sinners will generally be suspicious and reject in their hearts what they detect to be forced and unnatural. Your people long for reality. Be yourself, clothed with the Spirit, but be yourself. It is for our benefit and the benefit of our people that we seek to have this ongoing, realistic understanding and acceptance of our own identity both as men and as preachers. Resist all temptation to question, "Why did God put me together the way He did?" Ask Him that question when you get to heaven. Right now, He did it and you must live with it. I used to be tempted to ask God why He withheld certain influences from me when I most needed them, and as far as I can remember, really desired them. I wondered:

> Lord, why did You not bring wise men along at that critical period in my life to urge me to pursue a more solid, classical, theological training and go to a seminary and then from the seminary perhaps go on in further studies to focus on a given field of advanced studies that would have given me a more well-furnished mind?

Well, God did not do it, and I have to live with it, remembering the words of the apostle Paul, "forgetting what lies behind and straining forward to what lies ahead" (Phil. 3:13).

It is a liberating thing to live out the role God has designed for you, rather than to play the role men have mapped out for you, or that you may have desired. May God grant that as we continually come to grips with who and what we are as men and servants of God in the present, we will determine to live out to the hilt all the implications. May God make us, whoever and whatever we are, increasingly effective servants of our Lord Jesus.

CHAPTER 12

The Man of God in Relation to His Time and His Manifold Responsibilities

The Biblical Context of Self-Control

Before opening up this subject under three major headings, which I will call axioms as I always do, I want to place the subject in a biblical context. As I do, it seems to me that the single most appropriate, generic, biblical category under which to place it is the category of self-control. This will bring us into contact with the self-control family of words, namely, *enkráteia*, the noun, along with its corresponding verbal and adjectival forms (2 Pet. 1:6; 1 Cor. 7:9).

We will first look at Paul's teaching on the fruit of the Spirit, "But the fruit of the Spirit is love, joy, peace, patience, kindness, goodness, faithfulness, gentleness, self-control; against such things there is no law" (Gal. 5:22, 23). According to this text, wherever the Holy Spirit is present in His regenerating and indwelling presence in the life of a child of God, He will be active in producing His nine-fold fruit. In opposition to the works of the flesh, which in a very real sense could be described as the manifestations of self-indulgence, the Holy Spirit produces self-control.

For this reason, when Paul seeks to cut into the conscience of Felix, he underscores this virtue and its obvious absence in the life of that pagan ruler. He reasoned with him about self-control: "And as he reasoned about righteousness and self-control and the coming judgment, Felix was alarmed and said, 'Go away for the present. When I get an opportunity I will summon you'" (Acts 24:25). Peter exhorts us, in the way of conscious spiritual endeavor, to

> make every effort to supplement your faith with virtue, and virtue with knowledge, and knowledge with self-control, and self-control with steadfastness, and steadfastness with godliness, and godliness with brotherly affection, and brotherly affection with love (2 Pet. 1:5–7).

We naturally ask, "Is the presence and activity of this grace of self-control the Spirit's work, or is it our work?" The very language seems contradictory. The fruit of the *Spirit* is *self*-control. Where the Spirit is most present and active in the heart of the believer, there the believer is in most conscious control of himself. Where the control of the Spirit is present, self-control is evident in the heart of the child of God, and this is not a contradiction. It brings us into that New Testament doctrine of the Christian life which teaches that God's working is manifested in our working and our working is the fruit of His working. Paul said,

> Therefore, my beloved, as you have always obeyed, so now, not only as in my presence but much more in my absence, work out your own salvation with fear and trembling, for it is God who works in you, both to will and to work for his good pleasure (Phil. 2:12, 13).

The manifestation of God's in-working is my conscious out-working, and I need never fear that my out-working will outstrip His in-working. That is the great mystery of the theology of the Christian life, and this dynamic is dominant in this fruit of self-control.

The word *enkratē* (Titus 1:8) is listed as one of the character requirements for the office of an elder, and as with all other gifts and graces, we must never be content with a modicum of the grace that warrants our entrance into the office. We must aspire to the growth and development of those graces while in the office, so that, in the language of Paul to Timothy, our personal progress may be manifested for all to see. Few areas will more clearly indicate the measure of this grace than the structure and implementation of our daily schedules. To illustrate the vigor of this grace, consider its usage in the verbal form *enkrateuetai*. It is used of athletic mastery, "Every athlete *exercises self-control* in all things. They do it to receive a perishable wreath, but we an imperishable" (1 Cor. 9:25, *emphasis mine*). The man who wants the wreath of the victor in the Grecian games gears every facet of his life toward the attainment of that wreath of victory. His sleep schedule, his eating schedule, his exercise schedule, and his sexual appetite, are all brought under the virtuous discipline of self-control.

The vigor of this grace of self-control, embodied in the many uses of this verbal form, make it clear that we are dealing with a matter of crucial biblical importance in relationship to the man of God. It is wishful thinking to suppose that you will have any sustained effectiveness in pastoral preaching or in the pastoral government and shepherding of God's people, if you do not have an increasing measure of self-mastery, particularly as it relates to your daily schedule and manifold responsibilities.

Now let us proceed to consider the three basic axioms, and some concluding practical suggestions for implementing those axioms.

Understand and Commit to God-Given Ministerial Responsibilities

The first axiom is that *we must acquire and maintain a clear understanding of and a religious commitment to our God-given ministerial duties.*

We must *acquire.* God is not going to send down a sheet of paper on the day of our ordination which says, "My son and my servant, here is your job description." It does not work that way. It does not come automatically. We must put conscious thought and prayerful effort to the acquisition of a clear understanding of our God-given ministerial duties. Then, we must not only acquire, we must *maintain* this clear understanding. I emphasized this before in other lectures, and I keep emphasizing it because these elements, so critical to ministerial usefulness, are not static. The circumstances are constantly changing, in ourselves, in our families, in our church situations, and in all of the things that impinge upon us. These changing circumstances necessarily influence what we do with the twenty-four hours of any given day, and here I must give vent to an irritation. I am irritated when mere theorists, who have never known the manifold pressures of real pastoral experience, write their books and give their canons as to how we should organize our time. It is similar to men who write books about preaching who know little or nothing of the weekly, monthly, yearly, disciplined labor required to produce edifying sermons for the people of God that will encourage, mold, and shape them into a vibrant New Covenant community.

We must acquire *and then maintain a clear understanding* that is a rational, cognitive perception of our God-given ministerial duties. We must continue to feed that understanding by the various streams that flow into our lives, and make a religious commitment to them. These issues must become matters of conscience before God. That is what I mean by a religious commitment. It is the *God-given* ministerial duties, those laid upon us *by the Word of God*, and not things laid on us by the expectations of men or by the past traditions in our situation. It will be by continuous, periodic perusal of such passages as Paul's charge to the Ephesian elders in Acts 20 that we gain this understanding of our God-given ministerial duties. Also, we must give habitual attention to Ephesians 4:11–16, 1 Peter 5:1–5, 1 Thessalonians 2, and of course, the pastoral epistles generally. These are the main passages from which we derive our understanding of ministerial duties. We will pray, "Lord, help me to readjust my understanding of the tasks that You have laid upon me by these portions of the Word of God." I suggest that you take an occasional day to concentrate on these passages with the express purpose of strengthening your understanding and renewing your commitment to these God-given responsibilities. We must be able to cut through ecclesiastical traditions, current ministerial fads, our local consensus of expectations, and the carnal inclinations of our own remaining sin, and in all of these things keep these words before us, "You were bought with a price; do not become slaves of men" (1 Cor. 7:23).

Now, what are some of the major ministerial duties set forth in the Word of God? I now identify six of them in summary form.

The first duty consists of *the disciplines essential to the maintenance of a vital and growing piety.*

There are two texts here that should be emblazoned upon the walls of our minds. Paul exhorted the Ephesian elders, "pay careful attention to yourselves and to all the flock, in which the Holy Spirit has made you overseers, to care for the church of God, which he obtained with his own blood" (Acts 20:28). Paul exhorts Timothy, "keep a close watch on yourself and on the teaching. Persist in this, for by so doing you will save both yourself and your hearers" (1 Tim. 4:16). It is my great responsibility under God to keep a close watch on the state of my soul since nothing else will make as great an impact upon my ministry.

The second duty consists of *the disciplines essential to the maintenance of intellectual vigor and balance.*

God says, "and I will give you shepherds after my own heart, who will feed you with knowledge and understanding" (Jer. 3:15). An elder "must hold firm to the trustworthy word as taught, so that he may be able to give instruction in sound doctrine and also to rebuke those who contradict it" (Titus 1:9). We gave careful consideration to this matter under the section on the pastor's intellectual development, a development which ought to mark the man of God until he breathes his last.

The third duty consists of *the disciplines essential for adequate preparation for our public ministries.*

Paul says, "Do your best to present yourself to God as one approved, a worker who has no need to be ashamed, rightly handling the word of truth" (2 Tim. 2:15). Basic disciplines involving study habits in general, and exegetical habits in particular, are called for by this directive from Paul.

The fourth duty consists of *the disciplines essential for the demands of the individual care of the sheep of Christ.*

This duty is stated in Acts 20:28 which was quoted above under the first discipline of maintaining growing piety. This passage also focuses on taking care of the flock. Paul said, "Him we proclaim, warning everyone and teaching everyone with all wisdom, that we may present everyone mature in Christ" (Col. 1:28).

The fifth duty consists of *the disciplines essential to wise administration of the life of the people of God.*

Peter points to the administrative aspect of pastoral oversight, "Shepherd the flock of God that is among you, exercising oversight, not under compulsion, but willingly, as God would have you; not for shameful gain, but eagerly" (1 Pet. 5:2). Paul points to the requirement of the man of God to "care for God's church" (1 Tim. 3:5). We are called upon to take care of God's people as a large household over which God has given household managers to function as spiritual fathers.

The sixth duty consists of *the disciplines essential to the maintenance of good emotional and physical health.*

There are two important passages here. Paul said, "For while bodily training is of some value, godliness is of value in every way, as it holds promise for the present life and also for the life to come" (1 Tim. 4:8). Mark records the words of Jesus, "And he said to them, 'Come away by yourselves to a desolate place and rest a while.' For many were coming and going, and they had no leisure even to eat" (Mark 6:31, 32). These passages point us in the direction of the discipline to which I am referring, consisting of proper exercise and rest.

This list is not exhaustive, but it is enough to underscore the fact that such demanding duties will not be performed with any degree of consistency or efficiency if a man does not have a clear understanding of and a religious commitment to his God-given ministerial duties. Furthermore, the factors which determine the precise nature of one's own particularized

The Man of God

or customized ministerial duties are not static, but dynamic and fluid. We really need periodic reviews of where we are in relationship to these things.

Understand and Commit to God-Given General or Ordinary Responsibilities

The second axiom that we need to understand is that *you must acquire and maintain a clear understanding of and religious commitment to your God-given generic or ordinary Christian responsibilities.*

Each of us, in addition to the demands of our preaching and overseeing office, have other responsibilities given to us by God as stewardships. Each one comes with a demand on our time and energy. I am referring to those that are given to us simply as Christian men. I want to repeat the principle that I mentioned in a previous lecture: *God never gives to any man specific responsibilities as a minister to excuse him from any general responsibility as a Christian man.* Never does God call upon a man to do something as a minister which can only be done if he forfeits his commitment to his duty as a Christian man.

If married, you have duties as a *husband,* and God did not make you a minister in order to exempt you from those duties. Consider what I am saying in light of what Paul said,

> Husbands, love your wives, as Christ loved the church and gave himself up for her, that he might sanctify her, having cleansed her by the washing of water with the word, so that he might present the church to himself in splendor, without spot or wrinkle or any such thing, that she might be holy and without blemish. In the same way husbands should love their wives as their own bodies. He who loves his wife loves himself. For no one ever hated his own flesh, but nourishes and cherishes it, just as Christ does the church (Eph. 5:25–29).

Is it even conceivable that the God who spoke these words would be pleased with a pastor who ignored or sidelined this command so that he could "do the work of the ministry"?

I found that principle so helpful when Marilyn was diagnosed with cancer and, at the time, given eighteen months to live. God let her live for six years. I had to come back to that passage and apprise my fellow-elders and say,

> For forty-two years Marilyn held me with an open hand and was such a support in every way to my life and ministry. She is going to need

my nourishing and cherishing, my dwelling with her according to knowledge more now than ever in all of our forty plus years of marriage.

So I apprised my fellow-elders and said, "Insofar as I can continue to fill all my responsibilities as a pastor I am committed to do so, but not at the expense of failure to nourish and cherish this woman who is my own flesh." Less than two months before Marilyn went home to be with her Lord, she reluctantly said to me one day, "Dear, I am fearful now when you leave the house." I said, "That is it. I am taking an indefinite leave of absence until the Lord either raises her off her death bed or takes her home." Why? Because I had bound my conscience with this principle that I had a responsibility as a Christian man that was not to be negated or suspended in the light of my duties as a Christian minister.

Remember also that demonstrable competence in your domestic life is a prerequisite for the eldership (1 Tim. 3:4). What this means in your daily program will vary in terms of another man's daily program. What are your wife's particular needs as you dwell with her according to knowledge? Perhaps she has a weak constitution and taking care of little ones is more taxing for her than for other women her age. Perhaps your wife, when she is pregnant, has to end up in the hospital with IVs because she gets dehydrated from vomiting. Obviously, what you must do in that setting, compared to a man who has a wife who is never healthier than when she is pregnant, will be different. So again, you cannot set up a wooden list of *This is What a Preacher Should Do in Caring For His Wife.* Yet nonetheless, all of our God-given duties as husbands are not suspended or in any way to be neutered because of what we have in the way of duties as men of God and pastors.

We find the same principle operating as *fathers.* First Timothy 3, Titus 1, and Ephesians 6:4, all point in the direction that exemplary fulfillment of our paternal responsibilities is one of the non-negotiable requirements of an elder. What that demands also varies with the number, the age, the personality, and other variables in our children. Then when we become grandparents, the scope of our domestic responsibilities increases even more.

We have responsibilities as *friends,* and nurturing and maintaining those friendships will demand an investment of time in correspondence and in phone calls. God may open up various doors of opportunity for you, but none of your God-given responsibilities as a pastor should ever be allowed to undermine the fulfillment of your responsibilities as a Christian man even in this area of the cultivation of godly friendships.

No one just automatically fills all of these roles and administers these multi-faceted stewardships by simply following his instincts, or "flying by the seat of his pants." We must carefully and continually give due consideration to these responsibilities in framing our daily, weekly, and monthly patterns of activity.

I underscore again that these things are always in a state of flux, and just when you have gotten into a good groove, along comes another child, or one of the children becomes chronically sick, or one of the children enters a period of rebellion against God and begins seeking to overthrow the restraints of family government. In cases like these, the time that must be invested has to be increased. So we must continually keep before us the necessity of acquiring and maintaining a clear understanding of, and the same religious commitment to, our God-given general or ordinary responsibilities.

Establish a Structured Schedule

The third axiom that we need to understand *is that we ought prayerfully to establish a structured schedule which reflects a commitment to fulfill all of our ministerial and generic Christian duties.*

By establishing a structured schedule, I mean choosing a definite plan which can be utilized in the divinely ordained structures of time. God has established days and weeks and months and years. We utilize these structures to enable us to accomplish our stewardships. There are many resources available in our day to help us in this matter of our yearly, monthly, weekly, and daily planning. What works best for one man may not work for another, so you must find what helps you the most and enables you to have a good conscience in fulfilling both ordinary and ministerial duties. Now, in establishing such a schedule of activities, let me set before you four things that should mark your scheduling.

The first characteristic of scheduling is that *it should be realistic.*

God does not make supermen. The psalmist said, "As a father shows compassion to his children, so the LORD shows compassion to those who fear him. For he knows our frame; he remembers that we are dust" (Ps. 103:13, 14). Remembering that we are dust will send us back to one of the positive injunctions of the Sixth Commandment, which is that we are to preserve our own life and the life of others. And what is forbidden? Anything that contributes to the taking away of life, such as, in this case, unrealistic planning and involvements. Therefore, in establishing and constantly readjusting our schedule as we put it down, somewhere, somehow, in some form, to keep us on track, it should be with this realistic view governing all of our choices.

The second characteristic of scheduling is that *it should be comprehensive*.

There is enough time to do the will of God for you, but surely not enough time to do what others may do, and what others may expect you to do. I most strongly assert that there is enough time in every day, week, month, and year to do the will of God for you. Remember, if you are serious about serving God, you will be tempted to allow ministerial duties to crowd out other duties, such as duties toward your wife, to your children, and to your relatives. Never forget God's indictment given by the prophet Samuel to Saul, "And Samuel said, 'Has the LORD as great delight in burnt offerings and sacrifices, as in obeying the voice of the LORD? Behold, to obey is better than sacrifice, and to listen than the fat of rams'" (1 Sam. 15:22).

We have a most searching passage in Proverbs, "If one turns away his ear from hearing the law, even his prayer is an abomination" (Prov. 28:9). God's law demands that we as Christian men nurture our wives and our children, and also that we be good sons, grandsons, neighbors, and citizens. To say, "No, I just do not have time for these because I am serving God," is turning our ear away from the law. Our prayers at that point become an abomination. Oh, please remember this truth! There is always enough time to do the will of God if we are prayerfully realistic and God-fearing in our scheduling.

The third characteristic of scheduling is that *it should be tenaciously pursued*.

What has been carefully, prayerfully, and rationally planned should not be at the mercy of the whims of others or the impulses of our own flesh. Those are the two great enemies of this tenacious resolve. I am referring to the expectations of others and the impulses of our own flesh.

Now what do I mean by those things? Suppose you have Thursday blocked out for preparation for the Lord's Day and you get a phone call from one of the sheep saying, "Oh pastor, I must see you." We live in the age of instant gratification. You have every right to lovingly say, "My dear Mrs. So-and-So, (or) my dear brother, would you mind telling me what makes seeing me today that urgent?" And lo and behold, there is no real urgency. It is just that he or she has an itch and he or she wants you to scratch it. But the itch will wait until you take out your day planner and say, "I am sorry, Mrs. So-and-So, I have no real opportunity for counseling until next Tuesday afternoon. Would that work for you?" You are not to put yourself at the mercy of her assessment of "must." Now granted, there are some situations where you will have to drop what you have planned in order to respond to the need of a sheep that needs immediate attention. That will be the sheep in the ditch, and you really must go help her out at that time. Here is the key. Do not let people make that judgment for you. Make that judgment before God, rationally and prayerfully.

If Tuesday is your day for general or theological reading, does it really matter if you feel dull? The impulses of your own flesh ought not to determine whether you remain tenacious about your schedule. The last thing you feel like doing is picking up that book of systematic theology that you have prayerfully determined you ought to read. Even though it is the last thing we may feel like doing, we commit to the schedule which we have established. Naturally, there are exceptions to this determined pursuit of a schedule, such as unusually long counseling sessions or pastoral meetings that throw our schedule off at times, or emergencies that have come up in the church or family. Tenacious pursuit is how self-control works in the great Christian duty of self-denial.

The fourth characteristic of scheduling is that *it should be reasonably flexible.*

Granted, there are texts that inveigh against the sluggard in the wisdom books (Prov. 13:4; 20:4, 13; Eccl. 10:18). On the other hand, there are times when we need to hear our Lord say to us, "Come away by yourselves to a desolate place and rest a while" (Mark 6:31). We see the flexibility in our Lord when, after a day of teaching, and time to send the crowd away, He ministered to them instead (Mark 6:33–36). In Christian ministry, funerals will intrude into our schedules. Distressed sheep will need our attention in a very concentrated way, and your schedule for several days may be totally disrupted. The benefit is that you will know where it was disrupted and know how to get back on track again. This is an added benefit of having that structure.

Now let me say a few things about the practical implementation of these things. If we are to keep this axiom in order to maintain maximum faithfulness in ministerial and general stewardship responsibilities, then there are some things we must master in the strength of Christ.

First, we must be master of *ourselves.*

Galatians 5:23 calls us to self-control because it is a fruit of the Spirit. First Corinthians 9:27 calls us to the discipline of our bodies. There the apostle Paul does not say that the *Lord* keeps his body under subjection, but that *he himself* does it. Now he also tells us that he can do all things through Christ who strengthens him (Phil. 4:13), and that encourages and energizes us in the pursuit of self-mastery. We must master sloth and laziness and put off the spirit of the sluggard.

Second, you must be master of your *home*.

Your ministerial schedule is so intertwined with your family life that if you are not ruling and governing well, you will not be able to stick to those commitments. The solemn requirement which you met in 1 Timothy 3:4, 5 remains as a constant requirement for continuance in the ministry.

Third, you must be master of your *phones*.

You were bought with a price, so do not become the slaves of men who get to you by means of a fiber-optic line or a digital signal to the smart phone in your shirt pocket. I was not in the ministry long when my fellow-elder said something to me for which I am profoundly grateful. He said, "Pastor, the phone is your servant, never let it become your master." So I worked out that imagery of the servant and I said to myself,

> Now, if I were wealthy enough to have a servant who would greet anyone who comes to my front door desiring to see me, and I said to my servant, "Look, anyone who comes between seven and nine-thirty today, tell them if they want to see me they will have to wait till nine-thirty. I am occupied with business that cannot be interrupted, because that is my time to meet with God, read my Bible, and pray." Now suppose my servant was indifferent to my directive and came knocking at my door at eight o'clock? If such actions became a pattern, it would not be long before he would no longer be in my employ.

Yet the telephone gives people access to come right into your study and intrude upon your commitments, no matter what you are doing. It gives them the ability to disrupt your structured time for family worship and family fun times. We must not allow people to do that. Nobody has an unlimited, unqualified right to intrude into your schedule, and anyone who did it physically would be considered socially boorish. The telephone just enables them to do it in a more refined way.

Thankfully we have voice mail and other messaging capabilities. Yet I know there are men, and I have been in their company, who are slaves to their phones. I have been engaged in very fruitful and enjoyable conversation with them, and then their cellphone rings, "Oh, excuse me, I must answer that." Now, if you have told one of your church members who has a relative in the emergency room, "Once the doctors have assessed your loved ones' condition, please call me and let me know what the situation is. I will leave my phone on so that I may check my caller ID and answer you immediately." Answering your phone in that situation is an entirely different thing from allowing people to feel that they have an unrestricted right of access to you at any time and regardless of the situation in which you may be when they call. We need to get out from under the tyranny of technology or we will never have a schedule that is meaningful.

Finally, I will lump together a number of other areas which we need to bring under subjection. We must master our use of the Internet, television, social media, the newspaper, and magazines. We must be master of the pillow and of the blankets. We must be master of our hobbies and avocations, as legitimate as they may be. When there is a place for mental relaxation and general browsing of substantive blogs, put those times into your schedule, but make sure that you do not exceed the time apportioned for them.

If we would keep to a pattern of responsible, structured existence for useful service, we will need, wisely and graciously, to instruct others whose lives and whose needs impinge upon ours. We must instruct and secure the cooperation of our wives. They are helpers answering to our needs, and therefore we will need to help them understand these things. When they find that the track on the cabinet drawer is stuck, it will be best for them to find an appropriate time to tell us rather than right in the middle of sermon preparation time. This is mostly applicable to those who have their studies in the home, but even those who do not will need to deal with similar issues connected with family responsibilities and emergencies.

You will need to instruct and secure cooperation all the way from your children to your fellow-elders and the deacons. Instruct and secure the cooperation of your flock. Most of them have no idea how you spend your hours, and your ministry will be aided by some gentle reminders of the sacredness of the hours for prayer and the study of the Word. They will recognize that you are about your Master's business in those restricted times, and they will also know that at other times they have free access to you. Tell them, "Anytime you want to call me before such and such an hour, please call me. I am here for you." Then explain, if you feel the need, to give a simple snapshot of what is involved in your work. If they are true friends, they will love you for it, and they will not be upset.

I urge you, therefore, in this final word of exhortation, to realistically assess before God all of your responsibilities as a minister and as an ordinary Christian man, and commit yourself to the establishment of a realistic, comprehensive, tenaciously pursued and reasonably flexible schedule that enables you to fulfill those responsibilities in the power of the Spirit.

I close with a quote from Blaikie's work on the public ministry of our Lord:

> That our Lord worked by system, and could not otherwise have got through His work, is plain as noonday to all who know the difference between systematic and random working. It may be thought a mechanical way of work; hours and laws, we may be told, were made for slaves; and it may be extolled as a higher life where one obeys the impulse of the hour, and is free to catch and follow whatever gales of inspiration may at any time come upon one. No doubt, one may be bound by lines too hard and too fast; and—for our part we deem a little elasticity an advantage in any system,—a power of adapting it to emergencies as they arise. But those who are habitually systematic will probably find that they come to be comparatively independent of fitful impulses and inspirations, and that their faculties come to them, to use Milton's phrase, as nimble servitors whenever their aid is sought.
>
> We hold then that we may well claim our Lord as showing the value of system as an aid to the spirit of industry in labour. And partly no doubt through this habit, He was habitually *beforehand* in His work. He was always ready. His discourses have a wonderfully finished air, as if they had been matured before they were spoken. His very answers to casual objectors were marvellously clean-cut and finished. He was never disconcerted or at a loss how to answer or to act. His presence of mind never deserted Him. And what is very remarkable, He never allowed one thing to jostle another in His mind, however full it may have been of projects, and however burdened with anxieties.[1]

May God help us in this to be more and more like our Savior.

---

1. William G. Blaikie, *The Public Ministry of Christ* (Minneapolis, MN: Klock & Klock, 1984), 63, 64.

CHAPTER 13

---○───────────────○---

The Man of God in Relation to His Domestic Responsibilities (1)

The Axiom Stated and Explained

We will approach this subject of the man of God in relationship to his domestic responsibilities as we have done before, by stating an axiom.

The axiom is that *the man of God must manifest exemplary competence as a husband and a father.*

Note that I am not saying that we must manifest *perfection* as husbands and fathers. Nor am I saying that we must manifest the *highest level* of competence among the entire membership of the church. There may be better husbands and better fathers, and yet you still may fulfill your pastoral duties with a grip on the consciences of your people because, by the grace of God, you are displaying the measure of competence in these two areas which is required by the scriptures. We will explore *the necessity for domestic competence, ministerial temptations to domestic incompetence,* and *practical counsels for maintaining domestic competence.*

The Necessity for Domestic Competence

If you are to preach and effectively shepherd your people in a pastoral context, it is necessary for you to possess a pattern of biblically defined domestic competence. Every minister ought to seek competence as a father and a husband simply because this is a demand of generic Christian duty. I stated in the last lecture that our ministerial responsibilities neither negate nor lessen our domestic responsibilities nor our other stewardships as Christian men. The main passages which teach this duty are Ephesians 5:25–33, 1 Peter 3:7, Ephesians 6:4, and 1 Timothy 5:8. Every Christian man who is a husband and a father should have his soul saturated with the clear directives of these passages and seek to live them out through the power and presence of the Spirit of Christ in his life.

In addition to this general Christian duty incumbent upon all Christian men, there are three *specific* things which establish the necessity for domestic competence in the servant of Christ who labors in the work of the gospel.

The first specific thing is *the explicit biblical requirements for all who assume the office of an elder.*

We opened up these biblical requirements in Unit 1 on the call to the ministry. I am assuming you have read that material and are therefore familiar with the content, the meaning, and the weight of those requirements. In the specimen list of requirements found in 1 Timothy 3 and Titus 1, various aspects of the domestic requirements are repeatedly brought forward. The aspirant must be a one-woman man, manage his own household well, and be given to hospitality. It is highly significant that the only requirement for which the apostle gives his own commentary as to the importance and relationship to the function of the office is the domestic (1 Tim. 3:5).

What is involved in managing one's own house well? Some of the particulars are mentioned in the Timothy and Titus passages. Children are to be in subjection with proper respect. Children are not to be justly accused of being wild and disobedient. By implication, it is to be evident that a man is leading his wife in that wonderful fusion and proper tension of authority and graciousness. To rule one's own house well means that a man sees the full spectrum of what needs to be done and the best and most judicious means to attain those ends. He must then show that he is competent to administer that domestic government.

Ruling well means that a man is not inflicted with short-sightedness in terms of what the household needs are. It means that he will obtain divine wisdom to understand the best way to administer the accurate, broad assessment of what ruling his household involves. It also means that he has both the will and the God-given strength to stick with the relevant issues consistently in pursuit of this household order.

Do you see the distinct parallels between a well-ordered home and a well-ordered church, and why Paul draws these two together? Who wants to be part of a church where the elders only see the church in terms of doctrinal integrity but not in terms of the necessity of unity, peace, and moral and ethical integrity? Who wants to be in a church where the elders only see the necessity of well-ordered practical concerns and have no vision for broad spiritual perspectives? No, ordering the life of God's people well means that those in leadership see the full spectrum of the life of the church in the Word of God and are given spiritual wisdom to take the best steps to attain the holy ends of a well-ordered church. They are men who have the courage, the wisdom, and the grace to shepherd the flock, watching over the flock so that the flock will be healthy and useful. So, the Bible explicitly and clearly requires a degree of competence in domestic rule as an essential element in anyone who can take the office with any degree of confidence that Christ has put him there.

Let me apply this necessity for domestic competence in the strongest terms possible. What would you think of a man who said he aspires to the office of an overseer while being utterly indifferent to acquiring some basic understanding of the full spectrum of systematic theology, hermeneutics, exegesis, and the quality control of historical theology? How could such a man fulfill the requirement of being "able to teach" (1 Tim. 3:2) and "able to give instruction in sound doctrine and also to rebuke those who contradict it" (Titus 1:9)? You would say that such a man is deluded. The sooner someone throws a bucket of cold water on his head and tells him to get in touch with reality, the better off a church would be, because it should not receive such an incompetent and ignorant man to be a safe guide. Likewise, what would you think of the man who does give himself to the acquisition of all of those theological disciplines but is indifferent to the attainment and maintenance of biblical competence in the domestic sphere? The graces and gifts essential to ordering one's household well are, in principle, an application and an extension of the ordering of the life of all of God's people.

A man must learn how to exert authority without squelching and shriveling the lives of those whom he is governing. Is that not true in the church of Christ? Who wants to see a church where everyone goes about restricted and intimidated by an overpowering tyrant of an elder? On the other hand, who wants to be in a church where everyone is so free-spirited and expressive that you bite your nails wondering what kind of kooky thing is going to be said the next time any opportunity is given to say it? Gracious and assertive household government develops the full potential of one's wife and children, and graces will be present which will enable the people of God to come to maturity in Christ under such a man's pastoral labors.

Can a man govern well his own household if he does not know the difference between one of his children absentmindedly picking his nose, and another child who looks up at his mother and father and sticks out his lower lip and says, "No, I won't do it"? If you punish a child for absentmindedly picking his nose with the same intensity as you would when he rears back on his hind legs and says "No," you are not ruling well your own house. Anyone who would do this is failing to discern degrees of culpability in the actions of these children. Many a church suffers from men who cannot make the distinction between a little careless ecclesiastical nose-picking and blatant defiance of the rule of Christ. We could list such contrasting parallels *ad infinitum*, but that is why the apostle Paul joined those two things by asserting so emphatically, "for if someone does not know how to manage his own household, how will he care for God's church?" (1 Tim. 3:5).

There is indeed a necessity for domestic competence if we hope to preach with effectiveness as pastors. The biblical requirements for the office of elder demand that you work at acquiring the tools to be a competent guide in the scriptures (Titus 1:9). You must with equal diligence give yourself to becoming competent domestic leaders.

I long for the day when elders, ordination counsels, denominational ordination committees and presbyteries will think in a biblically balanced way so that they will not lay hands upon a man who does not have proven competence in the rule of his household any more than they would lay hands on a man who did not have a proven ability to exegete and apply the Word of God to God's people. According to the scriptures, both are disqualified, the man who is not "able to teach" as well as the man who does not "manage his own household."

When I have insisted upon this necessity for domestic competence in various ministries around the world, I have actually had people say to me, "But Brother Martin, if we took that standard seriously we would empty half our pulpits and significantly reduce the number of our lay elders!" My answer to this objection has been, "If the Bible empties them, then let them be empty, and when word gets around that half the pulpits of the land are empty and someone asks why, the answer will be, 'It is because people are taking the Bible seriously.'" It might be the beginning of a revival if we were determined to say, "No one is going to preach in our pulpit nor sit with our session or our board of elders who cannot come through the filter of 1 Timothy 3 and Titus 1 with their dominant emphasis upon domestic competence." What happens when the pulpits are open to doctrinal heretics? That heresy filters down and curses churches and denominations. What happens when pulpits are open to domestic incompetence? That incompetence filters down and brings a moral and ethical plague upon the church. A thoughtful person must wonder which has done more harm!

The second specific thing which establishes the necessity for domestic competence is *the position which we occupy as examples to the flock*.

All of the people of God are called to live exemplary lives. This fact is made plain in the words of the apostle Paul, "Do all things without grumbling or questioning, that you may be blameless and innocent, children of God without blemish in the midst of a crooked and twisted generation, among whom you shine as lights in the world" (Phil. 2:14, 15). The Bible knows nothing of a double standard, one for the laity and another for the clergy.

However, the Bible does know of an intensified standard for those who aspire to the eldership. In Peter's charge to the elders in the churches of Asia Minor, his capstone directive is that they are not to be "domineering over those in your charge, but being examples to the flock" (1 Pet. 5:3). While all Christians ought to be exemplary in their overall lifestyle and domestic functions, elders must have attained a good degree of exemplary Christian godliness in general, and domestic competence in particular, if they are to maintain a grip on the consciences of those to whom they minister.

In addressing the subject of domestic competence I am speaking about fulfilling a role of assertive but gracious leadership. When anyone tries to tell you that the role and function of an elder is primarily to generate "wise catalytic action," that is nonsense. Yet that is an emphasis that has a tremendous groundswell in our day where leadership in Christ's Church is basically viewed as standing on the sidelines as a catalyst to encourage God's people to lead themselves by their Bibles and by the Holy Spirit. Scriptural pastors are more than that.

Be sure that this assertive leadership is not lording it over the flock. Instead of the translation "not domineering over those in your charge" (1 Pet. 5:3), Phillips paraphrases, "aim not at being 'little tin gods.'" Notice the contrast. He does not say, by humble or gracious leadership guide the flock, but he says, "being examples to the flock" (1 Pet. 5:3). You will find that there is a relationship between a man's carnal, lordly leadership style and the absence of a consistent, exemplary life. What men lack in possessing a lifestyle that gives them a grip over others, they will often seek to make up with their tight fist and carnal, lordly bearing.

We find this emphasis on the necessity for an exemplary life in Paul's directives to Timothy and Titus. Neither of these men was a pastor in the strict meaning of that word. They were apostolic representatives and charged to perform tasks which are now tasks that have become part and parcel of the pastoral office. It is therefore right that we follow the injunctions given by Paul to Timothy and Titus, not in one-to-one parallels, but in terms of basic principles.

You will notice how this emphasis is patent in Paul's words to his spiritual son Timothy. Paul was conscious that Timothy would have certain liabilities as a young man. People would tend to think lightly of his leadership because of his youth, so he says, "Let no one despise you for your youth" (1 Tim. 4:12). Then, as though anticipating Timothy's question, "Paul, how am I to overcome this liability of my youth?" Paul's answer is, "set the believers an example in speech, in conduct, in love, in faith, in purity" (1 Tim. 4:12). "Let the maturation and the consistent patterns of godliness in your life cause people to forget your youth. They will see in you the patterns of godliness so that they will find it safe to follow your leadership even though you do not have a grey hair on your head."

Likewise, Titus is charged by the apostle to give instructions to old men, young men, all ages, and all classes, while never forgetting that he must "show [himself] in all respects to be a model of good works, and in [his] teaching show integrity, dignity, and sound speech that cannot be condemned" (Titus 2:7, 8). In both the Timothy and Titus passages, the Greek word is *typos*, from which we get our English word *type*. The *typos* is the pattern by which we are to cut the curves and angles of our own life. You are that *typos*; you are that pattern.

It is a vital aspect of both general and special revelation that God has so made us as creatures in His image that we learn by a process of modeling or imitation. That reality is captured in the word *typos*. It captures what Jesus said, "It is enough for the disciple to be like his teacher, and the servant like his master" (Matt. 10:25). It is not that the disciple is merely to think as his teacher, as though the relationship between disciple and teacher were merely cerebral. No, it is enough that the disciple *be like* his teacher. The end for which the teacher instructs is that he might mold the character into the very form of that teaching which the teacher supremely embodies. That is the biblical concept of pedagogy, and Matthew 10:25 is one of the greatest statements of biblical pedagogy in the Bible. Paul therefore can say, "be imitators of me, as I am of Christ" (1 Cor. 11:1). He can say to the Ephesian elders, "in all things I have shown you that by working hard in this way we must help the weak and remember the words of the Lord Jesus" (Acts 20:35).

It is our duty to be examples in all things in general, but surely no specific area is more vital than the domestic. The Bible reveals that, next to the church, no institution is of greater importance in the advancement of the Kingdom of God than is the family. It is a fact of biblical and general revelation that God calls many of His elect in family lines. God has ordained to form noble character in the context of family life and experience. We must therefore be exemplary in these matters. When people observe us relating to our wives and children up close in our homes, one of two things will happen. After two to three hours in our homes, they will listen to us the following Lord's Day with even greater attachment and respect to our persons, as well as with a deeper commitment to our credibility, or they will have to struggle over a barrier of some emerging question mark as to whether or not we are what we profess to be. Is it not a beautiful thing to go into a well-ordered home? We will come away saying, "This is the way it ought to be." Well, that is the climate you are called upon to create.

One of the saddest as well as one of the most humbling things that ever happened to me is when one of our dearest saints who had been with us at Trinity for twenty-four years came to me and said, "You know, Pastor Martin, I was scared to death the first time you invited me into your home." I said, "Why were you scared? Did I intimidate you?" She said, "No, just the opposite. I had grown to respect and love you like I never had respected and loved any servant of Christ in all my years." I asked again, "Why were you scared?" She said, "I thought it would all vaporize once I got in your home because my previous experience was that when I got into the home of some men I had begun to respect, the respect eroded and I could no longer sit and listen to the man's ministry with confidence." What a tragedy! Will people say that about you? I tell you this from the crucible of my own experience and because what I am talking about actually happens.

The third specific thing which establishes the necessity for domestic competence is that *the particular circumstances of our generation especially demand it.*

Each generation, culture, and period of history has its own peculiarly aggravated manifestations of sinfulness and human depravity. The potential for every form of wickedness is always latent in the heart of each individual and in the collective heart of any society. However, there are times when the latent becomes patent and obvious. A classic example of this in the New Testament is what Paul said about the Cretans, "One of the Cretans, a prophet of their own, said, 'Cretans are always liars, evil beasts, lazy gluttons.' This testimony is true" (Titus 1:12, 13).

Paul was saying, "Look Timothy, you are ministering in Crete, and you had better be aware of the peculiarly aggravated manifestations of human sinfulness in that city. One of their own prophets has stated it accurately, that Cretans 'are always liars, evil beasts, lazy gluttons.'" Now, when the restraints of common and special grace are removed so that certain sins become dominant in a society at any point in history, it is at those points that the people of God must be especially concerned to manifest the radical ethical implications and fruits of the gospel. Where Satan has established his strongholds, the gospel must establish its brightest beacons.

Unless you have been away on an extended vacation on the moon, or have been living with your eyes closed, you know that among our national sins in this present hour, few are more glaring than those which touch the sanctity, stability, and glory of the marriage institution and the family. You know the sad story as well as I. Therefore, those of us who profess to be concerned with the establishment of the reign of Christ in the hearts and lives of men through the gospel must manifest the reality and implications of that reign in this most crucial area.

I remember a time when many unconverted people had good stable marriages and stable homes. Common grace was so operative that people knew who the leader was and they welcomed it. There was structure. There was love. There was discipline. There was order. Responsibility was taught. There was collective common grace where I grew up in Stamford, Connecticut. If any one of us "neighborhood gang of kids" did anything out of line that was witnessed by anyone in the neighborhood, our parents were told and took that report to heart. You were hedged up with discipline and structure in the whole neighborhood. If you did something in somebody else's backyard thinking your own mother would never know what you had done, the other kid's mama told your mama, and she believed her and did not come to your defense. There was an assumption in the neighborhood that "together we are committed to teach these kids respect for authority, honesty, and integrity." That has eroded, except for pockets in some rural areas and a few ethnically and culturally insulated urban centers in our country. For the most part, convictions concerning the sanctity of marriage as a God-given institution involving a mutual covenant of lifetime commitment have all but been swept away into an ocean of irrelevance. The same is true with respect to the biblical teaching concerning the respective roles of men and women, fathers and mothers, the necessity of parental discipline, and authority.

Imagine a society where drunkenness and alcohol abuse is the dominant societal sin. Could a man preach in that context with any grip on the consciences of his hearers if there were the slightest legitimate question about his abuse of alcohol? In such a situation, it might be practical wisdom for him to voluntarily make it known that he was a teetotaler. Do you see my application? In a society that is drunk with the horrible fruits of a humanistic approach to family life and marriage, and where assigned roles and responsibilities have been jettisoned as common beliefs, if ever we needed to make it evident that we are committed to the standards of the Word of God, it is in this crucial area.

I close this lecture by pleading with you, my brother, to pray in the biblical teaching on the necessity for domestic competence. Make this a matter of earnest prayer and entreaty, and pursue the outworking of this kind of domestic life passionately, for the glory of God, the integrity of the Christian ministry, and the good and growth of the bride of Christ.

The Man of God in Relation to His Domestic Responsibilities (2)

Ministerial Temptations to Domestic Incompetence

I begin this lecture by reminding you that there are advantages for us in our domestic life as men in the ministry. Though the work of the ministry is demanding and time-consuming, and Christian ministers should work hard at fulfilling their stewardships, there is a measure of flexibility that allows us to be present at times when it is beneficial for the family. Yet this also presents certain temptations I would like to address.

The first temptation to domestic incompetence peculiar to Christian ministers is *to rationalize our domestic failures by successes in the realm of ministerial usefulness.*

Whatever successes God may be pleased to give us in our pastoral labors, our successes must never become our saviors. This would be to set apparent blessing in one area as a neutralizer of our evident sins and failures in another area. Only the blood of Christ cleanses from sin, and only the grace of the Spirit enables us to overcome sin. So we must never think to neutralize the seriousness of our personal sins and failures with our ministerial successes.

The Lord indicted the Pharisees as domestic failures, "But you say, 'If anyone tells his father or his mother, "What you would have gained from me is given to God," he need not honor his father.' So for the sake of your tradition you have made void the word of God" (Matt. 15:5, 6). The Lord insisted they are hypocrites when they say that what ought to be given to parents suddenly becomes dedicated to God. I, too, am guilty when time that my wife or children ought to have, I piously give to God and rationalize away my pre-existing, established, divine obligations by simply and sinfully saying, "Well, I am doing the work of God." No! God calls that service hypocritical. It is a wicked excuse, rationalization, and ultimately a self-generated choice. He wants nothing of that service. "To obey is better than sacrifice" (1 Sam. 15:22).

When an ordinary Christian chooses between an evening with his family and an evening at the local pub, the issues are quite clear, and his conscience should scream at him if he chooses the pub. On the other hand, when a servant of Christ makes the choice between an evening of fun and games with his children or visiting a distressed saint, the issue is blurred. He can very easily justify neglecting the promised evening with the children because "the work of the ministry demands that I minister to this distressed sheep." In this scenario, domestic competence is often sacrificed upon the altar of official ministerial duties. "I sacrificed that time with my family for the sake of the gospel." No, you did not. You set one duty against another, and you caused a ministerial duty to kill a domestic duty.

God is not in the business of killing duty with duty. Here again is the answer of the Word of God to this mentality: "To obey is better than sacrifice" (1 Sam. 15:22). You are called upon to sacrifice privileges, luxuries, and liberties, but never to sacrifice duties. You either perform or neglect your duties. The same God who has laid upon you the care of the flock has charged you with the care of the little flock of your family. He has explicitly commanded us, "Fathers, do not provoke your children to anger, but bring them up in the discipline and instruction of the Lord" (Eph. 6:4).

The rationalizing comes to light not only in the apportionment of our time but in the toleration and justification of unchristian attitudes and actions. The man who comes home from the office where he has been working among the ungodly, if he carries the spirit of quick and sharp speech into his Christian home, ought to have a conscience that will scream at him. He should say, "Dear children, forgive me, but Daddy has been around people all day who curse one another and speak harshly to one another, and something of that has rubbed off on my own spirit. I am sorry that I spoke sharply to you a few minutes ago. Will you forgive me?"

Perhaps in the course of your pastoral labors you come from a day of dealing with someone who has entrenched himself in an area of gross and grievous carnality. You have been pouring out your soul in seeking to deal faithfully with the muck and the filth of the sin of this individual. Maybe you have been insulted and have experienced tremendous emotional pressures from the ministry. Let us suppose you come home from this and you are short-tempered and quick with the children and your wife. What should you do then? Should you say, "Well, Daddy is not quite what he ought to be. The burden of the ministry has gotten to me." Well, is that how the Lord assesses it? Does the Bible say that the fruit of the ministry is anger and wrath, or does it say that the works of the flesh produce anger and wrath? Our task is to be like Christ, and if the burdens of the ministry have left us with little emotional energy, and we do not appropriate the grace available to us in Christ, let us call this sin! Let us never blame the sacred task of shepherding the flock of God! "Whoever conceals his transgressions will not prosper, but he who confesses and forsakes them will obtain mercy" (Prov. 28:13).

The second temptation is *the temptation to be insensitive to the special pressures brought upon our wives and children because we are pastors.* This leads to the following two major headings.

Incompetence in Relation to Our Wives

Let us consider our wives first of all. The Scripture tells us, "Likewise, husbands, live with your wives in an understanding way, showing honor to the woman as the weaker vessel, since they are heirs with you of the grace of life, so that your prayers may not be hindered" (1 Pet. 3:7). It does not call us to despise her because she is weaker, but, surprisingly, to give her special honor because she is weaker.

Think for a moment about the *emotional* pressures that are brought to bear upon your wife because she chose to marry you. Pastors' wives have varying levels of involvement with the most difficult emotional aspects of our work. You may be one who shields your wife from most or all of that emotional pressure which comes to you in the ministry. Or, you may be one who shares much or all of those things with her, except those matters concerning which it would be a sinful breach of ministerial confidentiality. You may need that and she may be very willing to bear that load with you. Yet even when there are confidential matters involved in pastoral ministry, we may still be able to give our wives a general description of situations without violating principles of confidentiality. Whether she enters in at a very deep level to the particulars of your labor or whether she simply stands by your side as a blotter absorbing some of the emotional heat, the fact that you are an elder in Christ's flock means that the emotional pressures brought to bear upon you will, to some degree, be shared by your wife.

Coupled with that pressure, it is often the case that your position puts her in a place where she cannot have the normal circle of intimate friends that an ordinary member of the flock can have. Now I did not say that this comes about of necessity, but that it often works out that way. One of the areas where a pastor's wife pays a tremendous price is in the area of loneliness. Circumstances may be such that it is not expedient for her to develop intimate friendships which make it possible for her to share her deepest burdens, frustrations, joys and sorrows. What happens then? She has additional pressures coming from the direction of her identity with you. She does not have the normal outlets and consolations that come because of her position at your side. She has a two-fold emotional vice, two jaws pressing in upon her.

Many a preacher, so utterly taken up with his "great ministry," is insensitive to those emotional pressures. He does not dwell with his wife according to knowledge. He does not seek to make up the lack of intimate friendship by being her trusted confidante and her emotional blotter. He does not seek to give her those outlets and diversions that will result in her emotional healing. Consequentially, she may become resentful. She may become vulnerable to a man who seems to be sensitive to her needs. The average woman, Christian or not, is lured into a man's bed not primarily by his face or his body, but by his soul. I once spoke to a woman who said to me,

> A man could be five feet two inches tall and weigh two hundred pounds, but if for five minutes he just looked at me and listened as if my feelings mattered, I feel I would be emotionally vulnerable to be an adulteress. I would not care what he looked like. If there was just a male soul that showed an interest in me emotionally, I would feel that temptation.

When I hear that preachers' wives have entered adulterous relationships, I cannot help but wonder if it could be that there was insensitivity to those emotional pressures that left her vulnerable to a caring, listening, and sensitive man.

There are also *physical* pressures upon the minister's wife. An elder is to be given to hospitality, but who bears the brunt of that ministry, making sure the house looks as it ought to look, and that the occasion of hospitality is all that it needs to be? So, what does your wife have to do? More than once, I have had to sit on my hands when I wanted to grab a man and shake him. There he is, sitting in the living room discussing theology, while I notice his wife out in the kitchen needing another set of hands as she tries to prepare the meal. There are times, when if the husband did not get the message, that I just excused myself, went out right in his presence, and said to his wife, "May I help you?" I did that with no hesitation. I am going to be like

Christ even if her husband is not. And if it shows him up, let it show him up. If he does not get the message, then perhaps it is time to take seriously the clear directive of Galatians 6:1. Or maybe when I leave, his wife will say, "You know, it was so nice to have the pastor come and help me." I have had preachers come to me and say, "My brother, you got me in trouble." I have said in response, "What did I do?" They said, "Well, after you left, my wife said, 'Pastor Martin helped fix the meal and helped wash the dishes. Why don't you do that?'" And I said, "Yes, why don't you?" Are we not to provoke one another unto love and good works?

I know that in certain cultures you would insult the man's wife if you did that. I am fully aware of those differences. I have had to learn how to be sensitive to them in different cultural settings, but the basic principle is to dwell with your wife according to knowledge. Do not be intemperate in your expectations of what she can do on any given day.

Be sensitive to this in terms of your intimate sexual life as well. Remember, most of your work is mental and hers is a combination of mental and physical. After you have been holed up with your books all day and then you feel her warm flesh close to you at night, you are ready for a time of holy eroticism. She feels worn and washed out and just a nice peck on the cheek and a thank you for the things she has done in the day is all she wants and all she has left. In the kind of setting I have just described, do not start quoting 1 Corinthians 7 to her about rendering to you her due!

Seek to relieve her by a periodic break from the pressures brought upon her because she is a pastor's wife. When my wife had little ones at home, even before she drove, there were times when I thought that I must give her a break. Ten dollars was a lot of money in our budget, or in anybody's budget in the early 1960s when our three children were born; yet, to help her I would occasionally give her ten dollars, drop her off at the local mall and say to her, "I am coming back in four hours, and I do not want you to spend a dime of that ten dollars on me or on the children." If I did not charge her to do that, she would have spent every last cent on us. "Do anything you want with it short of sin. You just have a good time, and I will pick you up in a few hours." She would come back home like a new person.

The temptation is always there to be insensitive to the pressures brought upon her *spiritually*. Because she stands with you in the eyes of the congregation, she is always on a pedestal by virtue of being the pastor's wife. She just wants to be an ordinary wife and a mother, but in the eyes of the people, she is the pastor's wife and mother of the pastor's children. That brings peculiar spiritual pressures upon her; therefore, you must be a priest to her.

Abraham Booth gives a moving and extensive warning about this whole matter:

> *Take heed*, I will venture to add, *take heed to your second self, in the person of your wife.* As it is of high importance for a young minister in single life, to behave with the utmost delicacy in all his intercourse with female friends, treating with peculiar caution those of them that are unmarried; and as it behooves him to pay the most conscientious regard to religious character, when choosing a companion for life; so, when in the conjugal state, his tenderest attention is due to the domestic happiness and the spiritual interests of his wife. This obligation, my brother, manifestly devolves upon you; as being already a husband and a father. Next after your own soul, therefore, your wife and your children evidently claim the most affectionate, conscientious, and pious care.
>
> Nor can it be reasonably doubted, that many a devout and amiable woman has given her hand to a minister of the gospel, in preference to a private Christian, though otherwise equally deserving, in sanguine expectation, by so doing, of enjoying peculiar spiritual advantages in the matrimonial relation. But, alas! there is much reason to apprehend, that not a few individuals among those worthy females, have often reflected to the following effect:
>
> > "I have, indeed, married a preacher of the gospel; but I do not find in him the affectionate domestic instructor, for either myself, or my children. My husband is much esteemed among his religious acquaintance, as a respectable Christian character; but his example at home is far from being delightful. Affable, condescending, and pleasing, in the parlours of religious friends; but, frequently, either trifling and unsavoury, or imperious and unsocial, in his own family. Preferring the opportunity of being entertained at a plentiful table, and of conversing with the wealthy, the polite, and the sprightly, to the homely fare of his own family, and the company of his wife and children, he often spends his afternoons and evenings from home, until so late an hour, that domestic worship is either omitted, or performed in a hasty and slovenly manner, with scarcely the appearance of devotion.—Little caring for my soul, or for the management of our growing offspring, he seems concerned for hardly any thing more, than keeping fair with his people: relative to which, I have often calmly

remonstrated, and submissively entreated, but all in vain. Surrounded with little ones, and attended with straits; destitute of the sympathies, the instructions, the consolations, which might have been expected from the affectionate heart of a pious husband, connected with the gifts of an evangelical minister, I pour out my soul to God, and mourn in secret." Such, there is ground of apprehension, has been the sorrowful soliloquy of many a minister's pious, dutiful, and prudent wife. Take heed, then, to the best interests of your *second-self*.[1]

I always sought to ask myself the following questions whenever my wife has been present when I preach: "Can I preach into my wife's eyes as I move my eyes across the congregation with as much grip upon her conscience as I hope I can with respect to the conscience of the person sitting next to her in the congregation?" "Does she find it a delight or a source of pain to hear me preach what a godly husband and father ought to be?" "Does she know me to be what others are saying to her about me?"

God's people come to your wife and say, "Oh, how thankful we are that God brought your husband to be our pastor. He is such a wise counselor. I came to him last week, and he helped me sort out a problem that I had." Does she stand there and say, "Would to God I knew what she was talking about. It must be nice"? Does she know you to be to her what others say you are to them? When others say, "How thankful I am to know that your husband prays for us," can your wife say, "I know; my husband prays for me!"? When they say, "How good it is to have a pastor who is a consistent example of selfless concern and of true, practical, biblical godliness," can she say, "Ah, if you knew what I know, you would say that with a lot more conviction"? Or is she sorely tempted to say, "If you knew what I know, you would take back your words"? There are tremendous spiritual pressures on our wives. Brethren, we must beware of the temptation to be insensitive to them.

Be mindful of the temptation *to submit to demands made upon you by your wife when she is not yet fully aware of the demands made upon you in connection with your labors as a minister of the gospel.*[2] A woman must grow into her understanding of what is demanded of you. She must grow in

---

1. Abraham Booth, "Pastoral Cautions," in *The Christian Pastor's Manual*, ed. John Brown (Ligonier, PA: Soli Deo Gloria Publications, 1991), 74, 75.

2. See my booklet, *Encouragement for Pastors' Wives*, published by Chapel Library, www.chapellibrary.org

her understanding of how crucial uninterrupted times are, especially if your study is at home. There are many benefits to having our studies at home. Many pastors are successful in maintaining the necessary disciplines essential to their maximum productivity working at home. You must lovingly and patiently train your family concerning why and how they must cooperate with you in protecting your working hours from unnecessary intrusions.

When you are wrestling with the organization of your sermon headings and you feel like things are just at the point of clarification in your own mind, this is not a good time for your wife to come into the study or call on the phone about an inconsequential household matter. It may be necessary for you to speak to her about things like that. Sometimes men are afraid that their wives are going to react and they capitulate, and before long the wife's demands increase until the minister becomes the lackey of his wife's every whim.

Can you imagine Mrs. Elijah, just before Elijah goes out on Mount Carmel, saying, "Elijah! Take out the garbage"? Marilyn had a very subtle way of making it known when the garbage needed to be taken out. When the garbage bin with the plastic bag inside it was full she would neatly tie it up and place it just inside the kitchen door, so that when it was convenient I knew it was ready to be carried out. But she would not have thought of knocking on the door of my study and saying, "Honey, the garbage should be taken out."

Incompetence in Relation to Our Children

Next, consider direct and indirect temptations with respect to our children.

The first direct temptation is that *the inordinate attention heaped upon them because they are your children can lead to their pride and general brattiness if you are not careful.*

Based on my observation, this potential problem is not quite the same in a larger church where there are so many children and usually other men in leadership who have children, so that your children do not receive quite the same high profile. However, most of you will commence your ministries in a relatively small church. Perhaps for a period of time you will be the only elder. Either out of ignorance of what fawning praise can do, or in a misguided way of showing their love for you, your people will heap attention upon your children. You will need to monitor that very carefully. Be sensitive to the vulnerability it creates to pride and their having a distorted view of themselves and their own importance. Furthermore, people may indulge your children contrary to your own standards, not willfully, but because you have not made your standards known to them. If necessary, at a special congregational meeting, tell your congregation about rules in your house. For example, you might say, "Our family's rule is no sweets before meals, therefore we would appreciate it if you do not give our children Lifesavers, bubblegum, and such things." Be candid with your people. Do it with a smile and say it sweetly, but tell them. You want your children to be surrounded with consistent standards of discipline and conduct.

The second direct temptation is *for them to have an inflated view of themselves and to set themselves over their peers, a temptation to "big-shot-itis" because they always see you in a prominent role.*

You must seek to neutralize this temptation to prevent your children from developing a kind of shared clerical swagger and importance.

Then there are the indirect and more subtle temptations, and this is where I want to park for a bit.

First of all, *understand that your children will be more vulnerable to bitterness and resentment because of the special demands made upon your time.*

In many ways we are like physicians and our children are like the children of physicians. Plans are made and they have to be scrapped because of unavoidable "professional duties." You do not schedule people's deaths. You plan a family outing, or an evening to spend with the children, and at four-thirty you get the news that one of the sheep in the congregation has just gone to glory, or a loved one has just been admitted to the special care unit. Just like the physician, you must leave at the expense of your family plans.

You must beware of being insensitive to the temptation that the children face at times like these, and do everything possible to neutralize any legitimate grounds for bitterness and resentment. Make it plain to them that you do not like those interruptions.

In light of this, it is good to make some fairly inflexible rules regarding family times. When our children were growing up, I made it known to the congregation that from five-thirty to seven-thirty each evening our telephone would be turned off. This was back in the days when there was one phone in the average home. They had their daddy from five-thirty to seven-thirty every night except Wednesday, Saturday, and Sunday. Your children will appreciate that they really are important to you when they see you marking out time, setting up some walls, and protecting that time for them. They see you do it with regard to preparation for worship and ministering to God's people. It encourages them to see that they also are a priority in your life. If you do not manifest your love in these practical ways, you will leave them vulnerable to bitterness and resentment.

They may face another subtle temptation, if you are not careful, which is *to resent being disciplined for the wrong motives.*

We are commanded to train and discipline our children for God's glory and for their good, and that is enough. Do not tell them, "Now you must do this because Daddy is a minister." They will begin to resent the fact that you are a minister because you are more strict or severe with them than you should be. Just do what is right as you "bring them up in the discipline and instruction of the Lord" (Eph. 6:4).

Another subtle temptation is resentment because of *unrealistic standards and expectations which others have simply because they are elders' kids.*

Warn your people about setting up a double standard for children, one for those of ordinary church members and another for yours, just because you are a pastor. "Oh, a *preacher's* kid must not do that!" What is there about being an elder's kid that makes him something halfway between an angel and a human being? Not a thing. You must see to it that your people do not impose unrealistic standards upon your children.

The fourth temptation that your children may have is *the temptation to frame a wrong conception of their daddy as a man of God.*

Most of our serious reading and praying is done in the prayer closet and in the study. If the study is not at home, they see mommy reading her Bible and going to pray, but they only see daddy reading the newspaper and perhaps a news magazine, listening to the radio, or watching a ball game on the television. They may subtly think that Daddy's faith is his profession, but the real daddy is the daddy who hollers when his favorite team scores a touchdown and who sits reading his magazine. So what must you do? Well, you must try to put yourself behind the eyeballs of your children and ask yourself, "What image are they receiving of me?" It may be, if for no other reason than their benefit, you may want to do some of your spiritual reading at home so they will see Daddy reading a godly biography or *Pilgrim's*

Progress. It would also be good if they hear Daddy listening to recorded sermons to feed his own soul. The image they have of you is the one they receive from their personal observation of you. As they get older, they will know you in a more sophisticated way, but while they are younger, they will not.

The last major temptation that I want to speak about in relation to your children is *the temptation to grow weary of the burden of constant leadership in spiritual matters.*

In the church, you must be the leader and be giving your judgment about many things. Your people will ask you questions, and you are called upon to give your understanding of particular Scripture passages, theological issues, and general problems they face which might be handled better with pastoral input. They are looking to you for guidance. There are times at home when the phone rings and people call with this and that problem and you feel like saying, "If I could just have relief from the burden of leadership for a few hours, it would be so wonderful!"

You must also lead in family worship. I confess, family worship was my greatest problem when my children were younger. The weariness I felt at the end of the day after bearing people's burdens placed the temptation before me of wanting to pass the buck and stop. I was tired of hearing my own voice. I would have loved to have had somebody come in and lead family worship for me. It was not that I was indisposed to the Bible and to prayer. I was just tired of having to be the one to do the leading, the thinking, breaking this down, and making it interesting and accessible to children of different ages. We often grow weary of that, and the place where you will break down is in fulfilling your spiritual responsibilities to your wife and children.

Beware of that temptation. Just lift up your weary heart to God and say,

Lord, You have said, "Fathers, do not provoke your children to anger, but bring them up in the discipline and instruction of the Lord." I am to be the priest in this home. Please give me grace, Lord. May the weariness not show on my face or in the tone of my voice so that my children will not get the idea that this is just a burdensome ritual that Daddy is imposing on us. Lord, give me enthusiasm, even if I do not feel an ounce of it.

God will lead you. I have found quickening at the table in family worship just like the quickening that comes to a weary mind and body in the pulpit. The weariness is not sinful in itself. It is a reminder that you have the treasure in an earthen vessel. Never forget the apostolic exhortation, "do not grow weary in doing good" (2 Thess. 3:13). Weariness in well-doing, leading to the negation of duty, is sin. "They who wait for the LORD shall renew their strength; they shall mount up with wings like eagles; they shall run and not be weary; they shall walk and not faint" (Isa. 40:31).

Now I want to give you four very brief yet practical counsels for maintaining domestic competence.

Practical Counsels for Maintaining Domestic Competence

First, *pray in and periodically refresh your conviction concerning the unyielding necessity for exemplary domestic competence.*

Make 1 Timothy 3 and Titus 1 your constant companions. When you are in the work of the ministry, periodically set aside half a morning to pray over one of these passages, to pray it in and say to yourself, looking yourself in the mirror with genuine Judgment Day honesty, "If you fail as father and husband, you are through as far as the ministry is concerned." Tell yourself that. Load your conscience with that until it becomes as deep a conviction as the conviction that the Bible is the Word of God and that Christ is the Son of God. "I must be a man of God before my wife and my children, or my mouth is shut and the office is vacated." Now, if that becomes a visceral conviction, you are on your way to being a competent father and husband.

Second, *seek the periodic assessment of competent observers regarding your domestic competence.*

Eventually this will be realized through your fellow-elders. Develop a climate of trust and openness with them. Be frank with each other in your evaluation of each other's performance as husbands and fathers. Wrestle these things through and develop a relational atmosphere in which you do not feel buried and threatened or defensive when someone says,

> Look, brother, I really believe that you have some areas of insensitivity. Remember when we were together the other night, three or four times I saw your wife just waiting to get a word in edge-wise, but you so dominated the conversation that she could not say a word. Were you aware of that?

Your brother may say, "I never even thought of it." You say, "Alright, let me remind you." This is the kind of thing I am talking about. Then the brother whom you exhorted will go home and say to his wife, "Honey, the other night, when we were together with such and such, I was very insensitive to you by dominating the conversation. Please forgive me. Please set up some hand signals for me to help me if I fall into that sin in the future."

Third, *periodically evaluate your domestic life with your wife and children.*

Sit down with your wife periodically and say, "Honey, if there is anything you could change in me, what would it be?" Then after she has told you, consider what she has said and see whether what she said is rooted in Scripture. Then make the changes in heart and ear and mouth and hand that you need to make. This is no little part of the virtue of humility which the Scripture requires of us. The practical steps which I have recommended are a means of grace. Sit your children down and do a similar thing, appropriate to their age. "If you could change anything in Daddy, what would you change?" Then work through their suggestions and see whether they are talking about things that ought legitimately to be changed because they are issues of insensitivity or sin.

With my children, it was my serious countenance. I was born with a wrinkled brow. I am naturally a serious person. I have a very active sense of humor as all my friends and confidants know, but I was put together a serious person. When God got hold of me in grace, He immediately laid some very weighty responsibilities on me. Those responsibilities were God's knife by which He cut out of me that typical rah-rah college stage of development between ages eighteen and twenty-two. After I was married and given children, that inclination to a serious life was such that at times I apparently created a climate of heaviness in my home. From time to time, my children would comment, "Daddy, you sometimes look sad." I thought, "What a terrible testimony." So I had my children give me input to help me cultivate the grace of greater cheerfulness and to let it show in my countenance and overall demeanor, no matter how heavy and pressing the issues were that were an inescapable part of my life and labors as a pastor. Knowing that little children are not drawn to sad-looking adults, I was always conscious about maintaining an approachable and cheerful spirit in the presence of the children who were part of the church family. However, in the more relaxed atmosphere of my own home, I was not exercising the same discipline to maintain an evident cheerfulness.

Fourth, *bind yourself to some inescapable pressure to keep attending persistently to this area of domestic competence.*

I give a personal reference once again. Early in our marriage my wife and I made a solemn vow to one another in certain areas which we believed were crucial to the cultivation of a healthy and God-honoring marital relationship. I had her make something short of a formal vow, but just as binding, that if she ever saw anything in my life in the area of personal or domestic incompetence or sin in general, that she would address it directly with me. If she did not see me making tangible efforts to deal with it in a reasonable timeframe, she was to go directly over my head to my fellow-elders and tell them exactly what she saw. Marilyn would have done that if it ever became necessary. She would have done it for the sake of my soul and for the sake of the souls of the people of God.

I was always thankful for that pressure. It was just one more barrier to resist the rationalization and the erosion that can come with a horrible fury, alas, even in our middle and later years. In the light of these realities, I urge you that early in your ministerial experience you bind yourself to some wholesome but inescapable pressures to attain and maintain domestic competence with growing grace and exemplary dignity.

The central burden of this unit of our studies in pastoral theology is captured in some of the opening words of the first lecture. *Sustained effectiveness in pastoral ministry is generally realized in proportion to the health and vigor of the pastor in his relationship to God, his people, himself, the management of his time and his manifold responsibilities, and his family.* In opening up that axiom, we covered considerable biblical and practical turf, seeking to establish the validity of each of the affirmations contained in it. I trust that the issues addressed have been presented in such a way that you will never doubt the validity of the old aphorism that "the life of the minister is the life of his ministry."

> Our Father, once again we have wrestled with matters that make great demands upon us, and left to ourselves we would again cry out, "Who is sufficient for these things?" But we believe that all that is necessary to be fruitful in the work to which You have called us is available to us in Christ. Help us, then, to lay hold of that grace, and to be responsible, self-controlled men, and fruitful in our labors. Hear us, and answer us we plead, in Jesus' Name. Amen.

Scripture Index

Topical Index

Author Index